P9-CFQ-751

MCGRAW-HILL
ONLINE RESOURCES

IMPORTANT:

HERE IS YOUR REGISTRATION CODE TO ACCESS
YOUR PREMIUM McGRAW-HILL ONLINE RESOURCES.

For key premium online resources you need THIS CODE to gain access. Once the code is entered, you will be able to use the Web resources for the length of your course.

If your course is using **WebCT** or **Blackboard**, you'll be able to use this code to access the McGraw-Hill content within your instructor's online course.

Access is provided if you have purchased a new book. If the registration code is missing from this book, the registration screen on our Website, and within your WebCT or Blackboard course, will tell you how to obtain your new code.

Registering for McGraw-Hill Online Resources

TO gain access to your McGraw-Hill web resources simply follow the steps below:

1. USE YOUR WEB BROWSER TO GO TO: **http://www.mhhe.com/santrockld9**

2. CLICK ON **FIRST TIME USER**.

3. ENTER THE REGISTRATION CODE* PRINTED ON THE TEAR-OFF BOOKMARK ON THE RIGHT.

4. AFTER YOU HAVE ENTERED YOUR REGISTRATION CODE, CLICK **REGISTER**.

5. FOLLOW THE INSTRUCTIONS TO SET-UP YOUR PERSONAL UserID AND PASSWORD.

6. WRITE YOUR UserID AND PASSWORD DOWN FOR FUTURE REFERENCE.
   KEEP IT IN A SAFE PLACE.

TO GAIN ACCESS to the McGraw-Hill content in your instructor's **WebCT** or **Blackboard** course simply log in to the course with the UserID and Password provided by your instructor. Enter the registration code exactly as it appears in the box to the right when prompted by the system. You will only need to use the code the first time you click on McGraw-Hill content.

Thank you, and welcome to your McGraw-Hill online Resources!

 Higher Education

mauritania-23169860

REGISTRATION CODE

 Higher Education

* YOUR REGISTRATION CODE CAN BE USED ONLY ONCE TO ESTABLISH ACCESS. IT IS NOT TRANSFERABLE.

0-07-282049-7 SANTROCK: LIFE-SPAN DEVELOPMENT, 9E

Life-Span Development

NINTH EDITION

John W. Santrock
University of Texas at Dallas

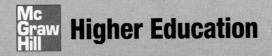
Higher Education

Boston   Burr Ridge, IL   Dubuque, IA   Madison, WI   New York   San Francisco   St. Louis
Bangkok   Bogotá   Caracas   Kuala Lumpur   Lisbon   London   Madrid   Mexico City
Milan   Montreal   New Delhi   Santiago   Seoul   Singapore   Sydney   Taipei   Toronto

Higher Education

LIFE-SPAN DEVELOPMENT, NINTH EDITION

Published by McGraw-Hill, a business unit of The McGraw-Hill Companies, Inc., 1221 Avenue of the Americas, New York, NY 10020. Copyright © 2004, 2002, 1999, 1997 by The McGraw-Hill Companies, Inc. All rights reserved. No part of this publication may be reproduced or distributed in any form or by any means, or stored in a database or retrieval system, without the prior written consent of The McGraw-Hill Companies, Inc., including, but not limited to, in any network or other electronic storage or transmission, or broadcast for distance learning.

Some ancillaries, including electronic and print components, may not be available to customers outside the United States.

This book is printed on recycled, acid-free paper containing 10% postconsumer waste.

International   1 2 3 4 5 6 7 8 9 0 QPD/QPD 0 9 8 7 6 5 4 3
Domestic   1 2 3 4 5 6 7 8 9 0 QPD/QPD 0 9 8 7 6 5 4 3

ISBN 0-07-282049-7
ISBN 0-07-121393-7 (ISE)

Vice president and editor-in-chief: *Thalia Dorwick*
Publisher: *Stephen D. Rutter*
Senior sponsoring editor: *Rebecca H. Hope*
Senior developmental editor: *Judith Kromm*
Marketing manager: *Melissa Caughlin*
Senior project manager: *Marilyn Rothenberger*
Manager, New book production: *Sandra Hahn*
Media technology producer: *Ginger Bunn*
Design coordinator: *Gino Cieslik*
Interior designer: *Ellen Pettengell*
Art editor: *Robin Mouat*
Illustrators: *John and Judy Waller*
Photo research coordinator: *Alexandra Ambrose*
Photo researcher: *LouAnn Wilson*
Senior supplement producer: *David A. Welsh*
Compositor: *GAC—Indianapolis*
Typeface: *9.5/12 Meridian*
Printer: *Quebecor World Dubuque, IA*

The credits section for this book begins on page C-1 and is considered an extension of the copyright page.

Library of Congress Cataloging-in-Publication Data

Santrock, John W.
   Life-span development / John W. Santrock.— 9th ed.
      p. cm.
   Includes bibliographical references and indexes.
   ISBN 0-07-282049-7 (alk. paper) — ISBN 0-07-121393-7 (ISE : alk. paper)
   1. Developmental psychology. I. Title.

BF713 .S26 2004
155—dc21

                                                                                    2003514125

INTERNATIONAL EDITION ISBN 0-07-121393-7
Copyright © 2004. Exclusive rights by The McGraw-Hill Companies, Inc., for manufacture and export. This book cannot be re-exported from the country to which it is sold by McGraw-Hill. The International Edition is not available in North America.

www.mhhe.com

With special appreciation to my parents,
Ruth and John Santrock

About the Author

John W. Santrock

John Santrock received his Ph.D. from the University of Minnesota in 1973. He taught at the University of Charleston and the University of Georgia before joining the Program in Psychology and Human Development at the University of Texas at Dallas, where he currently teaches a number of undergraduate courses. In 1982, John created the life-span development course at UT–Dallas and has taught it every year since then.

John has been a member of the editorial boards of Child Development and Developmental Psychology. His research on father custody is widely cited and used in expert witness testimony to promote flexibility and alternative considerations in custody disputes. John also has authored these exceptional McGraw-Hill texts: Psychology (7th edition), Child Development (9th edition), Children (7th edition), Adolescence (9th edition), and Educational Psychology (2nd edition).

For many years, John was involved in tennis as a player, teaching professional, and coach of professional tennis players. He has been married for more than 35 years to his wife, Mary Jo, who is a realtor. He has two daughters—Tracy, who is a technology specialist at Nortel in Raleigh, North Carolina, and Jennifer, who is a medical sales specialist at Medtronic. He has one granddaughter, Jordan, age 9. Tracy recently completed the New York Marathon, and Jennifer was in the top 100 ranked players on the Women's Professional Tennis Tour. In the last decade, John also has spent time painting expressionist art.

John Santrock, teaching in his undergraduate course in life-span development.

Brief Contents

SECTION 1

The Life-Span Developmental Perspective 3

1 Introduction 5
2 The Science of Life-Span Development 41

SECTION 2

Beginnings 77

3 Biological Beginnings 79
4 Prenatal Development and Birth 111

SECTION 3

Infancy 145

5 Physical Development in Infancy 147
6 Cognitive Development in Infancy 181
7 Socioemotional Development in Infancy 205

SECTION 4

Early Childhood 231

8 Physical and Cognitive Development in Early Childhood 233
9 Socioemotional Development in Early Childhood 267

SECTION 5

Middle and Late Childhood 299

10 Physical and Cognitive Development in Middle and Late Childhood 301
11 Socioemotional Development in Middle and Late Childhood 335

SECTION 6

Adolescence 365

12 Physical and Cognitive Development in Adolescence 367
13 Socioemotional Development in Adolescence 403

SECTION 7

Early Adulthood 437

14 Physical and Cognitive Development in Early Adulthood 439
15 Socioemotional Development in Early Adulthood 477

SECTION 8

Middle Adulthood 511

16 Physical and Cognitive Development in Middle Adulthood 513
17 Socioemotional Development in Middle Adulthood 541

SECTION 9

Late Adulthood 565

18 Physical Development in Late Adulthood 567
19 Cognitive Development in Late Adulthood 597
20 Socioemotional Development in Late Adulthood 623

SECTION 10

Endings 651

21 Death and Grieving 653

Contents

Preface xv

To The Student xxx

SECTION 1

Life-Span Developmental Perspective 3

CHAPTER 1

Introduction 5

Images of Life-Span Development
How Did Ted Kaczynski Become Ted Kaczynski and Alice Walker Become Alice Walker? 6

The Life-Span Perspective 6
What Is Life-Span Development? 7
The Historical Perspective 7
Characteristics of the Life-Span Perspective 9
Careers in Life-Span Development
K. Warner Schaie, Professor of Human Development 10
Some Contemporary Concerns 11
Careers in Life-Span Development
Luis Vargas, Child Clinical Psychologist 12
Sociocultural Worlds of Development
Women's Struggle for Equality: An International Journey 15

Developmental Processes and Periods 18
Biological, Cognitive, and Socioemotional Processes 18
Periods of Development 19
Age and Happiness 20
Conceptions of Age 21

Developmental Issues 23
Nature and Nurture 23
Continuity and Discontinuity 23
Stability and Change 24
Evaluating the Developmental Issues 25

Reach Your Learning Goals 26

APPENDIX Careers in Life-Span Development 29

CHAPTER 2

The Science of Life-Span Development 41

Images of Life-Span Development
The Childhoods of Erikson and Piaget 42

Theories of Development 43
Psychoanalytic Theories 44
Cognitive Theories 47
Sociocultural Worlds of Development
Cultural and Gender Bias in Freud's Theory 48
Behavioral and Social Cognitive Theories 51
Ethological Theory 53
Ecological Theory 55
An Eclectic Theoretical Orientation 57

Research in Life-Span Development 58
Types of Research 59
Time Span of Research 63

Facing Up to Research Challenges 67
Conducting Ethical Research 67
Minimizing Bias 69
Careers in Life-Span Development
Pam Reid, Educational and Developmental Psychologist 70

Reach Your Learning Goals 72

SECTION 2
Beginnings 77

CHAPTER 3
Biological Beginnings 79

Images of Life-Span Development
The Jim and Jim Twins 80

The Evolutionary Perspective 81
Natural Selection and Adaptive Behavior 81
Evolutionary Psychology 81

Genetic Foundations 83
What Are Genes? 83
Mitosis and Meiosis 84
Genetic Principles 84
Behavior Genetics 88
Molecular Genetics 88
Chromosome and Gene-Linked Abnormalities 90
Careers in Life-Span Development
Holly Ishmael, Genetic Counselor 92

Reproduction Challenges and Choices 94
Prenatal Diagnostic Tests 94
Infertility 95
Adoption 96

Heredity-Environment Interaction 98
Intelligence 98
Sociocultural Worlds of Development
The Abecedarian Intervention Program 101
Heredity-Environment Correlations 102
Shared and Nonshared Environmental Experiences 103
Conclusions About Heredity-Environment Interaction 103

Reach Your Learning Goals 106

CHAPTER 4
Prenatal Development and Birth 111

Images of Life-Span Development
Tanner Roberts' Birth: A Fantastic Voyage 112

Prenatal Development 113
The Course of Prenatal Development 113
Teratology and Hazards to Prenatal Development 117
Prenatal Care 124
Careers in Life-Span Development
Rachel Thompson, Obstetrician/Gynecologist 125
Cultural Beliefs About Pregnancy 125
Positive Prenatal Development 126

Birth 127
The Birth Process 127
Careers in Life-Span Development
Linda Pugh, Perinatal Nurse 130
Low-Birthweight Infants 131
Measures of Neonatal Health and Responsiveness 134

The Postpartum Period 135
What Is the Postpartum Period? 135
Physical Adjustments 136
Emotional and Psychological Adjustments 137
Bonding 137
Careers in Life-Span Development
Diane Sanford, Clinical Psychologist and Postpartum Expert 138

Reach Your Learning Goals 140

SECTION 3
Infancy 145

CHAPTER 5
Physical Development in Infancy 147

Images of Life-Span Development
Bottle- and Breast-Feeding in Africa 148

Physical Growth and Development in Infancy 148
Cephalocaudal and Proximodistal Patterns 149
Height and Weight 149
The Brain 150
Sleep 155
Nutrition 157

Sociocultural Worlds of Development
A Healthy Start 159
Careers in Life-Span Development
T. Berry Brazelton, Pediatrician 160
Toilet Training 160

Motor Development 161
Reflexes 161
Gross and Fine Motor Skills 163
Dynamic Systems Theory 167

Sensory and Perceptual Development 168
What Are Sensation and Perception? 168
The Ecological View 169

Visual Perception 169
Other Senses 172
Intermodal Perception 174
Perceptual-Motor Coupling and Unification 175

Reach Your Learning Goals 176

CHAPTER 6
Cognitive Development in Infancy 181

Images of Life-Span Development
Laurent, Lucienne, and Jacqueline 182

Piaget's Theory of Infant Development 183
The Sensorimotor Stage of Development 183
Understanding Physical Reality 185
Evaluating Piaget's Sensorimotor Stage 186

Learning and Remembering 188
Conditioning 188
Habituation and Dishabituation 188
Imitation 189
Memory 190

Individual Differences in Intelligence 191
Careers in Life-Span Development
Toosje Thyssen VanBeveren, Infant Assessment Specialist 193

Language Development 194
What Is Language? 194
How Language Develops 194
Biological Foundations of Language 197
Behavioral and Environmental Influences 198

Sociocultural Worlds of Development
Language Environment, Poverty, and Language Development 199

Reach Your Learning Goals 200

CHAPTER 7
Socioemotional Development in Infancy 205

Images of Life-Span Development
The Story of Tom's Fathering 206

Emotional and Personality Development 206
Emotional Development 206
Temperament 210
Personality Development 213

Attachment 215
What Is Attachment? 215
Individual Differences 217
Caregiving Styles and Attachment Classification 218
Attachment, Temperament, and the Wider Social World 219

Social Contexts 220
The Family 220
Day Care 222
Sociocultural Worlds of Development
Child-Care Policy Around the World 223
Careers in Life-Span Development
Rashmi Nakhre, Day-Care Director 224

Reach Your Learning Goals 226

SECTION 4
Early Childhood 231

CHAPTER 8
Physical and Cognitive Development in Early Childhood 233

Images of Life-Span Development
Teresa Amabile and Her Creativity 234

Physical Changes 234
Body Growth and Change 235
Motor Development 237
Nutrition 238
Illness and Death 238
Careers in Life-Span Development
Barbara Deloin, Pediatric Nurse 241

Cognitive Changes 242
Piaget's Preoperational Stage 242
Vygotsky's Theory 246

Information Processing 249
Careers in Life-Span Development
Helen Schwe, Developmental Psychologist and Toy Designer 253

Language Development 254

Early Childhood Education 256
The Child-Centered Kindergarten 256
The Montessori Approach 256
Developmentally Appropriate and Inappropriate Practice in Education 257
Does Preschool Matter? 257
Sociocultural Worlds of Development
Early Childhood Education in Japan 259
Careers in Life-Span Development
Yolanda Garcia, Director of Children's Services/Head Start 260
Education for Children Who Are Disadvantaged 260

Reach Your Learning Goals 262

CHAPTER 9

Socioemotional Development in Early Childhood 267

Images of Life-Span Development
Sara and Her Developing Moral Values 268

Emotional and Personality Development 268
The Self 268
Emotional Development 269
Moral Development 270
Gender 272

Families 276

Parenting 276
Careers in Life-Span Development
Darla Botkin, Marriage and Family Therapist 281
Sibling Relationships and Birth Order 281
The Changing Family in a Changing Society 282
Sociocultural Worlds of Development
Acculturation and Ethnic Minority Parenting 286

Peer Relations, Play, and Television 287
Peer Relations 287
Play 288
Television 291

Reach Your Learning Goals 294

SECTION 5
Middle and Late Childhood 299

CHAPTER 10

Physical and Cognitive Development in Middle and Late Childhood 301

Images of Life-Span Development
Jessica Dubroff, Child Pilot 302

Physical Changes and Health 302
Body Growth and Proportion 302
Motor Development 303
Exercise and Sports 303
Health, Illness, and Disease 305
Careers in Life-Span Development
Sharon McLeod, Child Life Specialist 305

Children with Disabilities 306
Who Are Children with Disabilitites? 306
Learning Disabilities 307
Attention Deficit Hyperactivity Disorder (ADHD) 308
Educational Issues 309
Sociocultural Worlds of Development
Family-Centered and Culture-Centered Approaches to Working with a Child Who Has a Disability 310

Cognitive Changes 311
Piaget's Theory 311
Information Processing 314
Careers in Life-Span Development
Laura Martin, Science Museum Educator and Research Specialist 316
Intelligence 317
Careers in Life-Span Development
Sterling Jones, Supervisor of Gifted and Talented Education 324
Creativity 324

Language Development 326
Vocabulary and Grammar 326
Reading 326

Bilingualism 327
Careers in Life-Span Development
Salvador Tamayo, Bilingual Education Teacher 328

Reach Your Learning Goals 330

CHAPTER 11

Socioemotional Development in Middle and Late Childhood 335

Images of Life-Span Development
The Stories of Lafayette and Pharoah: The Tragedy of Poverty and Violence 336

Emotional and Personality Development 337
The Self 337
Emotional Development 339
Moral Development 340
Gender 344

Families 349
Parent-Child Issues 349
Societal Changes in Families 350

Peers 352
Friends 352
Peer Statuses 353
Social Cognition 353
Bullying 354

Schools 355
The Transition to Elementary School 355
Socioeconomic Status and Ethnicity 356
Sociocultural Worlds of Development
The Global Lab 358
Careers in Life-Span Development
James Comer, Child Psychiatrist 359
Cross-Cultural Comparisons of Achievement 359

Reach Your Learning Goals 362

SECTION 6
Adolescence 367

CHAPTER 12

Physical and Cognitive Development in Adolescence 369

Images of Life-Span Development
The Best of Times and the Worst of Times for Today's Adolescents 370

The Nature of Adolescence 370

Puberty and Sexuality 372
Pubertal Changes 372
Adolescent Sexuality 376
Careers in Life-Span Development
Lynn Blankinship, Family and Consumer Science Educator 380

Adolescent Problems and Health 381
Substance Use and Abuse 381
Eating Problems and Disorders 384
Adolescent Health 385

Adolescent Cognition 386
Piaget's Theory 386
Adolescent Egocentrism 388
Information Processing 389

Schools 390
The Transition to Middle or Junior High School 390
Effective Schools for Young Adolescents 391
High School 392
Careers in Life-Span Development
Armando Ronquillo, High School Guidance Counselor/ College Advisor 394
Sociocultural Worlds of Development
Cross-Cultural Comparisons of Secondary Schools 395
Service Learning 396

Reach Your Learning Goals 398

CHAPTER 13

Socioemotional Development in Adolescence 403

Images of Life-Span Development
A 15-Year-Old Girl's Self-Description 404

Self-Esteem and Identity 404
Self-Esteem 404
Identity 405

Families 410
Autonomy and Attachment 410
Parent-Adolescent Conflict 411

Peers 413
Friendships 414
Peer Groups 414
Dating and Romantic Relationships 416

Culture and Adolescent Development 419
Cross-Cultural Comparisons 419
Ethnicity 421
Careers in Life-Span Development
Carola Suarez-Orozco, Lecturer, Researcher, and Co-Director of Immigration Projects 422
Sociocultural Worlds of Development
El Puente and Quantum 423

Adolescent Problems 424
Juvenile Delinquency 424
Careers in Life-Span Development
Rodney Hammond, Health Psychologist 427
Depression and Suicide 428
The Interrelation of Problems and Successful Prevention/Intervention Programs 429
Careers in Life-Span Development
Peter Benson, Director, Search Institute 431

Reach Your Learning Goals 432

SECTION 7
Early Adulthood 437

CHAPTER 14

Physical and Cognitive Development in Early Adulthood 439

Images of Life-Span Development
Florence Griffith Joyner 440

The Transition from Adolescence to Adulthood 440

Becoming an Adult 440
The Transition from High School to College 441
Careers in Life-Span Development
Grace Leaf, College/Career Counselor 444

Physical Development 445
The Peak and Slowdown in Physical Performance 445
Eating and Weight 446

Careers in Life-Span Development

Judith Rodin, University Professor, Health Psychology Researcher, and University President 448

Regular Exercise 449

Substance Abuse 450

Sexuality 454

Sexual Orientation 454

Sexually Transmitted Diseases 456

Forcible Sexual Behavior and Sexual Harassment 458

Cognitive Development 459

Cognitive Stages 459

Creativity 460

Careers in Life-Span Development

Mihaly Csikszentmihalyi, University Professor and Researcher 463

Careers and Work 464

Developmental Changes 464

Personality Types 464

Values and Careers 465

Monitoring the Occupational Outlook 465

Finding the Right Career 467

Work 467

Sociocultural Worlds of Development

Juggling Roles 470

Reach Your Learning Goals 472

CHAPTER 15

Socioemotional Development in Early Adulthood 477

Images of Life-Span Development

Edith, Phil, and Sherry—Searching for Love 478

Continuity and Discontinuity from Childhood to Adulthood 478

Temperament 479

Attachment 480

Attraction, Love, and Close Relationships 481

Attraction 481

The Faces of Love 483

Loneliness 487

Marriage and the Family 489

The Family Life Cycle 489

Marriage 490

Sociocultural Worlds of Development

Marriage Around the World 492

Parental Roles 495

Careers in Life-Span Development

Janis Keyser, Parent Educator 496

The Diversity of Adult Lifestyles 497

Single Adults 497

Cohabiting Adults 498

Divorced Adults 499

Remarried Adults 501

Gay and Lesbian Adults 502

Gender, Relationships, and Self-Development 503

Women's Development 503

Men's Development 504

Reach Your Learning Goals 506

SECTION 8
Middle Adulthood 511

CHAPTER 16

Physical and Cognitive Development in Middle Adulthood 513

Images of Life-Span Development

Time Perspectives 514

Changing Middle Age 514

Physical Development 516

Physical Changes 516

Health and Disease 518

Culture, Personality, Relationships, and Health 519

Sociocultural Worlds of Development

Health Promotion in African Americans, Latinos, Asian Americans, and Native Americans 520

Mortality Rates 522

Sexuality 522

Cognitive Development 525

Intelligence 525

Information Processing 527

Careers, Work, and Leisure 529

Work in Midlife 529

Job Satisfaction 529

Career Challenges and Changes 530

Leisure 530

Religion and Meaning in Life 532

Religion and Adult Lives 532

Religion and Health 532

Careers in Life-Span Development

Alice McNair, Pastoral Counselor 534

Meaning in Life 534

Reach Your Learning Goals 536

CHAPTER 17
Socioemotional Development in Middle Adulthood 541

Images of Life-Span Development
Middle-Age Variations 542

Personality Theories and Development 542
Adult Stage Theories 543
The Life-Events Approach 546
Contexts of Midlife Development 547

Stability and Change 551
Longitudinal Studies 551
Conclusions 553

Close Relationships 554
Love and Marriage at Midlife 554
The Empty Nest and Its Refilling 555
Parenting Conceptions 556
Sibling Relationships and Friendships 556
Intergenerational Relationships 557
Sociocultural Worlds of Development
Intergenerational Relationships in Mexican American Families—The Effects of Immigration and Acculturation 558
Careers in Life-Span Development
Lillian Troll, Professor of Psychology and Life-Span Development and Researcher on Families and Aging Women 559

Reach Your Learning Goals 560

SECTION 9
Late Adulthood 565

CHAPTER 18
Physical Development in Late Adulthood 567

Images of Life-Span Development
Learning to Age Successfully 568

Longevity 569
Life Expectancy and Life Span 569
The Young-Old, the Old-Old, and the Oldest-Old 571
Sociocultural Worlds of Development
Living Longer in Okinawa 572
Biological Theories of Aging 574

The Course of Physical Development in Late Adulthood 576
The Aging Brain 576
Physical Appearance and Movement 578
Sensory Development 579
The Circulatory System 580
The Respiratory System 581
Sexuality 581

Health 582
Health Problems 582
The Robust Oldest-Old 584
Exercise, Nutrition, and Weight 585
Health Treatment 588
Careers in Life-Span Development
Deborah Radomski, Geriatric Nurse 590

Reach Your Learning Goals 592

CHAPTER 19
Cognitive Development in Late Adulthood 597

Images of Life-Span Development *Sister Mary 598*

Cognitive Functioning in Older Adults 598
Multidimensionality and Multidirectionality 598
Education, Work, and Health 604
Use It or Lose It 605
Training Cognitive Skills 606
Careers in Life-Span Development
Sherry Willis, Professor of Human Development and Researcher 606

Work and Retirement 608
Work 608
Retirement in the United States and Other Countries 609
Adjustment to Retirement 609
Sociocultural Worlds of Development
Work and Retirement in Japan, the United States, England, and France 610

Mental Health 611
Depression 611
Dementia, Alzheimer's Disease, and Other Afflictions 612
Careers in Life-Span Development
Jan Weaver, Director of the Alzheimer's Association of Dallas 614
Fear of Victimization, Crime, and Elder Maltreatment 615
Meeting the Mental Health Needs of Older Adults 615

Religion 616

Reach Your Learning Goals 618

CHAPTER 20
Socioemotional Development in Late Adulthood 623

Images of Life-Span Development
Bob Cousy 624

Theories of Socioemotional Development 625
Erikson's Theory 625

Disengagement Theory 627
Activity Theory 627
Socioemotional Selectivity Theory 627
Selective Optimization with Compensation Theory 628
Careers in Life-Span Development
*Laura Carstensen, Psychology Professor and Director of Women's
Studies Program 629*
The Self and Society 631
The Self 631
Older Adults in Society 633
Families and Social Relationships 637
The Aging Couple 637

Grandparenting 637
Friendship 640
Social Support and Social Integration 640
Ethnicity, Gender, and Culture 641
Ethnicity 641
Gender 642
Culture 642
Sociocultural Worlds of Development
Being Female, Ethnic, and Old 643
Successful Aging 644
Reach Your Learning Goals 646

SECTION 10
Endings 651

CHAPTER 21
Death and Grieving 653
Images of Life-Span Development
Princess Diana's Death 654
Defining Death and Life/Death Issues 654
Issues in Determining Death 654
Decisions Regarding Life, Death, and Health Care 655
Death and Sociohistorical, Cultural Contexts 658
Changing Historical Circumstances 658
Death in Different Cultures 658
A Developmental Perspective on Death 660
Causes of Death and Expectations About Death 660
Attitudes Toward Death at Different Points in the Life Span 660
Careers in Life-Span Development
Robert Kastenbaum, Geropsychologist 661

Facing One's Own Death 663
Kübler-Ross' Stages of Dying 663
Perceived Control and Denial 664
The Contexts in Which People Die 665
Coping with the Death of Someone Else 665
Communicating with the Dying Person 666
Grieving 666
Careers in Life-Span Development
Sara Wheeler, Certified College Grief Counselor 667
Making Sense of the World 669
Losing a Life Partner 669
Sociocultural Worlds of Development
*The Family and the Community in Mourning—
The Amish and Traditional Judaism 670*
Forms of Mourning and the Funeral 671
Reach Your Learning Goals 672

Epilogue E-1

Glossary G–1

References R–1

Credits C–1

Name Index N–1

Subject Index S–1

Preface

Preparing a new edition of *Life-Span Development* is both a joy and a challenge. I enjoy revising this text because the feedback from instructors and students on each edition has been consistently enthusiastic. The challenge of revising a successful text is always to continue meeting readers' needs and expectations, while keeping the material fresh and up to date. For the ninth edition of *Life-Span Development*, I have emphasized three kinds of revisions to meet this challenge. I have expanded coverage in key areas, incorporated the latest research and applications, and honed the elements of the book that make learning easier and more engaging. Here I describe the thrust of these changes in general terms. A list of chapter-by-chapter changes subsequently provides more detail.

CHANGES IN THE NINTH EDITION

> "I am a huge fan of John Santrock's style and textbooks. I thought the 8th edition was very good. The 9th edition promises to be even better."
>
> —JAMES REID, *Washington University in St. Louis*

Expanded Coverage of Adult Development, Aging, and Diversity

Instructors have said repeatedly that most life-span texts don't give enough attention to adult development and aging. In the ninth edition, I have significantly modified, expanded, and updated the content on adult development and aging, continuing a process I began some time ago. Examples of added coverage are new sections on stress in early adulthood (chapter 14), work in midlife (chapter 16), and self-esteem in late adulthood (chapter 20).

> "I continue to believe that this book remains the most comprehensive life-span text suitable for undergraduates now available. The major efforts made in the 8th edition to give greater coverage and depth to the 75 percent of the life span spent in adulthood and old age have been continued in this edition. Most other life-span texts still think of development as practically ending by adolescence or early adulthood and treat the remainder of the life course as an appendix "also to be mentioned." John Santrock makes the conscious effort to understand the early parts of life as prologue for the much longer period of adulthood. Thus, he conveys to the reader early-on that we must understand the beginnings of human development in order to understand what happens later."
>
> —K. WARNER SCHAIE, *Pennsylvania State University*

Diversity is another very important aspect of life-span development, one that has come under increasing scrutiny from researchers in recent years. Every effort was made to explore diversity issues in a sensitive manner in every chapter of this edition. In addition to weaving diversity into discussions of life-span topics, I've included a Sociocultural Worlds of Development box in each chapter to highlight a diversity topic related to the chapter's content. New coverage of diversity includes discussions of early childhood education in Japan (chapter 8), attitudes toward corporal punishment in different cultures (chapter 9), the relationship of gender and ethnicity to obesity (chapter 14), and why people live longer in Okinawa (chapter 18).

> "John Santrock seems to have a special manner about issues of culture and diversity. I have many different cultures represented in my classes and I have never had one express any difficulties with the manner in which these issues are discussed."
>
> —BARBA PATTON, *University of Houston–Victoria*

> "I find this text to be the most comprehensive and culturally inclusive text. The coverage of cultural issues allows me, without apology, to include lectures in my course covering cultural issues and human development."
>
> —YVETTE HARRIS, *Miami University*

Research and Applications

Above all, a text on life-span development must include a solid research foundation. This edition of *Life-Span Development* presents the latest, most contemporary research on each period of the human life span and includes more than 800 citations from the past three years. For example, in chapter 5, I discuss new research on the stressful aspects of co-sleeping (Hunsley & Thoman, 2002); chapter 11 presents recent studies on gender differences in brain structure and function in middle childhood (Frederikse & others, 2000; Halpern, 2001; Swaab & others, 2001); and chapter 16 covers new research on hormonal changes in middle-aged men and women (Sommer, 2001), as well as on hormone replacement therapy for menopausal women (Hlatky & others, 2002).

This edition also includes many more graphs and tables of research data, so that students can see how data from research studies can be visually presented. There are more than 60 new figures and tables of data in *Life-Span Development*, ninth edition. Special care was taken to make sure that these illustrations are designed clearly so that students can interpret and understand them.

It is important not only to present the scientific foundations of life-span development to students, but also to demonstrate that research has real-world applications, to include many applied examples of concepts, and to give students a sense that the field of life-span development has personal meaning for them. For example, a new addition to chapter 10 focuses on recommendations for helping children cope effectively with terrorist attacks.

In addition to giving special attention throughout the text to health, parenting, and educational applications, the ninth edition emphasizes careers. Every chapter has one or more Careers in Life-Span Development inserts that profile an individual whose career relates to the chapter's content. Most of these inserts include a photograph of the person at work. In addition, a new Careers in Life-Span appendix that follows chapter 1 describes a number of careers in the education/research, clinical/counseling, medical/nursing/ physical, and families/relationship categories. Numerous Web links provide students with opportunities to read about these careers in greater depth.

> "Careers in Life-Span Development is an excellent and exciting addition to the text. A presentation of career vignettes throughout the text will help spark career interest as well as create an atmosphere of the 'applicability' of the material they are learning."
>
> —CHRISTINE KERRES MALECKI, *Northern Illinois University*

Improved Accessibility and Interest

I strongly believe that students not only should be challenged to study hard and think more deeply and productively about life-span development, but also should be provided with an effective learning system. Instructors and students alike have commented on many occasions about how student-friendly this text is. However, I strive to keep making the learning system better, and I am truly excited about the improvements for this edition.

Now more than ever, students struggle to find the main ideas in their courses, especially in courses like life-span development, which includes so much material. The new learning headings and learning system center on learning goals that, together with the main text headings, keep the key ideas in front of the reader from the beginning to the end of a chapter. Each chapter has no more than six main headings and corresponding learning goals, which are presented side by side on the chapter-opening spread. At the end of each main section of a chapter, the learning goal is repeated in a new feature called Review and Reflect, which prompts students to review the key topics in the section and poses a question to encourage them to think critically about what they have read. At the end of the chapter, under the heading Reach Your Learning Goals, the learning goals guide students through the bulleted chapter review.

In addition to the verbal tools just described, maps that link up with the learning goals are presented at the beginning of each major section in the chapter. At the end of each chapter,

the section maps are assembled into a complete map of the chapter that provides a visual review guide. The complete learning system, including many additional features not mentioned here, is presented later in the Preface in a section titled To the Student.

> "The learning goals were very informative. They provide direction for the readers. The concept maps are very useful."
>
> —TORO SATO, *Shippensburg University*

As important as it is to provide students with an effective learning system, it is imperative to present theories and research at a level that students can understand them and are motivated to learn about them. In each edition of the book, I have carefully rewritten much of the material to make sure it is at a level that challenges students but is also clearly written so they can understand it. I also continually seek better examples of concepts and material that will interest students.

> "The prose is clear, direct, compelling, and authoritative."
>
> —MARIAN UNDERWOOD, *University of Texas at Dallas*

CHAPTER-BY-CHAPTER CHANGES

A number of changes were made in all 21 chapters of *Life-Span Development,* ninth edition. The highlights of these changes include:

CHAPTER 1
Introduction

- Deletion of section on Careers in Life-Span Development from chapter 1 and creation of a careers appendix that now follows chapter 1. The appendix provides considerably expanded coverage of life-span careers and is accompanied by a self-assessment on careers on the book's website. A large number of connections to websites on life-span careers have been added.
- Addition of research descriptions to each section of contemporary concerns: health and well-being, parenting, education, and sociocultural contexts. Each of the research studies described is from the twenty-first century.
- New figure 1.4, illustrating that the main differences in the home environments of children from different ethnic groups are due to poverty rather than ethnicity (Bradley & others, 2001).
- New figure 1.7, showing no differences in happiness across age groups.

> "I like the reorganization of the chapter. It should make teaching easier."
>
> —K. WARNER SCHAIE, *Pennsylvania State University*

CHAPTER 2

The Science of Life-Span Development

- Extensive reworking of section on research methods
- Reorganization of types of research; new headings are Descriptive Research, Correlational Research, and Experimental Research
- New discussion of naturalistic observation research (Crowley & others, 2001) and new figure 2.8, illustrating the results of this research
- Expanded and updated coverage of ethics
- Extensively revised discussion of Vygotsky's theory for better student understanding
- Two new photographs to illustrate how research might produce different results depending on how homogeneous or diverse the sample is

CHAPTER 3
Biological Beginnings

- Important new section, The Collaborative Gene, that discusses why DNA does not determine heredity in a completely independent manner (Gottlieb, 2002)
- Clear, improved discussion of mitosis and meiosis
- New section on genetic imprinting
- Expanded, updated coverage of sex-linked genes
- Updated description of test-tube babies with new recent research studies (Golombok, MacCallum, & Goodman, 2001; Hahn & DiPietro, 2001) and new figure 3.10 on research data
- Expanded, contemporary discussion of the Human Genome Project, including the finding that humans only have about 30,000 to 35,000 genes
- New high-interest figure 3.6: Exploring Your Genetic Future

CHAPTER 4

Prenatal Development and Birth

- Expanded coverage of teratogens in terms of dose, time of exposure, and genetic susceptibility
- Updated research on cocaine babies
- New teratology section on incompatibility of blood types
- New discussion of cultural variations in childbirth
- New coverage of small for date infants and their comparison to preterm infants
- New discussion of low-birthweight infant rates around the world and very up-to-date information about this topic, including new figure 4.7 (UNICEF, 2001).

CHAPTER 5

Physical Development in Infancy

- Considerable expansion of material on the development of the brain, including new figure 5.4 on synaptic pruning
- Extensive research updating of breast-feeding
- New figure 5.8 on plasticity in the human brain; also new, the fascinating story of Michael Rehbein's loss of his left hemisphere and how his right hemisphere started taking over the functions of speech
- New research on the stressful aspects of co-sleeping (Hunsley & Thoman, 2002)
- Expanded discussion of cultural variations in infants' motor skills

CHAPTER 6
Cognitive Development in Infancy

- New section on infants' understanding of physical reality, including new figure 6.3 on infants' knowledge of cause-and-effect
- New figure 6.5, illustrating the concepts of habituation and dishabituation with seven-hour-old infants
- Expanded, updated coverage of infant memory that focuses on Patricia Bower's recent research
- New section on language production and language comprehension

- New section on language sounds, including Patricia Kuhl's research; also new figure 6.7 on Kuhl's research showing EEG recording of a baby in her research on the transition from a universal to a specialized linguist
- New figure 6.9, summarizing language milestones in infancy
- New discussion of link between level of maternal language and vocabulary growth in infants, including new figure 6.10

> "This chapter is a very good one; excellent."
>
> —JULIA RUX, *Georgia Perimeter College*

CHAPTER 7
Socioemotional Development in Infancy

- New section on social referencing
- New section on self-regulation of emotion and coping in infancy
- New discussion of separation protest, including new figure 7.1, showing how separation protest peaks between 13 and 15 months of age in four different cultures
- Discussion of contextual influences on self-regulation of emotion in infancy
- Expanded coverage of the contemporary view of temperament in terms of positive affect and approach, negative affectivity, and effortful control (self-regulation)
- New section on gender, culture, and temperament including recent theory and research (Putnam, Sanson, & Rothbart, 2002)
- Expanded discussion of culture and attachment, including new figure 7.5 on infant attachment in the United States, Germany, and Japan

> "The sections on temperament and attachment are very good. In general, this chapter is very strong."
>
> —ALAN FOGEL, *University of Utah*

CHAPTER 8
Physical and Cognitive Development in Early Childhood

- Expansion of discussion on changes in the brain in early childhood, including recent research on neural circuits (Krimel & Golman-Rakic, 2001), and new figure 8.2 on the prefrontal cortex's role in attention and memory
- Expanded coverage of handedness, including new material on the origin and development of handedness, the brain and language, and links of handedness to other abilities
- Addition of recent research on the effects of environmental tobacco smoke on children's respiratory problems and levels of vitamin C (Maninno & others, 2001; Strauss, 2001)

- New figure 8.5, showing the main causes of death in young children in the United States (National Vital Statistics Reports, 2001)
- New discussion of recent study comparing children from a traditional school and children from a Vygotsky-based collaborative school (Matusov, Bell, & Rogoff, 2001)
- New study showing a link between speed of processing information and children's math and reading achievement (Hitch, Towse, & Hutton, 2001)
- Clearer presentation of theory of mind and new figure 8.15 on developmental changes in false belief (Wellman, Cross, & Watson, 2001)
- Expanded coverage of language development in young children

> "This is a textbook that I have used for a number of years, and I continue to use it because it is written in an approachable way and its heart is in the right place."
>
> —JEAN BERKO GLEASON, *Boston University*

CHAPTER 9
Socioemotional Development in Early Childhood

- New section on the development of self-conscious emotions, such as pride, shame, and guilt
- New section on co-parenting
- New section on punishment and discipline in discussion of parenting, including cross-cultural comparisons of punishment, and new figure 9.5 on recent cross-cultural research
- New figure 9.7 on Hetherington and Kelly's (2002) research on the effects of divorce on children's adjustment
- Extensive revision and updating of culture, ethnicity, and families, including recent research (Coll & Pachter, 2002; McAdoo, 2002)
- New Sociocultural Worlds of Development box, Acculturation and Ethnic Minority Parenting, based on Cynthia Garcia Coll and Lee Patcher's ideas
- New discussion of recent longitudinal study on the effects of watching educational TV programs on children's achievement and aggression (Anderson & others, 2001).

> "The coverage in this chapter is excellent and the new work on punishment and TV are welcome updates."
>
> —ROSS PARKE, *University of California–Riverside*

CHAPTER 10
Physical and Cognitive Development in Middle and Late Childhood

- Recent data on the percentage increase of U.S. children who are overweight (NHANES, 2001)

- New figure 10.1, showing the dramatic decrease in the percentage of children taking daily P.E. classes in the U.S. from 1969 to 1999 (Health Management Resources, 2001)
- New research on Ritalin, behavior management, and ADHD (Swanson & others, 2001)
- Updated, expanded discussion of whether there is evidence for general intelligence (Brody, 2001)
- Updated coverage of language development
- Substantial update of reading issues, including new figure 10.10 on the link between daily reading time and reading achievement
- Expanded coverage of bilingual education, including Kenji Hakuta's (2000) research on how long it takes for language minority students to learn to read and speak English
- New figure 10.11, showing the relation of age of arrival in the United States with grammar proficiency

"Overall, I think this is an excellent chapter. . . . All of the important topics in this area are covered and the topics are well-balanced."

—TORU SATO, *Shippensburg University*

CHAPTER 11
Socioemotional Development in Middle and Late Childhood

- New section on coping with stress, including recommendations on how to help children cope effectively with terrorist attacks, such as 9/11/01 (Gurwitch & others, 2001; La Greca & others, 2002)
- New material on gender differences in brain structure and function (Frederikse & others, 2001; Halpern, 2001; Swaab & others, 2001)
- New data presented from the National Assessment of Educational Progress (2001) on gender and science and gender and reading scores, including new figure 11.3 on reading
- Updated coverage of stepfamilies, including Hetherington's most recent findings (Hetherington & Kelly, 2002)
- New graph (figure 11.5) of bullying behaviors in the United States (Nansel & others, 2001)
- New graph of data (figure 11.6) of Stevenson's research on Asian and U.S. children's math achievement

"Very well done with extremely current reference material."

—MYRA MARCUS, *Florida Gulf Coast University*

CHAPTER 12
Physical and Cognitive Development in Adolescence

- Added recent cross-cultural data on the age of initiation of intercourse (Singh & others, 2000)

- New research on pathways to adversity in early childbearers (Jaffe, 2002)
- Revised and updated coverage of adolescent drug use (Johnston, O'Malley, & Bachman, 2001)
- New figure 12.7, Ecstasy and the adolescent's brain, including two brain scans, one of a normal adolescent brain, the other of an adolescent brain under the influence of Ecstasy
- New studies on links between parents, peers, and drug use in adolescence (National Center on Addiction and Substance Abuse, 2001; Simons-Morton & others, 2001). Also new longitudinal study focused on early childhood predictors of early onset of substance abuse in 10- to 12-year-olds (Kaplow & others, 2002)
- New overview of research on eating disorders in adolescents with descriptions of a number of recent studies (Dowda & others, 2001; Field & others, 2001; Graber & Brooks-Gunn, 2001), including new figure 12.8 on the dramatic increase in obesity in adolescence in the last 40 years
- New study on factors involved in binge eating in adolescent girls (Stice, Presnell, & Spangler, 2002)
- New graph (figure 12.9) on U.S. high school dropouts from different ethnic groups
- New section on how to improve U.S. high schools (Dornbusch & Kaufman, 2001; National Commission on the High School Senior Year, 2001)

"This chapter is so well written and the illustrations are so effective that I cannot add any suggestions to make it stronger."

—BARBA PATTON, *University of Houston–Victoria*

CHAPTER 13
Socioemotional Development in Adolescence

- New section on self-esteem, highlighting the decline in self-esteem during adolescence, especially for girls, including new figure 13.1 (Robins & others, in press)
- New discussion of gender differences in autonomy granting by parents based on recent research (Bumpus, Crouter, & McHale, 2001)
- Recent research comparing parent-adolescent conflict, autonomy, and peer orientation in Japanese and U.S. youth
- New research showing the link between active parental monitoring and guidance and more positive adolescent peer relations and lower drug use (Mounts, 2002)
- New figure 13.5 on developmental changes in the age of onset of romantic activity (Buhrmester, 2001)
- New coverage of research on dating and romantic involvement of Latinas (Raffaelli & Ontai, in press)
- New research on Fast Track, a intervention designed to prevent adolescent problems (The Conduct Problems Prevention Research Group, 2002)
- New research by Richard Savin-Williams (2001) showing that earlier statements about estimates of suicide by gay youth were exaggerated

- New research showing links between degree of acculturation and adolescent problems (Gonzales & others, in press; Roosa & others, 2002)

"The new additions to this chapter are excellent."

—Ross Parke, *University of California–Riverside*

CHAPTER 14
Physical and Cognitive Development in Early Adulthood

- Expanded discussion of emerging adulthood, including cross-cultural comparisons, and new figure 14.1 on self-perceptions of adult status
- Extensive new research on adapting to college, including stress in college, what makes college students very happy, the role of ethnicity and gender in health, and the roles of optimism and family factors in adapting to college (Brisette, Scheier, & Carver, 2002; Courtenay, McCreary, & Merighi, 2002; Diener & Seligman, 2002; Sax & others, 2001)
- Recent research on alcohol use during college and new coverage of cultural variations in alcohol use (Wechsler & others, 2002) and new figure 14.7 on the decline in substance use after college (Bachman & others, 2002)
- New figure 14.4 on the role of leptin in obesity
- New section on gender, ethnicity, and obesity
- Completely updated discussion of dual-career couples, including recent data on the increased time spent by men in family tasks; new figure 14.14 (Hyde & Barnett, 2001)

"This chapter rates an 'A.' The text covers the material very well. . . . The topics are most interesting and insightful. . . . The clarity is just what you would expect from John Santrock. . . . I have reviewed almost every other text available for this course and have not found one that I think would be comparable to John Santrock's text."

—Barba Patton, *University of Houston–Victoria*

CHAPTER 15
Socioemotional Development in Early Adulthood

- New figure 15.2 on the effects that mere exposure to someone has on the extent to which the person is liked
- New study on women's and men's views of love (Fehr & Broughton, 2001)
- Completely revamped discussion of loneliness, including new section on loneliness and technology
- New national survey on young adults' perceptions of marriage (Whitehead & Popenoe, 2001)
- New discussion of the anxiety that many childless, highly successful women have (Hewlett, 2002)

- New coverage of Hetherington's recent research on the six pathways that divorced adults follow (Hetherington & Kelly, 2002) and new discussion of recommended strategies for divorced adults

"This chapter covers a wider range of topics than some other texts and I consider that a strength."

—Cynthia Reed, *Tarrant County College*

CHAPTER 16
Physical and Cognitive Development in Middle Adulthood

- New coverage of recent research suggesting that many people in their sixties and even seventies say that they are in middle age (Lachman, Maier, & Budner, 2000; National Council on Aging, 2000)
- New discussion of George Vaillant's recent presentation of new data from his longitudinal study of aging and new figure 16.1 based on this study that focuses on the link between characteristics in middle age and successful aging at 75 to 80 years of age
- New figure 16.2 on the relation of age and gender to cardiovascular disease and new section on lungs, including figure 16.3 on the relation of lung capacity to age and cigarette smoking
- New figure 16.4 on self-rated health at different points in adulthood (National Center for Health Statistics, 1999)
- New research on links between personality factors and health in a large longitudinal study (Aldwin & others, 2001)
- Updated, revised discussion of menopause and hormone replacement therapy
- New discussion of researcher Denise Park's (2001) view on why working memory declines in middle age
- New section on work in midlife

"I was very impressed with the quality of this chapter. . . . It is well conceived, well-written, and attractive."

—James Birren, *University of California, Los Angeles*

CHAPTER 17
Socioemotional Development in Middle Adulthood

- New discussion of Vaillant's (2002) longitudinal study showing a link between generativity in middle age and marital quality at 75 to 80 years of age
- Discussion of recent longitudinal study of generativity and identity certainty from the thirties through the fifties (Stewart, Ostrove, & Helson, 2001), including two new figures, figure 17.1 and figure 17.2

- Updated information about the women in the Mills College study conducted by Ravenna Helson, who most recently were assessed in their fifties
- New research on link between earlier support by parents and later support of aging parents by adult children (Silverstein & others, 2002)
- New description of six characteristics in midlife, including purpose in life, autonomy, and environmental mastery, based on Ryff and Keyes' (1998) research, including new figure 17.5
- New discussion of recent study on gender differences in personality traits in 26 countries (Costa, Terracciano, & McCrae, 2001)
- Updated and expanded conclusions about stability and change in personality development in middle adulthood, including the view of Caspi and Roberts (2001) that stability increases in the fifties and sixties

"Both chapters 16 and 17 are great. . . . The coverage is very good."

—JAMES REID, *Washington University*

CHAPTER 18
Physical Development in Late Adulthood

- New Sociocultural Worlds of Development box on living longer in Okinawa, including new figure 18.2 (Willcox, Willcox, & Suzuki, 2002)
- New figure 18.4 on the decrease in brain lateralization in older adults based on recent research (Cabeza, 2002)
- New research from the McArthur Studies of Successful Aging on factors linked with improved physical functioning in older adults (Seeman & Chen, 2002)
- New discussion of ethnicity and U.S. death rates (Centers for Disease Control and Prevention, 2002)
- Recent data on the percentage of men from 65 to 80 and over 80 who have erection difficulties (Butler & Lewis, 2002)
- Expanded, updated discussion of calorie restriction and longevity (Goto & others, 2002; Johannes, 2002)
- Extensive updating of research on exercise and aging (Singh, 2002)
- New discussion of general slowdown in central nervous system functioning
- New dramatic figure 18.5 showing new brain cells generated in an adult male as a consequence of exercise and an enriched environment
- New research on the link between B vitamins and cognitive performance in older adults (Calvaresi & Bryan, 2001)

"In many ways, John Santrock has successfully translated the data on aging into terms that will be understandable to the undergraduate and has done an excellent job of presenting material that focuses on positive images of aging."

—SUSAN WHITBOURNE, *University of Massachusetts, Amherst*

CHAPTER 19
Cognitive Development in Late Adulthood

- New section on aging and attention that focuses on selective attention, divided attention, and sustained attention
- New section on prospective memory and the complexity of age changes involved
- New figure 19.2 on the relation of age to speed of processing as measured by reaction time and new research on the role of exercise in preventing cognitive decline in older adults (Yaffe & others, 2001)
- New discussion of longitudinal study on engaging in stimulating cognitive activities and its link to a lower incidence of Alzheimer's disease (Wilson & others, 2002)
- New research on the link between chronic mild depression in older adults and reduced immune system functioning (McGuire, Kiecolt-Glaser, & Glaser, 2002)
- New research on the link between gender, depression, and aging from 50 to 80, including new figure 19.5 (Barefoot & others, 2001)
- Discussion of new research on religiosity and church attendance in the last year of life (Idler, Stanislav, & Hays, 2001)

"This chapter provides a good overview of major issues and findings."

—JOANN MONTEPARE, *Emerson College*

CHAPTER 20
Socioemotional Development in Late Adulthood

- New figure 20.3 based on national study of changes in positive and negative emotions in older and younger adults
- New section on self-esteem, including discussion of recent large-scale study of developmental changes in self-esteem and new figure 20.5 (Robins & others, 2002)
- New section on changes in self-acceptance across the adult years, including new figure 20.6
- New section on personal control, highlighting Heckhausen's theory and research on primary and secondary control strategies and new figure 20.7 to illustrate developmental changes in these processes across the life span
- New material on links of depression and lower life satisfaction to not having a close friend as an older adult (Antonucci, Lansford, & Akiyama, 2001)

"This chapter has good coverage of major issues."

—JOANN MONTEPARE, *Emerson College*

CHAPTER 21
Death and Grieving

- New research on the economic consequences of widowhood in the U.S. and Germany (Hungerford, 2001)
- New research on the role of psychological and religious factors in the well-being of older adults after the death of a spouse (Fry, 2001)
- New discussion of palliative care (Chochinov, 2002)
- Update on Oregon's active euthanasia through 2001
- Increased coverage of end-of-death issues (Wilson & Truman, 2002)

> *"This chapter is another 'A.' It is very insightful about the last stanza of human life."*
>
> —BARBA PATTON, *University of Houston–Victoria*

ACKNOWLEDGMENTS

I very much appreciate the support and guidance provided to me by many people at McGraw-Hill. Steve Debow, President, and Thalia Dorwick, Editor-in-Chief, have been truly outstanding in their administration of the social sciences area of McGraw-Hill Higher Education. Steve Rutter, Publisher, has brought a wealth of publishing knowledge and vision to bear on improving this book. This is the second edition of *Life-Span Development* that Rebecca Hope has been the editor. She is a wonderful editor who has made very competent decisions and provided valuable advice about many aspects of the ninth edition. Judith Kromm, Senior Developmental Editor, orchestrated important changes in the manuscript. The new edition has considerably benefited also from the energy, organization, and wisdom of Kate Russillo, Editorial Assistant. Melissa Caughlin, Marketing Manager, has contributed in numerous creative ways to this book, as did Chris Hall, the former Marketing Manager. Marilyn Rothenberger was a superb project manager and Bea Sussman did a stellar job in copyediting the book.

EXPERT CONSULTANTS

Life-span development has become an enormous, complex field and no single author can possibly be an expert in all areas of the field. To solve this problem, beginning with the sixth edition, I have sought the input of leading experts in many different areas of life-span development. This tradition continues in the ninth edition. The experts have provided me with detailed recommendations on new research to include for every period of the life span.

The panel of experts who contributed to the ninth edition literally is a who's who register for the field of life-span development. Their photographs and biographies appear on pages xxvii through xxix. Here are the names and areas of expertise of those individuals, whose invaluable feedback and evaluations I gratefully acknowledge:

K. Warner Schaie, *Pennsylvania State University* One of the architects of the field of adulthood and aging

James Birren, *University of California, Los Angeles* A major contributor to the field of aging

Yvette R. Harris, *Miami University (Ohio)* An expert on the effects of ethnicity on cognitive, intellectual, academic, and occupational development

Ross Parke, *University of California at Riverside* One of the world's leading authorities on family processes and children's socioemotional development

Jean Berko Gleason, *Boston University* One of the world's leading experts on children's language development

Scott Miller, *University of Florida* An authority on children's cognitive development

Carolyn Saarni, *Sonoma State University* An expert on children's emotional development

Alan Fogel, *University of Utah* A leading figure in the study of infant development

Susan Whitbourne, *University of Massachusetts, Amherst* An expert on adult development and aging

James Reid, *Washington University* An expert on middle adulthood and aging

Marian Underwood, *University of Texas at Dallas* An expert on peer relations and socioemotional development

Gilbert Gottlieb, *University of North Carolina* A leading figure in biological foundations of development

Barba Patton, *University of Houston–Victoria* An expert on education

Bert Hayslip, *University of North Texas* An expert on the topics of death and grieving

GENERAL TEXT REVIEWERS

I also owe special gratitude to the instructors teaching the life-span course who have provided detailed feedback about the book. Many of the changes in *Life-Span Development*, ninth edition, are based on their feedback. In this regard, I thank these individuals:

Pre-Revision Reviewers

Leslie Ault, *Hostos Community College–CUNY*
Dana Davidson, *University of Hawaii at Manoa*
Marian S. Harris, *University of Illinois at Chicago*
Donna Henderson, *Wake Forest University*
Donna Horbury, *Appalachian State University*
Steven J. Kohn, *Nazareth College*
Christine Malecki, *Northern Illinois University*
Robert McLaren, *California State University at Fullerton*
Leslee Pollina, *Southeast Missouri State University*

Cynthia Reed, *Tarrant County College–Northeast Campus*
Edythe Schwartz, *California State University at Sacramento*

Ninth Edition Reviewers

John Biondo, *Community College of Allegheny County*
Michelle Boyer-Pennington, *Middle Tennessee State University*
Andrea Clements, *East Tennessee State University*
Caroline Gould, *Eastern Michigan University*
Tom Gray, *Laredo Community College*
Michele Gregoire, *University of Florida–Gainesville*
Gary Gute, *University of Northern Iowa*
Derek Isaacowitz, *Brandeis University*
Christina Jose-Kampfner, *Eastern Michigan University*
Amanda Kowal, *University of Missouri*
Myra Marcus, *Florida Gulf Coast University*
Joann Montepare, *Emerson College*
Kimberley Howe Norris, *Cape Fear Community College*
Laura Overstreet, *Tarrant County College–Northeast*
Julia Rux, *Georgia Perimeter College*
Gayla Sanders, *Community College of Baltimore County–Essex*
Toru Sato, *Shippensburg University*
Lisa Scott, *University of Minnesota*
Collier Summers, *Florida Community College*
Debbie Tindell, *Wilkes University*

EXPERT CONSULTANTS FOR PREVIOUS EDITIONS

Beginning with the sixth edition, expert consultants have provided extremely valuable feedback to me. These leading figures in the field of life-span development served as expert consultants on editions 6 through 8: **Toni C. Antonucci,** *University of Michigan, Ann Arbor;* **Paul Baltes,** *Max Planck Institute for Human development;* **Diana Baumrind,** *University of California, Berkeley;* **Carol Beal,** *University of Massachusetts at Amherst;* **Marc H. Bornstein,** *National Institute of Child Health & Development;* **Sue Bredekamp,** *National Association for the Education of Young Children;* **Urie Bronfenbrenner,** *Cornell University;* **Rosalind Charlesworth,** *Weber State University;* **Florence Denmark,** *Pace University;* **Joseph Durlack,** *Loyola University;* **Glen Elder,** *University of North Carolina, Chapel Hill;* **Tiffany Field,** *University of Miami;* **Julia Graber,** *Columbia University;* **Sandra Graham,** *University of California, Los Angeles;* **Jane Halonen,** *Alverno College;* **Algea O. Harrison-Hale,** *Oakland University;* **Craig Hart,** *Brigham Young University;* **Ravenna Helson,** *University of California, Berkeley;* **Cigdem Kagitcibasi,** *Koc University (Turkey);* **Robert Kastenbaum,** *Arizona State University;* **Gisela Labouvie-Vief,** *Wayne State University;* **Barry M. Lester,** *Women and Infant's Hospital;* **Jean M. Mandler,** *University of California—San Diego;* **James Marcia,** *Simon Fraser University;* **Phyllis Moen,** *Cornell University;* **K. Warner Schaie,** *Pennsylvania State University;* **Jan Sinnott,** *Towson State University;* **Margaret Beale Spencer,** *University of Pennsylvania;* **Ross A. Thompson,** *University of Nebraska—Lincoln.*

REVIEWERS OF PREVIOUS EDITIONS

I also remain indebted to the following individuals who reviewed previous editions and whose suggestions have been carried forward into the current edition: **Patrick K. Ackles,** *Michigan State University;* **Berkeley Adams,** *Jamestown Community College;* **Joanne M. Alegre,** *Yavajai College;* **Gary L. Allen,** *University of South Carolina;* **Lilia Allen,** *Charles County Community College;* **Susan E. Allen,** *Baylor University;* **Doreen Arcus,** *University of Massachusetts, Lowell;* **Frank R. Ashbury,** *Valdosta State College;* **Renee L. Babcock,** *Central Michigan University;* **Daniel R. Bellack,** *Trident Technical College;* **Helen E. Benedict,** *Baylor University;* **Alice D. Beyrent,** *Hesser College;* **James A. Blackburn,** *University of Wisconsin, Madison;* **Stephanie Blecharczyk,** *Keene State College;* **Belinda Blevin-Knabe,** *University of Arkansas, Little Rock;* **Karyn Mitchell Boutin,** *Massasoit Community College;* **Donald Bowers,** *Community College of Philadelphia;* **Saundra Y. Boyd,** *Houston Community College;* **Michelle Boyer-Pennington,** *Middle Tennessee State University;* **Ann Brandt-Williams,** *Glendale Community College;* **Jack Busky,** *Harrisburg Area Community College;* **Joan B. Cannon,** *University of Lowell;* **Jeri Carter,** *Glendale Community College;* **Vincent Castranovo,** *Community College of Philadelphia;* **Ginny Chappeleau,** *Muskingum Area Technical College;* **M. A. Christenberry,** *Augusta College;* **Meredith Cohen,** *University of Pittsburg;* **Diane Cook,** *Gainesville College;* **Ava Craig,** *Sacramento City College;* **Kathleen Crowley-Long,** *College of Saint Rose;* **Cynthia Crown,** *Xavier University;* **Diane Davis,** *Bowie State University;* **Tom L. Day,** *Weber State University;* **Doreen DeSantio,** *West Chester University;* **Jill De Villiers,** *Smith College;* **Darryl M. Dietrich,** *College of St. Scholastica;* **Mary B. Eberly,** *Oakland University;* **Margaret Sutton Edmonds,** *University of Massachusetts, Boston;* **Martha M. Ellis,** *Collin County Community College;* **Richard Ewy,** *Penn State University;* **Dan Fawaz,** *Georgia Perimeter College;* **Shirley Feldman,** *Stanford University;* **Roberta Ferra,** *University of Kentucky;* **Linda E. Flickinger,** *St. Claire Community College;* **Lynne Andreozzi Fontaine,** *Community College of Rhode Island;* **Tom Frangicetto,** *Northhampton Community College;* **Kathleen Corrigan Fuhs,** *J. Sargeant Reynolds Community College;* **J. Steven Fulks,** *Utah State University;* **Cathy Furlong,** *Tulsa Junior College;* **Duwayne Furman,** *Western Illinois University;* **John Gat,** *Humboldt State University;* **Marvin Gelman,** *Montgomery County College;* **Rebecca J. Glare,** *Weber State College;* **Jean Berko Gleason,** *Boston University;* **David Goldstein,** *Temple University;* **Judy Goodell,** *National University;* **Mary Ann Goodwyn,** *Northeast Louisiana University;* **Peter C. Gram,** *Pensacola Junior College;* **Dan Grangaard,** *Austin Community College;* **Michael Green,** *University of North Carolina;* **Rea Gubler,** *Southern Utah University;* **Laura Hanish,** *Arizona State University;* **Ester Hanson,** *Prince George's Community College;* **Amanda W. Harrist,** *Oklahoma State University;* **Robert Heavilin,** *Greater Hartford Community College;* **Debra Hollister,** *Valencia Community College;* **Heather Holmes-Lonergan,** *Metropolitan State College of Denver;* **Ramona O. Hopkins,** *Brigham Young University;* **Susan Horton,** *Mesa Community College;* **Sharon C. Hott,** *Allegany College of Maryland;* **Stephen Hoyer,** *Pittsburgh State University;*

Kathleen Day Hulbert, *University of Massachusetss, Lowell;* **Kathryn French Iroz,** *Utah Valley State College;* **Erwin Janek,** *Henderson State University;* **James Jasper-Jacobsen,** *Indiana University—Purdue;* **Ursula Joyce,** *St. Thomas Aquinas College;* **Seth Kalichman,** *Loyola University;* **Barbara Kane,** *Indiana State University;* **Kevin Keating,** *Broward Community College;* **James L. Keeney,** *Middle Georgia College;* **Elinor Kinarthy,** *Rio Hondo College;* **Karen Kirkendall,** *Sangamon State University;* **A. Klingner,** *Northwest Community College;* **Jane Krump,** *North Dakota State College of Science;* **Joseph C. LaVoie,** *University of Nebraska at Omaha;* **Jean Hill Macht,** *Montgomery County Community College;* **Salvador Macias,** *University of South Carolina—Sumter;* **Karen Macrae,** *University of South Carolina;* **Kathy Manuel,** *Bossier Parish Community College;* **Allan Mayotte,** *Riverland Community College;* **Susan McClure,** *Westmoreland Community College;* **Dorothy H. McDonald,** *Sandhills Community College;* **Robert C. McGinnis,** *Ancilla College;* **Clara McKinney,** *Barstow College;* **Sharon McNeeley,** *Northeastern Illinois University;* **Heather E. Metcalfe,** *University of Windsor;* **Karla Miley,** *Black Hawk College;* **Jessica Miller,** *Mesa State College;* **Teri M. Miller-Schwartz,** *Milwaukee Area Technical College;* **David B. Mitchell,** *Loyola University;* **Martin D. Murphy,** *University of Akron;* **Malinda Muzi,** *Community College of Philadelphia;* **Gordon K. Nelson,** *Pennsylvania State University;* **Michael Newton,** *Sam Houston State University;* **Beatrice Norrie,** *Mount Royal College;* **Jean O'Neil,** *Boston College;* **Pete Peterson,** *Johnson County Community College;* **Richard Pierce,** *Pennsylvania State University—Altoona;* **David Pipes,** *Caldwell Community College;* **Robert Poresky,** *Kansas State University;* **Christopher Quarto,** *Middle Tennessee State University;* **Bob Rainey,** *Florida Community College;* **Nancy Rankin,** *University of New England;* **H. Ratner,** *Wayne State University;* **Russell Riley,** *Lord Fairfax Community College;* **Mark P. Rittman,** *Cuyahoga Community College;* **Clarence Romeno,** *Riverside Community College;* **Paul Roodin,** *SUNY—Oswego;* **Ron Russac,** *University of North Florida;* **Nancy Sauerman,** *Kirkwood Community College;* **Cynthia Scheibe,** *Ithica College;* **Robert Schell,** *SUNY—Oswego;* **Owen Sharkey,** *University of Prince Edward Island;* **Elisabeth Shaw,** *Texarkana College;* **Susan Nakayama Siaw,** *California State Polytechnical University;* **Vicki Simmons,** *Univeristy of Victoria;* **Gregory Smith,** *University of Maryland;* **Jon Snodgrass,** *California State University—LA;* **Donald Stanley,** *North Dallas Community College;* **Jean A. Steitz,** *The University of Memphis;* **Barbara Thomas,** *National University;* **Stacy D. Thompson,** *Oklahoma State University;* **Stephen Truhon,** *Winston-Salem State University;* **James Turcott,** *Kalamazoo Valley Community College;* **Gaby Vandergiessen,** *Fairmount State College;* **Stephen Werba,** *The Community College of Baltimore County—Catonsville;* **B. D. Whetstone,** *Birmingham Southern College;* **Nancy C. White,** *Reynolds Community College;* **Lyn W. Wickelgren,** *Metropolitan State College;* **Ann M. Williams,** *Luzerne County Community College;* **Myron D. Williams,** *Great Lakes Bible College;* **Linda B. Wilson,** *Quincy College.*

SUPPLEMENTS

The ninth edition of *Life-Span Development* is accompanied by a comprehensive and fully integrated array of supplemental materials, both print and electronic, written specifically for instructors and students of life-span development. In addition, a variety of generic supplements are available to further aid in the teaching and learning of life-span development.

For the Instructor

Once again, based on comprehensive and extensive feedback from instructors, we spent considerable time and effort in expanding and improving the ancillary materials.

Instructor's Manual *Christine Malecki* This comprehensive manual provides a variety of useful tools for both seasoned instructors and those new to the life-span development course. The instructor's manual provides these tools, all of which are tied to the text's Learning Goals as appropriate:

- A focused introductory section on teaching life-span development. This section covers helpful material for new instructors, including course-planning ideas, teaching tips, and teaching resources.
- A Total Teaching Package Outline begins each chapter. It features a fully integrated outline to help instructors better use the many resources for the course. Most of the supplementary materials offered in conjunction with *Life-Span Development,* ninth edition, are represented in this outline and have been correlated to the main concepts in each chapter.
- Lecture suggestions, classroom activities, out-of-class activities, research projects, and critical thinking multiple-choice and essay exercises, all of which provide answers where appropriate.
- Classroom activities now provide logistics for required materials, such as accompanying handouts, varying group sizes, and time needed for completion.
- Greatly expanded chapter outlines and personal application projects where students can apply development topics to their own lives.
- Comprehensive transparency, film, and video resources, updated URLs for useful Internet sites, and chapter maps derived from the textbook that can be used for lecture aids.

Printed Test Bank *Angela Sadowski* This comprehensive Test Bank has once again been extensively revised to include over 2,400 multiple-choice and short-answer/brief essay questions for the text's 21 chapters. Each multiple-choice item is classified as factual, conceptual, or applied, as defined by Benjamin Bloom's taxonomy of educational objectives. New to this edition, each test question is now keyed to a chapter learning goal, and the test bank notes which learning goal each item addresses. In response to customer feedback, this Test Bank also provides page references that indicate where in the text the answer to each item can be found.

PowerPoint Slide Presentations The chapter-by-chapter PowerPoint lectures for this edition integrate the text's learning goals, and provide key text material and illustrations, as well as additional illustrations and images not found in the textbook. These presentations are designed to be useful in both small- and large-lecture settings, and are easily tailored to suit an individual instructor's lectures.

Computerized Test Bank on CD-ROM The computerized test bank contains all of the questions in the printed test bank and can be used in both Windows and Macintosh platforms. This CD-ROM provides a fully functioning editing feature that enables instructors to integrate their own questions, scramble items, and modify questions.

The McGraw-Hill Developmental Psychology Image Bank This set of 200 full-color images was developed using the best selection of our human development art and tables and is available online for both instructors and students on the text's Online Learning Center.

Online Learning Center The extensive website designed specifically to accompany Santrock, *Life-Span Development,* ninth edition, offers an array of resources for both instructor and student. For instructors, the website includes a full set of PowerPoint Presentations, hotlinks for the text's topical web links that appear in margins and for the Taking It to the Net exercises that appear at the end of each chapter. These resources and more can be found by logging on to the website at http://www.mhhe.com/santrockld9.

Annual Editions–Developmental Psychology Published by Dushkin/McGraw-Hill, this is a collection of articles on topics related to the latest research and thinking in human development. These editions are updated annually and contain helpful features including a topic guide, an annotated table of contents, unit overviews, and a topical index. An Instructor's Guide containing testing materials is also available.

Sources: Notable Selections in Human Development This volume presents a collection of more than 40 articles, book excerpts, and research studies that have shaped the study of human development and our contemporary understanding of it. The selections are organized topically around major areas of study within human development. Each selection is preceded by a headnote that establishes the relevance of the article or study and provides biographical information about the author.

Taking Sides This debate-style reader is designed to introduce students to controversial viewpoints on the field's most crucial issues. Each issue is carefully framed for the student, and the pro and con essays represent the arguments of leading scholars and commentators in their fields. An Instructor's Guide containing testing material is available.

For the Student

Student Study Guide *Barba Patton* The revised Study Guide provides a complete introduction for students on how best to use each of the various study aids plus invaluable strategies on setting goals, benefiting from class, reading for learning, taking tests, and memory techniques in the section "Being an Excellent Student." Each Study Guide chapter begins with an outline of the chapter that also directs students to additional resources available for the study of specific topics or concepts. Resources referenced include the text's Online Learning Center and Student CD-ROM. The Study Guide also now thoroughly integrates the learning goals provided in each text chapter. The self-test sections contain multiple-choice questions and comprehensive essays with suggested answers, all of which are keyed to the learning goals. Self-tests also include matching sets on key people found in the text and word scramblers on key terms found in the text. Finally, the Study Guide also includes out-of-class projects such as personal application projects and Internet exercises that complement the revised student research projects and allow for more effective student learning.

Interactive CD-ROM for Students This user-friendly CD-ROM gives students an opportunity to test their comprehension of the course material. Prepared specifically to accompany Santrock, *Life-Span Development,* ninth edition, this CD-ROM provides 25 multiple-choice questions for each chapter to help students further test their understanding of key concepts. Feedback is provided for each question's answer. In addition, the CD-ROM provides a Learning Assessment questionnaire to help students discover which type of learner they are, of the three types covered in the program.

Online Learning Center The extensive website designed specifically to accompany Santrock, *Life-Span Development,* ninth edition, offers an array of resources for instructors and students. For students, the website includes interactive quizzing and exercises as well as hotlinks for the text's topical web links that appear in the margins and for the *Taking It to the Net* exercises that appear at the end of each chapter. An important new feature in this edition is the inclusion of many self-assessments related to chapter topics. These resources and more can be found by logging on to the website at http://www.mhhe.com/santrockld9.

Guide to Life-Span Development for Future Educators and **Guide to Life-Span Development for Future Nurses** These new course supplements help students apply the concepts of human development to education. They contain information, exercises, and sample tests designed to help students prepare for certification and understand human development from a professional perspective.

Resources for Improving Human Development This informative booklet provides descriptions and contact information for organizations and agencies that can provide helpful information, advice, and support related to particular problems or issues in life-span development. Recommended books and journals are also described and included. The booklet is organized by chronological order of the periods of the life span.

Expert Consultants

K. Warner Schaie

K. Warner Schaie was one of the pioneers who created and shaped the field of life-span development. He continues to be one of the world's leading experts on adult development and aging. Schaie is currently the Evan Pugh Professor of Human Development and Psychology and Director of the Gerontology Center at the Pennsylvania State University. He also holds an appointment as Affiliate Professor of Psychiatry and Behavioral Science at the University of Washington. Schaie received his Ph.D. in psychology from the University of Washington and an honorary doctorate from the Friedrich-Schiller-University of Jena,

Germany. He was honored with the Kleemeier Award for Distinguished Research Contributions from the Gerontological Society of America and the Distinguished Scientific Contributions award from the American Psychological Association. He is author or editor of 32 books including the textbook *Adult Development and Aging* (with S. L. Willis) and the *Handbook of the Psychology of Aging* (with J. E. Birren), both of which are now in their fifth edition. He has directed the Seattle Longitudinal Study of cognitive aging since 1956 and is the author of more than 250 journal articles and chapters on the psychology of aging. His current research interest focuses on the life course of adult intelligence, its antecedents and modifiability, as well as methodological issues in the developmental sciences.

James E. Birren

James E. Birren is a pioneering figure in the field of life-span development and continues to be one of the world's leading experts on adult development and aging. He currently is Associate Director of the UCLA Center on Aging and is also Professor Emeritus of Gerontology and Psychology at the University of Southern California. Birren received his M.A. and Ph.D. from Northwestern University, and has been a Visiting Scientist at the University of Cambridge, England, and a Fellow at the Center for Advanced Study in the Behavioral Sciences at Stanford University. Birren's career includes serving as founding Executive Director and Dean of the Gerontology Center at the University of Southern

California, as well as Past President of the Gerontological Society of America, the Western Gerontological Society, and the Division on Adult Development and Aging of the American Psychological Association. In addition, he has served as Chief of the Section on Aging of the National Institutes of Mental Health. His awards include the Brookdale Foundation Award for Gerontological Research; honorary doctorates from the University of Gothenberg, Sweden, Northwestern University, and St. Thomas University, Canada; the Gerontological Society Award for Meritorious Research; the Sandoz Prize for Gerontological Research; and the Canadian Association of Gerontology Award for Outstanding Contribution to Gerontology. Birren is Series Editor of the internationally recognized *Handbooks on Aging* and has published more than 250 academic journal articles and books.

Yvette R. Harris

Yvette R. Harris is a leading expert on diversity. She received her Ph.D. from the University of Florida and is currently a faculty member in the Department of Psychology at Miami University in Oxford, Ohio. Harris, a cognitive-developmental psychologist, has authored and co-authored articles on African-

American children and academic achievement, and maternal-child learning interaction in African-American families. She has been the recipient of awards from the National Science Foundation and the Murray Research Center to support her research on maternal-child interaction.

Ross Parke

Ross Parke is one of the world's leading experts on socioemotional development. He currently is Distinguished Professor of Psychology and Director of the Center for Family Studies at the University of California, Riverside. Parke obtained his Ph.D. from the University of Waterloo, Ontario, Canada. He is a Past President of Division 7 (Developmental Psychology) of the American Psychological Association and has received the G. Stanley Hall Award from this APA division. He is a Fellow of the American Association for the Advancement of Science. Parke cur-

rently is editor of the *Journal of Family Psychology,* having previously served as editor of *Developmental Psychology* and as associate editor of *Child Development.* He is the author of *Fatherhood* and co-author of two books: *Throwaway Dads* and *Child Psychology,* fifth edition, revised. Park is also the co-editor of these books: *Family-Peer Relationships; Children in Time and Place;* and *Exploring Family Relationships with Other Social Contexts.* Parke is well known for his pioneering research on punishment, aggression, child abuse, and the father's role. His current work focuses on the links between family and peer social systems and on the impact of economic stress on families of diverse ethnic backgrounds.

Jean Berko Gleason

Jean Berko Gleason is one of the world's leading experts on child language. She is a Professor in the Department of Psychology at Boston University and also a faculty member and former director of Boston University's Graduate Program in Applied Linguistics. Berko Gleason has been a Visiting Scholar at Stanford University, Harvard, and the Linguistics Institute of the Hungarian Academy of Sciences in Budapest. She received her undergraduate and graduate degrees from Harvard/Radcliffe and has been President of the International Association for the Study of Child Language. Berko Gleason is the author and editor of leading textbooks on language development and psycholinguistics. Since writing her doctoral dissertation on how children learn to make plurals and past tenses in English, she has published over one hundred articles on aphasia, language attrition, language development in children, gender differences in parents' speech, and cross-cultural differences. Her work is frequently cited in the professional literature, and has been featured in the popular press and on television.

Carolyn Saarni

Carolyn Saarni is one of the world's leading experts on children's emotional development. She received her Ph.D. from the University of California at Berkeley and her first academic appointment was at New York University. Since 1980 Saarni has been a Professor and subsequently Chair of the Graduate Department of Counseling at Sonoma State University in California where she trains prospective marriage, family, child counselors and school counselors. Her research has focused on how children learn that they can adopt an *emotional front*—that is, what they express emotionally does not need to match what they really feel. She has also investigated how children use this knowledge strategically in their interpersonal relations with others as well as when coping with aversive feelings. Her research has been funded by the National Science Foundation and the Spencer Foundation, among others. Saarni has co-edited several books on children's emotional development and most recently published *The Development of Emotional Competence.* The thesis of this book is that the skills of emotional competence are contextualized by culture, including moral values and beliefs about "how emotion works." She has also authored numerous chapters and articles on children's emotional development and is regularly consulted by the popular media on topics concerning emotional development in children and youth.

Alan Fogel

Alan Fogel is one of the world's leading experts on infant development. He is currently a Professor of Psychology at the University of Utah in Salt Lake City and previously held a faculty position at Purdue University. Fogel obtained his undergraduate degree at the University of Miami (Florida), his masters degree at Columbia University, and his Ph.D. at the University of Chicago. He is a Fellow of the American Psychological Association and has been an active contributor to research on infant socioemotional development. He especially is known for his application of dynamic systems theory to the study of developmental change. Fogel's theoretical perspective is best summarized in two books he has authored: *Developing through Relationships* and *Infancy: Infant, Family, and Society,* fourth edition. Further information about Alan Fogel's perspective and research can be found at **http://www.psych.utah.edu/alan_fogels_infant_lab/**.

Susan Krauss Whitbourne

Susan Krauss Whitbourne is a leading expert on adult development and aging. She is currently a Professor of Psychology at the University of Massachusetts at Amherst. Whitbourne obtained her Ph.D. in developmental psychology from Columbia University and completed postdoctoral training in clinical psychology at University of Massachusetts. Prior to joining the University of Massachusetts faculty, she was a faculty member at the University of Rochester and SUNY College at Geneseo. Her teaching has been recognized with the College Outstanding Teacher Award and the University Distinguished Teaching Award. Over the past 25 years, Whitbourne has held a variety of elected and appointed positions in Division 20 (Adult Development and Aging) of the American Psychological Association (APA), including President. Whitbourne is also a Fellow of the Gerontological Society of America. Her publications include 14 published books and 2 in preparation, as well as nearly 100 articles and chapters in leading research journals and books. She has been a consulting editor for *Psychology and Aging,* and serves on the editorial board of the *Journal of Gerontology.* Whitbourne has made more than 175 presentations, including a number of invited addresses, at professional conferences.

Marion K. Underwood

Marion K. Underwood is a leading researcher in children's socioemotional development. She obtained her undergraduate degree from Wellesley College and her doctoral degree in clinical psychology from Duke University. Underwood began her faculty career at Reed College in Portland, Oregon, and is currently a Professor at the University of Texas at Dallas. Her research examines anger, aggression, and gender, with special attention to the development of social aggression among girls. Underwood's research has been published in numerous scientific journals and her research program has been supported by the National Institutes of Mental Heath. She authored the forthcoming book, *Ice and Fire: Social Aggression in Girls.* Underwood also received the 2001 University of Texas Chancellor's Council Outstanding Teacher of the Year Award.

Gilbert Gottlieb

Gilbert Gottlieb is one of the world's leading experts on early development. He currently is Research Professor of Psychology in the Center for Developmental Science at the University of North Carolina at Chapel Hill. He held positions at the University of North Carolina at Greensboro and Dorothea Dix Hospital in Raleigh, after receiving his Ph.D. from Duke University, where he was the first graduate from the joint Psychology-Zoology Graduate Training Program in Animal Behavior. Gottlieb helped to revive interest in the field of behavioral embryology by editing a volume by that name. His interest in the developmental basis of evolution resulted in the book, *Individual Development and Evolution.* Gottlieb summarized his career-long research and theoretical efforts in *Synthesizing Nature–Nurture* (1997), which won the 1998 Eleanor Maccoby Award of the Developmental Psychology Division of the American Psychological Association. In 1999 Clark University Press published his monograph, *Probabilistic Epigenesis and Evolution,* which is based upon the Heinz Werner Lectures he gave there. Gottlieb has been a recipient of research grants from the National Institutes of Mental Health and from Child Health and Human Development, as well as from the National Science Foundation. He is Past President of the International Society for Developmental Psychobiology, and he is a recipient of the Distinguished Scientific Contributions to Child Development Award from the Society for Research in Child Development.

Barba Patton

Barba Patton is a leading expert on education. She received her Ed.D. from the University of Houston and is currently a faculty member at the University of Houston-Victoria, where she is Director of the Center for Excellence. Patton presents her views on education each year at national, regional, and local conferences on child development, mathematics, and learning. She has extensively reviewed articles for journals and manuscripts for books. Patton enjoys teaching and the interaction it involves with students. She actively assists teachers in classrooms with students who have learning problems, especially in the area of mathematics and science. She is currently conducting research on dyscalculia.

Bert Hayslip, Jr.

Bert Hayslip, Jr. is a leading expert on death and grieving. He obtained his doctorate in experimental developmental psychology from the University of Akron. He was a faculty member at Hood College and currently is Regents Professor of Psychology at the University of North Texas. Hayslip is a Fellow of the American Psychological Association, the Gerontological Society of America, and the Association for Gerontology in Higher Education. He has held research grants from the National Institute of Aging and other agencies. Hayslip is currently editor of *The International Journal of Aging and Human Development* and associate editor of *Experimental Aging Research.* His research focuses on cognitive processes in aging, interventions to enhance cognitive functioning in later life, personality-ability linkages in older adults, grandparents who raise their grandchildren, grief and bereavement, hospice care, death anxiety, and mental health and aging. He is the co-author of *Hospice Care; Psychology and Aging: An Annotated Bibliography; Grandparents Raising Grandchildren; Adult Development and Aging,* third edition; *Working with Custodial Grandparents;* and *Historical Shifts in Attitudes Toward Death, Dying, and Bereavement.*

TO THE STUDENT

This book provides you with important study tools to help you more effectively learn about life-span development. Especially important is the learning goals system that is integrated throughout each chapter. In the visual walk-through of features, pay special attention to how the learning goals system works.

The Learning Goals System

Using the learning goals system will help you to learn more material more easily. Key aspects of the learning goals system are the learning goals, chapter maps, Review and Reflect, and Reach Your Learning Goals sections, which are all linked together.

At the beginning of each chapter, you will see a page that includes both a chapter outline and three to six learning goals that preview the chapter's main themes and underscore the most important ideas in the chapter. Then, at the beginning of

each major section of a chapter, you will see a mini–chapter map that provides you with a visual organization of the key topics you are about to read in the section. At the end of each section is Review and Reflect, in which the learning goal for the section is restated, a series of review questions related to the mini–chapter map are asked, and a question that encourages you to think critically about a topic related to the section appears. At the end of the chapter, you will come to a section titled Reach Your Learning Goals. This includes an overall chapter map that visually organizes all of the main headings, a restatement of the chapter's learning goals, and a summary of the chapter's content that is directly linked to the chapter outline at the beginning of the chapter and the questions asked in the Review part of Review and Reflect within the chapter. The summary essentially answers the questions asked in the within-chapter Review sections.

A visual presentation of the learning goals system is provided on this and the following pages.

Chapter Opening Outline and Learning Goals

The outline shows the organization of topics by headings. Primary topic headings are printed in blue capital letters. The Learning Goals highlight the main ideas in the chapter by section.

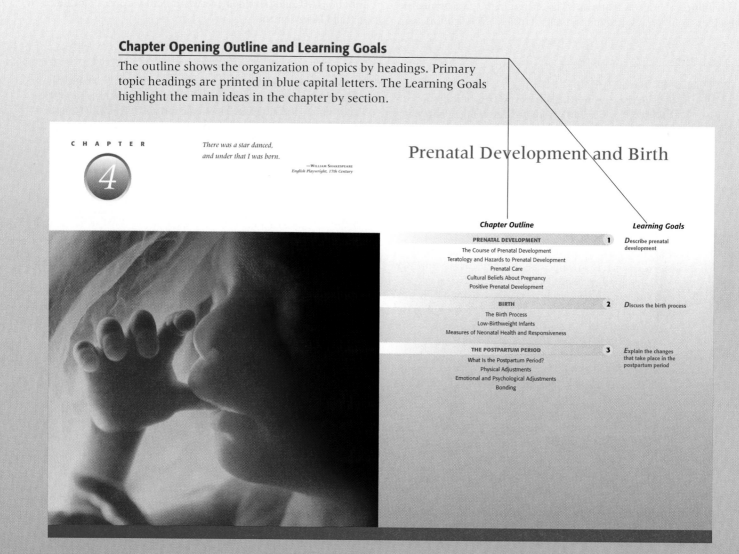

CHAPTER

4

There was a star danced,
and under that I was born.

—WILLIAM SHAKESPEARE
English Playwright, 17th Century

Prenatal Development and Birth

Chapter Outline

PRENATAL DEVELOPMENT
The Course of Prenatal Development
Teratology and Hazards to Prenatal Development
Prenatal Care
Cultural Beliefs About Pregnancy
Positive Prenatal Development

BIRTH
The Birth Process
Low-Birthweight Infants
Measures of Neonatal Health and Responsiveness

THE POSTPARTUM PERIOD
What Is the Postpartum Period?
Physical Adjustments
Emotional and Psychological Adjustments
Bonding

Learning Goals

1 *D*escribe prenatal development

2 *D*iscuss the birth process

3 *E*xplain the changes that take place in the postpartum period

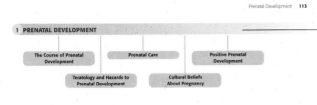

1 PRENATAL DEVELOPMENT

- The Course of Prenatal Development
- Teratology and Hazards to Prenatal Development
- Prenatal Care
- Cultural Beliefs About Pregnancy
- Positive Prenatal Development

Mini–Chapter Map

This visual preview displays the main headings and subheadings for each section of the chapter.

Imagine how Tanner Roberts came to be. Out of thousands of eggs and millions of sperm, one egg and one sperm united to produce him. Had the union of sperm and egg come a day or even an hour earlier or later, he might have been very different—maybe even of the opposite sex. Conception occurs when a single sperm cell from the male unites with an ovum (egg) in the female's fallopian tube in a process called fertilization. Remember from chapter 3 that the fertilized egg is called a zygote.

The Course of Prenatal Development

The course of prenatal development lasts approximately 266 days, beginning with fertilization and ending with birth. Prenatal development is divided into three periods: germinal, embryonic, and fetal.

The Germinal Period   The **germinal period** is the period of prenatal development that takes place in the first two weeks after conception. It includes the creation of the zygote, continued cell division, and the attachment of the zygote to the uterine wall. By approximately one week after conception, the differentiation of cells has already commenced, as inner and outer layers of the organism are formed. The **blastocyst** is the inner layer of cells that develops during the germinal period. These cells later develop into the embryo. The **trophoblast** is the outer layer of cells that develops during the germinal period. It later provides nutrition and support for the embryo. *Implantation*, the attachment of the zygote to the uterine wall, takes place about 10 to 14 days after conception. Figure 4.1 on page 114 illustrates some of the most significant ...

germinal period   The period of prenatal development that takes place in the first two weeks after conception. It includes the creation of the zygote, continued cell division...

Reach Your Learning Goals

This section includes a complete chapter map and a summary restating the Learning Goals and answering the bulleted review questions from the chapter. Use it as a guide to help you organize your study of the chapter, *not* as a substitute for reading and studying the chapter.

Reach Your Learning Goals

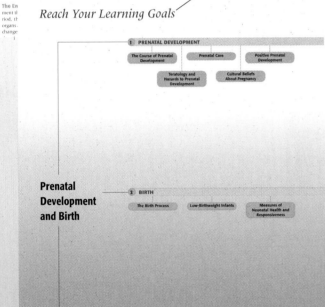

Prenatal Development and Birth

1 PRENATAL DEVELOPMENT

- The Course of Prenatal Development
- Teratology and Hazards to Prenatal Development
- Prenatal Care
- Cultural Beliefs About Pregnancy
- Positive Prenatal Development

2 BIRTH

- The Birth Process
- Low-Birthweight Infants
- Measures of Neonatal Health and Responsiveness

3 THE POSTPARTUM PERIOD

- What Is the Postpartum Period?
- Emotional and Psychological Adjustments
- Physical Adjustments
- Bonding

Summary

1 Describe prenatal development

- Prenatal development is divided into three periods: germinal (conception until 10 to 14 days later), which ends when the zygote (a fertilized egg) attaches to the uterine wall; embryonic (two to eight weeks after conception), during which the embryo differentiates into three layers, life-support systems develop, and organ systems form (organogenesis); and fetal (two months after conception until about nine months, or when the infant is born), a time when organ systems have matured to the point at which life can be sustained outside of the womb.
- Teratology is the field that investigates the causes of congenital (birth) defects. Any agent that causes birth defects is called a teratogen. The dose, time of exposure, and genetic susceptibility influence the severity of the damage to an unborn child and the type of defect that occurs. Prescription drugs that can be harmful include antibiotics, some depressants, and certain hormones. Nonprescription drugs that can be harmful include diet pills, aspirin, and coffee. Fetal alcohol syndrome (FAS) is a cluster of abnormalities that appear in offspring of mothers who drink heavily during pregnancy. When pregnant women drink moderately (one to two drinks a day), negative effects on their offspring have been found. Cigarette smoking by pregnant women has serious adverse effects on prenatal and child development (such as low birthweight). Illegal drugs that are potentially harmful to offspring include marijuana, cocaine, and heroin. Incompatibility of the mother's and the father's blood types can also be harmful to the fetus. Potential environmental hazards include radiation, environmental pollutants, toxic wastes, and prolonged exposure to heat in saunas and hot tubs. Rubella (German measles) can be harmful. Syphilis, genital herpes, and AIDS are other teratogens. A developing fetus depends entirely on its mother for nutrition. One nutrient that is especially important early in development is folic acid. High anxiety and stress in the mother are linked with less than optimal prenatal and birth outcomes. Maternal age can negatively affect the offspring's development if the mother is an adolescent or over 30. Paternal factors that can adversely affect prenatal development include exposure to lead, radiation, certain pesticides, and petrochemicals.
- Prenatal care varies extensively but usually involves medical care services with a defined schedule of visits.
- Specific actions in pregnancy are often determined by cultural beliefs. Certain behaviors are expected if a culture views pregnancy as a medical condition or a natural occurrence. For example, prenatal care may not be a priority for expectant mothers who view pregnancy as a natural occurrence.
- It is important to remember that, although things can and do go wrong during pregnancy, most of the time pregnancy and prenatal development go well. Avoiding teratogens helps ensure a positive outcome.

2 Discuss the birth process

- Childbirth occurs in three stages. The first stage, which lasts about 12 to 24 hours for a woman having her first child, is the longest stage. The cervix dilates to about 4 inches at the end of the first stage. The second stage begins when the baby's head moves through the cervix and ends with the baby's complete emergence. The third stage is afterbirth. Being born involves considerable stress for the baby, but the baby is well prepared and adapted to handle the stress. Anoxia—insufficient oxygen supply to the fetus/newborn—is a potential hazard. Childbirth strategies involve the childbirth setting and attendants. In many countries, a doula attends a childbearing woman. Methods of delivery include medicated, natural and prepared, and cesarean.
- Low-birthweight infants weigh less than 5½ pounds and they may be preterm (born three weeks or more before the pregnancy has reached full term) or small for date (also called small for gestational age, which refers to infants whose birthweight is below norm when the length of pregnancy is considered). Small for date infants may be preterm or full term. Although most low-birthweight infants are normal and healthy, as a group they have more health and developmental problems than normal-birthweight infants.
- For many years, the Apgar Scale has been used to assess the newborn's health. The Brazelton Neonatal Behavioral Assessment Scale examines the newborn's neurological development, reflexes, and reactions to people.

3 Explain the changes that take place in the postpartum period

- The postpartum period is the name given to the period after childbirth or delivery. In this period, the woman's body adjusts physically and psychologically to the process of childbearing. The period lasts for about six weeks or until the body has completed its adjustment.
- Physical adjustments in the postpartum period include fatigue, involution (the process by which the uterus returns to its prepregnant size [five or six weeks after birth]), hormonal changes, when to resume sexual intercourse, and exercises to recover body contour and strength.
- Emotional fluctuations on the part of the mother are common in this period, and they can vary a great deal from one mother to the next. The father also goes through a postpartum adjustment.
- Bonding is the formation of a close connection, especially a physical bond between parents and the newborn shortly after birth. Early bonding has not been found to be critical in the development of a competent infant.

140 / 141

Summary

Mexican American culture, the indigenous healer is called a *curandero*. In some Native American tribes, the medicine woman or man fulfills the healing role. Herbalists are often found in Asian cultures, and faith healers, root doctors, and spiritualists are sometimes found in African American culture. When health-care providers come into contact with expectant mothers, they need to assess whether such cultural practices pose a threat to the expectant mother and the fetus. If they pose no threat, there is no reason to try to change them. On the other hand, if certain cultural practices do pose a threat to the health of the expectant mother or the fetus, the health-care provider should consider a culturally sensitive way to handle the problem. For example, some Filipinos will not take any medication during pregnancy.

Positive Prenatal Development

Much of our discussion so far in this chapter has focused on what can go wrong with prenatal development. It is important to keep in mind that most of the time, prenatal development does not go awry and development occurs along the positive path that we described at the beginning of the chapter (Lester, 2000). That said, it is still important for prospective mothers and those who are pregnant to avoid the vulnerabilities to fetal development that we have described.

Review and Reflect

1 Describe prenatal development

REVIEW

- What is the course of prenatal development?
- What are some of the main hazards to prenatal development?
- What are some good prenatal care strategies?
- What are some cultural beliefs about pregnancy?
- Why is it important to take a positive approach to prenatal development?

REFLECT

- What can be done to convince women who are pregnant not to smoke or drink? Consider the role of health-care providers, the role of insurance companies, and specific programs targeted at women who are pregnant.

Review and Reflect

Review questions enable you to quiz yourself on the key ideas and find out whether you've met the learning goals for one section of a chapter before continuing to the next main topic. The question for reflection helps you to think about what you've just read and apply it. Answering these questions will help you to remember key points and concepts.

OTHER LEARNING SYSTEM FEATURES

Ted Kaczynski, the convicted Unabomber, traced his difficulties to growing up as a genius in a kid's body and not fitting in when he was a child.

Alice Walker won the Pulitzer Prize for her book *The Color Purple*. Like the characters in her book, Walker overcame pain and anger to triumph and celebrate the human spirit.

1 THE LIFE-SPAN PERSPECTIVE

Images of Life-Span Development
How Did Ted Kaczynski Become Ted Kaczynski and Alice Walker Become Alice Walker?

The intellectual Ted Kaczynski sprinted through high school, not bothering with his junior year and making only passing efforts at social contact. Off to Harvard at age 16, Kaczynski was a loner during his college years. One of his roommates at Harvard said that he had a special way of avoiding people by quickly shuffling by them and slamming the door behind him. After obtaining his Ph.D. in mathematics at the University of Michigan, Kaczynski became a professor at the University of California at Berkeley. His colleagues there remember him as hiding from social circumstances—no friends, no allies, no networking. After several years at Berkeley, Kaczynski resigned and moved to a rural area of Montana where he lived as a hermit in a crude shack for 25 years. Town residents described him as a bearded eccentric. Kaczynski traced his own difficulties to growing up as a genius in a kid's body and sticking out like a sore thumb in his surroundings as a child. In 1996, he was arrested and charged with being the notorious Unabomber, America's most wanted killer who sent sixteen mail bombs in 17 years that left 23 people wounded and maimed, and 3 people dead. In 1998, he pleaded guilty to the offenses and was sentenced to life in prison.

A decade before Kaczynski allegedly mailed his first bomb, Alice Walker, who would later win a Pulitzer Prize for her book *The Color Purple*, spent her days battling racism in Mississippi. She had recently won her first writing fellowship, but rather than use the money to follow her dream of moving to Senegal, Africa, she put herself

Images of Life-Span Development

Each chapter opens with a high-interest story that is linked to the chapter's content.

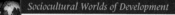

Sociocultural Worlds of Development

Women's Struggle for Equality: An International Journey

There are serious concerns about the educational and psychological conditions of women around the world (Maracek & others, 2003; United Nations, 2001). The countries with the fewest women being educated are in Africa, where in some areas women are receiving no education at all. Canada, the United States, and Russia have the highest percentages of educated women. In developing countries, 67 percent of women and 50 percent of men over the age of 25 have never been to school. At the beginning of the twenty-first century, 80 million more boys than girls were in primary and secondary educational settings around the world (United Nations, 2002).

Women in every country experience violence, often from someone close to them. Partner abuse occurs in one of every six households in the United States, with the vast majority of the abuse being directed at women by men (Walker, 2001). In a survey, "The New Woman Ethics Report," wife abuse was listed as number one among fifteen of the most pressing concerns facing society today (Johnson, 1990). Although most countries around the world now have battered women's shelters, beating women continues to be accepted and expected behavior in some countries.

In a study of depression in high-income countries, women were twice as likely as men to be diagnosed as depressed (Nolen-Hoeksema, 1990). In the United States, from adolescence through adulthood, females are more likely than males to be depressed (Davison & Neale, 2001; Hammen, 2003). Many sociocultural

inequities and experiences have contributed to the greater incidence of depression in females than males (Whiffen, 2001). Also, possibly more women are diagnosed with depression than actually have depression (Nolen-Hoeksema, 2001).

Around the world women too often are treated as burdens rather than assets in the political process. *What can be done to strengthen women's roles in the political process?*

Sociocultural Worlds of Development

Life-Span Development gives special attention to culture, ethnicity, and gender. Most chapters have a box that highlights the sociocultural dimensions of life-span development.

We will discuss sociocultural contexts in each chapter. In addition, a Sociocultural Worlds of Development box appears in most chapters. Look at the one above for a discussion of women's international struggle for equality.

Research on Children's Ethnicity, Poverty, and Type of Home Environment One study recently examined the home environments of three ethnic groups: European American, African American, and Latino (Bradley & others, 2001). The home environments were assessed (by a combination of observations and maternal interviews) at five points in children's lives from infancy through early adolescence. There were some ethnic differences, but the most consistent result involved poverty, which was a much more powerful indicator of the type of home environment children experienced than ethnicity was (see figure 1.4 on page 16).

Social Policy **Social policy** is a national government's course of action designed to promote the welfare of its citizens. The shape and scope of social policy is strongly tied to the political system. Our country's policy agenda and the welfare of the nation's citizens are influenced by the values held by individual lawmakers, by the nation's economic strengths and weaknesses, and by partisan politics.

Out of concern that policy makers are doing too little to protect the well-being of children and older adults, life-span researchers increasingly are undertaking studies that they hope will lead to effective social policy (Bogenschneider, 2002; Bornstein & Bradley, 2003; Maccoby, 2001; Zigler & Hall, 2000). When more than 15 percent of all children and almost half of all ethnic minority children are being raised in poverty, when 40 to 50 percent of all children can expect to spend at least 5 years in a single-parent home, when children and young adolescents are giving birth, when the use and

social poli
of action de
citizens.

Careers in Life-Span Development

Pam Reid, Educational and Developmental Psychologist

As a child, Pam Reid played with chemistry sets, and at the university she was majoring in chemistry, planning to become a medical doctor. Because some of her friends signed up for a psychology course as an elective, she decided to join them. She was so intrigued by learning more about how people think, behave, and develop that she changed her major to psychology. She says, "I fell in love with psychology." Dr. Reid went on to obtain her Ph.D. in educational psychology ◀▥ p. 31.

Today, Pamela Trotman Reid is a professor of education and psychology at the University of Michigan. She is also a research scientist for the UM Institute for Research on Women and Gender. Her main interest is how children and adolescents develop social skills, and especially how gender, socioeconomic status, and ethnicity are involved in development (Reid & Zalk, 2001). Because many psychological findings have been based on research with middle-socioeconomic-status non-Latino White populations, she believes it is important to study people from different ethnic groups. She stresses that by understanding the expectations, attitudes, and behavior of diverse groups, we enrich the theory and practice of psychology. Currently Dr. Reid is working with her graduate students on a project

involving middle school girls. She is interested in why girls, more often than boys, stop taking classes in mathematics.

Pam Reid (back row, center) with graduate students she is mentoring at the University of Michigan.

• How might research on topics of primary interest to females, such as relationships, feelings, and empathy, challenge existing theory? For example, in the study of moral development, the highest level has often been portrayed as based on a principle of "justice for the individual" (Kohlberg, 1976). However, more recent theorizing notes individuality and autonomy tend to be male concerns.

Careers in Life-Span Development

Every chapter has one or more Careers in Life-Span Development inserts, which feature a person working in a life-span field related to the chapter's content.

A Careers in Life-Span Development Appendix that describes a number of careers appears between Chapter 1 and Chapter 2.

Theories are part of the science of life-span development. Some individuals have difficulty thinking of life-span development as a science like physics, chemistry, and biology. Can a discipline that studies how parents nurture children, whether watching TV long hours is linked with being overweight, and the factors involved in life satisfaction among older adults be equated with disciplines that study the molecular structure of a compound and how gravity works? The answer is yes. Science is defined not by *what* it investigates, but by *how* it investigates. Whether you're studying photosynthesis, butterflies, Saturn's moons, or human development, it is the way you study that makes the approach scientific or not.

This chapter introduces the theories and methods that are the foundation of the science of life-span development. At the end of the chapter we will explore some of the ethical challenges and biases that researchers must guard against to protect the integrity of their results and respect the rights of the participants in their studies.

1 THEORIES OF DEVELOPMENT

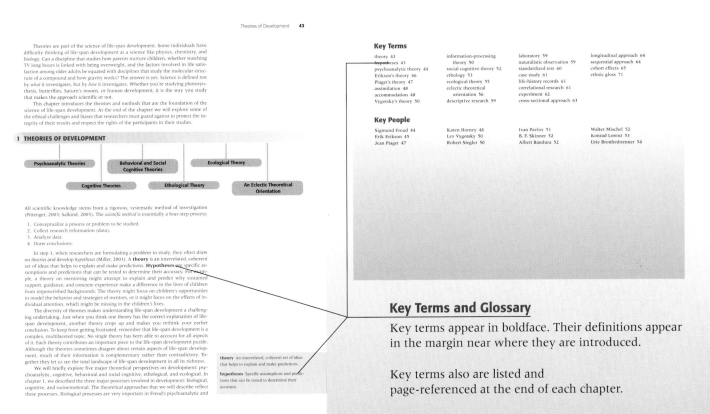

All scientific knowledge stems from a rigorous, systematic method of investigation (Pittenger, 2003; Salkind, 2003). The *scientific method* is essentially a four-step process:

1. Conceptualize a process or problem to be studied.
2. Collect research information (data).
3. Analyze data.
4. Draw conclusions.

In step 1, when researchers are formulating a problem to study, they often draw on *theories* and develop *hypotheses* (Miller, 2001). A **theory** is an interrelated, coherent set of ideas that helps to explain and make predictions. **Hypotheses** are specific assumptions and predictions that can be tested to determine their accuracy. For example, a theory on mentoring might attempt to explain and predict why sustained support, guidance, and concrete experience make a difference in the lives of children from impoverished backgrounds. The theory might focus on children's opportunities to model the behavior and strategies of mentors, or it might focus on the effects of individual attention, which might be missing in the children's lives.

The diversity of theories makes understanding life-span development a challenging undertaking. Just when you think one theory has the correct explanation of life-span development, another theory crops up and makes you rethink your earlier conclusion. To keep from getting frustrated, remember that life-span development is a complex, multifaceted topic. No single theory has been able to account for all aspects of it. Each theory contributes an important piece to the life-span development puzzle. Although the theories sometimes disagree about certain aspects of life-span development, much of their information is complementary rather than contradictory. Together they let us see the total landscape of life-span development in all its richness.

We will briefly explore five major theoretical perspectives on development: psychoanalytic, cognitive, behavioral and social cognitive, ethological, and ecological. In chapter 1, we described the three major processes involved in development: biological, cognitive, and socioemotional. The theoretical approaches that we will describe reflect these processes. Biological processes are very important in Freud's psychoanalytic and

theory An interrelated, coherent set of ideas that helps to explain and make predictions.

hypotheses Specific assumptions and predictions that can be tested to determine their accuracy.

Key Terms

theory 43	information-processing theory 50	laboratory 59	longitudinal approach 64
hypotheses 43	social cognitive theory 52	naturalistic observation 59	sequential approach 64
psychoanalytic theory 44	ethology 53	standardized test 60	cohort effects 65
Erikson's theory 46	ecological theory 55	case study 61	ethnic gloss 71
Piaget's theory 47	eclectic theoretical orientation 56	life-history records 61	
assimilation 48	descriptive research 59	correlational research 61	
accommodation 48		experiment 62	
Vygotsky's theory 50		cross-sectional approach 63	

Key People

Sigmund Freud 44	Karen Horney 48	Ivan Pavlov 51	Walter Mischel 52
Erik Erikson 45	Lev Vygotsky 50	B. F. Skinner 52	Konrad Lorenz 53
Jean Piaget 47	Robert Siegler 50	Albert Bandura 52	Urie Bronfenbrenner 54

Key Terms and Glossary

Key terms appear in boldface. Their definitions appear in the margin near where they are introduced.

Key terms also are listed and page-referenced at the end of each chapter.

Key terms are alphabetically listed, defined, and page-referenced in a Glossary at the end of the book.

---

opportunities for exercise, the infants often attain motor milestones earlier than infants whose caregivers have not provided these physical activities. For example, Jamaican mothers expect their infants to sit and walk alone two to three months earlier than English mothers do (Hopkins & Westra, 1990). Also, Jamaican mothers regularly massage their infants and stretch their arms and legs, and this is linked with advanced motor development (Hopkins, 1991). In the Gusii culture of Kenya, mothers encourage vigorous movement in their babies (Hopkins & Westra, 1988).

In developing countries, mothers often attempt to stimulate their infants' motor skills more than mothers in more advanced cultures (Hopkins, 1991). This stimulation of infants' motor skills in developing countries may be necessary to improve the infants' chances of survival. In some cases, the emphasis on early stimulation may occur because the caregivers recognize that motor skills are required for important jobs in the culture. Others factors such as climate and spiritual beliefs also may influence the way that caregivers guide their infants' motor development.

Although infants in some cultures, such as Jamaica, reach motor milestones earlier than infants in many cultures, nonetheless, regardless of how much practice takes place, infants around the world reach these motor milestones within the same age range. For example, Algonquin infants in Quebec, Canada, spend much of their first year strapped to a cradle board. Despite such inactivity, these infants still sit up, crawl, and walk within an age range similar to infants in other cultures who have much greater opportunity for activity. In sum, there are slight variations in the age at which infants reach motor milestones depending on their activity opportunities in different cultures, but the variations are not substantial and they are within normal ranges.

Fine Motor Skills Infants have hardly any control over fine motor skills at birth, although they have many components of what later become finely coordinated arm, hand, and finger movements (Rosenblith, 1992). The onset of reaching and grasping marks a significant achievement in infants' functional interactions with their surroundings (McCarty & Ashmead, 1999).

For many years it was believed that reaching for an object is visually guided—that is, the infant must continuously have sight of the hand and the target (White, Castle, & Held, 1964). However, in one study, Rachel Clifton and her colleagues (1993) demonstrated that infants do not have to see their own hands when reaching for an object. They concluded that, because the infants could not see their hand or arm in the dark in the experiment, proprioceptive (muscle, tendon, joint sense) cues, not sight of limb, guided the early reaching of the 4-month-old infants.

The development of reaching and grasping becomes more refined during the first two years of life. Initially, infants show only crude shoulder and elbow movements, but later they show wrist movements, hand rotation, and coordination of the thumb and forefinger. The maturation of hand-eye coordination over the first two years of life is reflected in the improvement of fine motor skills. Figure 5.12 on page 166 provides an overview of the development of fine motor skills in the first two years of life.

The infant's grasping system is very flexible and the environment plays a stronger role in grasping than previously thought. One way to show that the environment influences grasping is to vary the motor task and examine if this influences the infant's responses. This can be done by changing the size and shape of the objects for the infant to grasp. Indeed, infants vary their grip on

A baby is an angel whose wings decrease as his legs increase.

—French Proverb

(*Top*) In the Algonquin culture in Quebec, Canada, babies are strapped to a cradle board for much of their infancy. (*Bottom*) In Jamaica, mothers massage and stretch their infants' arms and legs. *To what extent do cultural variations infants activities influence the time at which they reach motor milestones?*

Quotations

These appear at the beginning of the chapter and occasionally in the margins to stimulate further thought about a topic.

Critical Thinking and Content Questions in Photograph Captions

Most photographs have a caption that ends with a critical thinking or knowledge question in italics to stimulate further thought about a topic.

Web Links

Web icons appear a number of times in each chapter. They signal you to go to the book's website where you will find connecting links that provide additional information on the topic discussed in the text. The labels under the Web icon appear as Web links at the Santrock *Life-Span Development,* ninth edition, website, under that chapter for easy access.

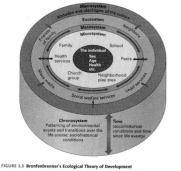

FIGURE 2.5 Bronfenbrenner's Ecological Theory of Development
Bronfenbrenner's ecological theory consists of five environmental systems: microsystem, mesosystem, exosystem, macrosystem, and chronosystem.

Ecological Theory

While ethological theory stresses biological factors, ecological theory emphasizes environmental factors. One ecological theory that has important implications for understanding life-span development was created by Urie Bronfenbrenner (1917–   ).
Ecological theory is Bronfenbrenner's (1986, 2000; Bronfenbrenner & Morris, 1998) environmental system of development. It consists of five environmental systems ranging from the fine-grained inputs of direct interactions with people to the broad-based inputs of culture (see figure 2.5).

Microsystem: The setting in which the individual lives. These contexts include the person's family, peers, school, and neighborhood ◀▦ p. 13. It is in the microsystem that the most direct interactions with social agents take place—with parents, peers, and teachers, for example. The individual is viewed as a passive recipient of experiences in these settings, but as someone who helps to construct the settings.

Mesosystem: Involves relations between microsystems or connections between contexts. Examples are the relation of family experiences to school experiences, school experiences to church experiences, and family experiences to peer experiences. For example, children whose parents have rejected them may have difficulty developing positive relations with teachers.

Exosystem: Is involved when experiences in another social setting—in which the individual does not have an active role—influence what the individual experiences in an immediate context. For example, work experiences can affect a

mhhe.com/santrockld9
Bronfenbrenner's Theory
Bronfenbrenner and a Multicultural Framework

ecological theory Bronfenbrenner's environmental systems theory that focuses on five environmental systems: microsystem, mesosystem, exosystem, macrosystem, and chronosystem.

Cross-Linkage

A specific page reference appears in the text with a backward-pointing arrow each time a key concept occurs in a chapter subsequent to its initial coverage. When you see the cross-linkage, go back to the page listed to obtain a foundation for the concept.

Online Learning Center

This directs you to the Online Learning Center for this book, where you will find many learning activities to improve your knowledge and understanding of the chapter. A new feature in this edition is the inclusion of a number of self-assessments.

Key People

The most important theorists and researchers in the chapter are listed and page-referenced at the end of each chapter.

Key Terms

theory 43	information-processing theory 50	laboratory 59	longitudinal approach 64
hypotheses 43	social cognitive theory 52	naturalistic observation 59	sequential approach 64
psychoanalytic theory 44	ethology 53	standardized test 60	cohort effects 65
Erikson's theory 46	ecological theory 55	case study 61	ethnic gloss 71
Piaget's theory 47	eclectic theoretical orientation 56	life-history records 61	
assimilation 48	descriptive research 59	correlational research 61	
accommodation 48		experiment 62	
Vygotsky's theory 50		cross-sectional approach 63	

Key People

Sigmund Freud 44	Karen Horney 48	Ivan Pavlov 51	Walter Mischel 52
Erik Erikson 45	Lev Vygotsky 50	B. F. Skinner 52	Konrad Lorenz 53
Jean Piaget 47	Robert Siegler 50	Albert Bandura 52	Urie Bronfenbrenner 54

mhhe.com/santrockld9   Taking It to the Net

1. Like many students of life-span psychology, Ymelda has a hard time with Freud's theory, insisting that it is "all about sex." Is that the extent of Freud's theoretical perspective?
2. Juan's life-span psychology teacher asked the class to read about Albert Bandura's famous "Bobo" doll experiment and determine if there were any gender differences in the responses of boys and girls who (a) saw aggressive behavior rewarded and (b) who saw aggressive behavior punished. What should Juan's conclusions be?
3. A requirement for Wanda's methods course is to design and

carry out an original research project. Among the many decisions she must make is what type of data she will collect. She decides to research adapting to college life. Her instructor asks if she will use an interview or a survey. What are the distinctions between surveys and interviews, and what are the benefits and difficulties of each?

Connect to www.mhhe.com/santrockld9 to research the answers and complete these exercises.

mhhe.com/santrockld9   E-Learning Tools

To help you master the material in this chapter, you'll find a number of valuable study tools on the Student CD-ROM that accompanies this book. In addition, visit the Online Learning Center for *Life-Span Development,* ninth edition, where you'll find these valuable resources for chapter 2, "The Science of Life-Span Development."

• Complete the self-assessment, *Models and Mentors in My Life,* to help you evaluate the role models and mentors who have

played an important part in your life and think about the type of role model you want to be.
• View video clips of key developmental psychology experts discussing their views on research methods, developmental theories, and ethics in research.
• Build your decision-making skills by trying your hand at the parenting and education "Scenarios."

Life-Span Development

The Life-Span Developmental Perspective

All the world's a stage. And all the men and women merely players. They have their exits and their entrances. And one man in his time plays many parts. . .
—WILLIAM SHAKESPEARE
English Playwright, 17th Century

This book is about human development—its universal features, its individual variations, its nature. Every life is distinct, a new biography in the world. Examining the shape of human development allows us to understand it better. *Life-Span Development* is about the rhythm and meaning of people's lives, about turning mystery into understanding, and about weaving a portrait of who each of us was, is, and will be. In Section 1, you will read two chapters: "Introduction" (chapter 1) and "The Science of Life-Span Development" (chapter 2).

We reach backward to our parents and forward to our children, and through their children to a future we will never see, but about which we need to care.

—CARL JUNG
*Swiss Psychiatrist,
20th Century*

Introduction

Chapter Outline

THE LIFE-SPAN PERSPECTIVE

What Is Life-Span Development?

The Historical Perspective

Characteristics of the Life-Span Perspective

Some Contemporary Concerns

DEVELOPMENTAL PROCESSES AND PERIODS

Biological, Cognitive, and Socioemotional Processes

Periods of Development

Age and Happiness

Conceptions of Age

DEVELOPMENTAL ISSUES

Nature and Nurture

Continuity and Discontinuity

Stability and Change

Evaluating the Developmental Issues

Learning Goals

1 **D**iscuss the life-span perspective of development

2 **I**dentify the most important developmental processes and periods

3 **D**escribe three key developmental issues

Images of Life-Span Development
How Did Ted Kaczynski Become Ted Kaczynski and Alice Walker Become Alice Walker?

Ted Kaczynski, the convicted Unabomber, traced his difficulties to growing up as a genius in a kid's body and not fitting in when he was a child.

Alice Walker won the Pulitzer Prize for her book *The Color Purple*. Like the characters in her book, Walker overcame pain and anger to triumph and celebrate the human spirit.

The intellectual Ted Kaczynski sprinted through high school, not bothering with his junior year and making only passing efforts at social contact. Off to Harvard at age 16, Kaczynski was a loner during his college years. One of his roommates at Harvard said that he had a special way of avoiding people by quickly shuffling by them and slamming the door behind him. After obtaining his Ph.D. in mathematics at the University of Michigan, Kaczynski became a professor at the University of California at Berkeley. His colleagues there remember him as hiding from social circumstances—no friends, no allies, no networking. After several years at Berkeley, Kaczynski resigned and moved to a rural area of Montana where he lived as a hermit in a crude shack for 25 years. Town residents described him as a bearded eccentric. Kaczynski traced his own difficulties to growing up as a genius in a kid's body and sticking out like a sore thumb in his surroundings as a child. In 1996, he was arrested and charged with being the notorious Unabomber, America's most wanted killer who sent sixteen mail bombs in 17 years that left 23 people wounded and maimed, and 3 people dead. In 1998, he pleaded guilty to the offenses and was sentenced to life in prison.

A decade before Kaczynski allegedly mailed his first bomb, Alice Walker, who would later win a Pulitzer Prize for her book *The Color Purple*, spent her days battling racism in Mississippi. She had recently won her first writing fellowship, but rather than use the money to follow her dream of moving to Senegal, Africa, she put herself into the heart and heat of the civil rights movement. Walker grew up knowing the brutal effects of poverty and racism. Born in 1944, she was the eighth child of Georgia sharecroppers who earned $300 a year. When Walker was 8, her brother accidentally shot her in the left eye with a BB gun. By the time her parents got her to the hospital a week later (they had no car), she was blind in that eye and it had developed a disfiguring layer of scar tissue. Despite the counts against her, Walker went on to become an essayist, a poet, an award-winning novelist, a short-story writer, and a social activist who, like her characters (especially the women), has overcome pain and anger.

What leads one individual, so full of promise, to commit brutal acts of violence and another to turn poverty and trauma into a rich literary harvest? If you have ever wondered why people turn out the way they do, you have asked yourself the central question we will explore in this book.

1 THE LIFE-SPAN PERSPECTIVE

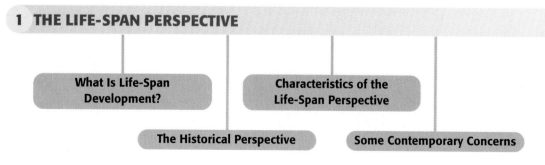

- What Is Life-Span Development?
- The Historical Perspective
- Characteristics of the Life-Span Perspective
- Some Contemporary Concerns

Why study life-span development? Perhaps you are or will be a parent or teacher, and responsibility for children is or will be a part of your everyday life. The more you learn about children, the better you can guide them. Perhaps you hope to gain an understanding of your own history—as an infant, a child, an adolescent, or a young adult.

Perhaps you want to know what your life will be like as you grow into middle age or old age. Or perhaps you accidentally came across the course description and found it intriguing. Whatever your reasons, you will discover that the study of life-span development is provocative, intriguing, and informative. The life-span perspective offers insights into who we are, how we came to be this way, and where our future will take us.

This chapter previews the themes and issues that we will consider throughout our study of life-span development. First, we will familiarize ourselves with the life-span perspective, then we will explore the processes and periods that characterize human development. Finally, we will examine the primary issues that developmentalists debate, issues that will come up repeatedly in this text.

What Is Life-Span Development?

Development is the pattern of movement or change that begins at conception and continues throughout the human life span. Most development involves growth, although it also includes decline brought on by aging and dying. Thus, we will explore development from the point in time when life begins until the time when it ends. You will see yourself as an infant, as a child, and as an adolescent, and be stimulated to think about how those years influenced the kind of individual you are today. And you will see yourself as a young adult, as a middle-aged adult, and as an adult in old age, and be stimulated to think about how your experiences today will influence your development through the remainder of your adult years.

Life-span development is linked with many different areas of psychology. Neuroscience/biological psychology, cognitive psychology, abnormal psychology, social psychology, and virtually all other areas of psychology explore how people develop in these areas. For example, how memory works is a key aspect of cognitive psychology. In this book you will read about how memory develops from infancy through old age.

The Historical Perspective

Interest in the development of children has a long and rich history, but interest in adults began to develop seriously only in the latter half of the twentieth century. Prior to that time, the number of people living into their sixties and seventies in the United States was small compared with the rest of the population, and development was considered to be something that happened only during childhood. Although development in childhood is very important, a complete view of development now requires that we also consider developmental changes in the adult years. In this section, we will look briefly at how the prevailing view of children and adults has changed.

Child Development   Throughout history, philosophers have speculated about the nature of children and how they should be reared. Three influential philosophical views are based on the ideas of original sin, tabula rasa, and innate goodness:

- In the **original sin view,** especially advocated during the Middle Ages, children were perceived as being basically bad, born into the world as evil beings. The goal of child rearing was salvation, which was believed to remove sin from the child's life.
- Toward the end of the seventeenth century, the **tabula rasa view** was proposed by English philosopher John Locke. He argued that children are not innately bad. Instead they are like a "blank tablet," a "tabula rasa" as he called it. They acquire their characteristics through experience. Locke believed that childhood experiences are important in determining adult characteristics. He advised parents to spend time with their children and help them become contributing members of society.
- In the eighteenth century, the **innate goodness view** was presented by Swiss-born French philosopher Jean-Jacques Rousseau. He stressed that children are inherently good. Rousseau said that because children are basically good,

development The pattern of change that begins at conception and continues through the life cycle.

original sin view Advocated during the Middle Ages, the belief that children were born into the world as evil beings and were basically bad.

tabula rasa view The idea, proposed by John Locke, that children are like a "blank tablet."

innate goodness view The idea, presented by Swiss-born philosopher Jean-Jacques Rousseau, that children are inherently good.

they should be permitted to grow naturally with little parental monitoring or constraint.

During the past century and a half, interest in the nature of children and ways to improve their well-being have continued to be important concerns of our society (Booth & Crouter, 2000; Graham, 2001; Wertlieb, 2003). We now conceive of childhood as a highly eventful and unique period of life that lays an important foundation for the adult years and is highly differentiated from them. In most approaches to childhood, distinct periods are identified in which special skills are mastered and new life tasks are confronted. Childhood is no longer seen as an inconvenient "waiting" period during which adults must suffer the incompetencies of the young. We now value childhood as a special time of growth and change, and we invest great resources in caring for and educating our children. We protect them from the stresses and responsibilities of adult work through strict child labor laws. We treat their crimes against society under a special system of juvenile justice. We also have government provisions for helping them when ordinary family support systems fail or when families seriously interfere with the child's well-being.

As we see next, although development in childhood is important, a complete view of development requires that we also consider developmental changes in the adult years.

Life-Span Development   The *traditional approach* to the study of development emphasizes extensive change from birth to adolescence, little or no change in adulthood, and decline in old age. Infancy is especially thought to be a time of considerable change. In contrast, the *life-span approach* emphasizes developmental change throughout adulthood as well as childhood (Birren & Schaie, 2001; Overton, 2003; Salthouse, 2000).

In 1900, human life expectancy in the United States was 47 years. It took 5,000 years to extend human life expectancy from 18 to 41 years of age (see figure 1.1). Then, in the twentieth century alone, life expectancy increased by 30 years. Improvements in sanitation, nutrition, and medical knowledge led to this amazing increase in life expectancy. Today, for most individuals, childhood and adolescence represent only about one-fourth of the life span (Schaie, 2000; Schaie & Willis, 2001).

How much has the older adult population grown in the United States? Figure 1.2 reveals a dramatic increase in the over-65 age group since 1900 and projects continued increases through 2040. A significant increase also will occur in the number of individuals in the 85-and-over and in the 100-and-over age categories. Currently, fewer than 50,000 Americans are 100 years of age or older; in 2050, the projected number is more than 800,000. A baby girl born today has a 1-in-3 chance of living to be 100 years of age!

Although we are living longer, on the average, than we did in the past, the maximum life span of humans has not changed since the beginning of recorded history. The upper boundary of the life span is approximately 120 years, and, as indicated in figure 1.3, our only competition from other species for the maximum recorded life span is the Galápagos turtle.

For too long we believed that development was something that happened only to children. To be sure, growth and development are dramatic in the first two decades of life, but a great deal of change goes on in the next five or six decades of life, too. Consider these descriptions of adult development:

> The next five or six decades are every bit as important,
> not only to those adults who are passing through them
> but to their children, who must live with and
> understand parents and grandparents. The changes
> in body, personality, and abilities through these
> later decades is great. Developmental tasks are
> imposed by marriage and parenthood, by the

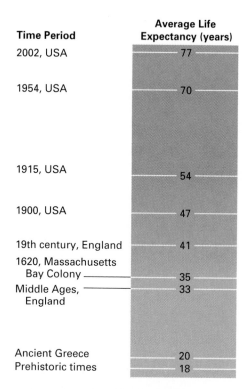

Time Period	Average Life Expectancy (years)
2002, USA	77
1954, USA	70
1915, USA	54
1900, USA	47
19th century, England	41
1620, Massachusetts Bay Colony	35
Middle Ages, England	33
Ancient Greece	20
Prehistoric times	18

FIGURE 1.1 Human Life Expectancy at Birth from Prehistoric to Contemporary Times

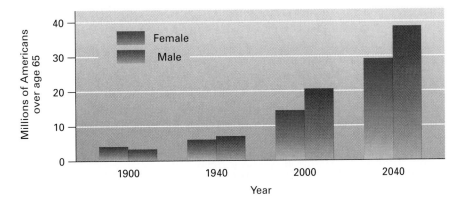

FIGURE 1.2 The Aging of America
Millions of Americans over age 65 from 1900 to the present and projected to the year 2040.

waxing and waning of physical prowess and of some intellectual capacities, by the children's flight from the nest, by the achievement of an occupational plateau, and by retirement and the prospect of final extinction. Parents have always been fascinated by their children's development, but it is high time adults began to look objectively at themselves, to examine the systematic changes in their own physical, mental, and emotional qualities, as they pass through the life span, and to get acquainted with the limitations and assets they share with so many others of their age.
(Sears & Feldman, 1973, pp. v–vi)

As the older population continues to increase in the twenty-first century, there is concern about the increasing number of older adults who will be without either a spouse or children (traditionally the main sources of support for older adults). In recent decades, American adults were less likely to be married, more likely to be childless, and more likely to be living alone than earlier in the twentieth century. As these individuals become older, their need for social relationships, networks, and supports is increasing at the same time as the supply is dwindling.

Characteristics of the Life-Span Perspective

The belief that development is lifelong is central to the life-span perspective, but according to life-span development expert Paul Baltes (1987, 2000), the **life-span perspective** includes several additional characteristics. Baltes describes the life-span perspective as lifelong, multidimensional, multidirectional, plastic, multidisciplinary, and contextual, and involves growth, maintenance, and regulation. Let's look at each of these concepts.

Development Is Lifelong In the life-span perspective, early adulthood is not the endpoint of development; rather, no age period dominates development. Researchers increasingly study the experiences and psychological orientations of adults at different points in their development. Later in this chapter we will describe the age periods of development and their characteristics.

Development Is Multidimensional Development consists of biological, cognitive, and socioemotional dimensions. Even within a dimension, such as intelligence, there

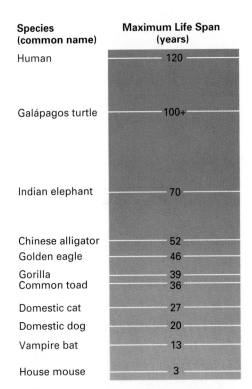

Species (common name)	Maximum Life Span (years)
Human	120
Galápagos turtle	100+
Indian elephant	70
Chinese alligator	52
Golden eagle	46
Gorilla	39
Common toad	36
Domestic cat	27
Domestic dog	20
Vampire bat	13
House mouse	3

FIGURE 1.3 Maximum Recorded Life Spans for Different Species

life-span perspective The view that development is lifelong, multidimensional, multidirectional, plastic, multidisciplinary, involves growth, maintenance, and regulation, and is contextual.

are many components, such as abstract intelligence, nonverbal intelligence, and social intelligence. K. Warner Schaie is one of the leading theorists and researchers who has studied intellectual development in the adulthood years. You can read further about him in the Careers in Life-Span Development insert.

Development Is Multidirectional   Some dimensions or components of a dimension expand and others shrink. In language development, when one language (such as English) is acquired early in development, the capacity for acquiring second and third languages (such as French and Spanish) decreases later in development, especially after early childhood (Levelt, 1989). In socioemotional development, heterosexual individuals begin to have more relationships with opposite-sex peers during adolescence. As they establish intimate relationships with opposite-sex peers their relationships with same-sex peers might decrease. In cognitive development, older adults might become wiser by being able to call on experience to guide their intellectual decision making (Baltes, 2000). However, they perform more poorly on tasks that require speed in processing information (Madden, 2001; Salthouse, 2000).

mhhe●com/
santrockld9

Exploring Aging Issues
National Aging Information Center
Global Resources on Aging

Careers in Life-Span Development

K. Warner Schaie, Professor of Human Development

K. Warner Schaie is a professor of human development and psychology at Pennsylvania State University, where he teaches and conducts research on adult development and aging. He also directs the Gerontology Center there. He is one of the pioneering psychologists who helped to create the life-span perspective. He is the author or editor of more than 25 books and more than 250 journal articles and book chapters on adult development and aging. Dr. Schaie conducted the Seattle Longitudinal Study of intellectual development, a major research investigation which revealed that many intellectual skills are maintained or even increase in middle age. *To what extent do you think that your intelligence will change during the remainder of your adult years?*

Life-span developmentalist K. Warner Schaie *(right)* with two older adults who are actively using their cognitive skills.

Development Is Plastic   A key developmental research agenda is the search for plasticity and its constraints (Maurer, 2001). *Plasticity* means the degree to which characteristics change or remain stable. For example, can intellectual skills still be improved through education for individuals in their seventies or eighties? Or might these intellectual skills be fixed by the time people are in their thirties so that further improvement is impossible? In one research study, the reasoning abilities of older adults were improved through retraining (Willis & Schaie, 1994). However, developmentalists debate how much plasticity people have at different points in their development; possibly we possess less capacity for change when we become old (Baltes, 2000). Later in the chapter we will discuss the issue of stability and change in development, which has close ties with the concept of plasticity.

Development Is Multidisciplinary   Psychologists, sociologists, anthropologists, neuroscientists, and medical researchers all study human development and share an interest in unlocking the mysteries of development through the life span. Research questions that cut across disciplines include:

- What constraints on intelligence are set by the individual's heredity and health status?
- How universal are cognitive and socioemotional changes?
- How do environmental contexts influence intellectual development?

Development Is Contextual   The individual continually responds to and acts on contexts, which includes a person's biological makeup, physical environment, cognitive processes, historical contexts, social contexts, and cultural contexts. In the contextual view, individuals are thought of as changing beings in a changing world.

Baltes and other life-span developmentalists (Baltes, 2000; Baltes, Reese, & Lipsitt, 1980; Schaie, 1996, 2000) believe that three important sources of contextual influences are (1) normative age-graded influences, (2) normative history-graded influences, and (3) nonnormative life events.

Normative age-graded influences are biological and environmental influences that are similar for individuals in a particular age group. These influences include biological processes such as puberty and menopause. They also include sociocultural, environmental processes such as entry into formal education (usually at about age 6 in most cultures) and retirement (which takes place in the fifties and sixties in most cultures).

Normative history-graded influences are common to people of a particular generation because of the historical circumstances they experience. Examples include economic changes (such as the Great Depression in the 1930s), war (such as World War II in the 1940s), the changing role of women, the technology revolution we currently are experiencing, and political upheaval and change (such as the decrease in hard-line communism in the 1990s and into the twenty-first century) (Modell & Elder, 2002).

Nonnormative life events are unusual occurrences that have a major impact on the individual's life and usually are not applicable to many people. These events might include the death of a parent when a child is young, pregnancy in early adolescence, a disaster (such as a fire that destroys a home), or an accident. Nonnormative life events also can include positive events (such as winning the lottery or getting an unexpected career opportunity with special privileges). An important aspect of understanding the role of nonnormative life events is to focus on how people adapt to them.

Development Involves Growth, Maintenance, and Regulation   Baltes and his colleagues (Baltes, 2000; Baltes, Staudinger, & Lindenberger, 1999) believe that the mastery of life often involves conflicts and competition among three goals of human development: growth, maintenance, and regulation. As individuals age into middle and late adulthood, the maintenance and regulation of their capacities takes center stage away from growth. Thus, for many individuals, the goal is not to seek growth in intellectual capacities (such as memory) or physical capacities (such as physical strength), but to maintain those skills or minimize their deterioration. In Section 9, "Late Adulthood," we will discuss these ideas about maintenance and regulation in greater depth.

Earlier in the chapter, we examined life-span development from a historical perspective. As you will see next, the life-span perspective also addresses a number of contemporary concerns from infancy through old age.

Some Contemporary Concerns

Consider some of the topics you read about every day in newspapers and magazines: genetic research, child abuse, mental retardation, parenting, intelligence, career changes, divorce, addiction and recovery, the increasing ethnic minority population, gender issues, homosexuality, midlife crises, stress and health, retirement, and aging. What life-span experts are discovering in each of these areas has direct and significant consequences for understanding children and adults and our decisions as a society about how they should be treated.

Of particular interest in this textbook are the roles that health and well-being, parenting, education, and sociocultural contexts play in life-span development, and their importance in social policy. Here we will preview these themes and highlight a research study pertaining to each one.

Health and Well-Being   Health and well-being have been important goals for just about everyone for most of human history. Asian physicians in 2600 B.C. and Greek physicians in 500 B.C. recognized that good habits are essential for good health. They did not blame the gods for illness or think that magic would cure it—they realized that people have some control over their health and well-being. A physician's role became that of a guide, assisting patients to restore a natural physical and emotional balance.

mhhe.com/
santrockld9

Adult Development and Aging
The Gerontological Society of America
Geropsychology Resources

In the twenty-first century, we once again recognize the power of lifestyles and psychological states in health and well-being (Baum, Revenson, & Singer, 2001; Brown, Steele, & Walsh-Childers, 2002; Hahn & Payne, 2003; Siegler, Bosworth, & Poon, 2003). In every chapter of this book, issues of health and well-being are integrated into our discussion of life-span development. They also are highlighted in the Internet connections that appear with World Wide Web icons throughout the book.

Careers in Life-Span Development

Luis Vargas, Child Clinical Psychologist

Luis Vargas is Director of the Clinical Child Psychology Internship Program and a professor in the Department of Psychiatry at the University of New Mexico Health Sciences Center. He also is Director of Psychology at the University of New Mexico Children's Psychiatric Hospital.

Dr. Vargas obtained an undergraduate degree in psychology from St. Edwards University in Texas, a master's degree in psychology from Trinity University in Texas, and a Ph.D. in clinical psychology from the University of Nebraska–Lincoln.

His main interests are cultural issues and the assessment and treatment of children, adolescents, and families. He is motivated to find better ways to provide culturally responsive mental health services. One of his special interests is the treatment of Latino youth for delinquency and substance abuse. He recently coauthored (with Joan Koss-Chioino) *Working with Latino Youth* (Koss-Chioino & Vargas, 1999), which spells out effective strategies for improving the lives of at-risk Latino youth. *Do you have an interest in helping children and adolescents cope more effectively with problems in their lives? If so, how do you think you could accomplish this goal?*

Luis Vargas *(left)* conducting a child therapy session.

The topics on health and well-being we will discuss include:

- Drug and alcohol use during pregnancy
- Genetic counseling
- Breast- versus bottle-feeding
- Early intervention
- School health programs
- At-risk adolescents
- Women's health issues
- Exercise
- Addiction and recovery
- Loneliness
- Adaptive physical skills in aging adults
- Coping with death

Clinical psychologists are among the health professionals who help people improve their well-being. Luis Vargas is a child clinical psychologist who has a deep concern about helping adolescents who have become juvenile delinquents and/or substance abusers get their lives on track. You can read further about Luis Vargas and his work in the Careers in Life-Span Development insert.

Research on Premature Infants Tiffany Field's (2001) research focuses on how massage therapy can facilitate weight gain in premature infants. In their original research, Field and her colleagues (1986) found that massage therapy conducted three times per day for 15 minutes with preterm infants led to 47 percent greater weight gain than standard medical treatment. The massaged infants also showed improved social and motor skills. The same positive results for massage therapy has been found in the Philippines and Israel (Goldstein-Ferber, 1997; Jinon, 1996). We will further discuss Field's massage therapy research in chapter 4, "Prenatal Development and Birth."

Parenting We hear a lot about pressures on the contemporary family (Borwkowsi, Ramey, & Bristol-Power, 2002; Cowen & Cowen, 2002; Fitzgerald & others, 2003; Maccoby, 2002; Pruett & Jackson, 2001). In later chapters, we will evaluate issues related to family functioning and parenting. Some of the topics we will consider are:

- Day care
- Working parents and latchkey children
- Effects of divorce on children
- The best way to parent
- Child maltreatment
- Support systems for families

- Marital relationships
- Intergenerational relations
- Aging parents

Research on Family and Peer Relations   One issue that interests researchers who study families and parents focuses on links between family and peer functioning. In one recent study of maltreated children (children who have been abused) and nonmaltreated children, the maltreated children were more likely to be repeatedly rejected across the childhood and adolescent years (Bolger & Patterson, 2001). The main reason for the rejection was the high rate of aggressive behavior shown by the children who had been abused by their parents. Why do you think the abuse by parents resulted in more aggression toward their peers by the children? We will have more to say about maltreated children in chapter 9, "Socioemotional Development in Early Childhood."

Education   In the past decade the American educational system has come under attack (Johnson & others, 2002; McCombs, 2003; Rogoff, Turkanis, & Bartlett, 2001; Sadker & Sadker, 2003). A national committee appointed by the Office of Education concluded that children are being poorly prepared for the increasingly complex future they will face. The educational topics we will explore include these:

Children learn to love when they are loved

- Variations in early childhood education
- Ethnicity, poverty, and schools
- Programs to improve children's critical thinking
- School and family coordination
- Cooperative learning
- How to avoid stifling children's creativity
- Bilingual education
- The best schools for adolescents

Research on Mentoring   Mentoring programs are increasingly being advocated as a strategy for improving the achievement of children and adolescents who are at risk for academic failure. One study focused on 959 adolescents who had applied to the Big Brothers/Big Sisters program (Rhodes, Grossman, & Resch, 2000). Half of the adolescents were mentored through extensive discussions about school, careers, and life, as well as participation in leisure activities with other adolescents. The other half were not mentored. Mentoring led to reduced unexcused absences from school, improvements in classroom performance, and better relationships with parents.

Health Links
Prevention Programs
AskERIC
Diversity
Social Policy
Trends in the Well-Being of Children and Youth

Sociocultural Contexts   The tapestry of American culture has changed dramatically in recent years. Nowhere is the change more dramatic than in the increasing ethnic diversity of America's citizens. This changing demographic tapestry promises not only the richness that diversity produces, but also difficult challenges in extending the American dream to all individuals (Fuligni & Yoshikawa, 2003).

Sociocultural contexts include four important concepts: context, culture, ethnicity, and gender. A **context** is the setting in which development occurs. This setting is influenced by historical, economic, social, and cultural factors. Contexts include homes, schools, peer groups, churches, cities, neighborhoods, university laboratories, countries, and many others. Each of these settings has meaningful historical, economic, social, and cultural legacies (Matsumoto, 2001; Triandis, 2001).

Culture encompasses the behavior patterns, beliefs, and all other products of a particular group of people that are passed on from generation to generation. Culture results from the interaction of people over many years. A cultural group can be as large as the United States or as small as an African hunter-gatherer group. Whatever

context The settings, influenced by historical, economic, social, and cultural factors, in which development occurs.

culture The behavior patterns, beliefs, and all other products of a group that are passed on from generation to generation.

Two Korean-born children on the day they became United States citizens. Asian American and Latino children are the fastest-growing immigrant groups in the United States. *How diverse are the students in this class on life-span development that you now are taking? How are their experiences in growing up likely similar to or different than yours?*

its size, the group's culture influences the behavior of its members (Saraswathi & Mistry, 2003; Shiraev & Levy, 2001; Valsiner, 2000). **Cross-cultural studies** involve a comparison of a culture with one or more other cultures. The comparison provides information about the degree to which development is similar, or universal, across cultures, or is instead culture-specific. For example, the United States is an achievement-oriented culture with a strong work ethic. However, recent cross-cultural studies of American and Japanese children showed that Japanese children are better at math, spend more time working on math at school, and do more math homework than American children (Stevenson, 1995, 2000). The topics on culture that we will discuss include:

- Child-care policy around the world
- Vygotsky's sociocultural cognitive theory
- Gender roles in Egypt and China
- Cross-cultural comparisons of secondary schools
- Marriage around the world
- Death and dying in different cultures

Race and ethnicity are sometimes misrepresented. *Race* is a controversial classification of people according to real or imagined biological characteristics such as skin color and blood group membership (Corsini, 1999). An individual's ethnicity can include his or her race but also many other characteristics. Thus, an individual might be White (a racial category) and a fifth-generation Texan who is a Catholic and speaks English and Spanish fluently.

Ethnicity (the word *ethnic* comes from the Greek word for "nation") is rooted in cultural heritage, nationality characteristics, race, religion, and language. Not only is there diversity within a culture such as found in the United States, there also is diversity within each ethnic group. These groups include African Americans, Latinos, Asian Americans, Native Americans, Polish Americans, Italian Americans, and so on. Not all African Americans live in low-income circumstances. Not all Latinos are Catholics. Not all Native Americans are high school dropouts. It is easy to fall into the trap of stereotyping an ethnic group by thinking that all of its members are alike. A more accurate ethnic group portrayal is diversity (Cushner, 2003; Eccles, 2001; Jenkins & others, 2003; McLoyd, 2000).

Among the ethnicity topics we will examine in later chapters are:

- Similarities, differences, and diversity
- Immigration
- Support systems for ethnic minority individuals
- Ethnicity and schooling
- Value conflicts
- Being old, female, and ethnic

Gender involves the psychological and sociocultural dimensions of being female or male. *Sex* refers to the biological dimension of being female or male. Few aspects of our development are more central to our identity and social relationships than gender (Eagly, 2001; Maracek & others, 2003; Worell, 2001). Our society's attitudes about gender are changing. But how much? The gender-related topics we will discuss include these:

- The mother's role and the father's role
- Parental and peer roles in gender development
- Gender similarities and differences
- Femininity, masculinity, and androgyny
- Carol Gilligan's care perspective
- Gender communication patterns
- Family work
- Gender and aging

cross-cultural studies Comparisons of one culture with one or more other cultures. These provide information about the degree to which development is similar, or universal, across cultures, and to the degree to which it is culture-specific.

ethnicity A characteristic based on cultural heritage, nationality characteristics, race, religion, and language.

gender The social dimension of being male or female.

Women's Struggle for Equality: An International Journey

There are serious concerns about the educational and psychological conditions of women around the world (Maracek & others, 2003; United Nations, 2001). The countries with the fewest women being educated are in Africa, where in some areas women are receiving no education at all. Canada, the United States, and Russia have the highest percentages of educated women. In developing countries, 67 percent of women and 50 percent of men over the age of 25 have never been to school. At the beginning of the twenty-first century, 80 million more boys than girls were in primary and secondary educational settings around the world (United Nations, 2002).

Women in every country experience violence, often from someone close to them. Partner abuse occurs in one of every six households in the United States, with the vast majority of the abuse being directed at women by men (Walker, 2001). In a survey, "The New Woman Ethics Report," wife abuse was listed as number one among fifteen of the most pressing concerns facing society today (Johnson, 1990). Although most countries around the world now have battered women's shelters, beating women continues to be accepted and expected behavior in some countries.

In a study of depression in high-income countries, women were twice as likely as men to be diagnosed as depressed (Nolen-Hoeksema, 1990). In the United States, from adolescence through adulthood, females are more likely than males to be depressed (Davison & Neale, 2001; Hammen, 2003). Many sociocultural inequities and experiences have contributed to the greater incidence of depression in females than males (Whiffen, 2001). Also, possibly more women are diagnosed with depression than actually have depression (Nolen-Hoeksema, 2001).

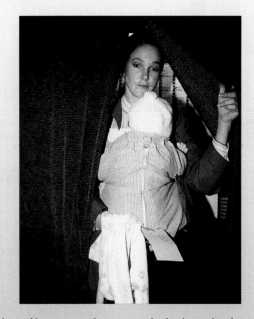

Around the world women too often are treated as burdens rather than assets in the political process. *What can be done to strengthen women's roles in the political process?*

We will discuss sociocultural contexts in each chapter. In addition, a Sociocultural Worlds of Development box appears in most chapters. Look at the one above for a discussion of women's international struggle for equality.

Research on Children's Ethnicity, Poverty, and Type of Home Environment One study recently examined the home environments of three ethnic groups: European American, African American, and Latino (Bradley & others, 2001). The home environments were assessed (by a combination of observations and maternal interviews) at five points in children's lives from infancy through early adolescence. There were some ethnic differences, but the most consistent result involved poverty, which was a much more powerful indicator of the type of home environment children experienced than ethnicity was (see figure 1.4 on page 16).

Social Policy **Social policy** is a national government's course of action designed to promote the welfare of its citizens. The shape and scope of social policy is strongly tied to the political system. Our country's policy agenda and the welfare of the nation's citizens are influenced by the values held by individual lawmakers, by the nation's economic strengths and weaknesses, and by partisan politics.

Out of concern that policy makers are doing too little to protect the well-being of children and older adults, life-span researchers increasingly are undertaking studies that they hope will lead to effective social policy (Bogenschneider, 2002; Bornstein & Bradley, 2003; Maccoby, 2001; Zigler & Hall, 2000). When more than 15 percent of all children and almost half of all ethnic minority children are being raised in poverty, when 40 to 50 percent of all children can expect to spend at least 5 years in a single-parent home, when children and young adolescents are giving birth, when the use and

social policy A national government's course of action designed to promote the welfare of its citizens.

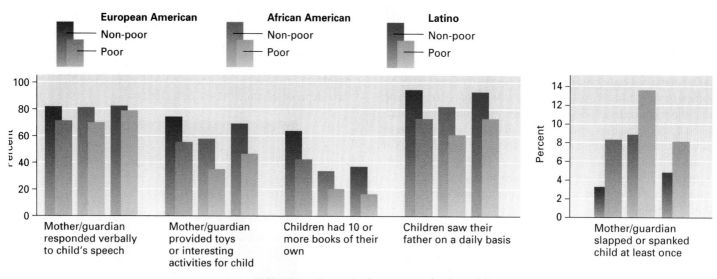

FIGURE 1.4 Home Environments of Infants by Ethnicity and Poverty Status

These data are based on home observations and maternal interviews obtained in the first three years of children's lives. Although there are some differences across ethnic groups, the most consistent differences were found between families classified as poor and non-poor. For example, regardless of their ethnic group, children growing up in non-poor home environments were more likely to have their speech responded to, be provided with toys or interesting activities, have ten or more books of their own, see their father on a daily basis, and be less likely to be slapped or spanked. Similar findings occurred when children were older.

abuse of drugs is widespread, when the specter of AIDS is present, and when the provision of health care for older adults is inadequate, our nation needs revised social policy.

Marian Wright Edelman, president of the Children's Defense Fund, has been a tireless advocate of children's rights (Children's Defense Fund, 2002). Especially troublesome to Edelman (1997) are the indicators of social neglect that place the United States at or near the lowest rank for industrialized nations in the treatment of children. Edelman says that parenting and nurturing the next generation of children is our society's most important function and that we need to take it more seriously than we have in the past. She points out that we hear a lot from politicians these days about "family values," but that when we examine our nation's policies for families, they don't reflect the politicians' words.

Marian Wright Edelman, president of the Children's Defense Fund (shown here interacting with young children), has been a tireless advocate of children's rights and has been instrumental in calling attention to the needs of children. *What are some of these needs?*

At the other end of the life span, our aging society and older persons' status in this society raise policy issues about the well-being of older adults. Special concerns are escalating health-care costs and the access of older adults to adequate health care (Hill & others, 2002).

The need for social welfare resources is far greater than policy makers have seen fit to provide. Then who should get the bulk of government dollars for improved well-being? Children? Their parents? Older adults? **Generational inequity,** a social policy concern, is the condition in which an aging society is being unfair to its younger members. It occurs because older adults pile up advantages by receiving disproportionately large allocations of resources, such as Social Security and Medicare. Generational inequity raises questions about whether the young should have to pay to care for the old and whether an "advantaged" older population is using up resources that should go to disadvantaged children. The argument is that older adults are advantaged because they have publicly financed pensions, health care, food stamps, housing subsidies, tax breaks, and other benefits that younger groups do not have. While the trend of greater services for the elderly has been occurring, the percentage of children in poverty has been rising.

Bernice Neugarten (1988) says the problem should be viewed not as one of generational inequity, but rather as a major shortcoming of our broader economic and social policies. She believes we need to develop a spirit of support for improving the range of options for all people in our society. Also, it is important to keep in mind that children will one day become older adults and will in turn be supported by the efforts of their children (Williams & Nussbaum, 2001). If there were no Social Security system, many adult children would have to bear the burden of supporting their aging parents and spend less of their resources on educating their children (Schaie, 2000).

Research on How Children Acquire Democratic Values If a democracy like the United States is to remain secure and stable, each new generation of citizens must believe in the system and believe it works for people like them. Research by Constance Flanagan and her colleagues (Flanagan & Faison, 2001; Flanagan, Gill, & Galley, 1998) with different ethnic groups of American youth points to the pivotal role of teaching in this regard (Flanagan, Gill, & Galley, 1998). They have found that the extent to which teachers ensure that all students are treated equally and listen to and respect each other is related to the students' endorsement of democracy.

Maggie Kuhn, founder of the Gray Panthers, an international advocacy group that began in 1970 with five older women committed to improving the social conditions of older adults.

Review and Reflect

1 Discuss the life-span perspective of development

REVIEW
- What is meant by the term *life-span development?*
- What is the historical background of life-span development?
- What are seven main characteristics of the life-span perspective?
- What are some contemporary concerns in life-span development?

REFLECT
- Imagine what your development would have been like in a culture that offered fewer or distinctly different choices than your own. How might your development have been different if your family had been significantly richer or poorer than it was?

Earlier in the chapter we described Paul Baltes' view of the life-span perspective's characteristics. Next, we will further explore the nature of development, examining in greater detail some of the concepts Baltes presented along with other ways of thinking about development.

generational inequity An aging society's being unfair to its younger members because older adults pile up advantages by receiving inequitably large allocations of resources.

2 DEVELOPMENTAL PROCESSES AND PERIODS

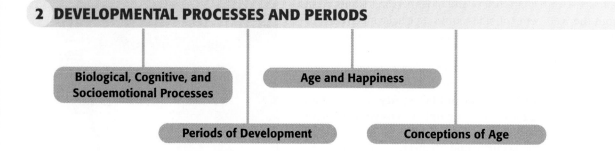

Biological, Cognitive, and Socioemotional Processes

Age and Happiness

Periods of Development

Conceptions of Age

Each of us develops partly like all other individuals, partly like some other individuals, and partly like no other individuals. Most of the time, our attention is directed to an individual's uniqueness. But psychologists who study life-span development are drawn to our shared characteristics as well as what makes us unique. As humans, we all have traveled some common paths. Each of us—Leonardo da Vinci, Joan of Arc, George Washington, Martin Luther King, Jr., you—walked at about 1 year, engaged in fantasy play as a young child, and became more independent as a youth. Each of us, if we live long enough, will experience hearing problems and the deaths of family members and friends.

At the beginning of the chapter, we defined *development* as the pattern of movement or change that begins at conception and continues through the life span. The pattern of movement is complex because it is the product of biological, cognitive, and socioemotional processes.

Biological, Cognitive, and Socioemotional Processes

Biological processes produce changes in an individual's physical nature. Genes inherited from parents, the development of the brain, height and weight gains, changes in motor skills, the hormonal changes of puberty, and cardiovascular decline all reflect the role of biological processes in development.

One area of biological research that has immense importance for development seeks to extend the human life span. Although researchers have not yet succeeded, they are making significant strides in understanding the cellular processes that might enable people to live longer (Aisner, Wright, & Shay, 2001; Shay & Wright, 2000). We will have more to say about the biological processes involved in aging in chapter 18, "Physical Development in Late Adulthood."

Cognitive processes refer to changes in the individual's thought, intelligence, and language. Watching a colorful mobile swinging above the crib, putting together a two-word sentence, memorizing a poem, imagining what it would be like to be a movie star, and solving a crossword puzzle all involve cognitive processes.

Researchers have found that the responsiveness of caregivers provides important support for children's advances in cognitive development. In one recent study, the mother's responsiveness was linked with a number of language milestones in children's development (Tamis-LeMonda, Bornstein, & Baumwell, 2001). Children with responsive mothers (such as mothers who respond to a child's bids for attention and to a child's play) spoke their first words earlier and combined parts of speech earlier than children whose mothers responded to them infrequently. We will have much more to say about language development, including how to talk with babies and toddlers, in chapter 6, "Cognitive Development in Infancy."

Socioemotional processes involve changes in the individual's relationships with other people, changes in emotions, and changes in personality. An infant's smile in response to her mother's touch, a young boy's aggressive attack on a playmate, a girl's development of assertiveness, an adolescent's joy at the senior prom, and the affection of an elderly couple all reflect the role of the socioemotional processes in development.

biological processes Changes in an individual's physical nature.

cognitive processes Changes in an individual's thought, intelligence, and language.

socioemotional processes Changes in an individual's relationships with other people, emotions, and personality.

One socioemotional process that interests researchers is marital relations. In a number of research studies, John Gottman and his colleagues (Gottman, 1994; Gottman & others, 2002) found that an important factor in whether wives or husbands felt satisfied with the sex, romance, and passion in their marriage was the quality of the couple's friendship. We will have more to say about marital relations and Gottman's research in chapter 15, "Socioemotional Development in Early Adulthood."

Biological, cognitive, and socioemotional processes are inextricably intertwined. For example, consider a baby smiling in response to its mother's touch. This response depends on biological processes (the physical nature of touch and responsiveness to it), cognitive processes (the ability to understand intentional acts), and socioemotional processes (the act of smiling often reflects a positive emotional feeling and smiling helps to connect us in positive ways with other human beings).

Also, in many instances biological, cognitive, and socioemotional processes are bidirectional. For example, biological processes can influence cognitive processes and vice versa. In Section 9, "Late Adulthood," you will read about how poor health (a biological process) is linked to lower intellectual functioning (a cognitive process). You also will read about how positive thinking about the ability to control one's environment (a cognitive process) can have a powerful effect on an individual's health (a biological process).

Thus, although usually we will study the different processes (biological, cognitive, and socioemotional) in separate locations, keep in mind that we are talking about the development of an integrated individual with a mind and body that are interdependent (see figure 1.5).

Periods of Development

The concept of *developmental period* refers to a time frame in a person's life that is characterized by certain features. For the purposes of organization and understanding, we commonly describe development in terms of these periods. The most widely used classification of developmental periods involves this sequence: prenatal period, infancy, early childhood, middle and late childhood, adolescence, early adulthood, middle adulthood, and late adulthood. Approximate age ranges are listed here for the periods to provide a general idea of when a period begins and ends.

The *prenatal period* is the time from conception to birth. It involves tremendous growth—from a single cell to an organism complete with brain and behavioral capabilities, produced in approximately a nine-month period.

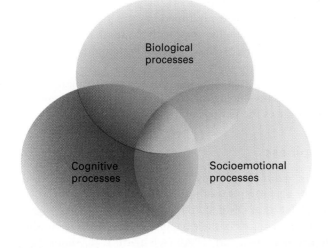

FIGURE 1.5 Developmental Changes Are the Result of Biological, Cognitive, and Socioemotional Processes

These processes interact as individuals develop.

One's children's children's children. Look back to us as we look to you; we are related by our imaginations. If we are able to touch, it is because we have imagined each other's existence, our dreams running back and forth along a cable from age to age.

—ROGER ROSENBLATT
American Writer, 20th Century

Infancy is the developmental period from birth to 18 or 24 months. Infancy is a time of extreme dependence upon adults. Many psychological activities are just beginning—language, symbolic thought, sensorimotor coordination, and social learning, for example.

Early childhood is the developmental period from the end of infancy to about 5 or 6 years. This period is sometimes called the "preschool years." During this time, young children learn to become more self-sufficient and to care for themselves, develop school readiness skills (following instructions, identifying letters), and spend many hours in play with peers. First grade typically marks the end of early childhood.

Middle and late childhood is the developmental period from about 6 to 11 years of age, approximately corresponding to the elementary school years. This period is sometimes called the "elementary school years." The fundamental skills of reading, writing, and arithmetic are mastered. The child is formally exposed to the larger world and its culture. Achievement becomes a more central theme of the child's world, and self-control increases.

Adolescence is the developmental period of transition from childhood to early adulthood, entered at approximately 10 to 12 years of age and ending at 18 to 22 years of age. Adolescence begins with rapid physical changes—dramatic gains in height and weight, changes in body contour, and the development of sexual characteristics such as enlargement of the breasts, development of pubic and facial hair, and deepening of the voice. At this point in development, the pursuit of independence and an identity are prominent. Thought is more logical, abstract, and idealistic. More time is spent outside the family.

Early adulthood is the developmental period that begins in the late teens or early twenties and lasts through the thirties. It is a time of establishing personal and economic independence, career development, and, for many, selecting a mate, learning to live with someone in an intimate way, starting a family, and rearing children.

Middle adulthood is the developmental period from approximately 40 years of age to about 60. It is a time of expanding personal and social involvement and responsibility; of assisting the next generation in becoming competent, mature individuals; and of reaching and maintaining satisfaction in a career.

Late adulthood is the developmental period that begins in the sixties or seventies and lasts until death. It is a time of adjustment to decreasing strength and health, life review, retirement, and adjustment to new social roles.

Life-span developmentalists increasingly distinguish between two age groups in late adulthood: the *young old,* or *old age* (65 to 74 years of age), and the *old old,* or *late old age* (75 years and older). Still others distinguish the *oldest old* (85 years and older) from younger older adults (Pearlin, 1994). Beginning in the sixties and extending to more than 100 years of age, late adulthood has the longest span of any period of development. Combining this lengthy span with the dramatic increase in the number of adults living to older ages, we will see increased attention given to differentiating the late adulthood period.

The periods of the human life span are shown in figure 1.6, along with the processes of development—biological, cognitive, and socioemotional. The interplay of these processes produces the periods of the human life span.

Age and Happiness

When individuals report how happy they are and how satisfied they are with their lives, no particular age group says they are happier or more satisfied than any other age group (Diener, Lucas, & Oishi, 2002). When nearly 170,000 people in 16 countries were surveyed, no differences in their happiness from adolescence into the late adulthood years were found (Inglehart, 1990) (see figure 1.7). About the same percentage of people in each age group—slightly less than 20 percent—reported that they were "very happy."

Periods of Development

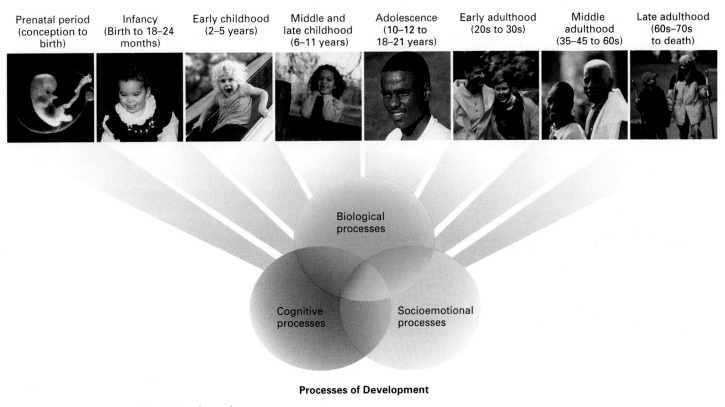

| Prenatal period (conception to birth) | Infancy (Birth to 18–24 months) | Early childhood (2–5 years) | Middle and late childhood (6–11 years) | Adolescence (10–12 to 18–21 years) | Early adulthood (20s to 30s) | Middle adulthood (35–45 to 60s) | Late adulthood (60s–70s to death) |

Biological processes

Cognitive processes

Socioemotional processes

Processes of Development

FIGURE 1.6 Processes and Periods of Development

The unfolding of life's periods of development is influenced by the interaction of biological, cognitive, and socioemotional processes.

Why might older people report just as much happiness and life satisfaction as younger people? Every period of the life span has its stresses, pluses and minuses, hills and valleys. Although adolescents must cope with developing an identity, feelings of insecurity, mood swings, and peer pressure, the majority of adolescents develop positive perceptions of themselves, feelings of competence about their skills, positive relationships with friends and family, and an optimistic view of their future. And while older adults face a life of reduced income, less energy, decreasing physical skills, and concerns about death, they are also less pressured to achieve and succeed, have more time for leisurely pursuits, and have accumulated many years of experience that help them adapt to their lives with a wisdom they may not have had in their younger years. Because growing older is a certain outcome of living, we can derive considerable pleasure from knowing that we are likely to be just as happy as older adults as when we were younger.

Conceptions of Age

In our description of the periods of the life span, we associated approximate age ranges with the periods. However, life-span expert Bernice Neugarten (1988) believes we are rapidly becoming an age-irrelevant society. She says we are already familiar with the 28-year-old mayor, the 35-year-old grandmother, the 65-year-old father of a preschooler, the 55-year-old widow who starts a business, and the 70-year-old student. Neugarten stresses that choices and dilemmas do not spring forth at

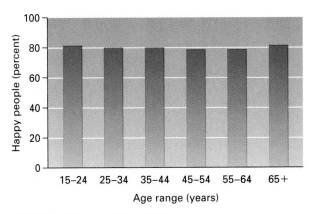

FIGURE 1.7 Age and Happiness

Analysis of surveys of nearly 170,000 people in 16 countries found no age differences in happiness from adolescence into the late adulthood years.

How old would you be if you didn't know how old you were?

—SATCHEL PAIGE
American Baseball Pitcher, 20th Century

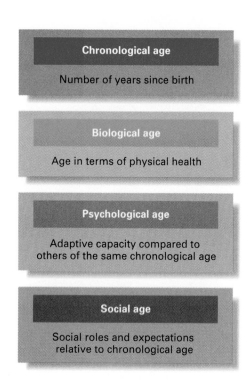

FIGURE 1.8 **Conceptions of Age**

10-year intervals. Decisions are not made and then left behind as if they were merely beads on a chain. Neugarten argues that most adulthood themes appear and reappear throughout the human life span. The issues of intimacy and freedom can haunt couples throughout their relationship. Feeling the pressure of time, reformulating goals, and coping with success and failure are not the exclusive property of adults of a particular age.

Neugarten's ideas raise questions about how age should be conceptualized. Some of the ways in which age has been conceptualized are as chronological age, biological age, psychological age, and social age (Hoyer, Rybash, & Roodin, 1999):

- **Chronological age** is the number of years that have elapsed since birth. Many people consider chronological age to be synonymous with the concept of age. However, some developmentalists argue that chronological age is not very relevant to understanding a person's psychological development (Botwinick, 1978). A person's age does not cause development. Time is a crude index of many events and experiences, and it does not cause anything.
- **Biological age** is a person's age in terms of biological health. Determining biological age involves knowing the functional capacities of a person's vital organs. One person's vital capacities may be better or worse than those of others of comparable age. The younger the person's biological age, the longer the person is expected to live, regardless of chronological age.
- **Psychological age** is an individual's adaptive capacities compared with those of other individuals of the same chronological age. Thus, older adults who continue to learn, are flexible, are motivated, control their emotions, and think clearly are engaging in more adaptive behaviors than their chronological agemates who do not continue to learn, are rigid, are unmotivated, do not control their emotions, and do not think clearly.
- **Social age** refers to social roles and expectations related to a person's age. Consider the role of "mother" and the behaviors that accompany the role (Huyck & Hoyer, 1982). In predicting an adult woman's behavior, it may be more important to know that she is the mother of a 3-year-old child than to know whether she is 20 or 30 years old. We still have some expectations for when certain life events—such as getting married, having children, becoming a grandparent, and retiring—should occur. However, as Neugarten concluded, chronological age has become a less accurate predictor of these life events in our society.

From a life-span perspective, an overall age profile of an individual involves more than just chronological age. It also consists of biological age, psychological age, and social age (see figure 1.8). For example, a 70-year-old man (chronological age) might be in good physical health (biological age), be experiencing memory problems and not be coping well with the demands placed on him by his wife's recent hospitalization (psychological age), and have a number of friends with whom he regularly golfs (social age).

chronological age The number of years that have elapsed since a person's birth; what is usually meant by "age."

biological age A person's age in terms of biological health.

psychological age An individual's adaptive capacities compared to those of other individuals of the same chronological age.

social age Social roles and expectations related to a person's age.

Review and Reflect

2 Identify the most important developmental processes and periods

REVIEW

- What are three key developmental processes?
- What are eight main developmental periods?
- How is age related to happiness?
- What are four ways age can be conceptualized?

REFLECT

- Do you think there is a best age to be? If so, what is it? Why?

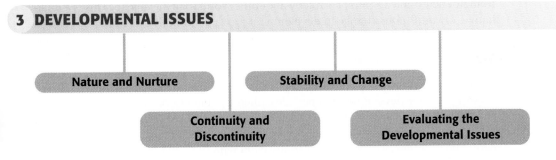

3 DEVELOPMENTAL ISSUES

- Nature and Nurture
- Stability and Change
- Continuity and Discontinuity
- Evaluating the Developmental Issues

The most important issues in the study of development include nature and nurture, continuity and discontinuity, and stability and change.

Nature and Nurture

The **nature-nurture issue** involves the debate about whether development is primarily influenced by nature or by nurture. *Nature* refers to an organism's biological inheritance, *nurture* to its environmental experiences. "Nature" proponents claim that the most important influence on development is biological inheritance. "Nurture" proponents claim that environmental experiences are the most important influence.

According to the nature advocates, just as a sunflower grows in an orderly way—unless defeated by an unfriendly environment—so does the human grow in an orderly way. The range of environments can be vast, but the nature approach argues that a genetic blueprint produces commonalities in growth and development. We walk before we talk, speak one word before two words, grow rapidly in infancy and less so in early childhood, experience a rush of sexual hormones in puberty, reach the peak of our physical strength in late adolescence and early adulthood, and then physically decline. The nature proponents acknowledge that extreme environments—those that are psychologically barren or hostile—can depress development. However, they believe that basic growth tendencies are genetically wired into humans.

By contrast, other psychologists emphasize the importance of nurture, or environmental experiences, in development. Experiences run the gamut from the individual's biological environment (nutrition, medical care, drugs, and physical accidents) to the social environment (family, peers, schools, community, media, and culture).

Continuity and Discontinuity

Think about your own development for a moment. Did you become the person you are gradually, like the seedling that slowly, cumulatively grows into a giant oak? Or did you experience sudden, distinct changes in your growth, like the caterpillar that changes into a butterfly (see figure 1.9 on page 24)? For the most part, developmentalists who emphasize nurture usually describe development as a gradual, continuous process. Those who emphasize nature often describe development as a series of distinct stages.

The **continuity-discontinuity issue** focuses on the extent to which development involves gradual, cumulative change (continuity) or distinct stages (discontinuity). In terms of continuity, as the oak grows from seedling to giant oak, it becomes *more* oak—its development is continuous. Similarly, a child's first word, though seemingly an abrupt, discontinuous event, is actually the result of weeks and months of growth and practice. Puberty, another seemingly abrupt, discontinuous occurrence, is actually a gradual process occurring over several years.

In terms of discontinuity, each person is described as passing through a sequence of stages in which change is qualitatively rather than quantitatively different. As the caterpillar changes to a butterfly, it is not just more caterpillar, it is a *different kind* of organism—its development is discontinuous. Similarly, at some point a child moves

nature-nurture issue *Nature* refers to an organism's biological inheritance, *nurture* to environmental influences. The "nature" proponents claim biological inheritance is the most important influence on development; the "nurture" proponents claim that environmental experiences are the most important.

continuity-discontinuity issue The issue regarding whether development involves gradual, cumulative change (continuity) or distinct stages (discontinuity).

FIGURE 1.9 Continuity and Discontinuity in Development

Is our development like that of a seedling gradually growing into a giant oak? Or is it more like that of a caterpillar suddenly becoming a butterfly?

stability-change issue The issue of whether development is best described as involving stability or as involving change. This issue involves the degree to which we become older renditions of our early experience or instead develop into someone different from who we were at an earlier point in development.

from not being able to think abstractly about the world to being able to. This is a qualitative, discontinuous change in development, not a quantitative, continuous change.

Stability and Change

Another important developmental topic is the **stability-change issue,** which addresses whether development is best described by stability or change. The stability-change issue involves the degree to which we become older renditions of our early experience or whether we develop into someone different from who were at an earlier point in development. Will the shy child who hides behind the sofa when visitors arrive be a wallflower at college dances, or will the child become a sociable, talkative individual? Will the fun-loving, carefree adolescent have difficulty holding down a 9-to-5 job as an adult or become a straitlaced, serious conformist?

The stability-change issue is linked with Paul Baltes' (1987, 2000) belief, which we discussed earlier, that plasticity or change is an important life-span issue. Recall that in the life-span perspective, plasticity or change is possible throughout the life span, although experts such as Baltes argue that older adults often show less capacity for change than younger adults.

One of the reasons why adult development was ignored by researchers until fairly recently was the predominant belief for many years that nothing much changes in adulthood. The major changes were believed to take place in childhood, especially during the first 5 years of life. Today, most developmentalists believe that some change is possible throughout the human life span, although they disagree, sometimes vehemently, about just how much change can take place, and how much stability there is.

An important dimension of the stability-change issue is the extent to which early experiences (especially in infancy) or later experiences determine a person's development. That is, if infants experience negative, stressful circumstances in their lives, can the effects of those experiences be counteracted by later, more positive experiences? Or are the early experiences so critical, possibly because they are the infant's first, prototypical experiences, that they cannot be overridden by an enriched environment later in development?

The early-later experience issue has a long history and continues to be hotly debated among developmentalists (Gottlieb, 2002). Some believe that unless infants experience warm, nurturant caregiving in the first year or so of life, their development will not likely be optimal (Waters & others, 2000). Plato was sure that infants who were rocked frequently became better athletes. Nineteenth-century New England ministers told parents in Sunday sermons that the way they handled their infants would determine their children's future character. The emphasis on the importance of early experience rests on the belief that each life is an unbroken trail on which a psychological quality can be traced back to its origin (Kagan, 1992, 1998, 2000).

The early-experience doctrine contrasts with the later-experience view that development, like a river, ebbs and flows continuously. The later-experience advocates argue that children are malleable throughout development and that later sensitive caregiving is just as important as earlier sensitive caregiving. A number of life-span developmentalists stress that too little attention has been given to later experiences in development (Baltes, 2000; Birren & Schaie, 2001). They argue that early experiences are important contributors to development, but no more important than later experiences. Jerome Kagan (2000) points out that even children who show the qualities of an inhibited temperament, which is linked to heredity, have the capacity to change their behavior. In his research, almost one-third of a group of children who had an inhibited temperament at 2 years of age were not unusually shy or fearful when they were 4 years of age.

People in Western cultures, especially those steeped in the Freudian belief that the key experiences in development are children's relationships with their parents in the first 5 years of life, have tended to support the idea that early experiences are more important than later experiences. But the majority of people in the world do not share this belief. For example, people in many Asian countries believe that experiences occurring after about 6 to 7 years of age are more important to development than earlier experiences. This stance stems from the long-standing belief in Eastern cultures that children's reasoning skills begin to develop in important ways in the middle childhood years.

One recent book—*The Myth of the First Three Years*—supports the later experience argument (Bruer, 1999). The argument is made, based on the available research evidence, that learning and cognitive development do not occur only in the first 3 years of life but rather are lifelong. The author concludes that too many parents act as though a switch goes off when a child turns 3, after which further learning either does not take place or is greatly diminished. That is not to say experiences in the first 3 years are unimportant, but rather that later experiences are too. This book has been highly controversial, with early-experience advocates being especially critical of it (Bornstein, 2000).

Evaluating the Developmental Issues

It is important to keep in mind that most life-span developmentalists do not take extreme positions on the three developmental issues. They acknowledge that development is not all nature or all nurture, not all continuity or all discontinuity, and not all stability or all change (Lerner, 2002). Nature and nurture, continuity and discontinuity, and stability and change characterize development throughout the human life span. With respect to the nature-nurture issue, then, the key to development is the *interaction* of nature and nurture rather than either factor alone (Rutter, 2002). For instance, an individual's cognitive development is the result of heredity-environment interaction, not heredity or environment alone. (Much more about heredity-environment interaction appears in chapter 3.)

Although most developmentalists do not take extreme positions on these three important issues, there is spirited debate regarding how strongly development is influenced by each of these factors (Waters, 2001). Are girls less likely to do well in math because of their "feminine" nature, or because of society's masculine bias? How extensively can the elderly be trained to reason more effectively? How much, if at all, does our memory decline in old age? Can techniques be used to prevent or reduce the decline? Can enriched experiences in adolescence remove "deficits" resulting from childhood experiences of poverty, neglect by parents, and poor schooling? The answers given by developmentalists to such questions depend on their stances regarding the issues of nature and nurture, continuity and discontinuity, and stability and change. The answers to these questions also have a bearing on public policy decisions about children, adolescents, and adults, and consequently, on each of our lives.

What is the nature of the early- and later-experience issue in development?

Review and Reflect

3 **Describe three key developmental issues**

REVIEW

- What is the nature and nurture issue?
- What is the continuity and discontinuity issue?
- What is the stability and change issue?
- What is a good strategy for evaluating the developmental issues?

REFLECT

- Can you identify an early experience that you believe contributed in important ways to your development? Can you identify a recent or current (later) experience that you think had (is having) a strong influence on your development?

Reach Your Learning Goals

Reach Your Learning Goals

Introduction

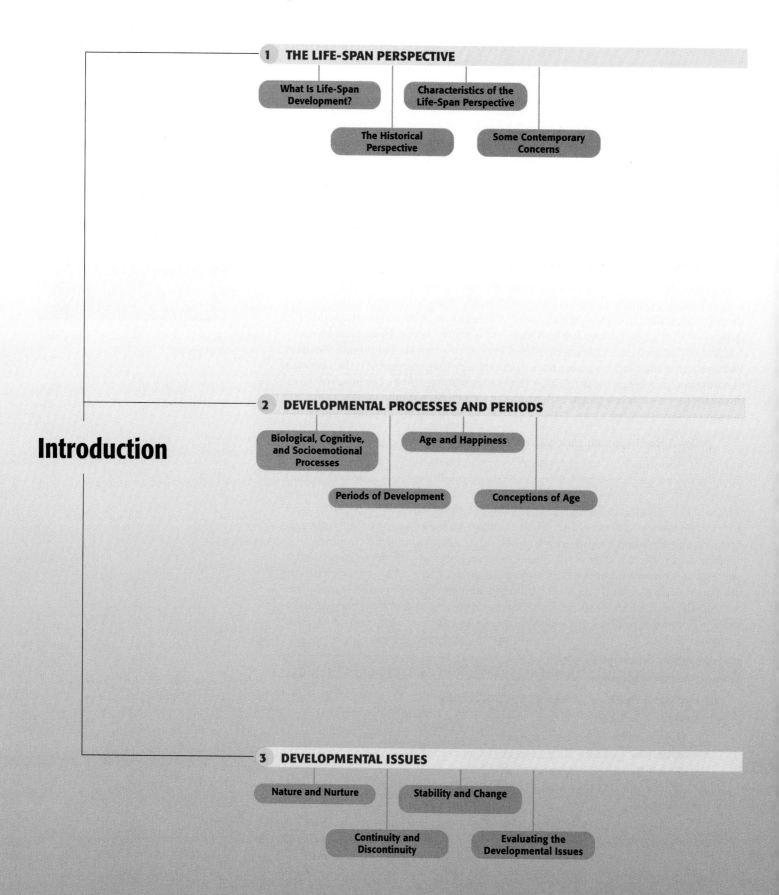

1   THE LIFE-SPAN PERSPECTIVE

- What Is Life-Span Development?
- The Historical Perspective
- Characteristics of the Life-Span Perspective
- Some Contemporary Concerns

2   DEVELOPMENTAL PROCESSES AND PERIODS

- Biological, Cognitive, and Socioemotional Processes
- Periods of Development
- Age and Happiness
- Conceptions of Age

3   DEVELOPMENTAL ISSUES

- Nature and Nurture
- Continuity and Discontinuity
- Stability and Change
- Evaluating the Developmental Issues

Summary

1 Discuss the life-span perspective of development

- Development is the pattern of movement or change that begins at conception and continues through the human life span. Development includes growth and decline.
- Interest in children has a long and rich history. Prior to the mid-nineteenth century, philosophical views of childhood were prominent, including the notions of original sin, tabula rasa, and innate goodness. The traditional approach to the study of development emphasizes extensive change in childhood but stability in adulthood; the life-span perspective emphasizes that change is possible throughout the life span. In the twentieth century alone, life expectancy increased by 30 years.
- The life-span perspective includes these basic conceptions: Development is lifelong, multidimensional, multidirectional, plastic, multidisciplinary, and contextual, and involves growth, maintenance, and regulation. Three important sources of contextual influences are (1) normative age-graded influences, (2) normative history-graded influences, and (3) nonnormative life events.
- Today, the development and well-being of children and adults capture the interest of the public, scientists, and policy makers. Among the important contemporary concerns are parenting, education, sociocultural contexts, and social policy. Three important sociocultural contexts are culture, ethnicity, and gender.

2 Identify the most important developmental processes and periods

- Development is influenced by an interplay of biological, cognitive, and socioemotional processes.
- The life-span is commonly divided into these periods of development: prenatal, infancy, early childhood, middle and late childhood, adolescence, early adulthood, middle adulthood, and late adulthood.
- In studies covering adolescence through old age, people report that they are not happier at one point in development than at others.
- Some experts on life-span development believe too much emphasis is placed on chronological age. Neugarten believes we are moving toward a society in which age is a weaker predictor of development in adulthood. However, we often think of age only in terms of chronological age. Nonetheless, a full evaluation of age requires consideration of four dimensions of age: chronological, biological, psychological, and social.

3 Describe three key developmental issues

- The nature-nurture issue focuses on the extent to which development is mainly influenced by nature (biological inheritance) or nurture (experience).
- Developmentalists describe development as continuous (gradual, a cumulative change) or as discontinuous (abrupt, a sequence of stages).
- The stability-change issue focuses on the degree to which we become older renditions of our early experience or develop into someone different from who we were earlier in development. A special aspect of the stability-change issue is the extent to which development is determined by early versus later experiences.
- Most developmentalists recognize that extreme positions on the nature-nurture, continuity-discontinuity, and stability-change issues are unwise. Despite this consensus, there is still spirited debate on these issues.

Key Terms

development 7
original sin view 7
tabula rasa view 7
innate goodness view 8
life-span perspective 9
context 13

culture 13
cross-cultural studies 14
ethnicity 14
gender 14
social policy 15
generational inequity 17

biological processes 18
cognitive processes 18
socioemotional processes 18
chronological age 22
biological age 22
psychological age 22

social age 22
nature-nurture issue 23
continuity-discontinuity
  issue 23
stability-change issue 24

Key People

John Locke 7
Jean-Jacques Rousseau 8
Paul Baltes 9

Marian Wright Edelman 16
Bernice Neugarten 17, 21
Jerome Kagan 24

Taking It to the Net

1. Janice plans to join a small family-practice group upon completion of her medical school pediatrics residency. Why should Janice, as a pediatrician, be involved in detecting and helping to prevent violence in the lives of her young patients?
2. Derrick has heard about a recent book that has stirred up a lot of controversy about the role of parents and peers in development. What is the book, what is its premise, and why has it generated so many strong feelings?

3. Carmen is completing her Ph.D. in clinical psychology. She is interested in geropsychology. What are some of the areas in which geropsychologists might conduct research and practice?

Connect to www.mhhe.com/santrockld9 to research the answers and complete these exercises.

E-Learning Tools

To help you master the material in this chapter, you'll find a number of valuable study tools on the Student CD-ROM that accompanies this book. In addition, visit the Online Learning Center for *Life-Span Development,* ninth edition, where you'll find these valuable resources for chapter 1, "Introduction."

- Learn more about your career options by completing the self-assessment, *Evaluating My Interest in a Career in Life-Span Development.*

- View video clips of key developmental psychology experts discussing their views on the nature-nurture controversy and the concept of understanding contexts of development.
- Build your decision-making skills by trying your hand at the parenting and education "Scenarios."

Appendix *Careers in Life-Span Development*

Some of you may be quite sure about what you plan to make your life's work. Others of you might not have decided on a major yet and might be uncertain about which career path you want to follow. Each of us wants to find a rewarding career and enjoy the work we do. The field of life-span development offers an amazing breadth of career options that can provide extremely satisfying work.

If you decide to pursue a career in life-span development, what career options are available to you? Many. College and university professors teach courses in many different areas of life-span development, education, family development, nursing, and medicine. Teachers impart knowledge, understanding, and skills to children and adolescents. Counselors, clinical psychologists, nurses, and physicians help people of different ages to cope more effectively with their lives and improve their well-being. Various professionals work with families to improve the quality of family functioning.

Although an advanced degree is not absolutely necessary in some areas of life-span development, you usually can considerably expand your opportunities (and income) by obtaining a graduate degree. Many careers in life-span development pay reasonably well. For example, psychologists earn well above the median salary in the United States. Also, by working in the field of life-span development, you can guide people in improving their lives, understand yourself and others better, possibly advance the state of knowledge in the field, and have an enjoyable time while you are doing these things.

If you are considering a career in life-span development, would you prefer to work with infants? children? adolescents? older adults? As you go through this term, try to spend some time with people of different ages. Observe their behavior. Talk with them about their lives. Think about whether you would like to work with people of this age in your life's work.

Another important aspect of exploring careers is to talk with people who work in various jobs. For example, if you have some interest in becoming a school counselor, call a school, ask to speak with a counselor, and set up an appointment to discuss the counselor's career and work. If you have an interest in becoming a nurse, think about whether you would rather work with babies, children, adolescents, or older adults. Call the nursing department at a hospital and set up an appointment to speak with the nursing coordinator about a nursing career.

Something else that should benefit you is to work in one or more jobs related to your career interests while you are in college. Many colleges and universities have internships or work experiences for students who major in such fields as life-span development. Some of these opportunities are for course credit or pay; others are strictly on a volunteer basis. Take advantage of these opportunities. They can provide you with valuable experiences to help you decide if this is the right career area for you, and they can help you get into graduate school, if you decide you want to go.

In the upcoming sections, we will profile a number of careers in four areas: education/research; clinical/counseling; medical/nursing/physical; and families/relationships. These are not the only career options in life-span development, but they should provide you with an idea of the range of opportunities available and information about some of the main career avenues you might pursue. In profiling these careers, we will address the amount of education required, the nature of the training, and a description of the work.

By going to the website for this book, you can obtain more detailed career information about the various careers in life-span development described in this appendix.

EDUCATION/RESEARCH

There are numerous career opportunities in life-span development that involve education and/or research. These range from being a college professor to day-care director to school psychologist.

College/University Professor

Courses in life-span development are taught in many different programs and schools in colleges and universities, including psychology, education, nursing, child and family studies, social work, and medicine. A Ph.D. or master's degree almost always is required to teach in some area of life-span development in a college or university. Obtaining a doctoral degree usually takes 4 to 6 years of graduate work. A master's degree requires approximately 2 years of graduate work. The professional job might be at a research university with one or more master's or Ph.D. programs in life-span development, at a 4-year college with no graduate programs, or at a community college.

The training involves taking graduate courses, learning to conduct research, and attending and presenting papers at professional meetings. Many graduate students work as teaching or research assistants for professors in an apprenticeship relationship that helps them to become competent teachers and researchers. The work that college professors do includes teaching courses either at the undergraduate or graduate level (or both), conducting research in a specific area, advising students and/or directing their research, and serving on college or university committees. Some college instructors do not conduct research as part of their job but instead focus mainly on teaching. However, research is part of the job description at most universities with master's and Ph.D. programs.

If you are interested in becoming a college or university professor, you might want to make an appointment with your instructor in this class on life-span development to learn more about their profession and what their work is like.

Researcher

Some individuals in the field of life-span development work in research positions. Most have either a master's or a Ph.D. in some area of life-span development. They might work at a university, in some cases in a university professor's research program, in government at such agencies as the National Institute of Mental Health, or in private industry. Individuals who have full-time research positions in life-span development generate innovative research ideas, plan studies, and carry out the research by collecting data, analyzing the data, and then interpreting it. Then, they will usually attempt to publish the research in a scientific journal. A researcher often works in a collaborative manner with other researchers on a project and may present the research at scientific meetings, where she or he also learns about other research. One researcher might spend much of his or her time in a laboratory; another researcher might work out in the field, such as in schools, hospitals, and so on.

Elementary or Secondary School Teacher

Becoming an elementary or secondary school teacher requires a minimum of an undergraduate degree. The training involves taking a wide range of courses with a major or concentration in education as well as completing a supervised practice teaching internship. The work of an elementary or secondary school teacher involves teaching in one or more subject areas, preparing the curriculum, giving tests, assigning grades, monitoring students' progress, conducting parent-teacher conferences, and attending in-service workshops.

Exceptional Children (Special Education) Teacher

Becoming a teacher of exceptional children requires a minimum of an undergraduate degree. The training consists of taking a wide range of courses in education and a concentration of courses in educating children with disabilities or children who are gifted. The work of a teacher of exceptional children involves spending concentrated time with individual children who have a disability or are gifted. Among the children a teacher of exceptional children might work with include children with learning disabilities, ADHD, mental retardation, or a physical disability such as cerebral palsy. Some of this work will usually be done outside of the student's regular classroom; some of it will be carried out when the student is in the regular classroom. The exceptional children teacher works closely with the student's regular classroom teacher and parents to create the best educational program for the student. Teachers of exceptional children often continue their education after obtaining their undergraduate degree and attain a master's degree.

Early Childhood Educator

Early childhood educators work on college faculties and have a minimum of a master's degree in their field. In graduate school, they take courses in early childhood education and receive supervisory training in day care or early childhood programs. Early childhood educators usually teach in community colleges that award an associate degree in early childhood education.

Preschool/Kindergarten Teacher

Preschool teachers teach mainly 4-year-old children, and kindergarten teachers primarily teach 5-year-old children. They usually have an undergraduate degree in education, specializing in early childhood education. State certification to become a preschool or kindergarten teacher usually is required. These teachers direct the educational activities of young children.

Family and Consumer Science Educator

Family and consumer science educators may specialize in early childhood education or instruct middle and high school students about such matters as nutrition, interpersonal relationships, human sexuality, parenting, and human development. Hundreds of colleges and universities throughout the United States offer 2- and 4-year degree programs in family and consumer science. These programs usually include an internship requirement. Additional education courses may be needed to obtain a teaching certificate. Some family and consumer educators go on to graduate school for further training, which provides a background for possible jobs in college teaching or research.

Educational Psychologist

An educational psychologist most often teaches in a college or university and conducts research in such areas of educational psychology as learning, motivation, classroom management, and assessment. Most educational psychologists have a doctorate in education, which takes 4 to 6 years of graduate work. They help train students who will take various positions in education, including educational psychology, school psychology, and teaching.

School Psychologist

School psychologists focus on improving the psychological and intellectual well-being of elementary, middle/junior, and high school students. They usually have a master's or doctoral degree in school psychology. In graduate school, they take courses in counseling, assessment, learning, and other areas of education and psychology. School psychologists may work in a centralized office in a school district or in one or more schools. They give psychological tests, interview students and their parents, consult with teachers, and may provide counseling to students and their families.

Gerontologist

Gerontologists usually work in research in some branch of the federal or state government. They specialize in the study of aging with a particular focus on government programs for older adults, social policy, and delivery of services to older adults. In their research, gerontologists define problems to be studied, collect data, interpret the results, and make recommendations for social policy. Most gerontologists have a master's or doctoral degree and have taken a concentration of course work in adult development and aging.

CLINICAL/COUNSELING

There are a wide variety of clinical and counseling jobs that are linked with life-span development. These range from child clinical psychologist to adolescent drug counselor to geriatric psychiatrist.

Clinical Psychologist

Clinical psychologists seek to help people with psychological problems. They work in a variety of settings, including colleges and universities, clinics, medical schools, and private practice. Clinical psychologists have either a Ph.D. (which involves clinical and research training) or a Psy.D. degree (which only involves clinical training). This graduate training usually takes 5 to 7 years and includes courses in clinical psychology and a 1-year supervised internship in an accredited setting toward the end of the training. In most cases, they must pass a test to become licensed in a state and to call themselves a clinical psychologist. Some clinical psychologists only conduct psychotherapy, others do psychological assessment and psychotherapy, and some also do research.

In regard to life-span development, clinical psychologists might specialize in a particular age group, such as children (child clinical psychologist) or older adults (often referred to a geropsychologist). Many geropsychologists pursue a year or two of postdoctoral training.

Psychiatrist

Psychiatrists obtain a medical degree and then do a residency in psychiatry. Medical school takes approximately 4 years, and the psychiatry residency another 3 to 4 years. Unlike psychologists (who do not go to medical school), psychiatrists can administer drugs to clients.

Like clinical psychologists, psychiatrists might specialize in working with children (child psychiatry) or with older adults (geriatric psychiatry). Psychiatrists might work in medical schools in teaching and research roles, in a medical clinic, or in private practice. In addition to administering drugs to help improve the lives of people with psychological problems, psychiatrists also may conduct psychotherapy.

Counseling Psychologist

Counseling psychologists go through much of the same training as clinical psychologists, although in a graduate program in counseling rather than clinical psychology. Counseling psychologists have either a master's degree or a doctoral degree. They also must go through a licensing procedure. One type of master's degree in counseling leads to the designation of licensed professional counselor. They work in the same settings as clinical psychologists, and may do psychotherapy, teach, or conduct research. Many counseling psychologists do not do therapy with individuals who have more severe mental disorders, such as schizophrenia.

School Counselor

School counselors help identify students' abilities and interests, guide students in developing academic plans, and explore career options with students. They may help students cope with adjustment problems. They may work with students individually, in small groups, or even in a classroom. They often consult with parents, teachers, and school administrators when trying to help students with their problems. School counselors usually have a master's degree in counseling.

High school counselors advise students on choosing a major, admissions requirements for college, taking entrance exams, applying for financial aid, and on appropriate vocational and technical training. Elementary school counselors are mainly involved in counseling students about social and personal problems. They may observe children in the classroom and at play as part of their work.

Career Counselor

Career counselors help individuals to identify what the best career options are for them and guide them in applying for jobs. They may work in private industry or at a college or university. They usually interview individuals and give them vocational and/or psychological tests to help provide students with information about appropriate careers that fit their interests and abilities. Sometimes they help individuals to create professional resumes or conduct mock interviews to help them feel comfortable in a job interview. They might create and promote job fairs or other recruiting events to help individuals obtain jobs.

Social Worker

Many social workers are involved in helping people with social or economic problems. They may investigate, evaluate, and attempt to rectify reported cases of abuse, neglect, endangerment, or domestic disputes. They can intervene in families if necessary and provide counseling and referral services to individuals and families. They have a minimum of an undergraduate degree from a school of social work that includes course work in various areas of sociology and psychology. Some social workers also have a master's or doctoral degree. They often work for publicly funded agencies at the city, state, or national level, although increasingly they work in the private sector in areas such as drug rehabilitation and family counseling.

In some cases, social workers specialize in a certain area, as is true of a medical social worker, who has a master's degree in social work (M.S.W.). This involves graduate coursework and supervised clinical experiences in medical settings. A medical social worker might coordinate a variety of support services to people with a severe or long-term disability. Family-care social workers often work with families with children or an older adult who needs support services.

Drug Counselor

Drug counselors provide counseling to individuals with drug-abuse problems. They may work on an individual basis with a substance abuser or conduct group therapy sessions. At a minimum, drug counselors go through an associate's or certificate program. Many have an undergraduate degree in substance-abuse counseling, and some have master's and doctoral degrees. They may work in private practice, with a state or federal government agency, with a company, or in a hospital setting. Some drug counselors specialize in working with adolescents or older adults. Most states provide a certification procedure for obtaining a license to practice drug counseling.

MEDICAL/NURSING/PHYSICAL

This third main area of careers in life-span development includes a wide range of careers in the medical and nursing areas, as well as jobs pertaining to improving some aspect of the person's physical development.

Obstetrician/Gynecologist

An obstetrician/gynecologist prescribes prenatal and postnatal care and performs deliveries in maternity cases. The individual also treats diseases and injuries of the female reproductive system. Becoming an obstetrician/gynecologist requires a medical degree plus 3 to 5 years of residency in obstetrics/gynecology. Obstetricians may work in private practice, in a medical clinic, a hospital, or in a medical school.

Pediatrician

A pediatrician monitors infants' and children's health, works to prevent disease or injury, helps children attain optimal health, and treats children with health problems. Pediatricians have attained a medical degree and then do a 3- to 5-year residency in pediatrics.

Pediatricians may work in private practice, in a medical clinic, in a hospital, or in a medical school. As a medical doctor, they can administer drugs to children and may counsel parents and children on ways to improve the children's health. Many pediatricians on the faculty of medical schools also teach and conduct research on children's health and diseases.

Geriatric Physician

A geriatric physician has a medical degree and has specialized in geriatric medicine by doing a 3- to 5-year residency. Geriatric physicians diagnose medical problems of older adults, evaluate treatment options, and make recommendations for nursing care or other arrangements. As with other doctors, they may work in private practice, in a medical clinic, in a hospital, or in a medical school. They also may primarily treat the diseases and health problems of older adults, but geriatric physicians in medical school settings also may teach future physicians and conduct research.

Neonatal Nurse

A neonatal nurse is involved in the delivery of care to the newborn infant. The neonatal nurse may work to improve the health and well-being of infants born under normal circumstances or be involved in the delivery of care to premature and critically ill neonates. A minimum of an undergraduate degree in nursing with a specialization in the newborn is required. This training involves coursework in nursing and the biological sciences, as well as supervisory clinical experiences.

Nurse-Midwife

A nurse-midwife formulates and provides comprehensive care to selected maternity patients, cares for the expectant mother as she prepares to give birth and guides her through the birth process, and cares for the postpartum patient. The nurse-midwife also may provide care to the newborn, counsel parents on the infant's development and parenting, and provide guidance about health practices. Becoming a nurse-midwife generally requires an undergraduate degree from a school of nursing. A nurse-midwife most often works in a hospital setting.

Pediatric Nurse

Pediatric nurses have a degree in nursing that takes 2 to 5 years to complete. Some also may go on to obtain a master's or doctoral degree in pediatric nursing. Pediatric nurses take courses in biological sciences, nursing care, and pediatrics, usually in a school of nursing. They also undergo supervised clinical experiences in medical settings. They monitor infants' and children's health, work to prevent disease or injury, and help children attain optimal health. They may work in hospitals, schools of nursing, or with pediatricians in private practice or at a medical clinic.

Geriatric Nurse

Geriatric nurses seek to prevent or intervene in the chronic or acute health problems of older adults. They take courses in a school of nursing and obtain a degree in nursing. This takes anywhere from 2 to 5 years. As in the case of a pediatric nurse, a geriatric nurse also may obtain a master's or doctoral degree in his or her specialty. Geriatric nurses take courses in biological sciences, nursing care, and mental health. They also experience supervised clinical training in geriatric settings. They may work in hospitals, nursing homes, schools of nursing, or with geriatric medical specialists or psychiatrists in a medical clinic or in private practice.

Physical Therapist

Physical therapists usually have an undergraduate degree in physical therapy and are licensed by a state. They take courses and experience supervised training in physical therapy. Many physical therapists work with people of all ages, although some specialize in working with a specific age group, such as children or older adults. They work directly with these individuals who have a physical problem either due to disease or injury to help them function as competently as possible. They may consult with other professionals and coordinate services for the individual.

Rehabilitation Counselor

Rehabilitation counselors work directly with individuals who have a physical disability that may have developed because of a disease or an injury. They try to help them function as competently as possible. In their efforts, they consult with other professionals and coordinate services.

Becoming a rehabilitation counselor requires a master's or Ph.D. degree in rehabilitation counseling. This includes graduate coursework, clinical training, training in physical therapy, and possibly research training.

Occupational Therapist

Occupational therapists may have an associate, bachelor's, master's, and/or doctoral degree with education ranging from two to six years. Training includes occupational therapy courses in a specialized program. National certification is required and licensing/registration is required in some states. Occupational Therapy is a health and rehabilitation profession that helps people regain, develop, and build skills that are important for independent functioning, health, well-being, security and happiness. The Occupational Therapist (OTR) initiates the evaluation of clients and manages the treatment process for clients with various impairments.

Therapeutic/Recreation Therapist

Therapeutic/recreation therapists maintain or improve the quality of life for people with special needs through intervention, leisure education, and recreation participation. They work in hospitals, rehabilitation centers, local government agencies, at-risk youth programs, as well as other settings. Becoming a therapeutic/recreation therapist requires an undergraduate degree with coursework in leisure studies and a concentration in therapeutic recreation. National certification is usually required. Coursework in anatomy, special education, and psychology are beneficial.

Audiologist

An audiologist has a minimum of an undergraduate degree in hearing science. This includes courses and supervisory training. Audiologists assess and identify the presence and severity of hearing loss, as well as problems in balance. Some audiologists also go on to obtain a master's or doctoral degree. They may work in a medical clinic, with a physician in private practice, in a hospital, or in a medical school.

Speech Therapist

Speech therapists are health-care professionals who are trained to identify, assess, and treat speech and language problems. They may work with physicians, psychologists, social workers, and other health-care professionals in a team approach to helping individuals with physical or psychological problems in which speech and language are involved in the problem. Speech pathologists have a minimum of an undergraduate degree in speech and hearing science or communications disorders area. They may work in private practice, in hospitals and medical schools, and in government agencies with individuals of any age. Some may specialize in working with children, others with the elderly, or in a particular type of speech disorder.

Genetic Counselor

Genetic counselors are health professionals with specialized graduate degrees and experience in the areas of medical genetics and counseling. Most enter the field after majoring in undergraduate school in such disciplines as biology, genetics, psychology, nursing, public health, and social work.

Genetic counselors work as members of a health-care team, providing information and support to families who have members with birth defects or genetic disorders and to families who may be at risk for a variety of inherited conditions. They identify families at risk and provide supportive counseling. They serve as educators and resource people for other health-care professionals and the public. Almost one-half work in university medical centers, and another one-fourth work in private hospital settings.

FAMILIES/RELATIONSHIPS

A number of careers and jobs are available for working with families and relationship problems across the life span. These range from being a home health aide to working as a marriage and family therapist.

Home Health Aide

No education is required for this position. There is brief training by an agency. A home health aide provides direct services to older adults in the older adults' homes, providing assistance in basic self-care tasks.

Child Welfare Worker

A child welfare worker is employed by the Child Protective Services unit of each state. The child welfare worker protects the child's rights, evaluates any maltreatment of the child, and may have the child removed from the home if necessary. A child social worker has a minimum of an undergraduate degree in social work.

Child Life Specialist

Child life specialists work with children and their families when the child needs to be hospitalized. They monitor the child's activities, seek to reduce the child's stress, help the child cope effectively, and assist the child in enjoying the hospital experience as much as possible. Child life specialists may provide parent education and develop individualized treatment plans based on an assessment of the child's development, temperament, medical plan, and available social supports. Child life specialists have an undergraduate degree, and they take courses in child development and education, as well as usually taking additional courses in a child life program.

Marriage and Family Therapist

Marriage and family therapists work on the principle that many individuals who have psychological problems benefit when psychotherapy is provided in the context of a marital or family relationship. Marriage and family therapists may provide marital therapy, couple therapy to individuals in a relationship who are not married, and family therapy to two or more members of a family.

Marriage and family therapists have a master's or doctoral degree. They go through a training program in graduate school similar to a clinical psychologist but with the focus on marital and family relationships. In most states, it is necessary to go through a licensing procedure to practice marital and family therapy.

WEBSITE CONNECTIONS FOR CAREERS IN LIFE-SPAN DEVELOPMENT

By going to the website for this book, you can obtain more detailed career information about the various careers in life-span development described in this Appendix. Go to the Web connections in the Career Appendix section, where you will read about a description of the websites. Then click on the title and you will be able to go directly to the website described. Here are the website connections:

Education/Research

Careers in Psychology
Elementary and Secondary School Teaching
Exceptional Children Teachers
Early Childhood Education
Family and Consumer Science Education
Educational Psychology
School Psychology

Clinical Counseling

Clinical Psychology
Psychiatry
Counseling Psychology
School Counseling
Social Work
Drug Counseling
Gerontology

Medical/Nursing/Physical Development

Obstetrics and Gynecology
Pediatrics
Nurse-Midwife
Neonatal Nursing
Pediatric Nursing
Gerontological Nursing
Physical Therapy
Occupational Therapy
Therapeutic/Recreation Therapy
Audiology and Speech Pathology
Genetic Counseling

Families/Relationships

Child Welfare Worker
Child Life Specialist
Marriage and Family Therapist

There is nothing quite so practical as a good theory.

—KURT LEWIN
American Social Psychologist, 20th Century

The Science of Life-Span Development

Chapter Outline

THEORIES OF DEVELOPMENT

Psychoanalytic Theories

Cognitive Theories

Behavioral and Social Cognitive Theories

Ethological Theory

Ecological Theory

An Eclectic Theoretical Orientation

RESEARCH IN LIFE-SPAN DEVELOPMENT

Types of Research

Time Span of Research

FACING UP TO RESEARCH CHALLENGES

Conducting Ethical Research

Minimizing Bias

Learning Goals

1 *D*escribe theories of life-span development

2 *E*xplain how research on life-span development is conducted

3 *D*iscuss research challenges in life-span development

Images of Life-Span Development
The Childhoods of Erikson and Piaget

Imagine that you have developed a major theory of development. What would influence you to construct this theory? A person interested in developing such a theory usually goes through a long university training program that culminates in a doctoral degree. As part of the training, the future theorist is exposed to many ideas about a particular area of life-span development, such as biological, cognitive, or socioemotional development. Another factor that could explain why someone develops a particular theory is that person's life experiences. Two important developmental theorists, whose views will be described later in the chapter, are Erik Erikson and Jean Piaget. Let's examine a portion of their lives as they were growing up to discover how their experiences might have contributed to the theories they developed.

Erik Homberger Erikson (1902–1994) was born near Frankfurt, Germany, to Danish parents. Before Erik was born, his parents separated, and his mother left Denmark to live in Germany. At age 3, Erik became ill, and his mother took him to see a pediatrician named Homberger. Young Erik's mother fell in love with the pediatrician, married him, and named Erik after his new stepfather.

Erik attended primary school from the ages of 6 to 10 and then the gymnasium (high school) from 11 to 18. He studied art and a number of languages. Erik did not like the atmosphere of formal schooling, and this attitude was reflected in his grades. Rather than going to college at age 18, the adolescent Erikson wandered around Europe, keeping a diary about his experiences. After a year of travel through Europe, he returned to Germany and enrolled in art school, became dissatisfied, and enrolled in another. Later he traveled to Florence, Italy. Psychiatrist Robert Coles described Erikson at this time:

> To the Italians he was the young, tall, thin Nordic expatriate with long, blond hair. He wore a corduroy suit and was seen by his family and friends as not odd or "sick" but as a wandering artist who was trying to come to grips with himself, a not unnatural or unusual struggle. (Coles, 1970, p. 15)

Contrast Erikson's experiences with those of Jean Piaget. Piaget (1896–1980) was born in Neuchâtel, Switzerland. Jean's father was an intellectual who taught young Jean to think systematically. Jean's mother was also very bright. His father had an air of detachment from his mother, whom Piaget described as prone to frequent outbursts of neurotic behavior.

In his autobiography, Piaget detailed why he chose to study cognitive development rather than social or abnormal development:

> I started to forego playing for serious work very early. Indeed, I have always detested any departure from reality, an attitude which I relate to . . . my mother's poor health. It was this disturbing factor which at the beginning of my studies in psychology made me keenly interested in psychoanalytic and pathological psychology. Though this interest helped me to achieve independence and widen my cultural background, I have never since felt any desire to involve myself deeper in that particular direction, always much preferring the study of normalcy and of the workings of the intellect to that of the tricks of the unconscious. (Piaget, 1952a, p. 238)

These snapshots of Erikson and Piaget illustrate how personal experiences might influence the direction in which a particular theorist goes. Erikson's wanderings and search for self contributed to his theory of identity development, and Piaget's intellectual experiences with his parents and schooling contributed to his emphasis on cognitive development.

Theories are part of the science of life-span development. Some individuals have difficulty thinking of life-span development as a science like physics, chemistry, and biology. Can a discipline that studies how parents nurture children, whether watching TV long hours is linked with being overweight, and the factors involved in life satisfaction among older adults be equated with disciplines that study the molecular structure of a compound and how gravity works? The answer is yes. Science is defined not by *what* it investigates, but by *how* it investigates. Whether you're studying photosynthesis, butterflies, Saturn's moons, or human development, it is the way you study that makes the approach scientific or not.

This chapter introduces the theories and methods that are the foundation of the science of life-span development. At the end of the chapter we will explore some of the ethical challenges and biases that researchers must guard against to protect the integrity of their results and respect the rights of the participants in their studies.

1 THEORIES OF DEVELOPMENT

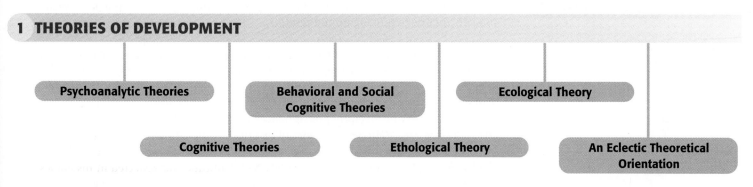

All scientific knowledge stems from a rigorous, systematic method of investigation (Pittenger, 2003; Salkind, 2003). The *scientific method* is essentially a four-step process:

1. Conceptualize a process or problem to be studied.
2. Collect research information (data).
3. Analyze data.
4. Draw conclusions.

In step 1, when researchers are formulating a problem to study, they often draw on *theories* and develop *hypotheses* (Miller, 2001). A **theory** is an interrelated, coherent set of ideas that helps to explain and make predictions. **Hypotheses** are specific assumptions and predictions that can be tested to determine their accuracy. For example, a theory on mentoring might attempt to explain and predict why sustained support, guidance, and concrete experience make a difference in the lives of children from impoverished backgrounds. The theory might focus on children's opportunities to model the behavior and strategies of mentors, or it might focus on the effects of individual attention, which might be missing in the children's lives.

The diversity of theories makes understanding life-span development a challenging undertaking. Just when you think one theory has the correct explanation of life-span development, another theory crops up and makes you rethink your earlier conclusion. To keep from getting frustrated, remember that life-span development is a complex, multifaceted topic. No single theory has been able to account for all aspects of it. Each theory contributes an important piece to the life-span development puzzle. Although the theories sometimes disagree about certain aspects of life-span development, much of their information is complementary rather than contradictory. Together they let us see the total landscape of life-span development in all its richness.

We will briefly explore five major theoretical perspectives on development: psychoanalytic, cognitive, behavioral and social cognitive, ethological, and ecological. In chapter 1, we described the three major processes involved in development: biological, cognitive, and socioemotional. The theoretical approaches that we will describe reflect these processes. Biological processes are very important in Freud's psychoanalytic and

theory An interrelated, coherent set of ideas that helps to explain and make predictions.

hypotheses Specific assumptions and predictions that can be tested to determine their accuracy.

Sigmund Freud, the pioneering architect of psychoanalytic theory. *How did Freud believe each individual's personality is organized?*

Freud's Theory

psychoanalytic theory Describes development as primarily unconscious and heavily colored by emotion. Behavior is merely a surface characteristic and the symbolic workings of the mind have to be analyzed to understand behavior. Early experiences with parents are emphasized.

ethological theory, cognitive processes in Piaget's, Vygotsky's, information-processing, and social cognitive theories. Socioemotional processes are important in Freud's and Erikson's psychoanalytic theories, Vygotsky's sociocultural cognitive theory, behavioral and social cognitive theories, and ecological theory. You will read more about these theories and processes at different points in later chapters in the book.

Psychoanalytic Theories

Psychoanalytic theory describes development as primarily unconscious (beyond awareness) and colored by emotion. Psychoanalytic theorists believe that behavior is merely a surface characteristic and that a true understanding of development requires analyzing the symbolic meanings of behavior and the deep inner workings of the mind. Psychoanalytic theorists also stress that early experiences with parents extensively shape development. These characteristics are highlighted in the main psychoanalytic theory, that of Sigmund Freud.

Freud's Psychosexual Theory Freud (1856–1939) developed his ideas about psychoanalytic theory while working with mental patients. He was a medical doctor who specialized in neurology. He spent most of his years in Vienna, though he moved to London near the end of his career because of Nazi anti-Semitism.

Freud (1917) believed that personality has three structures: the id, the ego, and the superego. The *id*, he said, consists of instincts, which are an individual's reservoir of psychic energy. In Freud's view, the id is totally unconscious; it has no contact with reality. As children experience the demands and constraints of reality, a new part of personality emerges—the *ego*, the Freudian personality structure that deals with the demands of reality. The ego is called the executive branch of personality because it uses reasoning to make decisions. The id and the ego have no morality. They do not take into account whether something is right or wrong. The *superego* is the Freudian structure of personality that is the moral branch of personality. The superego decides whether something is right or wrong. Think of the superego as what we often refer to as our "conscience." You probably are beginning to sense that both the id and the superego make life rough for the ego. Your ego might say, "I will have sex only occasionally and be sure to take the proper precautions because I don't want the intrusion of a child in the development of my career." However, your id is saying, "I want to be satisfied; sex is pleasurable." Your superego is at work, too: "I feel guilty about having sex."

As Freud listened to, probed, and analyzed his patients, he became convinced that their problems were the result of experiences early in life. Freud believed that we go through five stages of psychosexual development, and that at each stage of development we experience pleasure in one part of the body more than in others.

Freud thought that our adult personality is determined by the way we resolve conflicts between these early sources of pleasure—the mouth, the anus, and then the genitals—and the demands of reality. When these conflicts are not resolved, the individual may become fixated at a particular stage of development. Fixation occurs when the individual remains locked in an earlier developmental stage because needs are under- or overgratified. For example, a parent might wean a child too early, be too strict in toilet training the child, punish the child for masturbation, or "smother" the child with too much attention. Figure 2.1 illustrates the five Freudian stages.

The *oral stage* is the first Freudian stage of development, occurring during the first 18 months of life, in which the infant's pleasure centers around the mouth. Chewing, sucking, and biting are the chief sources of pleasure. These actions reduce tension in the infant.

The *anal stage* is the second Freudian stage of development, occurring between 1½ and 3 years of age, in which the child's greatest pleasure involves the anus or the eliminative functions associated with it. In Freud's view, the exercise of anal muscles reduces tension.

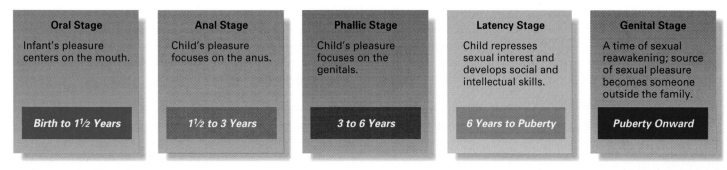

Oral Stage	Anal Stage	Phallic Stage	Latency Stage	Genital Stage
Infant's pleasure centers on the mouth.	Child's pleasure focuses on the anus.	Child's pleasure focuses on the genitals.	Child represses sexual interest and develops social and intellectual skills.	A time of sexual reawakening; source of sexual pleasure becomes someone outside the family.
Birth to 1½ Years	*1½ to 3 Years*	*3 to 6 Years*	*6 Years to Puberty*	*Puberty Onward*

FIGURE 2.1 Freudian Stages

The *phallic stage* is the third Freudian stage of development. The phallic stage occurs between the ages of 3 and 6; its name comes from the Latin word *phallus,* which means "penis." During the phallic stage, pleasure focuses on the genitals as both boys and girls discover that self-manipulation is enjoyable.

In Freud's view, the phallic stage has a special importance in personality development because it is during this period that the Oedipus complex, appears. This name comes from Greek mythology, in which Oedipus, the son of the King of Thebes, unwittingly kills his father and marries his mother. The *Oedipus complex* according to Freudian theory, is the young child's development of an intense desire to replace the same-sex parent and enjoy the affections of the opposite-sex parent.

How is the Oedipus complex resolved? At about 5 to 6 years of age, children recognize that their same-sex parent might punish them for their incestuous wishes. To reduce this conflict, the child identifies with the same-sex parent, striving to be like him or her. If the conflict is not resolved, though, the individual may become fixated at the phallic stage.

The *latency stage* is the fourth Freudian stage of development, which occurs between approximately 6 years of age and puberty. During this period, the child represses all interest in sexuality and develops social and intellectual skills. This activity channels much of the child's energy into emotionally safe areas and helps the child forget the highly stressful conflicts of the phallic stage.

The *genital stage* is the fifth and final Freudian stage of development, occurring from puberty onward. The genital stage is a time of sexual reawakening; the source of sexual pleasure now becomes someone outside of the family. Freud believed that unresolved conflicts with parents reemerge during adolescence. When these conflicts have been resolved, the individual is capable of developing a mature love relationship and functioning independently as an adult.

Freud's theory has undergone significant revisions by a number of psychoanalytic theorists (Eagle, 2000). Many contemporary psychoanalytic theorists place less emphasis on sexual instincts and more emphasis on cultural experiences as determinants of an individual's development. Unconscious thought remains a central theme, but most contemporary psychoanalysts believe that conscious thought makes up more of the mind than Freud envisioned. Next, we will explore the ideas of an important revisionist of Freud's ideas—Erik Erikson.

Erikson's Psychosocial Theory   Erik Erikson recognized Freud's contributions but believed that Freud misjudged some important dimensions of human development. For one thing, Erikson (1950, 1968) said we develop in *psychosocial* stages, rather than in *psychosexual* stages, as Freud maintained. For Freud, the primary motivation for human behavior was sexual in nature, for Erikson it was social and reflected a desire to affiliate with other people. Erikson emphasized developmental change throughout the human life span, whereas Freud argued that our basic personality is shaped in the first five years of life. In **Erikson's theory,** eight stages of development unfold as we go

Erikson's Theory

Erikson's theory Includes eight stages of human development. Each stage consists of a unique developmental task that confronts individuals with a crisis that must be faced.

Erikson's Stages	Developmental Period
Integrity versus despair	Late adulthood (60s onward)
Generativity versus stagnation	Middle adulthood (40s, 50s)
Intimacy versus isolation	Early adulthood (20s, 30s)
Identity versus identity confusion	Adolescence (10 to 20 years)
Industry versus inferiority	Middle and late childhood (elementary school years, 6 years to puberty)
Initiative versus guilt	Early childhood (preschool years, 3 to 5 years)
Autonomy versus shame and doubt	Infancy (1 to 3 years)
Trust versus mistrust	Infancy (first year)

FIGURE 2.2 Erickson's Eight Life-Span Stages

through the life span (see figure 2.2). Each stage consists of a unique developmental task that confronts individuals with a crisis that must be resolved. According to Erikson, this crisis is not a catastrophe but a turning point of increased vulnerability and enhanced potential. The more successfully an individual resolves the crises, the healthier development will be (Hopkins, 2000).

Trust versus mistrust is Erikson's first psychosocial stage, which is experienced in the first year of life. A sense of trust requires a feeling of physical comfort and a minimal amount of fear and apprehension about the future. Trust in infancy sets the stage for a lifelong expectation that the world will be a good and pleasant place to live.

Autonomy versus shame and doubt is Erikson's second stage of development. This stage occurs in late infancy and toddlerhood (1 to 3 years). After gaining trust in their caregivers, infants begin to discover that their behavior is their own. They start to assert their sense of independence, or autonomy. They realize their *will*. If infants are restrained too much or punished too harshly, they are likely to develop a sense of shame and doubt.

Initiative versus guilt, Erikson's third stage of development, occurs during the preschool years. As preschool children encounter a widening social world, they are challenged more than when they were infants. Active, purposeful behavior is needed to cope with these challenges. Children are asked to assume responsibility for their bodies, their behavior, their toys, and their pets. Developing a sense of responsibility increases initiative. Uncomfortable guilt feelings may arise, though, if the child is irresponsible and is made to feel too anxious. Erikson has a positive outlook on this stage. He believes that most guilt is quickly compensated for by a sense of accomplishment.

Industry versus inferiority is Erikson's fourth developmental stage, occurring approximately in the elementary school years. Children's initiative brings them in contact with a wealth of new experiences. As they move into middle and late childhood, they direct their energy toward mastering knowledge and intellectual skills. At no other time is the child more enthusiastic about learning than at the end of early childhood's period of expansive imagination. The danger in the elementary school years is that the child can develop a sense of inferiority—feeling incompetent and unproductive. Erikson believed that teachers have a special responsibility for children's development of industry. Teachers should "mildly but firmly coerce children into the adventure of finding out that one can learn to accomplish things which one would never have thought of by oneself" (Erikson, 1968, p. 127).

Identity versus identity confusion is Erikson's fifth developmental stage, which individuals experience during the adolescent years. At this time, individuals are faced with finding out who they are, what they are all about, and where they are going in life. Adolescents are confronted with many new roles and adult statuses—vocational and romantic, for example. Parents need to allow adolescents to explore many different roles and different paths within a particular role. If the adolescent explores such roles in a healthy manner and arrives at a positive path to follow in life, then a positive identity will be achieved. If an identity is pushed on the adolescent by parents, if the adolescent does not adequately explore many roles, and if a positive future path is not defined, then identity confusion reigns.

Intimacy versus isolation is Erikson's sixth developmental stage, which individuals experience during the early adulthood years. At this time, individuals face the developmental task of forming intimate relationships with others. Erikson describes intimacy as finding oneself yet losing oneself in another. If the young adult forms healthy friendships and an intimate relationship with another individual, intimacy will be achieved; if not, isolation will result.

Generativity versus stagnation is Erikson's seventh developmental stage, which individuals experience during middle adulthood. A chief concern is to assist the younger generation in developing and leading useful lives—this is what Erikson means by generativity. The feeling of having done nothing to help the next generation is stagnation.

Integrity versus despair is Erikson's eighth and final stage of development, which individuals experience in late adulthood. During this stage, a person reflects on the past and either pieces together a positive review or concludes that life has not been spent well. Through many different routes, the older person may have developed a positive outlook in most or all of the previous stages of development. If so, the retrospective glances will reveal a picture of a life well spent, and the person will feel a sense of satisfaction—integrity will be achieved. If the older adult resolved many of the earlier stages negatively, the retrospective glances likely will yield doubt or gloom—the despair Erikson talks about.

Erikson did not believe that the proper solution to a stage crisis is always completely positive. Some exposure or commitment to the negative side of the person's conflict is sometimes inevitable—you cannot trust all people under all circumstances and survive, for example. Nonetheless, in the healthy solution to a stage crisis, the positive resolution dominates. We will discuss Erikson's theory again on a number of occasions in the chapters on socioemotional development in this book.

Evaluating the Psychoanalytic Theories   The contributions of psychoanalytic theories include these factors:

- Early experiences play an important part in development.
- Family relationships are a central aspect of development.
- Personality can be better understood if it is examined developmentally.
- The mind is not all conscious; unconscious aspects of the mind need to be considered.
- Changes take place in adulthood as well as the childhood (Erikson).

These are some criticisms of psychoanalytic theories:

- The main concepts of psychoanalytic theories have been difficult to test scientifically.
- Much of the data used to support psychoanalytic theories come from individuals' reconstruction of the past, often the distant past, and are of unknown accuracy.
- The sexual underpinnings of development are given too much importance (especially in Freud's theory).
- The unconscious mind is given too much credit for influencing development.
- Psychoanalytic theories present an image of humans that is too negative (especially Freud).
- Psychoanalytic theories are culture- and gender-biased. To read about culture and gender bias, see the Sociocultural Worlds of Development box on page 48.

Erik Erikson with his wife, Joan, an artist. Erikson generated one of the most important developmental theories of the twentieth century. *Which stage of Erikson's theory are you in? Does Erikson's description of this stage characterize you?*

Cognitive Theories

Whereas psychoanalytic theories stress the importance of unconscious thoughts, cognitive theories emphasize conscious thoughts. Three important cognitive theories are Piaget's cognitive developmental theory, Vygotsky's sociocultural cognitive theory, and the information-processing theory.

Piaget's theory will be covered in detail later in this book, when we discuss cognitive development in infancy, early childhood, middle and late childhood, and adolescence. Here we briefly present the main ideas of his theory.

Piaget's Cognitive Developmental Theory   **Piaget's theory** states that children actively construct their understanding of the world and go through four stages of cognitive development. Two processes underlie this cognitive construction of the world: organization and adaptation. To make sense of our world, we organize our experiences. For example, we separate important ideas from less important ideas. We connect one idea to another. In addition to organizing our observations and

Piaget's theory States that children actively construct their understanding of the world and go through four stages of cognitive development.

Cultural and Gender Bias in Freud's Theory

The Oedipus conflict was one of Freud's most influential concepts. Freud's view that the young child desires to replace the same-sex parent and gain the affections of the opposite-sex parent was developed during the Victorian era of the late nineteenth century when the male was dominant and the female was passive, and when sexual interests were repressed.

Many psychologists believe Freud overemphasized behavior's biological determinants and did not give adequate attention to sociocultural influences. In particular his view on the differences between males and females has a strong biological flavor and focuses on anatomical differences. That is, Freud argued that because they have a penis, boys develop a dominant, powerful personality, and that girls, because they do not have a penis, develop a submissive, weak personality. In basing his view of male/female differences in personality development on anatomical differences, Freud ignored the enormous impact of culture and experience in determining the personalities of the male and the female (Nolen-Hoeksema, 2001).

Three-quarters of a century age, English anthropologist Bronislaw Malinowski (1927) observed the behavior of the Trobriand Islanders of the Western Pacific. He found that the Oedipus complex, is not universal but depends on culture. The family pattern of the Trobriand Islanders is different than in many cultures. In the Trobriand Islands, the biological father is not the head of the household. This role is reserved for the mother's brother, who acts as a disciplinarian. Thus, the Trobriand Islanders tease apart the roles played by the same person in Freud's Vienna and in many other cultures. In Freud's view, this different family constellation should make no difference. The Oedipus complex should still emerge, in which the father is the young boy's hated rival for the mother's love. However, Malinowski found no indication of conflict between fathers and sons in the Trobriand Islanders. Instead, he observed some negative feelings directed by the boy toward the maternal uncle.

The first feminist-based criticism of Freud's theory was proposed by psychoanalytic theorist Karen Horney (1987). She developed a model of women with positive feminine qualities and self-evaluation. Her critique of Freud's theory included reference to a male-dominant society and culture efforts to eliminate the male bias in psychoanalytic theory continues today.

Karen Horney developed the first feminist-based criticism of Freud's theory. Horney's view emphasizes women's positive qualities and self-evaluation. *Where did Horney think Freud was off base?*

---

mhhe●com/
santrockld9

Horney's Theory
Piaget's Theory

assimilation Occurs when individuals incorporate new information into their existing knowledge.

accommodation Occurs when individuals adjust to new information.

experiences, we *adapt* our thinking to include new ideas because additional information furthers understanding.

Piaget (1954) believed that we adapt in two ways: assimilation and accommodation. **Assimilation** occurs when individuals incorporate new information into their existing knowledge. **Accommodation** occurs when individuals adjust to new information. Consider a circumstance in which a 9-year-old girl is given a hammer and nails to hang a picture on the wall. She has never used a hammer, but from observation and vicarious experience she realizes that a hammer is an object to be held, that it is swung by the handle to hit the nail, and that it is usually swung a number of times. Recognizing each of these things, she fits her behavior into the information she already has (assimilation). However, the hammer is heavy, so she holds it near the top. She swings too hard and the nail bends, so she adjusts the pressure of her strikes. These adjustments reveal her ability to alter slightly her conception of the world (accommodation).

Piaget thought that assimilation and accommodation operate even in the very young infant's life. Newborns reflexively suck everything that touches their lips (assimilation), but, after several months of experience, they construct their understanding of the world differently. Some objects, such as fingers and the mother's breast, can be sucked, but others, such as fuzzy blankets, should not be sucked (accommodation).

Piaget also believed that we go through four stages in understanding the world (see figure 2.3). Each of the stages is age-related and consists of distinct ways of thinking. Remember, it is the *different* way of understanding the world that makes one stage more advanced than another; knowing *more* information does not make the child's thinking more advanced, in the Piagetian view. This is what Piaget meant when he said the child's cognition is *qualitatively* different in one stage compared to another (Vidal, 2000). What are Piaget's four stages of cognitive development like?

The *sensorimotor stage,* which lasts from birth to about 2 years of age, is the first Piagetian stage. In this stage, infants construct an understanding of the world by coordinating sensory experiences (such as seeing and hearing) with physical, motoric actions—hence the term *sensorimotor.* At the beginning of this stage, newborns have little more than reflexive patterns with which to work. At the end of the stage, 2-year-olds have complex sensorimotor patterns and are beginning to operate with primitive symbols.

The *preoperational stage,* which lasts from approximately 2 to 7 years of age, is the second Piagetian stage. In this stage, children begin to represent the world with words, images, and drawings. Symbolic thought goes beyond simple connections of sensory information and physical action. However, although preschool children can symbolically represent the world, according to Piaget, they still lack the ability to perform *operations,* the Piagetian term for internalized mental actions that allow children to do mentally what they previously did physically.

The *concrete operational stage,* which lasts from approximately 7 to 11 years of age, is the third Piagetian stage. In this stage, children can perform operations, and logical reasoning replaces intuitive thought as long as reasoning can be applied to specific or concrete examples. For instance, concrete operational thinkers cannot imagine the steps necessary to complete an algebraic equation, which is too abstract for thinking at this stage of development.

The *formal operational stage,* which appears between the ages of 11 and 15 and continues through adulthood, is the fourth and final Piagetian stage. In this stage, individuals move beyond concrete experiences and think in abstract and more logical terms. As part of thinking more abstractly, adolescents develop images of ideal circumstances. They might think about what an ideal parent is like and compare their parents to this ideal standard. They begin to entertain possibilities for the future and are fascinated with what they can be. In solving problems, formal operational thinkers

Jean Piaget, the famous Swiss developmental psychologist, changed the way we think about the development of children's minds. *What are some key ideas in Piaget's theory?*

Sensorimotor Stage	**Preoperational Stage**	**Concrete Operational Stage**	**Formal Operational Stage**
The infant constructs an understanding of the world by coordinating sensory experiences with physical actions. An infant progresses from reflexive, instinctual action at birth to the beginning of symbolic thought toward the end of the stage.	The child begins to represent the world with words and images. These words and images reflect increased symbolic thinking and go beyond the connection of sensory information and physical action.	The child can now reason logically about concrete events and classify objects into different sets.	The adolescent reasons in more abstract, idealistic, and logical ways.
Birth to 2 Years of Age	*2 to 7 Years of Age*	*7 to 11 Years of Age*	*11 Years of Age through Adulthood*

FIGURE 2.3 Piaget's Four Stages of Cognitive Development

There is considerable interest today in Lev Vygotsky's sociocultural cognitive theory of child development. *What were Vygotsky's three basic claims about children's development?*

mhhe●com/
santrockld9

Vygotsky's Theory

Vygotsky's theory A sociocultural cognitive theory that emphasizes how culture and social interaction guide cognitive development.

information-processing theory Emphasizes that individuals manipulate information, monitor it, and strategize about it. Central to this theory are the processes of memory and thinking.

are more systematic, developing hypotheses about why something is happening the way it is, then testing these hypotheses in a deductive manner. We will examine Piaget's cognitive developmental theory further in chapters 6, 8, 10, 12, and 14.

Vygotsky's Sociocultural Cognitive Theory Like Piaget, the Russian developmentalist Lev Vygotsky (1896–1934) also believed that children actively construct their knowledge. However, Vygotsky gave social interaction and culture far more important roles in cognitive development than Piaget did. **Vygotsky's theory** is a sociocultural cognitive theory that emphasizes how culture and social interaction guide cognitive development. Vygotsky was born the same year as Piaget, but he died much earlier, at the age of 37. Both Piaget's and Vygotsky's ideas remained virtually unknown to American scholars until the 1960s. In the past several decades, American psychologists and educators have shown increased interest in Vygotsky's (1962) views.

Vygotsky portrayed the child's development as inseparable from social and cultural activities. He believed that the development of memory, attention, and reasoning involves learning to use the inventions of society, such as language, mathematical systems, and memory strategies. In one culture, this might consist of learning to count with the help of a computer. In another, it might consist of counting on one's fingers or using beads.

Vygotsky's theory has stimulated considerable interest in the view that knowledge is *situated* and *collaborative* (Greeno, Collins, & Resnick, 1996; John-Steiner & Mahn, 2003; Kozulin, 2000; Rogoff, Turkanis, & Bartlett, 2001). In this view, knowledge is not generated from within the individual but rather is constructed through interaction with other people and objects in the culture, such as books. This suggests that knowing can best be advanced through interaction with others in cooperative activities.

Vygotsky believed that children's social interaction with more-skilled adults and peers is indispensable in advancing cognitive development. It is through this interaction that less-skilled members of the culture learn to use the tools that will help them adapt and be successful in the culture. For example, when a skilled reader regularly helps a child learn how to read, this not only advances a child's reading skills but also communicates to the child that reading is an important activity in the culture.

Vygotsky articulated unique and influential ideas about cognitive development. In chapter 8, "Physical and Cognitive Development in Early Childhood," we will further explore Vygotsky's contributions to our understanding of children's development.

The Information-Processing Theory **Information-processing theory** emphasizes that individuals manipulate information, monitor it, and strategize about it. Central to this theory are the processes of memory and thinking. According to the information-processing theory, individuals develop a gradually increasing capacity for processing information, which allows them to acquire increasingly complex knowledge and skills (Bjorklund & Rosenbaum, 2000; Chen & Siegler, 2000; Siegler, 2001). Unlike Piaget's cognitive developmental theory, the information-processing theory does not describe development as stagelike.

Although a number of factors stimulated the growth of the information-processing theory, none was more important than the computer, which demonstrated that a machine could perform logical operations. Psychologists began to wonder if the logical operations carried out by computers might tell us something about how the human mind works. They drew analogies to computers to explain the relation between cognition or thinking and the brain. The physical brain is said to be analogous to the computer's hardware, cognition is said to be analogous to its software. Although computers and software are not perfect analogies for brains and cognitive activities, the comparison contributed to our thinking about the mind as an active information-processing system.

Robert Siegler (1998), a leading expert on children's information processing, believes that thinking is information processing. He says that when individuals perceive, encode, represent, store, and retrieve information, they are thinking. Siegler especially thinks that an important aspect of development is to learn good strategies for processing information. For example, becoming a better reader might involve learning to monitor the key themes of the material being read.

Evaluating the Cognitive Theories These are some contributions of cognitive theories:

- The cognitive theories present a positive view of development, emphasizing conscious thinking.
- The cognitive theories (especially Piaget's and Vygotsky's) emphasize the individual's active construction of understanding.
- Piaget's and Vygotsky's theories underscore the importance of examining developmental changes in children's thinking.
- The information-processing theory offers detailed descriptions of cognitive processes.

These are some criticisms of cognitive theories:

- There is skepticism about the pureness of Piaget's stages.
- The cognitive theories do not give adequate attention to individual variations in cognitive development.
- The information-processing theory does not provide an adequate description of developmental changes in cognition.
- Psychoanalytic theorists argue that the cognitive theories do not give enough credit to unconscious thought.

Behavioral and Social Cognitive Theories

Behavioral and Social Cognitive Theories

Behaviorists essentially believe that scientifically we can study only what can be directly observed and measured. At about the same time as Freud was interpreting patients' unconscious minds through their early childhood experiences, Ivan Pavlov and John B. Watson were conducting detailed observations of behavior in controlled laboratory settings. Out of the behavioral tradition grew the belief that development is observable behavior that can be learned through experience with the environment. The three versions of the behavioral approach that we will explore are Pavlov's classical conditioning, Skinner's operant conditioning, and social cognitive theory.

Pavlov's Classical Conditioning In the early 1900s, the Russian physiologist Ivan Pavlov (1927) knew that dogs innately salivate when they taste food. He became curious when he observed that dogs salivate to various sights and sounds before eating their food. For example, when an individual paired the ringing of a bell with the food, the bell ringing subsequently elicited the salivation response from the dogs when it was presented by itself. With this experiment, Pavlov discovered the principle of *classical conditioning,* in which a neutral stimulus (in our example, ringing a bell) acquires the ability to produce a response originally produced by another stimulus (in our example, food).

In the early twentieth century, John Watson wanted to show that Pavlov's concept of classical conditioning could be applied to human beings. He showed an infant named Albert a white rat to see if he was afraid of it. He was not. As Albert played with the rat, a loud noise was sounded behind his head. As you might imagine, the noise caused little Albert to cry. After several pairings of the loud noise and the white rat, Albert began to fear the rat even when the noise was not sounded (Watson & Rayner, 1920).

B. F. Skinner was a tinkerer who liked to make new gadgets. The younger of his two daughters, Deborah, was raised in Skinner's enclosed Air-Crib, which he invented because he wanted to control her environment completely. The Air-Crib was sound-proofed and temperature controlled. Debbie, shown here as a child with her parents, is currently a successful artist, is married, and lives in London. *What do you think about Skinner's Air-Crib?*

Albert Bandura has been one of the leading architects of social cognitive theory. *What is the nature of his theory?*

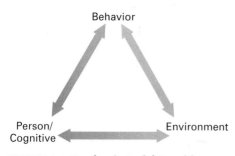

FIGURE 2.4 Bandura's Social Cognitive Model

The arrows illustrate how relations between behavior, person (cognitive), and environment are reciprocal rather than unidirectional.

Albert Bandura

social cognitive theory The view of psychologists who emphasize behavior, environment, and cognition as the key factors in development.

Today, we could not ethically conduct such an experiment, for reasons that we will discuss later in the chapter.

Many of our fears—fear of the dentist from a painful experience, fear of driving from being in an automobile incident, fear of heights from falling off a high chair when we were infants, and fear of dogs from being bitten—can be learned through classical conditioning.

Skinner's Operant Conditioning   In B. F. Skinner's (1938) *operant conditioning*, the consequences of a behavior produce changes in the probability of the behavior's occurrence. If a behavior is followed by a rewarding stimulus it is more likely to recur, but if a behavior is followed by a punishing stimulus it is less likely to recur. For example, when a person smiles at a child after the child has done something, the child is more likely to engage in the activity than if the person gives the child a nasty look.

For Skinner, such rewards and punishments shape individuals' development. For example, Skinner's approach argues that shy people learned to be shy as a result of experiences they had while growing up. It follows that modifications in an environment can help a shy person become more socially oriented.

Social Cognitive Theory   Some psychologists believe that the behaviorists basically are right when they say development is learned and is influenced strongly by environmental interactions. However, they believe that Skinner went too far in declaring that cognition is unimportant in understanding development. **Social cognitive theory** is the view of psychologists who emphasize behavior, environment, and cognition as the key factors in development.

American psychologists Albert Bandura (1986, 2000, 2001) and Walter Mischel (1973, 1995) are the main architects of social cognitive theory's contemporary version, which Mischel (1973) initially labeled *cognitive* social learning theory. Both Bandura and Mischel believe that cognitive processes are important mediators of environment-behavior connections. Bandura's early research program focused heavily on observational learning, learning that occurs through observing what others do. Observational learning is also referred to as imitation or modeling. What is *cognitive* about observational learning in Bandura's view? Bandura (1925–   ) believes that people cognitively represent the behavior of others and then sometimes adopt this behavior themselves. For example, a young boy might observe his father's aggressive outbursts and hostile interchanges with people; when observed with his peers, the young boy's style of interaction is highly aggressive, showing the same characteristics as his father's behavior. A girl might adopt the dominant and sarcastic style of her teacher. When observed interacting with her younger brother, she says, "You are so slow. How can you do this work so slowly?" Social cognitive theorists believe that people acquire a wide range of such behaviors, thoughts, and feelings through observing others' behavior and that these observations form an important part of life-span development.

Bandura's (1986, 1998, 2001) most recent model of learning and development involves behavior, the person/cognition, and the environment. An individual's confidence that he or she can control his or her success is an example of a person factor, and thinking is an example of a cognitive factor. As shown in figure 2.4, behavior, person/cognitive, and environmental factors operate interactively. Behavior can influence person factors and vice versa. The person's cognitive activities can influence the environment, the environment can change the person's cognition, and so on.

Let's consider how Bandura's model might work in the case of a college student's achievement behavior. As the student diligently studies and gets good grades, her behavior produces positive thoughts about her abilities. As part of her effort to make good grades, she plans and develops a number of strategies to make her studying more efficient. In these ways, her behavior has influenced her thought and her thought has influenced her behavior. At the beginning of the term, her college made a special effort to involve students in a study skills program. She decided to join. Her success, along with that of other students who attended the program, has led the college to expand the program next semester. In these ways, environment influenced behavior, and behavior changed the environment. And the college administrators' expectations that the study skills program would work made it possible in the first place. The program's success has spurred expectations that this type of program could work in other colleges. In these ways, cognition changed the environment, and the environment changed cognition.

Evaluating the Behavioral and Social Cognitive Theories   Contributions of the behavioral and social cognitive theories include:

- The importance of scientific research
- The environmental determinants of behavior
- The importance of observational learning (Bandura)
- Person and cognitive factors (social cognitive theory)

Criticisms of the behavioral and social cognitive theories include:

- Too little emphasis on cognition (Pavlov, Skinner)
- Too much emphasis on environmental determinants
- Inadequate attention to developmental changes
- Too mechanical and inadequate consideration of the spontaneity and creativity of humans

Behavioral and social cognitive theories emphasize the importance of environmental experiences in human development. Next we turn our attention to a theory that underscores the importance of biological foundations of development—ethological theory.

Exploring Ethology

Ethological Theory

Ethology stresses that behavior is strongly influenced by biology, is tied to evolution, and is characterized by critical or sensitive periods. Ethologists believe that the presence or absence of certain experiences at particular times in the life span influences individuals well beyond the time they first occur and that most psychologists underestimate the importance of these special time frames in early development. Ethologists also stress the powerful roles that evolution and biological foundations play in development (Rosenzweig, 2000).

ethology Stresses that behavior is strongly influenced by biology, is tied to evolution, and is characterized by critical or sensitive periods.

Konrad Lorenz, a pioneering student of animal behavior, is followed through the water by three imprinted greylag geese. Describe Lorenz's experiment with the geese. *Do you think his experiment would have the same results with human babies? Explain.*

Ethology emerged as an important view because of the work of European zoologists, especially Konrad Lorenz (1903–1989). Working mostly with greylag geese, Lorenz (1965) studied a behavior pattern that was considered to be programmed within the birds' genes. A newly hatched gosling seemed to be born with the instinct to follow its mother. Observations showed that the gosling was capable of such behavior as soon as it hatched. Lorenz proved that it was incorrect to assume that such behavior was programmed in the animal. In a remarkable set of experiments, Lorenz separated the eggs laid by one goose into two groups. One group he returned to the goose to be hatched by her. The other group was hatched in an incubator. The goslings in the first group performed as predicted. They followed their mother as soon as they hatched. However, those in the second group, which saw Lorenz when they first hatched, followed him everywhere, as though he were their mother. Lorenz marked the goslings and then placed both groups under a box. Mother goose and "mother" Lorenz stood aside as the box lifted. Each group of goslings went directly to its "mother." Lorenz called this process *imprinting,* the rapid, innate learning within a limited critical period of time that involves attachment to the first moving object seen.

The ethological view of Lorenz and the European zoologists forced American developmental psychologists to recognize the importance of the biological basis of behavior. However, ethological research and theory lacked some ingredients that would elevate it to the ranks of the other theories discussed so far in this chapter. In particular, there was little or nothing in the classical ethological view about the nature of social relationships across the human life span, something that any major theory of development must explain. Also, its concept of *critical period,* a fixed time period very early in development during which certain behaviors optimally emerge, seemed to be overdrawn. Classical ethological theory was weak in stimulating studies with humans. Recent expansion of the ethological view has improved its status as a viable developmental perspective.

One of the most important applications of ethological theory to human development involves John Bowlby's (1969, 1989) theory of attachment. Bowlby argued that attachment to a caregiver over the first year of life has important consequences throughout the life span. In his view, if this attachment is positive and secure, the individual will likely develop more positively in childhood and adulthood. If the attachment is negative and insecure, life-span development will likely not be optimal. In chapter 7, "Socioemotional Development in Infancy," we will explore the concept of infant attachment in much greater detail.

Contributions of ethological theory include:

- Increased focus on the biological and evolutionary basis of development
- Use of careful observations in naturalistic settings
- Emphasis on sensitive periods of development

These are some criticisms of ethological theory:

- The concepts of critical and sensitive periods might be too rigid
- Too strong an emphasis on biological foundations
- Inadequate attention to cognition
- The theory has been better at generating research with animals than with humans

Another theory that emphasizes the biological aspects of human development—evolutionary psychology—will be presented in chapter 3, "Biological Beginnings," along with views on the role of heredity in development. Also, we will examine a number of biological theories of aging in chapter 18, "Physical Development in Late Adulthood."

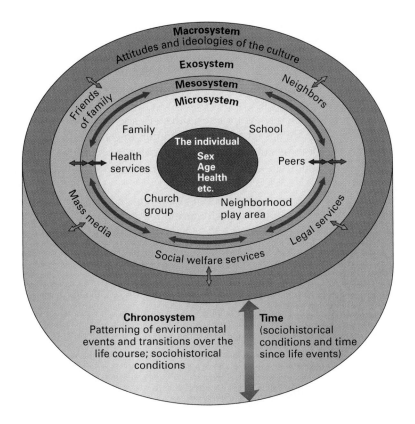

FIGURE 2.5 Bronfenbrenner's Ecological Theory of Development

Bronfenbrenner's ecological theory consists of five environmental systems: microsystem, mesosystem, exosystem, macrosystem, and chronosystem.

Ecological Theory

While ethological theory stresses biological factors, ecological theory emphasizes environmental factors. One ecological theory that has important implications for understanding life-span development was created by Urie Bronfenbrenner (1917–   ).

Ecological theory is Bronfenbrenner's (1986, 2000; Bronfenbrenner & Morris, 1998) environmental system of development. It consists of five environmental systems ranging from the fine-grained inputs of direct interactions with people to the broad-based inputs of culture (see figure 2.5).

- *Microsystem:* The setting in which the individual lives. These contexts include the person's family, peers, school, and neighborhood ◀▥ p. 13. It is in the microsystem that the most direct interactions with social agents take place—with parents, peers, and teachers, for example. The individual is viewed not as a passive recipient of experiences in these settings, but as someone who helps to construct the settings.
- *Mesosystem:* Involves relations between microsystems or connections between contexts. Examples are the relation of family experiences to school experiences, school experiences to church experiences, and family experiences to peer experiences. For example, children whose parents have rejected them may have difficulty developing positive relations with teachers.
- *Exosystem:* Is involved when experiences in another social setting—in which the individual does not have an active role—influence what the individual experiences in an immediate context. For example, work experiences can affect a

Bronfenbrenner's Theory

Bronfenbrenner and a Multicultural Framework

ecological theory Bronfenbrenner's environmental systems theory that focuses on five environmental systems: microsystem, mesosystem, exosystem, macrosystem, and chronosystem.

Urie Bronfenbrenner developed ecological theory, a perspective that is receiving increased attention. His theory emphasizes the importance of both micro and macro dimensions of the environment in which the child lives.

woman's relationship with her husband and their child. The mother might receive a promotion that requires more travel, which might increase marital conflict and change patterns of parent-child interaction. Another example is the federal government through its role in the quality of medical care and support systems for older adults.

- *Macrosystem:* The culture in which individuals live. Remember from chapter 1 that culture refers to the behavior patterns, beliefs, and all other products of a group of people that are passed on from generation to generation ◀▭▭▭ p. 13. Remember also that cross-cultural studies—the comparison of one culture with one or more other cultures—provide information about the generality of development.

- *Chronosystem:* The patterning of environmental events and transitions over the life course, as well as sociohistorical circumstances. For example, in studying the effects of divorce on children, researchers have found that the negative effects often peak in the first year after the divorce. The effects also are more negative for sons than for daughters (Hetherington, 1993). By two years after the divorce, family interaction is less chaotic and more stable. With regard to sociocultural circumstances, women today are much more likely to be encouraged to pursue a career than they were 20 or 30 years ago.

Bronfenbrenner (2000; Bronfenbrenner & Morris, 1998) has added biological influences to his theory and now describes it as a bioecological theory. Nonetheless, ecological, environmental contexts still predominate in Bronfenbrenner's theory (Ceci, 2000).

The contributions of ecological theory include:

- A systematic examination of macro and micro dimensions of environmental systems
- Attention to connections between environmental settings (mesosystem)
- Consideration of sociohistorical influences on development (chronosystem)

These are some criticisms of ecological theory:

- Even with the added discussion of biological influences in recent years, there is still too little attention to biological foundations of development
- Inadequate attention to cognitive processes

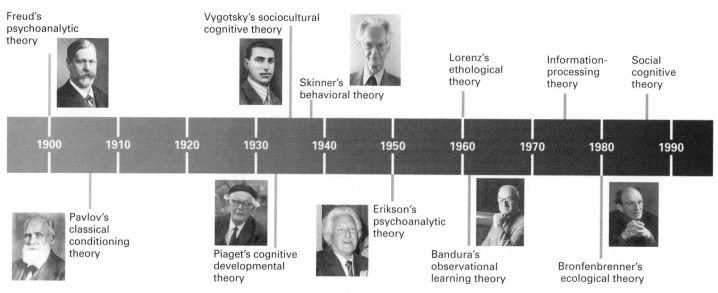

FIGURE 2.6 Time Line for Major Developmental Theories

An Eclectic Theoretical Orientation

An **eclectic theoretical orientation** does not follow any one theoretical approach, but rather selects from each theory whatever is considered its best features. No single theory described in this chapter can explain entirely the rich complexity of life-span development. Each of the theories has made important contributions to our understanding of development, but none provides a complete description and explanation. Psychoanalytic theory best explains the unconscious mind. Erikson's theory best describes the changes that occur in adult development. Piaget's, Vygotsky's, and the information-processing views provide the most complete description of cognitive development. The behavioral and social cognitive and ecological theories have been the most adept at examining the environmental determinants of development. The ethological theories have made us aware of biology's role and the importance of sensitive periods in development. It is important to recognize that, although theories are helpful guides, relying on a single theory to explain development is probably a mistake.

An attempt was made in this chapter to present five theoretical perspectives objectively. The same eclectic orientation will be maintained throughout the book. In this way, you can view the study of development as it actually exists—with different theorists making different assumptions, stressing different empirical problems, and using different strategies to discover information.

The theories that we have discussed were conceived at different points in the twentieth century. For a chronology of when these theories were proposed, see figure 2.6 on page 56. Figure 2.7 compares the main theoretical perspectives in terms of how they view important developmental issues in life-span development.

eclectic theoretical orientation An orientation that does not follow any one theoretical approach, but rather selects from each theory whatever is considered the best in it.

Theory	Issues		
	Continuity/discontinuity, early versus later experiences	Biological and environmental factors	Importance of cognition
Psychoanalytic	Discontinuity between stages—continuity between early experiences and later development; early experiences very important; later changes in development emphasized in Erikson's theory	Freud's biological determination interacting with early family experiences; Erikson's more balanced biological-cultural interaction perspective	Emphasized, but in the form of unconscious thought
Cognitive	Discontinuity between stages in Piaget's theory; continuity between early experiences and later development in Piaget's and Vygotsky's theory; no stages in Vygotsky's theory or information-processing theory	Piaget's emphasis on interaction and adaptation; environment provides the setting for cognitive structures to develop; information-processing view has not addressed this issue extensively but mainly emphasizes biological-environmental interaction	The primary determinant of behavior
Behavioral and social cognitive	Continuity (no stages); experience at all points of development important	Environment viewed as the cause of behavior in both views	Strongly deemphasized in the behavioral approach but an important mediator in social cognitive theory
Ethological	Discontinuity but no stages; critical or sensitive periods emphasized; early experiences very important	Strong biological view	Not emphasized
Ecological	Little attention to continuity/discontinuity; change emphasized more than stability	Strong environmental view	Not emphasized

FIGURE 2.7 A Comparison of Theories and Issues in Life-Span Development

Review and Reflect

1 Describe theories of life-span development

REVIEW

- What is the relationship between a theory and hypotheses? What are two main psychoanalytic theories? What are some strengths and weaknesses of the psychoanalytic theories?
- What are three main cognitive theories? What are some strengths and weaknesses of the cognitive theories?
- What are three main behavioral and social cognitive theories? What are some strengths and weaknesses of the behavioral and social cognitive theories?
- What is the nature of ethological theory? What are some strengths and weaknesses of the theory?
- What is an eclectic theoretical orientation?

REFLECT

- Which of the life-span theories do you think best explains your own development? Why?

2 RESEARCH IN LIFE-SPAN DEVELOPMENT

Types of Research   **Time Span of Research**

Generally, research in life-span development is designed to test hypotheses, which in some cases, are derived from the theories just described. Through research, theories are modified to reflect new data and occasionally new theories arise. What types of research are conducted in life-span development? If researchers want to study people of different ages, what research designs can they use? These are the questions that we will examine next.

In this research study, mother-child interaction is being videotaped. Later, researchers will code the interaction using precise categories.

Types of Research

This section describes the major methods used to gather data about life-span development. For this purpose, there are three basic types of research: descriptive, correlational, and experimental. Each has strengths and weaknesses.

Descriptive Research   Some important theories have grown out of **descriptive research,** which has the purpose of observing and recording behavior. For example, a psychologist might observe the extent to which people are altruistic or aggressive toward each other. By itself, descriptive research cannot prove what causes some phenomenon, but it can reveal important information about people's behavior and attitudes. Descriptive research methods include observation, surveys and interviews, standardized tests, case studies, and life-history records.

Observation   Scientific observation requires an important set of skills (McMillan & Wergin, 2002). Unless we are trained observers and practice our skills regularly, we might not know what to look for, we might not remember what we saw, we might not realize that what we are looking for is changing from one moment to the next, and we might not communicate our observations effectively.

For observations to be effective, they have to be systematic (Elmes, Kantowitz, & Roedinger, 2003). We have to have some idea of what we are looking for. We have to know whom we are observing, when and where we will observe, and how the observations will be made. In what form they will be recorded: In writing? Tape recording? Video?

Where should we make our observations? We have two choices: the laboratory and the everyday world.

When we observe scientifically, we often need to control certain factors that determine behavior but are not the focus of our inquiry (Hoyle & Judd, 2002). For this reason, some research in life-span development is conducted in a **laboratory,** a controlled setting with many of the complex factors of the "real world" removed.

An experiment conducted by Albert Bandura (1965) found that children behaved more aggressively after observing a model being rewarded for aggression. Bandura conducted this study in a laboratory with adults the child did not know. Thus, he controlled when the child witnessed aggression, how much aggression the child saw, and what form the aggression took. Bandura would not have had as much control over the experiment, or as much confidence in the results, if the study had been conducted in the children's homes and if familiar people had been present, such as the child's parents, siblings, or friends.

Laboratory research does have some drawbacks. First, it is almost impossible to conduct research without the participants' knowing they are being studied. Second, the laboratory setting is unnatural and therefore can cause the participants to behave unnaturally.

Another drawback of laboratory research is that people who are willing to come to a university laboratory may not fairly represent groups from diverse cultural backgrounds. Those who are unfamiliar with university settings, and with the idea of "helping science," may be intimidated by the setting.

Still another problem is that some aspects of life-span development are difficult if not impossible to examine in the laboratory. Laboratory studies of certain types of stress may even be unethical.

Naturalistic observation provides insights that we sometimes cannot achieve in the laboratory (Billman, 2003; Langston, 2002). **Naturalistic observation** means observing behavior in real-world settings, making no effort to manipulate or control the situation. Life-span researchers conduct naturalistic observations at sporting events, day-care centers, work settings, malls, and other places people live in and frequent. Suppose that you wanted to study the level of civility on your campus. Most likely, you would want to include some naturalistic observation of how people treat one another in places like the cafeteria or the library reading room.

Science refines everyday thinking.

—**Albert Einstein**
German-born American Physicist, 20th Century

descriptive research Has the purpose of observing and recording behavior.

laboratory A controlled setting in which many of the complex factors of the "real world" are removed.

naturalistic observation Observing behavior in real-world settings.

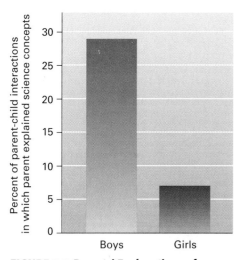

FIGURE 2.8 Parents' Explanations of Science to Sons and Daughters at a Science Museum

In a naturalistic observation study at a children's science museum, parents were three times more likely to explain science to boys than to girls (Crowley & others, 2001). The gender difference occurred regardless of whether the father, the mother, or both parents were with the child, although the gender difference was greatest for fathers' science explanations to sons and daughters.

"Would you say Attila is doing an excellent job, a good job, a fair job, or a poor job?"

standardized test A test with uniform procedures for administration and scoring. Many standardized tests allow a person's performance to be compared with the performance of other individuals.

Naturalistic observation was used in one study that focused on conversations in a children's science museum (Crowley & others, 2001). Parents were three times as likely to engage boys than girls in explanatory talk while visiting different exhibits at the science museum, suggesting a gender bias that encourages boys more than girls in science (see figure 2.8). In another study, Mexican American parents who had completed high school used more explanations with their children when visiting a science museum than Mexican American parents who had not completed high school (Tenenbaum & others, 2002).

Surveys and Interviews Sometimes the best and quickest way to get information about people is to ask them for it. One technique is to *interview* them directly. A related method that is especially useful when information from many people is needed is the *survey,* sometimes referred to as a questionnaire. A standard set of questions is used to obtain peoples' self-reported attitudes or beliefs about a particular topic. In a good survey, the questions are clear and unbiased, allowing respondents to answer unambiguously.

Surveys and interviews can be used to study a wide range of topics from religious beliefs to sexual habits to attitudes about gun control to beliefs about how to improve schools. Surveys and interviews can be conducted in person or over the telephone. In addition, some surveys are now being conducted over the Internet.

Some survey and interview questions are unstructured and open-ended, such as "Could you elaborate on your optimistic tendencies?" or "How fulfilling would you say your marriage is?" They allow for unique responses from each person surveyed. Other survey and interview questions are more structured and ask about more specific things. For example, one national poll on beliefs about what needs to be done to improve U.S. schools asked: "Of the following four possibilities, which one do you think offers the most promise for improving public schools in the community: a qualified, competent teacher in every classroom; free choice for parents among a number of private, church-related, and public schools; rigorous academic standards; the elimination of social promotion; or don't know? (Rose & Gallup, 2000). More than half of the respondents said that the most important way to improve schools is to have a qualified, competent teacher in every classroom.

One problem with surveys and interviews is the tendency of participants to answer questions in a way that they think is socially acceptable or desirable rather than telling what they truly think or feel (Best & Kahn, 2003). For example, on a survey or in an interview some individuals might say that they do not take drugs even though they do.

Standardized Tests A **standardized test** has uniform procedures for administration and scoring. Many standardized tests allow a person's performance to be compared with the performance of other individuals (Aiken, 2003). One widely used standardized test in psychology is the Stanford-Binet intelligence test, which is described in chapter 10, "Physical and Cognitive Development in Middle and Late Childhood."

Scores on standardized tests are often stated in percentiles. Suppose you scored in the 92nd percentile on the SAT. This score would mean that 92 percent of a large group of individuals who previously took the test received scores lower than yours.

The main advantage of standardized tests is that they provide information about individual differences among people. One problem with standardized tests is that they do not always predict behavior in non-test situations. Another problem is that standardized tests are based on the belief that a person's behavior is consistent and stable, yet personality and intelligence—two primary targets of standardized testing—can vary with the situation. For example, a person may perform poorly on a standardized intelligence test in an office setting but score much higher at home, where he or she is less anxious.

This criticism is especially relevant for members of minority groups, some of whom have been inaccurately classified as mentally retarded on the basis of their scores on intelligence tests (Valencia & Suzuki, 2001). In addition, cross-cultural psychologists caution that many psychological tests developed in Western cultures might not be appropriate in other cultures (Cushner & Brislin, 1995). People in other cultures may have had experiences that cause them to interpret and respond to questions much differently from the people for whom the test was standardized.

Case Studies   A **case study** is an in-depth look at a single individual. Case studies are performed mainly by mental health professionals when, for either practical or ethical reasons, the unique aspects of an individual's life cannot be duplicated and tested in other individuals (Dattilio, 2001). A case study provides information about one person's fears, hopes, fantasies, traumatic experiences, upbringing, family relationships, health, or anything that helps the psychologist understand the person's mind and behavior.

Mahatma Gandhi was the spiritual leader of India in the middle of the twentieth century. Erik Erikson conducted an extensive case study of his life to determine what contributed to his identity development. *What are some limitations of the case study approach?*

An example of a case study is Erik Erikson's (1969) analysis of India's spiritual leader Mahatma Gandhi. Erikson studied Gandhi's life in great depth to gain insights into how his positive spiritual identity developed, especially during his youth. In putting the pieces of Ghandi's identity development together, Erikson described the contributions of culture, history, family, and various other factors that might affect the way other people develop an identity.

Other vivid case studies appear in later chapters. One involves Michael Rehbein, who had much of the entire left side of his brain removed at 7 years of age to end severe epileptic seizures. Another concerns a modern-day wild child named Genie, who lived in near isolation during her childhood.

Case histories provide dramatic, in-depth portrayals of people's lives, but remember that we must be cautious when generalizing from this information. The subject of a case study is unique, with a genetic makeup and personal history that no one else shares. In addition, case studies involve judgments of unknown reliability. Psychologists who conduct case studies rarely check to see if other psychologists agree with their observations.

Life-History Records   **Life-history records** are records of information about a lifetime chronology of events and activities. They often involve a combination of data records on education, work, family, and residence. These records may be generated with information from archival materials (public records or historical documents) or interviews, which might include obtaining a life calendar from the respondent. Life calendars record the age (year and month) at which transitions occur in a variety of activity domains and life events, thus portraying an unfolding life course. In compiling life-history records, researchers increasingly use a wide array of materials, including written and oral reports from the subject, vital records, observation, and public documents (Clausen, 1993). One of the advantages of the multiple-materials approach is that information from varied sources can be compared and discrepancies sometimes can be resolved, resulting in a more accurate life-history record.

Correlational Research   In **correlational research,** the goal is to describe the strength of the relationship between two or more events or characteristics. The more strongly the two events are correlated (or related or associated), the more effectively we can predict one event from the other (Whitley, 2002). For example, if researchers find that low-involved, permissive parenting is correlated with a child's lack of self-control, it suggests that low-involved, permissive parenting might be one source of the lack of self-control. This form of research is a key method of data analysis, which you may recall, is the third step in the scientific method.

mhhe●com/
santrockld9

Correlational Research
Experimental Research

case study   An in-depth look at a single individual.

life-history records   Records of information about a lifetime chronology of events and activities that often involve a combination of data records on education, work, family, and residence.

correlational research   The goal is to describe the strength of the relationship between two or more events or characteristics.

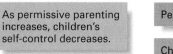

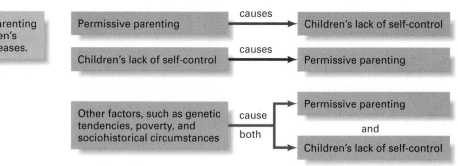

FIGURE 2.9 Possible Explanations for Correlational Data

An observed correlation between two events cannot be used to conclude that one event caused the other. Some possibilities are that the second event caused the first event or that a third, unknown event caused the correlation between the first two events.

A caution is in order, however. *Correlation does not equal causation.* The correlational finding just mentioned does not mean that permissive parenting necessarily causes low self-control in children. It could mean that, but it also could mean that a child's lack of self-control caused the parents to simply throw up their arms in despair and give up trying to control the child. It also could mean that other factors, such as heredity or poverty, caused the correlation between permissive parenting and low self-control in children. Figure 2.9 illustrates these possible interpretations of correlational data.

Throughout this book you will read about numerous correlational research studies. Keep in mind how easy it is to assume causality when two events or characteristics merely are correlated.

Experimental Research   An **experiment** is a carefully regulated procedure in which one or more factors believed to influence the behavior being studied are manipulated while all other factors are held constant. If the behavior under study changes when a factor is manipulated, we say that the manipulated factor has caused the behavior to change (Kirk, 2003). In other words, the experiment has demonstrated cause and effect. The cause is the factor that was manipulated. The effect is the behavior that changed because of the manipulation. Nonexperimental research methods (descriptive and correlational research) cannot establish cause and effect because they do not involve manipulating factors in a controlled way.

Independent and Dependent Variables   Experiments include two types of changeable factors, or variables: independent and dependent. An *independent variable* is a manipulated, influential, experimental factor. It is a potential cause. The label "independent" is used because this variable can be manipulated independently of other factors to determine its effect. Researchers have a vast array of options open to them in selecting independent variables, and one experiment may include several independent variables.

A *dependent variable* is a factor that can change in an experiment, in response to changes in the independent variable. As researchers manipulate the independent variable, they measure the dependent variable for any resulting effect.

Experimental and Control Groups   Experiments can involve one or more experimental groups and one or more control groups.

An *experimental group* is a group whose experience is manipulated. A *control group* is a comparison group that is as much like the experimental group as possible and that is treated in every way like the experimental group except for the manipulated factor (independent variable). The control group serves as a baseline against which the effects of the manipulated condition can be compared.

experiment A carefully regulated procedure in which one or more of the factors believed to influence the behavior being studied are manipulated while all other factors are held constant.

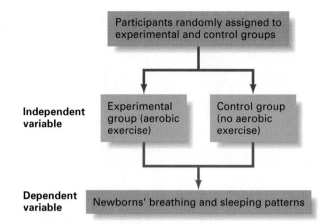

FIGURE 2.10 Principles of Experimental Research

Imagine that you decide to conduct an experimental study of the effects of aerobic exercise by pregnant women on their newborns' breathing and sleeping patterns. You would randomly assign pregnant women to experimental and control groups. The experimental group women would engage in aerobic exercise over a specified number of sessions and weeks. The control group would not. Then, when the infants are born, you would assess their breathing and sleeping patterns. If the breathing and sleeping patterns of newborns whose mothers were in the experimental group are more positive than those of the control group, you would conclude that aerobic exercise caused the positive effects.

Random assignment is an important principle for deciding whether each participant will be placed in the experimental group or in the control group (Shaughnessy, Zechmeister, & Zechmeister, 2003). *Random assignment* means that researchers assign participants to experimental and control groups by chance. It reduces the likelihood that the experiment's results will be due to any preexisting differences between groups. Figure 2.10 illustrates the nature of experimental research.

Time Span of Research

A special concern of developmentalists is the time span of a research investigation. Studies that focus on the relation of age to some other variable are common in life-span development. We have several options: Researchers can study different individuals of different ages and compare them; they can study the same individuals as they age over time; or they can use some combination of these two approaches.

Cross-Sectional Approach The **cross-sectional approach** is a research strategy in which individuals of different ages are compared at one time. A typical cross-sectional study might include a group of 5-year-olds, 8-year-olds, and 11-year-olds. Another might include a group of 15-year-olds, 25-year-olds, and 45-year-olds. The different groups can be compared with respect to a variety of dependent variables: IQ, memory, peer relations, attachment to parents, hormonal changes, and so on. All of this can be accomplished in a short time. In some studies data are collected in a single day. Even in large-scale cross-sectional studies with hundreds of subjects, data collection does not usually take longer than several months to complete.

The main advantage of the cross-sectional study is that the researcher does not have to wait for the individuals to grow up or become older. Despite its time efficiency, the cross-sectional approach has its drawbacks. It gives no information about how individuals change or about the stability of their characteristics. The increases and decreases of development—the hills and valleys of growth and development—can become obscured in the cross-sectional approach. For example, in a cross-sectional approach to perceptions of life satisfaction, average increases and decreases might be revealed. But the study would not show how the life satisfaction of individual adults

cross-sectional approach A research strategy in which individuals of different ages are compared at one time.

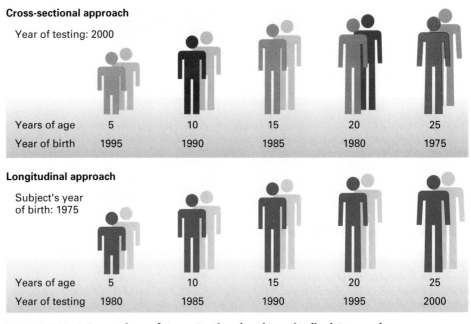

FIGURE 2.11 A Comparison of Cross-Sectional and Longitudinal Approaches

waxed and waned over the years. It also would not tell us whether adults who had positive or negative perceptions of life satisfaction as young adults maintained their relative degree of life satisfaction as middle-aged or older adults.

Longitudinal Approach   The **longitudinal approach** is a research strategy in which the same individuals are studied over a period of time, usually several years or more. For example, if a study of life satisfaction were conducted longitudinally, the same adults might be assessed periodically over a 70-year time span—at the ages of 20, 35, 45, 65, and 90, for example. Figure 2.11 compares the cross-sectional and longitudinal approaches.

Although longitudinal studies provide a wealth of information about such important issues as stability and change in development and the importance of early experience for later development, they are not without their problems (Raudenbush, 2001). They are expensive and time-consuming. The longer the study lasts, the more participants drop out—they move, get sick, lose interest, and so forth. Participants can bias the outcome of a study, because those who remain may be dissimilar to those who drop out. Those individuals who remain in a longitudinal study over a number of years may be more compulsive and conformity-oriented, for example, or they might have more stable lives.

Sequential Approach   Sometimes developmentalists also combine the cross-sectional and longitudinal approaches to learn about life-span development (Schaie, 1993). The **sequential approach** is the combined cross-sectional, longitudinal design. In most instances, this approach starts with a cross-sectional study that includes individuals of different ages. A number of months after the initial assessment, the same individuals are tested again—this is the longitudinal aspect of the design. At this later time, a new group of participants is assessed at each age level. The new groups at each level are added at the later time to control for changes that might have taken place in the original group—some might have dropped out of the study, or retesting might have improved their performance, for example. The sequential approach is complex, expensive, and time-consuming, but it does provide information that is impossible to obtain from cross-sectional or longitudinal approaches alone. The

longitudinal approach A research strategy in which the same individuals are studied over a period of time, usually several years or more.

sequential approach A combined cross-sectional, longitudinal design.

a.

b.

c.

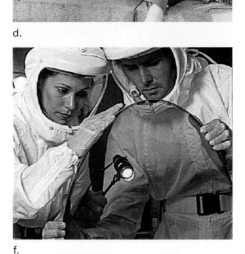
d.

e.

f.

FIGURE 2.12 Cohort Effects

Cohort effects are due to a person's time of birth or generation but not actually to age. Think for a moment about growing up in (a) the Roaring Twenties, (b) the Great Depression, (c) the 1940s and World War II, (d) the 1950s, (e) the late 1960s, and (f) today. *How might your development be different depending on which of these time frames has dominated your life? your parents' lives? your grandparents' lives?*

sequential approach has been especially helpful in examining cohort effects in life-span development, which we will discuss next.

Cohort Effects A *cohort* is a group of people who are born at a similar point in history and share similar experiences as a result, such as living through the Great Depression of the 1930s or growing up in the same city around the same time. For example, cohorts can differ in years of education, child-rearing practices, health, attitudes toward sex, religious values, and economic status (see figure 2.12). In life-span development research, **cohort effects** are due to a person's time of birth or

cohort effects Effects due to a person's time of birth or generation but not to actual age.

Research Method	Theory
Observation	• All theories emphasize some form of observation. • Behavioral and social cognitive theories place the strongest emphasis on laboratory observation. • Ethological theory places the strongest emphasis on naturalistic observation.
Survey/interview	• Psychoanalytic and cognitive studies (Piaget, Vygotsky) often use interviews. • Behavioral, social cognitive, and ethological theories are the least likely to use surveys or interviews.
Standardized test	• None of the theories discussed emphasize the use of this method.
Case study	• Psychoanalytic theories (Freud, Erikson) are the most likely to use this method.
Life-history record	• This method is most likely to be advocated by ecological theory and psychoanalytic theories.
Correlational research	• All of the theories use this research method, although psychoanalytic theories are the least likely to use it.
Experimental research	• The behavioral and social cognitive theories and the information-processing theories are the most likely to use the experimental method. • Psychoanalytic theories are the least likely to use it.
Cross-sectional/ longitudinal/ sequential methods	• No theory described uses these methods more than any other. • The sequential method is the least likely to be used by any theory.

FIGURE 2.13 Connections of Research Methods to Theories

generation but not to actual age. Cohort effects are important because they can powerfully affect the dependent measures in a study ostensibly concerned with age. Researchers have shown it is especially important to be aware of cohort effects in the assessment of adult intelligence (Schaie, 1996). Individuals born at different points in time—such as 1920, 1940, and 1960—have had varying opportunities for education, while individuals born in earlier years had less access ◀▥ p. 11.

Cross-sectional studies can show how different cohorts respond but they can confuse age changes and cohort effects. Longitudinal studies are effective in studying age changes but only within one cohort. With sequential studies, both age changes in one cohort can be examined and compared with age changes in another cohort.

A point that is important to make is that theories often are linked with a particular research method or methods. Thus, method(s) researchers use are associated with their particular theoretical approach. Figure 2.13 illustrates the connections between research methods and theories.

Review and Reflect

2 **Explain how research on life-span development is conducted**

REVIEW

- How is research on life-span development conducted?
- What are some ways that researchers study the time span of people's lives?

REFLECT

- You have learned that correlation does not equal causation. Develop an example of two variables (two sets of observations) that are correlated but that you believe almost certainly have no causal relationship.

3 FACING UP TO RESEARCH CHALLENGES

Conducting Ethical Research   **Minimizing Bias**

The scientific foundation of research in life-span development helps to minimize the effect of individual researcher's biases and to maximize the objectivity of the results. Still, some subtle challenges remain to be fully resolved. One is to ensure that research is conducted in an ethical way; another is to recognize, and try to overcome, researchers' deeply buried personal biases.

Conducting Ethical Research

Ethics is an important part of your understanding of the science of life-span development. Even if you have no formal exposure to life-span development beyond this course, you will find that scientific research in this field and related disciplines affects our everyday life. For one thing, decision makers in business, government, schools, and many other institutions use the results of research in life-span development to help people lead happier, healthier, more productive lives.

The explosion in technology has forced society to grapple with looming ethics questions that were unimaginable only a few decades ago. The same line of research that enables previously sterile couples to have children might also let prospective parents "call up and order" the characteristics they prefer in their children and someday tip the balance of males and females in the world. Should embryos left over from procedures for increasing fertility be saved or discarded? The line of research that enables previously sterile couples to have children has also led to the spectacle of frozen embryos being passed about in the courts as a part of divorce settlements.

Ethics in research may affect you more personally if you serve at some point, as is quite likely, as a participant in a study. In that event, you need to know about your rights as a participant and about the responsibilities researchers have in assuring that these rights are safeguarded. The failure to consider participants' well-being can have life-altering consequences for them. For example, one investigation of young dating couples asked them to complete a questionnaire that coincidentally stimulated some of the participants to think about potentially troublesome issues (Rubin & Mitchell, 1976). One year later, when the researchers followed up with the original sample, 9 of 10 participants said they had discussed their answers with their dating partner. In most instances, the discussions helped to strengthen the relationships. In some cases, though, the participants used the questionnaire as a springboard to discuss previously

**mhhe com/
santrockld9**

Psychologists' Ethical Principles

hidden problems or concerns. One participant said, "The study definitely played a role in ending my relationship with Larry." In this case, the couple had different views about how long they expected to be together. She was thinking of a short-term dating relationship only, while he was thinking in terms of a lifetime. Their answers to the questions brought the disparity in their views to the surface and led to the end of their relationship. Researchers have a responsibility to anticipate the personal problems their study might cause and to at least inform the participants of the possible fallout.

If you ever become a researcher in life-span development yourself, you will need an even deeper understanding of ethics. You may never become a researcher in the field of psychology, but you may carry out one or more experimental projects in psychology courses. Even smart, conscientious students frequently do not consider the rights of the participants who serve in their experiments. A student might think, "I volunteer in a home for the mentally retarded several hours per week. I can use the residents of the home in my study to see if a particular treatment helps improve their memory for everyday tasks." But without proper permissions the most well-meaning, kind, and considerate studies still violate the rights of the participants.

Ethics Guidelines Safeguarding the rights of research participants is a challenge because the potential harm is not always obvious (Gall, Borg, & Gall, 2003). At first glance, you might not imagine that a questionnaire on dating relationships among college students would have any substantial impact or that an experiment involving treatment of memory loss in older adults would be anything but beneficial. But researchers increasingly recognize that lasting harm might come to the participants in a study of life-span development.

Today colleges and universities have review boards that evaluate the ethical nature of research conducted at their institutions. Proposed research plans must pass the scrutiny of a research ethics committee before the research can be initiated.

In addition, the American Psychological Association (APA) has developed ethics guidelines for its members. The code of ethics instructs psychologists to protect their participants from mental and physical harm. The participants' best interests need to be kept foremost in the researcher's mind (Rosnow, 1995). APA's guidelines address four important issues:

- *Informed Consent* All participants must know what their participation will involve and what risks might develop. For example, participants in a study on dating should be told beforehand that a questionnaire might stimulate thoughts about issues in their relationship that they have not considered. Participants also should be informed that in some instances a discussion of the issues might improve their relationship, but in others might worsen the relationship and even end it. Even after informed consent is given, participants must retain the right to withdraw from the study at any time and for any reason.
- *Confidentiality* Researchers are responsible for keeping all of the data they gather on individuals completely confidential and when possible, completely anonymous.
- *Debriefing* After the study has been completed, participants should be informed of its purpose and the methods that were used. In most cases, the experimenter also can inform participants in a general manner beforehand about the purpose of the research without leading participants to behave in a way they think that the experimenter is expecting. When preliminary information about the study is likely to affect the results, participants can at least be debriefed after the study has been completed.
- *Deception* This is an ethical issue that researchers debate extensively (Hoyle & Judd, 2002). In some circumstances, telling the participant beforehand what the research study is about substantially alters the participant's behavior and invalidates the researcher's data. In all cases of deception, however, the psychologist must ensure that the deception will not harm the participant and that the partic-

Look at these two photographs, one of all White males, the other of a diverse group of females and males from different ethnic groups, including some White individuals. Consider a topic in psychology, such as parenting, love, or cultural values. *If you were conducting research on this topic, might the results of the study be different depending on whether the participants in your study were the individuals in the photograph on the left or those on the right?*

ipant will be told the complete nature of the study (debriefed) as soon as possible after the study is completed.

Minimizing Bias

Studies of life-span development are most useful when they are conducted without bias or prejudice toward any particular group of people. Of special concern is bias based on gender and bias based on culture or ethnicity ◀▥ p. 14.

Gender Bias For decades, society has had a strong gender bias, a preconceived notion about the abilities of women and men that prevented individuals from pursuing their own interests and achieving their potential. Gender bias also has had a less obvious effect within the field of life-span development (Etaugh & Bridges, 2001; Palvdi, 2002; Shields & Eyssell, 2001). For example, it is not unusual for conclusions to be drawn about females' attitudes and behaviors from research conducted with males as the only participants (Maracek & others, 2003).

Florence Denmark and her colleagues (1988) argue as well that when gender differences are found, they sometimes are unduly magnified. For example, a researcher might report in a study that 74 percent of the men had high achievement expectations versus only 67 percent of the women and go on to talk about the differences in some detail. In reality, this might be a rather small difference. It also might disappear if the study were repeated or the study might have methodological problems that don't allow such strong interpretations.

Researchers giving females equal rights in research have raised some new questions (Tetreault, 1997):

* How might gender bias influence the choice of hypotheses, participants, and research design? For example, the most widely known theory of moral development was proposed by a male (Lawrence Kohlberg) in a male-dominant society (the United States), and males were the main participants in research used to support the theory for many years.

Careers in Life-Span Development

Pam Reid, Educational and Developmental Psychologist

As a child, Pam Reid played with chemistry sets, and at the university she was majoring in chemistry, planning to become a medical doctor. Because some of her friends signed up for a psychology course as an elective, she decided to join them. She was so intrigued by learning more about how people think, behave, and develop that she changed her major to psychology. She says, "I fell in love with psychology." Reid went on to obtain her Ph.D. in educational psychology ◀||||| p. 31.

Today, Pamela Trotman Reid is a professor of education and psychology at the University of Michigan. She is also a research scientist for the UM Institute for Research on Women and Gender. Her main interest is how children and adolescents develop social skills, and especially how gender, socioeconomic status, and ethnicity are involved in development (Reid & Zalk, 2001). Because many psychological findings have been based on research with middle-socioeconomic-status non-Latino White populations, She believes it is important to study people from different ethnic groups. She stresses that by understanding the expectations, attitudes, and behavior of diverse groups, we enrich the theory and practice of psychology. Currently Dr. Reid is working with her graduate students on a project involving middle school girls. She is interested in why girls, more often than boys, stop taking classes in mathematics.

Pam Reid (*back row, center*) with graduate students she is mentoring at the University of Michigan.

- How might research on topics of primary interest to females, such as relationships, feelings, and empathy, challenge existing theory? For example, in the study of moral development, the highest level has often been portrayed as based on a principle of "justice for the individual" (Kohlberg, 1976). However, more recent theorizing notes individuality and autonomy tend to be male concerns, and suggest that a principle based on relationships and connections with others be added to our thinking about high-level moral development (Gilligan, 1982, 1998).

- How has research that has exaggerated gender differences between females and males influenced the way the people think about females? For example, some researchers believe that gender differences in mathematics have often been exaggerated and have been fueled by societal bias (Hyde & Mezulis, 2001; Hyde & Plant, 1995). Such exaggeration of differences can lead to negative expectations for females' math performance.

Cultural and Ethnic Bias   The realization that research on life-span development needs to include more people from diverse ethnic groups has also been building (Graham, 1992). Historically, people from ethnic minority groups (African American, Latino, Asian American, and Native American) have been discounted from most research in the United States and simply thought of as variations from the norm or average. Because their scores don't always fit the norm, minority individuals have been viewed as confounds or "noise" in data. Consequently, researchers have deliberately excluded them from the samples they have selected. Given the fact that individuals from diverse ethnic groups were excluded from research on life-span development for so long, we might reasonably conclude that people's real lives are perhaps more varied than research data have indicated in the past (Ponterotto & others, 2001; Stevenson, 1995).

Researchers also have tended to overgeneralize about ethnic groups (Jenkins & others, 2003; Trimble, 1989). **Ethnic gloss** is using an ethnic label such as African American or Latino in a superficial way that portrays an ethnic group as being more homogeneous than it really is. For example, a researcher might describe a research sample like this: "The participants were 20 Latinos and 20 Anglo-Americans." A more complete description of the Latino group might be something like this: "The 20 Latino participants were Mexican Americans from low-income neighborhoods in the southwestern area of Los Angeles. Twelve were from homes in which Spanish is the dominant language spoken, 8 from homes in which English is the main language spoken. Ten were born in the United States, 10 in Mexico. Ten described themselves as Mexican American, 5 as Mexican, 3 as American, 2 as Chicano, and 1 as Latino." Ethnic gloss can cause researchers to obtain samples of ethnic groups that are not representative of the group's diversity, which can lead to overgeneralization and stereotyping.

Pam Reid is a leading researcher who studies gender and ethnic bias in development. To read about Pam's interests, see the Careers in Life-Span Development insert on page 70.

Review and Reflect

3 **Discuss research challenges in life-span development**

REVIEW

- What are researchers' ethical responsibilities to the people they study?
- How can gender, cultural, and ethnic bias affect the outcome of a research study?

REFLECT

- Imagine that you are conducting a research study on the sexual attitudes and behaviors of adolescents? What ethical safeguards should you use in conducting the study?

ethnic gloss Using an ethnic label such as African American or Latino in a superficial way that portrays an ethnic group as being more homogeneous than it really is.

Reach Your Learning Goals

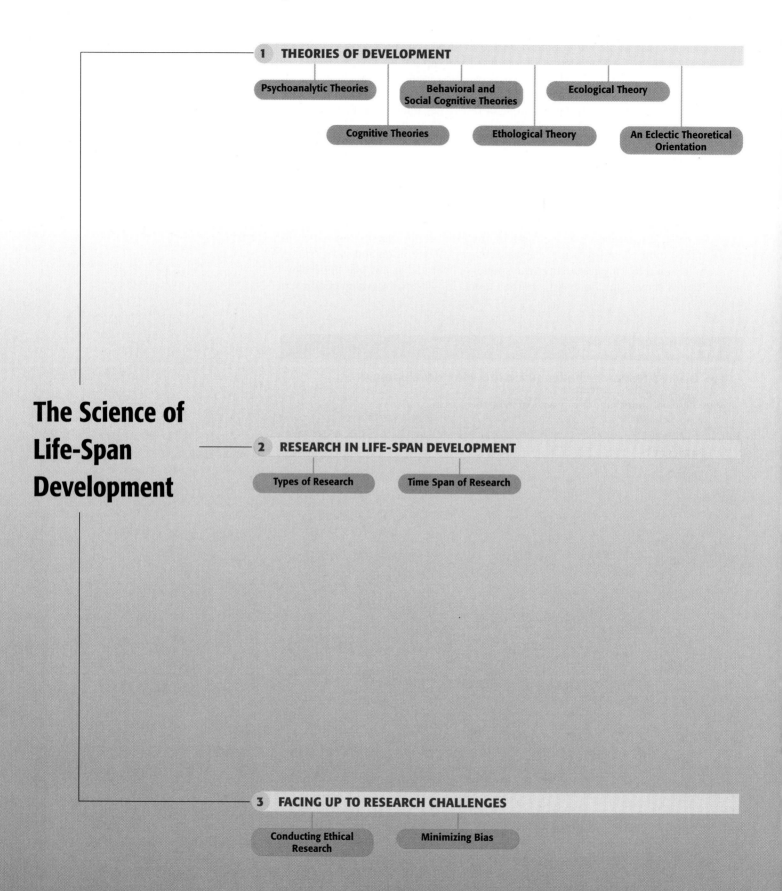

The Science of Life-Span Development

1 THEORIES OF DEVELOPMENT

- Psychoanalytic Theories
- Cognitive Theories
- Behavioral and Social Cognitive Theories
- Ethological Theory
- Ecological Theory
- An Eclectic Theoretical Orientation

2 RESEARCH IN LIFE-SPAN DEVELOPMENT

- Types of Research
- Time Span of Research

3 FACING UP TO RESEARCH CHALLENGES

- Conducting Ethical Research
- Minimizing Bias

Summary

1 Describe theories of life-span development

- The scientific method involves four main steps: (1) conceptualize a problem, (2) collect data, (3) analyze data, and (4) draw conclusions. Theory is often involved in conceptualizing a problem. A theory is an interrelated, coherent set of ideas that helps to explain and to make predictions. Hypotheses are specific assumptions and predictions, often derived from theory, that can be tested to determine their accuracy.
- Psychoanalytic theory describes development as primarily unconscious and as heavily colored by emotion. Psychoanalytic theorists believe that behavior is merely a surface characteristic and that early experiences with parents shape development. Freud said that personality is made up of three structures—id, ego, and superego. The conflicting demands of these structures produce anxiety. Freud also believed that individuals go through five psychosexual stages—oral, anal, phallic, latency, and genital. Erikson's theory emphasizes these eight psychosocial stages of development: trust vs. mistrust, autonomy vs. shame and doubt, initiative vs. guilt, industry vs. inferiority, identity vs. identity confusion, intimacy vs. isolation, generativity vs. stagnation, and integrity vs. despair. Contributions of psychoanaytic theories include an emphasis on a developmental framework. One criticism is that they often lack scientific support.
- Cognitive theories emphasize conscious thoughts. Piaget proposed a cognitive developmental theory in which children use the processes of organization and adaptation (assimilation and accommodation) to understand their world. In Piaget's theory, children go through four cognitive stages: sensorimotor, preoperational, concrete operational, and formal operational. Vygotsky's sociocultural cognitive theory emphasizes how culture and social interaction guide cognitive development. The information-processing theory emphasizes that individuals manipulate information, monitor it, and strategize about it. Contributions of cognitive theories include an emphasis on the active construction of understanding. One criticism is that they give too little attention to individual variations.
- Three versions of the behavioral approach are Pavlov's classical conditioning, Skinner's operant conditioning, and Bandura's social cognitive theory. In Pavlov's classical conditioning, a neutral stimulus acquires the ability to produce a response originally produced by another stimulus. In Skinner's operant conditioning, the consequences of a behavior produce changes in the probability of the behavior's occurrence. In Bandura's social cognitive theory, observational learning is a key aspect of life-span development. Bandura emphasizes reciprocal interactions among the person (cognition), behavior, and environment. Contributions of the behavioral and social cognitive theories include an emphasis on scientific research. One criticism is that they give inadequate attention to developmental changes.

- Ethology stresses that behavior is strongly influenced by biology, is tied to evolution, and is characterized by critical or sensitive periods. Contributions of ethological theory include a focus on the biological and evolutionary basis of development. Criticisms include a belief that the critical and sensitive period concepts might be too rigid.
- Ecological theory is Bronfenbrenner's environmental systems view of development. It consists of five environmental systems: microsystem, mesosystem, exosystem, macrosystem, and chronosystem. Contributions of the theory include a systematic examination of macro and micro dimensions of environmental systems. One criticism is that it gives inadequate attention to biological and cognitive factors.
- An eclectic theoretical orientation does not follow any one theoretical approach, but rather selects from each theory whatever is considered the best in it.

2 Explain how research on life-span development is conducted

- Three main types of research are (1) descriptive, (2) correlational, and (3) experimental. Five types of descriptive research are observation (in a laboratory or a naturalistic setting), survey (questionnaire) or interview, standardized test, case study, and life-history record. In correlational research, the goal is to describe the strength of the relationship between two or more events or characteristics. Experimental research involves conducting an experiment, which can determine cause and effect. An independent variable is the manipulated, influential, experimental factor. A dependent variable is a factor that can change in an experiment, in response to changes in the independent variable. Experiments can involve one or more experimental groups and control groups. In random assignment, researchers assign participants to experimental and control groups by chance.
- When researchers decide about the time span of their research, they can conduct cross-sectional, longitudinal, or sequential studies. Life-span researchers are especially concerned about cohort effects.

3 Discuss research challenges in life-span development

- Researchers' ethical responsibilities include seeking participants' informed consent, ensuring their confidentiality, debriefing them about the purpose and potential personal consequences of participating, and avoiding unnecessary deception of participants.
- Researchers need to guard against gender, cultural, and ethnic bias in research. Every effort should be made to make research equitable for both females and males. More individuals from ethnic minority backgrounds need to be included as participants in life-span research. A special concern is ethnic gloss.

Key Terms

theory 43
hypotheses 43
psychoanalytic theory 44
Erikson's theory 45
Piaget's theory 47
assimilation 48
accommodation 48
Vygotsky's theory 50

information-processing
  theory 50
social cognitive theory 52
ethology 53
ecological theory 55
eclectic theoretical
  orientation 56
descriptive research 59

laboratory 59
naturalistic observation 59
standardized test 60
case study 61
life-history records 61
correlational research 61
experiment 62
cross-sectional approach 63

longitudinal approach 64
sequential approach 64
cohort effects 65
ethnic gloss 71

Key People

Sigmund Freud 44
Erik Erikson 45
Jean Piaget 47

Karen Horney 48
Lev Vygotsky 50
Robert Siegler 50

Ivan Pavlov 51
B. F. Skinner 52
Albert Bandura 52

Walter Mischel 52
Konrad Lorenz 53
Urie Bronfenbrenner 54

Taking It to the Net

1. Like many students of life-span psychology, Ymelda has a hard time with Freud's theory, insisting that it is "all about sex." Is that the extent of Freud's theoretical perspective?

2. Juan's life-span psychology teacher asked the class to read about Albert Bandura's famous "Bobo" doll experiment and determine if there were any gender differences in the responses of boys and girls who (a) saw aggressive behavior rewarded and (b) who saw aggressive behavior punished. What should Juan's conclusions be?

3. A requirement for Wanda's methods course is to design and carry out an original research project. Among the many decisions she must make is what type of data she will collect. She decides to research adapting to college life. Her instructor asks if she will use an interview or a survey. What are the distinctions between surveys and interviews, and what are the benefits and difficulties of each?

Connect to www.mhhe.com/santrockld9 to research the answers and complete these exercises.

E-Learning Tools

To help you master the material in this chapter, you'll find a number of valuable study tools on the Student CD-ROM that accompanies this book. In addition, visit the Online Learning Center for *Life-Span Development*, ninth edition, where you'll find these valuable resources for chapter 2, "The Science of Life-Span Development."

- Complete the self-assessment, *Models and Mentors in My Life*, to help you evaluate the role models and mentors who have played an important part in your life and think about the type of role model you want to be.

- View video clips of key developmental psychology experts discussing their views on research methods, developmental theories, and ethics in research.

- Build your decision-making skills by trying your hand at the parenting and education "Scenarios."

Beginnings

What endless questions vex the thought, of whence and whither, when and how.
—SIR RICHARD BURTON
English Explorer, 19th Century

The rhythm and meaning of life involve beginnings. Questions are raised about how, from so simple a beginning, endless forms develop and grow and mature. What was this organism, what will this organism be? Section 2 contains two chapters: "Biological Beginnings" (chapter 3) and "Prenatal Development and Birth" (chapter 4). In these chapters we address questions about our beginnings.

C H A P T E R

3

There are one hundred and ninety-three living species of monkeys and apes. One hundred and ninety-two of them are covered with hair. The exception is the naked ape, self-named Homo sapiens.

—DESMOND MORRIS
British Zoologist, 20th Century

Biological Beginnings

Chapter Outline

THE EVOLUTIONARY PERSPECTIVE

Natural Selection and Adaptive Behavior

Evolutionary Psychology

GENETIC FOUNDATIONS

What Are Genes?

Mitosis and Meiosis

Genetic Principles

Behavior Genetics

Molecular Genetics

Chromosome and Gene-Linked Abnormalities

REPRODUCTION CHALLENGES AND CHOICES

Prenatal Diagnostic Tests

Infertility

Adoption

HEREDITY-ENVIRONMENT INTERACTION

Intelligence

Heredity-Environment Correlations

Shared and Nonshared Environmental Experiences

Conclusions About Heredity-Environment Interaction

Learning Goals

1 *D*iscuss the evolutionary perspective

2 *D*escribe the genetic foundations of development

3 *I*dentify important reproduction challenges and choices

4 *E*xplain heredity-environment interaction

Images of Life-Span Development
The Jim and Jim Twins

Jim Springer and Jim Lewis are identical twins. They were separated at 4 weeks of age and did not see each other again until they were 39 years old. Both worked as part-time deputy sheriffs, vacationed in Florida, drove Chevrolets, had dogs named Toy, and married and divorced women named Betty. One twin named his son James Allan, and the other named his son James Alan. Both liked math but not spelling, enjoyed carpentry and mechanical drawing, chewed their fingernails down to the nubs, had almost identical drinking and smoking habits, had hemorrhoids, put on 10 pounds at about the same point in development, first suffered headaches at the age of 18, and had similar sleep patterns.

Jim Lewis (*left*) and Jim Springer (*right*).

But Jim and Jim have some differences. One wears his hair over his forehead, the other slicks it back and has sideburns. One expresses himself best orally; the other is more proficient in writing. But, for the most part, their profiles are remarkably similar.

Another pair, Daphne and Barbara, are called the "giggle sisters" because, after being reunited, they were always making each other laugh. A thorough search of their adoptive families' histories revealed no gigglers. And the identical sisters handled stress by ignoring it, avoided conflict and controversy whenever possible, and showed no interest in politics.

Two other identical twin sisters were separated at 6 weeks and reunited in their fifties. Both had nightmares, which they describe in hauntingly similar ways: both dreamed of doorknobs and fishhooks in their mouths as they smothered to death! The nightmares began during early adolescence and stopped within the past 10 to 12 years. Both women were bed wetters until about 12 or 13 years of age, and their educational and marital histories are remarkably similar.

These sets of twins are part of the Minnesota Study of Twins Reared Apart, directed by Thomas Bouchard and his colleagues. The study brings identical twins (identical genetically because they come from the same fertilized egg) and fraternal twins (dissimilar genetically because they come from different fertilized eggs) from all over the world to Minneapolis to investigate their lives. There the twins complete a number of personality tests and provide detailed medical histories, including information about diet and smoking, exercise habits, chest X-rays, heart stress tests, and EEGs (brain-wave tests). The twins are interviewed and asked more than 15,000 questions about their family and childhood environment, personal interests, vocational orientation, values, and aesthetic judgments. They also are given ability and intelligence tests (Bouchard & others, 1990).

Critics of the Minnesota identical twins study point out that some of the separated twins were together for several months prior to their adoption, that some of the twins had been reunited prior to their testing (in some cases, a number of years earlier), that adoption agencies often place twins in similar homes, and that even strangers who spend several hours together and start comparing their lives are likely to come up with some coincidental similarities (Adler, 1991). Still, the Minnesota study of identical twins indicates the increased interest scientists have recently shown in the genetic basis of human development and points to the need for further research on genetic and environmental factors (Bouchard, 1995).

The examples of Jim and Jim, the giggle sisters, and the identical twins who had the same nightmares stimulate us to think about our genetic heritage and the biological foundations of our existence. Organisms are not like billiard balls, moved by simple, external forces to predictable positions on life's pool table. Environmental experiences and biological foundations work together to make us who we are. Our coverage of life's biological beginnings in this chapter focuses on evolution, genetic foundations, reproduction challenges and choices, and the interaction of heredity and environment.

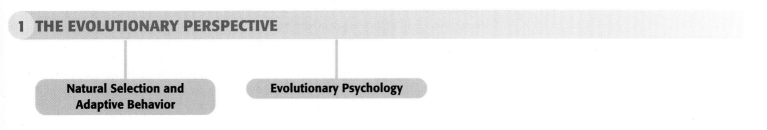

1 THE EVOLUTIONARY PERSPECTIVE

Natural Selection and Adaptive Behavior

Evolutionary Psychology

In evolutionary time, humans are relative newcomers to Earth, yet we have established ourselves as the most successful and dominant species. If we consider evolutionary time as a calendar year, humans arrived here in the last moments of December (Sagan, 1977). As our earliest ancestors left the forest to feed on the savannahs, and finally to form hunting societies on the open plains, their minds and behaviors changed. How did this evolution come about?

Natural Selection and Adaptive Behavior

Natural selection is the evolutionary process that favors individuals of a species that are best adapted to survive and reproduce. To understand natural selection, let's return to the middle of the nineteenth century, when the British naturalist Charles Darwin was traveling around the world, observing many different species of animals in their natural surroundings. Darwin, who published his observations and thoughts in *On the Origin of Species* (1859), noted that most organisms reproduce at rates that would cause enormous increases in the population of most species and yet populations remain nearly constant. He reasoned that an intense, constant struggle for food, water, and resources must occur among the many young born each generation, because many of the young do not survive. Those that do survive pass on their genes to the next generation. Darwin believed that those who do survive to reproduce are probably superior in a number of ways to those who do not. In other words, the survivors are better adapted to their world than are the nonsurvivors (Raven & others, 2002). Over the course of many generations, organisms with the characteristics needed for survival would comprise a larger percentage of the population. Over many, many generations, this could produce a gradual modification of the whole population. If environmental conditions change, however, other characteristics might become favored by natural selection, moving the process in a different direction.

To understand the role of evolution in behavior, we need to understand the concept of adaptive behavior. In evolutionary conceptions of psychology, *adaptive behavior* is behavior that promotes an organism's survival in the natural habitat. Adaptive behavior involves the organism's modification of its behavior to include its likelihood of survival (Cosmides & others, 2003). All organisms must adapt to particular places, climates, food sources, and ways of life. Natural selection designs an adaptation to perform a certain function. An example of adaptation is an eagle's claws, designed by natural selection to facilitate predation. In the human realm, attachment is a system designed by natural selection to ensure an infant's closeness to the caregiver for feeding and protection from danger.

Evolutionary Psychology

Although Darwin introduced the theory of evolution by natural selection in 1859, his ideas about evolution only recently have emerged as a popular framework for explaining behavior. Psychology's newest approach, **evolutionary psychology,**

Evolution
Evolution and Behavior
Evolutionary Psychology
Handbook of Evolutionary Psychology
Evolutionary Psychology Resources

evolutionary psychology A contemporary approach that emphasizes the importance of adaptation, reproduction, and "survival of the fittest" in explaining behavior.

emphasizes the importance of adaptation, reproduction, and "survival of the fittest" in explaining behavior. Evolution favors organisms that are best adapted to survive and reproduce in a particular environment. The evolutionary psychology approach focuses on conditions that allow individuals to survive or to fail. In this view, the evolutionary process of natural selection favors behaviors that increase organisms' reproductive success and their ability to pass their genes to the next generation (Bjorklund & Bering, 2001; Caporael, 2001; Cosmides & others, 2003; Durrant & Ellis, 2003).

David Buss' (1995, 1999, 2000; Larsen & Buss, 2002) ideas on evolutionary psychology have ushered in a whole new wave of interest in how evolution can explain human behavior. He believes that just as evolution shapes our physical features, such as body shape and height, it also pervasively influences how we make decisions, how aggressive we are, our fears, and our mating patterns.

Evolution and Life-Span Development According to life-span developmentalist Paul Baltes (1996; Baltes, Staudinger, & Lindenberger, 1999), the benefits of evolutionary selection decrease with age. Why do the later years of life benefit less from the optimizing power of evolutionary selection pressure than the younger years? The main reason is reproductive fitness, which primarily extends from conception through the earlier part of adulthood. As a consequence, says Baltes, selection operates mainly during the first half of life. Also, given the much shorter life span in early human evolution, selection pressure could not function as often in the later years of life. Most individuals died before possible negative genetic attributes were activated or their negative consequences appeared.

A concrete example of a decrease in the benefits of evolutionary selection in older adults involves Alzheimer's disease, a progressive, irreversible brain disorder characterized by gradual deterioration. This disease typically does not appear until age 70 or older. Possibly diseases like Alzheimer's emerge in later life because evolutionary pressures based on reproductive fitness were not able to select against it.

While Baltes believes that the benefits of evolutionary selection decrease following the decline in reproductive capacity, he argues that the need for culture increases (see figure 3.1). Some of the cultural factors needed by older adults are cognitive skills, motivation, socialization, literacy, and medical technology. In other words, as older adults weaken biologically, they need culture-based resources (material, social, economic, psychological). For example, for cognitive skills to continue into old age at levels of performance comparable to those experienced earlier in adulthood, cognitive support and training are needed (Hoyer, Rybash, & Roodin, 2003). And as we indicated in chapter 1, Baltes also stresses that there is a life-span shift in the allocation of resources away from growth and toward maintenance and the regulation of loss.

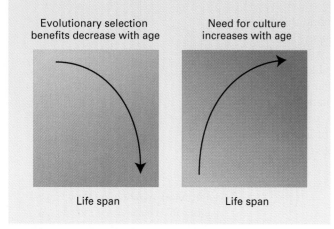

FIGURE 3.1 Baltes' View of Evolution and Culture Across the Life Span

Evaluating Evolutionary Psychology Albert Bandura (1998), whose social cognitive theory was described in chapter 2, addressed the "biologizing" of psychology and evolution's role in social cognitive theory ◀▥ p. 52. Bandura acknowledges the important influence of evolution on human adaptation and change. However, he rejects what he calls "one-sided evolutionism," which sees social behavior as the product of evolved biology, in favor of a bidirectional view. According to this view, evolutionary pressures created changes in biological structures for the use of tools, which enabled organisms to manipulate, alter, and construct new environmental conditions. Environmental innovations of increasing complexity produced, in turn, new selection pressures for the evolution of specialized biological systems for consciousness, thought, and language.

Human evolution gave us bodily structures and biological potentialities—in other words, not behavioral dictates. Having evolved, advanced biological capacities can be used to produce diverse cultures: aggressive, pacific, egalitarian, or autocratic. As American scientist

Steven Jay Gould (1981) concluded, in most domains of human functioning, biology allows a broad range of cultural possibilities. The Russian American Theodore Dobzhansky (1977) also reminds us that the human species has been selected for the ability to learn and for plasticity—for the capacity to adapt to diverse contexts, not for biologically fixed behavior. Bandura (1998) points out that the pace of social change shows that biology does permit a range of possibilities.

Review and Reflect

1 **Discuss the evolutionary perspective**

REVIEW

- How can natural selection and the concept of adaptive behavior be defined?
- What is evolutionary psychology and how has it been criticized?

REFLECT

- Are you more inclined to support the views of evolutionary psychologists or their critics? Why?

2 GENETIC FOUNDATIONS

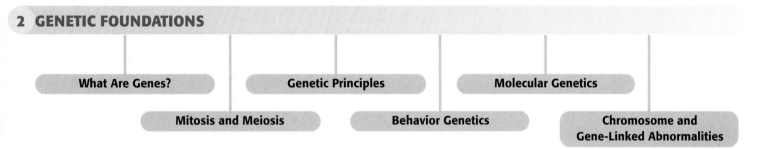

What Are Genes?   Genetic Principles   Molecular Genetics

Mitosis and Meiosis   Behavior Genetics   Chromosome and Gene-Linked Abnormalities

Every species must have a mechanism for transmitting characteristics from one generation to the next. This mechanism is explained by the principles of genetics (Cummings, 2003; Livesley, Jang, & Vernon, 2003). Each of us carries a genetic code that we inherited from our parents. This code is located within every cell in our bodies. Our genetic codes are alike in one important way—they all contain the human genetic code. Because of the human genetic code, a fertilized human egg cannot grow into an egret, eagle, or elephant.

What Are Genes?

Each of us began life as a single cell weighing about one twenty-millionth of an ounce! This tiny piece of matter housed our entire genetic code—information about who we would become. These instructions orchestrated growth from that single cell to a person made of trillions of cells, each containing a perfect replica of the original genetic code (Wilson, 2003).

The nucleus of each human cell contains 46 **chromosomes,** which are threadlike structures that come in 23 pairs, one member of each pair coming from each parent. Chromosomes are made up of deoxyribonucleic acid, or **DNA,** a complex molecule that contains genetic information. DNA's "double helix" shape looks like a spiral staircase. **Genes,** the units of hereditary information, are short segments of DNA. Genes carry information that enables cells to reproduce and manufacture the proteins needed to sustain life. Chromosomes, DNA, and genes can be mysterious. To gain a better understanding of this mystery, see figure 3.2 on page 84.

chromosomes Threadlike structures that come in 23 pairs, one member of each pair coming from each parent. Chromosomes are made up of the genetic substance DNA.

DNA A complex molecule that contains genetic information.

genes Units of hereditary information composed of DNA. Genes carry information that enables cells to reproduce themselves and manufacture the proteins that maintain life.

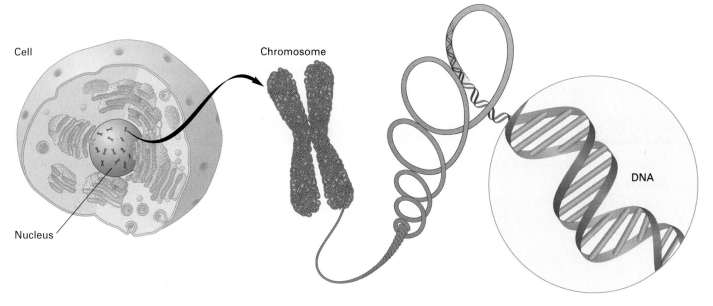

Cell

Nucleus

Chromosome

DNA

FIGURE 3.2 Cells, Chromosomes, Genes, and DNA

(*Left*) The body contains trillions of cells, which are the basic structural units of life. Each cell contains a central structure, the nucleus. (*Middle*) Chromosomes and genes are located in the nucleus of the cell. Chromosomes are made up of threadlike structures composed of DNA molecules. (*Right*) A gene, a segment of DNA that contains the hereditary code. The structure of DNA is a spiraled double chain.

Mitosis and Meiosis

Mitosis and meiosis are processes of cellular reproduction by which DNA is distributed to new cells. **Mitosis** is the process of cell division by which each chromosome in the cell's nucleus duplicates itself. The resulting 46 chromosomes move to the opposite sides of the cell, then the cell separates, and two new cells are formed with each now containing 46 chromosomes. Thus the process of mitosis allows DNA to duplicate itself.

A specialized division of chromosomes occurs during the formation of reproductive cells. **Meiosis** is the process by which cells in the reproductive organs divide into gametes (sperm in males, eggs in females), which have half the genetic material of the parent cell. Mitosis and meiosis differ in these ways:

- In mitosis, the focus is on cell growth and repair, whereas meiosis involves sexual reproduction.
- In mitosis, the number of chromosomes present in the new cells remains the same as in the original cell (the chromosomes copy themselves), whereas in meiosis, the number of chromosomes is cut in half.
- In mitosis, two daughter cells are formed from the dividing cell; in meiosis four daughter cells are produced as a result of two meiotic divisions.

Each human gamete has 23 unpaired chromosomes. The process of human **reproduction** begins when a female gamete, or ovum (egg), is fertilized by a male gamete, or sperm (see figure 3.3). A **zygote** is the single cell formed through fertilization. In the zygote, two sets of unpaired chromosomes combine to form one set of paired chromosomes—one member of each pair from the mother and the other member from the father. In this manner, each parent contributes 50 percent of the offspring's genes.

Genetic Principles

Genetic determination is a complex affair, and much is still unknown about the way genes work (Lewis, 2003). The known genetic principles include dominant-recessive

mitosis The process of cell division by which each chromosome in a cell's nucleus duplicates itself.

meiosis The process by which cells in the reproductive organs divide into gametes (sperm in males, eggs in females), which have half of the genetic material of the parent cell.

reproduction The process that, in humans, begins when a female gamete (ovum) is fertilized by a male gamete (sperm).

zygote A single cell formed through fertilization.

genes, sex-linked genes, genetic imprinting, polygenic inheritance, reaction range, and canalization.

Dominant-Recessive Genes Principle   According to the *dominant-recessive genes principle,* some genes are dominant and will always override so-called recessive genes. In other words, if one gene of a pair is dominant and one is recessive, the dominant gene will be expressed in the characteristic it governs. A recessive gene exerts its influence only if the two genes of a pair are both recessive. If you inherit a recessive gene for a trait from each of your parents, you will show the trait. If you inherit a recessive gene from only one parent, you may never know you carry the gene.

Brown hair and dimples rule over blond hair and freckles in the world of dominant-recessive genes. Can two brown-haired parents have a blond-haired child? Yes, they can. Suppose that in each parent the gene pair that governs hair color includes a dominant gene for brown hair and a recessive gene for blond hair. Since dominant genes override recessive genes, the parents have brown hair, but both are carriers of blondness and can pass on their recessive genes for blond hair. With no dominant gene to override them, if a child receives a gene for blond hair from each parent, the pair of recessive genes will make the child's hair blond. Figure 3.4 illustrates the dominant-recessive genes principle.

Sex-Linked Genes   For thousands of years, people wondered what determined whether we become male or female. Aristotle believed that the father's arousal during intercourse determines the offspring's sex. The more excited the father was, the more likely it would be a son, he reasoned. Of course, he was wrong, but it was not until the 1920s that researchers confirmed the existence of human sex chromosomes, 2 of the 46 chromosomes human beings normally carry. Ordinarily females have two X chromosomes, so-named for their shape, and males have one X and a smaller Y chromosome. Figure 3.5 on page 86, shows the chromosome makeup of a male and a female.

A number of disorders have been traced to the sex chromosomes. *X-linked inheritance* is the term used to describe the inheritance of a defective or mutated gene that is carried on the X chromosome (Trappe & others, 2001). Because males have only one X chromosome, when there is a mutant gene on the X chromosome, males have no "backup" copy and therefore may carry an X-linked disease. Females will be less likely to have an X-linked problem because their second X chromosome is not likely to carry

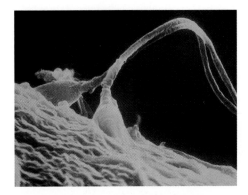

FIGURE 3.3   Union of Sperm and Egg

mhhe●com/
santrockld9

**Landmarks in the History
of Genetics
Heredity Resources
Genetics Journals and News**

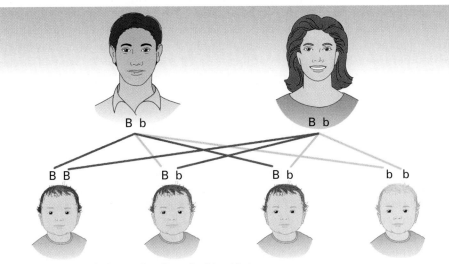

B = Gene for brown hair   b = Gene for blond hair

FIGURE 3.4   How Brown-Haired Parents Can Have a Blond-Haired Child

Although both parents have brown hair, each parent can have a recessive gene for blond hair. In this example, both parents have brown hair, but each parent carries the recessive gene for blond hair. Therefore, the odds of their child having blond hair are one in four—the probability the child will receive a recessive gene (*b*) from each parent.

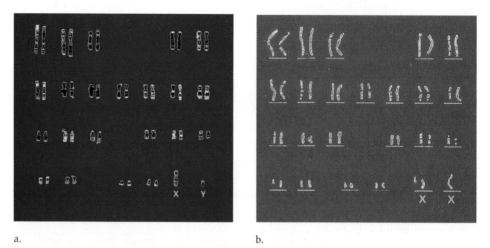

a.   b.

FIGURE 3.5 The Genetic Difference Between Males and Females

Set (*a*) shows the chromosome structure of a male, and set (*b*) shows the chromosome structure of a female. The last pair of 23 pairs of chromosomes is in the bottom right box of each set. Notice that the Y chromosome of the male is smaller than the X chromosome of the female. To obtain this kind of chromosomal picture, a cell is removed from a person's body, usually from the inside of the mouth. The chromosomes are stained by chemical treatment, magnified, and then photographed.

the altered gene. Thus, most individuals who have X-linked diseases are males. Females who have one changed copy of the X gene are known as "carriers," and they usually do not show any signs of the X-linked disease. Hemophilia and fragile X syndrome, which we will discuss later in the chapter, are examples of X-linked inheritance (Gonzales-del Angel & others, 2000).

Genetic Imprinting   *Genetic imprinting* is a mechanism in which genes have been modified in one of the parents and have differing effects depending on whether they are transmitted to the offspring through the egg or sperm (Jirtle, Sander, & Barret, 2000). An imprinted gene dominates one that has not been imprinted. Genetic imprinting may explain why individuals who inherit Huntington disease from their father show symptoms of the disease at an earlier age than when they inherit from their mother (Navarrette, Martinez, & Salamanca, 1994). Also, when individuals inherit Turner syndrome (which is characterized by underdeveloped sex organs) from their father, they tend to show better cognitive and social skills than when they inherit the disorder from their mother (Martinez-Pasarell & others, 1999). We will discuss Huntington disease and Turner syndrome later in the chapter.

Polygenic Inheritance   Genetic transmission is usually more complex than the simple examples we have examined thus far (Lewis, 2003). *Polygenic inheritance* is the genetic principle by which many genes can interact to produce a particular characteristic. Few psychological characteristics are associated with single pairs of genes. Most are related to the interaction of many different genes. There are about 30,000 to 35,000 genes in the human genome, so you can imagine that possible combinations of these are staggering in number. Traits affected by this mixing of genes are said to be polygenically determined.

No one possesses all the characteristics that our genetic structure makes possible. A **genotype** is the person's genetic heritage, the actual genetic material. However, not all of this genetic material is apparent in our observed and measurable characteristics. A **phenotype** is the way an individual's genotype is expressed in observable and measurable characteristics. Phenotypes include physical traits (such as height, weight, eye color, and skin pigmentation) and psychological characteristics (such as intelligence, creativity, personality, and social tendencies).

genotype A person's genetic heritage; the actual genetic material.

phenotype The way an individual's genotype is expressed in observed and measurable characteristics.

Calvin and Hobbes — by Bill Watterson

For each genotype, a range of phenotypes can be expressed. Imagine that we could identify all of the genes that would make a person introverted or extraverted. Would measured introversion-extraversion be predictable from knowledge of the specific genes? The answer is no, because, even if our genetic model were adequate, introversion-extraversion is a characteristic shaped by experience throughout life. For example, parents may push an introverted child into social situations and encourage the child to become more gregarious.

To understand how introverted a child is, think about a series of genetic codes that predispose the child to develop in a particular way, and imagine environments that are responsive or unresponsive to this development. For instance, the genotype of some persons may predispose them to be introverted in an environment that promotes a turning inward of personality, yet, in an environment that encourages social interaction and outgoingness, these individuals may become more extraverted. However, it would be unlikely for the individual with this introverted genotype to become a strong extravert.

Reaction Range The **reaction range** is the range of possible phenotypes for each genotype. The actual phenotype depends on an environment's restrictiveness or richness. Sandra Scarr (1984) explains reaction range this way: Each of us has a range of potential. For example, an individual with "medium-tall" genes for height who grows up in a poor environment may be shorter than average; however, in an excellent nutritional environment, the individual may grow up to be taller than average. No matter how well fed a person is, though, someone with "short" genes will never be taller than average. Scarr believes that characteristics such as intelligence and introversion work the same way. That is, there is a range within which the environment can modify intelligence, but intelligence is not completely malleable. Reaction range gives us an estimate of how modifiable intelligence is.

Canalization Although some traits have a wide reaction range, others are somewhat immune to extensive changes in the environment. These characteristics seem to stay on a particular developmental course, regardless of the environmental assaults on them (Waddington, 1957). **Canalization** is the term used to describe the narrow path, or developmental course, that certain characteristics take. Apparently, preservative forces help to protect, or buffer, a person from environmental extremes. For example, research by Jerome Kagan (1984) indicates that Guatemalan infants who had experienced extreme malnutrition as infants showed normal social and cognitive development later in childhood.

Although the genetic influence of canalization keeps organisms on a particular developmental path, genes alone do not directly determine human behavior. Developmentalist Gilbert Gottlieb (2000, 2002) points out that genes are an integral part of the organism but that their activity (genetic expression) can be affected by the organism's environment. For example, hormones that circulate in the blood make their way into

reaction range The range of possible phenotypes for each genotype, suggesting the importance of an environment's restrictiveness or richness.

canalization The process by which characteristics take a narrow path, or developmental course. Apparently, preservative forces help to protect a person from environmental extremes.

the cell, where they influence the cell's activity by turning genes "on" and "off." The flow of hormones themselves can be affected by environmental events, such as light, day length, nutrition, and behavior.

Behavior Genetics

Behavior genetics is the study of the degree and nature of behavior's hereditary basis. Behavior geneticists assume that behaviors are jointly determined by the interaction of heredity and environment (Maxson, 2003; Rowe, 2001; Wahlsten, 2000).

At the beginning of the chapter, we described the Minnesota Study of Twins Reared Apart. In their research on the link between heredity and behavior, behavior geneticists often conduct either twin studies or adoption studies. In the most common type of **twin study,** the behavioral similarity of identical twins is compared with the behavioral similarity of fraternal twins. *Identical twins* (called monozygotic twins) develop from a single fertilized egg that splits into two genetically identical replicas, each of which becomes a person. *Fraternal twins* (called dizygotic twins) develop from separate eggs and separate sperm, making them genetically no more similar than ordinary siblings. Although fraternal twins share the same womb, they are no more alike genetically than are non-twin brothers and sisters, and they may be of different sexes. By comparing groups of identical and fraternal twins, behavior geneticists capitalize on the basic knowledge that identical twins are more similar genetically than are fraternal twins (Jacob & others, 2001). In one twin study, 7,000 pairs of Finnish identical and fraternal twins were compared on the personality traits of extraversion and neuroticism (psychological instability) (Rose & others, 1998). On both of these personality traits, the identical twins were much more similar than the fraternal twins were, suggesting that heredity plays a role in both traits. However, several issues crop up as a result of twin studies. Adults might stress the similarities of identical twins more than those of fraternal twins, and identical twins might perceive themselves as a "set" and play together more than fraternal twins do. If so, observed similarities in identical twins could be environmentally influenced.

In an **adoption study,** investigators seek to discover whether, in behavior and psychological characteristics, adopted children are more like their adoptive parents, who have provided a home environment, or more like their biological parents, who have contributed their heredity. Another type of adoption study compares adoptive and biological siblings. In one investigation, the educational levels attained by the biological parents were better predictors of the adopted children's IQ scores than were the IQs of the children's adoptive parents (Scarr & Weinberg, 1983). Because of the genetic relation between the adopted children and their biological parents, the implication is that heredity influences children's IQ scores. However, keep in mind that adoption studies are correlational, so we cannot conclude that heredity alone causes variations in the behavior of adopted and biological children.

Molecular Genetics

In contrast to behavior geneticists who study the effects of heredity on behavior at a global level, molecular genetics is studied at microscopic level (Klug & Cummings, 2003). Today, there is a great deal of enthusiasm about the use of molecular genetics to discover the specific locations on genes that are linked to an individual's susceptibility to many diseases and other aspects of health and well-being (Lewis, 2003).

The Human Genome Project The Human Genome Project, begun in the 1970s, has made stunning progress in mapping all of the estimated 30,000 to 35,000 genes in the human genome (U.S. Department of Energy, 2001). The Human Genome Project has already linked specific DNA mutations with the increased risk of a number of

mhhe●com/
santrockld9

Behavior Genetics

Twin Research

Human Genome Project

behavior genetics The study of the degree and nature of behavior's basis in heredity.

twin study A study in which the behavioral similarity of identical twins is compared with the behavioral similarity of fraternal twins.

adoption study A study in which investigators seek to discover whether, in behavior and psychological characteristics, adopted children are more like their adoptive parents, who provided a home environment, or more like their biological parents, who contributed their heredity. Another form of the adoption study is to compare adoptive and biological siblings.

diseases and conditions, including Huntington disease (in which the central nervous system deteriorates), some forms of cancer, asthma, diabetes, hypertension, and Alzheimer's disease (Davies, 2001; Goodstadt & Ponting, 2001).

Every individual carries a number of DNA mutations that might lead to serious physical disease or mental disorder. Identifying the mutations could enable doctors to predict an individual's disease risks, recommend healthy lifestyle regimens, and prescribe the safest and most effective drugs. A decade or two from now, parents of a newborn baby may be able to leave the hospital with a full genomic analysis that would tell them which diseases the infant is at risk for.

However, mining DNA mutations to discover health risks might increasingly threaten an individual's ability to land and hold jobs, obtain insurance, and keep their genetic profile private. For example, should an airline pilot or neurosurgeon who one day will develop a hereditary disorder that makes their hands shake be required to leave that job early? To think further about such issues, see figure 3.6.

The Collaborative Gene   The hope of many biologists was that the Human Genome Project would demonstrate virtually a one-to-one connection between genes and behavior. I remember a conversation I had in the late 1990s with a biologist who had mapped the identity of several genes as part of the Human Genome Project. He strongly believed that the behavior of his two adolescents was solely due to the genes they inherited and was completely unrelated to the myriad of experiences they had while they were growing up.

One of the big surprises in the Human Genome Project was the recent finding that humans have only about 30,000 to 35,000 genes (U.S. Department of Energy, 2001). Previously, biologists were sure that humans had 50,000 to 100,000 or more genes. They also believed that there was a one-to-one correspondence between the number of genes and the number of proteins produced in the human body; that is, each gene was responsible for the synthesis of only one protein. However, it is now accepted that humans have far more proteins (300,000 to 500,000) than they have genes and, thus, there cannot be a one-to-one correspondence between them (Commoner, 2002; Moore, 2001).

	Yes	No	Undecided
1. Would you want you or your loved one to be tested for a gene that increases your risk for a disease, but does not determine whether you will actually develop the disease?	☐	☐	☐
2. Would you want you and your mate to be tested before having offspring to determine your risk for having a child who is likely to contract various diseases?	☐	☐	☐
3. Should testing of unborn children be restricted to traits that are commonly considered to have negative outcomes, such as disease?	☐	☐	☐
4. Should altering a newly conceived person's genes to improve qualities such as intelligence, appearance, and strength be allowed?	☐	☐	☐
5. Should employers be permitted access to your genetic information?	☐	☐	☐
6. Should life insurance companies have access to your genetic information?	☐	☐	☐

FIGURE 3.6 Exploring Your Genetic Future

These athletes, many of whom have Down syndrome, are participating in a Special Olympics competition. Notice the distinctive facial features of the individuals with Down syndrome, such as a round face and a flattened skull. *What causes Down syndrome?*

Developmental psychologist David Moore (2001) titled his recent book *The Dependent Gene* to underscore the concept that DNA does not determine traits in an independent manner. Rather, genes and the environment together influence our characteristics. DNA contains the genetic instructions needed for growth and development. However, DNA information can be modified within the cell as small pieces of DNA are mixed, matched, and linked with RNA (ribonucleic acid) in a process called *RNA editing.* RNA transmits the information for further processing in protein synthesis.

DNA clearly exerts an important influence on inheritance, but it acts only in collaboration with many protein-based processes that prevent and repair incorrect sequences, transform proteins into an active form, and provide genetic information beyond that originating in the gene itself (Commoner, 2002; Gottlieb, 1998). Numerous studies have shown that external sensory and internal neural events can excite or inhibit gene expression (Gottlieb, Wahlsten, & Lickliter, 1998; Mauro & others, 1994; Rusak & others, 1990). In sum, according to an increasing number of developmental psychologists who study molecular genetics, no single gene is solely responsible for a given protein and therefore for the inherited trait (Gottlieb, 2001; Moore, 2001). Rather than being an independent gene, DNA is a collaborative gene.

Most molecular biologists operate under the assumption that DNA is the secret of life. However, environmental scientist Barry Commoner (2002) argues that DNA likely did not create life but instead life created DNA. He concluded that when life was first formed on Earth, proteins must have appeared before DNA because, unlike DNA, proteins have the ability to generate the chemical energy necessary to assemble small molecules into larger ones like DNA. According to Commoner, DNA is a mechanism created by the cell to store information produced in the cell. Once produced by the primitive cell, DNA could become a stable place to store information about the cell's chemistry. Thus, in Commoner's view, the fundamental unit of life is not DNA but rather the cell of which DNA is a component.

Chromosome and Gene-Linked Abnormalities

Earlier in this chapter, we saw that abnormal genes are linked with a number of disorders. Here we will examine some of the abnormalities that can occur in chromosomes and genes.

Chromosome Abnormalities   When gametes are formed, the 46 chromosomes do not always divide evenly. In this case, the resulting sperm or ovum does not have the normal 23 chromosomes. The most notable outcomes of this error are Down syndrome and abnormalities of the sex chromosomes (see figure 3.7).

Down Syndrome   **Down syndrome** is a chromosomally transmitted form of mental retardation that is caused by the presence of an extra (47th) chromosome. An individual with Down syndrome has a round face, a flattened skull, an extra fold of skin over the eyelids, a protruding tongue, short limbs, and retardation of motor and mental abilities. It is not known why the extra chromosome is present, but the health of the male sperm or female ovum may be involved (Davison, Gardiner, & Costa, 2001; MacLean, 2000). Women between the ages of 18 and 38 are less likely to give birth to a child with Down syndrome than are younger or older women. Down syndrome appears approximately once in every 700 live births but rarely in African American children.

mhhe ●com/
santrockld9

Genetic Disorders
Prenatal Testing and Down Syndrome

Down syndrome A form of mental retardation, caused by the presence of an extra (47th) chromosome.

Name	Description	Treatment	Incidence
Down syndrome	An extra chromosome causes mild to severe retardation and physical abnormalities.	Surgery, early intervention, infant stimulation, and special learning programs	1 in 1,900 births at age 20 1 in 300 births at age 35 1 in 30 births at age 45
Klinefelter syndrome	An extra X chromosome causes physical abnormalities.	Hormone therapy can be effective	1 in 800 males
Fragile X syndrome	An abnormality in the X chromosome can cause mental retardation, learning disabilities, or short attention span.	Special education, speech and language therapy	More common in males than in females
Turner syndrome	A missing X chromosome in females can cause mental retardation and sexual underdevelopment.	Hormone therapy in childhood and puberty	1 in 2,500 female births
XYY syndrome	An extra Y chromosome can cause above-average height.	No special treatment required	1 in 1,000 male births

FIGURE 3.7 Some Chromosome Abnormalities

Note: Treatment does not necessarily erase the problem but may improve the individual's adaptive behavior and quality of life.

Some individuals have developed special programs to help children with Down syndrome. One such program was developed by Janet Marchese, an adoptive mother of a Down syndrome baby. She began putting the parents of children with Down syndrome together with couples who wanted to adopt the children. Her adoption network has placed more than 1,500 Down syndrome children and has a waiting list of couples who want to adopt.

Abnormalities of the Sex Chromosomes   Each newborn has at least one X chromosome. However, approximately 1 in every 500 infants either is missing a second X chromosome, or has an X chromosome that is combined with two more sex chromosomes. Four such sex-linked chromosomal disorders are Klinefelter syndrome, fragile X syndrome, Turner syndrome, and XYY syndrome (Baum, 2000).

Klinefelter syndrome is a disorder in which males have an extra X chromosome, making them XXY instead of XY (Lowe & others, 2001). Males with this disorder have undeveloped testes, and they usually have enlarged breasts and become tall. Klinefelter syndrome occurs approximately once in every 800 live male births.

Fragile X syndrome is a disorder that results from an abnormality in the X chromosome, which becomes constricted and tends to break. Mental deficiency often accompanies fragile X syndrome, but its form varies considerably (mental retardation, learning disability, short attention span) (Lewis, 2003). This disorder occurs more frequently in males than in females, possibly because the second X chromosome in females overrides the disorder's negative effects.

Turner syndrome is a disorder in females in which either an X chromosome is missing, making the person XO instead of XX, or the second X chromosome is partially deleted (Bramswig, 2001). These females are short in stature and have a webbed neck. They might be infertile and have difficulty in mathematics, but their verbal ability is often facilitated. Turner syndrome occurs in approximately 1 of every 2,500 live female births.

The **XYY syndrome** is a disorder in which the male has an extra Y chromosome. Early interest in this syndrome focused on the belief that the extra Y chromosome found in some males contributed to their aggression and violence. It was then reasoned that if a male had an extra Y chromosome he would likely be extremely aggressive and possibly develop a violent personality. However, researchers

Klinefelter syndrome A disorder in which males have an extra X chromosome, making them XXY instead of XY.

fragile X syndrome A disorder involving an abnormality in the X chromosome, which becomes constricted and, often, breaks.

Turner syndrome A disorder in females in which either an X chromosome is missing, making the person XO instead of XX, or the second X chromosome is partially deleted.

XYY syndrome A disorder in which males have an extra Y chromosome.

Careers in Life-Span Development

Holly Ishmael, Genetic Counselor

Holly Ishmael is a genetic counselor at Children's Mercy Hospital in Kansas City. She obtained an undergraduate degree in psychology from Sarah Lawrence College and then a master's degree in genetic counseling from the same college. She uses many of the principles discussed in this chapter in her genetic counseling work.

Genetic counselors have specialized graduate degrees in the areas of medical genetics and counseling ◀▥▥ p. 36. They enter graduate school in these areas with undergraduate backgrounds from a variety of disciplines, including biology, genetics, psychology, public health, and social work. Genetic counselors, like Ishmael, work as members of a health-care team, providing information and support to families with birth defects or genetic disorders. They identify families at risk by analyzing inheritance patterns and explore options with the family. Genetic counselors may serve as educators and resource people for other health-care professionals and the public. Some genetic counselors also work in administrative positions or conduct research. Some genetic counselors, like Ishmael, become specialists in prenatal and pediatric genetics; others might specialize in cancer genetics or psychiatric genetic disorders.

Holly says, "Genetic counseling is a perfect combination for people who want to do something science-oriented, but

need human contact and don't want to spend all of their time in a lab or have their nose in a book."

There are approximately thirty graduate genetic counseling programs in the United States. If you are interested in this profession, you can obtain further information from the National Society of Genetic Counselors at this website: http://www.nsgc.org.

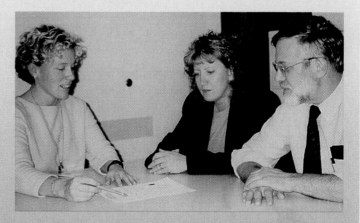

Holly Ishmael (*left*) in a genetic counseling session.

---

subsequently found that XYY males are no more likely to commit crimes than are XY males (Witkin & others, 1976).

Gene-Linked Abnormalities Not only can abnormalities be produced by an uneven number of chromosomes, but they also can result from harmful genes (Croyle, 2000). More than 7,000 such genetic disorders have been identified, although most of them are rare.

Phenylketonuria (PKU) is a genetic disorder in which the individual cannot properly metabolize a substance needed for production of proteins in the body. Phenylketonuria is now easily detected, but, if it is left untreated, mental retardation and hyperactivity result. The disorder is treated by diet to prevent an excess accumulation of the substance, phenylalanine. Phenylketonuria involves a recessive gene and occurs about once in every 10,000 to 20,000 live births. Phenylketonuria accounts for about 1 percent of institutionalized mentally retarded individuals, and it occurs primarily in Whites.

The story of phenylketonuria has important implications for the nature-nurture issue. Although phenylketonuria is a genetic disorder (nature), how or whether a gene's influence in phenylketonuria is played out can depend on environmental influences since the disorder can be treated (nurture). That is, restricting the individual's diet (environment) prevents mental retardation. Thus, phenylketonuria is an excellent example of the interaction of heredity and environment (Luciana, Sullivan, & Nelson, 2001; Merrick, Aspler, & Schwartz, 2001).

Sickle-cell anemia, which occurs most often in African Americans, is a genetic disorder that deforms the body's red blood cells. A red blood cell is usually shaped like

phenylketonuria (PKU) A genetic disorder in which an individual cannot properly metabolize a substance needed for production of proteins in the body. PKU is now easily detected but, if left untreated, results in mental retardation and hyperactivity.

sickle-cell anemia A genetic disorder that affects the red blood cells and occurs most often in people of African descent.

a disk, but in sickle-cell anemia, a change in a recessive gene modifies its shape to a hook-shaped "sickle." These cells die quickly, causing anemia, crippling pain in bones and joints, and early death of the individual because they cannot carry oxygen to other cells in the body. About 1 in 400 African American babies is born with sickle-cell anemia. One in 10 African Americans is a carrier, as is 1 in 20 Latin Americans. Treatment of individuals with sickle-cell anemia starts with early diagnosis, preferably in the newborn period and includes penicillin. Treatment of complications often includes antibiotics, pain management, and blood transfusions.

Other genetic abnormalities include cystic fibrosis, diabetes, hemophilia, spina bifida, and Tay-Sachs disease. Figure 3.8 provides information about these conditions.

Some genetic disorders, such as Huntington disease and Tay-Sachs disease, are hereditary. Others, such as spina bifida, can be diagnosed before birth. Genetic counselors, usually physicians or biologists who are well-versed in the field of medical genetics, are familiar with the kinds of problems just described, the odds of encountering them, and helpful strategies for offsetting some of their effects. To read about the career and work of a genetic counselor, see the Careers in Life-Span Development insert on page 92.

During a physical examination for a college football tryout, Jerry Hubbard, 32, learned that he carried the gene for sickle-cell anemia. Daughter Sara is healthy but daughter Avery (in the flowered dress) has sickle-cell anemia. *If you were a genetic counselor, would you recommend that this family have more children? Explain.*

Name	Description	Treatment	Incidence
Cystic fibrosis	Glandular dysfunction that interferes with mucus production; breathing and digestion are hampered, resulting in a shortened life span.	Physical and oxygen therapy, synthetic enzymes, and antibiotics; most individuals live to middle age.	1 in 2,000 births
Diabetes	Body does not produce enough insulin, which causes abnormal metabolism of sugar.	Early onset can be fatal unless treated with insulin.	1 in 2,500 births
Hemophilia	Delayed blood clotting causes internal and external bleeding.	Blood transfusions/injections can reduce or prevent damage due to internal bleeding.	1 in 10,000 males
Huntington disease	Central nervous system deteriorates, producing problems in muscle coordination and mental deterioration.	Doesn't usually appear until age 35 or older; death likely 10 to 20 years after symptoms appear.	1 in 20,000 births
Phenylketonuria (PKU)	Metabolic disorder that, left untreated, causes mental retardation.	Special diet can result in average intelligence and normal life span.	1 in 14,000 births
Sickle-cell anemia	Blood disorder that limits the body's oxygen supply; it can cause joint swelling, as well as heart and kidney failure.	Penicillin, medication for pain, antibiotics, and blood transfusions groups.	1 in 400 African American children (lower among other
Spina bifida	Neural tube disorder that causes brain and spine abnormalities.	Corrective surgery at birth, orthopedic devices, and physical/medical therapy.	2 in 1,000 births
Tay-Sachs disease	Deceleration of mental and physical development caused by an accumulation of lipids in the nervous system.	Medication and special diet are used, but death is likely by 5 years of age.	One in 30 American Jews is a carrier.

FIGURE 3.8 Some Gene-Linked Abnormalities

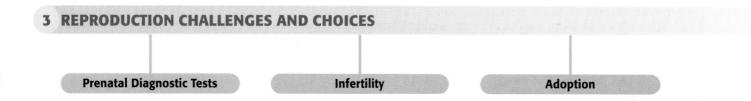

Review and Reflect

2 **Describe the genetic foundations of development**

REVIEW

- What are genes?
- What are mitosis and meiosis?
- What are some important genetic principles?
- What is behavior genetics?
- What is molecular genetics? What is the nature of the collaborative gene?
- What are some key chromosome- and gene-linked abnormalities?

REFLECT

- What are some possible ethical issues regarding genetics and development that might arise in the future?

3 REPRODUCTION CHALLENGES AND CHOICES

| Prenatal Diagnostic Tests | Infertility | Adoption |

Earlier in this chapter we discussed several principles of genetics, including the role of meiosis in reproduction. Having also examined a number of genetic abnormalities that can occur, we now have some background to consider some of the challenges and choices facing prospective parents.

Prenatal Diagnostic Tests

mhhe ● com/
santrockld9

Amniocentesis
Obstetric Ultrasound
Chorionic Villi Sampling
Genetic Counseling

Scientists have developed a number of tests to determine whether a fetus is developing normally, among them amniocentesis, ultrasound sonography, chorionic villi sampling, and the maternal blood test.

Amniocentesis is a prenatal medical procedure in which a sample of amniotic fluid is withdrawn by syringe and tested for any chromosome or metabolic disorders (Tercyak & others, 2001). The amnionic fluid is in the amnion, a thin, membraneous sac in which the embryo is suspended. Amniocentesis is performed between the 12th and 16th weeks of pregnancy. The later amniocentesis is performed, the better its diagnostic potential. The earlier it is performed, the more useful it is in deciding whether to terminate a pregnancy. There is a small risk of miscarriage when amniocentesis is performed; about 1 woman in every 200 to 300 miscarries after amniocentesis.

Ultrasound sonography is a prenatal medical procedure in which high-frequency sound waves are directed into the pregnant woman's abdomen. The echo from the sounds is transformed into a visual representation of the fetus' inner structures. This technique can detect such disorders as microencephaly, a form of mental retardation involving an abnormally small brain. Ultrasound sonography is often used in conjunction with amniocentesis to determine the precise location of the fetus in the

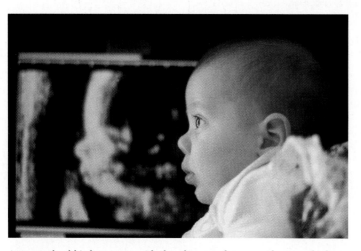

A 6-month-old infant poses with the ultrasound sonography record taken four months into the baby's prenatal development. *What is ultrasound sonography?*

mother's abdomen. When ultrasound sonography is used five or more times, the risk of low birth weight may be increased.

As scientists have searched for more accurate, safer assessments of high-risk prenatal conditions, they have developed a new test. *Chorionic villi sampling* is a prenatal medical procedure in which a small sample of the placenta (the vascular organ that links the fetus to the mother's uterus) is removed at some point between the 8th and 11th weeks of pregnancy (Zoppi & others, 2001). Diagnosis takes approximately 10 days. Chorionic villi sampling allows a decision about abortion to be made near the end of the first 12 weeks of pregnancy, a point when abortion is safer and less traumatic than after amniocentesis. Chorionic villi sampling has a slightly higher risk of miscarriage than amniocentesis and is linked with a slight risk of limb deformities. Both techniques provide valuable information about the presence of birth defects, but they also raise issues pertaining to whether an abortion should be obtained if birth defects are present.

The *maternal blood test (alpha-fetoprotein—AFP)* is a prenatal diagnostic technique that is used to assess blood alphaprotein level, which is associated with neural-tube defects. This test is administered to women 14 to 20 weeks into pregnancy only when they are at risk for bearing a child with defects in the formation of the brain and spinal cord.

Infertility

Approximately 10 to 15 percent of couples in the United States experience *infertility,* which is defined as the inability to conceive a child after 12 months of regular intercourse without contraception. The cause of infertility can rest with the woman or the man (Paseh, 2001). The woman may not be ovulating (releasing eggs to be fertilized), she may be producing abnormal ova, her fallopian tubes by which ova normally reach the womb may be blocked, or she may have a disease that prevents implantation of the ova. The man may produce too few sperm, the sperm may lack motility (the ability to move adequately), or he may have a blocked passageway (Oehnigner, 2001). In one study, long-term use of cocaine by men was related to low sperm count, low motility, and a higher number of abnormally formed sperm (Bracken & others, 1990). Cocaine-related infertility appears to be reversible if users stop taking the drug for at least one year.

In some cases, surgery may correct the cause of infertility. In others, hormone-based drugs may improve the probability of having a child. However, in some instances, fertility drugs have caused superovulation, producing three or more babies at a time. A summary of some of infertility's possible causes and solutions is presented in figure 3.9 on page 96.

In the United States, more than 2 million couples seek help for infertility every year. Of those, about 40,000 try high-tech assisted reproduction. The five most common techniques are these:

- *In vitro fertilization (IVF)*. An egg and a sperm are combined in a laboratory dish. If the egg is fertilized, the resulting embryo is transferred into the woman's uterus or womb. The success rate is just under 20 percent.
- *Gamete intrafallopian transfer (GIFT)*. A doctor inserts eggs and sperm directly into a woman's fallopian tube. The success rate is almost 30 percent.
- *Intrauterine insemination (IUI)*. Frozen sperm—that of the husband or an unknown donor—is placed directly into the uterus. The success rate is 10 percent.

The McCaughey septuplets, born in 1997. *Why has there been such a dramatic increase in multiple births?*

Men

Problem	Possible causes	Treatment
Low sperm count	Hormone imbalance, varicose vein in scrotum, possibly environmental pollutants Drugs (cocaine, marijuana, lead, arsenic, some steroids and antibiotics) Y chromosome gene deletions	Hormone therapy, surgery, avoiding excessive heat
Immobile sperm	Abnormal sperm shape Infection Malfunctioning prostate	None Antibiotics Hormones
Antibodies against sperm	Problem in immune system	Drugs

Women

Problem	Possible causes	Treatment
Ovulation problems	Pituitary or ovarian tumor Underactive thyroid	Surgery Drugs
Antisperm secretions	Unknown	Acid or alkaline douche, estrogen therapy
Blocked fallopian tubes	Infection caused by IUD or abortion or by sexually transmitted disease	Eggs surgically removed from ovary and placed in uterus
Endometriosis (tissue buildup in uterus)	Delayed parenthood until the thirties	Hormones, surgical removal of uterine tissue buildup

FIGURE 3.9 Fertility Problems, Possible Causes, and Treatments

- *Zygote intrafallopian transfer (ZIFT).* This is a two-step procedure. First, eggs are fertilized in the laboratory. Then, any resulting zygotes are transferred to a fallopian tube. The success rate is approximately 25 percent.
- *Intracytoplasmic sperm injection (ICSI).* A doctor uses a microscopic pipette to inject a single sperm from a man's ejaculate into an egg in a laboratory dish. The zygote is returned to the uterus. The success rate is approximately 25 percent.

The creation of families by means of the new reproductive technologies raises important questions about the psychological consequences for children. Studies support the idea that "test-tube" babies function well and typically do not differ from naturally conceived children in various behaviors and psychological characteristics (Golombok, MacCallum, & Goodman, 2001; Hahan & Dipietro, 2001) (see figure 3.10).

One consequence of fertility treatments is an increase in multiple births. Twenty-five to 30 percent of pregnancies achieved by fertility treatments—including in vitro fertilization—now result in multiple births. Though parents may be thrilled at the prospect of having children, they also face serious risks. Any multiple birth increases the likelihood that the babies will have life-threatening and costly problems, such as extremely low birthweight.

Adoption

Although surgery and fertility drugs can sometimes solve an infertility problem, another choice is to adopt a child (Moody, 2001). Adoption is the social and legal process by which a parent-child relationship is established between persons unrelated at birth. Researchers have found that adopted children and adolescents often show more psychological and school-related problems than nonadopted children (Brodzinsky & others, 1984; Brodzinsky, Lang, & Smith, 1995). Adopted adolescents are referred to psychological treatment two to five times as often as their nonadopted peers (Grotevant & McRoy, 1990).

In one study of 4,682 adopted adolescents and the same number of nonadopted adolescents, adoptees showed lower levels of adjustment (Sharma, McGue, & Benson, 1996). In another study, adopted adolescents had more school adjustment problems, were more likely to use illicit drugs, and were more likely to engage in delinquent behavior (Sharma, McGue, & Benson, 1998). However, adopted siblings were less withdrawn and engaged in more prosocial behavior (such as being altruistic, caring, and supportive of others) than nonadopted siblings. In one study of 1,587 adopted and 87,165 nonadopted adolescents, the adopted adolescents were at higher risk for all of the domains sampled, including school achievement and problems, substance abuse, psychological well-being, and physical health (Miller & others, 2000). In this study, the effects of adoption were more negative when the adopted parents had low levels of education. Also, in this study, when a subsample consisting of the most negative problem profiles was examined, the differences between adopted and nonadopted even widened with the adopted adolescents far more likely to have the most problems.

In one of these studies, the later adoption occurred, the more problems the adoptees had. Infant adoptees had the fewest adjustment difficulties; those adopted after they were 10 years of age had the most problems (Sharma, McGue, & Benson, 1996). Other research has documented that early adoption often has better outcomes for the child than later adoption. At age 6, children adopted from an orphanage in the first 6 months of their lives showed no lasting negative effects of their early experience. However, children from the orphanage who were adopted after they were 6 months of age had abnormally high levels of cortisol, a stress-regulating hormone, indicating that their stress regulation had not developed adequately (Chisholm, 1998).

These results have policy implications, especially for the thousands of children who are relegated to the foster care system after infancy. Most often, older children are put up for adoption due to parental abuse or neglect. The process of terminating the birth parents' parental rights can be lengthy. In the absence of other relatives, children are turned over to the foster care system, where they must wait for months or even years to be adopted.

A question that virtually every adoptive parent wants answered is, "Should I tell my adopted child that he or she is adopted? If so, when?" Most psychologists believe that adopted children should be told that they are adopted, because they will eventually find out anyway. Many children begin to ask where they came from when they are approximately 4 to 6 years of age. This is a natural time to begin to respond in simple ways to children about their adopted status. Clinical psychologists report that one problem that sometimes surfaces is the desire of adoptive parents to make life too perfect for the adoptive child and to present a perfect image of themselves to the child. The result too often is that adopted children feel that they cannot release any angry feelings and openly discuss problems (Warshak, 2001).

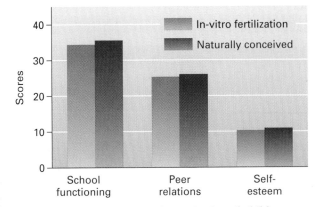

FIGURE 3.10 Socioemotional Functioning of Children Conceived Through In-Vitro Fertilization or Naturally Conceived

In one study, comparisons of the socioemotional functioning of young adolescents who had either been conceived through in-vitro fertilization (IVF) or naturally conceived revealed no differences between the two groups (Golombok & others, 2001). Although the means for the naturally conceived group were slightly higher, this is likely due to chance. The mean scores shown for the different measures are in the normal range of functioning.

Review and Reflect

3 **Identify important reproduction challenges and choices**

REVIEW

- What are some common prenatal diagnostic tests?
- What are some causes of infertility?
- How does adoption affect children's development?

REFLECT

- We discussed a number of studies indicating that adoption is linked with negative outcomes for children. Does that mean that all adopted children have more negative outcomes than all nonadopted children? Explain.

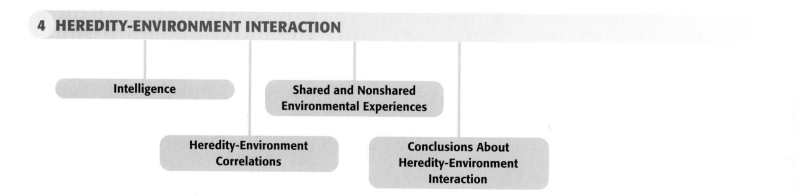

4 HEREDITY-ENVIRONMENT INTERACTION

In our discussion of adoption, we indicated that children who are adopted later in their development often have more problems than those who are adopted very early in their lives. This finding suggests that the environment plays an important role in children's development. Indeed, heredity and environment interact to produce development (McGuire, 2001). To explore this interaction, we will focus on one important area of development—intelligence—and then explore other aspects of heredity-environment interaction.

Intelligence

One of the hottest areas in the study of intelligence centers on the extent to which intelligence is influenced by genetics and the extent to which it is influenced by environment. Although it is difficult to tease apart these influences, that has not kept psychologists from trying to unravel them.

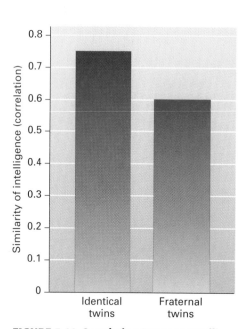

FIGURE 3.11 Correlation Between Intelligence Test Scores and Twin Status

The graph represents a summary of research findings that have compared the intelligence test scores of identical and fraternal twins. An approximate .15 difference has been found with a higher correlation for identical twins (.75) and a lower correlation for fraternal twins (.60).

Heredity   Arthur Jensen (1969) sparked a lively, and at times, hostile debate when he presented his thesis that intelligence is primarily inherited. Jensen believes that environment and culture play only a minimal role in intelligence. Jensen reviewed the research on intelligence, much of which involved comparisons of identical and fraternal twins. Identical twins have exactly the same genetic makeup. If intelligence is genetically determined, Jensen reasoned, identical twins' IQs should be similar. Fraternal twins and ordinary siblings are less similar genetically, so their IQs should be less similar.

The studies on intelligence in identical twins that Jensen reviewed had an average correlation of .82, a very high positive association. Investigations of fraternal twins, however, produced an average correlation of .50, a moderately high positive correlation. A difference of .32 is substantial.

Many scholars have criticized Jensen's work. One criticism concerns his definition of intelligence itself. Jensen believes that IQ as measured by standardized intelligence tests is a good indicator of intelligence. Critics argue that IQ tests tap only a narrow range of intelligence. Everyday problem solving, work, and social adaptability, say the critics, are important aspects of intelligence not measured in the traditional IQ tests used in Jensen's review of studies. A second criticism is that most investigations of heredity and environment do not include environments that differ radically. Thus, it is not surprising that many heredity studies show environment to be a fairly weak influence on intelligence. Further, in a much more recent review than Jensen's, the difference in intelligence between identical and fraternal twins was only .15, substantially less than what Jensen found (Grigorenko, 2000) (See figure 3.11).

The controversy about heredity and intelligence was fueled by the publication of *The Bell Curve: Intelligence and Class Structure in American Life* (1994) by Richard Herrnstein and Charles Murray. They argued that America is rapidly evolving a huge

underclass of intellectually deprived individuals whose cognitive abilities will never match the future needs of most employers. The authors believe that members of this underclass, a large percentage of whom are African American, might be doomed by their shortcomings to welfare dependency, poverty, crime, and lives devoid of hope of ever reaching the American dream.

Herrnstein and Murray believe that IQ can be quantitatively measured and that IQ test scores vary across ethnic groups. They point out that, in the United States, Asian Americans score several points higher than Whites, while African Americans score about 15 points lower than Whites. They also argue that these IQ differences are at least partly due to heredity and that government money spent on education programs such as Project Head Start is wasted, helping only the government's bloated bureaucracy.

Why do Herrnstein and Murray call their book *The Bell Curve*? A bell curve is a normal distribution graph, which has the shape of a bell—bulging in the middle and thinning out at the edges (see figure 3.12). Normal distribution graphs are used to represent large numbers of people, who are sorted according to a shared characteristic, such as weight, exposure to asbestos, taste in clothing, or IQ.

Herrnstein and Murray often refer to bell curves to make a point: that predictions about any individual based exclusively on the person's IQ are useless. Weak correlations between intelligence and job success have predictive value only when they are applied to large groups of people. Within such large groups, say Herrnstein and Murray, the pervasive influence of IQ on human society becomes apparent.

Significant criticisms have been leveled at *The Bell Curve* (Block, 2002; Moore, 2001). Experts on intelligence generally agree that African Americans score lower than Whites on IQ tests. However, many of these experts raise serious questions about

mhhe○com/
santrockld9

Two Views of *The Bell Curve*
Sternberg's Critique of *The Bell Curve*

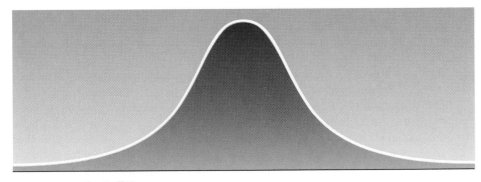

FIGURE 3.12 The Bell Curve

The term *bell curve* is used to describe a normal distribution graph, a symmetrical shape that looks like a bell—bulging in the middle and thinning out at the edges.

the accuracy of IQ tests as a measure of a person's intelligence. Critics contend that IQ tests are culturally biased against African Americans and Latinos (Ogbu, 2002). In 1971, the U.S. Supreme Court endorsed such criticisms and ruled that tests of general intelligence, in contrast to tests that solely measure fitness for a particular job, are discriminatory and cannot be administered as a condition of employment.

How strong is the correlation between parental IQ and children's IQ? The concept of heritability seeks to separate the effects of heredity and environment in a population. **Heritability** refers to the fraction of the variance in IQ in a population that is attributed to genetics. The heritability index is computed using correlational statistical techniques. Thus, the highest degree of heritabilty is 1.00 and correlations of .70 and above suggest a strong genetic influence. A committee of respected researchers convened by the American Psychological Association concluded that by late adolescence, the heritability of intelligence is about .75, which reflects a strong genetic influence (Neisser & others, 1996).

Interestingly, researchers have found that the heritability of intelligence increases from childhood to adulthood (from as low as 35 percent in childhood to as high as 75 percent in adulthood) (McGue & others, 1993). Why might hereditary influences on intelligence increase with age? Possibly as we grow older, our interactions with the environment are shaped less by the influence of others and the environment on us and more by our ability to choose our environments to allow the expression of genetic tendencies we have inherited (Neisser & others, 1996). For example, sometimes parents push children into environments that are not compatible with their genetic inheritance (wanting to be a doctor or an engineer, for example), but as adults these individuals may make their own choices about career and intellectual interests.

It is important to keep in mind that heritability refers to groups (populations), not to individuals (Okagaki, 2000). Researchers rely on the concept of heritability to describe why people differ, not to explain the effects of heredity on a single individual's intelligence.

Environment   Today, most researchers agree that heredity does not determine intelligence to the extent Jensen and Hernnstein and Murray claimed (Moore, 2001; Sternberg & Grigorenko, 2001). For most people, this means modifications in environment can change their IQ scores considerably. It also means that programs designed to enrich a person's environment can have a considerable impact, improving school achievement and fostering the acquisition of skills needed for employment. While genetic endowment may always influence a person's intellectual ability, the environmental influences and opportunities we provide children and adults do make a difference.

Researchers increasingly are interested in manipulating the early environment of children who are at risk for impoverished intelligence (Ramey, Ramey, & Lanzi, 2001). Their emphasis is on prevention rather than remediation. Many low-income parents have difficulty providing an intellectually stimulating environment for their children. Programs that educate parents to be more sensitive caregivers and train them to be better teachers, as well as support services, such as high quality child-care programs, can make a difference in a child's intellectual development. To read about one such early intervention program, see the Sociocultural Worlds of Development box.

Studies of schooling also reveal effects on intelligence (Ceci & Gilstrap, 2000; Christian, Bachnan, & Morrison, 2001). The biggest effects have been found when large groups of children have been deprived of formal education for an extended period of time, resulting in lower intelligence. In one study, the intellectual functioning of Indian children in South Africa whose schooling was delayed for four years because of the unavailability of teachers was investigated (Ramphal, 1962). Compared with children in nearby villages who had teachers, the Indian children whose entry into school was delayed by four years experienced a decrement of 5 IQ points for every year of delay.

heritability A concept that refers to the fraction of variance in IQ in a population that is attributed to genetics.

Sociocultural Worlds of Development

The Abecedarian Intervention Program

Each morning a young mother waited with her child for the bus that would take the child to school. The unusual part of this is that the child was only 2 months old and "school" was an experimental program at the University of North Carolina at Chapel Hill. There the child experienced a number of interventions designed to improve her intellectual development—everything from bright objects dangled in front of her eyes while she was a baby to language instruction and counting activities when she was a toddler (Wickelgren, 1999).

This child was part of the Abecedarian Intervention Program conducted by Craig Ramey and his associates (Ramey & Campbell, 1984; Ramey & Ramey, 1998; Ramey, Ramey, & Lanzi, 2001). They randomly assigned 111 young children from low-income, poorly educated families either to an intervention group, which experienced full-time, year-round day care along with medical and social work services, or to a control group, which got medical and social benefits but no day care. The day-care program included gamelike learning activities aimed at improving language, motor, social, and cognitive skills. The success of the program in improving IQ was evident by the time the children were 3 years old, at which time the children in the experimental group showed normal IQs averaging 101, a 17-point advantage over the control group. Recent follow-up results suggest that the effects are long-lasting. More than a decade later, at age 15, children from the intervention group still maintained an IQ advantage of 5 points over the control group children (97.7 to 92.6) (Ramey, Campbell, & Blair, 2001; Ramey & others, 2000). They also did better on standardized tests of reading and math, and they were less likely to be held back a year in school (see figure 3.13). The greatest IQ gains were in the children whose mothers had especially low IQs—below 70. At age 15, these children showed a 10-point IQ advantage over a group of children whose mothers had IQs below 70 but did not experience the day-care intervention.

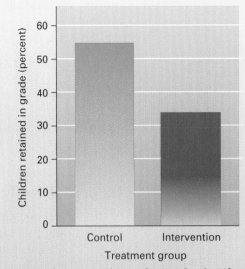

FIGURE 3.13 Early Intervention and Retention in School

When the children in the Abecedarian program were 15 years of age, those who experienced the preschool intervention were less likely to have been retained in a grade than the children in the control group.

Another possible effect of education on intelligence can be seen in rapidly rising IQ test scores around the world (Flynn, 1999). Scores on these tests have been rising so fast that a high percentage of people regarded as having average intelligence in the early 1900s would be considered below average in intelligence today (Howard, 2001) (see figure 3.14 on page 102). If a representative sample of people today took an intelligence test in 1932, about one-fourth would be defined as having very superior intelligence, a label usually accorded to fewer than 3 percent of the population. Because the change has taken place in a relatively short period of time, it can't be due to heredity, but rather may be due to increasing levels of education attained by a much greater percentage of the world's population or to other environmental factors, such as the explosion of information to which people are exposed. The worldwide increase in intelligence test scores that has occurred over a short time frame has been called the *Flynn effect*, after the researcher who discovered it—James Flynn.

Keep in mind that environmental influences are complex. Growing up with all the "advantages," for example, does not necessarily guarantee success. Children from wealthy families may have easy access to excellent schools, books, travel, and tutoring, but they may take such opportunities for granted and fail to develop the motivation to learn and to achieve. By the same token, "poor" or "disadvantaged" does not automatically equal "doomed." Many impoverished children and youth make the best of the opportunities available to them and learn to seek out advantages that can help them improve their lives.

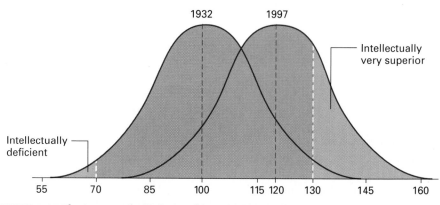

FIGURE 3.14 The Increase in IQ Scores from 1932 to 1997

As measured by the Stanford-Binet intelligence test, American children seem to be getting smarter. Scores of a group tested in 1932 fell along a bell-shaped curve with half below 100 and half above. Studies show that if children took that same test today, half would score above 120 on the 1932 scale. Very few of them would score in the "intellectually deficient" end, on the left side, and about one-fourth would rank in the "very superior" range.

Heredity-Environment Correlations

The notion of heredity-environment correlations involves the concept that individuals' genes influence the types of environments to which they are exposed. That is, individuals inherit environments that are related or linked to their genetic propensities (Plomin & others, 2001). Behavior geneticist Sandra Scarr (1993) described three ways that heredity and environment are correlated: passively, evocatively, and actively (see figure 3.15).

- **Passive genotype-environment correlations** occur because biological parents provide an environment that matches their own genetic tendencies and their children inherit genetic tendencies from their parents. For example, the parents might have a genetic predisposition to be intelligent and read skillfully. Because they read well and enjoy reading, they provide their children with books to read. The likely outcome is that their children, given their own inherited predispositions from their parents, will become skilled readers.

- **Evocative genotype-environment correlations** occur because a child's genotype elicits certain types of physical and social environments. For example, active, smiling children receive more social stimulation than passive, quiet children do. Cooperative, attentive adolescents evoke more pleasant and instructional responses from the adults around them than uncooperative, distractible adolescents do. Athletically inclined youth tend to elicit encouragement to engage in school sports. As a consequence, these adolescents tend to be the ones who try out for sport teams and go on to participate in athletically oriented environments.

- **Active (niche-picking) genotype-environment correlations** occur when children seek out environments that they find compatible and stimulating. Niche-picking refers to finding a niche or setting that is suited to one's abilities. Adolescents select from their surrounding environment some aspect that they respond to, learn about, or ignore. Their active selections of environments are related to their particular genotype. For example, attractive adolescents tend to seek out attractive peers. Adolescents who are musically inclined are likely to select musical environments in which they can successfully perform their skills.

passive genotype-environment correlations Correlations that occur because biological parents provide an environment that matches their own genetic tendencies and their children inherit genetic tendencies from their parents.

evocative genotype-environment correlations Correlations that exist when the child's genotype elicits certain types of physical and social environments.

active (niche-picking) genotype-environment correlations Correlations that exist when children seek out environments they find compatible and stimulating.

Heredity-Environment Correlation	Description	Examples
Passive	Children inherit genetic tendencies from their parents and parents also provide an environment that matches their own genetic tendencies.	Musically inclined parents usually have musically inclined children and they are likely to provide an environment rich in music for their children.
Evocative	The child's genetic tendencies elicit stimulation from the environment that supports a particular trait. Thus genes evoke environmental support.	A happy, outgoing child elicits smiles and friendly responses from others.
Active (niche-picking)	Children actively seek out "niches" in their environment that reflect their own interests and talents and are thus in accord with their genotype.	Libraries, sports fields, and a store with musical instruments are examples of environmental niches children might seek out if they have intellectual interests in books, talent in sports, or musical talents, respectively.

FIGURE 3.15 Exploring Heredity-Environment Correlations

Scarr believes that the relative importance of the three genotype-environment correlations changes as children develop from infancy through adolescence. In infancy, much of the environment that children experience is provided by adults. Thus, passive genotype-environment correlations are more common in the lives of infants and young children than they are for older children and adolescents who can extend their experiences beyond the family's influence and create their environments to a greater degree.

Shared and Nonshared Environmental Experiences

Behavior geneticists also believe that another way the environment's role in heredity-environment interaction is to consider the experiences that children have common with other children living in the same home, as well as experiences that are not shared (Feinberg & Hetherington, 2001; Plomin, Ashbury, & Dunn, 2001). **Shared environmental experiences** are children's common experiences, such as their parents' personalities or intellectual orientation, the family's socioeconomic status, and the neighborhood in which they live. Behavior geneticist Robert Plomin (1993) has found that common rearing, or shared environment, accounts for little of the variation in children's personality or interests. In other words, even though two children live under the same roof with the same parents, their personalities are often very different.

Nonshared environmental experiences are a child's unique experiences, both within the family and outside the family, that are not shared with another sibling. Thus, experiences occurring within the family can be part of the "nonshared environment." Parents often interact differently with each sibling, and siblings interact differently with parents (Hetherington, Reiss, & Plomin, 1994; Reiss & others, 2000). Siblings often have different peer groups, different friends, and different teachers at school.

Conclusions About Heredity-Environment Interaction

Both genes and environment are necessary for a person to even exist. Without genes, there is no person; without environment, there is no person (Scarr & Weinberg, 1980). Heredity and environment operate together—or cooperate—to produce a person's intelligence, temperament, height, weight, ability to pitch a baseball, ability to read, and so on (Gottlieb, 2001, 2002; Gottlieb, Wahlsten, & Lickliter, 1998) ◀▥ p. 23. If an attractive, popular, intelligent girl is elected president of her senior class in high

shared environmental experiences Children's common environmental experiences that are shared with their siblings, such as their parents' personalities and intellectual orientation, the family's social class, and the neighborhood in which they live.

nonshared environmental experiences The child's own unique experiences, both within the family and outside the family, that are not shared by another sibling. Thus, experiences occurring within the family can be part of the "nonshared environment."

*T*he interaction of heredity and environment is so extensive that to ask which is more important, nature or nurture, is like asking which is more important to a rectangle, height or width.

—WILLIAM GREENOUGH
Contemporary Developmental Psychologist, University of Illinois at Urbana

Genes and Parenting

What is the theme of Judith Harris' controversial book, The Nurture Assumption? *What is the nature of the controversy?*

school, is her success due to heredity or to environment? Of course, the answer is both. Because the environment's influence depends on genetically endowed characteristics, we say the two factors *interact* (Mader, 2002).

The relative contributions of heredity and environment are not additive. That is, we can't say that such-and-such a percentage of nature and such-and-such a percentage of experience make us who we are. That's the old view. Nor is it accurate to say that full genetic expression happens once, around conception or birth, after which we carry our genetic legacy into the world to see how far it takes us. Genes produce proteins throughout the life span, in many different environments. Or they don't produce these proteins, depending on how harsh or nourishing those environments are.

The emerging view is that many complex behaviors likely have some genetic loading that gives people a propensity for a particular developmental trajectory (Plomin & others, 2001). However, the actual development requires more: an environment. And that environment is complex, just like the mixture of genes we inherit (Sternberg & Grigorenko, 2001). Environmental influences range from the things we lump together under "nurture" (such as parenting, family dynamics, schooling, and neighborhood quality) to biological encounters (such as viruses, birth complications, and even biological events in cells) (Greenough, 1997, 1999; Greenough & others, 2001).

Imagine for a moment that there is a cluster of genes somehow associated with youth violence. (This example is hypothetical because we don't know of any such combination.) The adolescent who carries this genetic mixture might experience a world of loving parents, regular nutritious meals, lots of books, and a series of masterful teachers. Or the adolescent's world might include parental neglect, a neighborhood where gunshots and crime are everyday occurrences, and inadequate schooling. In which of these environments are the adolescent's genes likely to manufacture the biological underpinnings of criminality?

The most recent nature-nurture controversy erupted when Judith Harris (1998) published *The Nurture Assumption*. In this provocative book, she argued that what parents do does not make a difference in their children's and adolescents' behavior. Yell at them. Hug them. Read to them. Ignore them. Harris says it won't influence how they turn out. She argues that genes and peers are far more important than parents in children's and adolescents' development.

Harris is right that genes matter and she is right that peers matter, although her descriptions of peer influences do not take into account the complexity of peer contexts and developmental trajectories (Hartup, 1999). In addition to not adequately considering peer complexities, Harris is wrong that parents don't matter. For example, in the early child years parents play an important role in selecting children's peers and indirectly influencing children's development (Baumrind, 1999).

Child development expert T. Berry Brazelton (1998) commented, "*The Nurture Assumption* is so disturbing it devalues what parents are trying to do. . . . Parents might say, 'If I don't matter, why should I bother?' That's terrifying and it's coming when children and youth need a stronger home base." Even Jerome Kagan (1998), a champion of the view that biology strongly influences development, when commenting about Harris' book, concluded that whether children are cooperative or competitive, achievement-oriented or not, they are strongly influenced by their parents for better or for worse.

There is a huge parenting literature with many research studies documenting the importance of parents in children's development (Collins & others, 2000, 2001; Maccoby, 2002). We will discuss parents' important roles throughout this book.

Review and Reflect

4 **Explain heredity-environment interaction**

REVIEW

- How is intelligence influenced by heredity and how is it influenced by environment?
- What are three types of heredity-environment correlations? Give your own example of each.
- What are shared and nonshared experiences?
- What conclusions can be reached about heredity-environment interaction?

REFLECT

- Someone tells you that they have analyzed their genetic background and environmental experiences and reached the conclusion that environment definitely has had little influence on their intelligence. What would you say to this person about their ability to make this self-diagnosis?

Reach Your Learning Goals

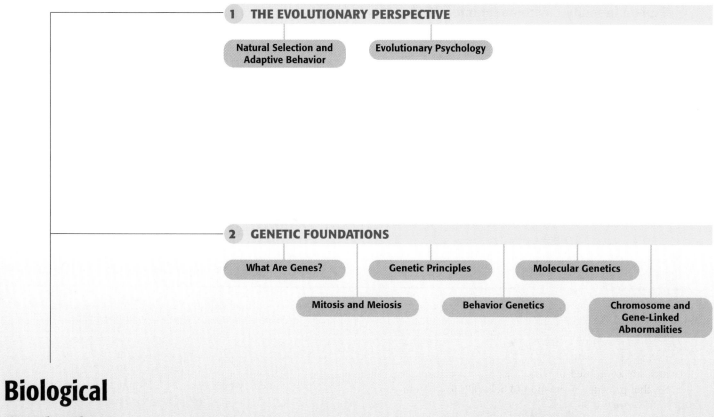

1 THE EVOLUTIONARY PERSPECTIVE

Natural Selection and Adaptive Behavior

Evolutionary Psychology

2 GENETIC FOUNDATIONS

What Are Genes?

Genetic Principles

Molecular Genetics

Mitosis and Meiosis

Behavior Genetics

Chromosome and Gene-Linked Abnormalities

Biological Beginnings

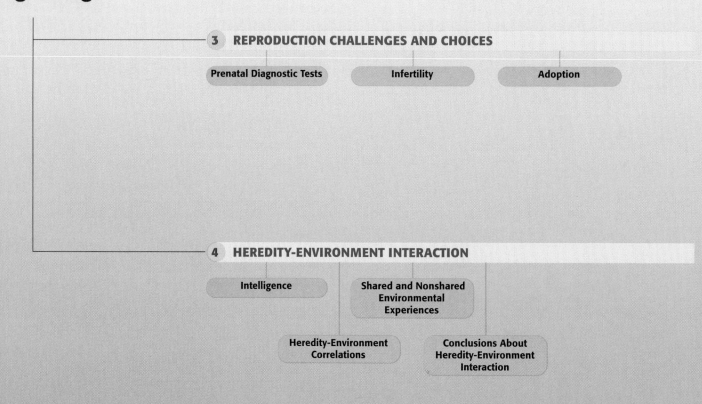

3 REPRODUCTION CHALLENGES AND CHOICES

Prenatal Diagnostic Tests

Infertility

Adoption

4 HEREDITY-ENVIRONMENT INTERACTION

Intelligence

Shared and Nonshared Environmental Experiences

Heredity-Environment Correlations

Conclusions About Heredity-Environment Interaction

Summary

1 **Discuss the evolutionary perspective**

- Natural selection is the process that favors the individuals of a species that are best adapted to survive and reproduce. The process of natural selection was originally described by Charles Darwin. In evolutionary theory, adaptive behavior is behavior that promotes the organism's survival in a natural habitat. Biological evolution shaped human beings into a culture-making species.
- Evolutionary psychology is the view that adaptation, reproduction, and "survival of the fittest" are important in explaining behavior. According to Baltes, the benefits of evolutionary selection decrease with age mainly because of a decline in reproductive fitness. While evolutionary selection benefits decrease with age, cultural needs increase. Social cognitive theorist Albert Bandura acknowledges evolution's important role in human adaptation and change but argues for a bidirectional view that enables organisms to alter and construct new environmental conditions. Biology allows for a broad range of cultural possibilities.

2 **Describe the genetic foundations of development**

- The nucleus of each human cell contains 46 chromosomes, which are composed of DNA. Genes are short segments of DNA that provide information to help cells to reproduce and manufacture proteins that sustain life.
- Mitosis is the process of cell division in which each chromosome duplicates itself so that the two daughter cells each have 46 identical chromosomes. Genes are transmitted from parents to offspring by gametes, or sex cells, which contain only half the full complement of chromosomes (23). Gametes are formed by meiosis, a process by which one parent cell splits into four daughter cells. Reproduction takes place when a female gamete (ovum) is fertilized by male gamete (sperm) to create a single-celled zygote.
- Genetic principles include those involving dominant-recessive genes, sex-linked genes, genetic imprinting, polygenic inheritance, genotype-phenotype influences, reaction range, and canalization.
- Behavior genetics is the field concerned with the degree and nature of behavior's hereditary basis. Methods used by behavior geneticists include twin studies and adoption studies.
- The field of molecular genetics seeks to discover the precise locations of genes that determine an individual's susceptibility to various diseases and other aspects of health and well-being. The Human Genome Project has made stunning progress in mapping the human genome. It is important to recognize that there is not a one-to-one correspondence between a gene, a protein, and a human trait or behavior. A gene does not act independently to produce a trait or behavior. Rather, it acts collaboratively.
- Chromosome abnormalities occur when chromosomes do not divide evenly. Down syndrome is the result of a chromosomal abnormality caused by the presence of a 47th chromosome. Abnormalities of the sex chromosomes can result in disorders such as Klinefelter syndrome, fragile X syndrome, Turner syndrome, and XYY syndrome. Gene-linked disorders caused by harmful genes include phenylketonuria (PKU) and sickle-cell anemia.

3 **Identify important reproduction challenges and choices**

- Amniocentesis, ultrasound sonography, chorionic villi sampling, and the maternal blood test are used to determine the presence of defects once pregnancy has begun.
- Approximately 10 to 15 percent of U.S. couples have infertility problems, some of which can be corrected through surgery or fertility drugs. Additional options include in-vitro fertilization and other more recently developed techniques.
- Adopted children and adolescents have more problems than their nonadopted counterparts. When adoption occurs very early in development, the outcomes for the child are improved.

4 **Explain heredity-environment interaction**

- The extent to which intelligence is due to heredity or to environment has been the subject of controversy. Jensen's and Herrnstein and Murray's views that intelligence is strongly determined by heredity have prompted critics to attempt to dismantle their arguments. Genetic similarity might explain why identical twins show stronger correlations on intelligence tests than fraternal twins do. Many studies show that intelligence has a reasonably strong heritability component, although the heritabilty concept has been criticized. Environmental influences on intelligence have been demonstrated in studies of intervention programs for children at risk for having low IQs, research on schooling, and in investigations of sociohistorical changes. Intelligence test scores have risen considerably around the world in recent decades. This so-called the Flynn effect supports the idea that environment plays an important role in intelligence.
- Scarr argues that the environments parents select for their children depend on the parents' genotypes. Passive genotype-environment, evocative genotype-environment, and active (niche-picking) genotype-environment are three correlations. Scarr believes the relative importance of these three genotype-environment correlations changes as children develop.
- Behavior geneticists study shared and nonshared environmental experiences to help determine how heredity and environment contribute to development. Shared environmental experiences refer to siblings' common experiences. Nonshared environmental influences refer to the child's unique experiences.
- Many complex behaviors have some genetic loading that gives people a propensity for a particular developmental trajectory. Actual development also requires an environment and that environment is complex. The interaction of heredity and environment is extensive.

Key Terms

evolutionary psychology 81
chromosomes 83
DNA 83
genes 83
mitosis 84
meiosis 84
reproduction 84
zygote 84
genotype 86
phenotype 86

reaction range 87
canalization 87
behavior genetics 88
twin study 88
adoption study 88
Down syndrome 90
Klinefelter syndrome 91
fragile X syndrome 91
Turner syndrome 91
XYY syndrome 91

phenylketonuria (PKU) 92
sickle-cell anemia 92
heritability 100
passive genotype-environment
   correlations 102
evocative genotype-
   environment
   correlations 102

active (niche-picking)
   genotype-environment
   correlations 102
shared environmental
   experiences 103
nonshared environmental
   experiences 103

Key People

Thomas Bouchard 80
Charles Darwin 81
David Buss 82
Albert Bandura 82

Steven Jay Gould 83
Theodore Dobzhansky 83
Gilbert Gottlieb 87
David Moore 90

Barry Commoner 90
Arthur Jensen 98
Richard Herrnstein and
   Charles Murray 98

Craig Ramey 100
Sandra Scarr 102
Robert Plomin 103
Judith Harris 104

Taking It to the Net

1. Ahmahl, a biochemistry major, is writing a psychology paper on the potential dilemmas that society and scientists may face as a result of the decoding of the human genome. What are some of the main issues or concerns that Ahmahl should address in his class paper?

2. Brandon and Katie are thrilled to learn that they are expecting their first child. They are curious about the genetic make-up of their unborn child and want to know (a) what disorders might be identified through prenatal genetic testing, and

(b) which tests, if any, Katie should undergo to help determine this information?

3. Greg and Courtney have three boys. They would love to have a girl. Courtney read that there is a clinic in Virginia where you can pick the sex of your child. How successful are such efforts? Would you want to have this choice available to you?

Connect to www.mhhe.com/santrockld9 to research the answers and complete these exercises.

E-Learning Tools

To help you master the material in this chapter, you'll find a number of valuable study tools on the Student CD-ROM that accompanies this book. In addition, visit the Online Learning Center for *Life-Span Development,* ninth edition, where you'll find these valuable resources for chapter 3, "Biological Beginnings."

- Learn more about how genetic screening is done by reviewing the sample assessment, Prenatal Genetic Screening

Questionnaire. Then try your hand at developing a family health tree by completing the self-assessment, *My Family Health Tree.*

- View video clips of key researchers, including David Buss as he discusses the importance of evolutionary psychology.

- Build your decision-making skills by trying your hand at the parenting and education "Scenarios."

CHAPTER 4

*There was a star danced,
and under that I was born.*

—WILLIAM SHAKESPEARE
English Playwright, 17th Century

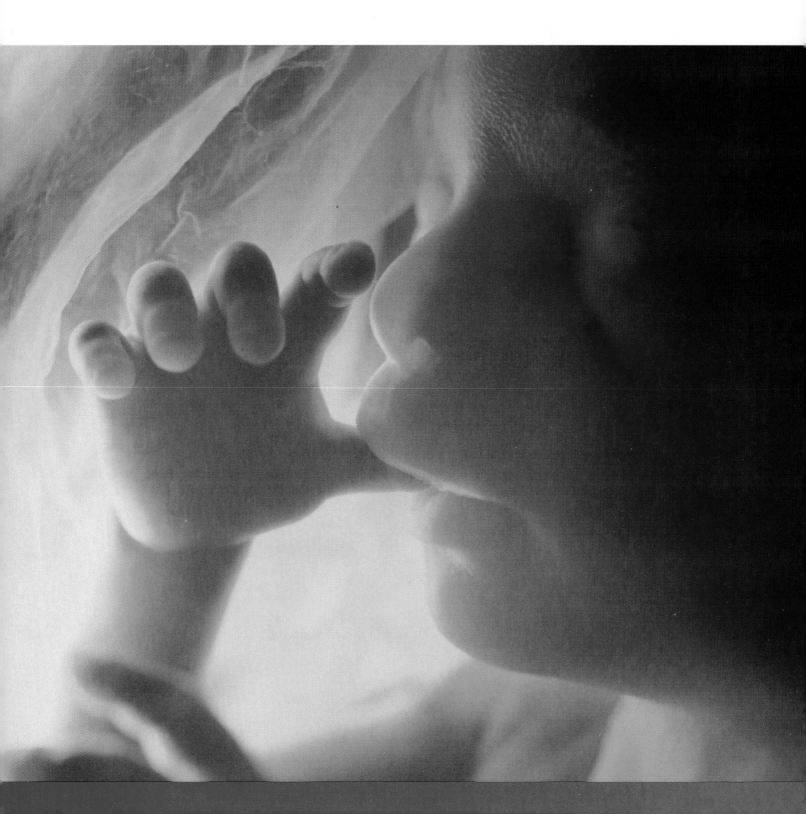

Prenatal Development and Birth

Chapter Outline

PRENATAL DEVELOPMENT

The Course of Prenatal Development
Teratology and Hazards to Prenatal Development
Prenatal Care
Cultural Beliefs About Pregnancy
Positive Prenatal Development

BIRTH

The Birth Process
Low-Birthweight Infants
Measures of Neonatal Health and Responsiveness

THE POSTPARTUM PERIOD

What Is the Postpartum Period?
Physical Adjustments
Emotional and Psychological Adjustments
Bonding

Learning Goals

1 Describe prenatal development

2 Discuss the birth process

3 Explain the changes that take place in the postpartum period

Images of Life-Span Development
Tanner Roberts' Birth: A Fantastic Voyage

Tanner Roberts was born in a suite at St. Joseph's Medical Center in Burbank, California (Warrick, 1992). Let's examine what took place in the hours leading up to his birth. It is day 266 of his mother Cindy's pregnancy. She is in the frozen-food aisle of a convenience store and feels a sharp pain, starting in the small of her back and reaching around her middle, which causes her to gasp. For weeks, painless Braxton Hicks spasms (named for the gynecologist who discovered them) have been flexing her uterine muscles. But these practice contractions were not nearly as intense and painful as the one she just experienced. After six hours of irregular spasms, her uterus settles into a more predictable rhythm.

At 3 A.M., Cindy and her husband, Tom, are wide awake. They time Cindy's contractions with a stopwatch. The contractions are now only six minutes apart. It's time to call the hospital. At the hospital, Cindy goes to a labor-delivery suite. The nurse puts a webbed belt and fetal monitor around Cindy's middle to measure the labor. The monitor picks up the fetal heart rate. With each contraction of the uterine wall, Tanner's heartbeat jumps from its resting state of about 140 beats to 160 to 170 beats per minute. When the cervix is dilated to more than 4 centimeters, or almost half open, Cindy is given her first medication. As Demerol begins to drip in her veins, she becomes more relaxed. Tanner's heart rate dips to 130 and then 120.

Contractions are now coming every three to four minutes, each one lasting about 25 seconds. The Demerol does not completely obliterate Cindy's pain. She hugs her husband as the nurse urges her to "relax those muscles. Breathe deep. Relax. You are almost done."

Each contraction briefly cuts off Tanner's source of oxygen. However, the minutes of rest between each contraction resupply the oxygen and Cindy's deep breathing helps rush fresh blood to the fetal heart and brain.

At 8 A.M., Cindy's obstetrician arrives and determines that her cervix is almost completely dilated. Using a tool made for the purpose, he reaches into the birth canal and tears the membranes of the amnio sac, and about half a liter of clear fluid flows out. Contractions are now coming every two minutes, and each one is lasting a full minute.

By 9 A.M., the labor suite has been transformed into a delivery room. Tanner's body is compressed by his mother's contractions and pushes. As he nears his entrance into the world, the compressions help press the fluid from his lungs in preparation for his first breath.

Squeezed tightly in the birth canal, the top of Tanner's head emerges. His face is puffy and scrunched. Although fiercely squinting because of the sudden light, Tanner's eyes are open. Tiny bubbles of clear mucus are on his lips. Before any more of his body emerges, the obstetrician cradles Tanner's head and suctions his nose and mouth. Tanner takes his first breath, a large gasp followed by whimpering, and then a loud cry. Tanner's body is wet but only slightly bloody as the doctor lifts him onto his mother's abdomen. The umbilical cord, still connecting Tanner with his mother, slows and stops pulsating. The obstetrician cuts it, severing Tanner's connection to his mother's womb. Now Tanner's blood flows not to his mother's blood for nourishment, but to his own lungs, intestines, and other organs. This chapter chronicles the truly remarkable developments from conception through birth. Imagine . . . at one time you were an organism floating in a sea of fluid in your mother's womb. Let's now explore what your development was like from the time you were conceived through the time you were born.

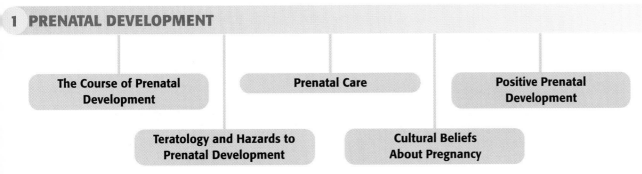

1 PRENATAL DEVELOPMENT

- The Course of Prenatal Development
- Teratology and Hazards to Prenatal Development
- Prenatal Care
- Cultural Beliefs About Pregnancy
- Positive Prenatal Development

Imagine how Tanner Roberts came to be. Out of thousands of eggs and millions of sperm, one egg and one sperm united to produce him. Had the union of sperm and egg come a day or even an hour earlier or later, he might have been very different—maybe even of the opposite sex. Conception occurs when a single sperm cell from the male unites with an ovum (egg) in the female's fallopian tube in a process called fertilization. Remember from chapter 3 that the fertilized egg is called a zygote.

The Course of Prenatal Development

The course of prenatal development lasts approximately 266 days, beginning with fertilization and ending with birth. Prenatal development is divided into three periods: germinal, embryonic, and fetal.

The Germinal Period   The **germinal period** is the period of prenatal development that takes place in the first two weeks after conception. It includes the creation of the zygote, continued cell division, and the attachment of the zygote to the uterine wall. By approximately one week after conception, the differentiation of cells has already commenced, as inner and outer layers of the organism are formed. The **blastocyst** is the inner layer of cells that develops during the germinal period. These cells later develop into the embryo. The **trophoblast** is the outer layer of cells that develops during the germinal period. It later provides nutrition and support for the embryo. *Implantation*, the attachment of the zygote to the uterine wall, takes place about 10 to 14 days after conception. Figure 4.1 on page 114 illustrates some of the most significant developments during the germinal period.

The Embryonic Period   The **embryonic period** is the period of prenatal development that occurs from two to eight weeks after conception. During the embryonic period, the rate of cell differentiation intensifies, support systems for cells form, and organs appear. As the zygote attaches to the uterine wall, the name of the mass of cells changes from *zygote* to *embryo* and three layers of cells are formed. The embryo's *endoderm* is the inner layer of cells, which will develop into the digestive and respiratory systems. The outer layer of cells is divided into two parts. The *ectoderm* is the outermost layer, which will become the nervous system, sensory receptors (ears, nose, and eyes, for example), and skin parts (hair and nails, for example). The *mesoderm* is the middle layer, which will become the circulatory system, bones, muscles, excretory system, and reproductive system. Every body part eventually develops from these three layers. The endoderm primarily produces internal body parts, the mesoderm primarily produces parts that surround the internal areas, and the ectoderm primarily produces surface parts.

As the embryo's three layers form, life-support systems for the embryo mature and develop rapidly. These life-support systems include the placenta, the umbilical cord, and the amnion. The **placenta** is a life-support system that consists of a disk-shaped group of tissues in which small blood vessels from the mother and the

germinal period The period of prenatal development that takes place in the first two weeks after conception. It includes the creation of the zygote, continued cell division, and the attachment of the zygote to the uterine wall.

blastocyst The inner layer of cells that develops during the germinal period. These cells later develop into the embryo.

trophoblast The outer layer of cells that develops in the germinal period. These cells provide nutrition and support for the embryo.

embryonic period The period of prenatal development that occurs two to eight weeks after conception. During the embryonic period, the rate of cell differentiation intensifies, support systems for the cells form, and organs appear.

placenta A life-support system that consists of a disk-shaped group of tissues in which small blood vessels from the mother and offspring intertwine.

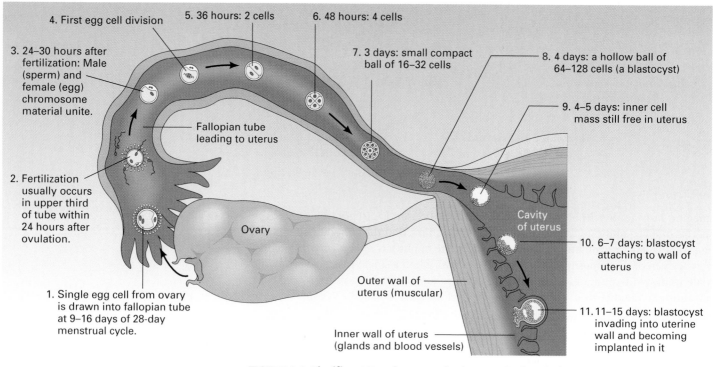

FIGURE 4.1 Significant Developments in the Germinal Period

The Visible Embryo

The Trimesters

offspring intertwine but do not join. The **umbilical cord** is a life-support system, containing two arteries and one vein, that connects the baby to the placenta. Very small molecules—oxygen, water, salt, food from the mother's blood, as well as carbon dioxide and digestive wastes from the embryo's blood—pass back and forth between the mother and infant. Large molecules cannot pass through the placental wall; these include red blood cells and harmful substances, such as most bacteria, maternal wastes, and hormones. The mechanisms that govern the transfer of substances across the placental barrier are complex and are still not entirely understood (Gielchinsky & others, 2002; Weeks & Mirembe, 2002). Figure 4.2 provides an illustration of the placenta, the umbilical cord, and the nature of blood flow in the expectant mother and developing child in the uterus. The **amnion**, a bag or an envelope that contains a clear fluid in which the developing embryo floats, is another important life-support system. Like the placenta and umbilical cord, the amnion develops from the fertilized egg, not from the mother's own body. At approximately 16 weeks, the kidneys of the fetus begin to produce urine. This fetal urine remains the main source of the amniotic fluid until the third trimester, when some of the fluid is excreted from the lungs of the growing fetus. Although the amniotic fluid increases in volume tenfold from the 12th to the 40th week of pregnancy, it is also removed in various ways. Some is swallowed by the fetus, and some is absorbed through the umbilical cord and the membranes covering the placenta. The amniotic fluid provides an environment that is temperature and humidity controlled, as well as shockproof.

Before most women even know they are pregnant, some important embryonic developments take place. In the third week, the neural tube that eventually becomes the spinal cord forms. At about 21 days, eyes begin to appear, and at 24 days the cells for the heart begin to differentiate. During the fourth week, the urogenital system becomes apparent, and arm and leg buds emerge. Four chambers of the heart take shape, and blood vessels appear. From the fifth to the eighth week, arms and legs differentiate further; at this time, the face starts to form but still is not very recognizable. The intestinal tract develops and the facial structures fuse. At eight weeks, the developing organism weighs about $1/30$ ounce and is just over 1 inch long. **Organogenesis** is the process of

umbilical cord A life-support system containing two arteries and one vein that connects the baby to the placenta.

amnion The life-support system that is a bag or envelope that contains a clear fluid in which the developing embryo floats.

organogenesis Organ formation that takes place during the first two months of prenatal development.

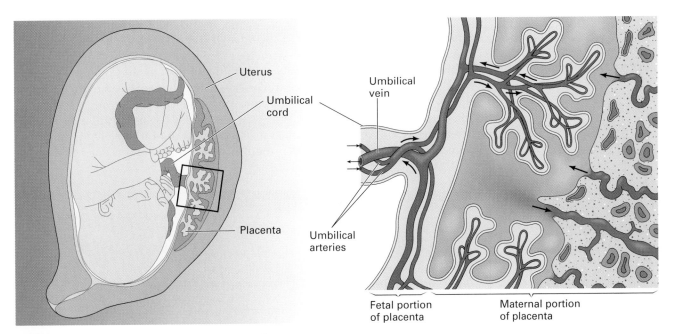

FIGURE 4.2 The Placenta and the Umbilical Cord

Maternal blood flows through the uterine arteries to the spaces housing the placenta, and it returns through the uterine veins to the maternal circulation. Fetal blood flows through the umbilical arteries into the capillaries of the placenta and returns through the umbilical veins to the fetal circulation. The exchange of materials takes place across the layer separating the maternal and fetal blood supplies, so the bloods never come into contact. *Note:* The area bound by the square is enlarged in the right half of the illustration. Arrows indicate the direction of blood flow.

organ formation that takes place during the first two months of prenatal development. When organs are being formed, they are especially vulnerable to environmental changes. Later in the chapter, we will describe the environmental hazards that can adversely affect organogenesis.

The Fetal Period The **fetal period** is the prenatal period of development that begins two months after conception and lasts for seven months, on the average. Growth and development continue their dramatic course during this time. Three months after conception, the fetus is about 3 inches long and weighs about 1 ounce. It has become active, moving its arms and legs, opening and closing its mouth, and moving its head. The face, forehead, eyelids, nose, and chin are distinguishable, as are the upper arms, lower arms, hands, and lower limbs. The genitals can be identified as male or female. By the end of the fourth month, the fetus has grown to 6 inches in length and weighs 4 to 7 ounces. At this time, a growth spurt occurs in the body's lower parts. Prenatal reflexes are stronger; arm and leg movements can be felt for the first time by the mother.

By the end of the fifth month, the fetus is about 12 inches long and weighs close to a pound. Structures of the skin have formed—toenails and fingernails, for example. The fetus is more active, showing a preference for a particular position in the womb. By the end of the sixth month, the fetus is about 14 inches long and has gained another half pound to a pound. The eyes and eyelids are completely formed, and a fine layer of hair covers the head. A grasping reflex is present and irregular breathing movements occur. By the end of the seventh month, the fetus is about 16 inches long, and having gained another pound, now weighs about 3 pounds. During the eighth and ninth months, the fetus grows longer and gains substantial weight—about another 4 pounds. At birth, the average American baby weighs 7½ pounds and is about 20 inches long. In these last two months, fatty tissues develop, and the functioning of various organ systems—heart and kidneys, for example—steps up.

Lines of communication should be open between the expectant mother and her partner during pregnancy. *What are some examples of good partner communication during pregnancy?*

fetal period The prenatal period of development that begins two months after conception and lasts for seven months, on the average.

We have described a number of changes in prenatal development in terms of germinal, embryonic, and fetal periods. Another way to divide prenatal development is in terms of equal periods of three months, called trimesters. An overview of some of the main changes in prenatal development in the three trimesters is presented in figure 4.3. Remember that the three trimesters are not the same as the three prenatal periods we have discussed—germinal, embryonic, and fetal. The germinal and embryonic periods occur in the first trimester. The fetal period begins toward the end of the first trimester and continues through the second and third trimesters. An important point that needs to be made is that the first time a fetus has a chance of surviving

First trimester (first 3 months)

Prenatal growth

Conception to 4 weeks
- Is less than 1/10 inch long
- Beginning development of spinal cord, nervous system, gastro-intestinal system, heart, and lungs
- Amniotic sac envelopes the preliminary tissues of entire body
- Is called a "zygote"

8 weeks
- Is less than 1 inch long
- Face is forming with rudimentary eyes, ears, mouth, and tooth buds
- Arms and legs are moving
- Brain is forming
- Fetal heartbeat is detectable with ultrasound
- Is called an "embryo"

12 weeks
- Is about 3 inches long and weighs about 1 ounce
- Can move arms, legs, fingers, and toes
- Fingerprints are present
- Can smile, frown, suck, and swallow
- Sex is distinguishable
- Can urinate
- Is called a "fetus"

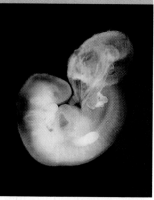

Second trimester (middle 3 months)

Prenatal growth

16 weeks
- Is about 5½ inches long and weighs about 4 ounces
- Heartbeat is strong
- Skin is thin, transparent
- Downy hair (lanugo) covers body
- Fingernails and toenails are forming
- Has coordinated movements; is able to roll over in amniotic fluid

20 weeks
- Is 10 to 12 inches long and weighs ½ to 1 pound
- Heartbeat is audible with ordinary stethoscope
- Sucks thumb
- Hiccups
- Hair, eyelashes, eyebrows are present

24 weeks
- Is 11 to 14 inches long and weighs 1 to 1½ pounds
- Skin is wrinkled and covered with protective coating (vernix caseosa)
- Eyes are open
- Waste matter is collected in bowel
- Has strong grip

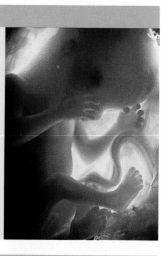

Third trimester (last 3 months)

Prenatal growth

28 weeks
- Is 14 to 17 inches long and weighs 2½ to 3 pounds
- Is adding body fat
- Is very active
- Rudimentary breathing movements are present

32 weeks
- Is 16½ to 18 inches long and weighs 4 to 5 pounds
- Has periods of sleep and wakefulness
- Responds to sounds
- May assume the birth position
- Bones of head are soft and flexible
- Iron is being stored in liver

36 to 38 weeks
- Is 19 inches long and weighs 6 pounds
- Skin is less wrinkled
- Vernix caseosa is thick
- Lanugo is mostly gone
- Is less active
- Is gaining immunities from mother

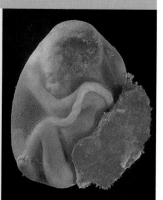

FIGURE 4.3 The Three Trimesters of Prenatal Development

outside of the womb is the beginning of the third trimester (at about seven months). Even when infants are born in the seventh month, they usually need assistance in breathing.

Teratology and Hazards to Prenatal Development

Some expectant mothers carefully tiptoe about in the belief that everything they do and feel has a direct effect on their unborn child. Others behave casually, assuming that their experiences will have little effect. The truth lies somewhere between these two extremes. Although living in a protected, comfortable environment, the fetus is not totally immune to the larger world surrounding the mother. The environment can affect the child in many well-documented ways. Thousands of babies born deformed or mentally retarded every year are the result of events that occurred in the mother's life, as early as one or two months before conception (Bailey, Forget, & Koren, 2002).

A **teratogen** (the word comes from the Greek word *tera* meaning "monster") is any agent that causes a birth defect. The field of study that investigates the causes of birth defects is called *teratology*. Teratogens include drugs, incompatible blood types, environmental pollutants, infectious diseases, nutritional deficiencies, maternal stress, and advanced maternal and paternal age. So many teratogens exist that practically every fetus is exposed to at least some teratogens. For this reason, it is difficult to determine which teratogen causes which birth defect. In addition, it may take a long time for the effects of a teratogen to show up. Only about half of all potential effects appear at birth.

The dose, the time of exposure to a particular agent, and genetic susceptibility influence the severity of the damage to an unborn child and the type of defect that occurs:

- *Dose* The dose effect is rather obvious—the greater the dose of an agent, such as a drug, the greater the effect.
- *Time of Exposure* Teratogens do more damage when they occur at some points in development rather than at others (Brent & Fawcett, 2000). In general, the embryonic period is a more vulnerable time than the fetal period. As figure 4.4 on page 118 shows, sensitivity to teratogens begins about three weeks after conception. The probability of a structural defect is greatest early in the embryonic period, when organs are being formed. After organogenesis is complete, teratogens are less likely to cause anatomical defects. Exposure later, during the fetal period, is more likely to stunt growth or to create problems in the way organs function. The precision of organogenesis is evident; teratologists point out that the vulnerability of the eyes is greatest at 24 to 40 days, the heart at 20 to 40 days, and the legs at 24 to 36 days.

  In chapter 2, we introduced the concept of *critical period* in our discussion of Lorenz' ethological theory. Recall that a critical period is a fixed time period very early in development during which certain experiences or events can have a long-lasting effect on development. As shown in figure 4.4, each body structure has its own critical period of formation. Thus, the critical period for the central nervous system (week 3) is earlier than for arms and legs (weeks 4 and 5).
- *Genetic Susceptibility* The type or severity of abnormalities caused by a teratogen is linked to the genotype of the pregnant woman and the genotype of the fetus. For example, variation in maternal metabolism of a particular drug can influence the degree to which the drug effects are transmitted to the fetus. Differences in placental membranes and placental transport also affect fetal exposure. The genetic susceptibility of the fetus to a particular teratogen can also affect the extent to which the fetus is vulnerable.

Prescription and Nonprescription Drugs Some pregnant women take prescription and nonprescription drugs without thinking about the possible effects on the fetus (Addis, Magrini & Mastroiacovo, 2001). Occasionally, a rash of deformed babies

The history of man for nine months preceding his birth would, probably, be far more interesting, and contain events of greater moment than all three score and ten years that follow it.

—Samuel Taylor Coleridge
English Poet, Essayist, 19th Century

Health and Prenatal Development

Exploring Teratology

High-Risk Situations

teratogen From the Greek word *tera*, meaning "monster." Any agent that causes a birth defect. The field of study that investigates the causes of birth defects is called teratology.

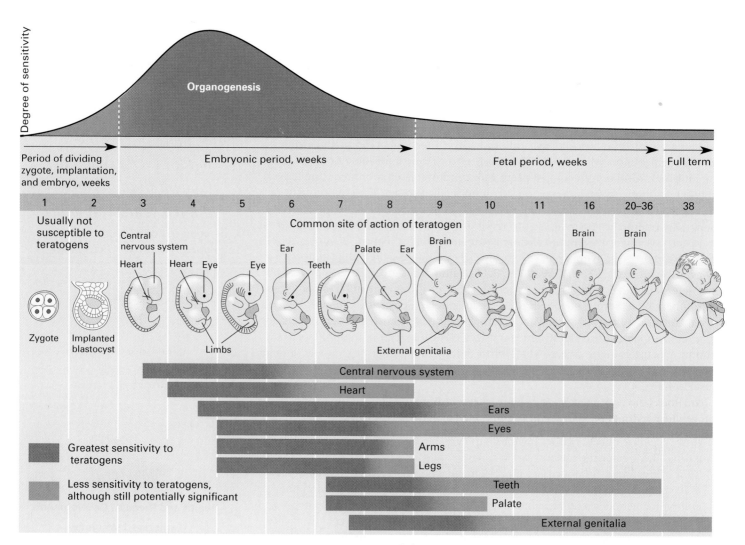

FIGURE 4.4 Teratogens and the Timing of Their Effects on Prenatal Development

The danger of structural defects caused by teratogens is greatest early in embryonic development. The period of organogenesis (red color) lasts for about six weeks. Later assaults by teratogens (blue-green color) mainly occur in the fetal period and instead of causing structural damage are more likely to stunt growth or cause problems of organ function.

is born, bringing to light the damage drugs can have on a developing fetus. This happened in 1961, when many pregnant women took a popular tranquilizer, thalidomide, to alleviate their morning sickness. In adults, the effects of thalidomide are mild; in embryos, however, they are devastating. Not all infants were affected in the same way. If the mother took thalidomide on day 26 (probably before she knew she was pregnant), an arm might not grow. If she took the drug two days later, the arm might not grow past the elbow. The thalidomide tragedy shocked the medical community and parents into the stark realization that the mother does not have to be a chronic drug user for the fetus to be harmed. Taking the wrong drug at the wrong time is enough to physically handicap the offspring for life (Sorokin, 2002).

Prescription drugs that can function as teratogens include antibiotics, such as streptomycin and tetracycline; some depressants; certain hormones, such as progestin and synthetic estrogen; and Accutane (which often is prescribed for acne) (Committee on Drugs, 2000).

Nonprescription drugs that can be harmful include diet pills, aspirin, and caffeine (Cnattingius & others, 2000). Let's explore the research on caffeine. A review of studies on caffeine consumption during pregnancy concluded that a small increase in the risks for spontaneous abortion and low birthweight occurs for pregnant women consuming more than 150 milligrams of caffeine (approximately two cups of brewed coffee or two to three 12-ounce cans of cola) per day (Fernandez & others, 1998). In one study, pregnant women who drank caffeinated coffee were more likely have preterm deliveries and newborns with a lower birthweight than their counterparts who did not drink caffeinated coffee (Eskenazi & others, 1999). In this study, no effects were found for pregnant women who drank decaffeinated coffee. Taking into account such results, the Food and Drug Administration recommends that pregnant women either not consume caffeine or consume it only sparingly.

Psychoactive Drugs   *Psychoactive drugs* are drugs that act on the nervous system to alter states of consciousness, modify perceptions, and change moods. A number of psychoactive drugs, including alcohol and nicotine, as well as illegal drugs such as cocaine, marijuana, and heroin have been studied to determine their links to prenatal and child development (Caulfield, 2001; Fogel, 2001).

Alcohol   Heavy drinking by pregnant women can be devastating to offspring (Barr & Streissguth, 2001; Enoch & Goldman, 2002; Committee on Substance Abuse, 2000). **Fetal alcohol syndrome (FAS)** is a cluster of abnormalities that appears in the offspring of mothers who drink alcohol heavily during pregnancy (Archibald & others, 2001). The abnormalities include facial deformities and defective limbs, face, and heart. Most of these children are below average in intelligence, and some are mentally retarded (Bookstein & others, 2002; Olson, 2000). Although many mothers of FAS infants are heavy drinkers, many mothers who are heavy drinkers do not have children with FAS or have one child with FAS and other children who do not have it. Figure 4.5 shows a child with fetal alcohol syndrome. Although no serious malformations such as those produced by FAS are found in infants born to mothers who are moderate drinkers, in one study, children whose mothers drank moderately (one to two drinks a day) during pregnancy were less attentive and alert, even at 4 years of age (Streissguth & others, 1984). In one study, prenatal alcohol exposure was a better predictor of adolescent alcohol use and its negative consequences than was family history of alcohol problems (Baer & others, 1998). And in another study, adults with fetal alcohol syndrome had a high incidence of mental disorders, such as depression or anxiety (Famy, Streissguth, & Unis, 1998).

Nicotine   Cigarette smoking by pregnant women can also adversely influence prenatal development, birth, and postnatal development. Fetal and neonatal deaths are higher among smoking mothers. There also are higher incidences of preterm births and lower birthweights (Bush & others, 2001; Wang & others, 2000).

In one study, urine samples from 22 of 31 newborns of smoking mothers contained substantial amounts of one of the strongest carcinogens (NNK) in tobacco smoke; the urine samples of the newborns whose mothers did not smoke were free of the carcinogen (Lackmann & others, 1999). In another study, prenatal exposure to cigarette smoking was related to poorer language and cognitive skills at 4 years of age (Fried & Watkinson, 1990). Respiratory problems and sudden infant death syndrome (also known as crib death) are more common among the offspring of mothers who smoked during pregnancy (Schoendorf & Kiely, 1992). Intervention programs designed to help pregnant women stop smoking can reduce some of smoking's negative behaviors, especially by raising birthweights (Klesges & others, 2001; Lightwood, Phibbs, & Glantz, 1999).

Illegal Drugs   Among the illegal drugs that have been studied to determine their effects on prenatal and child development are cocaine, marijuana, and heroin (Fifer & Grose-Fifer, 2001).

FIGURE 4.5 Fetal Alcohol Syndrome
Notice the wide-set eyes, flat bones, and thin upper lip.

mhhe●com/
santrockld9

Fetal Alcohol Syndrome
Smoking and Pregnancy

fetal alcohol syndrome (FAS) A cluster of abnormalities that appears in the offspring of mothers who drink alcohol heavily during pregnancy.

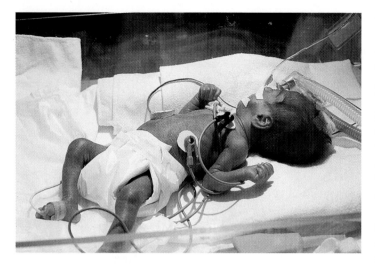

What do we know about the effects of cocaine on children's development?

Cocaine With the increased use of cocaine in the United States, there is concern about its effects on the embryos, fetuses, and infants of pregnant cocaine users (Hand & others, 2001). Cocaine use during pregnancy has recently attracted considerable attention because of possible harm to the developing embryo and fetus (Butz & others, 2001; Smith & others, 2001; Zeskind & others, 1999). The most consistent finding is that cocaine exposure during prenatal development is associated with reduced birthweight, length, and head circumference. Also, in one study, prenatal cocaine exposure was associated with impaired motor development at 2 years of age (Arendt & others, 1999).

Researchers increasingly are finding that fetal cocaine exposure is linked with impaired information processing (Singer, & others, 1999). In one study, prenatal cocaine exposure was moderately related to poor attentional skills through 5 years of age (Bandstra & others, 2000). In another study, prenatal cocaine exposure was related to impaired processing of auditory information after birth (Potter & others, 2000).

Although researchers are finding such deficits in children who are prenatally exposed to cocaine, a cautious interpretation of these findings is in order (Chavkin, 2001; Frank & others, 2001; Potter & others, 2000). Why? Because other factors (such as poverty, malnutrition, and other substance abuse) in the lives of pregnant women who use cocaine often cannot be ruled out as possible contributors to the negative effects on children (Kaugers & others, 2000). For example, cocaine users are more likely than nonusers to smoke cigarettes, use marijuana, drink alcohol, and take amphetamines. Teasing apart these potential influences from the effects of cocaine itself has not yet been adequately accomplished. Obtaining valid information about the frequency and type of drug use by mothers is complicated because many mothers fear prosecution and loss of child custody because of their drug use.

Indeed, there is still controversy about the effects on the offspring of cocaine use by women during pregnancy. One recent review concluded that prenatal exposure to cocaine by itself has not been demonstrated to have negative effects on the offspring (Frank & others, 2001).

Marijuana Marijuana use by pregnant women has detrimental effects on a developing fetus (Fried & Smith, 2001). Marijuana use by pregnant women is associated with increased tremors and startles among newborns and poorer verbal and memory development at 4 years of age (Fried & Watkinson, 1990).

Heroin It is well documented that infants whose mothers are addicted to heroin show several behavioral difficulties (Hulse & others, 2001). The young infants of these mothers are addicted and show withdrawal symptoms characteristic of opiate abstinence, such as tremors, irritability, abnormal crying, disturbed sleep, and impaired motor control. Behavioral problems are still often present at the first birthday, and attention deficits may appear later in the child's development. The most common treatment for heroin addiction, methadone, is associated with very severe withdrawal symptoms in newborns.

Incompatible Blood Types The incompatibility of the mother's and father's blood types is another risk to prenatal development. Variations in the surface structure of red blood cells distinguish different blood types. One type of surface marker borne by red blood cells identifies a person's blood group as A, B, O, or AB. The second type, called the *Rh factor*, is said to be positive if the Rh marker is present or negative if the individual's red blood cells do not carry this marker. If a pregnant woman is Rh negative and her partner is Rh positive, the fetus may be Rh positive (Weiss, 2001). When the fetus' blood is Rh positive and the mother's is Rh negative, the mother's immune system may produce antibodies that will attack the fetus. This can result in any number of problems, including miscarriage or stillbirth, anemia, jaundice, heart defects, brain damage, or death soon after birth (Narang & Jain, 2001).

Generally, the first Rh-positive baby of an Rh-negative mother is not at risk, but with each subsequent pregnancy the risk becomes greater. A vaccine (RhoGAM) may be given to the mother within three days of the child's birth to prevent her body from making antibodies that will attack future Rh-positive fetuses. Also, babies affected by Rh incompatibility can be given blood transfusions before or right after birth (Mannessier & others, 2000).

Environmental Hazards   Radiation, chemicals, and other hazards in our modern industrial world can endanger the fetus (Grigorenko, 2001; Ostrea, Whitehall, & Laken, 2000; Timins, 2001). For instance, radiation can cause a gene mutation (an abrupt, permanent change in genetic material). Chromosomal abnormalities are higher among the offspring of fathers exposed to high levels of radiation in their occupations (Schrag & Dixon, 1985). Radiation from X-rays also can affect the developing embryo and fetus, especially in the first several weeks after conception, when women do not yet know they are pregnant (Barnett & Maulik, 2001). It is important for women and their physicians to weigh the risk of an X-ray when an actual or potential pregnancy is involved (Shaw, 2001).

Environmental pollutants and toxic wastes are also sources of danger to unborn children. Researchers have found that various hazardous wastes and pesticides cause defects in animals exposed to high doses. Among the dangerous pollutants and wastes are carbon monoxide, mercury, and lead. Some children are exposed to lead because they live in houses in which lead-based paint flakes off the walls or near busy highways, where there are heavy automobile emissions from leaded gasoline. Researchers believe that early exposure to lead affects children's mental development (Markowitz, 2000). For example, in one study, 2-year-olds who prenatally had high levels of lead in their umbilical-cord blood performed poorly on a test of mental development (Bellinger & others, 1987).

Researchers also have found that manufacturing chemicals known as PCBs are harmful to prenatal development. In one study, the extent to which pregnant women ate PCB-polluted fish from Lake Michigan was examined, and subsequently their newborns were observed (Jacobson & others, 1984). The women who had eaten more PCB-polluted fish were more likely to have smaller, preterm infants who were more likely to react slowly to stimuli. And, in another study, prenatal exposure to PCBs was associated with problems in visual discrimination and short-term memory in 4-year-old children (Jacobson & others, 1992).

A current environmental concern is the low-level electromagnetic radiation emitted by computer monitors. The fear is that women who spend long hours in front of the monitors might risk adverse effects to their offspring, should they become pregnant. Researchers have not found exposure to computer monitors to be related to miscarriage (Schnorr & others, 1991).

Yet another recent environmental concern for expectant mothers is prolonged exposure to heat produced by saunas or hot tubs. By raising the mother's body temperature, a sauna or a hot tub can cause a fever that endangers the fetus. The high temperature of a fever may interfere with cell division and may cause birth defects or even fetal death if the fever occurs repeatedly for prolonged periods of time. If the expectant mother wants to take a sauna or bathe in a hot tub, prenatal experts recommend that she take her oral temperature while she is exposed to the heat. When the expectant mother's body temperature rises a degree or more, she should get out and cool down. Ten minutes is a reasonable length of time for expectant mothers to spend in a sauna or hot tub, since the body temperature does not usually rise in this length of time. If the expectant mother feels uncomfortably hot in a sauna or hot tub, she should get out, even if she has been there only for a short time.

An explosion at the Chernobyl nuclear power plant in the Ukraine produced radioactive contamination that spread to surrounding areas. Thousands of infants were born with health problems and deformities as a result of the nuclear contamination, including this boy whose arm did not form. *Other than radioactive contamination, what are some other types of environmental hazards to prenatal development?*

Other Maternal Factors So far we have discussed a number of drugs and environmental hazards that have harmful effects on prenatal and child development. Here we will explore these other potentially harmful maternal factors: infectious diseases, nutrition, emotional states and stress, and age.

Infectious Diseases Maternal diseases and infections can produce defects in offspring by crossing the placental barrier, or they can cause damage during the birth process itself (Iannucci, 2000). Rubella (German measles) is one disease that can cause prenatal defects. The greatest damage occurs if a mother contracts rubella in the third or fourth week of pregnancy, although infection during the second month is also damaging. A rubella outbreak in 1964–1965 resulted in 30,000 prenatal and neonatal (newborn) deaths, and more than 20,000 affected infants were born with malformations, including mental retardation, blindness, deafness, and heart problems. Elaborate preventive efforts ensure that rubella will never again have such disastrous effects. A vaccine that prevents German measles is now routinely administered to children, and women who plan to have children should have a blood test before they become pregnant to determine if they are immune to the disease (Signore, 2001; Ward, Lambert, & Lester, 2001).

Syphilis (a sexually transmitted disease) is more damaging later in prenatal development—four months or more after conception. Rather than affecting organogenesis, as rubella does, syphilis damages organs after they have formed. Damage includes eye lesions, which can cause blindness, and skin lesions. When syphilis is present at birth, problems can develop in the central nervous system and gastrointestinal tract (Hollier & others, 2001). Most states require that pregnant women be given a blood test to detect the presence of syphilis.

Another infection that has received widespread attention recently is genital herpes. Newborns contract this virus when they are delivered through the birth canal of a mother with genital herpes (Qutub & others, 2001). About one-third of babies delivered through an infected birth canal die; another one-fourth become brain damaged. If an active case of genital herpes is detected in a pregnant woman close to her delivery date, a cesarean section can be performed (in which the infant is delivered through an incision in the mother's abdomen) to keep the virus from infecting the newborn.

AIDS is a sexually transmitted disease that is caused by the human immunodeficiency virus (HIV), which destroys the body's immune system. In the early 1990s, before preventive treatments were available, 1,000 to 2,000 infants were born with HIV infection each year in the United States. Since then, dramatic reductions in the transmission of AIDS from mothers to the fetus/newborn have occurred. Only about one-third as many cases of newborns with AIDS appear today as in the early 1990s. This decline is due to the increase in counseling and voluntary testing of pregnant women for HIV and to the use of zidovudine (AZT) by infected women during pregnancy, and for the infant after birth (Bulterys, 2001; Centers for Disease Control and Prevention, 2000; Committee on Pediatric AIDS, 2000; Rovira & others, 2001).

A mother can infect her offspring with AIDS in three ways: (1) during gestation across the placenta, (2) during delivery through contact with maternal blood or fluids, and (3) postpartum (after birth) through breast-feeding. The transmission of AIDS through breast-feeding is especially a problem in many developing countries (Semba & Neville, 1999).

Babies born to HIV-infected mothers can be (1) infected and symptomatic (show AIDS symptoms), (2) infected but asymptomatic (not show AIDS symptoms), or (3) not infected at all. An infant who is infected and asymptomatic may still develop HIV symptoms up until 15 months of age.

Nutrition A developing fetus depends completely on its mother for nutrition, which comes from the mother's blood. The nutritional status of the fetus is determined by the mother's total caloric intake, and also by appropriate levels of proteins, vitamins, and minerals. The mother's nutrition even influences her ability to reproduce. In extreme instances of malnutrition, women stop menstruating, thus precluding conception. Children born to malnourished mothers are more likely to be malformed.

Researchers have also found that being overweight before and during pregnancy can be risk factors for the fetus and the child. In two recent studies, obese women had a significant risk of late fetal death, although the risk of preterm delivery was reduced in these women (Cnattingius & others, 1998; Kumari, 2001).

One aspect of maternal nutrition that is important for normal prenatal development is folic acid, a B-complex vitamin (Callender, Rickard, & Rinsky-Eng, 2001). A lack of folic acid is linked with neural tube defects in offspring, such as spina bifida (Honein & others, 2001). The U.S. Public Health Service now recommends that pregnant women consume a minimum of 400 micrograms of folic acid per day (that is about twice the amount the average woman gets in one day). Orange juice and spinach are examples of foods rich in folic acid.

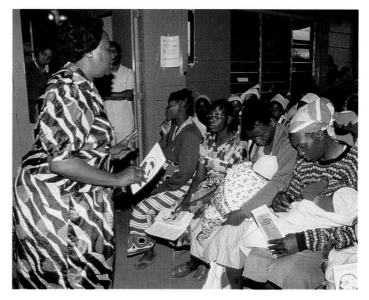

Because the fetus depends entirely on its mother for nutrition, it is important for the pregnant woman to have good nutritional habits. In Kenya, this government clinic provides pregnant women with information about how their diet can influence the health of their fetus and offspring. *What might the information about diet be like?*

Emotional States and Stress   Tales abound about how a pregnant woman's emotional state affects the fetus. For centuries it was thought that frightening experiences—such as a severe thunderstorm or a family member's death—leave birthmarks on the child or affect the child in more serious ways. Today we believe that the mother's stress can be transmitted to the fetus, but we have a better grasp of how this takes place (Monk & others, 2000; Relier, 2001). We now know that when a pregnant woman experiences intense fears, anxieties, and other emotions, physiological changes occur—among them, changes in respiration and glandular secretions. For example, producing adrenaline in response to fear restricts blood flow to the uterine area and can deprive the fetus of adequate oxygen.

The mother's emotional state during pregnancy can influence the birth process too. An emotionally distraught mother might have irregular contractions and a more difficult labor, which can cause irregularities in the baby's oxygen supply or can produce irregularities after birth. Babies born after extended labor also may adjust more slowly to their world and be more irritable.

Maternal anxiety during pregnancy is related to less than optimal outcomes (Brouwers, van Baar, & Pop, 2001). Circumstances that are linked with maternal anxiety during pregnancy include marital discord, death of a husband, and unwanted pregnancy (Field, 1990).

In studies on stress, prenatal development, and birth, Christine Dunkel-Schetter and her colleagues (1998; Dunkel-Schetter & others, 2001) have found that women under stress are about four times as likely to deliver their babies prematurely as are their low-stress counterparts. In another study, maternal stress increased the level of corticotrophin-releasing hormone (CRH) early in pregnancy (Hobel & others, 1999). CRH has been linked with premature delivery. There also is a connection between stress and unhealthy behaviors, such as smoking, drug use, and poor prenatal care (Dunkel-Schetter, 1999). Also, in one recent study, maternal depression was linked with increased fetal activity, possibly as a result of elevated stress hormones in the mother (Dieter & others, 2001). Further, researchers have found that pregnant women who are optimistic thinkers have less-adverse birth outcomes than pregnant women who are pessimistic thinkers (Loebel & Yali, 1999). Optimists believe that they have more control over the outcome of their pregnancy.

Maternal Age   Consideration of possible harmful effects of the mother's age on the fetus and infant focuses on adolescence and the thirties and beyond (Abel, Kruger, &

What are some of the risks for infants born to adolescent mothers?

Burd, 2002). Approximately one of every five births is to an adolescent; in some urban areas, the figure reaches as high as one in every two births. Infants born to adolescents are often premature (Ekwo & Moawad, 2000). In one recent study, low-birthweight delivery increased 11 percent and preterm delivery increased 14 percent for women 35 years and older (Tough & others, 2002). The mortality rate of infants born to adolescent mothers is double that of infants born to mothers in their twenties. Although such figures probably reflect the mothers' immature reproductive system, they also may involve poor nutrition, lack of prenatal care, and low socioeconomic status (Lenders, McElrath, & Scholl, 2000). Prenatal care decreases the probability that a child born to an adolescent girl will have physical problems. However, adolescents are the least likely of women in all age groups to obtain prenatal assistance from clinics, pediatricians, and health services.

Increasingly, women seek to establish their careers before beginning a family, delaying childbearing until their thirties. Down syndrome, a form of mental retardation, is related to the mother's age (Holding, 2002). A baby with Down syndrome rarely is born to a mother under the age of 30, but the risk increases after the mother reaches 30. By age 40, the probability is slightly over 1 in 100, and by age 50 it is almost 1 in 10. The risk also is higher before age 18.

Women also have more difficulty becoming pregnant after the age of 30. One study in a French fertility clinic focused on women whose husbands were sterile (Schwartz & Mayaux, 1982). To make it possible for the women to have a child, women were artificially inseminated once a month for one year. Each woman had 12 chances to become pregnant. Seventy-five percent of the women in their twenties became pregnant, 62 percent of the women 31 to 35 years old became pregnant, and only 54 percent of the women over 35 years old became pregnant.

We still have much to learn about the role of the mother's age in pregnancy and childbirth. As women remain active, exercise regularly, and are careful about their nutrition, their reproductive systems may remain healthier longer than was thought possible in the past.

Paternal Factors   So far, we have been considering maternal factors during pregnancy that can influence prenatal development and the development of the child. Might there also be some paternal risk factors? Indeed, there are several. Men's exposure to lead, radiation, certain pesticides, and petrochemicals may cause abnormalities in sperm that lead to miscarriage or diseases, such as childhood cancer (Lindbohm, 1991; Trasler, 2000; Trasler & Doerkson, 2000). When fathers have a diet low in vitamin C, their offspring have a higher risk of birth defects and cancer (Fraga & others, 1991). Also, it has been speculated that, when fathers take cocaine, it may attach itself to sperm and cause birth defects, but the evidence for this is not yet strongly established. In some studies, chronic marijuana use has been shown to reduce testosterone levels and sperm counts, although the results have been inconsistent (Fields, 1998; Nahas, 1984).

The father's smoking during the mother's pregnancy also can cause problems for the offspring. In one investigation, the newborns of fathers who smoked during their wives' pregnancy were 4 ounces lighter at birth for each pack of cigarettes smoked per day than were the newborns whose fathers did not smoke during their wives' pregnancy (Rubin & others, 1986). In another study, in China, the longer the fathers smoked, the stronger the risk was for their children to develop cancer (Ji & others, 1997). In such studies, it is very difficult to tease apart prenatal and postnatal effects.

As is the case with older mothers, older fathers also may place their offspring at risk for certain birth defects. These include Down syndrome (about 5 percent of these children have older fathers), dwarfism, and Marfan syndrome, which involves head and limb deformities.

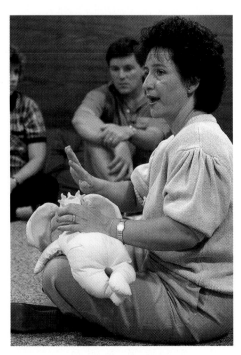

Early prenatal education classes focus on such topics as changes in the development of the fetus. Later classes focus on preparation for the birth and care of the newborn. *To what extent should fathers, as well as mothers, participate in these classes?*

Prenatal Care

Prenatal care varies enormously, but usually involves a package of medical care services in a defined schedule of visits (McCormick, 2001). In addition to medical care, prenatal care programs often include comprehensive educational, social, and nutritional services (Nichols & Humenick, 2000; Shiono & Behrman, 1995). Women who are pregnant can benefit from the information and advice they receive from health-care personnel, such as Rachel Thompson, an obstetrician/gynecologist whose work is described in the Careers in Life-Span Development insert.

Prenatal care usually includes screening for manageable conditions and/or treatable diseases that can affect the baby or the mother. The education an expectant woman receives about pregnancy, labor and delivery, and caring for the newborn can be extremely valuable, especially for first-time mothers (Cosey & Bechtel, 2001). Prenatal care is also very important for women in poverty because it links them with other social services. The legacy of prenatal care continues after birth, because women who receive this type of care are more likely to seek preventive care for their infants (Bates & others, 1994).

Inadequate prenatal care can occur for a variety of reasons, including the health-care system, provider practices, and individual and social characteristics (Howell, 2001). In one national study, 71 percent of low-income women experienced problems obtaining prenatal care (U.S. General Accounting Office, 1987). Lack of transportation and child care, as well as financial difficulties, were commonly cited as barriers to getting prenatal care. Motivating positive attitudes toward pregnancy is also important. Women who have unplanned or unwanted pregnancies, or who have negative attitudes about being pregnant, are more likely to delay prenatal care or to miss appointments (Joseph, 1989).

Despite the advances made in prenatal care and technology in the United States, the availability of high-quality medical and educational services still needs much improvement. Some countries, especially in Scandinavia and Western Europe, provide more consistent, higher-quality prenatal care than the United States does.

Cultural Beliefs About Pregnancy

A woman's behavior during pregnancy is often determined by cultural beliefs. Certain behaviors are expected if a culture views pregnancy as a medical condition, whereas other behaviors are expected if pregnancy is viewed as a natural occurrence. For example, prenatal care may not be a priority for expectant mothers who view pregnancy as a natural occurrence. Thus, health-care providers need to become aware of the health practices of various cultural groups, including health beliefs about pregnancy and prenatal development. Cultural assessment is an important dimension of providing adequate health care for expectant mothers from various cultural groups. Cultural assessment includes identifying the main beliefs, values, and behaviors related to pregnancy and childbearing. In particular, ethnic background, degree of affiliation with the ethnic group, patterns of decision making, religious preference, language, communication style, and common etiquette practices can significantly affect women's attitudes about the type of medical care needed during pregnancy.

Health-care practices during pregnancy are influenced by numerous factors, including the prevalence of traditional home care remedies and folk beliefs, the importance of indigenous healers, and the influence of professional health-care workers. Many Mexican American mothers are strongly influenced by their mothers and older

mhhe ●com/ santrockld9

Reproductive Health Links

Exploring Pregnancy

Childbirth Classes

Prenatal Care

Health-Care Providers

In India, a midwife checks on the size, position, and heartbeat of a fetus. Midwives deliver babies in many cultures around the world. *What are some cultural variations in prenatal care?*

women in their culture, often seeking and following their advice during pregnancy. In Mexican American culture, the indigenous healer is called a *curandero*. In some Native American tribes, the medicine woman or man fulfills the healing role. Herbalists are often found in Asian cultures, and faith healers, root doctors, and spiritualists are sometimes found in African American culture. When health-care providers come into contact with expectant mothers, they need to assess whether such cultural practices pose a threat to the expectant mother and the fetus. If they pose no threat, there is no reason to try to change them. On the other hand, if certain cultural practices do pose a threat to the health of the expectant mother or the fetus, the health-care provider should consider a culturally sensitive way to handle the problem. For example, some Filipinos will not take any medication during pregnancy.

Positive Prenatal Development

Much of our discussion so far in this chapter has focused on what can go wrong with prenatal development. It is important to keep in mind that most of the time, prenatal development does not go awry and development occurs along the positive path that we described at the beginning of the chapter (Lester, 2000). That said, it is still important for prospective mothers and those who are pregnant to avoid the vulnerabilities to fetal development that we have described.

Review and Reflect

1 Describe prenatal development

REVIEW

- What is the course of prenatal development?
- What are some of the main hazards to prenatal development?
- What are some good prenatal care strategies?
- What are some cultural beliefs about pregnancy?
- Why is it important to take a positive approach to prenatal development?

REFLECT

- What can be done to convince women who are pregnant not to smoke or drink? Consider the role of health-care providers, the role of insurance companies, and specific programs targeted at women who are pregnant.

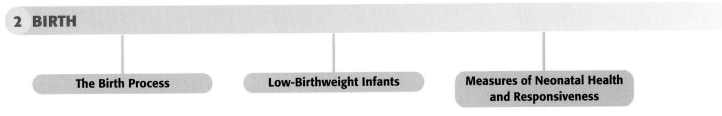

2 BIRTH

The Birth Process

Low-Birthweight Infants

Measures of Neonatal Health and Responsiveness

As we saw in the opening story about Tanner Roberts, many changes take place during the birth of a baby (Verklan, 2002). Let's further explore the birth process.

The Birth Process

Here we will examine the stages of birth, the transition from fetus to newborn, childbirth strategies, low-birthweight infants, and measures of neonatal (newborn) health and responsiveness.

Stages of Birth   Childbirth—or labor—occurs in three stages (see figure 4.6). For a woman having her first child, the first stage lasts an average of 12 to 24 hours; it is the longest of the three stages. In the first stage, uterine contractions are 15 to 20 minutes apart at the beginning and last up to a minute. These contractions cause the woman's cervix, the opening into the birth canal, to stretch and open. As the first stage progresses, the contractions come closer together, appearing every two to five minutes.

mhhe ● com/
santrockld9

Preparing for Birth

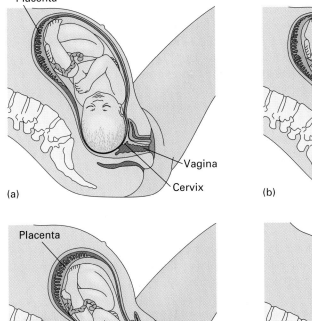

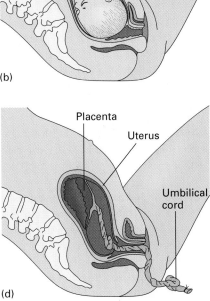

FIGURE 4.6 The Stages of Birth

(*a*) First stage: cervix is dilating; (*b*) late first stage (transition stage): cervix is fully dilated, and the amniotic sac has ruptured, releasing amniotic fluid; (*c*) second stage: birth of the infant; (*d*) third stage: delivery of the placenta (afterbirth).

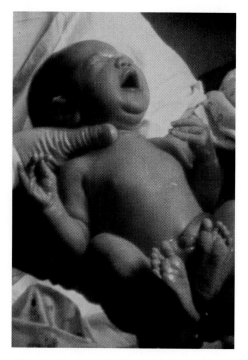

After the long journey of prenatal development, birth takes place. During birth the baby is on a threshold between two worlds. *What is the fetus/newborn transition like?*

*W*e must respect this instant of birth, this fragile moment. The baby is between two worlds, on a threshold, hesitating...

—FREDERICK LEBOYER
French Obstetrician, 20th Century

Their intensity increases too. By the end of the first birth stage, contractions dilate the cervix to an opening of about 4 inches, so that the baby can move from the uterus to the birth canal.

The second birth stage begins when the baby's head starts to move through the cervix and the birth canal. It terminates when the baby completely emerges from the mother's body. For a first birth, this stage lasts approximately 1½ hours. With each contraction, the mother bears down hard to push the baby out of her body. By the time the baby's head is out of the mother's body, the contractions come almost every minute and last for about a minute.

Afterbirth is the third stage, at which time the placenta, umbilical cord, and other membranes are detached and expelled. This final stage is the shortest of the three birth stages, lasting only minutes.

The Transition from Fetus to Newborn   Being born involves considerable stress for the baby. During each contraction, when the placenta and umbilical cord are compressed as the uterine muscles draw together, the supply of oxygen to the fetus is decreased. If the delivery takes too long, anoxia can develop (Mohan, Golding, & Paterson, 2001). *Anoxia* is the condition in which the fetus/newborn has an insufficient supply of oxygen. Anoxia can cause brain damage.

The baby has considerable capacity to withstand the stress of birth. Large quantities of adrenaline and noradrenalin, hormones that protect the fetus in the event of oxygen deficiency, are secreted in stressful circumstances. These hormones increase the heart's pumping activity, speed up heart rate, channel blood flow to the brain, and raise the blood-sugar level. Never again in life will such large amounts of these hormones be secreted. This circumstance underscores how stressful it is to be born and also how well prepared and adapted the fetus is for birth (Committee on Fetus and Newborn, 2000; Mishell, 2000; Van Beveren, 2002).

As we saw in the case of Tanner Roberts at the beginning of the chapter, the umbilical cord is cut immediately after birth, and the baby is on its own. Now 25 million little air sacs in the lungs must be filled with air. Until now, these air sacs have held fluid, but this fluid is rapidly expelled in blood. The first breaths may be the hardest ones an individual takes. Before birth, oxygen came from the mother via the umbilical cord, but now the baby has to be self-sufficient and breathe on its own.

At the time of birth, the baby is covered with what is called *vernix caseosa,* a protective skin grease. This vernix consists of fatty secretions and dead cells, thought to function in protecting the baby's skin against heat loss before and during birth. After the baby and mother have met and become acquainted with each other, the baby is taken to be cleaned, examined, weighed, and evaluated. Later in the chapter, we will discuss several measures that are used to examine the newborn's health and responsiveness.

Childbirth Strategies   Among the childbirth decisions that need to be made are what the setting will be, who the attendants will be, and which childbirth technique will be used. Here we will discuss the options available to expectant parents.

Childbirth Setting and Attendants   In the United States, 99 percent of births take place in hospitals, and more than 90 percent are attended by physicians (Ventura & others, 1997). Many hospitals now have birthing centers, where fathers or birth coaches may be with the mother during labor and delivery. Some people believe this so-called alternative birthing center offers a good compromise between a technological, depersonalized hospital birth (which cannot offer the emotional experience of a home birth) and a birth at home (which cannot offer the medical backup of a hospital). A birthing room approximates a home setting as much as possible and allows for a full range of birth experiences, from a totally unmedicated, natural birth to the most complex, intensive medical care. Some women with good medical histories and low risk for problem delivery choose a home delivery or a delivery in a freestanding birthing center, which is usually staffed by nurse-midwives (Wong, Perry, & Hockenberry, 2001).

Approximately 6 percent of women who deliver a baby in the United States are attended by a midwife (Ventura & others, 1997). Most midwives are nurses who have been specially trained in delivering babies (Oshio, Johnson, & Fullerton, 2002) ◄▐▐▐ p. 35. One study found that the risk of neonatal mortality (an infant death occurring in the first 28 days of life) was 33 percent lower and the risk of a low-birthweight baby was 31 percent lower for births attended by a certified nurse-midwife than for births attended by physicians (MacDorman & Singh, 1998). Compared to physicians, certified nurse-midwives generally spend more time with patients during prenatal visits, place more emphasis on patient counseling and education, provide more emotional support, and are more likely to be with the patient one-on-one during the entire labor and delivery process, which may explain the more positive outcomes for babies delivered by certified nurse-midwives.

In many countries around the world, babies are more likely to be delivered at home than they are in the United States. For example, in Holland, 35 percent of the babies are born at home, and more than 40 percent are delivered by midwives rather than doctors (Treffers & others, 1990).

In many countries, a doula attends a childbearing woman. *Doula* is a Greek word that means "a woman who helps." A **doula** is a caregiver who provides continuous physical, emotional, and educational support for the mother before, during, and after childbirth. Doulas remain with the mother throughout labor, assessing and responding to her needs. In one study, the mothers who received doula support reported less labor pain than the mothers who did not receive doula support (Klaus, Kennell, & Klaus, 1993). Doulas typically function as part of a "birthing team," serving as an adjunct to the midwife or the hospital obstetric staff (McGrath & others, 1999; Pascali-Bonaro, 2002).

In the United States, most doulas work as independent providers hired by the expectant woman. Managed care organizations are increasingly offering doula support as a part of regular obstetric care. In many cultures, the practice of a knowledgeable woman helping a mother in labor is not officially labeled "doula" support but is simply an ingrained, centuries-old custom.

In many cultures, several people attend the mother during labor and delivery. Which persons attend the mother may vary across cultures. In the East African Nigoni culture, men are completely excluded from the childbirth process. In this culture, women even conceal their pregnancy from their husband as long as possible. In the Nigoni culture, when a woman is ready to give birth, female relatives move into the woman's hut and the husband leaves, taking his belongings (clothes, tools, weapons, and so on) with him. He is not permitted to return until after the baby is born.

In some cultures, childbirth is a more open, community affair than in the United States. For example, in the Pukapukan culture in the Pacific Islands, women give birth in a shelter that is open for villagers to observe.

Methods of Delivery Among the methods of delivery are medicated, natural and prepared, and cesarean. The American Academy of Pediatrics recommends the least possible medication during delivery, although it is up to the mother or attending medical personnel to decide whether drugs are needed (Hotchner, 1997).

There are three basic kinds of drugs that are used for labor: analgesia, anesthesia, and oxytocics. *Analgesia* is used to relieve pain. Analgesics include tranquilizers, barbiturates, and narcotics (such as Demerol). *Anesthesia* is used in late first-stage labor and during expulsion of the baby to block sensation in an area of the body or to block consciousness. There is a trend toward not using general anesthesia, which blocks consciousness, in normal births because it can be transmitted through the placenta to the fetus. However, an epidural anesthesia does not cross the placenta. An *epidural block* is regional anesthesia that numbs the woman's body from the waist down. Even this drug, thought to be relatively safe, has come under recent criticism because it is

A woman in the African !Kung culture giving birth in a sitting position. Notice the help and support being given by another woman. *What are some cultural variations in childbirth?*

mhhe●com/
santrockld9

Childbirth Strategies
Childbirth Setting and Attendants
Midwifery
Doula
Fathers and Childbirth
Siblings and Childbirth

doula A caregiver who provides continuous physical, emotional, and educational support for the mother before, during, and after childbirth.

Linda Pugh, Perinatal Nurse

Perinatal nurses work with childbearing women to support health and growth during the childbearing experience ◀Ⅲ p. 35. Linda Pugh, Ph.D., R.N.C., is a perinatal nurse on the faculty at The Johns Hopkins University School of Nursing. She is certified as an inpatient obstetric nurse and specializes in the care of women during labor and delivery. She teaches undergraduate and graduate students, educates professional nurses, and conducts research. In addition, she consults with hospitals and organizations about women's health issues and topics we discuss in this chapter.

Her research interests include nursing interventions with low-income breast-feeding women, discovering ways to prevent and ameliorate fatigue during childbearing, and using breathing exercises during labor.

Linda Pugh (*right*), a perinatal nurse, with a mother and her newborn.

natural childbirth Developed in 1914 by Dick-Read, this method attempts to reduce the mother's pain by decreasing her fear through education about childbirth and relaxation techniques during delivery.

prepared childbirth Developed by French obstetrician Ferdinand Lamaze, this childbirth strategy is similar to natural childbirth but includes a special breathing technique to control pushing in the final stages of labor and a more detailed anatomy and physiology course.

associated with fever, extended labor, and increased risk for cesarean delivery (Ransjo-Arvidson & others, 2001). *Oxytocics* are synthetic hormones that are used to stimulate contractions. Pitocin is the most commonly used oxytocic (Carbonne, Tsatsarius, & Goffinet, 2001; Gard & others, 2002).

Predicting how a particular drug will affect an individual pregnant woman and the fetus is difficult. Though we have many commonalities as human beings, we also vary a great deal. Thus, a particular drug might have only a minimal effect on one fetus yet have a much stronger effect on another fetus. The drug's dosage also is a factor. Stronger doses of tranquilizers and narcotics given to decrease the mother's pain have a potentially more negative effect on the fetus than mild doses. It is important for the mother to assess her level of pain and have a voice in the decision of whether she should receive medication or not (Young, 2001).

Though the trend at one time was toward a natural childbirth without any medication, today the emphasis is on using some medication but keeping it to a minimum when possible. The emphasis today also is on broadly educating the pregnant woman so that she can be reassured and confident. The emphasis on education is reflected in the techniques of natural childbirth and prepared childbirth.

Natural childbirth was developed in 1914 by an English obstetrician, Grantley Dick-Read. Its purpose is to reduce the mother's pain by decreasing her fear through education about childbirth and by teaching her to use breathing methods and relaxation techniques during delivery. Dick-Read believed that the doctor's relationship with the mother is an important dimension of reducing her perception of pain. He said the doctor should be present during her active labor prior to delivery and should provide reassurance.

Prepared childbirth was developed by French obstetrician Ferdinand Lamaze. This childbirth strategy is similar to natural childbirth but includes a special breathing technique to control pushing in the final stages of labor, as well as a more detailed anatomy and physiology course. The Lamaze method has become very popular in the United States. The pregnant woman's husband or a friend usually serves as a coach, who attends childbirth classes with her and helps her with her breathing and relaxation during delivery.

Many other prepared childbirth techniques also have been developed (Samuels & Samuels, 1996). They usually include elements of Dick-Read's natural childbirth or Lamaze's method, plus one or more other components. For instance, the Bradley method places special emphasis on the father's role as a labor coach. Virtually all of the prepared childbirth methods emphasize some degree of education, relaxation and breathing exercises, and support. In recent years, new ways of teaching relaxation have been offered, including guided mental imagery, massage, and meditation. In sum, the current belief in prepared childbirth is that, when information and support are provided, women *know* how to give birth. To read about one nurse whose research focuses on discovering ways to prevent and reduce fatigue during childbearing and the use of breathing exercises during labor, see the Careers in Life-Span Development insert.

In a *cesarean delivery,* the baby is removed from the mother's uterus through an incision made in her abdomen. This method also is sometimes known as a cesarean section. A cesarean section is usually performed if the baby is in a **breech position,** which causes the baby's buttocks to be the first part to emerge from the vagina. Normally, the crown of the baby's head comes through the vagina first, but in 1 of every 25 deliveries, the baby's head is still in the uterus when the rest of the body is out. Breech births can cause respiratory problems.

Cesarean deliveries also are performed if the baby is lying crosswise in the uterus, if the baby's head is too large to pass through the mother's pelvis, if the baby develops complications, or if the mother is bleeding vaginally.

The benefits and risks of cesarean sections continue to be debated (Alexander, McIntire, & Leveno, 2001; Green & others, 2001; Peskin & Reine, 2002). Cesarean deliveries are safer than breech deliveries, but they involve a higher infection rate, longer hospital stay, and greater expense and stress that accompany any surgery.

Some critics believe that too many babies are delivered by cesarean section in the United States. More cesarean sections are performed in the United States than in any other country in the world. In the 1980s, births by cesarean section increased almost 50 percent in the United States, with almost one-fourth of babies delivered in this way. In the early 1990s, cesarean births decreased but recently have increased once again (National Center for Health Statistics, 2002).

Low-Birthweight Infants

A **low-birthweight infant** weighs less than 5½ pounds at birth. Two subgroups are those that are very low birthweight (under 3 pounds) and extremely low birthweight (under 2 pounds).

Another way of classifying low-birthweight babies involves whether they are preterm or small for date. **Preterm infants** are those born three weeks or more before the pregnancy has reached its full term. This means that the term "preterm" is given to an infant who is born 35 or less weeks after conception. Most preterm babies are also low-birthweight babies.

A short gestation period does not necessarily harm an infant. It is distinguished from retarded prenatal growth, in which the fetus has been damaged (Kopp, 1992). The neurological development of the preterm baby continues after birth on approximately the same timetable as if the infant were still in the womb. For example, consider a preterm baby born 30 weeks after conception. At 38 weeks, approximately two months after birth, this infant shows the same level of brain development as a 38-week fetus who is yet to be born.

Small for date infants (also called *small for gestational age infants*) are those whose birthweight is below normal when the length of the pregnancy is considered. Small for date infants may be preterm or full term. They weigh less than 90 percent of all babies of the same gestational age. Inadequate nutrition and smoking by pregnant women are among the main factors in producing small for date infants (Chan, Keane, & Robinson, 2001; England & others, 2001).

There has been an increase in low-birthweight infants in the United States in the last two decades (Hall, 2000). The increase is thought to be due to the increasing number of adolescents having babies, drug abuse, and poor nutrition. The incidence of low birthweight varies considerably from country to country (see figure 4.7 on page 132). As shown in figure 4.7, the U.S. low-birthweight rate of 7.6 percent is considerably higher than for many other developed countries (UNICEF, 2001). In the developing world, low birthweight stems mainly from the mother's poor health and nutrition. Diseases such as diarrhea and malaria, which are common in developing countries, can impair fetal growth if the mother becomes infected while she is pregnant. In developed countries, cigarette smoking during pregnancy is the leading cause of low birthweight (UNICEF, 2001). In both developed and developing countries, adolescents who give birth when their bodies have yet to fully mature are at risk for having low-birthweight babies.

Although most low-birthweight infants are normal and healthy, as a group they have more health and developmental problems than normal-birthweight infants

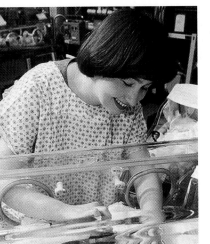

A "kilogram kid," weighing less than 2.3 pounds at birth. *What are some long-term outcomes for weighing so little at birth?*

breech position The baby's position in the uterus that causes the buttocks to be the first part to emerge from the vagina.

low-birthweight infant An infant that weighs less than 5½ pounds at birth.

preterm infants Those born three weeks or more before the pregnancy has reached its full term.

small for date infants Also called small for gestational age infants, these infants' birthweights are below normal when the length of pregnancy is considered. Small for date infants may be preterm or full term.

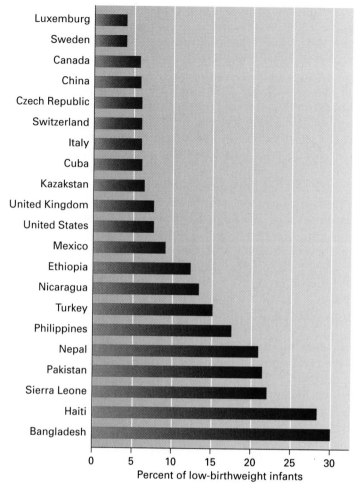

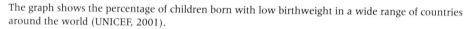

FIGURE 4.7 Low-Birthweight Rates by Country

The graph shows the percentage of children born with low birthweight in a wide range of countries around the world (UNICEF, 2001).

(Hack & others, 2002; Rickards & others, 2001). The number and severity of these problems increase as birthweight decreases (Kilbride, Thorstad, & Daily, 2000). With the improved survival rates for infants who are born very early and very small have come increases in severe brain damage (Yu, 2000). Cerebral palsy and other forms of brain injury are highly correlated with brain weight—the lower the brain weight, the greater the likelihood of brain injury (Watemberg & others, 2002). Approximately 7 percent of moderately low birthweight infants (3 pounds 5 ounces to 5 pounds 8 ounces) have brain injuries. This figure increases to 20 percent for the smallest newborns (1 pound 2 ounces to 3 pounds 5 ounces). Low-birthweight infants are also more likely than normal-birthweight infants to have lung or liver diseases.

At school age, children who were born low-birthweight infants are more likely than their normal-birthweight counterparts to have a learning disability, attention deficit disorder, or breathing problems such as asthma (Taylor, Klein, & Hack, 1994). Very low birthweight children have more learning problems and lower levels of achievement in reading and math than moderately low birthweight children. These problems are reflected in much higher percentages of low-birthweight children being enrolled in special education programs. Approximately 50 percent of all low-birthweight children are enrolled in special education programs.

Not all of these adverse consequences can be attributed solely to low birthweight. Some of the less severe but more common developmental and physical delays occur because many low-birthweight children come from disadvantaged environments (Fang, Madhaven, & Alderman, 1999).

Some of the devastating effects of low birthweight can be reversed (Blair & Ramey, 1996; Shino & Behrman, 1995). Intensive enrichment programs that provide medical and educational services for both the parents and the child have been shown to improve short-term developmental outcomes for low-birthweight children. Federal laws mandate that services for school-age children with a disability (which include medical, educational, psychological, occupational, and physical care) be expanded to include family-based care for infants. At present, these services are aimed at children born with severe congenital disabilities. The availability of services for moderately low birthweight children who do not have severe physical problems varies from state to state, but generally these services are not available.

Tiffany Field's (1998, 2001) research has led to a surge of interest in the role that massage might play in improving the developmental outcomes of low-birthweight infants. In her first study in this area, massage therapy conducted three times per day for 15-minute periods led to 47 percent greater weight gain than standard medical treatment (Field & others, 1986) (see figure 4.8). The massaged infants also were more active and alert, and they performed better on developmental tests. Field and her colleagues have also demonstrated the benefits of massage therapy with women in reducing their labor pain (Field & others, 1997), with cocaine babies (Scafidi & Field, 1996), and with the infants of depressed adolescent mothers (Field & others, 1996)

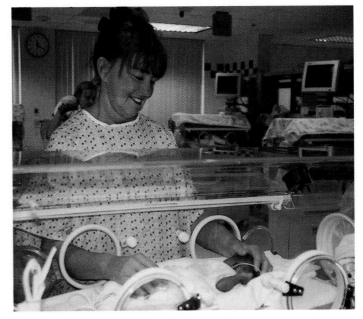

Shown here is Tiffany Field massaging a newborn infant. *What types of infants has massage therapy been shown to help?*

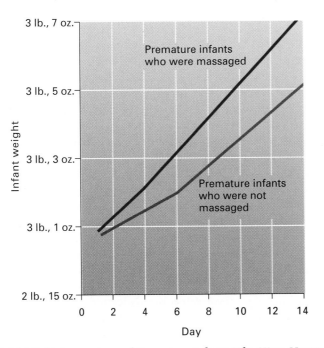

FIGURE 4.8 Weight Gain Comparison of Premature Infants Who Were Massaged or Not Massaged

The graph shows that the mean daily weight gain of premature infants who were massaged was greater than for premature infants who were not massaged.

Score	0	1	2
Heart rate	Absent	Slow—less than 100 beats per minute	Fast—100–140 beats per minute
Respiratory effort	No breathing for more than one minute	Irregular and slow	Good breathing with normal crying
Muscle tone	Limp and flaccid	Weak, inactive, but some flexion of extremities	Strong, active motion
Body color	Blue and pale	Body pink, but extremities blue	Entire body pink
Reflex irritability	No response	Grimace	Coughing, sneezing and crying

FIGURE 4.9 The Apgar Scale

Measures of Neonatal Health and Responsiveness

Almost immediately after birth, a newborn is weighed, cleaned up, and tested for signs of developmental problems that might require urgent attention. The **Apgar Scale** is widely used to assess the health of newborns at one and five minutes after birth. The Apgar Scale evaluates infants' heart rate, respiratory effort, muscle tone, body color, and reflex irritability. An obstetrician or a nurse does the evaluation and gives the newborn a score, or reading, of 0, 1, or 2 on each of these five health signs (see figure 4.9). A total score of 7 to 10 indicates that the newborn's condition is good. A score of 5 indicates there may be developmental difficulties. A score of 3 or below signals an emergency and indicates that the baby might not survive. The Apgar Scale is especially good at assessing the newborn's ability to respond to the stress of delivery, labor, and the new environment (Casey, McIntire, & Leveno, 2001). The Apgar Scale also identifies high-risk infants who need resuscitation.

To evaluate the newborn more thoroughly, the **Brazelton Neonatal Behavioral Assessment Scale** is performed within 24 to 36 hours after birth. This scale measures the newborn's neurological development, reflexes, and reactions to people. When the Brazelton is given, the newborn is treated as an active participant, and the score attained is based on the newborn's best performance. Sixteen reflexes, such as sneezing, blinking, and rooting, are assessed, along with reactions to circumstances, such as the infant's reaction to a rattle. (We will have more to say about reflexes in the next chapter, when we discuss physical development in infancy.) The examiner rates the newborn on each of 27 categories. As an indication of how detailed the ratings are, consider item 15: "cuddliness." Nine categories are involved in assessing this item, and scoring is done on a continuum that ranges from the infant's being very resistant to being held to the infant's being extremely cuddly and clinging. The Brazelton scale is used not only as a sensitive index of neurological competence in the week after birth, but also as a measure in many research studies on infant development. In scoring the Brazelton scale, T. Berry Brazelton and his colleagues (Brazelton, Nugent, & Lester, 1987) categorize the 27 items into four categories—physiological, motoric, state, and interaction. They also classify the baby in global terms, such as "worrisome," "normal," or "superior," based on these categories (Nugent & Brazelton, 2000).

A very low Brazelton score can indicate brain damage, or it can reflect stress to the brain that may heal in time. However, if an infant merely seems sluggish in responding to social circumstances, parents are encouraged to give the infant attention and become more sensitive to the infant's needs. Parents are shown how the newborn can respond to people and how to stimulate such responses. Researchers have found that the social interaction skills of both high-risk infants and healthy, responsive infants can be improved through such communication with parents (Worobey & Belsky, 1982).

Apgar Scale A widely used method to assess the health of newborns at one and five minutes after birth. The Apgar Scale evaluates infants' heart rate, respiratory effort, muscle tone, body color, and reflex irritability.

Brazelton Neonatal Behavioral Assessment Scale A test given several days after birth to assess newborns' neurological development, reflexes, and reactions to people.

Review and Reflect

2 **Discuss the birth process**

REVIEW

- What are the three main stages of birth? What is the transition from fetus to newborn like for the infant? What are some different birth strategies?
- What are the outcomes for children if they are born preterm or with a low birthweight?
- What are two measures of neonatal health and responsiveness?

REFLECT

- If you are a female, which birth strategy do you prefer? Why? If you are a male, how involved would you want to be in helping your partner through pregnancy and the birth of your baby?

3 THE POSTPARTUM PERIOD

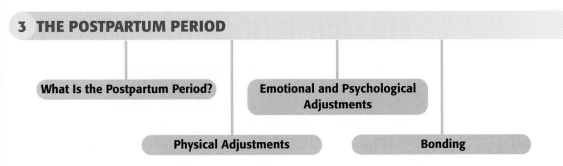

The weeks immediately following childbirth present a number of challenges for new parents and their offspring. Many health professionals believe that the best way to meet these challenges is with a family-centered approach that uses the family's resources to support an early and smooth adjustment to the newborn by all family members.

What Is the Postpartum Period?

The **postpartum period** is the period after childbirth or delivery. It is a time when the woman adjusts, both physically and psychologically, to the process of childbearing. It lasts for about six weeks or until the body has completed its adjustment and has returned to a nearly prepregnant state. Some health professionals refer to the postpartum period as the "fourth trimester." Though the time span of the postpartum period does not necessarily cover three months, the term of "fourth trimester" suggests continuity and the importance of the first several months after birth for the mother.

The postpartum period is influenced by what preceded it. During pregnancy, the woman's body gradually adjusted to physical changes, but now it is forced to respond quickly. The method of delivery and circumstances surrounding the delivery affect the speed with which the woman's body readjusts during the postpartum period.

The postpartum period involves a great deal of adjustment and adaptation (Plackslin, 2000). The baby has to be cared for; the mother has to recover from childbirth; the mother has to learn how to take care of the baby; the mother needs to learn to feel good about herself as a mother; the father needs to learn how to take care of his recovering wife; the father needs to learn how to take care of the baby; and the father needs to learn how to feel good about himself as a father.

postpartum period The period after childbirth when the mother adjusts, both physically and psychologically, to the process of childbirth. This period lasts for about six weeks or until her body has completed its adjustment and returned to a near prepregnant state.

Physical Adjustments

A woman's body makes numerous physical adjustments in the first days and weeks after childbirth. She may have a great deal of energy or feel exhausted and let down. Most new mothers feel tired and need rest. Though these changes are normal, the fatigue can undermine the new mother's sense of well-being and confidence in her ability to cope with a new baby and a new family life.

Involution is the process by which the uterus returns to its prepregnant size five or six weeks after birth. Immediately following birth, the uterus weighs 2 to 3 pounds. By the end of five or six weeks, the uterus weighs 2 to 3½ ounces. Nursing the baby helps contract the uterus at a rapid rate.

After delivery, a woman's body undergoes sudden and dramatic changes in hormone production. When the placenta is delivered, estrogen and progesterone levels drop steeply and remain low until the ovaries start producing hormones again. The woman will probably begin menstruating again in four to eight weeks if she is not breast-feeding. If she is breast-feeding, she might not menstruate for several months to a year or more, though ovulation can occur during this time. The first several menstrual periods following delivery might be heavier than usual, but periods soon return to normal.

Some women and men want to resume sexual intercourse as soon as possible after the birth. Others feel constrained or afraid. A sore perineum (the area between

mhhe●com/
santrockld9

Postpartum Adjustment

Postpartum Resources

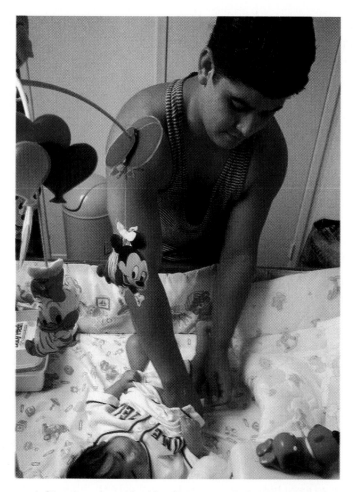

The postpartum period is a time of considerable adjustment and adaptation for both the mother and the father. Fathers can provide an important support system for mothers, especially in helping mothers care for young infants. *As part of supporting the mother, what kinds of tasks might the father of a newborn do?*

the anus and vagina in the female), a demanding baby, lack of help, and extreme fatigue affect a woman's ability to relax and to enjoy making love. Physicians often recommend that women refrain from having sexual intercourse for approximately six weeks following the birth of the baby.

If the woman regularly engaged in conditioning exercises during pregnancy, exercise will help her recover her former body contour and strength during the postpartum period. With a caregiver's approval, the new mother can begin some exercises as soon as one hour after delivery. In addition to recommending exercise in the postpartum period for women, health professionals also increasingly recommend that women practice the relaxation techniques they used during pregnancy and childbirth. Five minutes of slow breathing on a stressful day in the postpartum period can relax and refresh the new mother, as well as the new baby.

Emotional and Psychological Adjustments

Emotional fluctuations are common for mothers in the postpartum period. These emotional fluctuations may be due to any of a number of factors: hormonal changes, fatigue, inexperience or lack of confidence with newborn babies, or the extensive time and demands involved in caring for a newborn. For some women, the emotional fluctuations decrease within several weeks after the delivery and are a minor aspect of their motherhood. For others, they are more long-lasting and can produce feelings of anxiety, depression, and difficulty in coping with stress (Barnes, 2002; Troisi & others, 2002). Mothers who have such feelings, even when they are getting adequate rest, may benefit from professional help in dealing with their problems (Strass, 2002). Here are some of the signs that can indicate a need for professional counseling about postpartum adaptation:

- Excessive worrying
- Depression
- Extreme changes in appetite
- Crying spells
- Inability to sleep

The father also undergoes considerable adjustment in the postpartum period, although in many cases he will be away at work all day, whereas the mother will be at home, at least in the first few weeks. One of the most common reactions of the husband is the feeling that the baby comes first and gets all of the attention. In some marriages, the man may have had that relationship with his wife and now feels that he has been replaced by the baby.

One strategy to help the man's postpartum reaction is for the parents to set aside some special time to be together with each other. The father's postpartum reaction also likely will be improved if he has taken childbirth classes with his wife and is an active participant in caring for the baby.

Important factors for both the mother and the father are the time and thought that go into being a competent parent of a young infant (Cowan & Cowan, 2000; McVeigh, Baafi, & Williamson, 2002). It is important for both the mother and the father to become aware of the young infant's developmental needs—physical, psychological, and emotional. Both the mother and the father need to develop a sensitive, comfortable relationship with the baby.

Some health-care professionals specialize in the postpartum period. To read about the work and career of postpartum specialist Diane Sanford, see the Careers in Life-Span Development insert on page 138.

Bonding

A special component of the parent-infant relationship is **bonding,** the formation of a connection, especially a physical bond between parents and the newborn in the period

bonding The formation of a close connection, especially a physical bond between parents and their newborn in the period shortly after birth.

Careers in Life-Span Development

Diane Sanford, Clinical Psychologist and Postpartum Expert

The information you have read about postpartum adjustment is the focus of Diane Sanford's work. Sanford has a doctorate in clinical psychology and never set out to become a specialist in women's health ◀▥ p. 32. For many years she had a private practice in clinical psychology with a focus on marital and family issues. Then she began collaborating with a psychiatrist whose clients included women with postpartum depression.

For the last 14 years, she has specialized in postpartum problems and other related aspects of female development, including infertility, pregnancy loss, and menopause. Sanford provides clients with practical advice that she believes helps women effectively cope with their problems. She begins by guiding them to think about concrete steps they can take to ease their emotional turmoil during this important postpartum transition. For example, new mothers may need help in figuring out ways to get partners and others to help with their infants. Or they may just need to be reassured that they can handle the responsibilities they face as parents.

After years of practicing on her own, Sanford and a women's health nurse formed Women's Healthcare Partnership five years ago. In addition to the two partners, the staff now

includes a full-time counselor in marriage and family relationships, and a social worker. Nurse educators, a dietician, and a fitness expert work on a consulting basis. Dr. Sanford has also co-authored *Postpartum Survival Guide* (Dunnewold & Sanford, 1994), which reflects her strategies for helping women cope with postpartum issues.

Diane Sanford holding an infant of one of the mothers who comes to her for help in coping with postpartum issues.

shortly after birth. Some physicians believe that the period shortly after birth is critical in development. During this time, the parents and child need to form an important emotional attachment that provides a foundation for optimal development in years to come (Kennell & McGrath, 1999). Special interest in bonding stems from concern by pediatricians that the circumstances surrounding delivery often separate mothers and their infants, preventing or making difficult the development of a bond. The pediatricians argued that giving the mother drugs to make her delivery less painful can contribute to the lack of bonding. The drugs can make the mother drowsy, thus interfering with her ability to respond to and stimulate the newborn. Advocates of bonding also assert that preterm infants are isolated from their mothers to an even greater degree than are full-term infants, thereby increasing their difficulty in bonding.

Is there evidence that such close contact between mothers and newborns is critical for optimal development later in life? Although some research supports the bonding hypothesis (Klaus & Kennell, 1976), a body of research challenges the significance of the first few days of life as a critical period (Bakeman & Brown, 1980; Rode & others, 1981). Indeed, the extreme form of the bonding hypothesis—that the newborn must have close contact with the mother in the first few days of life to develop optimally—simply is not true.

Nonetheless, the weakness of the maternal-infant bonding research should not be used as an excuse to keep motivated mothers from interacting with their infants in the postpartum period. Such contact brings pleasure to many mothers. In some mother-infant pairs—including preterm infants, adolescent mothers, or mothers from disadvantaged circumstances—the practice of bonding may set in motion a climate for improved interaction after the mother and infant leave the hospital.

In recognition of the belief that bonding may have a positive effect on getting the parental-infant relationship off to a good start, many hospitals now offer a *rooming-in* arrangement, in which the baby remains in the mother's room most of the time during its hospital stay. However, if parents choose not to use this rooming-in arrangement, the weight of the research evidence suggests that it will not harm the infant emotionally (Lamb, 1994).

Review and Reflect

3 **Explain the changes that take place in the postpartum period**

REVIEW

- What does the postpartum period involve?
- What physical adjustments does the woman's body make in this period?
- What emotional and psychological adjustments characterize the postpartum period?
- Is bonding critical for optimal development?

REFLECT

- If you are a female, what can you do to adjust effectively in the postpartum period? If you are a male, what can you do to help in the postpartum period?

Reach Your Learning Goals

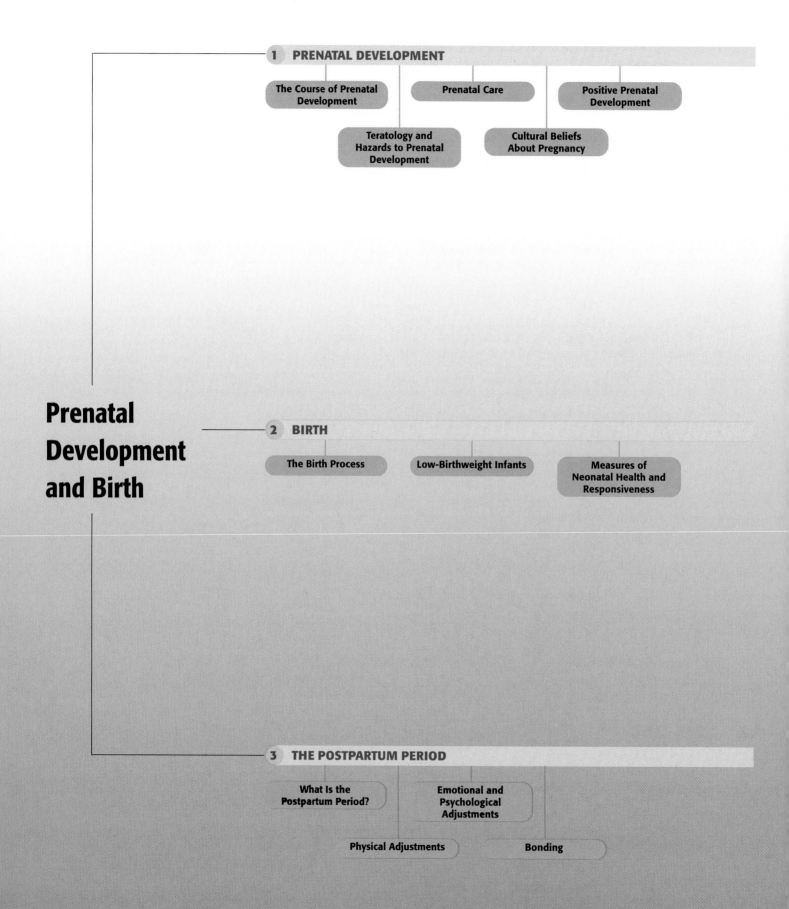

Prenatal Development and Birth

1 PRENATAL DEVELOPMENT

- The Course of Prenatal Development
- Teratology and Hazards to Prenatal Development
- Prenatal Care
- Cultural Beliefs About Pregnancy
- Positive Prenatal Development

2 BIRTH

- The Birth Process
- Low-Birthweight Infants
- Measures of Neonatal Health and Responsiveness

3 THE POSTPARTUM PERIOD

- What Is the Postpartum Period?
- Physical Adjustments
- Emotional and Psychological Adjustments
- Bonding

Summary

1 Describe prenatal development

- Prenatal development is divided into three periods: germinal (conception until 10 to 14 days later), which ends when the zygote (a fertilized egg) attaches to the uterine wall; embryonic (two to eight weeks after conception), during which the embryo differentiates into three layers, life-support systems develop, and organ systems form (organogenesis); and fetal (two months after conception until about nine months, or when the infant is born), a time when organ systems have matured to the point at which life can be sustained outside of the womb.
- Teratology is the field that investigates the causes of congenital (birth) defects. Any agent that causes birth defects is called a teratogen. The dose, time of exposure, and genetic susceptibility influence the severity of the damage to an unborn child and the type of defect that occurs. Prescription drugs that can be harmful include antibiotics, some depressants, and certain hormones. Nonprescription drugs that can be harmful include diet pills, aspirin, and coffee. Fetal alcohol syndrome (FAS) is a cluster of abnormalities that appear in offspring of mothers who drink heavily during pregnancy. When pregnant women drink moderately (one to two drinks a day), negative effects on their offspring have been found. Cigarette smoking by pregnant women has serious adverse effects on prenatal and child development (such as low birthweight). Illegal drugs that are potentially harmful to offspring include marijuana, cocaine, and heroin. Incompatibility of the mother's and the father's blood types can also be harmful to the fetus. Potential environmental hazards include radiation, environmental pollutants, toxic wastes, and prolonged exposure to heat in saunas and hot tubs. Rubella (German measles) can be harmful. Syphilis, genital herpes, and AIDS are other teratogens. A developing fetus depends entirely on its mother for nutrition. One nutrient that is especially important early in development is folic acid. High anxiety and stress in the mother are linked with less than optimal prenatal and birth outcomes. Maternal age can negatively affect the offspring's development if the mother is an adolescent or over 30. Paternal factors that can adversely affect prenatal development include exposure to lead, radiation, certain pesticides, and petrochemicals.
- Prenatal care varies extensively but usually involves medical care services with a defined schedule of visits.
- Specific actions in pregnancy are often determined by cultural beliefs. Certain behaviors are expected if a culture views pregnancy as a medical condition or a natural occurrence. For example, prenatal care may not be a priority for expectant mothers who view pregnancy as a natural occurrence.
- It is important to remember that, although things can and do go wrong during pregnancy, most of the time pregnancy and prenatal development go well. Avoiding teratogens helps ensure a positive outcome.

2 Discuss the birth process

- Childbirth occurs in three stages. The first stage, which lasts about 12 to 24 hours for a woman having her first child, is the longest stage. The cervix dilates to about 4 inches at the end of the first stage. The second stage begins when the baby's head moves through the cervix and ends with the baby's complete emergence. The third stage is afterbirth. Being born involves considerable stress for the baby, but the baby is well prepared and adapted to handle the stress. Anoxia—insufficient oxygen supply to the fetus/newborn—is a potential hazard. Childbirth strategies involve the childbirth setting and attendants. In many countries, a doula attends a childbearing woman. Methods of delivery include medicated, natural and prepared, and cesarean.
- Low-birthweight infants weigh less than $5\frac{1}{2}$ pounds and they may be preterm (born three weeks or more before the pregnancy has reached full term) or small for date (also called small for gestational age, which refers to infants whose birthweight is below norm when the length of pregnancy is considered). Small for date infants may be preterm or full term. Although most low-birthweight infants are normal and healthy, as a group they have more health and developmental problems than normal-birthweight infants.
- For many years, the Apgar Scale has been used to assess the newborn's health. The Brazelton Neonatal Behavioral Assessment Scale examines the newborn's neurological development, reflexes, and reactions to people.

3 Explain the changes that take place in the postpartum period

- The postpartum period is the name given to the period after childbirth or delivery. In this period, the woman's body adjusts physically and psychologically to the process of childbearing. The period lasts for about six weeks or until the body has completed its adjustment.
- Physical adjustments in the postpartum period include fatigue, involution (the process by which the uterus returns to its prepregnant size five or six weeks after birth), hormonal changes, when to resume sexual intercourse, and exercises to recover body contour and strength.
- Emotional fluctuations on the part of the mother are common in this period, and they can vary a great deal from one mother to the next. The father also goes through a postpartum adjustment.
- Bonding is the formation of a close connection, especially a physical bond between parents and the newborn shortly after birth. Early bonding has not been found to be critical in the development of a competent infant.

Key Terms

germinal period 113
blastocyst 113
trophoblast 113
embryonic period 113
placenta 113
umbilical cord 114

amnion 114
organogenesis 114
fetal period 115
teratogen 117
fetal alcohol syndrome
    (FAS) 119

doula 129
natural childbirth 130
prepared childbirth 130
breech position 131
low-birthweight infant 131
preterm infants 131

small for date infants 131
Apgar Scale 134
Brazelton Neonatal Behavioral
    Assessment Scale 134
postpartum period 135
bonding 137

Key People

Christine Dunkel-Schetter 123
Grantley Dick-Read 130

Ferdinand Lamaze 130
T. Berry Brazelton 134

Taking It to the Net

1. Denise's sister, Doreen, is pregnant for the first time. Doreen is not particularly known for her healthy lifestyle. What particular things can Denise encourage Doreen to do in order to give birth to a healthy baby?
2. Sienne told her fiancé, Jackson, that he had better stop smoking before they begin trying to conceive a child. Why is Sienne concerned about Jackson's smoking and its effect on their children before they have even started planning their family?

3. Hannah, who gave birth to a healthy baby boy—her first child—two weeks ago, appears to her husband Sean to be sad, lethargic, and is having trouble sleeping. How can Sean determine if Hannah is just going through a natural period of post-baby "blues" or if she might be suffering from postpartum depression?

Connect to www.mhhe.com/santrockld9 to research the answers and complete these exercises.

E-Learning Tools

To help you master the material in this chapter, you'll find a number of valuable study tools on the Student CD-ROM that accompanies this book. In addition, visit the Online Learning Center for *Life-Span Development*, ninth edition, where you'll find these valuable resources for chapter 4, "Prenatal Development and Birth."

- Learn how alcohol consumption might affect a pregnancy by completing the self-assessment, *Pregnancy Screening for Alcohol Use*.
- Build your decision-making skills by trying your hand at the parenting and education "Scenarios."

Infancy

Babies are such a nice way to start people.
—DON HEROLD
American Writer, 20th Century

As newborns, we were not empty-headed organisms. We had some basic reflexes, among them crying, kicking, and coughing. We slept a lot, and occasionally we smiled, although the meaning of our first smiles was not entirely clear. We ate and we grew. We crawled and then we walked, a journey of a thousand miles beginning with a single step. Sometimes we conformed, sometimes others conformed to us. Our development was a continuous creation of more complex forms. Our helpless kind demanded the meeting eyes of love. We juggled the necessity of curbing our will with becoming what we could will freely. Section 3 contains three chapters: "Physical Development in Infancy" (chapter 5), "Cognitive Development in Infancy" (chapter 6), and "Socioemotional Development in Infancy" (chapter 7).

A baby is the most complicated object made by unskilled labor.

—ANONYMOUS

Physical Development in Infancy

Chapter Outline

PHYSICAL GROWTH AND DEVELOPMENT IN INFANCY

Cephalocaudal and Proximodistal Patterns

Height and Weight

The Brain

Sleep

Nutrition

Toilet Training

MOTOR DEVELOPMENT

Reflexes

Gross and Fine Motor Skills

Dynamic Systems Theory

SENSORY AND PERCEPTUAL DEVELOPMENT

What Are Sensation and Perception?

The Ecological View

Visual Perception

Other Senses

Intermodal Perception

Perceptual-Motor Coupling and Unification

Learning Goals

1 *D*iscuss physical growth and development in infancy

2 *D*escribe infants' motor development

3 *E*xplain sensory and perceptual development in infancy

Images of Life-Span Development
Bottle- and Breast-Feeding in Africa

Latonya is a newborn baby in the African country of Ghana. The culture of the area in which she was born discourages breast-feeding. She has been kept apart from her mother and bottle-fed in her first days of infancy. Manufacturers of infant formula provide the hospital where she was born with free or subsidized milk powder. Her mother has been persuaded to bottle-feed rather than breast-feed her. When her mother bottle-feeds Latonya, she overdilutes the milk formula with unclean water. Latonya's feeding bottles also have not been sterilized. Latonya becomes very sick. She dies before her first birthday.

By contrast, Ramona lives in the African country of Nigeria. Her mother is breast-feeding her. Ramona was born at a Nigerian hospital where a "baby-friendly" program had been initiated. In this program, babies are not separated from their mothers when they are born, and the mothers are encouraged to breast-feed them. The mothers are told of the perils that bottle-feeding can bring because of unsafe water and unsterilized bottles. They also are informed about the advantages of breast milk, which include its nutritious and hygienic qualities, its ability to immunize babies against common illnesses, and its role in reducing the mother's risk of breast and ovarian cancer. At 1 year of age, Ramona is very healthy.

For the past 10 to 15 years, the World Health Organization and UNICEF have been trying to reverse the trend toward bottle-feeding of infants, which emerged in many impoverished countries. They have instituted the "baby-friendly" program in many countries. They also have persuaded the International Association of Infant Formula Manufacturers to stop marketing their baby formulas to hospitals in countries where the governments support the baby-friendly initiatives. For the hospitals themselves, costs actually will be reduced as infant formula, feeding bottles, and separate nurseries become unnecessary. For example, baby-friendly Jose Fabella Memorial Hospital in the Philippines already has reported saving 8 percent of its annual budget.

Hospitals play a vital role in getting mothers to breast-feed their babies. For many years, maternity units favored bottle-feeding and did not give mothers adequate information about the benefits of breast-feeding. With the initiatives of the World Health Organization and UNICEF, things are changing, but there still are many places in the world where the baby-friendly initiatives have not been implemented (Grant, 1993).

It is very important for infants to get a healthy start. In this chapter we will explore these aspects of the infant's development: physical growth, motor development, and sensory and perceptual development.

1 PHYSICAL GROWTH AND DEVELOPMENT IN INFANCY

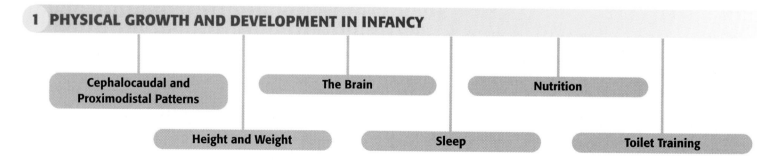

Cephalocaudal and Proximodistal Patterns • Height and Weight • The Brain • Sleep • Nutrition • Toilet Training

Infants' physical development in the first two years of life is extensive. At birth, neonates have a gigantic head (relative to the rest of the body), which flops around uncontrollably. They also possess reflexes that are dominated by evolutionary movements. In the span of 12 months, infants become capable of sitting anywhere, standing, stooping, climbing, and usually walking. During the second year, growth decelerates, but rapid increases in such activities as running and climbing take place. Let's now examine in greater detail the sequence of physical development in infancy.

Cephalocaudal and Proximodistal Patterns

The **cephalocaudal pattern** is the sequence in which the greatest growth always occurs at the top—the head—with physical growth in size, weight, and feature differentiation gradually working its way down from top to bottom (for example, shoulders, middle trunk, and so on). This same pattern occurs in the head area, because the top parts of the head—the eyes and brain—grow faster than the lower parts, such as the jaw. An extraordinary proportion of the total body is occupied by the head during prenatal development and early infancy (see figure 5.1). Later in the chapter you will see that sensory and motor development proceed according to the cephalocaudal principle. For example, infants see objects before they can control their trunk and they can use their hands long before they can crawl or walk.

The **proximodistal pattern** is the sequence in which growth starts at the center of the body and moves toward the extremities. An example of this is the early maturation of muscular control of the trunk and arms, as compared with that of the hands and fingers. Further, infants use their whole hand as a unit before they can control several fingers.

Height and Weight

The average North American newborn is 20 inches long and weighs 7½ pounds. Ninety-five percent of full-term newborns are 18 to 22 inches long and weigh between 5½ and 10 pounds.

In the first several days of life, most newborns lose 5 to 7 percent of their body weight before they learn to adjust to neonatal feeding. Once infants adjust to sucking, swallowing, and digesting, they grow rapidly, gaining an average of 5 to 6 ounces per week during the first month. They have doubled their birthweight by the age of 4

cephalocaudal pattern The sequence in which the greatest growth occurs at the top—the head—with physical growth in size, weight, and feature differentiation gradually working from top to bottom.

proximodistal pattern The sequence in which growth starts at the center of the body and moves toward the extremities.

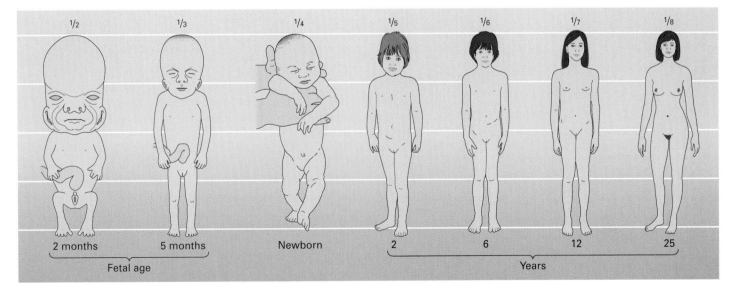

| 1/2 | 1/3 | 1/4 | 1/5 | 1/6 | 1/7 | 1/8 |

| 2 months | 5 months | Newborn | 2 | 6 | 12 | 25 |
| Fetal age | | | Years | | | |

FIGURE 5.1 Changes in Proportions of the Human Body During Growth

As individuals develop from infancy through adulthood, one of the most noticeable physical changes is that the head becomes smaller in relation to the rest of the body. The fractions listed refer to head size as a proportion of total body length at different ages.

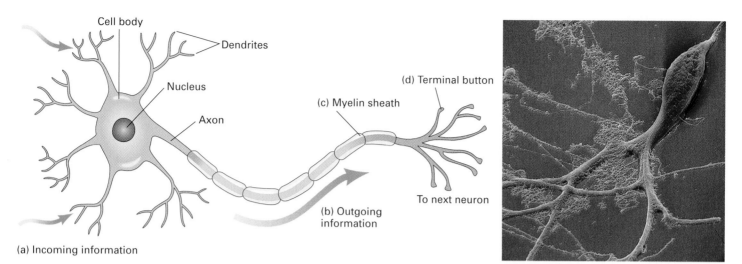

FIGURE 5.2 The Neuron

(*a*) The dendrites of the cell body receive information from other neurons, muscles, or glands through the axon. (*b*) Axons transmit information away from the cell body. (*c*) A myelin sheath covers most axons and speeds information transmission. (*d*) As the axon ends, it branches out into terminal buttons. At the right is an actual photograph of a neuron.

months and have nearly tripled it by their first birthday. Infants grow about 1 inch per month during the first year, reaching approximately 1½ times their birth length by their first birthday.

Infants' rate of growth is considerably slower in the second year of life. By 2 years of age, infants weigh approximately 26 to 32 pounds, having gained a quarter to half a pound per month during the second year; now they have reached about one-fifth of their adult weight. At 2 years of age, the average infant is 32 to 35 inches in height, which is nearly one-half of their adult height.

The Brain

As an infant walks, talks, runs, shakes a rattle, smiles, and frowns, changes are occurring in its brain. Consider that the infant began life as a single cell and nine months later was born with a brain and nervous system that contained approximately 100 billion nerve cells, or neurons. A **neuron** is a nerve cell that handles information processing at the cellular level (see figure 5.2). Indeed, at birth the infant probably has almost all of the neurons it will ever have.

The Brain's Development Among the most dramatic changes in the brain in the first two years of life are the spreading connections of dendrites to each other. Figure 5.3 illustrates these changes.

A *myelin sheath,* which is a layer of fat cells, encases most axons (see figure 5.2). Not only does the myelin sheath insulate nerve cells, but it also helps nerve impulses travel faster. *Myelination,* the process of encasing axons with fat cells, begins prenatally and continues after birth. Myelination for visual pathways occurs rapidly after birth, being completed in the first six months. Auditory myelination is not completed until 4 or 5 years of age. Some aspects of myelination continue even into adolescence.

In addition to dendritic spreading and the encasement of axons through myelination, another important aspect of the brain's development at the cellular level is the dramatic increase in connections between neurons (Ramey & Ramey, 2000). *Synapses* are tiny gaps between neurons where connections between axons and dendrites take place. As the infant develops, synaptic connections between axons and dendrites proliferate (Baudry, 2003).

neuron Nerve cell that handles information processing at the cellular level.

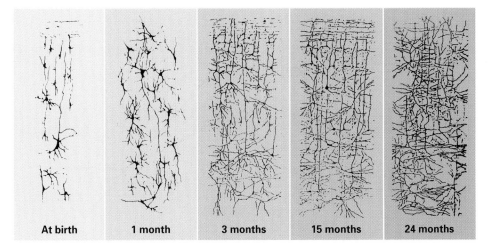

| At birth | 1 month | 3 months | 15 months | 24 months |

FIGURE 5.3 The Development of Dendritic Spreading
Note the increase in connectedness between neurons over the course of the first 2 years of life.

Neural Processes

Researchers have discovered an intriguing aspect of synaptic connections. Nearly twice as many of these connections are made as will ever be used (Huttenlocher & others, 1991; Huttenlocher & Dabholkar, 1997). The connections that are used become strengthened and survive while the unused ones are replaced by other pathways or disappear (Casey, Durston, & Fossella, 2001; Varoqueaux, 2003). That is, these connections will be "pruned," in the language of neuroscience. Figure 5.4 on page 152 vividly illustrates the dramatic growth and later pruning of synapses in the visual, auditory, and prefrontal cortex areas of the brain (Huttenlocher & Dabholkar, 1997). These areas are critical for higher-level cognitive functioning in areas like learning, memory, and reasoning.

As shown in figure 5.4, "blooming and pruning" vary considerably by brain region in humans (Thompson & Nelson, 2001). For example, the peak of synaptic overproduction in the visual cortex occurs at about the fourth postnatal month, followed by a gradual retraction until the middle to end of the preschool years (Huttenlocher & Dabholkar, 1997). In areas of the brain involved in hearing and language, a similar, though somewhat later, course is detected. However, in the prefrontal cortex (the area of the brain where higher-level thinking and self-regulation occur), the peak of overproduction takes place at about 1 year of age and it is not until middle to late adolescence that the adult density of synapses is achieved. Both heredity and environment are thought to influence the timing and course of synaptic overproduction and subsequent retraction.

Using the electroencephalogram (EEG), which measures the brain's electrical activity, researchers have found that a spurt in EEG activity occurs from about 1½ to 2 years of age (Fischer & Bidell, 1998; Fischer & Rose, 1995). Other spurts seem to take place at about 9, 12, 15, and 18 to 20 years of age. Researchers believe that these spurts of brain activity may coincide with important changes in cognitive development. For example, the increase in EEG brain activity at 1½ to 2 years of age is likely associated with an increase in conceptual and language growth.

At birth, the newborn's brain is about 25 percent of its adult weight. By the second birthday, the brain is about 75 percent of its adult weight. However, the brain's areas do not mature uniformly. Some areas, such as the primary motor areas, develop earlier than others, such as the primary sensory areas.

Studying the brain's development in infancy is not as easy as it might seem, because even the latest brain-imaging technologies can't make out fine details and they can't be used on the babies. Positron-emission tomography (PET) scans pose a

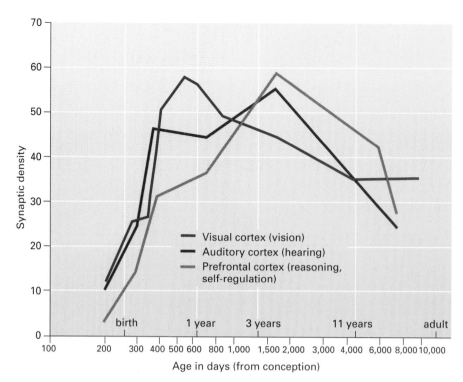

FIGURE 5.4 Synaptic Density in the Human Brain from Infancy to Adulthood

The graph shows the dramatic increase and then pruning in synaptic density for three regions of the brain: visual cortex, auditory cortex, and prefrontal cortex. Synaptic density is believed to be an important indication of the extent of connectivity between neurons.

radiation risk, and infants wriggle too much for magnetic resonance imaging, or an MRI (Marcus, Mulrine, & Wong, 1999). However, one researcher who is making strides in finding out more about the brain's development in infancy is Charles Nelson (1999; deHaan & Nelson, 1999), some of whose research involves attaching up to 128 electrodes to a baby's scalp (see figure 5.5). He has found that even newborns produce distinctive brain waves that reveal they can distinguish their mother's voices from another woman's, even while they are asleep. In other research, Nelson has found that by 8 months of age babies can distinguish the picture of a wooden toy they were allowed to feel, but not see, from pictures of other toys. This achievement coincides with the development of neurons in the brain's hippocampus (an important structure in memory), allowing the infant to remember specific items and events.

The Brain's Lobes and Hemispheres   The highest level of the brain is the forebrain. It consists of a number of structures, including the *cerebral cortex*, which makes up about 80 percent of the brain's volume and covers the lower portions of the brain like a cap. The cerebral cortex plays a critical role in many important human functions, such as perception, language, and thinking.

The cerebral cortex is divided into four main areas called lobes:

- the *frontal lobe* is involved in voluntary movement and thinking.
- the *occipital lobe* is involved in vision.
- the *temporal lobe* is involved in hearing.
- the *parietal lobe* is involved in processing information about body sensations.

The frontal lobe is immature in the newborn. However, as neurons in the frontal lobes become myelinated and interconnected during the first year of life, infants develop an ability to regulate their physiological states (such as sleep) and gain more control over their reflexes. Cognitive skills that require deliberate thinking don't

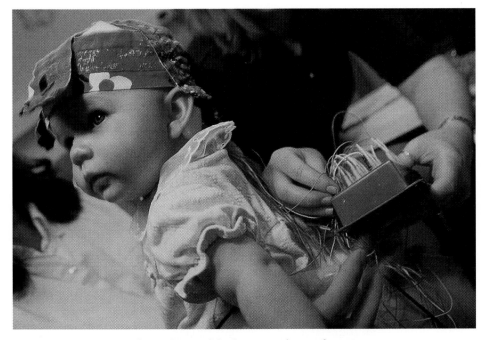

FIGURE 5.5 Measuring the Brain's Activity in Research on Infant Memory

In Charles Nelson's research, electrodes are attached to a baby's scalp to measure the brain's activity to determine its role in the development of an infant's memory. *Why is it so difficult to measure infants' brain activity?*

emerge until later (Bell & Fox, 1992). Indeed, as we saw earlier, the prefrontal region of the frontal lobe has the most prolonged development of any brain region with changes detectable at least into the adolescent years (Johnson, 2001).

The cerebral cortex is divided into two halves, or hemispheres (see figure 5.6). **Lateralization** is the specialization of function in one hemisphere of the cerebral cortex or the other. There continues to be considerable interest in the degree to which each is involved in various aspects of thinking, feeling, and behavior (Hellige, 2003).

The most extensive research on the brain's hemispheres has focused on language. At birth, the hemispheres already have started to specialize: Newborns show greater electrical brain activity in the left hemisphere than the right hemisphere when they are listening to speech sounds (Hahn, 1987). A common misconception is that virtually all language processing is carried out in the left hemisphere. Speech and grammar are localized to the left hemisphere in most people; however, some aspects of language such as appropriate language use in different contexts and the use of metaphor and humor involves the right hemisphere. Thus, language does not occur exclusively in the brain's left hemisphere (Johnson, 2000, 2001).

It is a popular myth that the left hemisphere is the exclusive location of logical thinking and the right hemisphere the exclusive location of creative thinking. However, most neuroscientists agree that complex functions, such as reading, performing music, and creating art, involve both hemispheres. They believe that labeling people as "left-brained" because they are logical thinkers and "right-brained" because they are creative thinkers does not correspond to the way the brain's hemispheres actually work. Such complex thinking in normal people is the outcome of communication between both sides of the brain.

Early Experience and the Brain   Until the middle of the twentieth century, scientists believed that the brain's development was determined almost exclusively by genetic factors. Researcher Mark Rosenzweig (1969) was curious about whether early experiences change the brain's development. He conducted a number of experiments with rats and other animals to investigate this possibility. Animals were randomly

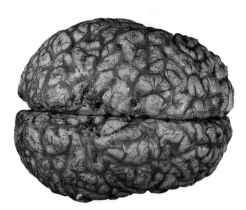

FIGURE 5.6 The Human Brain's Hemispheres

The two halves (hemispheres) of the human brain are clearly seen in this photograph.

lateralization Specialization of function in one hemisphere of the cerebral cortex or the other.

assigned to grow up in different environments. Animals in an enriched early environment lived in cages with stimulating features, such as wheels to rotate, steps to climb, levers to press, and toys to manipulate. In contrast, other animals had the early experience of growing up in standard cages or in barren, isolated conditions.

The results were stunning. The brains of the animals growing up in the enriched environment developed better than the brains of the animals reared in standard or isolated conditions. The brains of the "enriched" animals weighed more, had thicker layers, had more neuronal connections, and had higher levels of neurochemical activity.

Similar findings occurred when older animals were reared in vastly different environments, although the results were not as strong as for the younger animals. Such results give hope that enriching the lives of infants and young children who live in impoverished environments can produce positive changes in their development.

Depressed brain activity has recently been found in children who grow up in a deprived environment (Cicchetti, 2001). As shown in figure 5.7, a child who grew up in the unresponsive and unstimulating environment of a Romanian orphanage showed considerably depressed brain activity compared to a normal child (Begley, 1997).

Scientists also now know that, starting shortly after birth, a baby's brain produces trillions more connections between neurons than it can possibly use. The brain eliminates connections that are seldom or never used. This pruning of brain connections continues at least until about 10 years of age.

The profusion of connections provides the growing brain with flexibility and resilience. Consider 16-year-old Michael Rehbein. At age 4½, he began to experience uncontrollable seizures—as many as 400 a day. Doctors said the only solution was to remove the left hemisphere of his brain where the seizures were occurring. The first major surgery was at age 7 and another at age 10. Recovery was slow but his right hemisphere began to reorganize and take over functions that normally occur in the brain's left hemisphere. One of these functions was speech (see figure 5.8).

Neuroscientists believe that what wires the brain—or rewires it, in the case of Michael Rehbein—is repeated experience (Nash, 1997). Each time a baby tries to

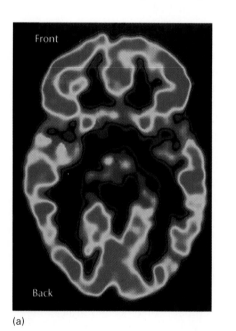 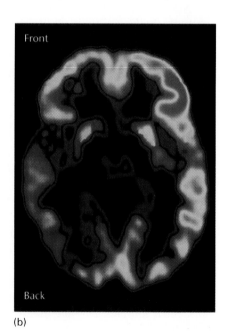

(a) (b)

FIGURE 5.7 Early Deprivation and Brain Activity

These two photographs are PET (positron-emission tomography) scans (which use radioactive tracers to image and analyze blood flow and metabolic activity in the body's organs) of the brains of (*a*) a normal child and (*b*) an institutionalized Romanian orphan who experienced substantial deprivation since birth. In PET scans, the highest to lowest brain activity is reflected in the colors of red, yellow, green, blue, and black, respectively. As can be seen, red and yellow show up to a much greater degree in the PET scan of the normal child than the deprived Romanian orphan.

touch an attractive object or gazes intently at a face, tiny bursts of electricity shoot through the brain, knitting together neurons into circuits. The results are some of the behavioral milestones we discuss in this and other chapters. For example, at about 2 months of age, the motor-control centers of the brain develop to the point at which infants can suddenly reach out and grab a nearby object. At about 4 months, the neural connections necessary for depth perception begin to form. And at about 12 months the brain's speech centers are poised to produce one of infancy's magical moments: when the infant utters its first word.

In sum, neural connections are formed early in life. The infant's brain literally is waiting for experiences to determine how connections are made (Greenough, 2001; Johnson, 2000, 2001). Before birth, it appears that genes mainly direct how the brain establishes basic wiring patterns. Neurons grow and travel to distant places awaiting further instructions. After birth, environmental experiences are important in the brain's development. The inflowing stream of sights, sounds, smells, touches, language, and eye contact help shape the brain's neural connections (Black, 2001).

Sleep

When we were infants, sleep consumed more of our time than it does now. Newborns sleep 16 to 17 hours a day, although some sleep more and others less. The range is from a low of about 10 hours to a high of about 21 hours, although the longest period of sleep is not always between 11 P.M. and 7 A.M. Although total sleep remains somewhat consistent for young infants, their sleep during the day does not always follow a rhythmic pattern. An infant might change from sleeping several long bouts of 7 or 8 hours to three or four shorter sessions only a few hours in duration. By about 1 month of age, many American infants have begun to sleep longer at night, and by about 4 months of age, they usually have moved closer to adultlike sleep patterns, spending the most time sleeping at night and the most time awake during the day (Daws, 2000).

There are cultural variations in infant sleeping patterns. For example, in the Kipsigis culture in the African country of Kenya, infants sleep with their mothers at night and are permitted to nurse on demand (Super & Harkness, 1997). During the day they are strapped to their mother's backs, accompanying them on their daily rounds of chores and social activities. As a result, the Kipsigis infants do not sleep through the night until much later than American infants do. During the first eight months of postnatal life, Kipsigis infants rarely sleep longer than three hours at a stretch, even at night. This contrasts with American infants, many of whom begin to sleep up to eight hours a night by 8 months of age.

REM Sleep   Researchers are intrigued by the various forms of infant sleep. They are especially interested in *REM (rapid eye movement) sleep*. Most adults spend about one-fifth of their night in REM sleep, and REM sleep usually appears about 1 hour after non-REM sleep. However, about one-half of an infant's sleep is REM sleep, and infants often begin their sleep cycle with REM sleep rather than non-REM sleep. By the time infants reach 3 months of age, the percentage of time they spend in REM sleep falls to about 40 percent, and REM sleep no longer begins their sleep cycle. The large amount of REM sleep may provide infants with added self-stimulation, since they spend less time awake than do older children (Zuk & Zuk, 2002). REM sleep also might promote the brain's development in infancy (McNamara, Lijowska, & Thach, 2002). Figure 5.9 on page 156 illustrates the average number of total hours spent in sleep and the amount of time spent in REM sleep, across the human life span. As can be seen, infants sleep far more than children and adults, and a much greater amount of time is taken up by REM sleep in infancy than at any other point in the life span.

Shared Sleeping   There is considerable variation across cultures in newborns' sleeping arrangements. Sharing a bed with a mother is a common practice in many

(a)

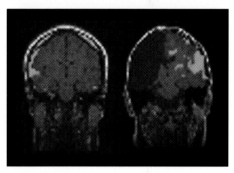
(b)

FIGURE 5.8 Plasticity in the Brain's Hemispheres

(*a*) Michael Rehbein at 14 years of age. (*b*) Michael's right hemisphere (*right*) has reorganized to take over the language functions normally carried out by corresponding areas in the left hemisphere of an intact brain (*left*). However, the right hemisphere is not as efficient as the left, and more areas of the brain are recruited to process speech.

mhhe ○ com/
santrockld9

Development of the Brain

Early Development of the Brain

Early Experience and the Brain

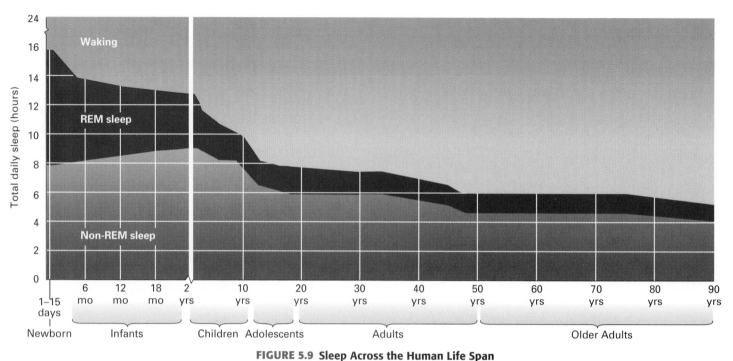

FIGURE 5.9 Sleep Across the Human Life Span

cultures, whereas in others newborns sleep in a crib, either in the same room as the parents or in a separate room. In the United States, sleeping in a crib in a separate room is the most frequent sleeping arrangement for an infant. In one cross-cultural study, American mothers said they have their infants sleep in a separate room to promote the infants' self-reliance and independence (Morelli & others, 1992). By contrast, Mayan mothers in rural Guatemala had infants sleep in their bed until the birth of a new sibling, at which time the infant would sleep with another family member or in a separate bed in the mother's room. The Mayan mothers believed that the co-sleeping arrangement with their infants enhanced the closeness of their relationship with the infants and were shocked when told that American mothers have their baby sleep alone.

Some child experts believe there are benefits to shared sleeping, such as promoting breast-feeding, responding more quickly to the baby's cries, and detecting potentially dangerous breathing pauses in the baby (McKenna, Mosko, & Richard, 1997). However, the American Academy of Pediatrics Task Force on Infant Positioning and SIDS (2000; Cohen, 2000) discourages shared sleeping. The Task Force concluded that in some instances bed sharing might lead to sudden infant death syndrome (SIDS), as could be the case if a sleeping mother rolls over on her baby. One recent study found physiological responses indicative of greater stress in co-sleeping infants than non-co-sleeping infants (Hunsley & Thoman, 2002). Thus, shared sleeping remains a controversial issue, with some experts recommending it, others arguing against it.

SIDS **Sudden infant death syndrome (SIDS)** is a condition that occurs when infants stop breathing, usually during the night, and suddenly die without an apparent cause. Since 1992, The American Academy of Pediatrics has recommended that infants be placed to sleep on their backs to reduce the risk of SIDS. Since that time, the frequency of prone sleeping has decreased from 70 percent to 20 percent of U.S. infants (American Academy of Pediatrics Task Force in Infant Positioning and SIDS, 2000). Some researchers now believe that an inability to swallow effectively in the prone (face down) sleeping position is an important reason SIDS occurs (Jeffery & others, 2000). Researchers have found that SIDS decreases when infants sleep on their backs rather than on their stomachs or sides (Smith & Hattersley, 2000). However,

sudden infant death syndrome (SIDS) A condition that occurs when an infant stops breathing, usually during the night, and suddenly dies without an apparent cause.

SIDS still remains the highest cause of infant death in the United States with nearly 3,000 infant deaths due to SIDS. Risk of SIDS is highest at 4 to 6 weeks of age.

Unfortunately, at this time there is no definitive way to predict which infants will become the victims of SIDS. However, researchers have found that these are risk factors for SIDS (American Academy of Pediatrics Task Force in Infant Positioning and SIDS, 2000; Goldwater, 2001; Kahn & others, 2002; Maas, 1998):

SIDS

- Low-birthweight infants are 5 to 10 times more likely to die of SIDS than are their normal-weight counterparts (Sowter & others, 1999).
- Infants whose siblings have died of SIDS are two to four times as likely to die of it (Lenoir, Mallet, & Calenda, 2000).
- Six percent of infants with sleep apnea, a temporary cessation of breathing in which the airway is completely blocked, usually 10 seconds or longer, die of SIDS (McNamara & Sullivan, 2000).
- African American and Eskimo infants are four to six times as likely as all others to die of SIDS (Pollock & Frohna, 2001).
- SIDS is more common in lower socioeconomic groups (Mitchell & others, 2000).
- SIDS is more common in infants who are passively exposed to cigarette smoke (Pollack, 2001).
- Soft bedding is not recommended (Flick & others, 2001).

Nutrition

Our coverage of infant nutrition begins with information about nutritional needs and eating behavior, then turns to the issue of breast- versus bottle-feeding, and concludes with an overview of malnutrition.

Nutritional Needs and Eating Behavior   The importance of adequate energy and nutrient intake consumed in a loving and supportive environment during the infant years cannot be overstated (Samour, Helm, & Lang, 2000). From birth to 1 year of age, human infants nearly triple their weight and increase their length by 50 percent. Individual differences among infants in terms of their nutrient reserves, body composition, growth rates, and activity patterns make defining actual nutrient needs difficult. However, because parents need guidelines, nutritionists recommend that infants consume approximately 50 calories per day for each pound they weigh—more than twice an adult's requirement per pound.

Some years ago, controversy surrounded the issue of whether a baby should be fed on demand or on a regular schedule. Behaviorist John Watson (1928) argued that scheduled feeding is superior because it increases the child's orderliness. An example of a recommended schedule for newborns was 4 ounces of formula every six hours. In recent years, demand feeding—in which the timing and amount of feeding are determined by the infant—has become more popular.

Today, Americans are extremely nutrition-conscious. Does the same type of nutrition that makes us healthy adults also make young infants healthy? Some affluent, well-educated parents almost starve their babies by feeding them the low-fat, low-calorie diet they eat themselves. Diets designed for adult weight loss and prevention of heart disease may actually retard growth and development in babies. Fat is very important for babies. Nature's food—breast milk—is not low in fat or calories. No child under the age of 2 should be consuming skim milk.

In one investigation, seven babies 7 to 22 months of age were found to be undernourished by their unwitting health-conscious parents (Lifshitz & others, 1987). In some instances, the parents had been fat themselves and were determined that their child was not going to be. The well-meaning parents substituted vegetables, skim milk, and other low-fat foods for what they called junk food. However, for growing infants, high-calorie, high-energy foods are part of a balanced diet.

Human milk, or an alternative formula, is a baby's source of nutrients for the first 4 to 6 months. The growing consensus is that breast-feeding is better for the baby's health, although controversy still swirls about the issue of breast- versus bottle-feeding. *Why is breast-feeding strongly recommended by pediatricians?*

Breast- Versus Bottle-Feeding Human milk or an alternative formula is the baby's source of nutrients and energy for the first 4 to 6 months of life. For years, debate has focused on whether breast-feeding is better for the infant than bottle-feeding. The growing consensus is that breast-feeding is better for the baby's health (Blum, 2000).

What are some of the benefits of breast-feeding? They include these benefits during the first 2 years of life and later (AAP Work Group on Breastfeeding, 1997; Eiger & Olds, 1999; London & others, 2000):

- Appropriate weight gain
- Fewer allergies (Arshad, 2001; Hoppu & others, 2001)
- Prevention or reduction of diarrhea, respiratory infections (such as pneumonia and bronchitis), bacterial and urinary tract infections, and otitis media (a middle ear infection) (AAP Work Group on Breastfeeding, 1997; Kramer & others, 2001; Silfverdal & others, 2002)
- Denser bones in childhood and adulthood (Gibson & others, 2000; Jones, Riley, & Dwyer, 2000)
- Reduced childhood cancer and reduced incidence of breast cancer in mothers and their female offspring (Bernier & others, 2000)
- Lower incidence of SIDS—in one study, for every month of exclusive breast-feeding, the rate of SIDS was cut in half (Fredrickson, 1993)
- Neurological and cognitive development (Brody, 1994)
- Visual acuity (Makrides & others, 1995)

Which women are least likely to breast-feed? They include mothers who work full-time outside of the home, mothers under age 25, mothers without a high school education, African American mothers, and mothers in low-income circumstances (Ryan, 1997). In one study of low-income mothers in Georgia, interventions (such as counseling focused on the benefits of breast-feeding and the free loan of a breast pump) increased the incidence of breast-feeding (Ahluwalia & others, 2000). Increasingly, mothers who return to work in the infant's first year of life use a breast pump to extract breast milk that can be stored for later feeding of the infant when the mother is not present.

The American Pediatric Association strongly endorses breast-feeding throughout the first year of life (AAP Work Group on Breastfeeding, 1997). Are there circumstances when mothers should not breast-feed? Yes, they are (1) when the mother is infected with AIDS, which can be transmitted through her milk, or has another infectious disease; (2) if she has active tuberculosis; or (3) she is taking any drug that might not be safe for the infant (AAP Committee on Drugs, 1994; AAP Work Group on Breastfeeding, 1997).

Some women cannot breast-feed their infants because of physical difficulties; others feel guilty if they terminate breast-feeding early (Mozingo & others, 2000). They might worry that they are depriving their infants of important emotional and psychological benefits. Some researchers have found that there are no psychological differences between breast-fed and bottle-fed infants (Ferguson, Harwood, & Shannon, 1987; Young, 1990). To read about a program that gives infants a healthy start in life, see the Sociocultural Worlds of Development box.

This Honduran child has kwashiorkor. Notice the tell-tale sign of kwashiorkor—a greatly expanded abdomen. *What are some other characteristics of kwashiorkor?*

Malnutrition in Infancy Early weaning from breast milk to inadequate nutrients, such as unsuitable and unsanitary cow's milk formula, can cause protein deficiency and malnutrition.

A Healthy Start

The Hawaii Family Support/Healthy Start Program began in 1985 (Allen, Brown, & Finlay, 1992). It was designed by the Hawaii Family Stress Center in Honolulu, which had been making home visits to improve family functioning and reduce child abuse for more than a decade. Participation is voluntary. Families of newborns are screened for family risk factors, including unstable housing, histories of substance abuse, depression, parents' abuse as children, late or no prenatal care, fewer than 12 years of schooling, poverty, and unemployment. Early identification workers screen and interview new mothers in the hospital. They also screen families referred by physicians, nurses, and others. Because the demand for services outstrips available resources, only families with a substantial number of risk factors can participate.

Each new participating family receives a weekly visit from a family support worker. Each of the program's eight home visitors works with approximately 25 families at a time. The worker helps the family cope with any immediate crisis, such as unemployment or substance abuse. The family also is linked directly with a pediatrician to ensure that the children receive regular health care. Infants are screened for developmental delays and are immunized on schedule. Pediatricians have been educated about the program. They are notified when a child is enrolled in Healthy Start and when a family at risk stops participating.

The Family Support/Healthy Start Program recently hired a child development specialist to work with families of children with special needs. And in some instances, the program's male family support worker visits a father to talk specifically about his role in the family. The support workers encourage parents to participate in group activities held each week at the program center located in a neighborhood shopping center.

Over time, parents are encouraged to assume more responsibility for their family's health and well-being. Families can participate in Healthy Start until the child is 5 and enters public school.

The Hawaii Family Support/Healthy Start Program provides many home-visitor services for overburdened families of newborns and young children. This program has been very successful in reducing abuse and neglect in families. *What are some examples of the home-visitor services in this program?*

Something that looks like milk but is not, usually a form of tapioca or rice, also might be used. In many of the world's developing countries, mothers used to breast-feed their infants for at least two years. To become more modern, they stopped breast-feeding much earlier and replaced it with bottle-feeding. Comparisons of breast-fed and bottle-fed infants in such countries as Afghanistan, Haiti, Ghana, and Chile document that the death rate of bottle-fed infants is as much as five times that of breast-fed infants (Grant, 1997).

Two life-threatening conditions that can result from malnutrition are marasmus and kwashiorkor. **Marasmus** is a wasting away of body tissues in the infant's first year, caused by severe protein-calorie deficiency. The infant becomes grossly underweight, and its muscles atrophy. **Kwashiorkor** is a condition caused by a deficiency in protein in which the child's abdomen and feet swell with water. This disease usually appears between 1 to 3 years of age. Kwashiorkor makes children sometimes appear to be well-fed even though they are not. Kwashiorkor causes a child's vital organs to collect the nutrients that are present and deprive other parts of the body of them. The child's hair also becomes thin, brittle, and colorless. And the child's behavior often becomes listless.

Even if not fatal, severe and lengthy malnutrition is detrimental to physical, cognitive, and social development (Grantham-McGregor, Ani & Fernald, 2001). In some cases, even moderate malnutrition can produce subtle difficulties in development. In one investigation, two groups of extremely malnourished 1-year-old South African infants were studied (Bayley, 1970). The children in one group were given adequate nourishment during the next six years; no intervention took place in the lives of the

marasmus A wasting away of body tissues in the infant's first year, caused by severe protein-calorie deficiency.

kwashiorkor A condition caused by a deficiency in protein in which the child's abdomen and feet become swollen with water.

Careers in Life-Span Development

T. Berry Brazelton, Pediatrician

T. Berry Brazelton is America's best-known pediatrician as a result of his numerous books, television appearances, and newspaper and magazine articles about parenting and children's health ◀▥ p. 34. He takes a family-centered approach to child development issues and communicates with parents in easy-to-understand ways.

Dr. Brazelton founded the Child Development Unit at Boston Children's Hospital and created the Brazelton Neonatal Behavioral Assessment Scale, a widely used measure of the newborn's health and well-being (which you read about in chapter 4). He also has conducted a number of research studies on infants and children and has been president of the Society for Research in Child Development, a leading research organization.

T. Berry Brazelton, pediatrician, with a young child.

**mhhe ● com/
santrockld9**

**Malnutrition in Infancy
Toilet Training**

other group. After the seventh year, the poorly nourished group of children performed much worse on tests of intelligence than did the adequately nourished group. Another study linked the diets of rural Guatemalan infants with their social development at the time they entered elementary school (Barrett, Radke-Yarrow, & Klein, 1982). Children whose mothers had been given nutritious supplements during pregnancy and who themselves had been given more nutritious, high-calorie foods in their first two years of life were more active, more involved, more helpful with their peers, less anxious, and happier than their counterparts who had not been given nutritional supplements. The results suggest how important it is for parents to be attentive to the nutritional needs of their infants.

In further research on early supplementary feeding and children's cognitive development, Ernesto Pollitt and his colleagues (1993) conducted a longitudinal investigation over two decades in rural Guatemala. They found that early nutritional supplements in the form of protein and increased calories can have positive long-term effects on cognitive development. The researchers also found that the relation of nutrition to cognitive performance is moderated both by the time period during which the supplement is given and by the sociodemographic context. For example, the children in the lowest socioeconomic groups benefited more than did the children in higher socioeconomic groups. Although there still was a positive nutritional influence when supplementation began after 2 years of age, the effect on cognitive development was less powerful.

To adequately develop physically, as well as cognitively and socioemotionally, children need a nurturant, supportive environment. One individual who has stood out as an advocate of caring for children is T. Berry Brazelton, who is featured in the Careers in Life-Span Development insert.

Toilet Training

The ability to control elimination depends on both muscular maturation and motivation (Schum & others, 2002). Children must be able to control their muscles to eliminate at the appropriate time, and they must want to eliminate in the toilet or potty, rather than in their pants. Many toddlers are physically able to do this by the time they are about 2 years of age (Bakker & others, 2002; Maizels, Rosenbaum, & Keating, 1999). When toilet training is initiated, it should be accomplished in a warm, relaxed, supportive manner (Michel, 2000).

Many parents today are being encouraged to use a "readiness" approach to toilet training—that is, wait until children show signs that they are ready for toilet training. Pediatricians note that toilet training is being delayed until an older age today more than in earlier generations (American Academy of Pediatrics, 2001). One recent study of almost 500 U.S. children found that 50 percent of the girls were toilet trained by 35 months and 50 percent of the boys by 39 months (Schum & others, 2001).

Some developmentalists argue that delaying toilet training until the twos and threes can make it a battleground because many children at these ages are pushing so strongly for autonomy. Another argument is that late toilet training can be difficult for children who go to day care, because older children in diapers or training pants can be stigmatized by peers.

Review and Reflect

1 Discuss physical growth and development in infancy

REVIEW

- What are cephalocaudal and proximodistal patterns?
- What changes in height and weight take place in infancy?
- What are some key features of the brain and its development in infancy?
- What changes occur in sleep during infancy?
- What are infants' nutritional needs?
- When should toilet training be instituted?

REFLECT

- What three pieces of advice about the infant's physical development would you want to give a friend who has just had a baby? Why those three?

2 MOTOR DEVELOPMENT

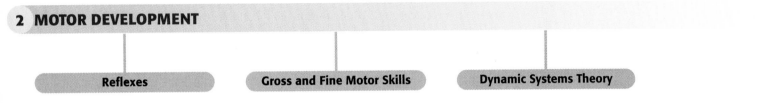

Reflexes   Gross and Fine Motor Skills   Dynamic Systems Theory

The study of motor development has seen a renaissance in the past decade. New insights are being made into the ways in which infants acquire motor skills. We will begin our exploration of motor development by examining reflexes, then turn our attention to gross and fine motor skills. To conclude, we will cover dynamic systems theory, which is responsible for the awakened interest in the ways in which infants acquire motor skills.

Reflexes

The newborn is not a passive, unresponsive organism. Among other things, it has some basic reflexes, which are genetically endowed survival mechanisms. For example, the newborn has no fear of water, naturally holding its breath and contracting its throat to keep water out if it is submerged in water. Reflexes can serve as important building blocks for subsequent purposeful motor activity.

Reflexes govern the newborn's movements, which are automatic and beyond the newborn's control. They are built-in reactions to stimuli. Reflexes provide infants adaptive responses to the environment before infants have had the opportunity to learn. Let's look at several of these reflexes:

- The **sucking reflex** occurs when newborns automatically suck an object placed in their mouth. The sucking reflex enables newborns to get nourishment before they have associated a nipple with food. The sucking reflex is an example of a reflex that is present at birth but later disappears.
- The **rooting reflex** occurs when the infant's cheek is stroked or the side of the mouth is touched. In response, the infant turns its head toward the side that was touched in an apparent effort to find something to suck. The sucking and rooting reflexes disappear when the infant is 3 to 4 months old. They are replaced by the infant's voluntary eating. The sucking and rooting reflexes have survival value for newborn mammals, who must find the mother's breast to obtain nourishment.

*T*he experiences of the first three years of life are almost entirely lost to us, and when we attempt to enter into a small child's world, we come as foreigners who have forgotten the landscape and no longer speak the native tongue.

—Selma Fraiberg
Developmentalist and Child Advocate, 20th Century

sucking reflex A newborn's built-in reaction of automatically sucking an object placed in its mouth. The sucking reflex enables the infant to get nourishment before it has associated a nipple with food.

rooting reflex A newborn's built-in reaction that occurs when the infant's cheek is stroked or the side of the mouth is touched. In response, the infant turns its head toward the side that was touched, in an apparent effort to find something to suck.

- The **Moro reflex** is a neonatal startle response that occurs in response to a sudden, intense noise or movement. When startled, the newborn arches its back, throws back its head, and flings out its arms and legs. Then the newborn rapidly closes its arms and legs to the center of its body. The Moro reflex is a vestige from our primate ancestry, and it also has survival value—it leads the newborn to grab for support while falling. This reflex, which is normal in all newborns, also tends to disappear at 3 to 4 months of age. Steady pressure on any part of the infant's body calms the infant after it has been startled. Holding the infant's arm flexed at the shoulder will quiet the infant.

- The **grasping reflex** occurs in the first three months of life when something touches the infant's palms. The infant responds by grasping tightly.

Some reflexes present in the newborn—coughing, blinking, and yawning, for example—persist throughout life. They are as important for the adult as they are for the infant. Other reflexes, though, disappear several months following birth, as the infant's brain functions mature, and voluntary control over many behaviors develops. The movements of some reflexes eventually become incorporated into more complex, voluntary actions. One example is the grasping reflex. By the end of the third month, the grasping reflex diminishes, and the infant displays a more voluntary grasp, which is often produced by visual stimuli. For example, when an infant sees a mobile whirling above its crib, it may reach out and try to grasp it. As its motor development becomes smoother, the infant will grasp objects, carefully manipulate them, and explore their qualities.

An overview of the main reflexes we have discussed, along with others, is given in figure 5.10.

Sucking is an especially important reflex: It is the infant's route to nourishment. The sucking capabilities of newborns vary considerably. Some newborns are efficient at forceful sucking and obtaining milk; others are not as adept and get tired before they are full. Most newborns take several weeks to establish a sucking style that is coordinated with the way the mother is holding the infant, the way milk is coming out of the bottle or breast, and the infant's sucking speed and temperament.

Moro reflex A neonatal startle response that occurs in reaction to a sudden, intense noise or movement. When startled, the newborn arches its back, throws its head back, and flings out its arms and legs. Then the newborn rapidly closes its arms and legs to the center of the body.

grasping reflex A neonatal reflex that occurs when something touches the infant's palms. The infant responds by grasping tightly.

Reflex	Stimulation	Infant's Response	Developmental Pattern
Blinking	Flash of light, puff of air	Closes both eyes	Permanent
Babinski	Sole of foot stroked	Fans out toes, twists foot in	Disappears after 9 months to 1 year
Grasping	Palms touched	Grasps tightly	Weakens after 3 months, disappears after 1 year
Moro (startle)	Sudden stimulation, such as hearing loud noise or being dropped	Startles, arches back, throws head back, flings out arms and legs and then rapidly closes them to center of body	Disappears after 3 to 4 months
Rooting	Cheek stroked or side of mouth touched	Turns head, opens mouth, begins sucking	Disappears after 3 to 4 months
Stepping	Infant held above surface and feet lowered to touch surface	Moves feet as if to walk	Disappears after 3 to 4 months
Sucking	Object touching mouth	Sucks automatically	Disappears after 3 to 4 months
Swimming	Infant put face down in water	Makes coordinated swimming movements	Disappears after 6 to 7 months
Tonic neck	Infant placed on back	Forms fists with both hands and usually turns head to the right (sometimes called the "fencer's pose" because the infant looks like it is assuming a fencer's position)	Disappears after 2 months

FIGURE 5.10 Infant Reflexes

A study by pediatrician T. Berry Brazelton (1956) involved observations of infants for more than a year to determine the incidence of their sucking when they were nursing and how their sucking changed as they grew older. Over 85 percent of the infants engaged in considerable sucking behavior unrelated to feeding. They sucked their fingers, their fists, and pacifiers. By the age of 1 year, most had stopped the sucking behavior.

Parents should not worry when infants suck their thumb, their fist, or even a pacifier. Many parents, though, do begin to worry when thumb sucking persists into the preschool and elementary school years. As much as 40 percent of children continue to suck their thumbs after they have started school (Kessen, Haith, & Salapatek, 1970). Most developmentalists do not attach a great deal of significance to this behavior and are not aware of parenting strategies that might contribute to it. Individual differences in children's biological makeup may be involved to some degree in the continuation of sucking behavior.

Gross and Fine Motor Skills

Gross motor skills involve large muscle activities, such as moving one's arms and walking. **Fine motor skills** involve more finely tuned movements, such as finger dexterity. Let's examine the changes in gross and fine motor skills in the first two years of life.

Gross Motor Skills   Ask any parents about their baby, and sooner or later you are likely to hear about one or more motor milestones, such as "Cassandra just learned to crawl," "Jesse is finally sitting alone," or "Shauna took her first step last week." It is no wonder that parents proudly announce such milestones. New motor skills are the most dramatic and observable changes in the infant's first year of life. These motor progressions transform babies from being unable to even lift their heads to being able to grab things off the grocery store shelf, to chase the cat, and to participate actively in the family's social life (Thelen, 1995).

At birth, infants have no appreciable coordination of the chest or arms, but in the first month they can lift their head from a prone position. At about 3 months, infants can hold their chest up and use their arms for support after being in a prone position. At 3 to 4 months, infants can roll over, and at 4 to 5 months they can support some weight with their legs. At about 6 months, infants can sit without support, and by 7 to 8 months they can crawl and stand without support. At approximately 8 months, infants can pull themselves up to a standing position, at 10 to 11 months they can walk using furniture for support (this is called cruising), and at 12 to 13 months they can walk without assistance. A summary of the developmental accomplishments in gross motor skills during the first year is shown in figure 5.11 on page 164. The actual month at which the milestones occur varies by as much as 2 to 4 months, especially among older infants. What remains fairly uniform, however, is the sequence of accomplishments. An important implication of these infant motor accomplishments is the increasing degree of independence they bring. Older infants can explore the environment more extensively and initiate social interaction with caregivers and peers more readily than when they were younger.

Although infants usually learn to walk about their first birthday, the neural pathways that control the leg alternation component of walking are thought to be in place from a very early age, possibly even at birth or before (Thelen, 2000). Infants engage in frequent alternating kicking movements throughout the first six months of life when they are lying on their backs. Also, when 1- to 2-month-olds are given support with their feet in contact with a motorized treadmill, they show well-coordinated, alternating steps.

If infants can produce forward stepping movements so early in their first year of life, why does it take them so long to learn to walk? The key skills in learning to walk appear to be stabilizing balance on one leg long enough to swing the other forward

gross motor skills Motor skills that involve large muscle activities, such as walking.

fine motor skills Motor skills that involve more finely tuned movements, such as finger dexterity.

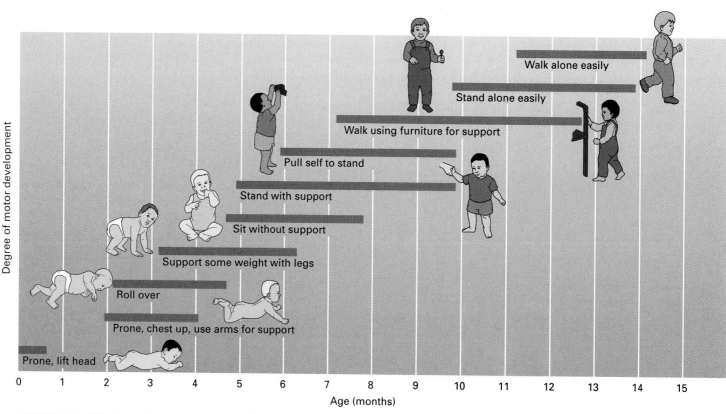

FIGURE 5.11 Milestones in Gross Motor Development

and shifting the weight without falling. This is a difficult biomechanical problem to solve, and it takes infants about a year to do it.

In the second year of life, toddlers become more motorically skilled and mobile. They are no longer content with being in a playpen and want to move all over the place. Child development experts believe that motor activity during the second year is vital to the child's competent development and that few restrictions, except for safety purposes, should be placed on their motoric adventures (Fraiberg, 1959).

By 13 to 18 months, toddlers can pull a toy attached to a string and use their hands and legs to climb up a number of steps. By 18 to 24 months, toddlers can walk quickly or run stiffly for a short distance, balance on their feet in a squat position while playing with objects on the floor, walk backward without losing their balance, stand and kick a ball without falling, stand and throw a ball, and jump in place.

With the increased interest of today's adults in aerobic exercise and fitness, some parents have tried to give their infants a head start on becoming physically fit and physically talented. However, most pediatricians recommend against structured exercise classes for babies. They are seeing more bone fractures and dislocations and more muscle strains in babies now than in the past. They point out that, when an adult is stretching and moving an infant's limbs, it is easy to go beyond the infant's physical limits without knowing it.

Physical fitness classes for infants range from passive fare—with adults putting infants through the paces—to programs called "aerobic" because they demand crawling, tumbling, and ball skills. However, exercise for infants cannot be aerobic, because infants cannot exercise with enough intensity to achieve aerobic benefits.

In most cultures, infants are not exposed to structured physical fitness classes like the ones that are showing up in the United States. However, when parents or other caregivers provide babies with physical guidance by physically handling them in special ways (such as stroking, massaging, or stretching) or providing them with

mhhe ● com/
santrockld9

**Developmental Milestones
Physical Development in Infancy**

opportunities for exercise, the infants often attain motor milestones earlier than infants whose caregivers have not provided these physical activities. For example, Jamaican mothers expect their infants to sit and walk alone two to three months earlier than English mothers do (Hopkins & Westra, 1990). Also, Jamaican mothers regularly massage their infants and stretch their arms and legs, and this is linked with advanced motor development (Hopkins, 1991). In the Gusii culture of Kenya, mothers encourage vigorous movement in their babies (Hopkins & Westra, 1988).

In developing countries, mothers often attempt to stimulate their infants' motor skills more than mothers in more advanced cultures (Hopkins, 1991). This stimulation of infants' motor skills in developing countries may be necessary to improve the infants' chances of survival. In some cases, the emphasis on early stimulation may occur because the caregivers recognize that motor skills are required for important jobs in the culture. Others factors such as climate and spiritual beliefs also may influence the way that caregivers guide their infants' motor development.

Although infants in some cultures, such as Jamaica, reach motor milestones earlier than infants in many cultures, nonetheless, regardless of how much practice takes place, infants around the world reach these motor milestones within the same age range. For example, Algonquin infants in Quebec, Canada, spend much of their first year strapped to a cradle board. Despite such inactivity, these infants still sit up, crawl, and walk within an age range similar to infants in other cultures who have much greater opportunity for activity. In sum, there are slight variations in the age at which infants reach motor milestones depending on their activity opportunities in different cultures, but the variations are not substantial and they are within normal ranges.

Fine Motor Skills Infants have hardly any control over fine motor skills at birth, although they have many components of what later become finely coordinated arm, hand, and finger movements (Rosenblith, 1992). The onset of reaching and grasping marks a significant achievement in infants' functional interactions with their surroundings (McCarty & Ashmead, 1999).

For many years it was believed that reaching for an object is visually guided—that is, the infant must continuously have sight of the hand and the target (White, Castle, & Held, 1964). However, in one study, Rachel Clifton and her colleagues (1993) demonstrated that infants do not have to see their own hands when reaching for an object. They concluded that, because the infants could not see their hand or arm in the dark in the experiment, proprioceptive (muscle, tendon, joint sense) cues, not sight of limb, guided the early reaching of the 4-month-old infants.

The development of reaching and grasping becomes more refined during the first two years of life. Initially, infants show only crude shoulder and elbow movements, but later they show wrist movements, hand rotation, and coordination of the thumb and forefinger. The maturation of hand-eye coordination over the first two years of life is reflected in the improvement of fine motor skills. Figure 5.12 on page 166 provides an overview of the development of fine motor skills in the first two years of life.

The infant's grasping system is very flexible and the environment plays a stronger role in grasping than previously thought. One way to show that the environment influences grasping is to vary the motor task and examine if this influences the infant's responses. This can be done by changing the size and shape of the objects for the infant to grasp. Indeed, infants vary their grip on

A baby is an angel whose wings decrease as his legs increase.
—FRENCH PROVERB

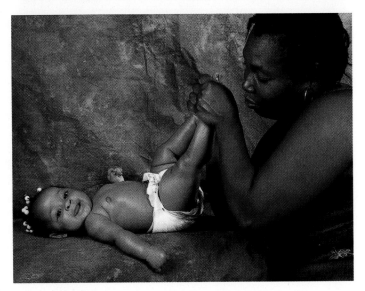

(*Top*) In the Algonquin culture in Quebec, Canada, babies are strapped to a cradle board for much of their infancy. (*Bottom*) In Jamaica, mothers massage and stretch their infants' arms and legs. *To what extent do cultural variations infants activities influence the time at which they reach motor milestones?*

Birth to 6 months	
2 months	Holds rattle briefly
2½ months	Glances from one object to another
3 to 4 months	Plays in simple way with rattle; inspects fingers; reaches for dangling ring; visually follows ball across table
4 months	Carries object to mouth
4 to 5 months	Recovers rattle from chest; holds two objects
5 months	Transfers object from hand to hand
5 to 6 months	Bangs in play; looks for object while sitting

6 to 12 months	
6 months	Secures cube on sight; follows adult's movements across room; immediately fixates on small objects and stretches out to grasp them; retains rattle
6½ months	Manipulates and examines an object; reaches for, grabs, and retains rattle
7 months	Pulls string to obtain an object
7½ to 8½ months	Grasps with thumb and finger
8 to 9 months	Persists in reaching for toy out of reach on table; shows hand preference, bangs spoon; searches in correct place for toys dropped within reach of hands; may find toy hidden under cup
10 months	Hits cup with spoon; crude release of object
10½ to 11 months	Picks up raisin with thumb and forefinger; pincer grasp; pushes car along
11 to 12 months	Puts three or more objects in a container

12 to 18 months	
	Places one 2-inch block on top of another 2-inch block (in imitation)
	Scribbles with a large crayon on large piece of paper
	Turns two to three pages in a large book with cardboard pages while sitting in an adult's lap
	Places three 1-inch cube blocks in a 6-inch diameter cup (in imitation)
	Holds a pencil and makes a mark on a sheet of paper
	Builds a four-block tower with 2-inch cube blocks (in imitation)

18 to 24 months	
	Draws an arc on a piece of unlined paper with a pencil after being shown how
	Turns a doorknob that is within reach, using both hands
	Unscrews a lid put loosely on a small jar after being shown how
	Places large pegs in a pegboard
	Connects and takes apart a pop bead string of five beads
	Zips and unzips a large zipper after being shown how

FIGURE 5.12 The Development of Fine Motor Skills in Infancy

an object depending on its size and shape, as well as the size of their own hands relative to the object's size. Infants grip small objects with their thumb and forefinger (and sometimes their middle finger too) while they grip large objects with all of the fingers of one hand or both hands.

In studies of grasping, age differences occur in regard to which perceptual system is most likely to be used in coordinating grasping. Four-month-olds rely more on touch to determine how they will grip an object; eight-month-olds are more likely to use vision as a guide (Newell & others, 1989). This developmental change is efficient because vision lets infants preshape their hands as they reach for an object. As we see next, such perceptual-motor coupling is an important aspect of dynamic systems theory.

Dynamic Systems Theory

The study of motor development has seen a renaissance in the last decade. Historically, researcher Arnold Gesell (1934), as well as others, gave rich descriptions of motor milestones, but they assumed that they were unfolding as a consequence of a genetic plan. In recent years, it has become recognized that motor development is not the result of nature alone or nurture alone. And there has been a shift to focus on *how* motor skills develop.

Esther Thelen (1995, 2000, 2001) has presented a new theory that reflects the new perspective in motor development. **Dynamic systems theory** seeks to explain how motor behaviors are assembled for perceiving and acting. In this theory, "assembly" means the coordination or convergence of a number of factors, such as the development of the nervous system, the body's physical properties and movement possibilities, the goal the infant is motivated to reach, and the environmental support for the skill. This theory also emphasizes that perception and action work together in the infant's mastery of a skill.

The dynamic systems view contrasts with the traditional maturational view by proposing that even the universal milestones, such as crawling, reaching, and walking are learned through a process of adaptation (Goldfield & Wolff, 2002). It emphasizes exploration and selection in finding solutions to new task demands. In other words, infants modify their movement patterns to fit a new task by exploring and selecting various configurations. The assumption is that the infant is motivated by the new challenge—a desire to get a new toy in one's mouth or to cross the room to join other family members. It is the new task, the challenge of the context, not a genetic program that represents the driving force for change.

Let's look at two babies—Gabriel and Hannah—to see how dynamic systems theory describes and explains their behavior and development (Bower, 1999). Each child improvises ways to reach out with one of their arms from a sitting position and wrap their fingers around a new toy. Gabriel and Hannah make all sorts of split-second adjustments to keep each reaching motion on course. Their rapid arm extension requires holding their bodies steady so that their arm and upper torso don't plow into the toy. Muscles in their arm and shoulder contract and stretch in a host of combinations and

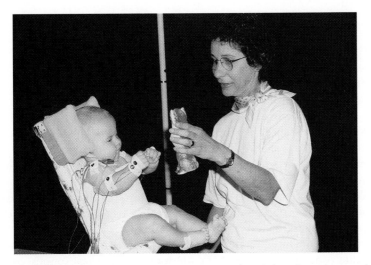

Esther Thelen is shown conducting an experiment to discover how infants learn to control their arms to reach and grasp for objects. A computer device is used to monitor the infant's arm movements and to track muscle patterns. Thelen's research is conducted from a dynamic systems perspective. *What is the nature of this perspective?*

dynamic systems theory The new perspective on motor development in infancy that seeks to explain how motor behaviors are assembled for perceiving and acting.

exert a variety of forces. Their arm movements are not exact, machinelike motions that can be precisely planned out in advance but rather adapt to the goal and context at hand—how to pick up the new toy.

Review and Reflect

2 Describe infants' motor development

REVIEW

- What are some reflexes that infants have?
- How do gross and fine motor skills develop in infancy?
- What is dynamic systems theory?

REFLECT

- Which view of infant motor development do you prefer—the traditional maturational view or the dynamic systems view? Why?

3 SENSORY AND PERCEPTUAL DEVELOPMENT

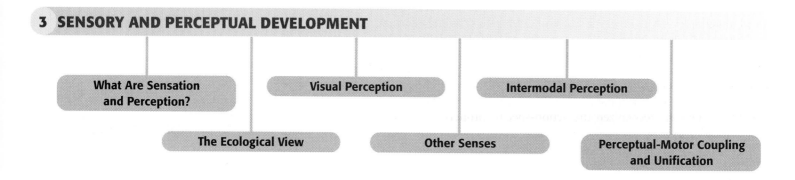

What Are Sensation and Perception?

The Ecological View

Visual Perception

Other Senses

Intermodal Perception

Perceptual-Motor Coupling and Unification

A key theme in the dynamic systems view that we just discussed is that perception and action are coupled when new skills are learned. Keep this idea in mind as you read about sensory and perceptual development (Slater, 2001).

What Are Sensation and Perception?

How does a newborn know that her mother's skin is soft rather than rough? How does a 5-year-old know what color his hair is? How does an 8-year-old know that summer is warmer than winter? How does a 10-year-old know that a firecracker is louder than a cat's meow? Infants and children "know" these things because of their senses. All information comes to the infant through the senses. Without vision, hearing, touch, taste, smell, and other senses, the infant's brain would be isolated from the world; the infant would live in dark silence, a tasteless, colorless, feelingless void.

Sensation occurs when information interacts with sensory receptors—the eyes, ears, tongue, nose, and skin. The sensation of hearing occurs when waves of pulsating air are collected by the outer ear and transmitted through the bones of the inner ear to the auditory nerve. The sensation of vision occurs as rays of light contact the eyes and become focused on the retina.

Perception is the interpretation of what is sensed. The information about physical events that contacts the ears may be interpreted as musical sounds, for example. The physical energy transmitted to the retinas may be interpreted as a particular color, pattern, or shape.

sensation The product of the interaction between information and the sensory receptors—the eyes, ears, tongue, nostrils, and skin.

perception The interpretation of what is sensed.

The Ecological View

In the past several decades, much of the research on perceptual development in infancy has been guided by the ecological view of Eleanor and James J. Gibson (E. J. Gibson, 1969, 1989, 2001; J. J. Gibson, 1966, 1979). They believe that we can directly perceive information that exists in the world around us: We do not have to build up representations of the world in our mind; information about the world is available in the environment. Thus, the **ecological view** states that perception functions to bring organisms in contact with the environment and increase adaptation. In ecological theory, perception is for action. Perception gives people such information as when to duck, when to turn their body through a narrow passageway, and when to put a hand up to catch something.

The Gibsons believe that if complex things can be perceived directly, perhaps they can be perceived even by young infants. Thus, the ecological view has inspired investigators to search for the competencies that young infants possess. Of course, ecological theorists do not deny that perception develops as infants and children develop. In fact, the ecological theorists stress that, as perceptual processes mature, the child becomes more efficient at discovering the properties of objects available to the senses.

For the Gibsons, all objects have **affordances,** which are opportunities for interaction offered by objects that are necessary to perform functional activities. For example, adults immediately know when a chair is appropriate for sitting, a surface is for walking, or an object is within reach. We directly and accurately perceive these affordances by sensing information from the environment—such as the light or sound reflected by the surfaces of the world—and from our own bodies through muscle receptors, joint receptors, skin receptors, and the like. The developmental question, though, is how these affordances are acquired. In one study, infants who were crawlers or walkers recognized the action-specific properties of surfaces (Gibson & others, 1987). When faced with a rigid plywood surface or a squishy waterbed, crawlers crossed both without hesitating. The toddlers, however, stopped and explored the waterbed, then chose to crawl rather than walk across it. Note the coupling of perception and action to adapt to a particular task demand in the world.

In another study, infants who were learning to walk were more cautious about descending a steep slope than younger infants were (Adolph, 1997). The older infants perceived that a slope *affords* the possibility not only for faster locomotion but also for falling.

Visual Perception

Can newborns see? How does visual perception develop in infancy?

Visual Acuity and Color Psychologist William James (1890/1950) called the newborn's perceptual world a "blooming, buzzing confusion." Was James right? A century later, we can safely say that he was wrong. The infant's perception of visual information is far more advanced than was once thought (Slater, 2001).

Just how well can infants see? The newborn's vision is estimated to be 20/400 to 20/800 on the well-known Snellen chart, with which you are tested when you have your eyes examined (Haith, 1991). This is about 10 to 30 times lower than normal adult vision (20/20). By 6 months of age, though, vision is 20/100 or better, and, by about the first birthday, the infant's vision approximates that of an adult (Banks & Salapatek, 1983). Figure 5.13 on page 170 shows a computer estimation of what a picture of a face looks like to an infant at different points in development from a distance of about 6 inches.

Can newborns see color? At birth, babies can distinguish between green and red (Adams, 1989). Adultlike functioning in all three types (red, blue, green) of color-sensitive receptors is present by 2 months of age.

mhhe com/
santrockld9

Perceptual Development

Newborns' Senses

Richard Aslin's Research

International Society on Infant Studies

The infant is by no means as helpless as it looks and is quite capable of some very complex and important actions.

—Herb Pick
Contemporary Developmental Psychologist, University of Minnesota

ecological view The view that perception functions to bring organisms in contact with the environment and to increase adaptation.

affordances Opportunities for interaction offered by objects that are necessary to perform functional activities.

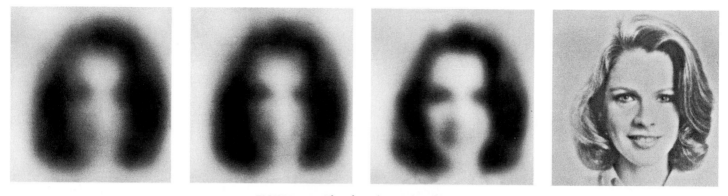

FIGURE 5.13 Visual Acuity During the First Months of Life

The four photographs represent a computer estimation of what a picture of a face looks like to a 1-month-old, 2-month-old, 3-month-old, and 1-year-old (which approximates that of an adult).

Visual Preferences   Robert Fantz (1963) is a pioneer in the study of visual perception in infants. Fantz made an important discovery that advanced the ability of researchers to investigate infants' visual perception: Infants look at different things for different lengths of time. Fantz placed infants in a "looking chamber," which had two visual displays on the ceiling above the infant's head. An experimenter viewed the infant's eyes by looking through a peephole. If the infant was fixating on one of the displays, the experimenter could see the display's reflection in the infant's eyes. This allowed the experimenter to determine how long the infant looked at each display. In figure 5.14, you can see Fantz's looking chamber and the results of his experiment. The infants preferred to look at patterns rather than at color or brightness. For example, they preferred to look at a face, a piece of printed matter, or a bull's-eye longer than at red, yellow, or white discs. In another experiment, Fantz found that younger infants—only 2 days old—look longer at patterned stimuli, such as faces and concentric circles, than at red, white, or yellow discs. Based on these results, it is likely that

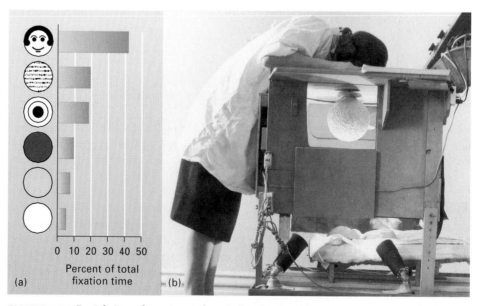

FIGURE 5.14 Fantz's Experiment on Infants' Visual Perception

(*a*) Infants 2 to 3 months old preferred to look at some stimuli more than others. In Fantz's experiment, infants preferred to look at patterns rather than at color or brightness. For example, they looked longer at a face, a piece of printed matter, or a bull's-eye than at red, yellow, or white discs. (*b*) Fantz used a "looking chamber" to study infants' perception of stimuli.

pattern perception has an innate basis, or at least is acquired after only minimal environmental experience. The newborn's visual world is not the blooming, buzzing confusion William James imagined.

Perception of Faces   The human face is perhaps the most important visual pattern for the newborn to perceive. The infant progresses through a sequence of steps to full perceptual appreciation of the face (Gibson, 1969). At about 3½ weeks the infant is fascinated with the eyes, perhaps because the infant notices simple perceptual features such as dots, angles, and circles. At 2 months of age and older, the infant begins to notice the mouth and pay attention to its movements. By 5 months of age the infant has detected other features of the face, such as its three-dimensional surface and the oval shape of the head. Beyond 6 months of age, the infant distinguishes familiar faces from unfamiliar faces—mother from stranger and masks from real faces, for example.

How do young infants scan the human face? In one study, researchers showed human faces to 1- and 2-month-old infants (Maurer & Salapatek, 1976). By use of a special mirror arrangement, the faces were projected as images in front of the infant's eyes so that the infant's eye movements could be photographed. Figure 5.15 shows the plotting of eye fixations of a 1-month-old and a 2-month-old infant. Notice that the 1-month-old scanned only a few portions of the entire face—a narrow segment of the chin and two spots on the head. The 2-month-old scanned a much wider area of the face—the mouth, the eyes, and a large portion of the head. The older infant also spent more time examining the internal details of the face, while the younger infant concentrated more on the outer contour of the face.

Depth Perception   How early can infants perceive depth? To investigate this question, infant perception researchers Eleanor Gibson and Richard Walk (1960) conducted a classic experiment. They constructed a miniature cliff with a drop-off covered by glass. The motivation for this experiment arose when Gibson was eating a picnic lunch on the edge of the Grand Canyon. She wondered whether an infant looking over the canyon's rim would perceive the dangerous drop-off and back up. In their laboratory, Gibson and Walk placed infants on the edge of a visual cliff and had their mothers coax them to crawl onto the glass (see figure 5.16). Most infants would not crawl out on the glass, choosing instead to remain on the shallow side, indicating that they could perceive depth. However, because the 6- to 14-month-old infants had extensive visual experience, this research did not answer the question of whether depth perception is innate.

Exactly how early in life does depth perception develop? Since younger infants do not crawl, this question is difficult to answer. Research with 2- to 4-month-old infants shows differences in heart rate when they are placed directly on the deep side of the visual cliff instead of on the shallow side (Campos, Langer, & Krowitz, 1970). However, an alternative interpretation is that young infants respond to differences in some visual characteristics of the deep and shallow cliffs, with no actual knowledge of depth.

Visual Expectations   Infants not only see forms and figures at an early age but also develop expectations about future events in their world by the time they are 3 months of age. Marshall Haith and his colleagues (Canfield & Haith, 1991; Haith, Hazen, & Goodman, 1988) studied whether babies would form expectations about where an interesting picture would appear. The pictures were presented to the infants in either a regularly

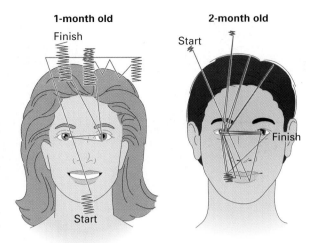

FIGURE 5.15 How 1- and 2-Month-Old Infants Scan the Human Face

FIGURE 5.16   Examining Infants' Depth Perception on the Visual Cliff

Eleanor Gibson and Richard Walk (1960) found that most infants would not crawl out on the glass, which indicated that they had depth perception.

FIGURE 5.17 The Young Infant's Knowledge of the Perceptual World

A 4-month-old in Elizabeth Spelke's infant perception laboratory is tested to determine if it knows that an object in motion will not stop in midair.

Elizabeth Spelke's Research

alternating sequence—such as left, right, left, right—or an unpredictable sequence—such as right, right, left, right. When the sequence was predictable, the 3-month-old infants began to anticipate the location of the picture, looking at the side on which it was expected to appear. The young infants formed this visual expectation in less than one minute. However, younger infants did not develop expectations about where a picture would be presented.

Elizabeth Spelke (1988, 1991) also has demonstrated that young infants form visual expectations. She placed babies before a puppet stage and showed them a series of unexpected actions—for example, a ball seemed to roll through a solid barrier, another seemed to leap between two platforms, and a third appeared to hang in midair (Spelke, 1979) (see figure 5.17). Spelke measured the babies' looking times and recorded longer intervals for unexpected than expected actions. She concluded that, by 4 months of age, even though infants do not yet have the ability to talk about objects, move around objects, manipulate objects, or even see objects with high resolution, they can recognize where a moving object is when it has left their visual field and can infer where it should be when it comes into their sight again.

Other Senses

Considerable development also takes place in other sensory systems during infancy. We will explore development in hearing, touch and pain, smell, and taste.

Hearing Can the fetus hear? What is the newborn's hearing like? What types of auditory stimulation should be used with infants at different points in the first year?

In the last few months of pregnancy, the fetus can hear sounds: the mother's voice, music, and so on (Kisilevsky, 1995). Given that the fetus can hear sounds, two psychologists wanted to find out if listening to Dr. Seuss' classic story *The Cat in the Hat*, while still in the mother's womb, would produce a preference for hearing the story after birth (DeCasper & Spence, 1986). Sixteen pregnant women read *The Cat in the Hat* to their fetuses twice a day over the last six weeks of their pregnancies. When the babies were born, their mothers read *The Cat in the Hat* or a story with a different rhyme and pace, *The King, the Mice and the Cheese* (which was not read to them during prenatal development). The infants sucked on a nipple in a different way when the mothers read *The Cat in the Hat*, suggesting that the infants recognized its pattern and tone (to which they had been exposed prenatally) (see figure 5.18).

Two important conclusions can be drawn from this investigation. First, it reveals how ingenious scientists have become at assessing the development not only of infants but of fetuses as well, in this case discovering a way to "interview" newborn babies who cannot yet talk. Second, it reveals the remarkable ability of an infant's brain to learn even before birth. However, conclusions from this study should not be overdrawn. It does not suggest that reading to an infant prenatally will produce a child who acquires language and cognitive development more rapidly.

Immediately after birth, infants can hear, although their sensory thresholds are somewhat higher than those of adults (Slater, Field, & Hernandez-Reif, 2002; Trehub & others, 1991). That is, a stimulus must be louder to be heard by a newborn than by an adult. Also, in one study, as infants aged from 8 to 28 weeks, they became more proficient at localizing sounds (Morrongiello, Fenwick, & Chance, 1990).

Babies are born into the world prepared to respond to the sounds of any human language. Even very young infants can discriminate subtle phonetic differences, such as those between the speech sounds of *ba* and *ga*. Young infants also will suck more

FIGURE 5.18 Hearing in the Womb

(*a*) Pregnant mothers read *The Cat in the Hat* to their fetuses during the last few months of pregnancy. (*b*) When they were born, the babies preferred listening to a recording of their mothers reading *The Cat in the Hat*, as evidenced by their sucking on a nipple that produced this recording, rather than another story, *The King, the Mice and the Cheese*.

rapidly on a nipple in order to listen to some sounds rather than others (Flohr & others, 2001; Mehler & others, 1988; Spence & DeCasper, 1987):

- A recording of their mother's voice is preferred to the voice of an unfamiliar woman.
- Their mother's native language is preferred to a foreign language.
- The classical music of Beethoven is preferred to the rock music of Aerosmith.

And an interesting developmental change occurs during the first year of life. Six-month-old infants can discriminate phonetic sound contrasts from languages to which they have never been exposed, but they lose this discriminative ability by their first birthday. This finding demonstrates that experience with a specific language is necessary for retaining this ability (Werker & LaLonde, 1988).

Touch and Pain   Do newborns respond to touch? Can newborns feel pain?

Touch   Newborns respond to touch. A touch to the cheek produces a turning of the head, whereas a touch to the lips produces sucking movements. An important ability that develops in infancy is to connect information about vision with information about touch. One-year-olds clearly can do this, and it appears that 6-month-olds can, too (Acredolo & Hake, 1982). Whether still younger infants can coordinate vision and touch is yet to be determined.

Pain   It once was thought that newborns are indifferent to pain, but we now know that is not true. The main research that has documented newborns' sensitivity to pain involves male infants' stressful reactions to being circumcised (Gunnar, Malone, & Fisch, 1987). For example, newborn males show a higher level of cortisol (a hormonal response to stress) after circumcision than prior to the surgery. As a consequence, anesthesia now is used in some cases of circumcision (Taddio & others, 1997).

For many years, doctors have performed operations on newborns without anesthesia. This medical practice was accepted because of the dangers of anesthesia and the supposition that newborns do not feel pain. Recently, as researchers have convincingly demonstrated that newborns can feel pain, the long-standing practice of operating on newborns without anesthesia is being challenged.

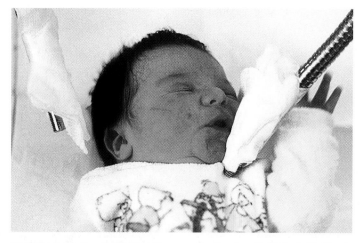

FIGURE 5.19 Newborns' Preference for the Smell of Their Mother's Breast Pad

In the experiment by MacFarlane (1975), 6-day-old infants preferred to smell their mother's breast pad rather than a clean one that had never been used, but 2-day-old infants did not show the preference, indicating that this odor preference requires several days of experience to develop.

Smell Newborns can differentiate odors. For example, by the expressions on their faces, they seem to indicate that they like the smell of vanilla and strawberry but do not like the smell of rotten eggs and fish (Steiner, 1979). In one investigation, young infants who were breast-fed showed a clear preference for smelling their mother's breast pad when they were 6 days old (MacFarlane, 1975) (see figure 5.19). However, when they were 2 days old, they did not show this preference (compared to a clean breast pad), indicating that they require several days of experience to recognize this odor.

Taste Sensitivity to taste might be present before birth. When saccharin was added to the amniotic fluid of a near-term fetus, increased swallowing was observed (Windle, 1940). In one study, even at only 2 hours of age, babies made different facial expressions when they tasted sweet, sour, and bitter solutions (Rosenstein & Oster, 1988) (see figure 5.20). At about 4 months of age, infants begin to prefer salty tastes, which as newborns they were averse to (Harris, Thomas, & Booth, 1990).

Intermodal Perception

Imagine yourself playing basketball or tennis. You are experiencing many visual inputs: the ball coming and going, other players moving around, and so on. You are also experiencing many auditory inputs: the sound of the ball bouncing or being hit, the grunts and groans, and so on. There is good correspondence between much of the visual and auditory information: When you see the ball bounce, you hear a bouncing sound; when a player stretches to hit a ball, you hear a groan.

We live in a world of objects and events that can be seen, heard, and felt. When mature observers simultaneously look and listen to an event, they experience a unitary episode. All of this is so commonplace that it scarcely seems worth mentioning, but consider the task of very young infants with little practice at perceiving. Can they put vision and sound together as precisely as adults do?

Intermodal perception is the ability to relate and integrate information about two or more sensory modalities, such as vision and hearing. To test intermodal perception, Elizabeth Spelke (1979) showed 4-month-old infants two films simultaneously. In each film, a puppet jumped up and down, but in one of the films the sound track matched the puppet's dancing movements; in the other film, it did not. By measuring the infants' gaze, Spelke found that the infants looked more at the puppet whose actions were synchronized with the sound track, suggesting that they recognized the visual-sound correspondence. Young infants can also coordinate visual-auditory information involving people (Condry, Smuth, & Spelke, 2001). In one study, infants as young as 3½ months old looked more at their mother when they also heard her voice and longer at their father when they also heard his voice (Spelke & Owsley, 1979).

Might auditory-visual relations be coordinated even in newborns? Newborns do turn their eyes and their head toward the sound of a voice or rattle when the sound is maintained for several seconds (Clifton & others, 1981), but the newborn can localize a sound and look at an object only in a crude way (Bechtold, Bushnell, & Salapatek, 1979). Improved accuracy at auditory-visual coordination likely requires a sharpening through experience with visual and auditory stimuli. Nonetheless, although at a crude level, auditory-visual intermodal perception appears to be present at birth, likely having evolutionary value.

In sum, crude exploratory forms of intermodal perception exist in newborns. These exploratory forms of intermodal perception become sharpened with experience in the first year of life. In the first 6 months, infants have difficulty forming mental representations that connect sensory input from different modes, but in the second half of the first year they show an increased ability to make this connection mentally.

intermodal perception The ability to relate and integrate information about two or more sensory modalities, such as vision and hearing.

Thus, babies come into the world with some innate abilities to perceive relations among sensory modalities, but their intermodal abilities improve considerably through experience. As with all aspects of development, in perceptual development, nature and nurture interact and cooperate.

Perceptual-Motor Coupling and Unification

For the most part our discussion of motor development and sensory/perceptual development have been separated in this chapter. Indeed, the main thrust of research in many studies has been to discover how perception guides action. A less well studied but important issue is how action shapes perception. Motor activities might be crucial because they provide the means for exploring the world and learning about its properties. Only by moving one's eyes, head, hands, and arms and by traversing from one location to another can individuals fully experience their environment and learn to effectively adapt to it.

The distinction between perceiving and doing has been a time-honored tradition in psychology. However, a number of contemporary experts on perceptual and motor development question this distinction (Bornstein & Arterberry, 1999; Lochman, 2000; Pick, 1997; Thelen, 2000, 2001). For example, Esther Thelen (1995) argues that individuals perceive in order to move and move in order to perceive. Thus, there is an increasing belief that perceptual and motor development do not occur in isolation from one another but, rather, are coupled.

Babies are continually coordinating their movements with concurrent perceptual information to learn how to maintain balance, reach for objects in space, and locomote across various surfaces and terrains (Thelen, 2001). To illustrate how infants are motivated to move by what they perceive, consider the sight of an attractive object across the room. In this situation, infants must perceive the current state of their bodies and learn how to use their limbs to get to the goal object. Although their movements at first are awkward and uncoordinated, babies soon learn to select patterns that are appropriate for reaching their goals. Equally important is the other part of the perception-action coupling: action educates perception. For example, watching an object while exploring it manually helps infants to visually discriminate its properties of texture, size, and hardness. Locomoting in the environment teaches babies how objects and people look from different perspectives or whether surfaces will support their weight.

Also think about how often during each day you need to coordinate perceptual input with motor actions to accomplish what you want to do. For example, right now I am looking at my computer screen (perceiving) to make sure the words are appearing accurately as I am typing them (motorically). We develop this ability by physically exploring the world revealed to us by sensation and perception, thus experiencing new sensations and perceptions to be explored.

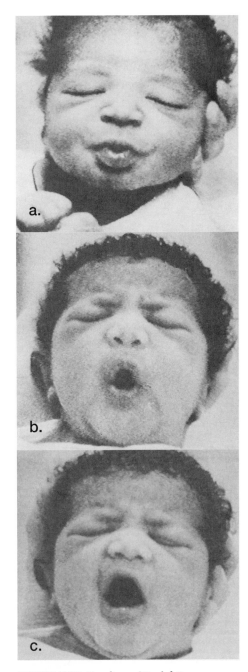

FIGURE 5.20 Newborns' Facial Responses to Basic Tastes

Facial expressions elicited by (*a*) a sweet solution, (*b*) a sour solution, and (*c*) a bitter solution.

Review and Reflect

3 **Explain sensory and perceptual development in infancy**

REVIEW

- What are sensation and perception?
- What is the ecological view of perception?
- How does visual perception develop in infancy?
- How do hearing, touch and pain, smell, and taste develop in infancy?
- What is intermodal perception?
- How is perceptual-motor development coupled and unified?

REFLECT

- How much sensory stimulation should caregivers provide for infants? A little? A lot? Could an infant be given too much sensory stimulation? Explain.

Reach Your Learning Goals

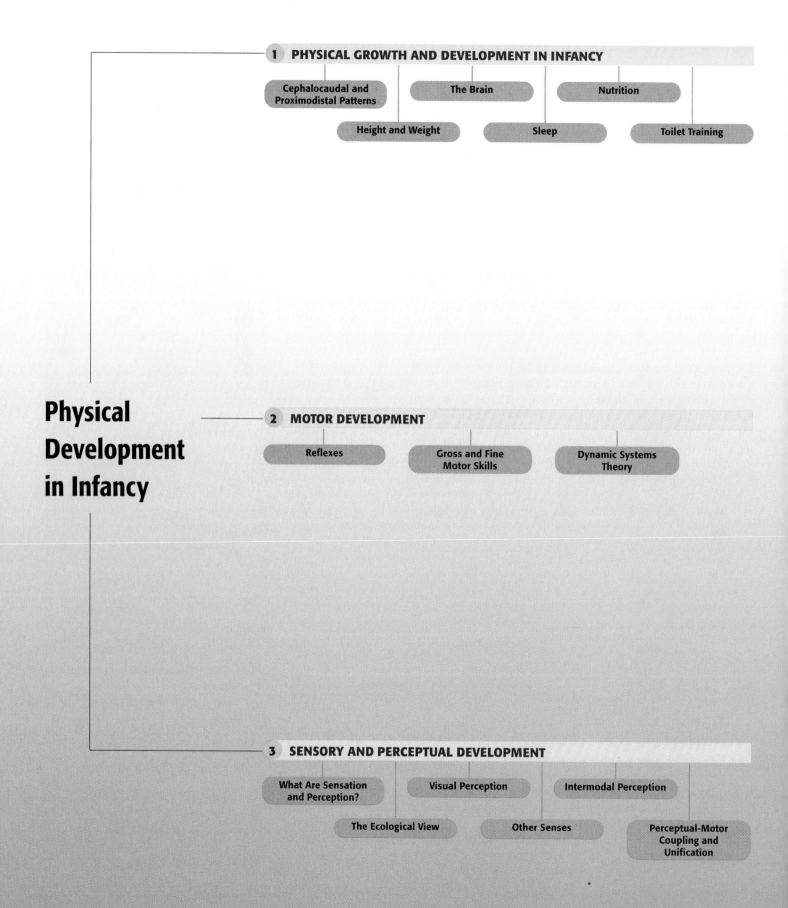

Physical Development in Infancy

1 PHYSICAL GROWTH AND DEVELOPMENT IN INFANCY

- Cephalocaudal and Proximodistal Patterns
- Height and Weight
- The Brain
- Sleep
- Nutrition
- Toilet Training

2 MOTOR DEVELOPMENT

- Reflexes
- Gross and Fine Motor Skills
- Dynamic Systems Theory

3 SENSORY AND PERCEPTUAL DEVELOPMENT

- What Are Sensation and Perception?
- The Ecological View
- Visual Perception
- Other Senses
- Intermodal Perception
- Perceptual-Motor Coupling and Unification

Summary

1 Discuss physical growth and development in infancy

- The cephalocaudal pattern is the sequence in which growth proceeds from top to bottom. The proximodistal pattern is the sequence in which growth starts at the center of the body and moves toward the extremities.
- The average North American newborn is 20 inches long and weighs 7½ pounds. Infants grow about 1 inch per month in the first year and nearly triple their weight by their first birthday. The rate of growth slows in the second year.
- One of the most dramatic changes in the brain in the first two years of life is dendritic spreading. Myelination continues through infancy and even into adolescence. The cerebral cortex has two hemispheres (left and right). Lateralization refers to the specialization of function in one hemisphere or the other. Research with animals suggests that the environment plays a key role in early brain development. Neural connections are formed early in an infant's life. Before birth, genes mainly direct neurons to different locations. After birth, the inflowing stream of sights, sounds, smells, touches, language, and eye contact help shape the brain's neural connections.
- Newborns usually sleep 16 to 17 hours a day. By 4 months of age, many American infants approach adultlike sleeping patterns. REM sleep—during which dreaming occurs—is present more in early infancy than in childhood and adulthood. Sleeping arrangements for infants vary across cultures. In America, infants are more likely to sleep alone than in many other cultures. Some experts believe shared sleeping can lead to sudden infant death syndrome (SIDS), a condition that occurs when a sleeping infant suddenly stops breathing and dies without an apparent cause.
- Infants need to consume about 50 calories per day for each pound they weigh. The growing consensus is that breast-feeding is superior to bottle-feeding. Severe infant malnutrition is still prevalent in many parts of the world. A special concern in impoverished countries is early weaning from breast milk.
- Toilet training is expected to be attained by about 3 years of age in North America. Toilet training should be carried out in a relaxed, supportive manner.

2 Describe infants' motor development

- The newborn is not a passive organism. Reflexes (automatic movements, such as the rooting reflex and the Moro reflex) govern the newborn's behavior. For infants, sucking is an especially important reflex because it provides a means of obtaining nutrition.
- Gross motor skills involve large muscle activities, such as moving one's arms and walking. A number of gross motor milestones occur in infancy although the actual month of these milestones may vary as much as 2 to 4 months, especially in older infants. Although, infants usually learn to walk by their first birthday, the neural pathways that allow walking begin to form earlier. Fine motor skills involve movements that are more finely tuned than gross motor skills. A number of fine motor milestones occur in infancy. The development of reaching and grasping becomes more refined during the first two years of life.
- Dynamic systems theory seeks to explain how motor behaviors are assembled for perceiving and acting. This approach emphasizes the importance of exploration and selection in finding solutions to new task demands. A key theme is that perception and action are coupled when new skills are learned.

3 Explain sensory and perceptual development in infancy

- Sensation occurs when information interacts with the sensory receptors—the eyes, ears, tongue, nose, and skin. Perception is the interpretation of what is sensed.
- In the ecological view, perception functions to bring organisms in contact with the environment and increase adaptation.
- William James was wrong in belief that the newborn's visual world is a "blooming, buzzing confusion." Newborns can see and can distinguish colors, and they prefer to look at patterns rather than at color or brightness. In Fantz's pioneering research, infants only 2 days old looked longer at patterned stimuli, such as faces, than at single-colored discs. The human face is one of the most important visual patterns for infants to perceive and they show developmental changes in how they perceive faces. A classic study by Gibson and Walk demonstrated through the use of the visual cliff that infants as young as 6 months of age have depth perception. Haith has demonstrated that infants develop expectations about future events in their world by the time they are 3 months of age.
- The fetus can hear in the last few months before birth. Immediately after birth, a newborn can hear, and its sensory threshold is higher than that of adults. Newborns respond to touch and can feel pain.
- Intermodal perception is the ability to relate and integrate information about two or more sensory modalities, such as vision and hearing. Spelke's research demonstrated that infants as young as 3½ months of age can link visual and auditory stimuli.
- A time-honored belief in psychology has been that perceptual and motor development are distinct. Increasingly, it is believed that perceptual-motor development is coupled and unified. For example, infants perceive in order to move and move in order to perceive. Babies are continually coordinating their movements with concurrent information to learn how to maintain balance, reach for objects, and locomote.

Key Terms

cephalocaudal pattern 149
proximodistal pattern 149
neuron 150
lateralization 153
sudden infant death syndrome
    (SIDS) 156

marasmus 159
kwashiorkor 159
sucking reflex 161
rooting reflex 161
Moro reflex 162
grasping reflex 162

gross motor skills 163
fine motor skills 163
dynamic systems theory 167
sensation 168
perception 168
ecological view 169

affordances 169
intermodal perception 174

Key People

Charles Nelson 152
Mark Rosenzweig 153
Ernesto Pollitt 159
T. Berry Brazelton 160, 163

Rachel Clifton 165
Esther Thelen 167, 175
Eleanor and James J.
    Gibson 169

William James 169
Robert Fantz 170
Richard Walk 171
Marshall Haith 171

Elizabeth Spelke 172, 174

Taking It to the Net

1. Professor Samuels asked his life-span psychology students to write a one-page report explaining how a child's brain develops during infancy and what role parents play in fostering maximal brain development. What should this report contain that would provide a comprehensive explanation of the research found to date?

2. Huy grew up in a traditional Chinese family, where co-sleeping until adolescence was the norm. He sees no problem with allowing his infant daughter to sleep with him and his wife. His wife, Lori, who was born and raised in the United States, is concerned that allowing her to sleep in their bed places her at risk for SIDS. Is co-sleeping a significant risk factor for SIDS? What else can Huy and Lori do to reduce the risk?

3. Marianne has landed a part-time job as a nanny for Jack, a 2-month-old boy. What can Marianne expect to see in terms of the child's sensory and motor development as she interacts with and observes Jack over the next six months?

Connect to www.mhhe.com/santrockld9 to research the answers and complete these exercises.

E-Learning Tools

To help you master the material in this chapter, you'll find a number of valuable study tools on the Student CD-ROM that accompanies this book. In addition, visit the Online Learning Center for *Life-Span Development*, ninth edition, where you'll find these valuable resources for chapter 5, "Physical Development in Infancy."

- What are your beliefs about an infant's physical development? Use the self-assessment, *My Beliefs About Nurturing a Baby's Physical Development*, to determine what your views are.

- View video clips of key researchers, including Charles Nelson as he discusses his research with infants.
- Build your decision-making skills by trying your hand at the parenting and education "Scenarios."

CHAPTER

6

I wish I could travel down by the road that crosses the baby's mind where reason makes kites of her laws and flies them....

—RABINDRANATH TAGORE
Bengali Poet, Essayist,
20th Century

Cognitive Development in Infancy

Chapter Outline

PIAGET'S THEORY OF INFANT DEVELOPMENT

The Sensorimotor Stage of Development

Understanding Physical Reality

Evaluating Piaget's Sensorimotor Stage

LEARNING AND REMEMBERING

Conditioning

Habituation and Dishabituation

Imitation

Memory

INDIVIDUAL DIFFERENCES IN INTELLIGENCE

LANGUAGE DEVELOPMENT

What Is Language?

How Language Develops

Biological Foundations of Language

Behavioral and Environmental Influences

Learning Goals

1 **S**ummarize Piaget's theory of infant development

2 **D**escribe how infants learn and remember

3 **D**iscuss the assessment of intelligence in infancy

4 **E**xplain language development in infancy

Images of Life-Span Development
Laurent, Lucienne, and Jacqueline

The Swiss psychologist Jean Piaget was a meticulous observer of his three children—Laurent, Lucienne, and Jacqueline. His books on cognitive development are filled with his observations. This list provides a glimpse of Piaget's observations of his children's cognitive development in infancy (Piaget, 1952).

- At 21 days of age, Laurent finds his thumb after three attempts; once he finds his thumb, prolonged sucking begins. But, when he is placed on his back, he doesn't know how to coordinate the movement of his arms with that of his mouth; his hands draw back, even when his lips seek them.
- During the third month, thumb sucking becomes less important to Laurent because of new visual and auditory interests. But, when he cries, his thumb goes to the rescue.
- Toward the end of Lucienne's fourth month, while she is lying in her crib, Piaget hangs a doll over her feet. Lucienne thrusts her feet at the doll and makes it move. Afterward, she looks at her motionless foot for a second, then kicks at the doll again. She has no visual control of her foot because her movements are the same whether she only looks at the doll or it is placed over her head. By contrast, she does have tactile control of her foot; when she tries to kick the doll and misses, she slows her foot movements to improve her aim.
- At 11 months, while seated, Jacqueline shakes a little bell. She then pauses abruptly so she can delicately place the bell in front of her right foot; then she kicks the bell hard. Unable to recapture the bell, she grasps a ball and places it in the same location where the bell was. She gives the ball a firm kick.
- At 1 year, 2 months, Jacqueline holds in her hands an object that is new to her: a round, flat box that she turns over and shakes; then she rubs it against her crib. She lets it go and tries to pick it up again. She succeeds only in touching it with her index finger, being unable to fully reach and grasp it. She keeps trying to grasp it and presses to the edge of her crib. She makes the box tilt up, but it nonetheless falls again. Jacqueline shows an interest in this result and studies the fallen box.
- At 1 year, 8 months, Jacqueline arrives at a closed door with a blade of grass in each hand. She stretches her right hand toward the doorknob but detects that she cannot turn it without letting go of the grass, so she puts the grass on the floor, opens the door, picks up the grass again, and then enters. But, when she wants to leave the room, things get complicated. She puts the grass on the floor and grasps the doorknob. Then she perceives that, by pulling the door toward her, she simultaneously chases away the grass that she had placed between the door and the threshold. She then picks up the grass and places it out of the door's range of movement.

For Piaget, these observations reflect important changes in the infant's cognitive development. Later in the chapter, you will learn that Piaget believed that infants go through six substages of development and that the behaviors you have just read about characterize those substages.

The excitement and enthusiasm about infant cognition have been fueled by an interest in what an infant knows at birth and soon after, by continued fascination about innate and learned factors in the infant's cognitive development, and by controversies about whether infants construct their knowledge (as Piaget believed) or whether they know their world more directly. In this chapter we will study Piaget's theory of infant development, learning and remembering, individual differences in intelligence, and language development.

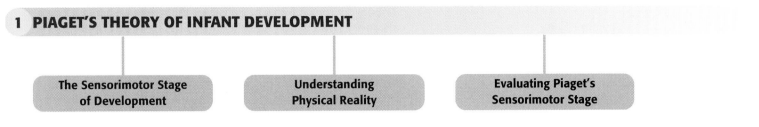

1   PIAGET'S THEORY OF INFANT DEVELOPMENT

| The Sensorimotor Stage of Development | Understanding Physical Reality | Evaluating Piaget's Sensorimotor Stage |

Poet Noah Perry once asked, "Who knows the thoughts of a child?" Piaget knew as much as anyone. Through careful, inquisitive interviews and observations of his own three children—Laurent, Lucienne, and Jacqueline—Piaget changed the way we think about children's conception of the world. Remember that we studied a general outline of Piaget's cognitive developmental theory in chapter 2 ◀▥ p. 47. You might want to review that discussion now.

Piaget believed that the child passes through a series of stages of thought from infancy to adolescence. Passage through these stages results from biological pressures to *adapt* to the environment (through assimilation and accommodation) and to structure thinking. Recall from chapter 2 that assimilation occurs when individuals incorporate new knowledge into existing knowledge and that accommodation takes place when individuals adjust to new information.

Another important concept in Piaget's theory is **scheme,** a cognitive structure that helps individuals organize and understand their experiences. Schemes change with age. Even newborns have schemes. For instance, they grasp reflexively anything that touches their hand. As children grow older and gain more experience, they gradually shift from using schemes based on physical activities to schemes based on internal mental activities such as strategies and plans. For example, later in infancy an action-based grasping scheme can become part of a plan for obtaining a desirable object.

Piaget's stages are *qualitatively* different from one another. The way children reason at one stage is qualitatively different from the way they reason at another stage. This contrasts with the quantitative assessments of intelligence made through the use of standardized intelligence tests—which focus on what the child knows, or how many questions the child can answer correctly. Remember from chapter 2 that Piaget believed there are four stages of cognitive development: sensorimotor, preoperational, concrete operational, and formal operational. Here our focus is on Piaget's stage of infant cognitive development. In later chapters (8, 10, and 12) we will explore the last three Piagetian stages.

The Sensorimotor Stage of Development

According to Piaget, the sensorimotor stage lasts from birth to about 2 years of age, corresponding to the period of infancy. During this time, mental development is characterized by considerable progression in the infant's ability to organize and coordinate sensations with physical movements and actions—hence the name *sensorimotor* (Piaget, 1952).

At the beginning of the sensorimotor stage, the infant has little more than reflexive patterns with which to work. By the end of the stage, the 2-year-old has complex sensorimotor patterns and is beginning to operate with a primitive system of symbols. Unlike other stages, the sensorimotor stage is subdivided into six substages, each of which involves qualitative changes in sensorimotor organization.

Within a developmental substage, there may be different schemes—sucking, rooting, and blinking in substage 1, for example. In substage 1, the schemes are basically

> *We are born capable of learning.*
> —Jean-Jacques Rousseau
> *Swiss-Born French Philosopher, 18th Century*

mhhe ○com/
santrockld9

Piaget's Stages
Sensorimotor Development

scheme In Piaget's theory, a cognitive structure that helps individuals organize and understand their experiences.

Simple reflexes

Infants are limited to exercising simple reflexes, such as rooting and sucking.

0 to 1 month of age

First habits and primary circular reactions

Infants' reflexes evolve into adaptive schemes that are more refined and coordinated.

1 to 4 months of age

Secondary circular reactions

Infants become more outwardly oriented, moving beyond self-preoccupation. They discover procedures for producing interesting events.

4 to 8 months of age

Coordination of secondary circular reactions

Infants combine and recombine earlier schemes and engage for the first time in truly intentional behavior. Infants can now separate means and end in trying to reach a goal.

8 to 12 months of age

Tertiary circular reactions, novelty, and curiosity

Infants start to vary schemes to produce new effects.

12 to 18 months of age

Internalization of schemes

Infants' capacity for symbolic thought emerges.

18 to 24 months of age

FIGURE 6.1 Piaget's Six Substages of Sensorimotor Development

reflexive. From substage to substage, the schemes change in organization. This change is at the heart of Piaget's description of the stages. The six substages of sensorimotor development are (see figure 6.1):

- **Simple reflexes** are the hallmarks of Piaget's first sensorimotor substage, which corresponds to the first month after birth. In this substage, the basic means of coordinating sensation and action is through reflexive behaviors. These include rooting and sucking, which the infant has at birth. In substage 1, the infant exercises these reflexes. More important, the infant develops an ability to produce behaviors that resemble reflexes in the absence of obvious reflexive stimuli. The newborn may suck when a bottle or nipple is only nearby, for example. When the baby was just born, the bottle or nipple would have produced the sucking pattern only when placed directly in its mouth or touched to the lips. Reflexlike actions in the absence of a triggering stimulus are evidence that the infant is initiating action and is actively structuring experiences in the first month of life.

- **First habits and primary circular reactions** characterize Piaget's second sensorimotor stage, which develops between 1 and 4 months of age. In this substage, infants' reflexes have evolved into adaptive schemes that are more refined and coordinated. A *habit* is a scheme based on a simple reflex, such as sucking, that has become completely separated from its eliciting stimulus. For example, an infant in substage 1 might suck when orally stimulated by a bottle or when visually shown the bottle. However, an infant in substage 2 might exercise the sucking scheme even when no bottle is present. A **primary circular reaction** is a scheme based on the infant's attempt to reproduce an interesting or a pleasurable event that initially occurred by chance. In a well-known Piagetian example, a child accidentally sucks his fingers when they are placed near his mouth. Later, he searches for his fingers to suck them again, but the fingers do not cooperate in the search because the infant cannot coordinate visual and manual actions. Habits and circular reactions are stereotyped, in that the infant repeats them the same way each time.

- **Secondary circular reactions** make up Piaget's third sensorimotor stage, which develops between 4 and 8 months of age. In this substage, the infant becomes more object-oriented or focused on the world, moving beyond the preoccupation with the self that characterizes sensorimotor interactions. By chance, the infant might shake a rattle. The infant will repeat this action for the sake of experiencing what it can do in the world. The infant imitates some simple actions of others, such as the baby talk or burbling of adults, and some physical gestures. However, these imitations are limited to actions the infant is already able to produce.

- **Coordination of secondary circular reactions** occurs in Piaget's fourth sensorimotor substage, which develops between 8 and 12 months of age. In this substage, several significant changes take place that involve the coordination of schemes and intentionality. Infants readily combine and recombine previously learned schemes in a *coordinated way*. They might look at an object and grasp it simultaneously, or they might visually inspect a toy, such as a rattle, and finger it simultaneously in obvious tactile exploration. Actions are even more outwardly directed than before. Related to this coordination is the second achievement—the presence of *intentionality,* the separation of means and goals in accomplishing simple feats. For example, infants might manipulate a stick (the means) to bring a desired toy within reach (the goal). They might knock over one block to reach and play with another one.

- **Tertiary circular reactions, novelty, and curiosity** distinguish Piaget's fifth sensorimotor substage, which develops between 12 and 18 months of age. In this substage, infants become intrigued by the variety of properties that objects possess and by the many things they can make happen to objects. A block can be made to fall, spin, hit another object, and slide across the ground. Tertiary circular reactions are schemes in which the infant purposely explores new possibilities with objects, continually changing what is done to them and exploring the results. Piaget says that this stage marks the developmental starting point for human curiosity and interest in novelty. Previously circular reactions were devoted exclusively to reproducing former events, with the exception of imitation of novel acts, which occurs as early as substage 4. The tertiary circular act is the first to be concerned with novelty.

- **Internalization of schemes** occurs in Piaget's sixth and final sensorimotor substage, which develops between 18 and 24 months of age. In this substage, the infant's mental functioning shifts from a purely sensorimotor plane to a symbolic plane, and the infant develops the ability to use primitive symbols. For Piaget, a *symbol* is an internalized sensory image or word that represents an event. Primitive symbols permit the infant to think about concrete events without directly acting them out or perceiving them. Moreover, symbols allow the infant to manipulate and transform the represented events in simple ways. In a favorite Piagetian example, Piaget's young daughter saw a matchbox being opened and closed. Sometime later, she mimicked the event by opening and closing her mouth. This was an obvious expression of her image of the event. In another example, a child opened a door slowly to avoid disturbing a piece of paper lying on the floor on the other side. Clearly, the child had an image of the unseen paper and what would happen to it if the door opened quickly.

Understanding Physical Reality

Piaget thought that children, even infants, are much like little scientists, examining the world to find out how it works. Developmentalists are interested in how infants' knowledge of the physical world develops (Bremner, 2002). Key aspects of infants' understanding of physical reality are object permanence and cause and effect.

Object Permanence   **Object permanence** is the Piagetian term for one of an infant's most important accomplishments: understanding that objects and events continue to exist even when they cannot directly be seen, heard, or touched. Imagine what thought would be like if you could not distinguish between yourself and your world. Your thinking would be chaotic, disorganized, and unpredictable. This is what the mental life of a newborn is like, according to Piaget. There is no self-world differentiation and no sense of object permanence. By the end of the sensorimotor period, however, both are present.

The principal way in which object permanence is studied is by watching an infant's reaction when an interesting object or event disappears (see figure 6.2 on page 186). If infants show no reaction, it is assumed they believe the object no longer exists. By contrast, if infants are surprised at the disappearance and search for the object, it is assumed they believe it continues to exist.

In one research study of object permanence, Renée Baillargeon (1986) showed 6- and 8-month-old infants a toy car that moved down an inclined track, disappeared behind a screen, and then reemerged at the other end, still on the track. After this same sequence was repeated several times, the infants then saw something different

simple reflexes Piaget's first sensorimotor substage, which corresponds to the first month after birth. In this substage, the basic means of coordinating sensation and action is through reflexive behaviors, such as rooting and sucking, which the infant has at birth.

first habits and primary circular reactions Piaget's second sensorimotor substage, which develops between 1 and 4 months of age. In this substage, infants' reflexes evolve into adaptive schemes that are more refined and coordinated.

primary circular reaction A scheme based on the infant's attempt to reproduce an interesting or a pleasurable event that initially occurred by chance.

secondary circular reactions Piaget's third sensorimotor substage, which develops between 4 and 8 months of age. In this substage, the infant becomes more object-oriented, or focused on the world, moving beyond preoccupation with the self in sensorimotor interactions.

coordination of secondary circular reactions Piaget's fourth sensorimotor substage, which develops between 8 and 12 months of age. In this substage, several significant changes take place involving the coordination of schemes and intentionality.

tertiary circular reactions, novelty, and curiosity Piaget's fifth sensorimotor substage, which develops between 12 and 18 months of age. In this substage, infants become intrigued by the variety of properties that objects possess and by the multiplicity of things they can make happen to objects.

internalization of schemes Piaget's sixth and final sensorimotor substage, which develops between 18 and 24 months of age. In this substage, the infant's mental functioning shifts from a purely sensorimotor plane to a symbolic plane, and the infant develops the ability to use primitive symbols.

object permanence The Piagetian term for one of an infant's most important accomplishments: understanding that objects and events continue to exist, even when they cannot directly be seen, heard, or touched.

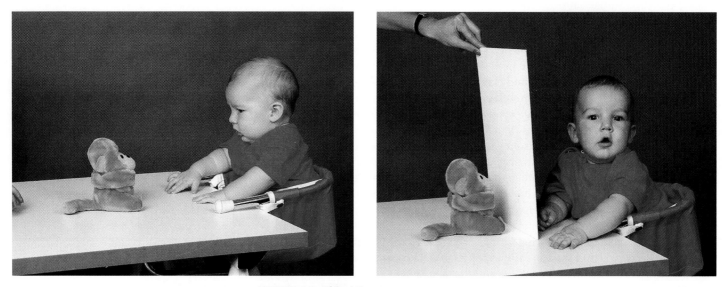

FIGURE 6.2 Object Permanence

Piaget thought that object permanence is one of infancy's landmark cognitive accomplishments. For this 5-month-old boy, "out-of-sight" is literally out of mind. The infant looks at the toy monkey (*left*), but, when his view of the toy is blocked (*right*), he does not search for it. Several months later, he will search for the hidden toy monkey, reflecting the presence of object permanence.

take place. A box was placed behind the screen, in one instance next to the track (a possible event), in another instance directly on the track (an impossible event). Then the infants watched the toy car go from one side of the screen to the other. Infants looked longer at the impossible event than at the possible event. This indicated they remembered not only that the box still existed (object permanence) but its location.

Causality Piaget was very interested in infants' knowledge of cause and effect. His conclusions about infants' understanding of cause and effect were based mainly on his observations of the extent to which infants acted to produce a desired outcome, such as pushing aside an obstacle to reach a goal.

One study on infants' understanding of causality found that even young infants comprehend the size of a moving object determines how far it will move a stationary object if it collides with it (Kotovsky & Baillargeon, 1994 (see figure 6.3). In this research, a cylinder rolls down a ramp and hits a toy bug that is located at the bottom of the ramp. By $5^1/2$ to $6^1/2$ months of age, infants understand that the bug will roll farther if it is hit by a large cylinder than if it is hit by a small cylinder after they have observed how far it will be pushed by a medium-sized cylinder. Thus, by the middle of the first year of life, these infants understood that the size of the cylinder was a causal factor in determining how far the bug would move when it was hit by the cylinder.

Evaluating Piaget's Sensorimotor Stage

Piaget opened up a whole new way of looking at infants by describing how their main task is to coordinate their sensory impressions with their motor activity. Piaget constructed his view of infancy mainly by observing the development of his own three children. Few laboratory techniques were available at the time. In the past several decades, sophisticated experimental techniques have been devised to study infants, and there have been a large number of research studies on infant development (Cohen & Cashon, 2003). Much of the new research suggests that the infant's cognitive world is not as neatly packaged as Piaget portrayed it (Gounin-Decarie, 1996; Meltzoff & Moore, 1999). The two research areas that have led researchers to a somewhat different understanding of infant development are (1) perceptual development and (2) conceptual development.

Perceptual Development   A number of theorists, such as Eleanor Gibson (2001) and Elizabeth Spelke (1991; Spelke & Newport, 1998), believe that infants' perceptual abilities are highly developed very early in development ◄▥ p. 169. For example, Spelke has demonstrated that infants as young as 4 months of age have intermodal perception—the ability to coordinate information from two or more sensory modalities, such as vision and hearing. Other research, by Renée Baillargeon (1995), documents that infants as young as 4 months expect objects to be substantial (in the sense that other objects cannot move through them) and permanent (in the sense that objects continue to exist when they are hidden). In sum, researchers believe that infants see objects as bounded, unitary, solid, and separate from their background, possibly at birth or shortly thereafter, but definitely by 3 to 4 months of age. Young infants still have much to learn about objects, but the world appears both stable and orderly to them and, thus, capable of being conceptualized. Infants are continually trying to structure and make sense of their world (Meltzoff & Gopnik, 1997).

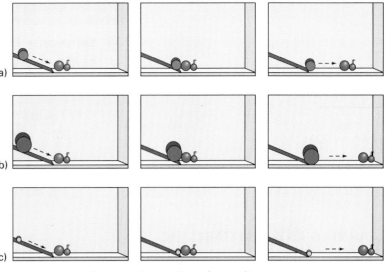

FIGURE 6.3 The Infants' Understanding of Causality

After young infants saw how far the medium-sized cylinder (*a*) pushed a toy bug, they showed more surprise at the event in (*c*) that showed a very small cylinder pushing the toy bug as far as the large cylinder (*b*). Their surprise, indicated by looking at (*c*) longer than (*b*), indicated that they understood the size of a cylinder was a causal factor in determining how far the toy bug would be pushed when it was hit by the cylinder.

Conceptual Development   It is more difficult to study what infants are thinking about than to study what they see. Still, researchers have devised ways to assess whether or not infants are thinking. One strategy is to look for symbolic activity, such as using a gesture to refer to something. Piaget (1952) used this strategy to document infants' motor recognition. For example, he observed his 6-month-old daughter make a gesture when she saw a familiar toy in a new location. She was used to kicking at the toy in her crib. When she saw it across the room, she made a brief kicking motion. However, Piaget did not consider this to be true symbolic activity because it was a motor movement, not a purely mental act. Nonetheless, Piaget suggested that his daughter was referring to, or classifying, the toy through her actions (Mandler, 1998). In a similar way, infants whose parents use sign language have been observed to start using conventional signs at about 6 to 7 months of age (Bonvillian, Orlansky, & Novack, 1983).

In summary, many of today's researchers believe that Piaget wasn't specific enough about how infants learn about their world and that infants are far more competent than Piaget envisioned (Meltzoff, 2000). Recent research on infants' perceptual and conceptual development suggests that infants have more sophisticated perceptual abilities and can begin to think earlier than Piaget envisioned. These researchers believe that infants either are born with or acquire these abilities early in their development (Mandler, 1990, 1998).

Piaget's view is a general, unifying story of how biology and experience sculpt the infant's cognitive development: assimilation and accommodation always take the infant to higher ground through a series of substages. And for Piaget, the motivation for change is general, an internal search for equilibrium. However, like much of the modern world, today the field of infant cognition is very specialized. There are many researchers working on different questions, with no general theory emerging that can connect all of the different findings (Nelson, 1999). Their theories are local theories, focused on specific research questions, rather than grand theories like Piaget's. If there is a unifying theme, it is that investigators in infant development struggle with the big issue of nature and nurture.

mhhe ●com/
santrockld9

Cognitive Milestones
Challenges to Piaget

Infants are creating concepts and organizing their world into conceptual domains that will form the backbone of their thought throughout life.

—Jean Mandler
Contemporary Psychologist,
University of California–San Diego

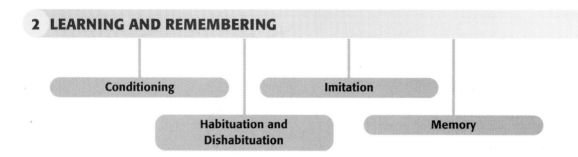

Review and Reflect

1 Summarize Piaget's theory of infant development

REVIEW

- What are some characteristics of Piaget's stage of sensorimotor development?
- What are two key aspects of infants' understanding of physical reality?
- What are some contributions and criticisms of Piaget's sensorimotor stage?

REFLECT

- What are some implications of Piaget's theory of infant development for parenting?

2 LEARNING AND REMEMBERING

Conditioning

Habituation and Dishabituation

Imitation

Memory

In this section, we will explore these aspects of how infants learn and remember: conditioning; habituation and dishabituation; imitation; and memory. In contrast to Piaget's theory, the approaches we will look at here do not describe infant development in terms of stages.

FIGURE 6.4 The Technique Used in Rovee-Collier's Investigation of Infant Memory

In Rovee-Collier's experiment, operant conditioning was used to demonstrate that infants as young as 2½ months of age can retain information from the experience of being conditioned.

Conditioning

In chapter 2, "The Science of Life-Span Development," we described Pavlov's classical conditioning and Skinner's operant conditioning ◀‖‖ p. 51. Both types of conditioning have been demonstrated in infants.

Here we will examine some aspects of operant conditioning (in which the consequences of the behavior produce changes in the probability of the behavior's occurrence) in infants. For example, if an infant's behavior is followed by a rewarding stimulus, the behavior is likely to recur.

Operant conditioning has especially been helpful to researchers in their efforts to determine what infants perceive. For example, infants will suck faster on a nipple when the sucking behavior is followed by a visual display, music, or a human voice (Rovee-Collier, 1987).

Carolyn Rovee-Collier (1987) has also demonstrated how infants can retain information from the experience of being conditioned. In a characteristic experiment, she places a 2½-month-old baby in a crib under an elaborate mobile. She then ties one end of a ribbon to the baby's ankle and the other end to the mobile. Subsequently, she observes that the baby kicks and makes the mobile move. The movement of the mobile is the reinforcing stimulus (which increases the baby's kicking behavior) in this experiment. Weeks later, the baby is returned to the crib, but its foot is not tied to the mobile. The baby kicks, which suggests it has retained the information that if it kicks a leg, the mobile will move (see figure 6.4).

Habituation and Dishabituation

If a stimulus—a sight or sound—is presented to infants several times in a row, they usually pay less attention to it each time. This response suggests they are bored with it. This is the process of **habituation**—repeated presentation of the same stimulus, which causes reduced attention to the stimulus. **Dishabituation** is an increase in responsiveness after a change in stimulation. Among the measures researchers use to study whether habituation is occurring are sucking behavior (sucking behavior stops when the young infant attends to a novel object), heart and respiration rates, and the length of time the infant looks at an object. Newborn infants can habituate to repetitive stimulation in virtually every stimulus modality—vision, hearing, touch, and so on (Rovee-Collier, 1987). Figure 6.5 shows the results of one study of habituation and dishabituation with newborns (Slater, Morison, & Somers, 1988).

Habituation can be used to tell us much about infants' perception, such as the extent to which they can see, hear, smell, taste, and experience touch (Cohen & Cashon, 2003; Slater, 2002). Habituation also can be used to tell whether infants recognize something they have previously experienced.

The extensive assessment of habituation in recent years has resulted in its use as a measure of an infant's maturity and well-being. Infants who have brain damage or have suffered birth traumas, such as insufficient oxygen, do not habituate well and might later have developmental and learning problems.

A knowledge of habituation and dishabituation can benefit parent-infant interaction. Infants respond to changes in stimulation. If stimulation is repeated often, the infant's response will decrease to the point that the infant no longer responds to the parent. In parent-infant interaction, it is important for parents to do novel things and to repeat them often until the infant stops responding. The wise parent senses when the infant shows an interest and that many repetitions of the stimulus may be necessary for the infant to process the information. The parent stops or changes behaviors when the infant redirects her attention (Rosenblith, 1992).

Imitation

Can infants imitate someone else's emotional expressions? If an adult smiles, will the baby follow with a smile? If an adult protrudes her lower lip, wrinkles her forehead, and frowns, will the baby show a sad face? If an adult opens his mouth, widens his eyes, and raises his eyebrows, will the baby follow suit? Can infants only a few days old do these things?

> **habituation** Repeated presentation of the same stimulus, which causes reduced attention to the stimulus.
>
> **dishabituation** An increase in responsiveness after a change in stimulation.

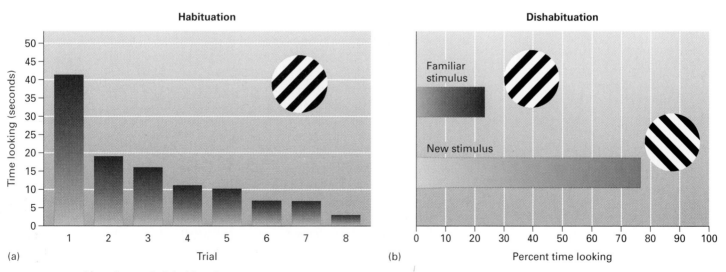

FIGURE 6.5 Habituation and Dishabituation

In the first part of one study, 7-hour-old newborns were shown the stimulus in (*a*). As indicated, the newborns looked at it an average of 41 seconds when it was first presented to them (Slater, Morison, & Somers, 1988). Over seven more presentations of the stimulus, they looked at it less and less. In the second part of study, infants were presented with both the familiar stimulus to which they had just become habituated (*a*) and a new stimulus (shown in *b*, which was rotated 90 degrees). The newborns looked at the new stimulus three times as much as the familiar stimulus.

FIGURE 6.6 Infant Imitation
Infant development researcher Andrew Meltzoff protrudes his tongue in an attempt to get the infant to imitate his behavior.

Infant development researcher Andrew Meltzoff (2000; Meltzoff & Moore, 1999) has conducted numerous studies of infants' imitative abilities. He believes infants' imitative abilities are biologically based, because infants can imitate a facial expression within the first few days after birth. This occurs before they have had the opportunity to observe social agents in their environment protruding their tongues and engaging in other behaviors. He also emphasizes that the infant's imitative abilities do not resemble what ethologists conceptualize as a hardwired, reflexive, innate releasing mechanism but, rather, involve flexibility, adaptability, and intermodal perception. In Meltzoff's observations of infants in the first 72 hours of life, the infants gradually displayed a full imitative response of an adult's facial expression, such as protruding the tongue or opening the mouth wide (see figure 6.6).

Not all experts on infant development accept Meltzoff's conclusions that newborns are capable of imitation. Some say that these babies were engaging in little more than automatic responses to a stimulus.

Meltzoff also has studied **deferred imitation,** which occurs after a time delay of hours or days. In one study, Meltzoff (1988) demonstrated that 9-month-old infants could imitate actions that they had seen performed 24 hours earlier. Each action consisted of an unusual gesture—such as pushing a recessed button in a box (which produced a beeping sound). Piaget believed that deferred imitation doesn't occur until about 18 months of age. Meltzoff's research suggested that it occurs much earlier.

Memory

Memory is a central feature of cognitive development that involves the retention of information over time. Sometimes information is retained only for a few seconds, and at other times it is retained for a lifetime.

Can infants remember? Some infant researchers, such as Carolyn Rovee-Collier, argue that infants as young as 2 to 6 months of age can remember some experiences through 1 1/2 to 2 years of age (Rovee-Collier, 2001; Rovee-Collier & Barr, 2002).

However, critics such as Jean Mandler (2000), a leading expert on infant cognition, argue that Rovee-Collier fails to distinguish between retention of a perceptual-motor variety that is involved in conditioning tasks (like that involved in kicking a mobile), often referred to as *implicit memory,* and the ability to consciously recall the past, often referred to as *explicit memory.* When people think about what memory is, they are referring to the latter, which most researchers find does not occur until the second half of the first year (Mandler & McDonough, 1995).

By 9 months of age, infants' explicit memory is readily apparent. For example, in one study, 9-month-old infants long-term recall of a two-step sequence (such as "Make Big Bird turn on the light") occurred (Carver & Bauer, 1999). Five weeks after experiencing such two-step sequences, 45 percent of the infants demonstrated their long-term memory by producing the two actions in the sequence. The other 55 percent did not show evidence of remembering the sequence of actions, reflecting individual differences in infant memory. Also, in a related assessment of these infants, researchers demonstrated changes in the brain activity of the infants as they engaged in recall of the sequences they had experienced five weeks earlier (Carver, Bauer, & Nelson, 2000).

While explicit memory emerges in the second half of the first year of life, the results of other research reveal that it undergoes substantial development and consolidation over the course of the second year of life (Carver & Bower, 2001). In one longitudinal study, infants were assessed several times during the second year of life (Bauer & others, 2000). These older infants showed more accurate memory and required fewer prompts to demonstrate their memory than infants under the age of 1.

*L*ife is all memory, except for the one present moment that goes by you so quick you hardly catch it going.

—TENNESSEE WILLIAMS
American Playwright, 20th Century

deferred imitation Imitation that occurs after a time delay of hours or days.

memory A central feature of cognitive development, pertaining to all situations in which an individual retains information over time.

Most adults cannot remember anything from the first three years of their life; this is referred to as *infantile amnesia*. When adults seem to be able to recall something from their infancy, it likely is something they have been told about by relatives or something they saw in a photograph or home movie. One explanation of infantile amnesia focuses on the maturation of the brain, especially in the frontal lobes, which occurs after infancy (Boyer & Diamond, 1992).

Review and Reflect

2 **Describe how infants learn and remember**

REVIEW

- How do infants learn through conditioning?
- How does infant learning involve habituation and dishabituation?
- How is imitation involved in infant learning?
- To what extent can infants remember?

REFLECT

- If someone said that they remember being abused by their parents when they were 2 years old, would you believe them? Explain your answer.

3 INDIVIDUAL DIFFERENCES IN INTELLIGENCE

So far, we have discussed how the cognitive development of infants generally progresses. We have emphasized what is typical of the largest number of infants or the average infant, but the results obtained for most infants do not apply to all infants. It is advantageous to know whether an infant is developing at a slow, normal, or advanced pace during the course of infancy. If an infant advances at an especially slow rate, then some form of enrichment may be necessary. If an infant develops at an advanced pace, parents may be advised to provide toys that stimulate cognitive growth in slightly older infants. Individual differences in infant cognitive development have been studied primarily through the use of developmental scales, or infant intelligence tests. For example, the Brazelton Neonatal Behavioral Assessment Scale, which we discussed in chapter 4, is widely used to evaluate newborns ◀▥ p. 134.

The infant testing movement grew out of the tradition of IQ testing of older children. However, the measures for assessing infants are necessarily less verbal than IQ tests that assess the intelligence of older children. The infant developmental scales contain far more perceptual motor items. They also include measures of social interaction.

The most important early contributor to the developmental testing of infants was Arnold Gesell (1934). He developed a measure that was used as a clinical tool to help distinguish potentially normal babies from abnormal ones. This was especially useful to adoption agencies, which had large numbers of babies awaiting placement. Gesell's examination was used widely for many years and is still frequently used by pediatricians to assess infants. The current version of the Gesell test has four categories of behavior: motor, language, adaptive, and personal-social. The **developmental quotient (DQ)** is an overall developmental score that combines subscores in motor, language, adaptive, and personal-social domains in the Gesell assessment of infants.

The **Bayley Scales of Infant Development,** developed by Nancy Bayley, are widely used in the assessment of infant development. The current version has three components: a mental scale, a motor scale, and an infant behavior profile. Unlike Gesell, whose scales were clinically motivated, Bayley (1969) wanted to develop scales that would assess infant behavior and predict later development. The early version of the Bayley scales covered only the first year of development. In the 1950s, the scales

developmental quotient (DQ) An overall developmental score that combines subscores in motor, language, adaptive, and personal-social domains in the Gesell assessment of infants.

Bayley Scales of Infant Development Scales developed by Nancy Bayley, which are widely used in the assessment of infant development. The current version has three components: a mental scale, a motor scale, and an infant behavior profile.

were extended to assess older infants. In 1993, the Bayley-II was published, with up-dated norms for diagnostic assessment at a younger age.

Because our discussion in this chapter centers on the infant's cognitive develop-ment, our primary interest is in Bayley's mental scale. It includes assessment of:

- Auditory and visual attention to stimuli
- Manipulation, such as combining objects or shaking a rattle
- Examiner interaction, such as babbling and imitation
- Relation with toys, such as banging spoons together
- Memory involved in object permanence, as when the infant finds a hidden toy
- Goal-directed behavior that involves persistence, such as putting pegs in a board
- Ability to follow directions and knowledge of objects' names, such as under-standing the concept of "one"

How well should a 6-month-old perform on the Bayley mental scale? The 6-month-old infant should be able to vocalize pleasure and displeasure, persistently search for objects that are just out of immediate reach, and approach a mirror that is placed in front of the infant by the examiner. How well should a 12-month-old per-form? By 12 months of age, the infant should be able to inhibit behavior when com-manded to do so, imitate words the examiner says (such as *Mama*), and respond to simple requests (such as "Take a drink").

Another assessment tool, the Fagan Test of Infant Intelligence, is increasingly be-ing used (Fagan, 1992). This test focuses on the infant's ability to process information, including encoding the attributes of objects, detecting similarities and differences be-tween objects, forming mental representations, and retrieving these representations. The Fagan test estimates babies' intelligence by comparing the amount of time they look at a new object with the amount of time they spend looking at a familiar object. This test elicits similar performances from infants in different cultures and is correlated with measures of intelligence in older children.

Tests of infant intelligence have been valuable in assessing the effects of malnutri-tion, drugs, maternal deprivation, and environmental stimulation on the development of infants. However, they do not correlate highly with IQ scores obtained later in childhood. This shortcoming is not surprising because the test items are considerably less verbal than the items on intelligence tests given to older children. Yet specific as-pects of infant intelligence are related to specific aspects of childhood intelligence. For example, in one study, infant language abilities assessed by the Bayley test predicted language, reading, and spelling ability at 6 to 8 years of age (Siegel, 1989). Infant perceptual-motor skills predicted visuospatial, arithmetic, and fine motor skills at 6 to 8 years of age. These results indicate that an item analysis of infant scales like Bayley's can provide information about the development of specific intellectual functions.

Toosje Thyssen VanBeveren is an infant assessment specialist who administers tests like the Bayley scales and the Fagan Test of Infant Intelligence. To read about her work with infants, see the Careers in Life-Span Development insert.

The explosion of interest in infant development has produced many new mea-sures, especially using tasks that evaluate the way infants process information. Evi-dence is accumulating that measures of habituation and dishabituation predict intelligence in childhood (McCall & Carriger, 1993). Less cumulative attention by an infant in the habituation situation and greater amounts of attention in the dishabitu-ation situation reflect more efficient information processing. Both types of attention—decrement and recovery—when measured in the first 6 months of infancy, are related to higher IQ scores on standardized intelligence tests given at various times between infancy and adolescence. In sum, more precise assessments of the infant's cognition with information-processing tasks involving attention have led to the conclusion that continuity between infant and childhood intelligence is greater than was previously believed.

It is important, however, not to go too far and think that the connections between early infant cognitive development and later childhood cognitive development are so

Careers in Life-Span Development

Toosje Thyssen VanBeveren, Infant Assessment Specialist

Toosje Thyssen VanBeveren is a developmental psychologist at the University of Texas Medical Center in Dallas. She has a master's degree in child clinical psychology and a Ph.D. in human development.

Currently, Dr. VanBeveren is involved in a program called New Connections. This 12-week program is a comprehensive intervention for young children (0 to 6 years of age) who were affected by substance abuse prenatally and for their caregivers.

In the New Connections program, VanBeveren conducts assessments of infants' developmental status and progress, identifying delays and deficits. She might refer the infants to a speech, physical, or occupational therapist and monitor the infants' therapeutic services and developmental progress. VanBeveren trains the program staff and encourages them to use the exercises she recommends. She also discusses the child's problems with the primary caregivers, suggests activities they can carry out with their children, and assists them in enrolling their infants in appropriate programs.

During her graduate work at the University of Texas at Dallas, Dr. VanBeveren was author John Santrock's teaching assistant in his undergraduate course on life-span development for four years. As a teaching assistant, she attended classes, graded exams, counseled students, and occasionally gave lectures. Each semester, VanBeveren returns to give a lecture on prenatal development and infancy in the life-span class. She also teaches part-time in the psychology department at UT-Dallas. She teaches an undergraduate course, "The Child in Society," and a graduate course, "Infant Development."

In Dr. VanBeveren's words, "My days are busy and full. The work is often challenging. There are some disappointments but mostly the work is enormously gratifying."

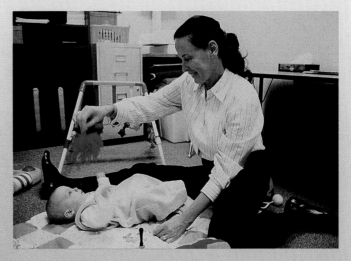

Toosje Thyssen VanBeveren conducting an infant assessment.

strong that no discontinuity takes place. Rather than asking whether cognitive development is continuous *or* discontinuous, perhaps we should be examining the ways cognitive development is both continuous and discontinuous. Some important changes in cognitive development take place after infancy, changes that underscore the discontinuity of cognitive development. We will describe these changes in cognitive development in subsequent chapters, which focus on later periods of development.

Review and Reflect

3 **Discuss the assessment of intelligence in infancy**

REVIEW

- How is infant intelligence measured?

REFLECT

- Parents have their 1-year-old infant assessed with a developmental scale and the infant does very well on it. How confident should they be that the infant is going to be a genius when he or she grows up?

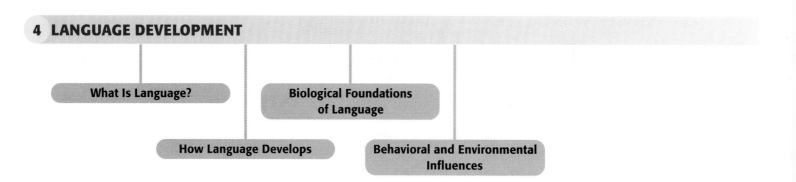

4 LANGUAGE DEVELOPMENT

In 1799, a nude boy was observed running through the woods in France. The boy was captured when he was 11 years old. He was called the Wild Boy of Aveyron and was believed to have lived in the woods alone for six years. When found, he made no effort to communicate. Even after a number of years, he never learned to communicate effectively. Sadly, a modern-day wild child named Genie was discovered in Los Angeles in 1970. Despite intensive intervention, Genie never acquired more than a primitive form of language. Both cases—the Wild Boy of Aveyron and Genie—raise questions about the biological and environmental determinants of language, topics that we will examine in greater detail later in this chapter. First, though, we need to define the term *language*.

What Is Language?

Language is a form of communication, whether spoken, written, or signed, that is based on a system of symbols. Think how important language is in our everyday lives. We need language in order to speak with others, listen to others, read, and write. Our language enables us to describe past events in detail and to plan for the future. Language lets us pass down information from one generation to the next and create a rich cultural heritage.

All human languages have some common characteristics. These include infinite generativity and organizational rules. **Infinite generativity** is the ability to produce an endless number of meaningful sentences using a finite set of words and rules. This quality makes language a highly creative enterprise.

How Language Develops

As infants develop, they reach a number of language milestones. At birth they communicate by crying, but by about 2 years of age, most can say approximately 200 words in the language their parents use. How does this remarkable ability develop?

Babbling and Other Vocalizations   Babies actively produce sounds from birth onward (Lock, 2002). The purpose of these early communications is to attract attention from caregivers and others in the environment. In the first year, the production of sound goes through this sequence:

- *Crying.* This is present even at birth and can signal distress. However, as you will discover in chapter 7, there are different types of cries that can signal different things.
- *Cooing.* This first occurs at about 1 to 2 months. These are *oo* sounds such as *coo* or *goo* that usually occur during interaction with the caregiver.
- *Babbling.* This first occurs in the middle of the first year and includes strings of consonant-vowel combinations.
- *Gestures.* Infants start using gestures, such as showing and pointing, at about 8 to 12 months of age. Some examples of gestures are waving bye-bye, nodding

language A form of communication based on a system of symbols. In humans language is characterized by infinite generativity and rule systems.

infinite generativity An individual's ability to generate an infinite number of meaningful sentences using a finite set of words and rules, which makes language a highly creative enterprise.

one's head to mean "yes," showing an empty cup to ask for more milk, and pointing to a dog to draw attention to it.

Deaf infants, born to deaf parents who use sign language, babble with their hands and fingers at about the same age as hearing children babble vocally (Bloom, 1998). Such similarities in timing and structure between manual and vocal babbling indicate the presence of a unified language capacity that underlies signed and spoken language (Petitto & Marnetette, 1991).

Recognizing Language Sounds Language is made up of basic sounds or phonemes. **Phonology** is a language's sound system. Phonological rules ensure that certain sound sequences occur (for example, *sp, ba,* or *ar*) and others do not (for example, *zx* or *qp*).

Phonology provides a basis for constructing a large and expandable set of words—all that are or ever will be in that language—out of two or three dozen phonemes. We do not need 500,000 phonemes, only a few dozen.

Patricia Kuhl's (1993, 2000) research reveals that long before they actually learn words, infants can sort through a number of spoken sounds in search of the ones that have meaning. Kuhl argues that from birth up to about 7 months of age, infants are "universal linguists" who are capable of distinguishing each of the 150 sounds that make up human speech. By about 11 months of age, they clearly have started to specialize in the speech sounds of their native language (see figure 6.7).

An important language task for infants is to pick out individual words from the nonstop stream of sound that comprises ordinary speech. To do so, they have to find the boundaries between words, which is very difficult for infants because adults don't pause between words when they speak (Jusczyk, 2002). Still, researchers have found that infants begin to detect word boundaries by 8 months of age. For example, in one study, 8-month-old infants listened at home to recorded stories that contained unusual words, such as *hornbill* and *python* (Jusczyk & Hohne, 1997). Two weeks later, the researchers tested the infants with two lists of words, one made up of words they had already heard in the stories, the other of new, unusual words that did not appear in the stories. The infants listened to the familiar words for a second longer, on average, than to new words.

Language Milestones
The Naming Explosion
Brain and Language Development

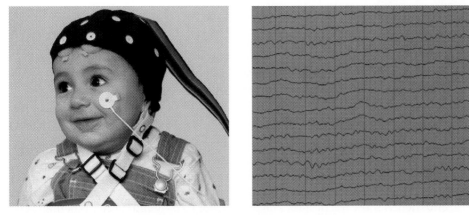

FIGURE 6.7 From Universal to Specialized Linguist
The people of the world speak thousands of languages and babies are born with the ability to learn any of them. In her research, Patricia Kuhl monitors infants' brain waves (an example of a brain wave recording is shown on the right) as they listen to different sounds. She has discovered that up to about the age of 7 months, infants can distinguish between two sounds in a language such as Mandarin Chinese—a subtle difference that English-speaking parents cannot detect. However, by 11 months of age, unused neuronal connections have begun to be pruned away. As infants' brains process a single language over time, they cease to be "universal linguists."

phonology A language's sound system.

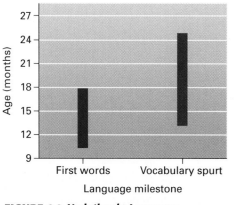

FIGURE 6.8 Variation in Language Milestones

First Words Spoken vocabulary begins when the infant utters its first word, a milestone eagerly anticipated by every parent. This event usually occurs at about 10 to 15 months of age. Many parents view the onset of language development as coincident with this first word. However, as we have seen, some significant language milestones have already occurred, such as cooing and babbling.

The infant's spoken vocabulary rapidly increases once the first word is spoken (Camaioni, 2002). The *vocabulary spurt* is a label that has been given to the rapid increase in an infant's vocabulary that begins to occur at approximately 18 months of age (Bloom, Lifter, & Broughton, 1985). The average 18-month-old can speak about 50 words, but by the age of 2 years can speak about 200 words.

A child's first words include those that name important people (*dada*), familiar animals (*kitty*), vehicles (*car*), toys (*ball*), food (*milk*), body parts (*eye*), clothes (*hat*), household items (*clock*), and greeting terms (*bye*). These were the first words of babies 50 years ago. They are the first words of babies today. At times it is hard to tell what these one-word utterances mean. One possibility is that they stand for an entire sentence in the infant's mind.

There is variation in the timing at which children say their first word and in their vocabulary spurt (Bloom, 1998). Figure 6.8 shows the range for these two language milestones in 14 children. The average ages of these children at the time they reached these milestones were: first word (13 months) and vocabulary spurt (19 months). However, the individual children ranged from 10 to 17 months for their first word and from 13 to 25 months for their vocabulary spurt.

Around the world, young children learn to speak in two-word utterances, in most cases, at about 18 to 24 months of age. *What are some examples of these two-word utterances?*

Two-Word Utterances By the time children are 18 to 24 months of age, they usually utter two-word statements. During this two-word stage, they quickly grasp the importance of expressing concepts and of the role that language plays in communicating with others. To convey meaning with two-word utterances, the child relies heavily on gesture, tone, and context. The wealth of meaning children can communicate with a two-word utterance includes (Slobin, 1972):

- Identification: "See doggie."
- Location: "Book there."
- Repetition: "More milk."
- Nonexistence: "All gone thing."
- Negation: "Not wolf."
- Possession: "My candy."
- Attribution: "Big car."
- Agent-action: "Mama walk."
- Action-direct object: "Hit you."
- Action-indirect object: "Give Papa."
- Action-instrument: "Cut knife."
- Question: "Where ball?"

These examples are from children whose first language is English, German, Russian, Finnish, Turkish, or Samoan. Although these two-word sentences omit many parts of speech, they are remarkably succinct in conveying many messages. In fact, in every language, a child's first combinations of words have this economical quality. **Telegraphic speech** is the use of short and precise words to communicate. When we send a telegram, we try to be short and precise, excluding any unnecessary words. As a result, articles, auxiliary verbs, and other connectives usually are omitted. Young children's two- and three-word utterances are characteristically telegraphic. Of course, telegraphic speech is not limited to two-word phrases. "Mommy give ice cream" and "Mommy give Tommy ice cream" also are examples of telegraphic speech. As children leave the two-word stage, they move rather quickly into three-, four-, and five-word combinations.

telegraphic speech The use of short and precise words to communicate; young children's two- and three-word utterances characteristically are telegraphic.

Language Production and Language Comprehension   A distinction is made between language production and language comprehension. *Language production* refers to the words and sentences that children use. *Language comprehension* refers to the language children understand. At about 8 to 12 months, infants often indicate their first word comprehension (Bloom, 1993). But recall that they don't say their first word (language production) until an average of about 13 months. On the average, infants understand about 50 words at about 13 months but can't say this many words until about 18 months (Menyuk, Liebergott, & Schultz, 1995). Thus, in infancy, receptive vocabulary (words the child understands) considerably exceeds spoken vocabulary (words the child uses).

We have discussed a number of language milestones in infancy. Figure 6.9 summarizes the time at which infants typically reach these milestones.

Age	Language Milestones
Birth	Crying
1 to 2 months	Cooing begins
6 months	Babbling begins
8 to 12 months	Use gestures, such as showing and pointing Comprehension of words appears
13 months	First word spoken
18 months	Vocabulary spurt starts
18 to 24 months	Uses two-word utterances Rapid expansion of understanding of words

FIGURE 6.9 Some Language Milestones in Infancy

Biological Foundations of Language

The strongest evidence for the biological basis of language is that children all over the world reach language milestones at about the same time developmentally and in about the same order. This occurs despite the vast variation in the language input they receive. For example, in some cultures, adults never talk to children under 1 year of age, yet these infants still acquire language. Also, there is no other convincing way to explain how *quickly* children learn language than through biological foundations.

With these thoughts in mind, let's now explore these questions about biological influences on language: How strongly is language influenced by biological evolution? Are humans biologically wired to learn language?

Biological Evolution   Estimates vary as to how long ago humans acquired language—about 100,000 years ago. In evolutionary time, then, language is a very recent acquisition. A number of experts believe that biological evolution undeniably shaped humans into linguistic creatures (Chomsky, 1957). The brain, nervous system, and vocal apparatus of our predecessors changed over hundreds of thousands of years. Physically equipped to do so, *Homo sapiens* went beyond grunting and shrieking to develop abstract speech. Language clearly gave humans an enormous edge over other animals and increased the chances of survival (Pinker, 1994).

Biological Prewiring   Linguist Noam Chomsky (1957) believes humans are biologically prewired to learn language at a certain time and in a certain way. He said that children are born into the world with a **language acquisition device (LAD),** a biological endowment that enables the child to detect certain language categories, such as phonology, syntax, and semantics. The LAD is a theoretical construct that flows from evidence about the biological basis of language.

Is there evidence for the existence of a LAD? Supporters of the LAD concept cite the uniformity of language milestones across languages and cultures, biological substrates for language, and evidence that children create language even in the absence of well-formed input. With regard to the last argument, most deaf children are the offspring of hearing parents. Some of these parents choose not to expose their deaf child to sign language, in order to motivate the child to learn speech while providing the child with a supportive social environment. Susan Goldin-Meadow (1979) has found that these children develop spontaneous gestures that are not based on their parents' gestures.

In the wild, chimps communicate through calls, gestures, and expressions, which evolutionary psychologists believe might be the roots of true language. *How strong is biology's role in language?*

language acquisition device (LAD) A biological endowment, hypothesized by Chomsky, that enables the child to detect certain language categories, such as phonology, syntax, and semantics.

Behavioral and Environmental Influences

Behaviorists view language as just another behavior, such as sitting, walking, and running. They argue that language represents chains of responses (Skinner, 1957) or imitation (Bandura, 1977). But many of the sentences we produce are novel; we have not heard them or spoken them before. For example, a child hears the sentence "The plate fell on the floor" and then says, "My mirror fell on the blanket," after dropping the mirror on the blanket. The behavioral mechanisms of reinforcement and imitation cannot completely explain this.

While spending long hours observing parents and their young children, child language researcher Roger Brown (1973) searched for evidence that parents reinforce their children for speaking in grammatical ways. He found that parents sometimes smile and praise their children for sentences they like. However, they also reinforce sentences that are ungrammatical. Brown concluded that no evidence exists to document that reinforcement is responsible for language's rule systems.

Another criticism of the behavioral view is that it fails to explain the extensive orderliness of language. The behavioral view predicts that vast individual differences should appear in children's speech development because of each child's unique learning history. But, as we have seen, a compelling fact about language is its structure and ever-present rule systems. All infants coo before they babble. All toddlers produce one-word utterances before two-word utterances. All state sentences in the active form before they state them in a passive form.

However, we do not learn language in a social vacuum. Most children are bathed in language from a very early age (Fernald, 2001; Hart & Risley, 1995). We need this early exposure to language to acquire competent language skills. The Wild Boy of Aveyron did not learn to communicate effectively after living in social isolation for years. Genie's language is rudimentary, even after years of extensive training.

Today most language acquisition researchers believe that children from a wide variety of cultural contexts acquire their native language without explicit teaching (Clark, 2000). In some cases, they do so without apparent encouragement. Thus, there appear to be very few aids that are necessary for learning a language. However, the support and involvement of caregivers and teachers greatly facilitate a child's language learning (Berko Gleason, 2000, 2001; Hoff, 2003; Hoff-Ginsberg & Lerner, 1999). Of special concern are children who grow up in impoverished circumstances and are not exposed to guided participation in language. To read about the effects that poverty has on language development, see the Sociocultural Worlds of Development box.

An intriguing aspect of the environment in the young child's acquisition of language is called **infant-directed speech.** This type of speech is often used by parents (in which case it sometimes is called "parentese") and other adults when they talk to babies. It has a higher than normal pitch and involves the use of simple words and sentences.

It is hard to talk this way when not in the presence of a baby, but as soon as you start talking to a baby, you immediately shift into it. Much of this is automatic and something adults often are unaware that they are even doing. Infant-directed speech has the important functions of capturing the infant's attention and maintaining communication. When parents are asked why they use infant-directed speech when talking to their baby, they point out that it is designed to teach their baby to talk. Older child peers and siblings also might use infant-directed speech or "baby talk" when communicating with an infant.

Are there strategies other than infant-directed speech that adults use to enhance the child's acquisition of language? Four candidates are recasting, echoing, expanding, and labeling. *Recasting* is rephrasing something the child has said in a different way, perhaps turning it into a question. For example, if the child says, "The dog was barking," the adult can respond by asking, "When was the dog barking?" The effects of recasting fit with suggestions that "following in order to lead" helps a child learn language. That is, letting a child initially indicate an interest and then proceeding to elaborate that interest—commenting, demonstrating, and explaining—improve

infant-directed speech Speech often used by parents (in which case it sometimes is called "parentese") and other adults when they talk to babies. It has a higher than normal pitch and involves the use of simple words and sentences.

Language Environment, Poverty, and Language Development

In a study conducted by Betty Hart and Todd Risley (1995), the language environments and language development of children from middle-income professional and welfare backgrounds were observed. All of the children developed normally in terms of learning to talk and acquiring all of the forms of English and basic vocabulary. However, there were enormous differences in the sheer amount of language the children were exposed to and the level of the children's language development. For example, in a typical hour, the middle-income professional parents spent almost twice as much time communicating with their children as the welfare parents did. The children from the middle-income professional families heard about 2,100 words an hour, their child counterparts in welfare families only 600 words an hour. The researchers estimated that by 4 years of age, the average welfare family child would have 13 million fewer words of cumulative language experience than the child in the average middle-income professional family. Amazingly, some of the 3-year-old children from middle-income professional families had a recorded vocabulary that exceeded the recorded vocabulary of some of the welfare parents!

In another study, the level of maternal speech to infants was carefully assessed (Huttenlocher & others, 1991). As shown in figure 6.10, mothers who used a higher level of language (more talkative and used far more words) when interacting with their infants had infants with markedly higher vocabularies. By the second birthday, vocabulary differences were substantial and linked to the level of language input provided by the mother.

In sum, the language environment of children is linked to their vocabulary development. When children grow up in impoverished circumstances, and when their parents do not use a large number of vocabulary words in communicating with them, their vocabulary development suffers.

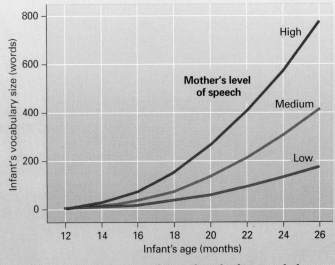

FIGURE 6.10 Level of Maternal Speech and Infant Vocabulary

communication and help language acquisition. In contrast, an overly active, directive approach to communicating with the child may be harmful.

Echoing is repeating what a child says, especially if it is an incomplete phrase or sentence. *Expanding* is restating, in a linguistically sophisticated form, what a child has said. *Labeling* is identifying the names of objects. Young children are forever being asked to identify the names of objects. Roger Brown (1986) identified this as "the great word game" and claimed that much of the early vocabulary acquired by children is motivated by this adult pressure to identify the words associated with objects.

The strategies just described—recasting, echoing, expanding, and labeling—are used naturally and in meaningful conversations. Parents do not (and should not) use any deliberate method to teach their children to talk. Even for children who are slow in learning language, the experts agree that intervention should occur in natural ways, with the goal of being able to convey meaning.

Review and Reflect

4 **Explain language development in infancy**

REVIEW

- What is language?
- How does language develop in infancy?
- What are some biological foundations of language?
- What are some behavioral and environmental influences on language?

REFLECT

- Would it be a good idea for parents to hold large flash cards of words in front of their infant to help the infant learn language? Why or why not? What do you think Piaget would say about this activity?

Reach Your Learning Goals

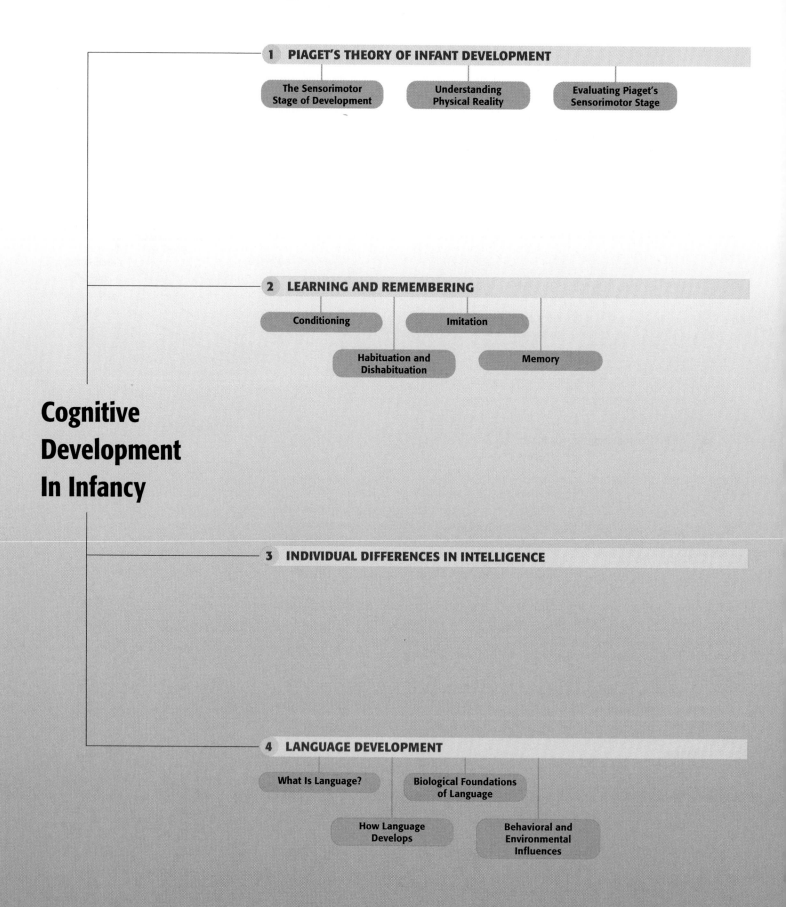

Cognitive Development In Infancy

1 PIAGET'S THEORY OF INFANT DEVELOPMENT

- The Sensorimotor Stage of Development
- Understanding Physical Reality
- Evaluating Piaget's Sensorimotor Stage

2 LEARNING AND REMEMBERING

- Conditioning
- Habituation and Dishabituation
- Imitation
- Memory

3 INDIVIDUAL DIFFERENCES IN INTELLIGENCE

4 LANGUAGE DEVELOPMENT

- What Is Language?
- How Language Develops
- Biological Foundations of Language
- Behavioral and Environmental Influences

Summary

1 **Summarize Piaget's theory of infant development**

- In Piaget's theory, there are four qualitatively different cognitive stages of development: sensorimotor, preoperational, concrete operational, and formal operational. Assimilation, accommodation, and schemes are important concepts that are involved in the individual's adaptation. In Piaget's first stage—sensorimotor development—the infant is able to organize and coordinate sensations with physical movements. This stage lasts from birth to about 2 years of age and is nonsymbolic throughout, according to Piaget. Sensorimotor development has six substages: simple reflexes; first habits and primary circular reactions; secondary circular reactions; coordination of secondary circular reactions; tertiary circular reactions, novelty, and curiosity; and internalization of schemes.
- Piaget and other developmentalists have been interested in the infant's understanding of physical reality. One aspect of this is reality is object permanence, the ability to understand that objects and events continue to exist even though the infant is no longer observing them. The other aspect involves infant's understanding of cause and effect.
- Piaget opened up a whole new way of looking at infant development in terms of coordinating sensory input with motoric actions. In the last three decades many research studies have suggested that revision of Piaget's view is needed. In perceptual development, researchers have found that a stable and differentiated perceptual world is formed earlier than Piaget envisioned. In conceptual development, researchers have found that memory and other forms of symbolic activity occur at least by the second half of the first year of life, much earlier than Piaget believed.

2 **Describe how infants learn and remember**

- Both classical and operant conditioning occur in infants. Operant conditioning techniques have especially been useful to researchers in demonstrating infants' perception and retention of information about perceptual-motor actions.
- Habituation is the repeated presentation of the same stimulus, causing reduced attention to the stimulus. If a different stimulus is presented and the infant pays increased attention to it, dishabituation is occurring. Newborn infants can habituate to repetitive stimulation.
- Meltzoff has shown that newborns can match their behaviors (such as protruding their tongue) to a model. His research also shows that deferred imitation occurs as early as 9 months of age.
- Memory is the retention of information over time. Infants as young as 2 months of age can retain information about perceptual-motor actions. However, many experts argue that what we commonly think of as memory (consciously remembering the past) does not occur until the second half of the first year of life.

3 **Discuss the assessment of intelligence in infancy**

- Developmental scales for infants grew out of the tradition of IQ testing of older children. These scales are less verbal than IQ tests. Gesell was an early developer of an infant test. His scale is still widely used by pediatricians; it provides a developmental quotient (DQ). The Bayley scales are the developmental scales that continue to be widely used today; developed by Nancy Bayley, they consist of a motor scale, a mental scale, and an infant behavior profile. Increasingly used, the Fagan test assesses how effectively the infant processes information. Global infant intelligence measures are not good predictors of childhood intelligence. However, specific aspects of infant intelligence, such as information-processing tasks involving attention, have been better predictors of childhood intelligence, especially in a specific area. There is both continuity and discontinuity between infant cognitive development and cognitive development later in childhood.

4 **Explain language development in infancy**

- Language is a form of communication, whether spoken, written, or signed, that is based on a system of symbols. Infinite generativity is the ability to produce an endless number of meaningful sentences using a finite set of words and rules.
- Among the milestones in infant language development are crying (birth), cooing (1 to 2 months), babbling (6 months), using gestures (8 to 12 months), comprehension of words (8 to 12 months), first word spoken (13 months), vocabulary spurt (18 months), rapid expansion of understanding words (18 to 24 months), and two-word utterances (18 to 24 months).
- The strongest evidence for a biological foundation for language is that children all over the world reach language milestones at about the same time developmentally despite vast variation in language input. In evolution, language clearly gave humans an enormous edge over other animals and increased their chance of survival. Chomsky proposed the concept of a language acquisition device (LAD) that flows from the evidence about the biological foundations of language.
- The behavioral view—that language reinforcement and imitation are the factors in language acquisition—has not been supported by research. Among the ways that adults teach language to children are infant-directed speech, recasting, echoing, expanding, and labeling. Parents should talk extensively with an infant, especially about what the baby is attending to. Talk primarily should be live talk, not mechanical talk.

Key Terms

scheme 183
simple reflexes 184
first habits and primary
   circular reactions 184
primary circular reaction 184
secondary circular
   reactions 184

coordination of secondary
   circular reactions 184
tertiary circular reactions,
   novelty, and curiosity 185
internalization of schemes 185
object permanence 185
habituation 189

dishabituation 189
deferred imitation 190
memory 190
developmental quotient
   (DQ) 191
Bayley Scales of Infant
   Development 191

language 194
infinite generativity 194
phonology 195
telegraphic speech 196
language acquisition device
   (LAD) 197
infant-directed speech 198

Key People

Jean Piaget 182, 183
Eleanor Gibson 187
Elizabeth Spelke 187
Renée Baillargeon 185, 187

Carolyn Rovee-Collier 188,
   190
Andrew Meltzoff 190
Jean Mandler 190

Arnold Gesell 191
Nancy Bayley 191
Noam Chomsky 197
Roger Brown 198, 199

Betty Hart and
   Todd Risley 199

Taking It to the Net

1. Toby must make a 15-minute class presentation on an important theorist who has significantly contributed to our understanding of human development. If Toby were to select
Piaget, what types of information (written, spoken, visual)
should he include in this presentation to his class?

2. Veronica works in an infant day-care center that serves
mothers who are participating in a welfare-to-work program,
advising the mothers about nutrition. What do these mothers
need to know about the effect of poor nutrition on their
child's cognitive development?

3. Taye is worried that his 1-year-old-cousin, Matthew, whom
he often baby-sits, is not on track with his language development as compared to his niece, Rita. By this age, what are
some of the language-related milestones or tasks that an
average child usually has achieved?

**Connect to www.mhhe.com/santrockld9 to research the
answers and complete these exercises.**

E-Learning Tools

To help you master the material in this chapter, you'll find a
number of valuable study tools on the Student CD-ROM that accompanies this book. In addition, visit the Online Learning Center
for *Life-Span Development,* ninth edition, where you'll find these
valuable resources for chapter 6, "Cognitive Development in
Infancy."

- What are your beliefs about nurturing an infant's cognitive
development? Use the self-assessment, *My Beliefs About
Nurturing a Baby's Mind,* to determine what your views are.
- Build your decision-making skills by trying your hand at the
parenting and education "Scenarios."

CHAPTER 7

We never know the love of our parents until we have become parents.

—HENRY WARD BEECHER
American Writer, 19th Century

Socioemotional Development in Infancy

Chapter Outline

EMOTIONAL AND PERSONALITY DEVELOPMENT

Emotional Development
Temperament
Personality Development

ATTACHMENT

What Is Attachment?
Individual Differences
Caregiving Styles and Attachment Classification
Attachment, Temperament, and the Wider Social World

SOCIAL CONTEXTS

The Family
Day Care

Learning Goals

1 *Discuss emotional and personality development in infancy*

2 *Describe how attachment develops in infancy*

3 *Explain how social contexts influence the infant's development*

Images of Life-Span Development
The Story of Tom's Fathering

Many fathers are spending more time with their infants.

TOM IS A 1-year-old infant who is being reared by his father during the day. His mother works full-time at her job away from home, and his father is a writer who works at home; they prefer this arrangement over putting Tom in day care. Tom's father is doing a great job of caring for him. Tom's father keeps Tom nearby while he is writing and spends lots of time talking to him and playing with him. From their interactions, it is clear that they genuinely enjoy each other.

Tom's father is a far cry from the emotionally distant, conformist, traditional-gender-role fathers of the 1950s. He looks to the future and imagines the Little League games Tom will play in and the many other activities he can enjoy with Tom. Remembering how little time his own father spent with him, he is dedicated to making sure that Tom has an involved, nurturing experience with his father. Of course, not all fathers in the 1950s behaved like Tom's father and not all fathers today are as emotionally involved with their children as Tom is.

When Tom's mother comes home in the evening, she spends considerable time with him. Tom shows a positive attachment to both his mother and his father. His parents have cooperated and successfully juggled their careers and work schedules to provide 1-year-old Tom with excellent child care.

In chapters 5 and 6, you read about how the infant perceives, learns, and remembers. Infants also are socioemotional beings, capable of displaying emotions and initiating social interaction with people close to them.

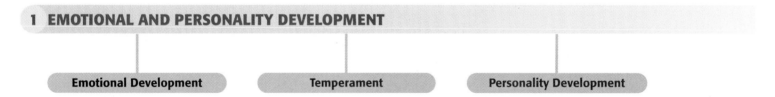

1 EMOTIONAL AND PERSONALITY DEVELOPMENT

Emotional Development   Temperament   Personality Development

Anyone who has been around infants for even a brief period of time detects that they are emotional beings. Not only do we notice infants' expressions of emotions, but we sense that they vary in their temperament. Some are shy and others are outgoing. Some are active and others much less so. Let's explore these and other aspects of emotional and personality development in infants.

Emotional Development

Infants can express a number of emotions. We will see what these are and how they develop, but first we need to define *emotion*.

Defining *emotion* is difficult because it is not easy to tell when a child or an adult is in an emotional state. Is a child in an emotional state when her heart beats fast, her palms sweat, and her stomach churns? Or is she in an emotional state when she smiles or grimaces? The body and face play important roles in understanding children's emotion. However, psychologists debate how important each is in determining whether a child is in an emotional state. For our purposes, we will define **emotion** as

emotion Feeling, or affect, that can involve physiological arousal (a fast heartbeat, for example), conscious experience (thinking about being in love with someone, for example), and behavioral expression (a smile or grimace, for example).

feeling, or affect, that can involve physiological arousal (a fast heartbeat, for example), conscious experience (thinking about being in love with someone, for example), and behavioral expression (a smile or grimace, for example). Psychologists debate which of these components is the most important aspect of emotion and how they mix to produce emotional experiences (Izard, 2000; Witherington, Campos, & Hertenstein, 2002).

When we think about children's emotions, a few dramatic feelings, such as rage, fear, and glorious joy, usually spring to mind. However, emotions can be subtle as well—the feeling a mother has when she holds her baby, the mild irritation of boredom, and the uneasiness of being in a new situation.

Affect in Parent-Child Relationships   Emotions are the first language with which parents and infants communicate before the infant acquires speech (Maccoby, 1992). Infants react to their parents' facial expressions and tone of voice. In return, parents "read" what the infant is trying to communicate, responding appropriately when their infants are either distressed or happy. Sensitive, responsive parents help their infants grow emotionally, whether the infants respond in distressed or happy ways (Campos, 2001; Thompson, 1998).

The initial aspects of infant attachment to parents are based on emotion-linked interchanges, as when an infant cries and the caregiver sensitively responds. By the end of the first year, a mother's facial expression—either smiling or fearful—influences whether an infant will explore an unfamiliar environment. And, when children hear their parents quarreling, they often react with distress and inhibit their play (Cummings, 1987). Exceptionally well-functioning families often include humor in their interactions, sometimes making each other laugh and developing light, pleasant mood states to defuse conflicts. And, when a positive mood has been induced in the child, the child is more likely to comply with a parent's directions.

Infant and adult affective communicative capacities make possible coordinated infant-adult interactions (Thompson, 1999). The face-to-face interactions of even 3-month-old infants and adults are bidirectional (mutually regulated). This coordination has led to the characterization of mother-infant interaction as "reciprocal" or "synchronous." These terms attempt to capture the quality of interaction when all is going well.

Crying   Crying is the most important mechanism newborns have for communicating with their world. This statement is true even for the first cry, which tells the mother and doctor the baby's lungs have filled with air. Cries also may tell physicians and researchers something about the central nervous system.

Babies don't have just one type of cry. They have at least three:

- **Basic cry:** a rhythmic pattern that usually consists of a cry, followed by a briefer silence, then a shorter inspiratory whistle that is somewhat higher in pitch than the main cry, then another brief rest before the next cry. Some infancy experts believe that hunger is one of the conditions that incite the basic cry.
- **Anger cry:** a variation of the basic cry in which more excess air is forced through the vocal cords.
- **Pain cry:** stimulated by a high-intensity stimulus, a sudden appearance of a long, initial loud cry followed by breath holding; no preliminary moaning is present.

Most parents, and adults in general, can determine whether an infant's cries signify anger or pain (Zeskind, Klein, & Marshall, 1992). Parents also can distinguish the cries of their own baby better than those of another baby.

To soothe or not to soothe—should a crying baby be given attention and soothed, or does this spoil the infant? Many years ago, the behaviorist John Watson (1928) argued that parents spend too much time responding to infant crying. As a consequence, he said, parents are actually rewarding infant crying and increasing its incidence. More

*Blossoms are scattered by the wind
And the wind cares nothing, but
The blossoms of the heart
No wind can touch.*

—Youshida Kenko
Buddhist Monk, 14th Century

mhhe.com/
santrockld9

Exploring Emotion
International Society for Research on Emotions

basic cry A rhythmic pattern usually consisting of a cry, a briefer silence, a shorter inspiratory whistle that is higher pitched than the main cry, and then a brief rest before the next cry.

anger cry A cry similar to the basic cry, with more excess air forced through the vocal chords.

pain cry A sudden appearance of loud crying without preliminary moaning and followed by an extended period of breath holding.

He who binds himself to joy
Does the winged life destroy;
But he who kisses the joy as it
Flies lives in eternity's sun rise.

—**William Blake**
English Poet, 19th Century

What are some developmental changes in emotion during infancy? What are some different types of crying that infants display?

mhhe●com/
santrockld9

Infant Crying

recently, behaviorist Jacob Gewirtz (1977) found that a caregiver's quick, soothing response to crying increased crying. In contrast, infancy experts Mary Ainsworth (1979) and John Bowlby (1989) stress that you can't respond too much to infant crying in the first year of life. They believe that the caregiver's quick, comforting response to the infant's cries is an important ingredient in the development of a strong bond between the infant and caregiver. In one of Ainsworth's studies, infants whose mothers responded quickly when they cried at 3 months of age cried less later in the first year of life (Bell & Ainsworth, 1972). We will examine Ainsworth's work in more detail later in this chapter.

Controversy, then, still characterizes the issue of whether parents should respond to an infant's cries (Lewis & Ramsay, 1999). However, developmentalists increasingly argue that an infant cannot be spoiled in the first year of life, which suggests that parents should soothe a crying infant rather than be unresponsive; as a result, infants will likely develop a sense of trust and secure attachment to the caregiver in the first year of life.

Smiling   Smiling is another important communicative affective behavior of the infant. Two types of smiling can be distinguished in infants:

- **Reflexive smile:** a smile that does not occur in response to external stimuli and appears during the first month after birth, usually during sleep.
- **Social smile:** a smile that occurs in response to an external stimulus, typically a face in the case of the young infant.

Social smiling does not occur until 2 to 3 months of age (Emde, Gaensbauer, & Harmon, 1976), although some researchers believe that infants grin in response to voices as early as 3 weeks of age (Sroufe & Waters, 1976). The power of the infant's smiles was appropriately captured by British theorist John Bowlby (1969): "Can we doubt that the more and better an infant smiles the better he is loved and cared for? It is fortunate for their survival that babies are so designed by nature that they beguile and enslave mothers."

reflexive smile A smile that does not occur in response to external stimuli. It happens during the month after birth, usually during irregular patterns of sleep, not when the infant is in an alert state.

social smile A smile in response to an external stimulus, which, early in development, typically is a face.

Fear   The most frequent expression of an infant's fear involves **stranger anxiety,** in which an infant shows a fear and wariness of strangers. This reaction tends to appear in the second half of the first year of life. There are individual variations in stranger anxiety, and not all infants show distress when they encounter a stranger. Stranger anxiety usually emerges gradually, first appearing at about 6 months of age in the form of wary reactions. By age 9 months, the fear of strangers is often more intense and continues to escalate through the infant's first birthday (Emde, Gaensbauer, & Harmon, 1976).

A number of factors can influence whether an infant shows stranger anxiety, including the social context and the characteristics of the stranger. In terms of the social context, infants show less stranger anxiety when they are in familiar settings. For example, in one study, 10-month-olds showed little stranger anxiety when they met a stranger in their own home but much greater fear when they encountered a stranger in a research laboratory (Sroufe, Waters, & Matas, 1974). Also, infants show less stranger anxiety when they are sitting on their mothers' laps than when placed in an infant seat several feet away from their mothers (Bohlin & Hagekull, 1993). Thus, it appears that, when infants have a sense of security, they are less likely to show stranger anxiety.

Who the stranger is and how the stranger behaves also influence stranger anxiety in infants. Infants are less fearful of child strangers than adult strangers. They also are less fearful of friendly, outgoing, smiling strangers than of passive, unsmiling strangers (Bretherton, Stolberg, & Kreye, 1981).

Another expression of the infant's fear is **separation protest,** the infant's distress over being separated from his or her caregiver. Separation protest tends to peak at about 15 months in U.S. infants. In one study, charted in figure 7.1, separation protest peaked at about 13 to 15 months in four different cultures (Kagan, Kearsley, & Zelazo, 1978). Although the percentage of infants who engaged in separation protest varied across cultures, the infants reached a peak of protest at about the same age—just before the middle of the second year of life.

Social Referencing   **Social referencing** involves "reading" emotional cues in others to help determine how to act in a particular situation. The development of social referencing helps infants to interpret ambiguous situations more accurately, as when they encounter a stranger and need to know whether to fear the person (Mumme, Fernald, & Herrera, 1996). Infants become better at social referencing in the second year of life. In their second year, they have a tendency to "check" with their mother before they act. That is, they look at her to see if she is happy, angry, or fearful. In one study, 14- to 22-month-old infants were more likely to look at their mother's face as a source of information about how to act in a situation than were 6- to 9-month-old infants (Walden, 1991).

Emotional Regulation and Coping   **Emotional regulation** consists of effectively managing arousal to adapt and reach a goal (Eisenberg & others, 2002). Arousal involves a state of alertness or activation, which can reach levels that are too high for effective functioning. Crying and anger are two emotions that often require regulation.

During the first year of life, the infant gradually develops an ability to inhibit, or minimize, the intensity and duration of emotional reactions (Eisenberg, 2001). At the same time, infants acquire a greater diversity of emotional responses. Examples of early emotional regulation are infants' soothing themselves by sucking and withdrawing from excessive stimulation. Caregivers play an important role in helping infants learn how to regulate their emotions by attending to their distress and providing them with comfort.

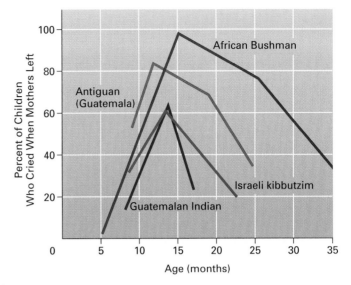

FIGURE 7.1 Separation Protest in Four Cultures

Note that separation protest peaked at about the same time in all four cultures in this study (13 to 15 months of age). However, a higher percentage (100 percent) of infants in an African Bushman culture engaged in separation protest compared to only about 60 percent of infants in Guatemalan Indian and Israeli kibbutzim cultures.

stranger anxiety An infant's fear and wariness of strangers; it tends to appear in the second half of the first year of life.

separation protest An infant's distress over being separated from his or her caregiver.

social referencing "Reading" emotional cues in others to help determine how to act in a particular situation.

emotional regulation Effectively managing arousal to adapt and reach a goal.

"Oh, he's cute, all right, but he's got the temperament of a car alarm."

From early in infancy, babies put their thumbs in their mouths as a self-soothing strategy. In the early part of infancy, infants mainly depend on caregivers to help them sooth their emotions by rocking them to sleep, singing lullabyes to them, gently stroking them, and so on. Many developmentalists believe it is a good strategy for a caregiver to soothe an infant before the infant gets into an intense, agitated, uncontrolled state (Thompson, 1994). Later in infancy, when they become aroused, infants sometimes redirect their attention to something else or distract themselves in order to reduce their arousal (Grolnick, Bridges, & Connell, 1996).

Contexts can influence emotional regulation (Kopp & Neufeld, 2002; Saarni, 1999). Infants are often affected by such factors as fatigue, hunger, time of day, the people around them, and where they are. Infants must learn to increasingly adapt to different contexts that require emotional regulation. Further, new context demands appear as the infant becomes older and parents modify their expectations. For example, a parent may not expect a 1½-year-old to scream loudly in a restaurant but may not have been as bothered by this when the infant was 6 months old.

By 2 years of age, toddlers can use language to define their feeling states and the context that is upsetting them (Kopp & Neufeld, 2002). A toddler might say, "Feel bad. Dog scare." The communication of this type of information about feeling states and context may help caregivers to more effectively assist the child in regulating emotion.

Temperament

Emotional responses to similar situations vary among infants. One infant might be cheerful and happy much of the time; another baby might cry a lot and more often display a negative mood. These behaviors reflect differences in temperament (Halpern & Brand, 1999; Rothbart & Putnam, 2002). Let's explore a definition of temperament, the ways in which it can be classified, and the implications of temperamental variations for parenting.

Defining and Classifying Temperament **Temperament** is an individual's behavioral style and characteristic way of emotionally responding. A widely debated issue is just what the key dimensions of temperament are. Psychiatrists Alexander Chess and Stella Thomas (Chess & Thomas, 1977; Thomas & Chess, 1991) believe there are three basic types, or clusters, of temperament:

- **Easy child:** This child is generally in a positive mood, quickly establishes regular routines in infancy, and adapts easily to new experiences.
- **Difficult child:** This child reacts negatively and cries frequently, engages in irregular daily routines, and is slow to accept new experiences.
- **Slow-to-warm-up child:** This child has a low activity level, is somewhat negative, and displays a low intensity of mood.

Various dimensions make up these three basic clusters of temperament. In their longitudinal investigation, Chess and Thomas found that 40 percent of the children they studied could be classified as easy, 10 percent as difficult, and 15 percent as slow to warm up (35 percent did not fit any of the three patterns). Researchers have found that these three basic clusters of temperament are moderately stable across the childhood years.

One way of classifying temperament involves comparing a shy, subdued, timid child with a sociable, extraverted, bold child. Jerome Kagan (1997, 2000, 2002; Kagan & Snidman, 1991) regards shyness with strangers, whether peers or adults, as one feature of a broader temperament category called *inhibition to the unfamiliar.* Inhibited

temperament An individual's behavioral style and characteristic way of emotionally responding.

easy child A child who is generally in a positive mood, who quickly establishes regular routines in infancy, and who adapts easily to new experiences.

difficult child A child who tends to react negatively and cry frequently, who engages in irregular daily routines, and who is slow to accept new experiences.

slow-to-warm-up child A child who has a low activity level, is somewhat negative, shows low adaptability, and displays a low intensity of mood.

children react to many aspects of unfamiliarity with initial avoidance, distress, or subdued affect, especially beginning about 7 to 9 months of age. Kagan has found that inhibition shows considerable stability across the infant and early childhood years.

New classifications of temperament continue to be forged (Bornstein, 2000; Rothbart & Putnam, 2002; Wachs & Bates, 2002; Wachs & Kohnstamm, 2001). In a review of temperament research, Mary Rothbart and John Bates (1998) concluded that the best framework for classifying temperament involves a revision of Chess and Thomas' categories of easy, difficult, and slow to warm up. The general classification of temperament now focuses more on:

- *Positive affect and approach.* This category is much like the personality trait of extraversion/introversion. This category fits Kagan's concept of uninhibited children.
- *Negative affectivity.* Children whose temperament is characterized by negative affectivity are easily distressed and may fret and cry often. Negative affectivity is closely related to the personality trait of introversion, a tendency toward shyness and inhibition. This category also fits Kagan's concept of inhibition.
- *Effortful control (self-regulation).* This category reflects the child's ability to control his or her emotions and matches the concept of emotional regulation that we discussed earlier in the chapter. Thus, infants who are high on effortful control show an ability to keep their arousal from getting too high and have strategies for soothing themselves. By contrast, children low on effortful control often show an inability to control their arousal and they become easily agitated and intensely emotional.

What are some ways that developmentalists have classified infants' temperaments? Which classification makes the most sense to you, based on your observations of infants?

A number of scholars conceive of temperament as a stable characteristic of newborns, which comes to be shaped and modified by the child's later experiences. This raises the question of heredity's role in temperament (Goldsmith, 1988). Twin and adoption studies have been conducted to answer this question (Plomin & others, 1994). The researchers have found a heritability index in the range of .50 to .60, suggesting a moderate influence of heredity on temperament. However, the strength of the association usually declines as infants become older (Goldsmith & Gottesman, 1981). This finding supports the belief that temperament becomes more malleable with experience. Alternatively, it may be that, as a child becomes older, behavior indicators of temperament are more difficult to spot.

Infant Temperament

Goodness of Fit   *Goodness of fit* refers to the match between a child's temperament and the environmental demands the child must cope with (Bates, 2001; Matheny & Phillips, 2001). Goodness of fit can be important to the child's adjustment. For example, consider an active child who is made to sit still for long periods of time or lives in a small apartment. Consider also a slow-to-warm-up child who is abruptly pushed into new situations on a regular basis. A bad fit between the child's temperament and these environmental demands can produce adjustment problems for the child. In our discussion of parenting and the child's temperament, many of the recommendations involve consideration of goodness of fit.

Parenting and the Child's Temperament   Many parents don't become believers in temperament's importance until the birth of their second child. They tend to view the first child's behavior as being solely a result of how they socialized the child. However, management strategies that worked with the first child might not be as effective

What are some good strategies for parents to adopt when responding to their infant's temperament?

with the second child. Problems experienced with the first child (such as those involved in feeding, sleeping, and coping with strangers) might not exist with the second child, but new problems might arise. Such experiences strongly suggest that nature as well as nurture influence the child's development, that children differ from each other from very early in life, and that these differences have important implications for parent-child interaction (Kwak & others, 1999).

What are the implications of temperamental variations for parenting? Although answers to this question necessarily are speculative because of the incompleteness of the research literature, these conclusions were reached by temperament expert Mary Rothbart and her colleagues (Putnam, Sanson, & Rothbart, 2002; Sanson & Rothbart, 1995):

- *Attention to and respect for individuality.* An important implication of taking children's individuality seriously is that it becomes difficult to generate prescriptions for "good parenting," other than possibly specifying that parents need to be sensitive and flexible. Parents need to be sensitive to the infant's signals and needs. A goal of parenting might be accomplished in one way with one child and in another way with another child, depending on the child's temperament.

    Some temperament characteristics pose more parenting challenges than others, at least in modern Western societies. Children's proneness to distress, as exhibited by frequent crying and irritability, can contribute to the emergence of avoidant or coercive parental responses. In one research study, though, extra support and training for mothers of distress-prone infants improved the quality of mother-infant interaction (van den Boom, 1989).
- *Structuring the child's environment.* Crowded, noisy environments can pose greater problems for some children (such as a "difficult child") than others (such as an "easygoing" child). We might also expect that a fearful, withdrawing child would benefit from slower entry into new contexts.
- *The "difficult child" and packaged parenting programs.* Some books and programs for parents focus specifically on temperament (Cameron, Hansen, & Rosen, 1989; Turecki & Tonner, 1989). These programs usually focus on children with "difficult" temperaments. Acknowledgment that some children are harder to parent is often helpful, and advice on how to handle particular difficult temperament characteristics can also be useful. However, weighted against these potential advantages are several disadvantages. Whether a particular characteristic is difficult depends on its fit with the environment, whereas the notion of difficult temperament suggests that the problem rests solely with the child. Labeling a child "difficult" risks becoming a self-fulfilling prophecy—that is, if a child is identified as "difficult," the labeling might lead adults to expect the child to behave in this way and contribute to the continuance of the difficult behavior.

A child's temperament needs to be taken into account when considering caregiving behavior (Kochanska, 1999). Research does not yet allow for many highly specific recommendations, but, in general, caregivers should (1) be sensitive to the individual characteristics of the child, (2) be flexible in responding to these characteristics, and (3) avoid negative labeling of the child.

Gender, Culture, and Temperament Parents might react differently to a child's temperament, depending on whether the child is a girl or a boy (Kerr, 2001). For example, in one study, mothers were more responsive to the crying of irritable girls than to the crying of irritable boys (Crockenberg, 1986).

Children's temperament also can vary across cultures (Putnam, Sanson, & Rothbart, 2002). For example, an active temperament might be valued in some cultures (such as the United States) but not in other cultures (such as China). Indeed, behavioral inhibition is more highly valued in China than in North America and researchers have found that Chinese infants have a more inhibited temperament than Canadian infants (Chen & others, 1998). The cultural differences in temperament were linked to parental attitudes and behaviors. Canadian mothers of inhibited 2-year-olds were less accepting of their infants' inhibited temperament while their Chinese mothers were more accepting.

Personality Development

We have explored some important aspects of emotional development and temperament, which reveal individual variations in infants. Let's now examine the characteristics that often are thought of as central to the infant's personality development: trust and the development of self and independence.

Trust According to Erik Erikson (1968), the first year of life is characterized by the trust-versus-mistrust stage of development ◀▥ p. 46. Following a life of regularity, warmth, and protection in the mother's womb, the infant faces a world that is less secure. Erikson believes that infants learn trust when they are cared for in a consistent, warm manner. If the infant is not well fed and kept warm on a consistent basis, a sense of mistrust is likely to develop.

Trust versus mistrust is not resolved once and for all in the first year of life. It arises again at each successive stage of development, which can have positive or negative outcomes. For example, children who enter school with a sense of mistrust may trust a particular teacher who has taken the time to make herself trustworthy. With this second chance, children overcome their early mistrust. By contrast, children who leave infancy with a sense of trust can still have their sense of mistrust activated at a later stage, perhaps if their parents are separated or divorced under conflicting circumstances.

The Developing Sense of Self and Independence Individuals carry with them a sense of who they are and what makes them different from everyone else. They cling to this identity and begin to feel secure in the knowledge that their identity is becoming more stable. Real or imagined, the sense of self is a strong motivating force in life. When does the individual begin to sense a separate existence from others?

The Self Infants are not "given" a self by their parents or the culture. Rather, they find and construct selves (Rochat, 2002). Studying the self in infancy is difficult mainly because infants are unable to describe with language their experiences of themselves.

To determine whether infants can recognize themselves, psychologists have used mirrors. In the animal kingdom, only the great apes learn to recognize their reflection in the mirror, but human infants accomplish this feat by about 18 months of age. How does the mirror technique work? The mother puts a dot of rouge on her infant's nose. The observer watches to see how often the infant touches its nose. Next, the infant is placed in front of a mirror, and observers detect whether nose touching increases. In two independent investigations in the second half of the second year of life, a majority of infants recognized their own image and coordinated the image they saw with the actions of touching their own body (Amsterdam, 1968; Lewis & Brooks-Gunn, 1979) (see figure 7.2).

Independence Not only does the infant develop a sense of self in the second year of life, but independence also becomes a more central theme in the infant's life. The theories of Margaret Mahler and Erik Erikson have important implications for both self-development and independence. Mahler (1979) believes that the child goes through a separation and then an individuation process. Separation involves the infant's movement away from the mother. Individuation involves the development of self.

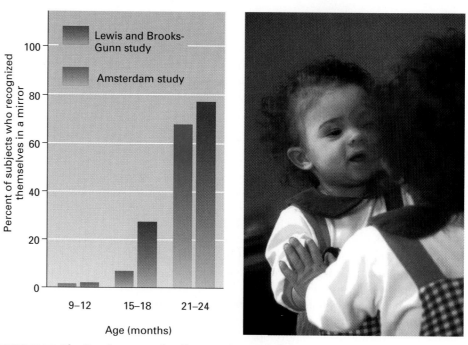

FIGURE 7.2 The Development of Self-Recognition in Infancy

The graph shows the findings of two studies in which infants less than 1 year of age did not recognize themselves in the mirror. A slight increase in the percentage of infant self-recognition occurred around 15 to 18 months of age and then by 2 years of age, a majority of children recognized themselves.

Erikson (1968), like Mahler, believed that independence is an important issue in the second year of life ◀▥ p. 46. Erikson describes the second stage of development as the stage of autonomy versus shame and doubt. Autonomy builds on the infant's developing mental and motor abilities. At this point in development, not only can infants walk, but they can also climb, open and close, drop, push and pull, and hold and let go. Infants feel pride in these new accomplishments and want to do everything themselves, whether it is flushing a toilet, pulling the wrapping off a package, or deciding what to eat. It is important for parents to recognize the motivation of toddlers to do what they are capable of doing at their own pace. Then they can learn to control their muscles and their impulses themselves. But when caregivers are impatient and do for toddlers what they are capable of doing themselves, shame and doubt develop. Every parent has rushed a child from time to time. It is only when parents consistently overprotect toddlers or criticize accidents (wetting, soiling, spilling, or breaking, for example) that children develop an excessive sense of shame and doubt about their ability to control themselves and their world.

Erikson also believed that the stage of autonomy versus shame and doubt has important implications for the development of independence and identity during adolescence. The development of autonomy during the toddler years gives adolescents the courage to be independent individuals who can choose and guide their own future.

mhhe●com/
santrockld9

Self-Development in Infancy
Seeking Independence

Review and Reflect

1 Discuss emotional and personality development in infancy
REVIEW
- What is the nature of an infant's emotions and how do they change?
- What is temperament and how does it develop in infancy?
- What are some important aspects of personality in infancy and how do they develop?

REFLECT

• How would you describe your temperament? Does it fit one of Chess and Thomas' three styles—easy, slow to warm up, or difficult? If you have siblings, is your temperament similar or different from theirs?

2 ATTACHMENT

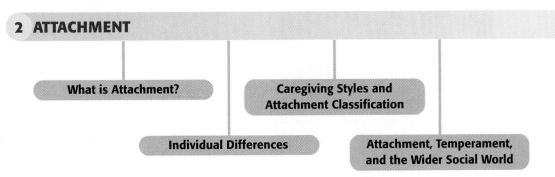

What is Attachment?

Caregiving Styles and Attachment Classification

Individual Differences

Attachment, Temperament, and the Wider Social World

A small curly-haired girl named Danielle, 12 months old, begins to whimper. After a few seconds, she begins to wail. The psychologist observing Danielle is conducting a research study on the nature of attachment between infants and their mothers. Subsequently, Danielle's mother enters the room, and Danielle's crying ceases. Quickly, Danielle crawls over to where her mother is seated and reaches out to be held. This situation is one of the main ways in which psychologists study the nature of attachment during infancy.

What Is Attachment?

In everyday language, attachment is a relationship between two individuals who feel strongly about each other and do a number of things to continue the relationship. Many pairs of people are attached: relatives, lovers, a teacher and student. In the language of developmental psychology, though, attachment is often restricted to a relationship between particular social figures and a particular phenomenon that is thought to reflect unique characteristics of the relationship. In this case, the developmental period is infancy, the social figures are the infant and one or more adult caregivers, and the phenomenon is a bond (Bowlby, 1969, 1989). To summarize, **attachment** is a close emotional bond between an infant and a caregiver.

There is no shortage of theories about infant attachment. Freud believed that infants become attached to the person or object that provides oral satisfaction. For most infants, this is the mother, since she is most likely to feed the infant.

Is feeding as important as Freud thought? A classic study by Harry Harlow (1958) reveals that the answer is no (see figure 7.3). Harlow evaluated whether feeding or contact comfort was more important to infant attachment. Infant monkeys were removed from their mothers at birth and reared for six months by surrogate (substitute) "mothers." One of the mothers was made of wire, the other of cloth. Half of the infant monkeys were fed by the wire mother, half by the cloth mother. Periodically, the amount of time the infant monkeys spent with either the wire or the cloth monkey was computed. Regardless of whether they were fed by the wire or the cloth mother, the infant monkeys spent far more time with the cloth mother. This study clearly demonstrated that feeding is not the crucial element in the attachment process and that contact comfort is important.

Erik Erikson (1968) believed that the first year of life is the key time frame for the development of attachment. Recall his proposal—also discussed in chapter 2—that the

mhhe●com/
santrockld9

Harry Harlow

attachment A close emotional bond between an infant and a caregiver.

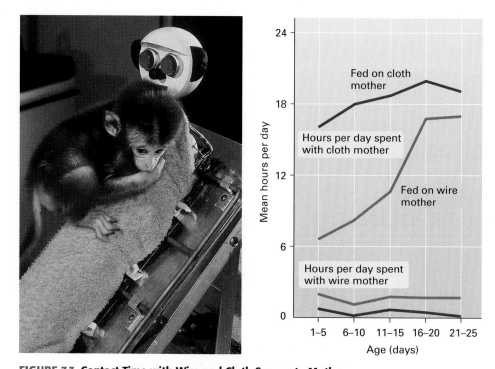

FIGURE 7.3 Contact Time with Wire and Cloth Surrogate Mothers
Regardless of whether the infant monkeys were fed by a wire or a cloth mother, they overwhelmingly preferred to spend contact time with the cloth mother.

first year of life represents the stage of trust versus mistrust ◀▥ p. 46. A sense of trust requires a feeling of physical comfort and a minimal amount of fear and apprehension about the future. Trust in infancy sets the stage for a lifelong expectation that the world will be a good and pleasant place to be. Erikson also believed that responsive, sensitive parenting contributes to an infant's sense of trust.

The ethological perspective of British psychiatrist John Bowlby (1969, 1989) also stresses the importance of attachment in the first year of life and the responsiveness of the caregiver. Bowlby believes that an infant and his or her primary caregiver form an attachment. He argues that the newborn is biologically equipped to elicit attachment behavior (Weizmann, 2000). The baby cries, clings, coos, and smiles. Later, the infant crawls, walks, and follows the mother. The infant's goal is to keep the primary caregiver nearby.

Attachment does not emerge suddenly but rather develops in a series of phases, moving from a baby's general preference for human beings to a partnership with primary caregivers. Here are four such phases based on Bowlby's conceptualization of attachment (Schaffer, 1996):

Phase 1:	Birth to 2 months	Infants instinctively direct their attachment to human figures. Strangers, siblings, and parents are equally likely to elicit smiling or crying from the infant.
Phase 2:	2 to 7 months	Attachment becomes focused on one figure, usually the primary caregiver, as the baby gradually learns to distinguish familiar from unfamiliar people.
Phase 3:	7 to 24 months	Specific attachments develop. With increased locomotor skills, babies actively seek contact with regular caregivers, such as the mother or father.

Phase 4: 24 months on A goal-corrected partnership is formed in which children become aware of others' feelings, goals, and plans and begin to take these into account in forming their own actions.

Individual Differences

Although attachment to a caregiver intensifies midway through the first year, isn't it likely that some babies have a more positive attachment experience than others? Mary Ainsworth (1979) thinks so. She says that, in **secure attachment,** infants use the caregiver, usually the mother, as a secure base of attachment from which to explore the environment. Ainsworth believes that secure attachment in the first year of life provides an important foundation for psychological development later in life. The caregiver's sensitivity to the infant's signals increases secure attachment (deWolff & van Ijzendoorn, 1997). The securely attached infant moves freely away from the mother but processes her location through periodic glances. The securely attached infant responds positively to being picked up by others and, when put back down, freely moves away to play. An insecurely attached infant, by contrast, avoids the mother or is ambivalent toward her, fears strangers, and is upset by minor, everyday separations. Ainsworth's concept of secure attachment has much in common with Erikson's ideas about the development of trust.

Ainsworth created the **Strange Situation,** an observational measure of infant attachment that requires the infant to move through a series of introductions, separations, and reunions with the caregiver and an adult stranger in a prescribed order (see figure 7.4). In using the Strange Situation, researchers hope that their observations will provide them with information about the infant's motivation to be near the caregiver and the degree to which the caregiver's presence provides the infant with security and confidence. For example, in the presence of their caregiver, securely attached infants explore the room and examine toys that have been placed in it. When the caregiver departs, securely attached infants might mildly protest, and when the caregiver returns these infants reestablish positive interaction with her, perhaps by smiling or climbing on her lap. Subsequently, the securely attached infant often resumes playing with the toys in the room.

Three types of insecurely attached infants have been described:

- **Insecure avoidant babies** show insecurity by avoiding the mother. In the Strange Situation, these babies engage in little interaction with the caregiver, often display distress by crying when she leaves the room, usually do not reestablish contact with her on her return, and may even turn their back on her at this point. If contact is established, the infant usually leans away or looks away.
- **Insecure resistant babies** often cling to the caregiver and then resist her by fighting against the closeness, perhaps by kicking or pushing away. In the Strange Situation, these babies often cling anxiously to the caregiver and don't explore the playroom. When the caregiver leaves, they often cry loudly and push away if she tries to comfort them on her return.
- **Insecure disorganized babies** show insecurity in being disorganized and disoriented. In the Strange Situation, these babies might appear dazed, confused, and fearful. To be classified as disorganized, strong patterns of avoidance and resistance must be shown or certain select behaviors, such as extreme fearfulness around the caregiver, must be present.

Although the Strange Situation has been used in a large number of studies of infant attachment, some critics believe that the isolated, controlled events of the setting might not necessarily reflect what would happen if infants were observed with their caregiver in a natural environment. The issue of using controlled, laboratory assessments versus naturalistic observations is widely debated in child development circles.

secure attachment The infant uses a caregiver as a secure base from which to explore the environment. Ainsworth believes that secure attachment in the first year of life provides an important foundation for psychological development later in life.

Strange Situation An observational measure of infant attachment that requires the infant to move through a series of introductions, separations, and reunions with the caregiver and an adult stranger in a prescribed order.

insecure avoidant babies Babies that show insecurity by avoiding the caregiver.

insecure resistant babies Babies that often cling to the caregiver, then resist her by fighting against the closeness, perhaps by kicking or pushing away.

insecure disorganized babies Babies that show insecurity by being disorganized and disoriented.

Episode	Persons present	Duration of episode	Description of setting
1	Caregiver, baby, and observer	30 seconds	Observer introduces caregiver and baby to experimental room, then leaves. (Room contains many appealing toys scattered about.)
2	Caregiver and baby	3 minutes	Caregiver is nonparticipant while baby explores; if necessary, play is stimulated after 2 minutes.
3	Stranger, caregiver, and baby	3 minutes	Stranger enters. First minute: Stranger is silent. Second minute: Stranger converses with caregiver. Third minute: Stranger approaches baby. After 3 minutes caregiver leaves unobtrusively.
4	Stranger and baby	3 minutes or less	First separation episode. Stranger's behavior is geared to that of baby.
5	Caregiver and baby	3 minutes or more	First reunion episode. Caregiver greets and/or comforts baby, then tries to settle baby again in play. Caregiver then leaves, saying "bye-bye."
6	Baby alone	3 minutes or less	Second separation episode.
7	Stranger and baby	3 minutes or less	Continuation of second separation. Stranger enters and gears behavior to that of baby.
8	Caregiver and baby	3 minutes	Second reunion episode. Caregiver enters, greets baby, then picks baby up. Meanwhile stranger leaves unobtrusively.

FIGURE 7.4 The Ainsworth Strange Situation

Mary Ainsworth (*left*) developed the Strange Situation to assess whether infants are securely or insecurely attached to their caregiver. The episodes involved in the Ainsworth Strange Situation are described here.

If early attachment to a caregiver is important, it should relate to a child's social behavior later in development. Researchers have found that for some children, early attachments seem to foreshadow later functioning (Schneider, Atkinson, & Tardif, 2001; Sroufe, Egeland, & Carlson, 1999). For other children, there is little continuity (Thompson, 2000). Consistency in caregiving over a number of years is likely an important factor in connecting early attachment and the child's functioning later in development.

Caregiving Styles and Attachment Classification

Attachment is defined as a close emotional bond between the infant and caregiver. Is the parent's caregiving style linked with this close emotional bond called attachment? Securely attached babies have caregivers who are sensitive to their signals and are consistently available to respond to their infants' needs (Gao, Elliot, & Waters, 1999; Main, 2000). These caregivers often let their babies have an active part in determining the onset and pacing of interaction in the first year of life.

How do the caregivers of insecurely attached babies interact with them? Caregivers of insecure avoidant babies tend to be unavailable or rejecting (Berlin & Cassidy, 2000). They often don't respond to their babies' signals and have little physical contact with them. When they do interact with their babies, they may behave in an angry and irritable way toward them. Caregivers of insecure resistant babies tend to be inconsistently available to their babies (Cassidy & Berlin, 1994). That is, sometimes they respond to their babies' needs, and sometimes they don't. In general, they tend not to be very affectionate with their babies and show little synchrony when interacting with them. Caregivers of insecure disorganized babies often neglect or physically abuse their babies (Barnett, Ganiban, & Cicchetti, 1999). In some cases, these caregivers also have depression (Field, 1992; Levy, 1999).

Attachment, Temperament, and the Wider Social World

Not all research reveals the power of infant attachment to predict subsequent development. In one longitudinal study, attachment classification in infancy did not predict attachment classification at 18 years of age (Lewis, 1997). In this study, the best predictor of attachment classification at 18 was the occurrence of parent divorce in intervening years.

Thus, not all developmentalists believe that attachment in infancy is the only path to competence in life. Indeed, some developmentalists believe that too much emphasis is placed on the importance of the attachment bond in infancy. Jerome Kagan (1987, 2000), for example, believes that infants are highly resilient and adaptive; he argues that they are evolutionarily equipped to stay on a positive developmental course, even in the face of wide variations in parenting. Kagan and others stress that genetic and temperament characteristics play a more important role in a child's social competence than the attachment theorists, such as Bowlby, Ainsworth, and Sroufe, are willing to acknowledge (Chaudhuri & Williams, 1999; Young & Shahinfar, 1995). For example, infants may have inherited a low tolerance for stress. This inherited characteristic, rather than an insecure attachment bond, may be responsible for their inability to get along with peers.

Also, researchers have found cultural variations in attachment. German and Japanese babies often show different patterns of attachment than American infants do. As shown in figure 7.5, German infants are more likely to show an avoidant attachment pattern and Japanese infants are less likely to show this pattern than U.S. infants (van Ijzendoorn & Kroonenberg, 1988). The avoidant pattern in German babies likely occurs because their caregivers encourage them to be more independent (Grossmann & others, 1985). Also as shown in figure 7.5, Japanese babies are more likely than American babies to be categorized as resistant. This may have more to do with the Ainsworth Strange Situation as a measure of attachment than with attachment insecurity itself. Japanese mothers rarely let anyone unfamiliar with their babies care for them. Thus, the Ainsworth Strange Situation might create considerably more stress for Japanese infants than for American infants, who are more accustomed to separation from their mothers (Takahashi, 1990). Even though there are cultural variations in attachment classification, the prevailing classification in every culture studied so far is secure attachment (van Ijzendoorn & Kroonenberg, 1988).

Another criticism of attachment theory is that it ignores the diversity of socializing agents and contexts that exists in an infant's world. In some cultures, infants show attachments to many people. Among the Hausa (who live in Nigeria), both grandmothers and siblings provide a significant amount of care for infants (Harkness & Super, 1995). Infants in agricultural societies tend to form attachments to older siblings, who are assigned a major responsibility for younger siblings' care. The attachments formed by infants in group care in Israeli kibbutzim provide another challenge to the singular attachment thesis.

Researchers recognize the importance of competent, nurturant caregivers in an infant's development (Maccoby, 1999; McHale & others, 2001; Parke, 2001). At issue, though, is whether or not secure attachment, especially to a single caregiver, is critical (Thompson, 2000).

What is the nature of secure and insecure attachment?

mhhe ○com/
santrockld9

Forming a Secure Attachment

Attachment Research

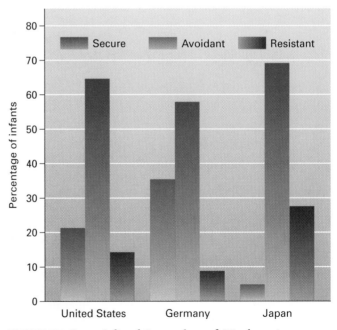

FIGURE 7.5 Cross-Cultural Comparison of Attachment

In one study, infant attachment in three countries—the United States, Germany, and Japan—was measured in the Ainsworth Strange Situation (van Ijzendoorn & Kroonenberg, 1988). The dominant attachment pattern in all three countries was secure attachment. However, German infants were more avoidant and Japanese infants were less avoidant and more resistant than U.S. infants.

Review and Reflect

2 **Describe how attachment develops in infancy**

REVIEW

- What is attachment?
- What are some individual variations in attachment?
- How are caregiving styles related to attachment classifications?
- What are some issues related to attachment?

REFLECT

- How might the infant's temperament be related to the way in which attachment is classified? Look at the temperament categories we described and reflect on how these might be more likely to show up in infants in some attachment categories than others.

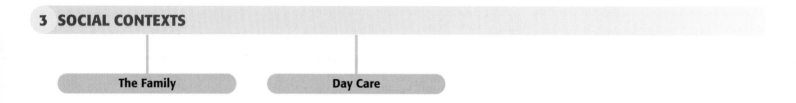

3 SOCIAL CONTEXTS

The Family   **Day Care**

Now that we have explored the infant's emotional and personality development and attachment, let's examine the social contexts in which these occur. We will begin by studying a number of aspects of the family and then turn to a social context in which infants increasingly spend time—day care.

The Family

Most of us began our lives in families and spent thousands of hours during our childhood interacting with our parents. Some of you are already parents; others of you may become parents. What is the transition to parenthood like?

mhhe●com/
santrockld9

The Transition to Parenting

The Transition to Parenthood   When people become parents through pregnancy, adoption, or stepparenting, they face disequilibrium and must adapt (Heincke, 2002; Klitzing, Simoni, & Burgin, 1999). Parents want to develop a strong attachment with their infant, but they still want to maintain strong attachments to their spouse and friends, and possibly continue their careers. Parents ask themselves how this new being will change their lives. A baby places new restrictions on partners; no longer will they be able to rush out to a movie on a moment's notice, and money may not be readily available for vacations and other luxuries. Dual-career parents ask, "Will it harm the baby to place her in day care? Will we be able to find responsible baby-sitters?"

In a longitudinal investigation of couples from late pregnancy until 3½ years after the baby was born, couples enjoyed more positive marital relations before the baby was born than after (Cowan & Cowan, 2000; Cowan & others, 1995). Still, almost one-third showed an increase in marital satisfaction. Some couples said that the baby had both brought them closer together *and* moved them farther apart. They commented that being parents enhanced their sense of themselves and gave them a new, more stable identity as a couple. Babies opened men up to a concern with intimate relationships, and the demands of juggling work and family roles stimulated women to manage family tasks more efficiently and pay attention to their own personal growth.

At some point during the early years of the child's life, parents face the difficult task of juggling their roles as parents and as self-actualizing adults. Until recently in our culture, nurturing our children and having a career were thought to be incompatible. Fortunately, we have come to recognize that the balance between caring and achieving, nurturing and working—although difficult to manage—can be accomplished (Hoffman & Youngblade, 1999).

Reciprocal Socialization For many years, socialization between parents and children was viewed as a one-way process: Children were considered to be the products of their parents' socialization techniques. Today, however, we view parent-child interaction as reciprocal (Hartup & Laursen, 1999). **Reciprocal socialization** is socialization that is bidirectional. That is, children socialize parents just as parents socialize children. For example, the interaction of mothers and their infants is symbolized as a dance or a dialogue in which successive actions of the partners are closely coordinated. This coordinated dance or dialogue can assume the form of mutual synchrony in which each person's behavior depends on the partner's previous behavior (Feldman, Greenbaum, & Yirmiya, 1999). Or it can be reciprocal in the sense that actions of the partners are matched, as when one partner imitates the other or when there is mutual smiling.

When reciprocal socialization has been studied in infancy, mutual gaze, or eye contact, plays an important role in early social interaction. In one investigation, the mother and infant engaged in a variety of behaviors while they looked at each other. By contrast, when they looked away from each other, the rate of such behaviors dropped considerably (Stern & others, 1977). In sum, the behaviors of mothers and infants involve substantial interconnection, mutual regulation, and synchronization.

An important form of reciprocal socialization is **scaffolding,** in which parents time interactions in such a way that the infant experiences turn-taking with the parents. Scaffolding involves parental behavior that supports children's efforts, allowing them to be more skillful than they would be if they were to rely only on their own abilities. In using scaffolding, caregivers provide a positive, reciprocal framework in which they and their children interact. For example, in the game peek-a-boo, the mother initially covers the baby. Then she removes the cover and registers "surprise" at the infant's reappearance. As infants become more skilled at peek-a-boo, pat-a-cake, and so on, there are other caregiver games that exemplify scaffolding and turn-taking sequences. In one study, infants who had more extensive scaffolding experiences with their parents (especially in the form of turn-taking) were more likely to engage in turn-taking when they interacted with their peers (Vandell & Wilson, 1988). Scaffolding is not confined to parent-infant interaction but can be used by parents to support children's achievement-related efforts in school by adjusting and modifying the amount and type of support that best suits the child's level of development.

The Family as a System As a social system, the family can be thought of as a constellation of subsystems defined in terms of generation, gender, and role (Kreppner, 2001; Minuchin, 2001). Divisions of labor among family members define particular subunits, and attachments define others. Each family member is a participant in several subsystems. Some are *dyadic* (involving two people), some *polyadic* (involving more than two people). The father and child represent one dyadic subsystem, the mother and father another. The mother-father-child represent one polyadic subsystem, the mother and two siblings another.

Jay Belsky (1981) proposed an organizational scheme that highlights the reciprocal influences of family members and family subsystems (see figure 7.6). Belsky believes that marital relations, parenting, and infant behavior and development can have both direct and indirect effects on each other. An example of a direct effect is the influence of the parents' behavior on the child. An example of an indirect effect is how the relationship between the spouses mediates the way a parent acts toward the child (McHale, Lauretti, & Kuerston-Hogan, 1999). For example, marital conflict might

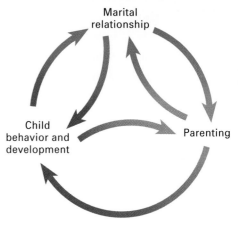

FIGURE 7.6 Interaction Between Children and Their Parents: Direct and Indirect Effects

reciprocal socialization Socialization that is bidirectional; children socialize parents, just as parents socialize children.

scaffolding Parents time interactions so that infants experience turn-taking with the parents.

reduce the efficiency of parenting, in which case marital conflict would indirectly affect the child's behavior.

Maternal and Paternal Infant Caregiving Can fathers take care of infants as competently as mothers can? Observations of fathers and their infants suggest that fathers have the ability to act sensitively and responsively with their infants (Parke, 1995, 2000, 2001, 2002). The strongest evidence of the plasticity of male caregiving abilities is based on male primates, which are notoriously low in their interest in offspring. When forced to live with infants whose female caregivers are absent, the adult male competently rears the infants. Remember, however, that, although fathers can be active, nurturant, involved caregivers with their infants, many do not choose to follow this pattern (Eggebeen & Knoester, 2001; Silverstein, 2001).

Do fathers behave differently toward infants than mothers do? Maternal interactions usually center on child-care activities—feeding, changing diapers, bathing. Paternal interactions are more likely to include play. Fathers engage in more rough-and-tumble play. They bounce infants, throw them up in the air, tickle them, and so on (Lamb, 1986, 2000). Mothers do play with infants, but their play is less physical and arousing than that of fathers.

In stressful circumstances, do infants prefer their mother or father? In one study, 20 12-month-olds were observed interacting with their parents (Lamb, 1977). With both parents present, the infants preferred neither their mother nor their father. The same was true when the infants were alone with the mother or the father. However, the entrance of a stranger, combined with boredom and fatigue, produced a shift in the infants' social behavior toward the mother. In stressful circumstances, then, infants show a stronger attachment to the mother.

In a more recent study, fathers were interviewed about their caregiving responsibilities when their children were 6, 15, 24, and 36 months of age (NICHD Early Child Care Research Network, 2000). A subset was videotaped during father-child play at 6 and 36 months. Caregiving activities (such as bathing, feeding, and dressing the child, and taking the child to day care) and sensitivity during play interactions (such as being responsive to the child's signals and needs, and expressing positive feelings) with their children were predicted by several factors. Fathers were more involved in caregiving when they worked fewer hours and mothers worked more hours, when fathers and mothers were younger, when mothers reported greater marital intimacy, and when the children were boys. Fathers who had less-traditional child-rearing beliefs and reported more marital intimacy were more sensitive during play.

Might the nature of parent-infant interaction be different in families that adopt nontraditional gender roles? This question was investigated by Michael Lamb and his colleagues (1982). They studied Swedish families in which the fathers were the primary caregivers of their firstborn, 8-month-old infants. The mothers were working full-time. In all observations, the mothers were more likely to discipline, hold, soothe, kiss, and talk to the infants than were the fathers. These mothers and fathers dealt with their infants differently, along the lines of American fathers and mothers following traditional gender roles. Having fathers assume the primary caregiving role did not substantially alter the way they interacted with their infants. This may be for biological reasons or because of deeply ingrained socialization patterns in cultures.

Day Care

Many parents worry whether day care will adversely affect their children. They fear that day care will reduce their infants' emotional attachment to them, retard the infants' cognitive development, fail to teach them how to control anger, and allow them to be unduly influenced by their peers. How extensive is day care? Are the worries of these parents justified?

Today far more young children are in day care than at any other time in history; about 2 million children currently receive formal, licensed day care, and more than

mhhe●com/
santrockld9

Family Resources
Maternal Resources
The Fatherhood Project

*W e have all the knowl-
edge necessary to provide
absolutely first-rate child
care in the United States.
What is missing is the
commitment and the will.*

—**Edward Zigler**
*Contemporary Developmental Psychologist,
Yale University*

Child-Care Policy Around the World

Sheila Kammerman (1989, 2000a, b) has conducted extensive examinations of parental leave policies around the world. Parental leaves were first enacted as maternity policies more than a century ago to protect the physical health of working women at the time of childbirth. More recently, child-rearing, parental, and paternity leaves were created in response not only to the needs of working women (and parents), but also because of concern for the child's well being. The European Union (EU) mandated a paid 14-week maternity leave in 1992 and a three-month parental leave in 1998.

Across cultures, policies vary in eligibility criteria, leave duration, benefit level, and the extent to which parents take advantage of these policies. The European policies just mentioned lead the way in creating new standards of parental leave. The United States is alone among advanced industrialized countries in the briefness of parental leave granted and among the few countries with unpaid leave (Australia and New Zealand are the others).

There are five different types of parental leave from employment:

- *Maternity Leave.* In some countries the pre-birth leave is compulsory as is a 6- to 10-week leave following birth.
- *Paternity Leave.* This is usually much briefer than maternity leave. It may be especially important when a second child is born and the first child requires care.
- *Parental Leave.* This is a gender-neutral leave that usually follows a maternity leave and allows either women or men to take advantage of the leave policy and share it or choose which of them will use it.
- *Child-Rearing Leave.* In some countries, this is a supplement to a maternity leave or a variation on a parental leave. A child-rearing leave is usually longer than a maternity leave and is typically paid at a much lower level.
- *Family Leave.* This covers reasons other than the birth of a new baby and can allow time off from employment to care for an ill child or other family members, time to accompany a child to school for the first time, or time to visit a child's school.

Sweden has one of the most extensive leave policies. Paid for by the government at 80 percent of wages, one year of parental leave is allowed (including maternity leave). Maternity leave may begin 60 days prior to expected birth of the baby and ends six weeks after birth. Another six months of parental leave can be used until the child's eighth birthday (Kammerman, 2000a). Virtually all eligible mothers take advantage of the leave policy and approximately 75 percent of eligible fathers take at least some part of the leave they are allowed. In addition, employed grandparents now also have the right to take time off to care for an ill grandchild.

Spain is an example of a relatively poor country that still provides substantial parental leave. Spain allows a 16-week paid maternity leave (paid at 100 percent of wages) at childbirth with up to 6 weeks prior to childbirth allowed. Fathers are permitted two days of leave.

---

5 million children attend kindergarten. Also, uncounted millions of children are cared for by unlicensed baby-sitters.

In Sweden, mothers or fathers are given paid maternity or paternity leave for up to one year. For this reason, day care for Swedish infants under 1 year of age is usually not a major concern. Sweden and many other European countries have well-developed child care policies. To learn about these policies, see the Sociocultural Worlds of Development box.

Because the United States does not have a policy of paid leave for child care, day care in the United States has become a major national concern. The type of day care that young children receive varies extensively (Burchinal & others, 1996; Scarr, 2000). Many day-care centers house large groups of children and have elaborate facilities. Some are commercial operations; others are nonprofit centers run by churches, civic groups, and employers. Child care is frequently provided in private homes, at times by child care professionals, at others by mothers who want to earn extra money.

A special contemporary interest of researchers is the role of poverty in the quality of day care (Chase-Lansdale, Coley, & Grining, 2001; Huston, McLoyd, & Coll, 1994). In one study, day-care centers that served high-income children delivered better-quality care than did centers that served middle- and low-income children (Phillips & others, 1994). The indices of quality (such as teacher-child ratios) in subsidized centers for the poor were fairly good, but the quality of observed teacher-child interaction was lower than in high-income centers.

What constitutes a high-quality day-care program for infants? The demonstration program developed by Jerome Kagan and his colleagues (Kagan, Kearsley, & Zelazo,

Careers in Life-Span Development

Rashmi Nakhre, Day-Care Director

Rashmi Nakhre has two master's degrees—one in psychology, the other in child development—and is director of the Hattie Daniels Day Care Center in Wilson, North Carolina. At a recent ceremony, "Celebrating a Century of Women," Nakhre received the Distinguished Women of North Carolina Award for 1999–2000.

Nakhre first worked at the day-care center soon after she arrived in the United States 25 years ago. She says that she took the job initially because she needed the money but "ended up falling in love with my job." Nakhre has turned the Wilson, North Carolina, day-care center into a model for other centers. The Center almost closed several years after she began working there because of financial difficulties. Dr. Nakhre played a major role in raising funds not only to keep it open but to improve it. The Center provides quality day care for the children of many Latino migrant workers.

Rashmi Nakhre, day-care director, working with some of the children at her center.

1978) at Harvard University is exemplary. The day-care center included a pediatrician, a nonteaching director, and an infant-teacher ratio of 3 to 1. Teachers' aides assisted at the center. The teachers and aides were trained to smile frequently, to talk with the infants, and to provide them with a safe environment, which included many stimulating toys. No adverse effects of day care were observed in this project. More information about what to look for in a quality day-care center is presented in figure 7.7. Using such criteria, one study discovered that children who entered low-quality child care as infants were least likely to be socially competent in early childhood (less compliant, less self-controlled, less task-oriented, more hostile, and less competent in peer interaction) (Howes, 1988). Unfortunately, children who come from families with few resources (psychological, social, and economic) are more likely to experience poor-quality day care than are children from more-advantaged backgrounds (Lamb, 1994). To read about one individual who provides quality day care to individuals from impoverished backgrounds, see the Careers in Life-Span Development insert.

Aware of the growing use of child care, the National Institute of Child Health and Human Development (NICHD) set out to develop a comprehensive, longitudinal study (a study that follows the same individuals over time, usually several years or more) that focuses on the child-care experiences of children and their development (Burchinal, 2001; Owen, 2001; Peth-Pierce, 1998). The study began in 1991, and data were collected on a diverse sample of almost 1,400 children and their families at 10 locations across the United States over a period of seven years. Researchers used multiple methods (trained observers, interviews, questionnaires, and testing) and measured many facets of children's development, including physical health, cognitive development, and socioemotional development. Here are some of the results of this extensive study to date:

- The infants from low-income families were more likely to receive low-quality child care than were their higher-income counterparts. Quality of care was based on such characteristics as group size, child–adult ratio, physical environment, caregiver characteristics (such as formal education, specialized training, and child-care experience), and caregiver behavior (such as sensitivity to children).
- Child care in and of itself neither adversely affected nor promoted the security of infants' attachments to their mothers. Certain child-care conditions, in combination with certain home environments, did increase the probability that infants would be insecurely attached to their mothers. The infants who received either poor quality of care or more than 10 hours per week of care, or were in more than one setting in the first 15 months of life, were more likely to be insecurely attached, but only if their mothers were less sensitive in responding to them.
- Child-care quality, especially sensitive and responsive attention from caregivers, was linked with fewer child problems. The higher the quality of child care over the first three years of life (more positive language stimulation and interaction between the child and the provider), the greater the child's language and cognitive abilities. No cognitive benefits were found for the children in the exclusive care of their mother.

What constitutes quality child care? These recommendations were made by the National Association for the Education of Young Children (1986). They are based on a consensus arrived at by experts in early childhood education and child development. It is especially important for parents to meet the adults who will care for their child. Caregivers are responsible for every aspect of the program's operation.

1. The adult caregivers

- The adults should enjoy and understand how infants and young children grow.
- There should be enough adults to work with a group and to care for the individual needs of children. The recommended ratios of adult caregivers to children of different ages are:

Age of children	Adult to children ratio
0 to 1 Year	1:3
1 to 2 Years	1:5
2 to 3 Years	1:6
3 to 4 Years	1:8
4 to 5 Years	1:10

- Caregivers should observe and record each child's progress and development.

2. The program activities and equipment

- The environment should foster the growth and development of young children working and playing together.
- A good center should provide appropriate and sufficient equipment and play materials and make them readily available.
- Infants and children should be helped to increase their language skills and to expand their understanding of the world.

3. The relation of staff to families and the community

- A good program should consider and support the needs of the entire family. Parents should be welcome to observe, discuss policies, make suggestions, and work in the activities of the center.
- The staff in a good center should be aware of and contribute to community resources. The staff should share information about community recreational and learning opportunities with families.

4. The design of the facility and the program to meet the varied demands of infants and young children, their families, and the staff

- The health of children, staff, and parents should be protected and promoted. The staff should be alert to the health of each child.
- The facility should be safe for children and adults.
- The environment should be spacious enough to accommodate a variety of activities and equipment. More specifically, there should be a minimum of 35 square feet of usable playroom floor space indoors per child and 75 square feet of play space outdoors per child.

FIGURE 7.7 What Is High-Quality Day Care?

**National Child Care
Information Center
NICHD Study of Early Child Care**

Review and Reflect

3 Explain how social contexts influence the infant's development

REVIEW

- What are some important family processes in infant development?
- How does day care influence infant development?

REFLECT

- Imagine that a friend of yours is getting ready to put her baby in day care. What advice would you give to her? Do you think she should stay home with the baby? Why or why not? What type of day care would you recommend?

Reach Your Learning Goals

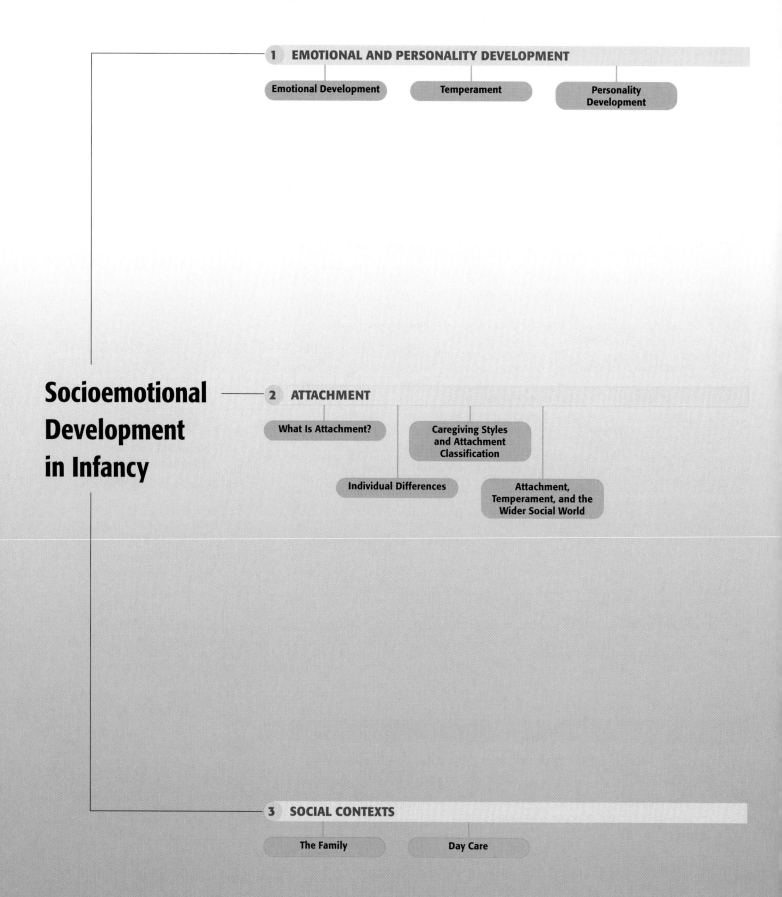

Socioemotional Development in Infancy

1 EMOTIONAL AND PERSONALITY DEVELOPMENT

- Emotional Development
- Temperament
- Personality Development

2 ATTACHMENT

- What Is Attachment?
- Individual Differences
- Caregiving Styles and Attachment Classification
- Attachment, Temperament, and the Wider Social World

3 SOCIAL CONTEXTS

- The Family
- Day Care

Summary

1 Discuss emotional and personality development in infancy

- Emotion is feeling or affect that can involve a mixture of physiological arousal, conscious experience, and overt behavior. Emotions are the way that parents and infants communicate before the infant acquires speech. Expressions of emotion make possible coordinated infant-adult interaction. Babies have at least three types of cries—basic cry, anger cry, and pain cry. Most parents, and adults in general, can tell whether an infant's cry signifies anger or pain. There is controversy about whether babies should be soothed when crying. An increasing number of development researchers support Bowlby and Ainsworth's belief that infant crying should be responded to immediately in the first year of life. Two types of smiles can be distinguished in infants: reflexive and social. Two fears that infants develop are stranger anxiety and separation protest. Social referencing increases in the second year of life. As infants develop it is important for them to engage in emotional regulation.

- Temperament is an individual's behavioral style and characteristic way of emotionally responding. Chess and Thomas classified infants as (1) easy, (2) difficult, or (3) slow to warm up. Kagan believes that inhibition to the unfamiliar is an important temperament category. Recent classifications focus more on (1) positive affect and approach, (2) negative affectivity, and (3) effortful control (self-regulation). Goodness of fit—the match between a child's temperament and the environmental demands the child must cope with—can be an important aspect of a child's adjustment. Although research evidence is sketchy at this point in time, some general recommendations are that caregivers should (1) be sensitive to the individual characteristics of the child, (2) be flexible in responding to these characteristics, and (3) avoid negative labeling of the child. Gender and culture are linked to variations in temperament.

- Erikson argued that an infant's first year is characterized by the stage of trust versus mistrust. At some point in the second half of the second year of life, the infant develops a sense of self. Independence becomes a central theme in the second year of life. Mahler argues that the infant separates herself from her mother and then develops individuation. Erikson stressed that the second year of life is characterized by the stage of autonomy versus shame and doubt.

2 Describe how attachment develops in infancy

- Attachment is a close emotional bond between the infant and caregiver. Feeding is not an important aspect of attachment, although contact comfort and trust are. Bowlby's ethological theory stresses that the caregiver and the infant instinctively form attachment. Attachment develops in four phases, beginning at birth and continuing past 24 months.

- Securely attached babies use the caregiver, usually the mother, as a secure base from which to explore the environment. Three types of insecure attachment are avoidant, resistant, and disorganized. Ainsworth argued that secure attachment in the first year of life is optimal for development. She created the Strange Situation, an observational measure of attachment.

- Caregivers of secure babies are sensitive to the babies' signals and are consistently available to meet their needs. Caregivers of insecure avoidant babies tend to be unavailable or rejecting. Caregivers of insecure resistant babies tend to be inconsistently available to their babies and usually are not very affectionate. Caregivers of insecure disorganized babies often neglect or physically abuse their babies.

- Some critics argue that attachment theorists have not given adequate attention to genetics and temperament. Other critics stress that they have not adequately taken into account the diversity of social agents and contexts. Cultural variations in attachment have been found, but in all cultures studied to date secure attachment is the most common classification.

3 Explain how social contexts influence the infant's development

- The transition to parenthood requires considerable adaptation and adjustment on the part of parents. Children socialize parents just as parents socialize children. Mutual regulation and scaffolding are important aspects of reciprocal socialization. Belsky's model describes direct and indirect effects. The mother's primary role when interacting with the infant is caregiving; the father's is playful interaction.

- Day care has become a basic need of the American family. More children are in day care now than at any earlier point in history. The quality of day care is uneven, and day care remains a controversial topic. Quality day care can be achieved and seems to have few adverse effects on children. In the NICHD child-care study, infants from low-income families were more likely to receive the lowest quality of care. Also, higher quality of child care was linked with fewer child problems.

Key Terms

emotion 206
basic cry 207
anger cry 207
pain cry 207
reflexive smile 208
social smile 208

stranger anxiety 209
separation protest 209
social referencing 209
emotional regulation 209
temperament 210
easy child 210

difficult child 210
slow-to-warm-up child 210
attachment 215
secure attachment 217
Strange Situation 217
insecure avoidant babies 217

insecure resistant babies 217
insecure disorganized
 babies 217
reciprocal socialization 221
scaffolding 221

Key People

John Watson 207
Jacob Gewirtz 208
Mary Ainsworth 208, 217
John Bowlby 208, 216

Alexander Chess and
 Stella Thomas 210
Mary Rothbart and
 John Bates 211

Erik Erikson 213, 215
Margaret Mahler 213
Harry Harlow 215
Jerome Kagan 219, 223

Jay Belsky 221

1. Catherine is conducting a class for new parents at a local clinic. What advice should Catherine give the parents about how parenting practices can affect a child's inborn temperament?

2. Janice is a researcher for a biotech firm. Her husband, Jeff, is a corporate attorney. Both of them have worked hard to establish themselves in their careers, and neither wants to stay home to take care of their 6-month-old daughter, Jessica. Although they are looking into various day-care programs,

both of them are concerned about the potential negative effects. According to the research, does day care have a negative effect on attachment or future development? Does the quality of the program or the amount of time in day care make a difference?

Connect to www.mhhe.com/santrockld9 to research the answers and complete these exercises.

To help you master the material in this chapter, you'll find a number of valuable study tools on the Student CD-ROM that accompanies this book. In addition, visit the Online Learning Center for *Life-Span Development,* ninth edition, where you'll find these valuable resources for chapter 7, "Socioemotional Development in Infancy."

- What are your beliefs about nurturing an infant's socioemotional development? Use the self-assessment, *My Beliefs About*

Nurturing a Baby's Socioemotional Development, to determine what your views are.

- View video clips of key researchers, including Alan Sroufe as he discusses his research on attachment.
- Build your decision-making skills by trying your hand at the parenting and education "Scenarios."

Early Childhood

You are troubled at seeing him spend his early years doing nothing. What! Is it nothing to be happy? Is it nothing to skip, to play, to run about all day long? Never in his life will he be so busy as now.
—JEAN-JACQUES ROUSSEAU
Swiss-Born Philosopher, 18th Century

In early childhood, our greatest untold poem was being only 4 years old. We skipped and ran and played all day long, never in our lives so busy, busy being something we had not quite grasped yet. Who knew our thoughts, which we worked up into small mythologies all our own? Our thoughts and images and drawings took wings. The blossoms of our heart, no wind could touch. Our small world widened as we discovered new refuges and new people. When we said "I," we meant something totally unique, not to be confused with any other. Section Four consists of two chapters: "Physical and Cognitive Development in Early Childhood" (chapter 8) and "Socioemotional Development in Early Childhood" (chapter 9).

*The greatest person
ever known
Is one all poets have
outgrown;
The poetry, innate and
untold,
Of being only four
years old.*

—CHRISTOPHER MORLEY
American Novelist, 20th Century

Physical and Cognitive Development in Early Childhood

Chapter Outline

Learning Goals

PHYSICAL CHANGES

1 *I*dentify physical changes in early childhood

Body Growth and Change

Motor Development

Nutrition

Illness and Death

COGNITIVE CHANGES

2 *D*escribe three views of the cognitive changes that occur in early childhood

Piaget's Preoperational Stage

Vygotksy's Theory

Information Processing

LANGUAGE DEVELOPMENT

3 *S*ummarize how language develops in early childhood

EARLY CHILDHOOD EDUCATION

4 *E*valuate different approaches to early childhood education

The Child-Centered Kindergarten

The Montessori Approach

Developmentally Appropriate and Inappropriate Practice in Education

Does Preschool Matter?

Education for Children Who Are Disadvantaged

Images of Life-Span Development
Teresa Amabile and Her Creativity

Teresa Amabile remembers that, when she was in kindergarten, she rushed in every day, excited and enthusiastic about getting to the easel and playing with all those bright colors and big paint brushes. Children also had free access to a clay table with all kinds of art materials on it. Teresa remembers going home every day and telling her mother she wanted to draw, paint, and play with crayons.

Teresa's kindergarten experience, unfortunately, was the high point of her artistic interest. The next year, she entered a traditional elementary school and things began to change. Instead of Teresa's having free access to art materials every day, art became just another subject, something she had for an hour and a half every Friday afternoon.

Week after week, all through elementary school, it was the same art class. According to Teresa, her elementary school art classes were very restricted and demoralizing. She recalls being given small reprints of painting masterpieces, a different one each week. For example, one week in the second grade, children were presented with Leonardo da Vinci's *Adoration of the Magi.* This was meant for art appreciation, but that's not how the teacher used it. Instead, the children were told to take out their art materials and try to copy the masterpiece. For Teresa, and the other children, this was an exercise in frustration. She says that young elementary school children do not have the skill development even to make all those horses and angels fit on the page, let alone make them look like the masterpiece. Teresa easily could tell that she was not doing well at what the teacher asked her to do.

The children were not given any help in developing their skills. Also, the teacher graded the children on the art they produced, adding evaluation pressure to the situation. Teresa was aware at that time that her motivation for doing artwork was being completely destroyed. She no longer wanted to go home and paint at the end of the day.

Teresa Amabile eventually obtained her Ph.D. in psychology and became one of the leading researchers on creativity. Her hope is that more elementary schools will not crush children's enthusiasm for creativity, the way hers did. So many young children, like Teresa, are excited about exploring and creating, but, by the time they reach the third or fourth grade, many don't like school, let alone have any sense of pleasure in their own creativity (Goleman, Kaufman, & Ray, 1993).

Parents and educators who clearly understand how young children develop can play an active role in creating programs that foster their natural interest in learning, rather than stifling it. We will explore different approaches to early childhood education in this chapter, following a discussion of the physical, cognitive, and language changes in young children.

1 PHYSICAL CHANGES

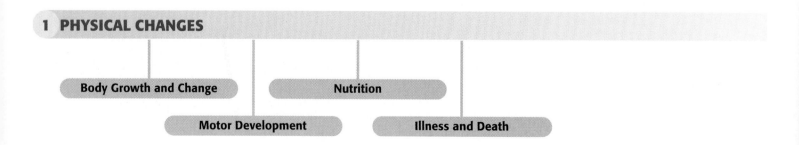

Remember from chapter 5 that an infant's growth in the first year is rapid and follows cephalocaudal and proximodistal patterns ◀▥ p. 149. Around their first birthday, most infants begin to walk. During an infant's second year, the growth rate begins to slow down, but both gross and fine motor skills progress rapidly. The infant develops a sense of mastery through increased proficiency in walking and running. Improvement in fine motor skills—such as being able to turn the pages of a book one at a time—also contributes to the infant's sense of mastery in the second year. The growth rate continues to slow down in early childhood. Otherwise, we would be a species of giants.

Body Growth and Change

Growth in height and weight is the obvious physical change that characterizes early childhood. Unseen changes in the brain and nervous system are no less significant in preparing children for advances in cognition and language.

Height and Weight   The average child grows 2¹/₂ inches in height and gains between 5 and 7 pounds a year during early childhood. As the preschool child grows older, the percentage of increase in height and weight decreases with each additional year. Girls are only slightly smaller and lighter than boys during these years, a difference that continues until puberty. During the preschool years, both boys and girls slim down as the trunks of their bodies lengthen. Although their heads are still somewhat large for their bodies, by the end of the preschool years most children have lost their top-heavy look. Body fat also shows a slow, steady decline during the preschool years. The chubby baby often looks much leaner by the end of early childhood. Girls have more fatty tissue than boys; boys have more muscle tissue.

Growth patterns vary individually. Think back to your preschool years. This was probably the first time you noticed that some children were taller than you, some shorter; some were fatter, some thinner; some were stronger, some weaker. Much of the variation is due to heredity, but environmental experiences are involved to some extent. A review of the height and weight of children around the world concluded that the two most important contributors to height differences are ethnic origin and nutrition (Meredith, 1978). The urban, middle-socioeconomic-status, and firstborn children were taller than rural, lower-socioeconomic-status, and later-born children. Children whose mothers smoked during pregnancy were half an inch shorter than the children whose mothers did not smoke during pregnancy. In the United States, African American children are taller than White children.

Why are some children unusually short? The possible culprits are congenital factors (genetic or prenatal problems), physical problems that develop in childhood, or emotional difficulties. An example of a congenital factor is having a mother who smoked regularly during pregnancy. The physical problem of being chronically sick can make a child shorter than age-mates who are rarely sick. Emotional difficulties among children who have been physically abused or neglected might inhibit the secretion of adequate growth hormone, which can restrict physical growth. In many cases, children with growth problems can be treated with hormones. Usually this treatment is directed at the pituitary gland, located at the base of the brain, which secretes growth-related hormones.

The Brain   One of the most important physical developments during early childhood is the continuing development of the brain and nervous system (Byrnes, 2001). The changes that occur during this period enable children to plan their actions, to attend to stimuli more effectively, and to make considerable strides in language development.

Brain Size and Growth   While the brain continues to grow in early childhood, it does not grow as rapidly as in infancy. The

**Preschool Growth
and Development
Development Milestones**

The bodies of 5-year-olds and 2-year-olds are different. Notice that the 5-year-old not only is taller and weighs more, but also has a longer trunk and legs than the 2-year-old. *Can you think of some other physical differences between 2- and 5-year-olds?*

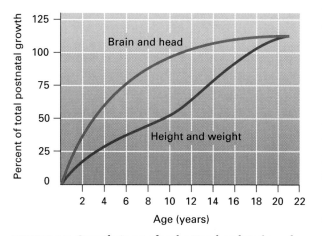

FIGURE 8.1 Growth Curves for the Head and Brain and for Height and Weight

The more rapid growth of the brain and head can easily be seen. Height and weight advance more gradually over the first two decades of life.

brain and the head grow more rapidly than any other part of the body. The top parts of the head, the eyes, and the brain grow faster than the lower portions, such as the jaw. Figure 8.1 reveals how the growth curve for the head and brain advances more rapidly than the growth curve for height and weight.

Changes in Neurons   Communication in the brain is characterized by the transmission of information between neurons, or nerve cells. Some of the brain's increase in size is due to the increase in the number and size of nerve endings within and between areas of the brain. These nerve endings continue to grow at least until adolescence.

Neurons communicate with each other through *neurotransmitters* (chemical substances) that carry information across *synapses* (gaps) between the neurons. The concentration of the neurotransmitter dopamine increases considerably from 3 to 6 years of age (Diamond, 2001). We will discuss the significance of this change shortly.

Some of the brain's increase in size also is due to an increase in **myelination,** the process by which nerve cells are covered and insulated with a layer of fat cells ◀▥ p. 150. This has the effect of increasing the speed of information traveling through the nervous system. Some developmentalists believe myelination is important in the maturation of a number of children's abilities. For example, myelination in the areas of the brain related to hand-eye coordination is not complete until about 4 years of age. Myelination in the areas of the brain related to focusing attention is not complete until the end of the middle or late childhood.

Changes in Brain Structures   Until recently, scientists have not had adequate technology to detect and map sensitive changes in the human brain as it develops. However, the creation of sophisticated brain-scanning techniques has allowed better detection of these changes (Blumenthal & others, 1999; Casey, 2002; Schalagar & others, 2002). Using these techniques, scientists recently have discovered that children's brains undergo dramatic anatomical changes between the ages of 3 and 15 (Thompson & others, 2000). By repeatedly obtaining brain scans of the same children for up to 4 years, they have found that children's brains experience rapid, distinct spurts of growth. The amount of brain material in some areas can nearly double in as little as a year, followed by a drastic loss of tissue as unneeded cells are purged and the brain continues to reorganize itself. The scientists found that the overall size of the brain did not increase dramatically from age 3 to 15. What did dramatically change were local patterns within the brain.

Researchers have found that from 3 to 6 years of age the most rapid growth takes place in the frontal lobe areas involved in planning and organizing new actions, and in maintaining attention to tasks. From age 6 through puberty, the most growth takes place in the temporal and parietal lobes, especially areas that play major roles in language and spatial relations.

The Brain and Cognitive Development   The increasing maturation of the brain, combined with opportunities to experience a widening world, contribute to children's emerging cognitive abilities. Consider a child who is learning to read aloud. Input from the child's eyes is transmitted to the child's brain, then passed through many brain systems, which translate (process) the patterns of black and white into codes for letters, words, and associations. The output occurs in the form of messages to the child's lips and tongue. The child's own gift of speech is possible because brain systems are organized in ways that permit language processing.

The brain is organized in many neural circuits, which consist of neurons with certain functions. One neural circuit has an important function in attention and working memory (a type of memory similar to short-term memory that is like a mental work-

myelination The process in which the nerve cells are covered and insulated with a layer of fat cells, which increases the speed at which information travels through the nervous system.

bench in performing many cognitive tasks) (Krimel & Goldman-Rakic, 2001). This neural circuit involves the *prefrontal cortex* and the neurotransmitter dopamine (Case, Durston, & Fossella, 2001; Diamond, 2001) (see figure 8.2).

In sum, scientists are beginning to chart connections between children's cognitive development (attention and memory, for example), brain structures (prefrontal cortex, for example), and the transmission of information at the level of the neuron (the neurotransmitter dopamine, for example). As advances in technology allow scientists to "look inside" the brain and observe its activity, we will likely understand more precisely how the brain functions in cognitive development.

Motor Development

Running as fast as you can, falling down, getting right back up and running just as fast as you can . . . building towers with blocks . . . scribbling, scribbling, and scribbling some more . . . cutting paper with scissors . . . During your preschool years, you probably developed the ability to perform all of these activities.

Gross Motor Skills   The preschool child no longer has to make an effort simply to stay upright and to move around. As children move their legs with more confidence and carry themselves more purposefully, moving around in the environment becomes more automatic.

At 3 years of age, children enjoy simple movements, such as hopping, jumping, and running back and forth, just for the sheer delight of performing these activities. They take considerable pride in showing how they can run across a room and jump all of 6 inches. The run-and-jump will win no Olympic gold medals, but for the 3-year-old the activity is a source of considerable pride and accomplishment.

At 4 years of age, children are still enjoying the same kind of activities, but they have become more adventurous. They scramble over low jungle gyms as they display their athletic prowess. Although they have been able to climb stairs with one foot on each step for some time, they are just beginning to be able to come down the same way.

At 5 years of age, children are even more adventuresome than when they were 4. It is not unusual for self-assured 5-year-olds to perform hair-raising stunts on practically any climbing object. Five-year-olds run hard and enjoy races with each other and their parents. A summary of development in gross motor skills during early childhood is shown in figure 8.3.

Fine Motor Skills   At 3 years of age, children are still emerging from the infant ability to place and handle things. Although they have had the ability to pick up the tiniest objects between their thumb and forefinger for some time, they are still somewhat

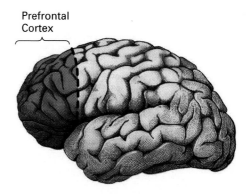

Prefrontal
Cortex

FIGURE 8.2 The Prefrontal Cortex
This evolutionarily advanced portion (shaded in purple) of the brain shows extensive development from 3 to 6 years of age and is believed to play important roles in attention and working memory.

37 to 48 Months	49 to 60 Months	61 to 72 Months
Throws ball underhanded (4 feet)	Bounces and catches ball	Throws ball (44 feet, boys; 25 feet, girls)
Pedals tricycle 10 feet	Runs 10 feet and stops	Carries a 16-pound object
Catches large ball	Pushes/pulls a wagon/doll buggy	Kicks rolling ball
Completes forward somersault (aided)	Kicks 10 inch´ ball toward target	Skips alternating feet
Jumps to floor from 12 inches	Carries 12-pound object	Roller skates
Hops three hops with both feet	Catches ball	Skips rope
Steps on footprint pattern	Bounces ball under control	Rolls ball to hit object
Catches bounced ball	Hops on one foot four hops	Rides bike with training wheels

FIGURE 8.3 The Development of Gross Motor Skills in Early Childhood
The skills are listed in the approximate order of difficulty within each age period.

37 to 48 Months	49 to 60 Months	61 to 72 Months
Approximates a circle in drawing	Strings and laces shoelace	Folds paper into halves and quarters
Cuts paper	Cuts following a line	Traces around hand
Pastes using pointer finger	Strings 10 beads	Draws rectangle, circle, square, and triangle
Builds three-block bridge	Copies figure X	
Builds eight-block tower	Opens and places clothespins (one-handed)	Cuts interior piece from paper
Draws 0 and +	Builds a five-block bridge	Uses crayons appropriately
Dresses and undresses doll	Pours from various containers	Makes clay object with two small parts
Pours from pitcher without spilling	Prints first name	Reproduces letters
		Copies two short words

Note: The skills are listed in the approximate order of difficulty within each age period.

FIGURE 8.4 The Development of Fine Motor Skills in Early Childhood

clumsy at it. Three-year-olds can build surprisingly high block towers, each block placed with intense concentration but often not in a completely straight line. When 3-year-olds play with a simple jigsaw puzzle, they are rather rough in placing the pieces. Even when they recognize the hole a piece fits into, they are not very precise in positioning the piece. They often try to force the piece in the hole or pat it vigorously.

By 4 years of age, children's fine motor coordination has improved substantially and become much more precise. Sometimes 4-year-old children have trouble building high towers with blocks because, in their desire to place each of the blocks perfectly, they may upset those already stacked. By age 5, children's fine motor coordination has improved further. Hand, arm, and body all move together under better command of the eye. Mere towers no longer interest the 5-year-old, who now wants to build a house or a church, complete with steeple, though adults might still need to be told what each finished project is meant to be. A summary of the development of fine motor skills in early childhood is shown in figure 8.4.

Handedness For centuries, left-handers have suffered unfair discrimination in a world designed for right-handers. For many years, teachers forced all children to write with their right hand, even if they had a left-hand tendency. Fortunately, today most teachers let children write with the hand they favor.

Origin and Development of Handedness What is the origin of hand preference? Genetic inheritance seems to be a strong influence. In one study, the handedness of adopted children was not related to the handedness of their adopted parents, but it was related to the handedness of their biological parents (Carter-Saltzman, 1980).

Right-handedness is dominant in all cultures (it appears in a ratio of about 9 right-handers to 1 left-hander) and it appears before the impact of culture. For example, in one study, ultrasound observations of fetal thumb sucking showed that 9 of 10 fetuses were more likely to be sucking their right hand's thumb (Hepper, Shahidullah, & White, 1990). Newborns also show a preference for one side of their body over the other. In one study, 65 percent of the infants turned their head to the right when they were lying on their back in a crib (Michel, 1981). Fifteen percent preferred to face toward the left and the remaining 20 percent showed no preference. These preferences for the right or the left were linked with handedness later in development.

Handedness, the Brain, and Language Approximately 95 percent of right-handed individuals primarily process speech in the brain's left hemisphere (Springer & Deutsch, 1985). However, left-handed individuals show more variation. More than one-half of left-handers process speech in their left hemisphere, just like right-handers. However, about one-fourth of left-handers process speech equally in both hemispheres (Knecht & others, 2000).

mhhe●com/
santrockld9

Handedness

Today, most teachers let children write with the hand they favor. *What are the main reasons children become left- or right-handed?*

Are there differences in the language development of left- and right-handers? The most consistent finding is that left-handers are more likely to have reading problems (Geschwind & Behan, 1984; Natsopoulos & others, 1998).

Handedness and Other Abilities Although there is a tendency for left-handers to have more reading problems than right-handers, left-handedness is more common among mathematicians, musicians, architects, and artists (Michelangelo, Leonardo da Vinci, and Picasso were all left-handed) (Schacter & Ransil, 1996). Architects and artists who are left-handed benefit from the tendency of left-handers to have unusually good visual-spatial skills and the ability to imagine spatial layouts (Holtzen, 2000). Also, in one study of more than 100,000 students taking the Scholastic Aptitude Test (SAT), 20 percent of the top-scoring group was left-handed, twice the rate of left-handedness found in the general population (10 percent) (Bower, 1985).

Nutrition

What are a preschool child's energy needs? What is a preschooler's eating behavior like?

Energy Needs Feeding and eating habits are important aspects of development during early childhood. What children eat affects their skeletal growth, body shape, and susceptibility to disease. Recognizing that nutrition is important for the child's growth and development, the federal government provides money for school lunch programs.

Energy requirements for individual children are determined by the **basal metabolism rate (BMR),** which is the minimum amount of energy a person uses in a resting state. An average preschool child requires 1,700 calories per day, but energy needs of individual children of the same age, sex, and size vary. Although the reasons for these differences are not known, differences in physical activity, basal metabolism, and the efficiency with which children use energy are possible explanations.

Eating Behavior Caregivers' special concerns involve the appropriate amount of fat in young children's diets (Troiano & Flegal, 1998). While some health-conscious parents may be providing too little fat in their infants' and children's diets, other parents are raising their children on diets in which the percentage of fat is far too high. Our changing lifestyles, in which we often eat on the run and pick up fast-food meals, contribute to the increased fat levels in children's diets. The American Heart Association recommends that the daily limit for calories from fat should be approximately 35 percent, and many fast-food meals have fat content that is too high for good health.

Might being overweight be associated with lower self-esteem, even in young children? In one recent study, the relation of weight status and self-esteem in 5-year-old girls was examined (Davison & Birth, 2001). The girls who were overweight had lower body self-esteem than those who were not overweight.

Being overweight can be a serious problem in early childhood (Behrman, Kliegman, & Jenson, 2000). Except for extreme cases of obesity, overweight preschool children are usually not encouraged to lose a great deal of weight but to slow their rate of weight gain so that they will grow into a more normal weight for their height by thinning out as they grow taller. Prevention of obesity in children includes helping children and parents see food as a way to satisfy hunger and nutritional needs, not as proof of love or as a reward for good behavior (Hill & Trowbridge, 1998). Routine physical activity should be a daily occurrence. The child's life should be centered on activity, not meals (Rothstein, 2001).

Illness and Death

What are the leading causes of death in young children in the United States? What are the greatest health risks for children today? How pervasive is death among young children around the world?

> *This would be a better world for children if parents had to eat the spinach.*
> —GROUCHO MARX
> *American Comedian, 20th Century*

basal metabolism rate (BMR) The minimum amount of energy a person uses in a resting state.

mhhe ● com/
santrockld9

Exploring Childhood Obesity

Helping an Overweight Child

Preschoolers' Health

Harvard Center for Children's Health

Child Health Guide

Causes of death	Deaths per 100,000

Accidents (unintentional injuries)
Motor vehicle **4.3**
Other accidents **8.2**   **12.5**

Congenital malformations,
deformations, and
chromosomal abnormalities   **3.6**

Malignant neoplasms   **2.8**

Assault (homicide)   **2.5**

Diseases of
the heart   **1.2**

Influenza and   **0.8**
pneumonia

**FIGURE 8.5 Main Causes of Death in
Children 1 through 4 Years of Age**

These figures are based on the number of deaths
per 100,000 children 1 through 4 years of age in
the United States in 1999 (National Vital Statistics Report, 2001).

The United States If a pediatrician who stopped practicing 50 years ago were to
study the illness and health records of young children today, the conclusion
might seem to be more like science fiction than medical fact (Elias, 1998). The story
of children's health in the past 50 years is a shift toward prevention and out-
patient care.

In recent decades, vaccines have nearly eradicated disabling bacterial meningitis
and have become available to prevent measles, rubella, mumps, and chicken pox.
From 1950 to the present, there has been a dramatic decline in deaths of children under the age of 5 from birth immaturity, birth defects, accidents, cancer, homicide, and
heart disease. The disorders most likely to be fatal during early childhood today are
birth defects, cancer, and heart disease. Although the dangers of many diseases for
children have been greatly diminished, it still is important for parents to keep young
children on an immunization schedule to prevent a resurgence of these contagious
diseases.

In the United States, accidents are the leading cause of death in young children
(National Vital Statistics Reports, 2001) (see figure 8.5). Motor vehicle accidents,
drowning, falls, and poisoning are high on the list of causes of death in young children
(Brenner & others, 2001).

Today, a special concern about children's illness and health is exposure to parental
smoking. An estimated 22 percent of children and adolescents in the United States are
exposed to tobacco smoke in the home. An increasing number of studies reach the
conclusion that children are at risk for health problems if they live in homes in which
a parent smokes (Ehrlich & others, 2001). In one study, if the mother smoked, her
children were twice as likely to have respiratory problems as the children of nonsmoking mothers (Etzel, 1988). Research studies have found that children exposed to
tobacco smoke in the home are more likely to experience wheezing symptoms and
asthma than children in nonsmoking homes (Jaakkola, Nafstad, & Magnus, 2001;
Mannino & others, 2001). Environmental tobacco smoke also affects the amount of
vitamin C, a key nutrient for the immune system, in children and adolescents. In a
recent study, when parents smoked at home their 4- to 18-year-old children and adolescents had significantly lower levels of vitamin C in their blood than their counterparts in nonsmoking homes (Strauss, 2001). And the more parents smoked, the less
vitamin C the children and adolescents had.

Another contemporary concern in the United States is the poor health status of
many young children from low-income families (Karns, 2001). Approximately 11 million preschool children in the United States are malnourished and therefore at risk for
health problems. Many have less resistance to diseases, including minor ones, such as
colds, and major ones, such as influenza, than other children.

In addition, an estimated 3 million children under 6 years of age are thought to be
at risk for lead poisoning (Chisolm, 2001; Geltman, Brown, & Cochran, 2001). Lead
can get into children's bloodstreams through food or water that is contaminated by
lead, from putting lead-contaminated fingers in their mouths, or from inhaling dust
from lead-based paint. The negative effects of high lead levels in children's blood are
lower intelligence and achievement, and attention deficit hyperactivity disorder
(Soong & others, 1999). Children in poverty are at higher risk for lead poisoning than
children living in higher-socioeconomic conditions.

Information about how to avoid environmental smoke, lead contamination, and
other hazards to children's health is available from pediatricians and pediatric nurses.
To read about the work of one pediatric nurse, Barbara Deloin, see the Careers in Life-
Span Development insert.

The State of Illness and Health of the World's Children One of every three
deaths in the world is that of a child under 5. Every week more than a quarter of a
million children die in developing countries. The most devastating effects occur in
countries where poverty rates are high. The poor are the majority in nearly one of
every five nations in the world (UNICEF, 2002). They often experience lives of hunger,

Careers in Life-Span Development

Barbara Deloin, Pediatric Nurse

Barbara Deloin is a pediatric nurse in Denver, Colorado. She practices nursing in the Pediatric Oral Feeding Clinic and is involved in research as part of an irritable infant study for the Children's Hospital in Denver. She also is on the faculty of nursing at the Colorado Health Sciences Center. Deloin previously worked in San Diego where she was coordinator of the Child Health Program for the County of San Diego.

Her research interests focus on children with special health-care needs, especially high-risk infants and children and promoting positive parent-child experiences. Deloin was elected president of the National Association of Pediatric Nurse Associates and Practitioners for the 2000–2001 term ◀‖‖ p. 35.

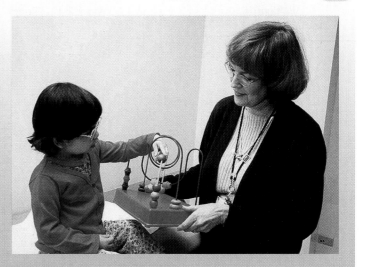

Barbara Deloin, working with a child with special health-care needs.

malnutrition, illness, inadequate access to health care, unsafe water, and inadequate protection from harm.

A leading cause of child death in impoverished countries is diarrhea produced by dehydration. Giving the child a large volume of water and liquids usually prevents dehydration. Measles, tetanus, and whooping cough also still lead to the deaths of many children around the world, although increased immunization programs in the last several decades have led to a decrease in deaths due to these diseases (Foege, 2000).

In the last decade, there has been a dramatic increase in the number of young children who have died because of HIV/AIDS transmitted to them by their parents (UNICEF, 2002). The uneducated are four times more likely to believe there is no way to avoid AIDS and three times more likely to be unaware that the virus can be transmitted from mother to child (UNICEF, 2002).

Review and Reflect

1 Identify physical changes in early childhood

REVIEW

- What is the nature of body growth and change?
- What changes take place in motor development?
- What role does nutrition play in early childhood?
- What are some causes of illness and death among young children in the United States and around the world?

REFLECT

- What were your eating habits as a young child? In what ways are they similar or different to your current eating habits? Were your early eating habits a forerunner of whether or not you have weight problems today?

2 COGNITIVE CHANGES

| Piaget's Preoperational Stage | Vygotksy's Theory | Information Processing |

The cognitive world of the preschool child is creative, free, and fanciful. Preschool children's imaginations work overtime, and their mental grasp of the world improves. Our coverage of cognitive development in early childhood focuses on three theories: Piaget's, Vygotsky's, and information processing.

Piaget's Preoperational Stage

Remember from chapter 6 that, during Piaget's sensorimotor stage of development, the infant progresses in the ability to organize and coordinate sensations and perceptions with physical movements and actions ◀▥ p. 183. What kinds of changes take place in the preoperational stage?

The preoperational stage stretches from approximately 2 to 7 years of age. It is a time when stable concepts are formed, mental reasoning emerges, egocentrism begins strongly and then weakens, and magical beliefs are constructed. The label *preoperational* emphasizes that the child at this stage cannot yet think something through without acting it out.

What are operations? **Operations** are internalized sets of actions that allow children to do mentally what before they did physically. Mentally adding and subtracting numbers are examples of operations.

Thought in the preoperational stage is flawed and not well organized. Preoperational thought is the beginning of the ability to reconstruct at the level of thought what has been established in behavior. Preoperational thought also involves a transition from primitive to more sophisticated use of symbols. Preoperational thought can be divided into two substages: the symbolic function substage and the intuitive thought substage.

Symbolic Function Substage The **symbolic function substage** is the first substage of preoperational thought, which occurs roughly between 2 and 4 years of age. In this substage, the young child gains the ability to mentally represent an object that is not present. The ability to engage in symbolic thought is called *symbolic function*, and it vastly expands the child's mental world. Young children use scribbled designs to represent people, houses, cars, clouds, and so on. Other examples of symbolism in early childhood are language and the prevalence of pretend play. In sum, the ability to think symbolically and to represent the world mentally predominates in this early substage of preoperational thought (DeLoache, 2001). However, although young children make distinct progress during this substage, their thought still has several important limitations, two of which are egocentrism and animism.

Egocentrism, the inability to distinguish between one's own perspective and someone else's, is an important feature of preoperational thought. This telephone conversation between 4-year-old Mary, who is at home, and her father, who is at work, typifies Mary's egocentric thought:

Father: Mary, is Mommy there?

Mary: (Silently nods)

Father: Mary, may I speak to Mommy?

Mary: (Nods again silently)

mhhe ● com/
santrockld9

Symbolic Thinking

operations In Piaget's theory, internalized sets of actions that allow children to do mentally what they formerly did physically.

symbolic function substage Piaget's first substage of preoperational thought, in which the child gains the ability to mentally represent an object that is not present (between 2 and 4 years of age).

egocentrism The inability to distinguish between one's own perspective and someone else's (salient feature of the first substage of preoperational thought).

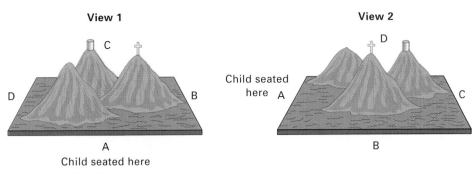

FIGURE 8.6 The Three Mountains Task

View 1 shows the child's perspective from where he or she is sitting. View 2 is an example of the photograph the child would be shown, mixed in with others from different perspectives. To correctly identify this view, the child has to take the perspective of a person sitting at spot (*b*). Invariably, a preschool child who thinks in a preoperational way cannot perform this task. When asked what a view of the mountains looks like from position (*b*), the child selects a photograph taken from location (*a*), the child's view at the time.

Mary's response is egocentric in that she fails to consider her father's perspective before replying. A nonegocentric thinker would have responded verbally.

Piaget and Barbel Inhelder (1969) studied young children's egocentrism by devising the three mountains task (see figure 8.6). The child walks around the model of the mountains and becomes familiar with what the mountains look like from different perspectives. During this walking tour, the child can see that there are different objects on the mountains. The child is then seated on one side of the table on which the mountains are placed. The experimenter moves a doll to different locations around the table, at each location asking the child to select, from a series of photos, the one photo that most accurately reflects the view the doll is seeing. Children in the preoperational stage often pick the view from where they are sitting, rather than the doll's view. Perspective-taking does not develop uniformly in preschool children, who frequently show perspective skills on some tasks but not others.

Animism, another limitation of preoperational thought, is the belief that inanimate objects have "lifelike" qualities and are capable of action. A young child might show animism by saying, "That tree pushed the leaf off, and it fell down," or "The sidewalk made me mad; it made me fall down." A young child who uses animism fails to distinguish the appropriate occasions for using human and nonhuman perspectives (Gelman & Opfer, 2002).

Possibly because young children are not very concerned about reality, their drawings are fanciful and inventive. Suns are blue, skies are yellow, and cars float on clouds in their symbolic, imaginative world. One 3½-year-old looked at a scribble he had just drawn and described it as a pelican kissing a seal (see figure 8.7a). The symbolism is simple but strong, like abstractions found in some modern art. As the famous twentieth-century artist Pablo Picasso commented, "I used to draw like Raphael but it has taken me a lifetime to draw like young children." In the elementary school years, a child's drawings become more realistic, neat, and precise (see figure 8.7b). Suns are yellow, skies are blue, and cars travel on roads (Winner, 1986).

Intuitive Thought Substage Tommy is 4 years old. Although he is starting to develop his own ideas about the world he lives in, his ideas are still simple, and he is not very good at thinking things out. He has difficulty understanding events he knows are taking place but which he cannot see. His fantasized thoughts bear little resemblance to reality. He cannot yet answer the question "What if . . . ?" in any reliable way. For example, he has only a vague idea of what would happen if a car were to hit him. He also has difficulty negotiating traffic because he cannot do the mental calculations necessary to estimate whether an approaching car will hit him when he crosses the road.

animism The belief that inanimate objects have "lifelike" qualities and are capable of action.

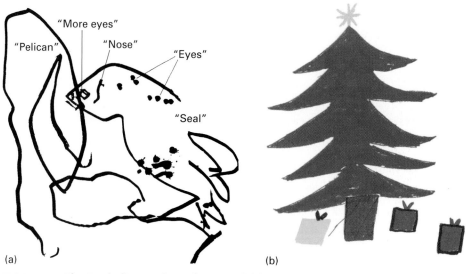

FIGURE 8.7 The Symbolic Drawings of Young Children

(*a*) A 3½-year-old's symbolic drawing. Halfway into this drawing, the 3½-year-old artist said it was "a pelican kissing a seal." (*b*) This 11-year-old's drawing is neater and more realistic but also less inventive.

The **intuitive thought substage** is the second substage of preoperational thought, which occurs between approximately 4 and 7 years of age. In this substage, children begin to use primitive reasoning and want to know the answers to all sorts of questions. Piaget called this time period *intuitive* because, on the one hand, young children seem so sure about their knowledge and understanding, yet they are so unaware of how they know what they know. That is, they say they know something but know it without the use of rational thinking.

An important characteristic of preoperational thought is **centration**—the focusing, or centering, of attention on one characteristic to the exclusion of all others. Centration is most clearly evidenced in young children's lack of **conservation**—awareness that altering an object's or a substance's appearance does not change its quantitative properties. To adults, it is obvious that a certain amount of liquid stays the same, regardless of a container's shape. But this is not at all obvious to young children. Instead, they are struck by the height of the liquid in the container. In the conservation task—Piaget's most famous test—a child is presented with two identical beakers, each filled to the same level with liquid (see figure 8.8). The child is asked if these beakers have the same amount of liquid, and she usually says yes. Then the liquid from one beaker is poured into a third beaker, which is taller and thinner than the first two. The child is then asked if the amount of liquid in the tall, thin beaker is equal to that which remains in one of the original beakers. Children who are less than 7 or 8 years old usually say no and justify their answers in terms of the differing height or width of the beakers. Older children usually answer yes and justify their answers appropriately ("If you poured the milk back, the amount would still be the same").

In Piaget's theory, failing the conservation of liquid task is a sign that children are at the preoperational stage of cognitive development. Passing this test is a sign that they are at the concrete operational stage. In Piaget's view, the preoperational child fails to show conservation not only of liquid but also of number, matter, length, volume, and area (figure 8.9 portrays several of these). Children often vary in their performance on different conservation tasks. Thus, a child might be able to conserve volume but not number.

The child's inability to mentally reverse actions is an important characteristic of preoperational thought. For example, in the conservation of matter shown in figure 8.9, preoperational children say that the longer shape has more clay because they

FIGURE 8.8 Piaget's Conservation Task

The beaker test is a well-known Piagetian test to determine whether a child can think operationally—that is, can mentally reverse actions and show conservation of the substance. (*a*) Two identical beakers are presented to the child. Then, the experimenter pours the liquid from B into C, which is taller and thinner than A or B. (*b*) The child is asked if these beakers (A and C) have the same amount of liquid. The preoperational child says "no". When asked to point to the beaker that has more liquid, the preoperational child points to the tall, thin beaker.

assume that "longer is more." Preoperational children cannot mentally reverse the clay-rolling process to see that the amount of clay is the same in both the shorter ball shape and the longer stick shape.

Some developmentalists do not believe Piaget was entirely correct in his estimate of when children's conservation skills emerge. For example, Rochel Gelman (1969) showed that, when the child's attention to relevant aspects of the conservation task is improved, the child is more likely to conserve. Gelman has also demonstrated that attentional training on one dimension, such as number, improves the preschool child's performance on another dimension, such as mass. Thus, Gelman believes that

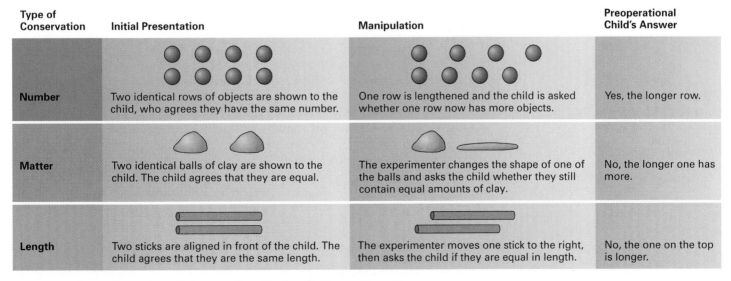

FIGURE 8.9 Some Dimensions of Conservation: Number, Matter, and Length

"I still don't have all the answer, but I'm beginning to ask the right questions."

Vygotsky on Language and Thought

Vygotsky: Revolutionary Scientist

zone of proximal development (ZPD) Vygotsky's term for tasks too difficult for children to master alone but that can be mastered with assistance.

scaffolding In cognitive development, Vygotsky used this term to describe the changing support over the course of a teaching session, with the more-skilled person adjusting guidance to fit the child's current performance level.

conservation appears earlier than Piaget thought and that attention is especially important in explaining conservation.

Yet another characteristic of preoperational children is that they ask a barrage of questions. Children's earliest questions appear around the age of 3, and by the age of 5 they have just about exhausted the adults around them with "why" questions. The child's questions yield clues about mental development and reflect intellectual curiosity. These questions signal the emergence of the child's interest in reasoning and figuring out why things are the way they are. Here are some samples of the questions children ask during the questioning period of 4 to 6 years of age (Elkind, 1976):

- "What makes you grow up?"
- "Why does a lady have to be married to have a baby?"
- "Who was the mother when everybody was a baby?"

Vygotsky's Theory

In chapter 2, we described some basic ideas about Vygotsky's theory. Here we expand on Vygotsky's theory of development, beginning with his unique ideas about the zone of proximal development ◀▥ p. 50.

The Zone of Proximal Development   The **zone of proximal development (ZPD)** is Vygotsky's term for the range of tasks that are too difficult for a child to master alone but that can be learned with the guidance and assistance of adults or more-skilled children. Thus, the lower limit of the ZPD is the level of problem solving reached by the child working independently. The upper limit is the level of additional responsibility the child can accept with the assistance of an able instructor (see figure 8.10). Vygotsky's emphasis on the ZPD underscores his belief in the importance of social influences, especially instruction, on children's cognitive development. An example of the ZPD is an adult helping a child put together a jigsaw puzzle.

The ZPD captures the child's cognitive skills that are in the process of maturing and can be mastered only with the assistance of a more-skilled person (Rowe & Wertsch, 2002). Vygotsky (1962) called these the "buds" or "flowers" of development, to distinguish them from the "fruits" of development, tasks that the child already can accomplish independently.

Scaffolding   In chapter 7, we discussed the concept of scaffolding in socioemotional development ◀▥ p. 221. Here we describe its role in cognitive development. Closely linked to the idea of zone of proximal development, **scaffolding** involves changing the level of support. Over the course of a teaching session, a more-skilled person adjusts the amount of guidance to fit the child's current performance level. When the task the student is learning is new, the more-skilled person may use direct instruction. As the student's competence increases, less guidance is given.

Language and Thought   Vygotsky (1962) believed that young children use language not only for social communication but also to plan, guide, and monitor their behavior in a self-regulatory fashion. The use of language for self-regulation is called *inner speech* or *private speech.* For Piaget, private speech is egocentric and immature, but for Vygotsky it is an important tool of thought during the early childhood years.

Vygotsky believed that language and thought initially develop independently of each other and then merge. He said that all mental functions have external, or social, origins. Children must use language to communicate with others before they can focus inward on their own thoughts. Children also must communicate externally and use language for a long period of time before the transition from external to internal speech takes place. This transition period occurs between the ages of 3 and 7 years of age and involves talking to oneself. After a while, the self-talk becomes second nature

Lee Vygotsky (1896–1934), shown here with his daughter, believed that children's cognitive development is advanced through social interaction with skilled individuals embedded in a sociocultural backdrop. *How is Vygotsky's theory different from Piaget's?*

to children, and they can act without verbalizing. When this occurs, children have internalized their egocentric speech in the form of inner speech, which becomes their thoughts. Vygotsky believed that children who use a lot of private speech are more socially competent than those who don't. He argued that private speech represents an early transition in becoming more socially communicative.

Vygotsky's view challenged Piaget's ideas on language and thought. Vygotsky said that language, even in its earliest forms, is socially based. By contrast, Piaget emphasized young children's egocentric and nonsocial speech. For Vygotsky, when young children talk to themselves, they are using language to govern their behavior and guide themselves. Piaget believed that such self-talk reflects immaturity. However, researchers have found support for Vygotsky's view of the positive role of private speech in children's development (Winsler, Diaz, & Montero, 1997).

Evaluating and Comparing Vygotsky's and Piaget's Theories Although Vygotsky and Piaget were contemporaries, Vygotsky's work was not translated until 1962, long after his death, so it has not yet been evaluated as thoroughly. Vygotsky's theory has been embraced by many teachers and has been successfully applied to education. His view of the importance of sociocultural influences on children's development fits with the current belief that it is important to evaluate the contextual factors in learning (Gojdamaschko, 1999). However, some critics say he overemphasizes the role of language in thinking.

We already have mentioned several comparisons of Vygotsky's and Piaget's theories, such as Vygotsky's emphasis on the role of inner speech in development and Piaget's view that such speech is immature. We also said earlier that both Vygotsky's and Piaget's theories are constructivist, emphasizing that children actively construct knowledge and understanding, rather than being passive receptacles.

Although both theories are constructivist, Vygotsky's is a **social constructivist approach,** which emphasizes the social contexts of learning and the mutual construction of knowledge. Piaget's theory does not have this social emphasis. These analogies reflect the differing degree of social emphasis in the theories. Moving from

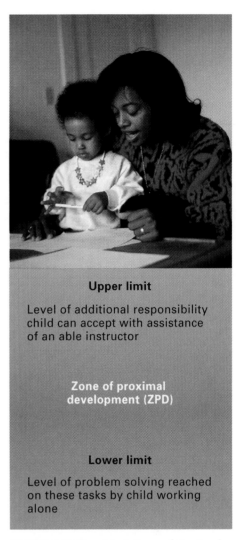

Upper limit

Level of additional responsibility child can accept with assistance of an able instructor

Zone of proximal development (ZPD)

Lower limit

Level of problem solving reached on these tasks by child working alone

FIGURE 8.10 Vygotsky's Zone of Proximal Development

Vygotsky's zone of proximal development has a lower limit and an upper limit. Tasks in the ZPD are too difficult for the child to perform alone. They require assistance from an adult or a skilled child. As children experience the verbal instruction or demonstration, they organize the information in their existing mental structures, so they can eventually perform the skill or task alone.

social constructivist approach An approach that emphasizes the social contexts of learning and that knowledge is mutually built and constructed. Vygotsky's theory reflects this approach.

Piaget to Vygotsky, the conceptual shift is from the individual to collaboration, social interaction, and sociocultural activity (John-Steiner & Mahn, 2003: Rogoff, 1998). For Piaget, children construct knowledge by transforming, organizing, and reorganizing previous knowledge. For Vygotsky, children construct knowledge through social interaction with others (Hogan & Tudge, 1999). The implication of Piaget's theory for teaching is that children need support to explore their world and discover knowledge. The main implication of Vygotsky's theory for teaching is that students need many opportunities to learn with the teacher and more-skilled peers. In both Piaget's and Vygotsky's theories, teachers serve as facilitators and guides, rather than as directors and molders of learning. Figure 8.11 compares Vygotsky's and Piaget's theories.

Teaching Strategies Based on Vygotsky's Theory   Here are some ways that Vygotsky's theory can be incorporated in the classroom:

- *Use the child's zone of proximal development in teaching.* Teaching should begin toward the zone's upper limit, where the child is able to reach the goal only through close collaboration with the instructor. With adequate continuing instruction and practice, the child organizes and masters the behavioral sequences required to perform the target skill. As the instruction continues, the performance transfers from the teacher to the child. The teacher gradually reduces the explanations, hints, and demonstrations until the student is able to perform the skill alone. Once the goal is achieved, it may become the foundation for the development of a new ZPD.
- *Use scaffolding.* Look for opportunities to use scaffolding when children need help with self-initiated learning activities (Elicker, 1996). Also use scaffolding to help children move to a higher level of skill and knowledge. Offer just enough assistance.

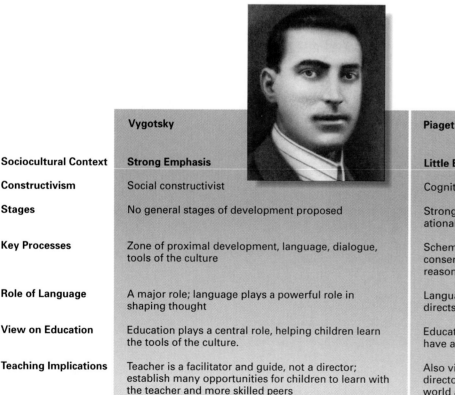

	Vygotsky	Piaget
Sociocultural Context	**Strong Emphasis**	**Little Emphasis**
Constructivism	Social constructivist	Cognitive constructivist
Stages	No general stages of development proposed	Strong emphasis on stages (sensorimotor, preoperational, concrete operational, and formal operational)
Key Processes	Zone of proximal development, language, dialogue, tools of the culture	Schema, assimilation, accommodation, operations, conservation, classification, hypothetical-deductive reasoning
Role of Language	A major role; language plays a powerful role in shaping thought	Language has a minimal role; cognition primarily directs language
View on Education	Education plays a central role, helping children learn the tools of the culture.	Education merely refines the child's cognitive skills that have already emerged.
Teaching Implications	Teacher is a facilitator and guide, not a director; establish many opportunities for children to learn with the teacher and more skilled peers	Also views teacher as a facilitator and guide, not a director; provide support for children to explore their world and discover knowledge

FIGURE 8.11 Comparison of Vygotsky's and Piaget's Theories

- *Use more-skilled peers as teachers.* Children can benefit from the support and guidance of more-skilled children, as well as from adults.
- *Monitor and encourage children's use of private speech.* Be aware of the developmental change from externally talking to oneself when solving a problem during the preschool years to privately talking to oneself in the early elementary school years. In the elementary school years, encourage children to internalize and self-regulate their talk to themselves.
- *Assess the child's ZPD, not IQ.* Like Piaget, Vygotsky did not believe that formal, standardized tests are the best way to assess children's learning. Rather, Vygotsky argued that assessment should focus on determining the child's zone of proximal development. The skilled helper presents the child with tasks of varying difficulty to determine the best level at which to begin instruction. The ZPD is a measure of learning potential.
- *Transform the classroom with Vygotskian ideas.* What does a Vygotskian classroom look like? In the Kamehameha Elementary Education Program (KEEP), which is based on Vygotsky's theory (Tharp, 1994), the zone of proximal development is the key element of instruction. Children might read a story and then interpret its meaning. Many of the learning activities take place in small groups. All children spend at least 20 minutes each morning in an activity setting called "Center One." In this context, scaffolding is used to improve children's literary skills. The instructor asks questions, responds to students' queries, and builds on the ideas that students generate. Thousands of low-income children have attended KEEP public schools in Hawaii, on an Arizona Navajo Indian reservation, and in Los Angeles. Compared with a control group of non-KEEP children, the KEEP children participate more actively in classroom discussion, are more attentive in class, and have higher reading achievement (Tharp & Gallimore, 1988).

In Vygotsky's theory, an important point is that children need to learn the skills that will help them do well in their culture. Vygotsky believed that this should be accomplished through interaction with more-skilled members of the culture, such as this Mexican-American girl learning to read with the guidance of her mother. *What are some other ways that skilled members of a society can interact with young children?*

In one recent study with a foundation in Vygotsky's theory, pairs of children from two U.S. public schools worked together (Matusov, Bell, & Rogoff, 2001). One member of the pair was always from a school with a traditional format involving only occasional opportunities for children to cooperate in their schoolwork. The other member of the pair was always from a school that emphasizes collaboration throughout the school day. The children with the collaborative school background more often built on each other's ideas in a collaborative way than did the children with the traditional school background. The traditional school children primarily used a "quizzing" form of guidance based on asking known-answer questions and withholding information to test learner's understanding.

Piaget's cognitive development theory and Vygotsky's sociocultural cognitive theory have provided important insights about the way young children think and how this thinking changes developmentally. Next, we will explore a third major view on children's thinking—information processing.

Information Processing

Not only can we study stages of cognitive development, as Piaget did, but we can also study young children's cognitive processes. Two important aspects of preschool children's thinking are attention and memory. What are the limitations and advances in attention and memory during the preschool years?

Attention In chapter 6, we discussed attention in the context of habituation, which is something like being bored ◀▥ p. 189. In habituation, the infant loses interest in a stimulus and no longer attends to it. Habituation involves a decrement in attention. Dishabituation is the recovery of attention. The importance of these aspects of attention in infancy for the preschool years was underscored by research showing that both decrement and recovery of attention, when measured in the first six months of infancy, were associated with higher intelligence in the preschool years (Bornstein & Sigman, 1986).

The child's ability to pay attention changes significantly during the preschool years in three ways:

- *Control of attention.* Toddlers wander around, shift attention from one activity to another, and seem to spend little time focused on any one object or event. By comparison, the preschool child might be observed watching television for a half hour. In one study, young children's attention to television in the natural setting of the home was videotaped (Anderson & others, 1985). In 99 families comprising 460 individuals who were observed for 4,672 hours, visual attention to television dramatically increased during the preschool years.
- *Salient versus relevant dimensions.* One deficit in attention during the preschool years concerns those dimensions that stand out, or are *salient,* compared with those that are relevant to solving a problem or performing well on a task. For example, a problem might have a flashy, attractive clown that presents the directions for solving a problem. Preschool children are influenced strongly by the features of the task that stand out, such as the flashy, attractive clown. After the age of 6 or 7, children attend more efficiently to the dimensions of the task that are relevant, such as the directions for solving a problem. Developmentalists believe this change reflects a shift to cognitive control of attention, so that children act less impulsively and reflect more.
- *Planfulness.* When experimenters ask children to judge whether two complex pictures are the same, preschool children tend to use a haphazard comparison strategy, not examining all of the details before making a judgment. By comparison, elementary school age children are more likely to systematically compare the details across the pictures, one detail at a time (Vurpillot, 1968) (see figure 8.12).

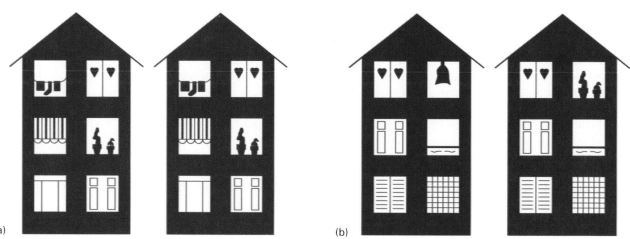

(a) (b)

FIGURE 8.12 The Planfulness of Attention

In one study, children were given pairs of houses to examine, like the ones shown here (Vurpillot, 1968). For three pairs of houses, what was in the windows was identical (*a*). For the other three pairs, the windows had different items in them (*b*). By filming the reflection in the children's eyes, it could be determined what they were looking at, how long they looked, and the sequence of their eye movements. Children under 6 examined only a fragmentary portion of each display and made their judgments on the basis of insufficient information. By contrast, older children scanned the windows in more detailed ways and were more accurate in their judgments of which windows were identical.

Memory Memory is a central process in children's cognitive development; it involves the retention of information over time. Conscious memory comes into play as early as 7 months of age, although children and adults have little or no memory of events experienced before the age of 3 ◀▥ p. 191. Among the interesting questions about memory in the preschool years are those involving short-term memory.

Short-Term Memory In **short-term memory,** individuals retain information for up to 30 seconds, assuming there is no rehearsal of the information. Using rehearsal (repeating information after it has been presented), we can keep information in short-term memory for a much longer period. One method of assessing short-term memory is the memory-span task. If you have taken an IQ test, you were probably exposed to one of these tasks. You simply hear a short list of stimuli—usually digits—presented at a rapid pace (one per second, for example). Then you are asked to repeat the digits. Research with the memory-span task suggests that short-term memory increases during early childhood. For example, in one investigation, memory span increased from about 2 digits in 2- to 3-year-old children to about 5 digits in 7-year-old children, yet, between 7 and 13 years of age, memory span increased only by 1½ digits (Dempster, 1981) (see figure 8.13). Keep in mind, though, that memory span varies from one individual to another; it is for this reason that IQ and various aptitude tests were developed.

Why are there differences in memory span because of age? Rehearsal of information is important; older children rehearse the digits more than younger children. Speed and efficiency of processing information are important, too, especially the speed with which memory items can be identified. For example, in one study, children were tested on their speed at repeating words presented orally (Case, Kurland, & Goldberg, 1982). Speed of repetition was a powerful predictor of memory span. Indeed, when the speed of repetition was controlled, the 6-year-olds' memory spans were equal to those of young adults.

The speed-of-processing explanation highlights a key point in the information-processing perspective: The speed with which a child processes information is an important aspect of the child's cognitive abilities (Schneider, 2002). In one recent study, faster processing speed on a memory-span task was linked with higher reading and mathematics achievement (Hitch, Towse, & Hutton, 2001).

How Accurate Are Young Children's Long-Term Memories? In chapter 6, we saw that most of an infant's memories are fragile and, for the most part, short-lived—except for the memory of perceptual-motor actions, which can be substantial (Mandler, 2000). Does their memory become more accurate when they grow into the early childhood years? Yes, it does. Young children can remember a great deal of information if they are given appropriate cues and prompts.

A current controversy focuses on whether young children should be allowed to testify in court. Increasingly, young children are being allowed to testify, especially if they are the only witnesses to abuse, a crime, and so forth. These conclusions have been reached about children as eyewitnesses (Bruck & Ceci, 1999):

- *Age differences in children's susceptibility to suggestion.* Preschoolers are more suggestible than older children and adults (Koriat, Goldsmith, & Pansky, 2000). Young children can be led, under certain circumstances, to incorporate false suggestions into their accounts of even intimate body touching by adults (Hyman & Loftus, 2001). Despite their greater resistance to suggestibility, there is concern, too, about the effects of suggestive interviews on older children.
- *Individual differences in susceptibility.* Some preschoolers are highly resistant to interviewers' suggestions, while others succumb immediately to the slightest suggestion.

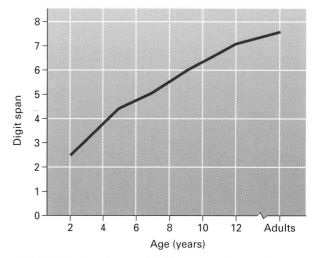

FIGURE 8.13 Developmental Changes in Memory Span

In one study, memory span increased about 3 digits from 2 years of age to 5 digits at 7 years of age (Dempster, 1981). By 12 years of age, memory span had increased on average another 1½ digits to 7 digits.

Children's Eyewitness Testimony

short-term memory The memory component in which individuals retain information for up to 30 seconds, assuming there is no rehearsal.

Four-year-old Jennifer Royal was the only eyewitness to one of her playmate's being shot to death. She was allowed to testify in open court and the clarity of her statements helped to convict the gunman. *What are some issues involved in whether young children should be allowed to testify in court?*

- *Young children's accuracy as eyewitnesses.* Despite the evidence that many young children's responses can be infuenced by suggestible interviews, they are capable of recalling much that is relevant about an event (Howe, 1997). Children are more likely to accurately recall an event when the interviewer has a neutral tone, does not use misleading questions, and they are not motivated to make a false report (Bruck & Ceci, 1999).

In sum, whether a young child's eyewitness testimony is accurate or not may depend on a number of factors such as the type, number, and intensity of the suggestive techniques the child has experienced. It appears that the reliability of young children's reports have as much to do with the skills and motivation of the interiewer as with any natural limitations on young children's memory.

Strategies   In chapter 2, we mentioned that an especially important aspect of information-processing theory is the use of good strategies ◀▥ p. 50. Strategies consist of deliberate mental activities to improve the processing of information. For example, rehearsing information and organizing it are two typical strategies that older children and adults use to remember more effectively. For the most part, young children do not use rehearsal and organization to remember (Miller & Seier, 1994).

Do young children use any strategies at all? Problem-solving strategies in young children were the focus of research by Zhe Chen and Robert Siegler (2000). They placed young children at a table where an attractive toy was placed too far away for the child to reach it (they were not allowed to crawl on the table). On the table, between the child and the toy, were six potential tools (see figure 8.14). Only one of them was likely to be useful in obtaining the toy. After initially assessing the young children's attempts to obtain the toy on their own, the experimenters either modeled how to obtain the toy (using the appropriate tool) or gave the child a hint (telling the child to use the particular tool). These 2-year-olds learned the strategy and subsequently mapped the strategy onto new problems. Admittedly, this is a rather simple problem-solving strategy—selecting the best tool to use to obtain a desired toy—but it does document that children as young as 2 years of age can learn a strategy.

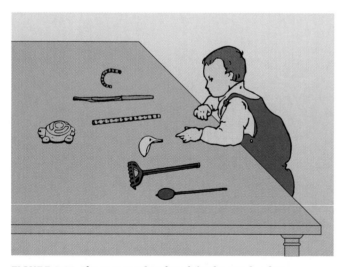

FIGURE 8.14 The Toy-Retrieval Task in the Study of Young Children's Problem-Solving Strategies

The child needed to choose the target tool (in this illustration, the toy rake) to pull in the toy (in this case, the turtle).

The Young Child's Theory of Mind   **Theory of mind** refers to awareness of one's own mental processes and the mental processes of others. Even young children are curious about the nature of the human mind, and developmentalists have shown a flurry of interest in children's thoughts about what the human mind is like (Flavell, 1999; McCormick, 2003; Wellman, 1997, 2000, 2002).

Children's theory of mind changes as they go through the early childhood years (Flavell, Miller, & Miller, 2002):

- *2 to 3 years of age.* Children begin to understand three mental states:

  Perceptions. The child realizes that another person sees what is in front of his or her eyes and not necessarily what is in front of the child's eyes.

  Desires. The child understands that if someone wants something, he or she will try to get it. A child might say, "I want my mommy."

  Emotions. The child can distinguish between positive (for example, happy) and negative (sad, for example) emotions. A child might say, "Tommy feels bad."

theory of mind Refers to the awareness of one's own mental processes and the mental processes of others.

Careers in Life-Span Development

Helen Schwe, Developmental Psychologist and Toy Designer

Helen Schwe obtained a Ph.D. from Stanford University in developmental psychology. She now spends her days talking with computer engineers and designing "smart" toys for children ◀||||| p. 30. Smart toys are designed to improve children's problem-solving and symbolic thinking skills.

During graduate school Dr. Schwe worked part-time for Hasbro Toys, testing its children's software on preschoolers. Her first job after graduate school was with Zowie Entertainment, which recently was purchased by LEGO.

While with Zowie and now LEGO, Dr. Schwe helped to design the pirate game called "Redbeard's Pirate Quest" and many other toys for children. She says that even in a toy's most primitive stage of development, you see children creatively responding to challenges and displaying their joy when they solve a problem. Along with conducting experiments and focus groups at different stages of a toy's development, She also helps assess the age-appropriateness of a toy. Most of her current work focuses on 3- to 5-year-old children. (Schlegel, 2000).

Helen Schwe, a developmental psychologist, with some of the toys she designed.

Despite these advances, at 2 to 3 years of age, children have only a minimal understanding of how mental life can be linked to behavior. They think that people are at the mercy of their desires and don't understand how beliefs influence behavior.

- *4 to 5 years of age.* Children come to understand that the mind can represent objects and events accurately or inaccurately. The realization that people can have *false beliefs*—beliefs that are not true—develops in a majority of children by the time they are 5 years old (Wellman, Cross, & Watson, 2001) (see figure 8.15). One study of false beliefs involved showing young children a Band-Aids box and asking them what was inside (Jenkins & Astington, 1996). To the children's surprise, the box actually contained pencils. When asked what a child who had never seen the box would think was inside, 3-year-olds typically responded "pencils." However, the 4- and 5-year-olds, grinning at the anticipation of other children's false beliefs who had not seen what was inside the box, were more likely to say "Band-Aids."

Some developmental psychologists use their training in areas such as cognitive development to pursue careers in applied areas. To read about the work of one individual who followed this path, see the Careers in Life-Span Development insert.

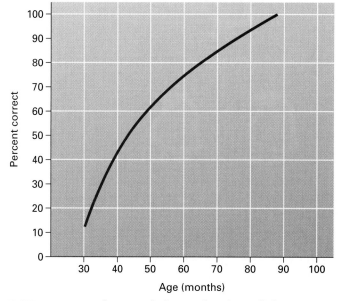

FIGURE 8.15 Developmental Changes in False-Belief Performance

False-belief performance dramatically increases from 2½ years of age through the middle of the elementary school years. In a summary of the results of many studies, 2½-year-olds gave incorrect responses about 80 percent of the time (Wellman, Cross, & Watson, 2001). At 3 years, 8 months, they were correct about 50 percent of the time, and after that, gave increasingly correct responses.

Review and Reflect

2 **Describe three views of the cognitive changes that occur in early childhood**

REVIEW

- What characterizes Piaget's stage of preoperational thought?
- What is Vygotsky's theory of children's cognitive development?
- What are some important ways that young children process information?

REFLECT

- Should children be allowed to develop such concepts as conservation naturally or should the concepts be taught to them? Explain.

3 LANGUAGE DEVELOPMENT

This is a wug.

Now there is another one.
There are two of them.
There are two _____.

FIGURE 8.16 Stimuli in Berko's Study of Young Children's Understanding of Morphological Rules

In Jean Berko's (1958) study, young children were presented cards, such as this one with a "wug" on it. Then the children were asked to supply the missing word; in supplying the missing word, they had to say it correctly too. "Wugs" is the correct response here.

Young children's understanding sometimes gets way ahead of their speech. One 3-year-old, laughing with delight as an abrupt summer breeze stirred his hair and tickled his skin, commented, "I got breezed!" Many of the oddities of young children's language sound like mistakes to adult listeners. However, from the children's point of view, they are not mistakes. They represent the way young children perceive and understand their world at that point in their development.

As children go through the early childhood years, their grasp of the rule systems that govern language increase (Hoff, 2003). These rule systems include phonology (the sound system) morphology (the rules for combining minimal units of meaning), syntax (rules for making sentences), semantics (the meaning system), and pragmatics (the rules for use in social settings).

Children become increasingly capable of producing all the sounds of their language. They can even produce complex consonant clusters.

By the time children move beyond two-word utterances, they demonstrate a knowledge of morphology rules. Children begin using the plural and possessive forms of nouns (such as *dogs* and *dog's*). They put appropriate endings on verbs (such as *-s* when the subject is third-person singular and *-ed* for the past tense. They use prepositions (such as *in* and *on*), articles (such as *a* and *the*), and various forms of the verb *to be* (such as "I *was* going to the store"). Some of the best evidence for changes in children's use of morphological rules occurs in their overgeneralization of the rules. Have you ever heard a preschool child say "foots" instead of "feet," or "goed" instead of "went"? If you do not remember hearing such usage, talk to parents who have young children or to the young children themselves. You will hear some interesting morphological errors.

In a classic experiment that was designed to study children's understanding of morphological rules, Jean Berko (1958) presented preschool children and first-grade children with cards such as the one shown in figure 8.16. Children were asked to look at the card while the experimenter read aloud the words on the card. Then the children were asked to supply the missing word. This might sound easy, but Berko was interested not just in the children's ability to recall the right word but also in their ability to say it "correctly" (with the ending that was dictated by morphological rules). "Wugs" would be the correct response for the card in figure 8.16.

Although the children's answers were not perfect, they were much better than chance. Moreover, the children demonstrated their knowledge of morphological rules,

How do children's language abilities develop during early childhood?

not only with the plural forms of nouns ("There are two wugs") but with possessive forms of nouns and the third-person singular and past-tense forms of verbs. What makes Berko's study impressive is that most of the words were made up for the experiment. Thus, the children could not base their responses on remembering past instances of hearing the words. Instead, they were forced to rely on *rules.*

Young children also learn to manipulate syntax. They can generate questions, passives, clauses, and all the major syntactical structures of their language.

As children move beyond the two-word stage, their knowledge of semantics or meanings also rapidly advances. The speaking vocabulary of a 6-year-old child ranges from 8,000 to 14,000 words. Assuming that word learning began when the child was 12 months old, this translates into a rate of 5 to 8 new word meanings a day between the ages of 1 and 6. After five years of word learning, the 6-year-old child does not slow down. According to some estimates, the average child of this age is moving along at the awe-inspiring rate of 22 words a day! How would you fare if you were given the task of learning 22 new words every day? It is truly miraculous how quickly children learn language.

Although there are many differences between a 2-year-old's language and a 6-year-old's language, the most dramatic differences pertain to pragmatics. A 6-year-old is simply a much better conversationalist than a 2-year-old. What are some of the changes in pragmatics that are made in the preschool years? At about 3 years of age, children improve in their ability to talk about things that are not physically present. That is, they improve their command of the characteristic of language known as "displacement." Children become increasingly removed from the "here and now" and are able to talk about things that are not physically present, as well as things that happened in the past, or may happen in the future. Preschoolers can tell you what they want for lunch tomorrow, something that would not have been possible at the two-word stage in infancy. Preschool children also become increasingly able to talk in different ways to different people.

The advances in language that take place in early childhood lay the foundation for later development in the elementary school years, which we will discuss in chapter 10.

mhhe●com/
santrockld9

**Language Development
Language Growth
Pragmatic Language**

Review and Reflect

3 **Summarize how language develops in early childhood**

REVIEW

- How does the grasp of language's rule systems change in early childhood?

REFLECT

- How are nature and nurture likely to be involved in the dramatic increase in a young child's spoken vocabulary?

4 EARLY CHILDHOOD EDUCATION

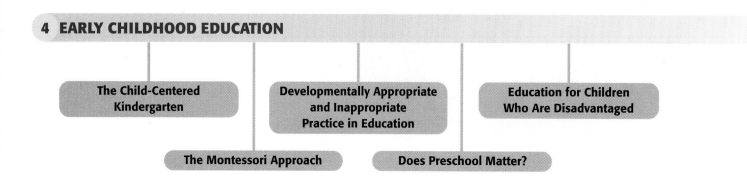

mhhe●com/
santrockld9

Early Childhood Education

Reggio Emilia

NAEYC

High/Scope: Active Learning

There are many variations in the ways young children are educated. First we will explore the child-centered kindergarten and the Montessori approach, then we will turn our attention to developmentally appropriate and inappropriate practice in education, whether preschool is necessary, and education for children who are disadvantaged.

The Child-Centered Kindergarten

Kindergarten programs vary a great deal (Roopnarine & Johnson, 2000). Some approaches place more emphasis on young children's social development, others on their cognitive development.

In the **child-centered kindergarten,** education involves the whole child and includes concern for the child's physical, cognitive, and socioemotional development. Instruction is organized around the child's needs, interests, and learning styles. The process of learning, rather than what is learned, is emphasized (White & Coleman, 2000). Each child follows a unique developmental pattern, and young children learn best through firsthand experiences with people and materials. Play is extremely important in the child's total development. *Experimenting, exploring, discovering,* and *trying out* are all words that describe excellent kindergarten programs.

The Montessori Approach

Montessori schools are patterned after the educational philosophy of Maria Montessori, an Italian physician-turned-educator, who crafted a revolutionary approach to young children's education at the beginning of the twentieth century (Wentworth, 1999). Although some Montessori schools provide programs for school-age children, most specialize in early childhood education.

In the **Montessori approach,** children are given considerable freedom and spontaneity in choosing activities. They are allowed to move from one activity to another as they desire. The teacher acts as a facilitator rather than a director of learning. The teacher shows the child how to perform intellectual activities, demonstrates interesting ways to explore curriculum materials, and offers help when the child requests it.

child-centered kindergarten Education that involves the whole child by considering both the child's physical, cognitive, and social development and the child's needs, interests, and learning styles.

Montessori approach An educational philosophy in which children are given considerable freedom and spontaneity in choosing activities and are allowed to move from one activity to another as they desire.

Some developmentalists favor the Montessori approach, but others believe that it neglects children's social development. For example, while Montessori fosters independence and the development of cognitive skills, it deemphasizes verbal interaction between the teacher and child and peer interaction. Montessori's critics also argue that it restricts imaginative play.

Developmentally Appropriate and Inappropriate Practice in Education

Developmentally appropriate practice is based on knowledge of the typical development of children within an age span (age-appropriateness) and the uniqueness of the child (individual-appropriateness). Developmentally appropriate practice contrasts with developmentally inappropriate practice, which ignores the concrete, hands-on approach to learning. Direct teaching largely through abstract paper-and-pencil activities presented to large groups of young children is believed to be developmentally inappropriate.

One of the most comprehensive documents addressing the issue of developmentally appropriate practice in early childhood programs is the position statement by the National Association for the Education of Young Children (NAEYC) (Bredekamp, 1987, 1997; National Association for the Education of Young Children, 1986). This document reflects the expertise of many of the foremost experts in the field of early childhood education. In figure 8.17 you can examine some of the NAEYC recommendations for developmentally appropriate practice. In one study, the children who attended developmentally appropriate kindergartens displayed more appropriate classroom behavior and had better conduct records and better work and study habits in the first grade than did the children who attended developmentally inappropriate kindergartens (Hart & others, 1993, 1998).

Does Preschool Matter?

Preschool is rapidly becoming a norm in early childhood education. Twenty-three states already have legislation pending to provide schooling for 4-year-old children, and there are many private preschool programs. The growth in preschool education may benefit many children, but is preschool really a good thing for all children?

According to developmental psychologist David Elkind (1988), parents who are exceptionally competent and dedicated and who have both the time and the energy can provide the basic ingredients of early childhood education in their home. If parents have the competence and resources to provide young children with a variety of learning experiences and exposure to other children and adults (possibly through neighborhood play groups), along with opportunities for extensive play, then home schooling may sufficiently educate young children. However, if parents do not have the commitment, the time, the energy, and the resources to provide young children with an environment that approximates a good early childhood program, then it *does* matter whether a child attends preschool. Thus, the issue is not whether preschool is important but whether home schooling can closely duplicate what a competent preschool program can offer.

There is a concern about preschool and early childhood programs that place too much emphasis on achievement. Researchers have documented that increased academic pressure can be stressful for young children. In one study, Diane Burts and her colleagues (1989) compared the frequencies of stress-related behaviors observed in young children in classrooms with developmentally appropriate instructional practices with those of children in classrooms with developmentally inappropriate instructional practices. They found that the children in the developmentally inappropriate classrooms exhibited more stress-related behaviors than the children in the developmentally appropriate classrooms. In another study, children in a highly academically oriented early childhood education program were compared with children in a low academically

Head Start Resources
Poverty and Learning
Early Childhood Care and Education Around the World

developmentally appropriate practice
Education that focuses on the typical developmental patterns of children (age-appropriateness) and the uniqueness of each child (individual-appropriateness).

Component	Appropriate practice	Inappropriate practice
Language development, literacy, and cognitive development	Children are provided many opportunities to see how reading and writing are useful before they are instructed in letter names, sounds, and word identification. Basic skills develop when they are meaningful to children. An abundance of these activities is provided to develop language and literacy: listening to and reading stories and poems; taking field trips; dictating stories; participating in dramatic play; talking informally with other children and adults; and experimenting with writing.	Reading and writing instruction stresses isolated skill development, such as recognizing single letters, reading the alphabet, singing the alphabet song, coloring within predefined lines, and being instructed in correct formation of letters on a printed line.
	Children develop an understanding of concepts about themselves, others, and the world around them through observation, interaction with people and real objects, and the seeking of solutions to concrete problems. Learning about math, science, social studies, health, and other content areas is integrated through meaningful activities.	Instruction stresses isolated skill development through memorization. Children's cognitive development is seen as fragmented in content areas, such as math or science, and times are set aside for each of these.
Physical development	Children have daily opportunities to use large muscles, including running, jumping, and balancing. Outdoor activity is planned daily so children can freely express themselves.	Opportunity for large muscle activity is limited. Outdoor time is limited because it is viewed as interfering with instructional time, rather than as an integral part of the children's learning environment.
	Children have daily opportunities to develop small muscle skills through play activities, such as puzzles, painting, and cutting.	Small motor activity is limited to writing with pencils, coloring predrawn forms, and engaging in similar structured lessons.
Aesthetic development and motivation	Children have daily opportunities for aesthetic expression and appreciation through art and music. A variety of art media are available.	Art and music are given limited attention. Art consists of coloring predrawn forms or following adult-prescribed directions.
	Children's natural curiosity and desire to make sense of their world are used to motivate them to become involved in learning.	Children are required to participate in all activities to obtain the teacher's approval; to obtain extrinsic rewards, such as stickers or privileges; or to avoid punishment.

FIGURE 8.17 NAEYC Recommendations for Developmentally Appropriate and Inappropriate Education

Early Childhood Education in Japan

At a time of low academic achievement by children in the United States, many Americans are turning to Japan, a country of high academic achievement, for possible answers. However, the answers provided by Japanese preschools are not the ones Americans expected to find. In most Japanese preschools, surprisingly little emphasis is put on academic instruction. In one study, 300 Japanese and 210 Americans preschool teachers, child development specialists, and parents were asked about various aspects of early childhood education (Tobin, Wu, & Davidson, 1989). Only 2 percent of the Japanese respondents listed "to give children a good start academically" as one of their top three reasons for a society to have preschools. In contrast, over half the American respondents chose this as one of their top three choices. To prepare children for successful careers in first grade and beyond, Japanese schools do not teach reading, writing, and mathematics but rather skills like persistence, concentration, and the ability to function as a member of a group. The vast majority of young Japanese children are taught to read at home by their parents.

In the comparison of Japanese and American parents, more than 60 percent of the Japanese parents said that the purpose of preschool is to give children experience being a member of the group compared to only 20 percent of the U.S. parents (Tobin, Wu, & Davidson, 1989) (see figure 8.18). Lessons in living and working together grow naturally out of the Japanese culture. In many Japanese kindergartens, children wear the same uniforms, including caps, which are of different colors to indicate the classrooms to which they belong. They have identical sets of equipment, kept in identical drawers and shelves. This is not intended to turn the young children into robots, as some Americans have observed, but to impress on them that other people, just like themselves, have needs and desires that are equally important (Hendry, 1986).

As in America, there is diversity in Japanese early childhood education. Some Japanese kindergartens have specific aims, such as early musical training or the practice of Montessori strategies. In large cities, some kindergartens are attached to universities that have elementary and secondary schools. Some Japanese parents believe that, if their young children attend a university-based program, it will increase the children's chances of eventually being admitted to top-rated schools and universities. Several more progressive programs have introduced free play as an antidote for the heavy intellectual orientation in some Japanese kindergartens.

In Japan, learning how to cooperate and participating in group experiences are viewed as extremely important reasons for early childhood education.

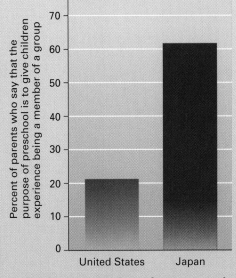

FIGURE 8.18 **Comparison of Japanese and U.S. Parents' Views on the Purpose of Preschool**

oriented early childhood education program (Hirsch-Pasek & others, 1989). No benefits appeared for children in the highly academically oriented early childhood education program, but some possible harmful effects were noted. Higher test anxiety, less creativity, and a less positive attitude toward school characterized more of the children in the highly academic program than in the low academic program.

In Japan, the goals of early childhood education are quite different from those of American programs. To read about the differences, see the Sociocultural Worlds of Development box.

Careers in Life-Span Development

Yolanda Garcia, Director of Children's Services/Head Start

Yolanda Garcia has worked in the field of early childhood education and family support for three decades. She has been the Director of the Children's Services Department for the Santa Clara, California, County Office of Education since 1980. As director, she is responsible for managing child development programs for 2,500 3- to 5-year-old children in 127 classrooms. Her training includes two master's degrees, one in public policy and child welfare from the University of Chicago and another in educational administration from San Jose State University.

Garcia has served on many national advisory committees that have resulted in improvements in the staffing of Head Start programs. Most notably, she served on the Head Start Quality Committee that recommended the development of Early Head Start and revised performance standards for Head Start programs. Garcia currently is a member of the American Academy of Science Committee on the Integration of Science and Early Childhood Education.

Yolanda Garcia, Director of Children's Services/Head Start, working with some Head Start children in Santa Clara, California.

Education for Children Who Are Disadvantaged

For many years, children from low-income families did not receive any education before they entered the first grade. In the 1960s, an effort was made to try to break the cycle of poverty and poor education for young children in the United States through compensatory education. **Project Head Start** is a government-funded program designed to provide children from low-income families the opportunity to acquire the skills and experiences important for success in school. Project Head Start began in the summer of 1965, funded by the Economic Opportunity Act, and it continues to serve disadvantaged children today.

Evaluations support the positive influence of quality early childhood programs on both the cognitive and social worlds of disadvantaged young children (Goelman & others, 2003; Reynolds, 1999). One high-quality early childhood education program (although not a Head Start program) is the Perry Preschool program in Ypsilanti, Michigan, a 2-year preschool program that includes weekly home visits from program personnel. In an analysis of the long-term effects of the program, young adults who attended the Perry Preschool have higher high school graduation rates, a higher employment rate, less need for welfare, a lower crime rate, and a lower teen pregnancy rate than in a control group from the same background who did not have the enriched early childhood education experience (Weikart, 1993).

Although educational intervention for children who are disadvanted is important, Head Start programs are not all created equal. One estimate is that 40 percent of the

Project Head Start A government-funded program that is designed to provide children from low-income families the opportunity to acquire the skills and experiences important for school success.

1,400 Head Start programs are of questionable quality (Zigler & Styfco, 1994). Developing consistently high-quality Head Start programs should be a national priority.

One individual who is strongly motivated to make Head Start a valuable learning experience for young children from disadvantaged backgrounds is Yolanda Garcia. To read about her work, see the Careers in Life-Span Development insert.

Review and Reflect

4 **Evaluate different approaches to early childhood education**

REVIEW

- What is child-centered kindergarten?
- What is the Montessori approach?
- How is developmentally appropriate practice different from developmentally inappropriate practice?
- Does preschool matter?
- What are the main efforts to educate young children who are disadvantaged?

REFLECT

- Might preschool be more beneficial to children from middle-income than low-income families? Why?

Reach Your Learning Goals

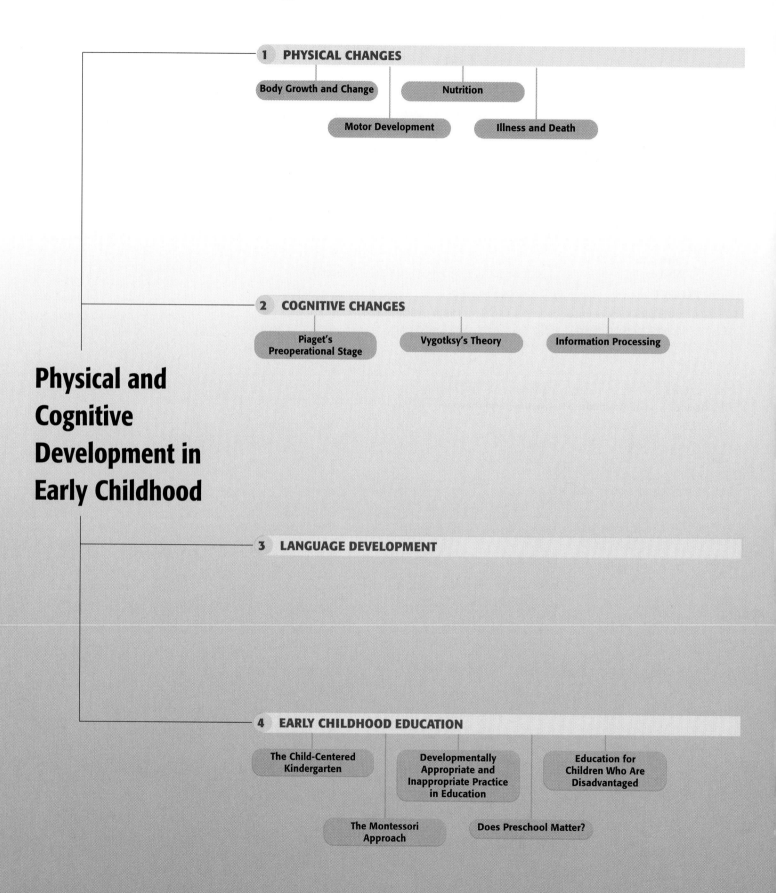

Physical and Cognitive Development in Early Childhood

1 PHYSICAL CHANGES

Body Growth and Change

Nutrition

Motor Development

Illness and Death

2 COGNITIVE CHANGES

Piaget's Preoperational Stage

Vygotksy's Theory

Information Processing

3 LANGUAGE DEVELOPMENT

4 EARLY CHILDHOOD EDUCATION

The Child-Centered Kindergarten

Developmentally Appropriate and Inappropriate Practice in Education

Education for Children Who Are Disadvantaged

The Montessori Approach

Does Preschool Matter?

Summary

1 Identify physical changes in early childhood

- The average child grows 2½ inches in height and gains between 5 and 7 pounds a year during early childhood. Growth patterns vary individually, though. Some children are unusually short because of congenital problems, a physical problem that develops in childhood, or emotional problems. Some of the brain's increase in size in early childhood is due to increases in the number and size of nerve endings, some to myelination. Recently, researchers have found that changes in local patterns in the brain occur between 3 and 15 years of age. These changes often involve spurts of brain activity. From 3 to 6 years of age, the most rapid growth occurs in the frontal lobes; from 6 to puberty, the most substantial changes take place in the temporal and parietal lobes, especially those areas involving language and spatial relations. Increasing brain maturation contributes to improved cognitive abilities.

- Gross motor skills increase dramatically during early childhood. Children become increasingly adventuresome as their gross motor skills improve. Fine motor skills also improve substantially during early childhood. At one point, all children were taught to be right-handed. In today's world, the strategy is to allow children to use the hand they favor. Left-handed children are as competent in motor skills and intellect as right-handed children, although left-handers have more reading problems. Both genetic and environmental explanations of handedness have been given.

- Energy requirements vary according to basal metabolism, rate of growth, and level of activity. A special concern is that too many young children are being raised on diets that are too high in fat. The child's life should be centered on activities, not meals.

- In recent decades, vaccines have virtually eradicated many diseases that once resulted in the deaths of many young children. The disorders still most likely to be fatal for young children are birth defects, cancer, and heart disease, but accidents are the leading cause of death in young children. A special concern is the poor health status of many young children in low-income families. They often have less resistance to disease, including colds and influenza, than do their higher-socioeconomic-status counterparts. One of every three deaths in the world is that of a child under 5. Every week, more than a quarter of a million children die in developing countries. The most common cause of children's death in developing countries is diarrhea. There has been a dramatic increase in HIV/AIDS in young children in developing countries in the last decade.

2 Describe three views of the cognitive changes that occur in early childhood

- Piaget's preoperational stage of thought is the beginning of the ability to reconstruct at the level of thought what has been established in behavior and a transition from primitive to more sophisticated use of symbols. In preoperational thought, the child's thoughts are flawed and not well organized. The symbolic function substage occurs between 2 and 4 years of age and is characterized by symbolic thought, egocentrism, and animism. The intuitive thought substage stretches from 4 to 7 years of age. It is called intuitive because children seem so sure about their knowledge yet are unaware of how they know what they know. The preoperational child lacks conservation and asks a barrage of questions.

- In Vygotsky's theory, the zone of proximal development (ZPD) describes the range of tasks that are too difficult for children to master alone but which can be learned with the guidance and assistance of adults or more-skilled children. Scaffolding involves changing the level of support over the course of a teaching session, with the more-skilled person adjusting guidance to fit the student's current performance level. Vygotsky believed that language plays a key role in guiding cognition. Comparisons of Vygotsky's and Piaget's theories involve constructivism, metaphors for learning, stages, key processes, role of language, views on education, and teaching implications. Vygotsky's theory is social constructivist, Piaget's cognitive constructivist. Applications of Vygotsky's theory in education focus on using the child's zone of proximal development, using scaffolding and more-skilled peers as teachers, monitoring and encouraging children's use of private speech, assessing the child's ZPD rather than IQ, and transforming the classroom with Vygotskian ideas.

- Information-processing theory emphasizes cognitive processes. The child's ability to attend to stimuli dramatically improves during early childhood. One deficit in attention in early childhood is that the child attends to the salient rather than the relevant features of a task. Significant improvement in short-term memory occurs during early childhood. With good prompts, young children's long-term memories can be accurate, although young children can be led into developing false memories. Young children usually don't use strategies to remember, but they can learn rather simple problem-solving strategies. Theory of mind is the awareness of one's own mental processes and the mental processes of others. Children begin to understand mental states involving perceptions, desires, and emotions at 2 to 3 years of age and at 4 to 5 years of age realize that people can have false beliefs.

3 Summarize how language develops in early childhood

- Young children increase their grasp of language's rule systems. These include phonology, morphology, syntax, semantics, and pragmatics. Berko's classic experiment demonstrated that young children understand morphological rules.

Evaluate different approaches to early childhood education

- The child-centered kindergarten emphasizes the education of the whole child, with particular attention to individual variation, the process of learning, and the importance of play in development.
- The Montessori approach, another well-known strategy for early childhood education, allows children to choose from a range of activities while teachers serve as facilitators.
- Developmentally appropriate practice focuses on the typical patterns of children (age-appropriateness) and the unique-

ness of each child (individual-appropriateness). Such practice contrasts with developmentally inappropriate practice, which ignores the concrete, hands-on approach to learning.
- A special concern is the view that education is a race and that an early academic start in preschool will help children win the race. Critics argue that too many preschools are academically oriented and stressful for young children.
- The U.S. government has tried to break the poverty cycle with programs such as Head Start. Model programs have been shown to have positive effects on children from poverty backgrounds.

Key Terms

myelination 236
basal metabolism rate (BMR) 239
operations 242
symbolic function substage 242
egocentrism 242

animism 243
intuitive thought substage 244
centration 244
conservation 244
zone of proximal development (ZPD) 246
scaffolding 246

social constructivist approach 247
short-term memory 251
theory of mind 252
child-centered kindergarten 256
Montessori approach 256

developmentally appropriate practice 258
Project Head Start 260

Key People

Teresa Amabile 234
Jean Piaget 242
Barbel Inhelder 243
Rochel Gelman 245

Lev Vygtosky 246
Zhe Chen and Robert Siegler 252

Jean Berko 254
Maria Montessori 256
David Elkind 258

1. Professor Jackson has asked his students to try and place Piaget's theories in the context of contemporary research. What should students know about how Piaget's theories stack up in relation to recent research findings?

2. Judith and Louis have a 3-year-old son, Mitchell. Many of their friends are enrolling their children in preschool. Judith and Louis do not think they can afford to enroll Mitchell in a preschool program, although both of them think that the benefits of preschool might justify the cost. Are there significant benefits associated with preschool programs? Are there particular types of preschools that seem more beneficial for children?

3. Beyonce, who is working in a prosecutor's office for her senior internship, has been asked to write a memo on the suggestibility of child witnesses and how likely a jury is to believe a child's testimony in court cases. How can she find information for the memo that provides research-based facts as well as guidelines for dealing with child witnesses that will be helpful for the prosecutors?

Connect to www.mhhe.com/santrockld9 to research the answers and complete these exercises.

To help you master the material in this chapter, you'll find a number of valuable study tools on the Student CD-ROM that accompanies this book. In addition, visit the Online Learning Center for *Life-Span Development*, ninth edition, where you'll find these valuable resources for chapter 8, "Physical and Cognitive Development in Early Childhood."

- What do you think are the most important aspects of early childhood education? Use the self-assessment, *What I Think Is Important in Early Childhood Education*, to solidify your opinions on the topic.

- View video clips of key researchers, including Steve Ceci as he discusses his research on child witness testimony.

- Build your decision-making skills by trying your hand at the parenting and education "Scenarios."

CHAPTER 9

Let us play, for it is
yet day
And we cannot go to
sleep;
Besides, in the sky
the little birds fly
And the hills are all
covered with sheep.

—WILLIAM BLAKE
English Poet, 19th Century

Socioemotional Development in Early Childhood

Chapter Outline

EMOTIONAL AND PERSONALITY DEVELOPMENT

    The Self

    Emotional Development

    Moral Development

    Gender

FAMILIES

    Parenting

    Sibling Relationships and Birth Order

    The Changing Family in a Changing Society

PEER RELATIONS, PLAY, AND TELEVISION

    Peer Relations

    Play

    Television

Learning Goals

1 Discuss emotional and personality development in early childhood

2 Explain how families can influence young children's development

3 Describe the roles of peers, play, and television in young children's development

Images of Life-Span Development
Sarah and Her Developing Moral Values

Like many children, Sara Newland loves animals. When she was just 4 years old, she turned that love into social activism. During a trip to the zoo, she learned about the plight of an endangered species and became motivated to help. With her mother's assistance, Sara baked cakes and cookies and sold them on the sidewalk near her apartment building in New York City. She was elated when she raised $35, which she promptly mailed to the World Wildlife Fund. A few weeks later, her smiles turned into tears when the fund wrote Sara asking for more money. Sara was devastated because she thought she had taken care of the animal problem. Her mother told Sara that the endangered species problem and many others are so big that they require continual help from lots of people. That explanation apparently worked because Sara, now 9 years old, helps out at an inner-city child-care center and regularly takes meals to homeless people in her neighborhood (Kantrowitz, 1991). Sara tells her friends not to be scared of homeless people. She says that some people wonder why she gives to them, then says, "If everyone gave food to them, they would all have decent meals."

Sensitive parents can make a difference in encouraging young children's sense of morality and values. Some experts on moral development believe that a capacity for goodness is present from the start, which reflects the "innate goodness" view of the child, which we discussed in chapter 1. But many developmentalists also believe that parents must nurture that goodness, just as they help their children become good readers, musicians, or athletes.

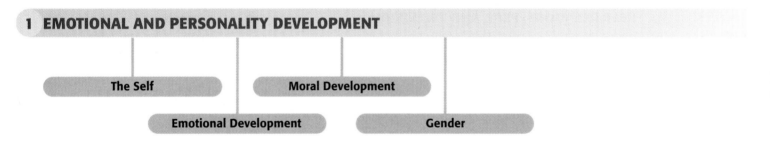

1 EMOTIONAL AND PERSONALITY DEVELOPMENT

In the story that opened the chapter, Sara displayed a positive sense of morality through her motivation to help an endangered species and the homeless. Let's further explore young children's moral development and other aspects of their emotional and personality development, beginning with the self.

The Self

We learned in chapter 7 that toward the end of the second year of life children develop a sense of self ◀Ⅲ p. 213. During early childhood, some important developments in the self take place. Among these developments are facing the issue of initiative versus guilt and enhancing self-understanding.

Initiative Versus Guilt According to Erik Erikson (1968), the psychosocial stage that characterizes early childhood is *initiative versus guilt*. By now, children have become convinced that they are a person of their own; during early childhood, they must discover what kind of person they will become. They intensely identify with their parents, who most of the time appear to them to be powerful and beautiful, although often unreasonable, disagreeable, and sometimes even dangerous. During early childhood, children use their perceptual, motor, cognitive, and language skills to make things happen. They have a surplus of energy that permits them to forget failures quickly and to approach new areas that seem desirable—even if they seem dangerous—with undiminished zest and some increased sense of direction. On their own *initiative*, then, children at this stage exuberantly move out into a wider social world.

The great governor of initiative is *conscience*. Children now not only feel afraid of being found out, but they also begin to hear the inner voice of self-observation, self-guidance, and self-punishment (Bybee, 1999). Their initiative and enthusiasm may bring them not only rewards but also punishments. Widespread disappointment at this stage leads to an unleashing of guilt that lowers the child's self-esteem.

Whether children leave this stage with a sense of initiative that outweighs their sense of guilt depends in large part on how parents respond to their children's self-initiated activities. Children who are given the freedom and opportunity to initiate motor play, such as running, bike riding, sledding, skating, tussling, and wrestling, have their sense of initiative supported. Initiative is also supported when parents answer their children's questions and do not deride or inhibit fantasy or play activity. In contrast, if children are made to feel that their motor activity is bad, that their questions are a nuisance, and that their play is silly and stupid, then they often develop a sense of guilt over self-initiated activities that may persist through life's later stages (Elkind, 1970).

Self-Understanding   **Self-understanding** is the child's representation of self, the substance and content of self-conceptions. For example, a 5-year-old girl understands that she is a girl, has blond hair, likes to ride her bicycle, has a friend, and is a swimmer. An 11-year-old boy understands that he is a student, a boy, a football player, a family member, a video-game lover, and a rock music fan. A child's self-understanding is based on the various roles and membership categories that define who children are. Though not the whole of personal identity, self-understanding provides its rational underpinnings (Damon & Hart, 1992).

The rudimentary beginning of self-understanding begins with self-recognition, which takes place by approximately 18 months of age. Since children can verbally communicate their ideas, research on self-understanding in childhood is not limited to visual self-recognition, as it was during infancy. Mainly by interviewing children, researchers have probed children's conceptions of many aspects of self-understanding (Moore & Lemmon, 2001). These include mind and body, self in relation to others, and pride and shame in self. In early childhood, children usually conceive of the self in physical terms. Most young children think the self is part of their body, usually their head. Young children usually confuse self, mind, and body. Because the self is a body part for them, they describe it along many material dimensions, such as size, shape, and color. Young children distinguish themselves from others through many different physical and material attributes. Says 4-year-old Sandra, "I'm different from Jennifer because I have brown hair and she has blond hair." Says 4-year-old Ralph, "I am different from Hank because I am taller, and I am different from my sister because I have a bicycle."

Researchers also believe that the *active dimension* is a central component of the self in early childhood (Keller, Ford, & Meacham, 1978). If we define the category *physical* broadly enough, we can include physical actions as well as body image and material possessions. For example, preschool children often describe themselves in terms of such activities as play. In sum, in early childhood, children frequently think of themselves in terms of a physical self or an active self.

Emotional Development

Children, like adults, experience many emotions during the course of a day. At times, children also try to make sense of other people's emotional reactions and feelings.

Young Children's Emotion Language and Understanding   Among the most important changes in emotional development in early childhood are the increased use of emotion language and the understanding of emotion (Kuebli, 1994). Preschoolers

self-understanding The child's cognitive representation of self, the substance and content of the child's self-conceptions.

Approximate Age of Child	Description
2 to 3 years	Increase emotion vocabulary most rapidly
	Correctly label simple emotions in self and others and talk about past, present, and future emotions
	Talk about the causes and consequences of some emotions and identify emotions associated with certain situations
	Use emotion language in pretend play
4 to 5 years	Show increased capacity to reflect verbally on emotions and to consider more complex relations between emotions and situations
	Understand that the same event may call forth different feelings in different people and that feelings sometimes persist long after the events that caused them
	Demonstrate growing awareness about controlling and managing emotions in accord with social standards

FIGURE 9.1 Some Characteristics of Young Children's Emotion Language and Understanding

become more adept at talking about their own and others' emotions. Between 2 and 3 years of age, children continue to increase the number of terms they use to describe emotion (Ridgeway, Waters, & Kuczaj, 1985). However, in the preschool years, children are learning more than just the "vocabulary" of emotion terms, they also are learning about the causes and consequences of feelings (Denham, 1998).

At 4 to 5 years of age, children show an increased ability to reflect on emotions. In this developmental time frame, they also begin to understand that the same event can elicit different feelings in different people. Moreover, they show a growing awareness about controlling and managing emotions to meet social standards (Bruce, Olen, & Jensen, 1999). A summary of the characteristics of young children's emotion language and understanding is shown in figure 9.1.

Self-Conscious Emotions *Self-conscious emotions* require that children be able to refer to themselves and be aware of themselves as distinct from others (Lewis, 1993, 1995, 2002). Pride, shame, embarrassment, and guilt are self-conscious emotions.

Recall from chapter 7, "Socioemotional Development in Infancy," that self-awareness appears in the last half of the second year of life. The self-conscious emotions do not appear to develop, at the very earliest, until this self-awareness is in place. Thus, emotions such as pride and guilt become more common in the early childhood years. They are especially influenced by parents' responses to children's behavior. For example, a young child may experience a twinge of guilt when a parent says, "You should feel bad about biting your sister." Shortly, we will further discuss guilt in the context of moral development.

Moral Development

Moral development involves the development of thoughts, feelings, and behaviors regarding rules and conventions about what people should do in their interactions with other people. Developmentalists study how children think, behave, and feel about such rules and regulations. We will begin our exploration of moral development in children by focusing on a cognitive view of moral development.

Piaget's View of Moral Reasoning Interest in how the child thinks about moral issues was stimulated by Jean Piaget (1932). He extensively observed and interviewed children from the age of 4 to 12. He watched them play marbles, seeking to learn how they used and thought about the game's rules. He also asked children questions about

moral development Development that involves thoughts, feelings, and actions regarding rules and conventions about what people should do in their interactions with other people.

ethical rules—theft, lies, punishment, and justice, for example. Piaget concluded that children think in two distinctly different ways about morality, depending on their developmental maturity:

- **Heteronomous morality** is the first stage of moral development in Piaget's theory, occurring from approximately 4 to 7 years of age. Justice and rules are conceived of as unchangeable properties of the world, removed from the control of people.
- **Autonomous morality** is the second stage of moral development in Piaget's theory, displayed by older children (about 10 years of age and older). The child becomes aware that rules and laws are created by people and that, in judging an action, one should consider the actor's intentions as well as the consequences.

Children 7 to 10 years of age are in a transition between the two stages, showing some features of both.

Let's consider Piaget's two stages of moral development further. The heteronomous thinker judges the rightness or goodness of behavior by considering the consequences of the behavior, not the intentions of the actor. For example, the heteronomous thinker says that breaking 12 cups accidentally is worse than breaking 1 cup intentionally while trying to steal a cookie. For the moral autonomist, the reverse is true. The actor's intentions assume paramount importance. The heteronomous thinker also believes that rules are unchangeable and are handed down by all-powerful authorities. When Piaget suggested that new rules be introduced into the game of marbles, the young children resisted. They insisted that the rules had always been the same and could not be altered. By contrast, older children—who were moral autonomists—accepted change and recognized that rules are merely convenient, socially agreed-upon conventions, subject to change by consensus.

The heteronomous thinker also believes in **imminent justice,** the concept that, if a rule is broken, punishment will immediately be meted out. The young child believes that the violation is connected in some automatic way to the punishment. Thus, young children often look around worriedly after committing a transgression, expecting inevitable punishment. Older children, the moral autonomists, recognize that punishment is socially mediated and occurs only if a relevant person witnesses the wrongdoing and that, even then, punishment is not inevitable.

Piaget argued that, as children develop, they become more sophisticated in thinking about social matters, especially about the possibilities and conditions of cooperation. Piaget believed that this social understanding comes about through the mutual give-and-take of peer relations. In the peer group, where all members have similar power and status, plans are negotiated and coordinated, and disagreements are reasoned about and eventually settled. Parent-child relations, in which parents have the power and the child does not, are less likely to advance moral reasoning, because rules are often handed down in an authoritarian way. Later, in chapter 11, we will discuss another highly influential cognitive view of moral development, that of Lawrence Kohlberg.

Moral Behavior The study of moral behavior is emphasized by behavioral and social cognitive theorists ◀‖‖ p. 51. The processes of reinforcement, punishment, and imitation are used to explain children's moral behavior. When children are rewarded for behavior that is consistent with laws and social conventions, they are likely to repeat that behavior. When models who behave morally are provided, children are likely to adopt their actions. And, when children are punished for immoral behavior, those behaviors are likely to be reduced or eliminated. However, because punishment may have adverse side effects, it needs to be used judiciously and cautiously.

Another important point needs to be made about the social cognitive view of moral development. Moral behavior is influenced extensively by the situation. What children do in one situation is often only weakly related to what they do in other situations. A child might cheat in math class but not in English class; a child might steal

heteronomous morality The first stage of moral development, in Piaget's theory, occurring from approximately 4 to 7 years of age. Justice and rules are conceived of as unchangeable properties of the world, removed from the control of people.

autonomous morality The second stage of moral development, in Piaget's theory, displayed by older children (about 10 years of age and older). The child becomes aware that rules and laws are created by people and that, in judging an action, one should consider the actor's intentions as well as the consequences.

imminent justice The concept that, if a rule is broken, punishment will be meted out immediately.

*W*hat is moral is what you feel good after and what is immoral is what you feel bad after.

—Ernest Hemingway
American Author, 20th Century

a piece of candy when others are not present but not steal it when they are present. More than half a century ago, morality's situational nature was observed in a comprehensive study of thousands of children in many different situations—at home, at school, and at church, for example. The totally honest child was virtually nonexistent; so was the child who cheated in all situations (Hartshorne & May, 1928–1930).

Social cognitive theorists also believe that the ability to resist temptation is closely tied to the development of self-control. Children must overcome their impulses toward something they want that is prohibited. To achieve this self-control, they must learn to be patient and to delay gratification. Social cognitive theorists believe that cognitive factors are important in the child's development of self-control (Bandura, 2002).

Moral Feelings In chapter 2, we discussed Sigmund Freud's psychoanalytic theory ◀‖‖ p. 44. It describes the *superego* as one of the three main structures of personality—the id and ego being the other two. In Freud's classical psychoanalytic theory, the child's superego—the moral branch of personality—develops as the child resolves the Oedipus conflict and identifies with the same-sex parent in the early childhood years. Among the reasons children resolve the Oedipus conflict is the fear of losing their parents' love and of being punished for their unacceptable sexual wishes toward the opposite-sex parent. To reduce anxiety, avoid punishment, and maintain parental affection, children form a superego by identifying with the same-sex parent. Through their identification with the same-sex parent, children internalize the parents' standards of right and wrong that reflect societal prohibitions. And the child turns inward the hostility that was previously aimed externally at the same-sex parent. This inwardly directed hostility is now felt self-punitively as guilt, which is experienced unconsciously (beyond the child's awareness). In the psychoanalytic account of moral development, the self-punitiveness of guilt is responsible for keeping the child from committing transgressions. That is, children conform to societal standards to avoid guilt.

Positive feelings, such as empathy, contribute to the child's moral development. *Empathy* is reacting to another's feelings with an emotional response that is similar to the other's feelings. Although empathy is experienced as an emotional state, it often has a cognitive component. The cognitive component is the ability to discern another's inner psychological states, or what is called "perspective taking." Young infants have the capacity for some purely empathic responses, but for effective moral action children need to learn how to identify a wide range of emotional states in others. They also need to learn to anticipate what kinds of action will improve another person's emotional state.

Gender

While sex refers to the biological dimension of being male or female, **gender** refers to the social and psychological dimensions of being male or female. Two aspects of gender bear special mention:

- **Gender identity** is the sense of being male or female, which most children acquire by the time they are 3 years old.
- **Gender role** is a set of expectations that prescribes how females or males should think, act, and feel.

Biological Influences In chapter 3, you learned that humans normally have 46 chromosomes arranged in pairs. The 23rd pair may have two X chromosomes to produce a female, or it may have an X and a Y chromosome to produce a male.

Just as chromosomes are important in understanding biological influences, so are hormones. The two main classes of sex hormones are estrogens and androgens. *Estrogens,* such as estradiol, influence the development of female physical sex characteristics. *Androgens,* such as testosterone, promote the development of male physical sex characteristics. In the first few weeks of gestation, female and male embryos look alike. Male sex organs start to differ from female sex organs when the Y chromosome in the male

gender The social and psychological dimension of being male or female.

gender identity The sense of being male or female, which most children acquire by the time they are 3 years old.

gender role A set of expectations that prescribes how females or males should think, act, and feel.

embryo triggers the secretion of androgens. Low levels of androgens in the female embryo allow the normal development of female sex organs.

In gender development, however, biology is not completely destiny. When gender attitudes and behavior are at issue, children's socialization experiences matter a great deal (Eccles, 2000; Lippa, 2002: Rice, 2002; Travis, 2001).

Social Influences In the United States, adults discriminate between the sexes shortly after the infant's birth. The "pink and blue" treatment might be applied to boys and girls before they leave the hospital. Soon afterward, differences in hairstyles, clothes, and toys become obvious. Adults and peers reward these differences throughout development. And boys and girls learn gender roles through imitation, or observational learning, by watching what other people say and do. In recent years, the idea that parents are the critical socializing agents in gender-role development has come under fire. Parents are only one of many sources through which the individual learns gender roles (Beal, 1994; Fagot, Rodgers, & Leinbach, 2000). Culture, schools, peers, the media, and other family members are others, yet it is important to guard against swinging too far in this direction because—especially in the early years of development—parents are important influences on gender development.

Psychoanalytic and Social Cognitive Theories Two prominent theories address the way children acquire masculine and feminine attitudes and behaviors from their parents:

- The **psychoanalytic theory of gender** stems from Freud's view that the preschool child develops a sexual attraction to the opposite-sex parent. At 5 or 6 years of age, the child renounces this attraction because of anxious feelings. Subsequently, the child identifies with the same-sex parent, unconsciously adopting the same-sex parent's characteristics. However, today many child developmentalists do not believe gender development proceeds on the basis of identification, at least not in terms of Freud's emphasis on childhood sexual attraction (Callan, 2001). Children become gender-typed much earlier than 5 or 6 years of age, and they become masculine or feminine even when the same-sex parent is not present in the family.
- The **social cognitive theory of gender** emphasizes that children's gender development occurs through observation and imitation of gender behavior, and through the rewards and punishments children experience for gender-appropriate and -inappropriate behavior. Unlike psychoanalytic theory, social cognitive theory argues that sexual attraction to parents is not involved in gender development. (A comparison of the psychoanalytic and social cognitive views is presented in figure 9.2) Parents often use rewards and punishments to teach their daughters to be feminine ("Karen, you are being a good girl when you play gently with your doll") and their sons to be masculine ("Keith, a boy as big as you is

Theory	Processes	Outcomes
Freud's psychoanalytic theory	Sexual attraction to opposite-sex parent at 3 to 5 years of age; anxiety about sexual attraction and subsequent identification with same-sex parent at 5 to 6 years of age	Gender behavior similar to that of same-sex parent
Social cognitive theory	Rewards and punishments of gender-appropriate and -inappropriate behavior by adults and peers; observation and initiation of models' masculine and feminine behavior	Gender behavior

FIGURE 9.2 A Comparison of the Psychoanalytic and Social Cognitive Views of Gender Development
Parents influence their children's development by action and example.

mhhe com/ santrockld9
Gender Resources

psychoanalytic theory of gender A theory deriving from Freud's view that the preschool child develops a sexual attraction to the opposite-sex parent, by approximately 5 or 6 years of age renounces this attraction because of anxious feelings, and subsequently identifies with the same-sex parent, unconsciously adopting the same-sex parent's characteristics.

social cognitive theory of gender A theory that emphasizes that children's gender development occurs through the observation and imitation of gender behavior and through the rewards and punishments children experience for gender-appropriate and -inappropriate behavior.

In childhood, boys and girls tend to gravitate toward others of their own sex. Boys' and girls' groups develop distinct cultures with different agendas.

—Eleanor Maccoby
Contemporary Developmental Psychologist, Stanford University

**mhhe ● com/
santrockld9**

Fathers and Sons

not supposed to cry"). Peers also extensively reward and punish gender behavior (Lott & Maluso, 2001). And, by observing adults and peers at home, at school, in the neighborhood, and on television, children are widely exposed to a myriad of models who display masculine and feminine behavior. Critics of the social cognitive view argue that gender development is not as passively acquired as it indicates. Later, we will discuss the cognitive views of gender development, which stress that children actively construct their gender world.

Parental Influences   Parents, by action and by example, influence their children's gender development. Both mothers and fathers are psychologically important in children's gender development. Mothers are more consistently given responsibility for nurturance and physical care. Fathers are more likely to engage in playful interaction and to be given responsibility for ensuring that boys and girls conform to existing cultural norms. And, whether or not they have more influence on them, fathers are more involved in socializing their sons than their daughters. Fathers seem to play an especially important part in gender-role development. They are more likely than mothers to act differently toward sons and daughters. Thus, they contribute more to distinctions between the genders (Huston, 1983).

Many parents encourage boys and girls to engage in different types of play and activities (Fagot, Leinbach, & O'Boyle, 1992). Girls are more likely to be given dolls to play with during childhood. When old enough, they are more likely to be assigned baby-sitting duties. Girls are encouraged to be more nurturant and emotional than boys. Fathers are more likely to engage in aggressive play with their sons than with their daughters.

Peer Influences   Parents provide the earliest discrimination of gender roles in development. Before long, though, peers join the societal process of responding to and modeling masculine and feminine behavior (Brannon, 2002). Children who play in sex-appropriate activities tend to be rewarded for doing so by their peers. Those who play in cross-sexed activities tend to be criticized by their peers or left to play alone. Children show a clear preference for being with and liking same-sex peers (Maccoby, 1993, 1998, 2002). This tendency usually becomes stronger during the middle and late childhood years. After extensive observations of elementary school playgrounds, two researchers characterized the play settings as "gender school." They said that boys teach one another the required masculine behavior and enforce it strictly (Luria &

As reflected in this tug-of-war battle between boys and girls, the playground in elementary school is like going to "gender school." Elementary school children show a clear preference for being with and liking same-sex peers. *Think back to when you were in elementary school. How much did you prefer being with peers who were the same sex as you?*

Herzog, 1985). Girls also pass on the female culture and congregate mainly with one another. Individual "tomboy" girls can join boys' activities without losing their status in the girls' groups; however, the reverse is not true for boys, reflecting our society's greater pressure for boys to conform to a traditional male role than for girls to conform to a traditional female role.

Cognitive Influences Developmentalists also recognize the important role that cognitive factors play in gender. Two cognitive theories of gender have been proposed:

- The **cognitive developmental theory of gender** states that children's gender typing occurs after they have developed a concept of gender. Once they consistently conceive of themselves as males or female, children often organize their world on the basis of gender. In this view, children use physical and behavioral clues to differentiate gender roles and to gender-type themselves early in their development. Initially proposed by Lawrence Kohlberg (1966), this theory argues that gender development proceeds in this way: A child realizes, "I am a girl. I want to do girl things. Therefore, the opportunity to do girl things is rewarding." Kohlberg said that gender constancy develops at about 6 or 7 years of age in concert with the development of children's conservation and categorization skills. After children consistently conceive of themselves as female or male, they begin to organize their world on the basis of gender, such as selecting same-sex models to imitate.
- **Gender schema theory** states that an individual's attention and behavior are guided by an internal motivation to conform to gender-based sociocultural standards and stereotypes. Note that a *schema* is a cognitive structure, a network of associations that organizes and guides an individual's perceptions. A *gender schema* organizes the world in terms of female and male. Gender schema theory suggests that "gender-typing" occurs when individuals are ready to encode and organize information along the lines of what is considered appropriate or typical for males and females in a society (Martin & Dinella, 2001; Sokal & Seifert, 2001). Whereas Kohlberg's cognitive developmental theory argues that a particular cognitive prerequisite—gender constancy—is necessary for gender-typing, *gender constancy* refers to the understanding that sex remains the same even though activities, clothing, and hairstyle might change (Ruble, 2000). Gender schema theory states that a general readiness to respond to and categorize information on the basis of culturally defined gender roles fuels children's gender-typing activities. A comparison of the cognitive developmental and gender schema theories is presented in figure 9.3.

Theory	Processes	Emphasis
Cognitive developmental theory	Development of gender constancy, especially around 6 to 7 years of age, when conservation skills develop; after children develop ability to consistently conceive of themselves as male or female, children often organize their world on the basis of gender, such as selecting same-sex models to imitate	Cognitive readiness facilitates gender identity
Gender schema theory	Sociocultural emphasis on gender-based standards and stereotypes; children's attention and behavior are guided by an internal motivation to conform to these gender-based standards and stereotypes, allowing children to interpret the world through a network of gender-organized thoughts	Gender schemas reinforce gender behavior

FIGURE 9.3 The Development of Gender Behavior According to the Cognitive Developmental and Gender Schema Theories of Gender Development

cognitive developmental theory of gender The theory that children's gender typing occurs after they have developed a concept of gender. Once they consistently conceive of themselves as male or female, children often organize their world on the basis of gender.

gender schema theory The theory that an individual's attention and behavior are guided by an internal motivation to conform to gender-based sociocultural standards and stereotypes.

Review and Reflect

1 **Discuss emotional and personality development in early childhood**

REVIEW

- What are changes in the self during early childhood?
- What changes take place in emotional development in early childhood?
- What are some key aspects of moral development in young children?
- How does gender develop in young children?

REFLECT

- Which theory of gender development do you like the best? What might an eclectic theoretical view of gender development be like? (You might want to review the discussion of an eclectic theoretical orientation in chapter 2).

2 FAMILIES

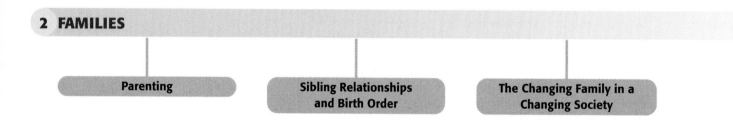

Parenting | Sibling Relationships and Birth Order | The Changing Family in a Changing Society

In chapter 7, we learned that attachment is an important aspect of family relationships during infancy ◀▥ p. 215. Remember that some experts believe attachment to a caregiver during the first several years of life is the key ingredient in the child's socioemotional development. We also learned that other experts believe secure attachment has been overemphasized and that the child's temperament, other social agents and contexts, and the complexity of the child's social world are also important in determining the child's social competence and well-being. Some developmentalists also emphasize that the infant years have been overdramatized as determinants of life-span development. They argue that social experiences in the early childhood years and later deserve more attention than they have sometimes been given.

In this chapter, we will discuss early childhood experiences beyond attachment. We will explore the different types of parenting styles, sibling relationships, and the ways in which more children are now experiencing socialization in a greater variety of family structures than at any other point in history.

Parenting

Parenting

An important dimension of parenting is the styles parents use when they interact with their children. Other considerations include punishment, child abuse, coparenting, and time and effort.

Parenting Styles Parents want their children to grow into socially mature individuals, and they may feel frustrated in trying to discover the best way to accomplish this. Developmentalists have long searched for the ingredients of parenting that promote competent socioemotional development (Bornstein, 2002; Brooks, 1999). For example, in the 1930s, John Watson argued that parents are too affectionate with their children. In the 1950s, a distinction was made between physical and psychological discipline. Psychological discipline, especially reasoning, was emphasized as the best way to rear a child. In the 1970s and beyond, the dimensions of competent parenting have become more precise (Lerner, 2000).

Calvin and Hobbes

Especially widespread is the view of Diana Baumrind (1971). She believes parents should be neither punitive nor aloof. Rather, they should develop rules for their children and be affectionate with them. She emphasizes four types of parenting styles:

- **Authoritarian parenting** is a restrictive, punitive style in which parents exhort the child to follow their directions and respect their work and effort. The authoritarian parent places firm limits and controls on the child and allows little verbal exchange. For example, an authoritarian parent might say, "You do it my way or else." Authoritarian parents also might spank the child frequently, enforce rules rigidly but not explain them, and show rage toward the child. Children of authoritarian parents are often unhappy, fearful, and anxious about comparing themselves with others, fail to initiate activity, and have weak communication skills.
- **Authoritative parenting** encourages children to be independent but still places limits and controls on their actions. Extensive verbal give-and-take is allowed, and parents are warm and nurturant toward the child. An authoritative parent might put his arm around the child in a comforting way and say, "You know you should not have done that. Let's talk about how you can handle the situation better next time." Authoritative parents show pleasure and support of children's constructive behavior. They also expect mature, independent, and age-appropriate behavior of children. Children whose parents are authoritative are often cheerful, self-controlled and self-reliant, achievement-oriented, maintain friendly relations with peers, cooperate with adults, and cope well with stress.
- **Neglectful parenting** is a style in which the parent is very uninvolved in the child's life. Children whose parents are neglectful develop the sense that other aspects of the parents' lives are more important than they are. These children tend to be socially incompetent. Many have poor self-control and don't handle independence well. They frequently have low self-esteem, are immature, and may be alienated from the family. In adolescence, they may show patterns of truancy and delinquency.
- **Indulgent parenting** is a style of parenting in which parents are highly involved with their children but place few demands or controls on them. Such parents let their children do what they want. The result is that the children never learn to control their own behavior and always expect to get their way. Some parents deliberately rear their children in this way because they believe the combination of warm involvement and few restraints will produce a creative, confident child. However, children whose parents are indulgent rarely learn respect for others and have difficulty controlling their behavior. They might be domineering, egocentric, noncompliant, and have difficulties in peer relations.

The four classifications of parenting just discussed involve combinations of acceptance and responsiveness on the one hand and demand and control on the other. How

authoritarian parenting A restrictive punitive style in which parents exhort the child to follow their directions and to respect work and effort. The authoritarian parent places firm limits and controls on the child and allows little verbal exchange. Authoritarian parenting is associated with children's social incompetence.

authoritative parenting A parenting style in which parents encourage their children to be independent but still place limits and controls on their actions. Extensive verbal give-and-take is allowed, and parents are warm and nurturant toward the child. Authoritative parenting is associated with children's social competence.

neglectful parenting A style of parenting in which the parent is very uninvolved in the child's life; it is associated with children's social incompetence, especially a lack of self-control.

indulgent parenting A style of parenting in which parents are highly involved with their children but place few demands or controls on them. Indulgent parenting is associated with children's social incompetence, especially a lack of self-control.

	Accepting, responsive	Rejecting, unresponsive
Demanding, controlling	Authoritative	Authoritarian
Undemanding, uncontrolling	Indulgent	Neglectful

FIGURE 9.4 Classification of Parenting Styles

The four types of parenting styles (authoritative, authoritarian, indulgent, and neglectful) involve the dimensions of acceptance and responsiveness, on the one hand, and demand and control on the other. For example, authoritative parenting involves being both accepting/responsive and demanding/controlling.

these dimensions combine to produce authoritarian, authoritative, neglectful, and indulgent parenting is shown in figure 9.4.

Punishment For centuries, corporal (physical) punishment, such as spanking, has been considered a necessary and even desirable method of disciplining children (Greven, 1991). Use of corporal punishment is legal in every state in America and it is estimated that 70 to 90 percent of American parents have spanked their children (Straus, 2001).

Despite the widespread use of corporal punishment, there have been surprisingly few research studies on physical punishment and those that have been conducted are correlational (Baumrind, Larzelere, & Cowan, 2002). Clearly, it would be highly unethical to randomly assign parents to either spank or not spank their children in an experimental study. Recall that cause and effect cannot be determined in a correlational study. In one correlational study, spanking by parents was linked with children's antisocial behavior, including cheating, telling lies, being mean to others, bullying, getting into fights, and being disobedient (Straus, Sugarman, & Giles-Sims, 1997). In a recent study of White, African American, and Latino families, spanking by parents predicted an increase in children's problems over time in all three groups (McLoyd & Smith, 2002). However, when parents showed strong emotional support of the child, the link between spanking and child problems was reduced.

A recent research review concluded that corporal punishment by parents is associated with children's higher levels of immediate compliance and aggression, and lower levels of moral internalization and mental health (Gershoff, 2002). Some critics, though, argue that the research evidence is not yet sound enough to warrant a blanket injunction against corporal punishment (Baumrind, Larzelere, & Cowan, 2002).

Here are some of the reasons why spanking or other forms of intense punishment with children should be avoided:

- When intense punishment, like yelling, screaming, or spanking is used, the adult is presenting the child with an out-of-control model for handling stressful situations. The children may imitate this aggressive, out-of-control behavior.
- Punishment can instill fear, rage, or avoidance in children. For example, spanking the child may cause the child to avoid being around the parent and fear the parent.
- Punishment tells children what not to do rather than what to do. When parents make punishing statements to children, such as "No, don't do that!" it should be accompanied by positive feedback, such as, "but why don't you try this?"
- Punishment can be abusive. When parents discipline their children, they might not intend to be abusive but become so aroused when they are punishing the child that they become abusive (Baumrind, Larzelere, & Cowan, 2002).

Because of reasons such as these, a law was passed in Sweden in 1979 forbidding parents to physically punish (spank or slap, for example) when disciplining their children. The law is still in effect and since it was enacted youth rates of juvenile delinquency, alcohol abuse, rape, and suicide have dropped in Sweden (Durrant, 2000). The improved picture for Swedish youth may have occurred for other reasons, such as changing societal attitudes and opportunities for youth. Nonetheless, the Swedish experience suggests that physical punishment of children may not be necessary to improve the well-being of youth. Joining Sweden in forbidding parents to physically punish their children, these countries have also passed anti-spanking laws: Finland (1984), Denmark (1986), Norway (1987), Austria (1989), Cyprus (1994), Latvia (1998), Croatia (1999), Germany (2000), and Israel (2000).

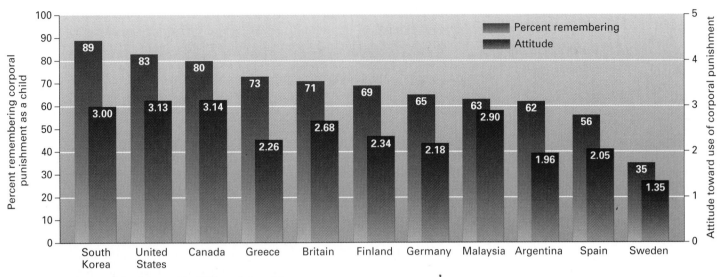

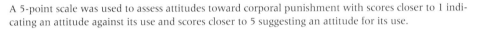

FIGURE 9.5 Corporal Punishment in Different Countries

A 5-point scale was used to assess attitudes toward corporal punishment with scores closer to 1 indicating an attitude against its use and scores closer to 5 suggesting an attitude for its use.

A recent cross-cultural comparison found that individuals in the United States and Canada were among the most favorable toward corporal punishment and remembered it being used by their parents (Curran & others, 2001) (see figure 9.5). People in Sweden especially had an unfavorable attitude toward corporal punishment and were less likely than people in the other countries to remember it being used by their parents.

Most child psychologists recommend reasoning with the child, especially explaining the consequences of the child's actions for others, as the best way to handle children's misbehaviors(Straus, 2003). Time-out, in which the child is removed from a setting where the child experiences positive reinforcement, can also be effective. For example, when the child has misbehaved, a parent might take away TV viewing for a specified period of time.

Child Abuse   Unfortunately, as we just mentioned, punishment sometimes leads to the abuse of infants and children. Child abuse is an increasing problem in the United States. Estimates of its incidence vary, but some authorities say that as many as 500,000 children are physically abused every year. Laws in many states now require doctors and teachers to report suspected cases of child abuse, yet many cases go unreported, especially those of battered infants.

Child abuse is such a disturbing circumstance that many people have difficulty understanding or sympathizing with parents who abuse or neglect their children. Our response is often outrage and anger directed at the parent. This outrage focuses our attention on parents as bad, sick, monstrous, sadistic individuals who cause their children to suffer. Experts on child abuse believe that this view is too simple and deflects attention away from the social context of the abuse and parents' coping skills. It is especially important to recognize that child abuse is a diverse condition, that it is usually mild to moderate in severity, and that it is only partially caused by the individual personality characteristics of parents (Azar, 2002; Field, 2000). The most common kind of abuser is not a raging, uncontrolled physical abuser but an overwhelmed single mother in poverty who neglects the child.

The Multifaceted Nature of Abuse   Whereas the public and many professionals use the term *child abuse* to refer to both abuse and neglect, developmentalists increasingly

Child maltreatment involves grossly inadequate and destructive aspects of parenting.

—DANTE CICCHETTI
Contemporary Developmental Psychologist, University of Rochester

Child Abuse Prevention Network

International Aspects of Child Abuse

National Clearinghouse on Child Abuse and Neglect

use the term *child maltreatment* (Cicchetti, 2001). This term does not have quite the emotional impact of the term *abuse* and acknowledges that maltreatment includes several different conditions. Among the different types of maltreatment are physical and sexual abuse; the fostering of delinquency; lack of supervision; medical, educational, and nutritional neglect; and drug or alcohol abuse. In one large survey, approximately 20 percent of the reported cases involved abuse alone, 46 percent neglect alone, 23 percent both abuse and neglect, and 11 percent sexual abuse (American Association for Protecting Children, 1986).

The Cultural Context of Abuse   The extensive violence that takes place in the American culture is reflected in the occurrence of violence in the family (Azar, 2002). A regular diet of violence appears on television screens, and parents often resort to power assertion as a disciplinary technique. In China, where physical punishment is rarely used to discipline children, the incidence of child abuse is reported to be very low. In the United States, many abusing parents report that they do not have sufficient resources or help from others. This may be a realistic evaluation of the situation experienced by many low-income families, who do not have adequate preventive and supportive services.

Family Influences   To understand abuse in the family, the interactions of all family members need to be considered, regardless of who actually performs the violent acts against the child. For example, even though the father may be the one who physically abuses the child, contributions by the mother, the child, and siblings also should be evaluated. Many parents who abuse their children come from families in which physical punishment was used. These parents view physical punishment as a legitimate way of controlling the child's behavior. Physical punishment may be a part of this sanctioning.

Were parents who abuse children abused by their own parents? About one-third of parents who were abused themselves when they were young abuse their own children (Cicchetti & Toth, 1998). Thus, some, but not a majority, of parents are locked into an intergenerational transmission of abuse. Mothers who break out of the intergenerational transmission of abuse often have at least one warm, caring adult in their background, have a close, positive marital relationship, and have received therapy (Egeland, Jacobivitz, & Sroufe, 1988).

Developmental Consequences of Abuse   Among the developmental consequences of child maltreatment are poor emotion regulation, attachment problems, problems in peer relations, difficulty in adapting to school, and other psychological problems (Azar, 2002; Shonk & Cicchetti, 2001). Difficulties in initiating and modulating positive and negative affect have been observed in maltreated infants (Cicchetti, Ganiban, & Barnett, 1991). Maltreated infants also may show excessive negative affect or blunted positive affect (Maughan & Cicchetti, 2002).

Maltreated children appear to be poorly equipped to develop successful peer relations, due to their aggressiveness, avoidance, and aberrant responses to both distress and positive approaches from peers (Bolger & Patterson, 2001; Mueller & Silverman, 1989).

Being physically abused has been linked with children's anxiety, personality problems, depression, conduct disorder, and delinquency (Shonk & Cicchetti, 2001; Toth, Manley, & Cicchetti, 1992). Later, during the adult years, maltreated children show increased violence toward other adults, dating partners, and marital partners, as well as increased substance abuse, anxiety, and depression (Malinosky-Rummell & Hansen, 1993). In sum, maltreated children are at risk for developing a wide range of problems and disorders (Bissada & Briere, 2002).

Coparenting   A dramatic increase in research on coparenting has occurred in the last two decades. The organizing theme of this research is that poor coordination, active undermining and disparagement of the other parent, lack of cooperation and warmth, and disconnection by one parenting partner—either alone or in combination with overinvolvement by the other—are conditions that place children at developmental risk (McHale & others, 2002). By contrast, parental cooperation and warmth show clear ties to children's prosocial behavior and competence in peer relations. For example, in one study, 4-year-old children from families characterized by low levels of mutuality and support in coparenting were more likely than their classmates to show difficulties in social adjustment when observed on the playground (McHale, Johnson, & Sinclair, 1999).

Good Parenting Takes Time and Effort   In today's society, there is an unfortunate theme which suggests that parenting can be done quickly and with little or no inconvenience (Sroufe, 2000). One example of this involves playing Mozart CDs in the hope that they will enrich infants' and young children's brains. Some of these parents might be thinking "I don't have enough time to spend with my children so I'll just play these intellectual CDs and then they won't need me as much." Judith Harris' book *The Nurture Assumption* (which states that heredity and peer relations are the key factors in children's development) fits into this theme that parents don't need to spend much time with their children ◀▥ p. 104. Why did it become so popular? To some degree some people who don't spend much time with their children saw it as supporting their neglect and reducing their guilt.

One-minute bedtime stories also are now being marketed successfully for parents to read to their children (Walsh, 2000). Most of these are brief summaries of longer stories. There are one-minute bedtime bear books, puppy books, and so on. These parents know it is good for them to read with their children, but they don't want to spend a lot of time doing it.

What is wrong with these quick-fix approaches to parenting? Good parenting takes a lot of time and a lot of effort. You can't do it in a minute here and a minute there. You can't do it with CDs.

Parents who do not spend enough time with their children or who have problems in child rearing can benefit from counseling and therapy. To read about the work of marriage and family counselor Darla Botkin, see the Careers in Life-Span Development insert.

Sibling Relationships and Birth Order

What are sibling relationships like? How extensively does birth order influence behavior?

Sibling Relationships   Any of you who have grown up with siblings (brothers or sisters) probably have a rich memory of aggressive, hostile interchanges. But sibling relationships also have many pleasant, caring moments (Zukow-Goldring, 2002). Children's sibling relationships include helping, sharing, teaching, fighting, and playing. Children can act as emotional

Careers in Life-Span Development

Darla Botkin, *Marriage and Family Therapist*

Darla Botkin, a marriage and family therapist who teaches, conducts research, and engages in therapy in the area of marriage and family therapy ◀▥ p. 37. She is on the faculty of the University of Kentucky. Botkin obtained a bachelor's degree in elementary education with a concentration in special education and then went on to receive a master's degree in early childhood education. She spent the next six years working with children and their families in a variety of settings, including day care, elementary school, and Head Start. These experiences led Botkin to recognize the interdependence of the developmental settings that children and their parents experience (such as home, school, and work). She returned to graduate school and obtained a Ph.D. in family studies from the University of Tennessee. She then became a faculty member in the Family Studies program at the University of Kentucky. Completing further coursework and clinical training in marriage and family therapy, she became certified as a marriage and family therapist.

Dr. Botkin's current interests include working with young children in family therapy, gender and ethnic issues in family therapy, and the role of spirituality in family wellness.

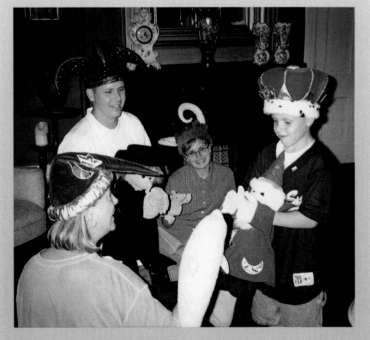

Darla Botkin (*left*), conducting a family therapy session.

The one-child family is becoming much more common in China because of the strong motivation to limit the population growth in the People's Republic of China. The policy is still new, and its effects on children have not been fully examined. *In general, what have researchers found the only child to be like?*

Big sisters are the crab grass in the lawn of life.

—CHARLES SCHULZ
American Cartoonist, 20th Century

supports, rivals, and communication partners. More than 80 percent of American children have one or more siblings. Because there are so many possible sibling combinations, it is difficult to generalize about sibling influences. Among the factors to consider are the number of siblings, the ages of siblings, birth order, age spacing, the sex of siblings, and whether sibling relationships are different from parent-child relationships (Teti, 2001).

Birth Order Birth order is a special interest of sibling researchers. When differences in birth order are found, they usually are explained by variations in interactions with parents and siblings associated with the unique experiences of being in a particular position in the family. This is especially true in the case of the firstborn child (Teti & others, 1993). Parents have higher expectations for firstborn children than for later-born children. They put more pressure on them for achievement and responsibility. They also interfere more with their activities (Rothbart, 1971).

Given the differences in family dynamics involved in birth order, it is not surprising that firstborns and later-borns have different characteristics (Zajonc, 2001). Firstborn children are more adult-oriented, helpful, conforming, anxious, and self-controlled than their siblings. Parents give more attention to firstborns and this is related to firstborns' nurturant behavior (Stanhope & Corter, 1993). Parental demands and high standards established for firstborns result in these children's excelling in academic and professional endeavors. Firstborns are overrepresented in *Who's Who* and Rhodes scholars, for example. However, some of the same pressures placed on firstborns for high achievement may be the reason they also have more guilt, anxiety, and difficulty in coping with stressful situations, as well as higher admission to child guidance clinics.

What is the only child like? The popular conception is that the only child is a "spoiled brat," with such undesirable characteristics as dependency, lack of self-control, and self-centered behavior. But researchers present a more positive portrayal of the only child, who often is achievement-oriented and displays a desirable personality, especially in comparison with later-borns and children from large families (Falbo & Poston, 1993; Jiao, Ji, & Jing, 1996).

Keep in mind, though, that birth order by itself often is not a good predictor of behavior. When factors such as age spacing, sex of the siblings, heredity, temperament, parenting styles, peer influences, school influences, sociocultural factors, and so forth are taken into account, they often are more important in determining a child's behavior than birth order.

The Changing Family in a Changing Society

More children are growing up in diverse family structures than ever before. Many mothers spend the greatest part of their day away from their children, even their infants. More than one of every two mothers with a child under the age of 5 is in the labor force; more than two of every three with a child from 6 to 17 years of age is. And the increasing number of children growing up in single-parent families is staggering. As shown in figure 9.6, the United States has the highest percentage of single-parent families, compared with virtually all other countries.

mhhe●com/
santrockld9

Working Parents
Family and the Workplace

Working Parents Because household operations have become more efficient and family size has decreased in America, it is not certain that when both parents work outside the home, children receive less attention than children in the past whose mothers were not employed. Outside employment—at least for parents with school-age children—might simply be filling time previously taken up by added household burdens and more children. It also cannot be assumed that, if the mother did not go to

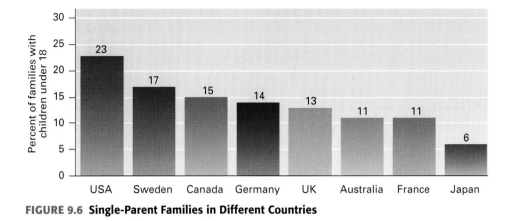

FIGURE 9.6 Single-Parent Families in Different Countries

work, the child would benefit from the time freed up by streamlined household operations and smaller families. Mothering does not always have a positive effect on the child. The educated, nonworking mother may overinvest her energies in her children. This can foster an excess of worry and discourage the child's independence. In such situations, the mother may give more parenting than the child can profitably handle.

As Lois Hoffman (1989) commented, maternal employment is a part of modern life. It is not an aberrant aspect of it but a response to other social changes. The needs of the growing child require the mother to loosen her hold on the child. This task may be easier for the working woman, whose job is an additional source of identity and self-esteem.

A number of researchers have found no detrimental effects of maternal employment on children's development (Gottfried, Gottfried, & Bathurst, 2002; Hoffman & Youngblade, 1999). However, in specific circumstances, work can produce positive or negative effects on parenting. In some families, work-related stress can spill over and harm parenting. In others, a greater sense of overall well-being produced by work can lead to more positive parenting.

Further, researchers are consistently finding when a child's mother works in the first year of life it can have a negative effect on the child's later development (Belsky & Eggebeen, 1991; Hill & others, 2001). For example, a recent major longitudinal study found that the 3-year-old children of mothers who went to work before the children were 9 months old had poorer cognitive outcomes than 3-year-old children who had stayed at home with their mothers in the first nine months of the child's life (Brooks-Gunn, Han, & Waldfogel, 2002). The negative effects of working mothers were less pronounced with the mothers worked less than 30 hours a week, the mothers were more sensitive (responsive and comforting) in their caregiving, and the child care the children received outside the home was higher in quality. Thus, when mothers do go back to work in the infant's first year of life, it clearly is important that they consider how many hours they are going to work, be sensitive in their caregiving, and get the best child care they can afford.

Effects of Divorce on Children   Let's examine some important questions about
the effects of divorce on children:

- *Are children better adjusted in intact, never-divorced families than in divorced families?*
  Most researchers agree that children from divorced families show poorer adjustment than their counterparts in nondivorced families (Amato & Keith, 1991; Hetherington & Kelly, 2002; Hetherington & Stanley-Hagan, 2002) (see figure 9.7). Those that have experienced multiple divorces are at greater risk. Children in divorced families are more likely than children in nondivorced families to have academic problems, to show externalized problems (such as acting out and delinquency) and internalized problems (such as anxiety and

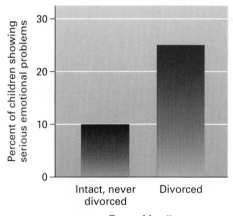

FIGURE 9.7 Divorce and Children's Emotional Problems

In Hetherington's research, 25 percent of children from divorced families showed serious emotional problems compared to only 10 percent of children from intact, never-divorced families. However, keep in mind that a substantial majority (75 percent) of the children from divorced families did not show serious emotional problems.

mhhe ● com/
santrockld9

Children and Divorce

Divorce and Family Ties

Divorce Resources

Father Custody

depression), to be less socially responsible, to have less competent intimate relationships, to drop out of school, to become sexually active at an early age, to take drugs, to associate with antisocial peers, and to have low self-esteem (Conger & Chao, 1996). Nonetheless, keep in mind that a majority of children in divorced families do not have significant adjustment problems (Buchanan, 2001).

- *Should parents stay together for the sake of the children?* Whether parents should stay in an unhappy or conflicted marriage for the sake of their children is one of the most commonly asked questions about divorce (Hetherington, 1999, 2000). If the stresses and disruptions in family relationships associated with an unhappy, conflictual marriage that erode the well-being of children are reduced by the move to a divorced, single-parent family, divorce can be advantageous. However, if the diminished resources and increased risks associated with divorce also are accompanied by inept parenting and sustained or increased conflict, not only between the divorced couple but also between the parents, children, and siblings, the best choice for the children would be for an unhappy marriage to be retained (Hetherington & Stanley-Hagan, 2002). These are "ifs," and it is difficult to determine how these will play out when parents either remain together in an acrimonious marriage or become divorced.

- *How much do family processes matter in divorced families?* Family processes matter a lot (Emery & others, 2001; Hetherington & Stanley-Hagan, 2002; Kelly, 2001). When divorced parents' relationship with each other is harmonious and when they use authoritative parenting, the adjustment of children improves (Hetherington, Bridges, & Insabella, 1998). A number of researchers have shown that a disequilibrium, which includes diminished parenting skills, occurs in the year following the divorce but that, by two years after the divorce, restabilization has occurred and parenting skills have improved (Hetherington, 1989).

- *What factors are involved in the child's individual risk and vulnerability in a divorced family?* Among the factors involved in the child's risk and vulnerability are the child's adjustment prior to the divorce, as well as the child's personality and temperament, gender, and custody situation (Hetherington & Stanley-Hagan, 2002). Children whose parents later divorce show poorer adjustment before the breakup (Amato & Booth, 1996).

Personality and temperament also play a role in children's adjustment in divorced families. Children who are socially mature and responsible, who show few behavioral problems, and who have an easy temperament are better able to cope with their parents' divorce. Children with a difficult temperament often have problems in coping with their parents' divorce (Hetherington, 1999).

Earlier studies reported gender differences in response to divorce, with divorce being more negative for girls than boys in mother-custody families. However, more recent studies have shown that gender differences are less pronounced and consistent than was previously believed. Some of the inconsistency may be due to the increase in father custody, joint custody, and increased involvement of noncustodial fathers, especially in their sons' lives. One recent analysis of studies found that children in joint-custody families were better adjusted than children

In Japan, only 6% of children live in single-parent families, compared to 23% in the United States. *What might explain this difference?*

in sole-custody families (Bauserman, 2002). Some studies have shown that boys adjust better in father-custody families, girls in mother-custody families, while other studies have not (Maccoby & Mnookin, 1992; Santrock & Warshak, 1979),

Cultural, Ethnic, and Socioeconomic Variations in Families   Parenting can be influenced by culture, ethnicity, and socioeconomic status. What have cross-cultural studies found about parenting?

Cross-Cultural Studies   Cultures vary on a number of issues involving families, such as what the father's role in the family should be, the extent to which support systems are available to families, and the ways in which children should be disciplined (Harkness & Super, 2002). Although there are cross-cultural variations in parenting (Whiting & Edwards, 1988), in one study of parenting behavior in 186 cultures around the world, the most common pattern was a warm and controlling style, one that was neither permissive nor restrictive (Rohner & Rohner, 1981). The investigators commented that the majority of cultures have discovered, over many centuries, a "truth" that only recently emerged in the Western world—namely, that children's healthy social development is most effectively promoted by love and at least some moderate parental control.

Ethnicity   Families within different ethnic groups in the United States differ in their size, structure, composition, reliance on kinship networks, and levels of income and education (Coll & Pachter, 2002; Parke & Buriel, 1998). Large and extended families are more common among minority groups than among the White majority. For example, 19 percent of Latino families have three or more children, compared with 14 percent of African American and 10 percent of White families. African American and Latino children interact more with grandparents, aunts, uncles, cousins, and more-distant relatives than do White children.

Single-parent families are more common among African Americans and Latinos than among White Americans (Weinraub, Houruath, & Gringlas, 2002). In comparison with two-parent households, single parents often have more limited resources of time, money, and energy (Gyamfi, Brooks-Gunn, & Jackson, 2001). Ethnic minority parents also are less educated and more likely to live in low-income circumstances than their White counterparts. Still, many impoverished ethnic minority families manage to find ways to raise competent children (Coll & Pachter, 2002).

Some aspects of home life can help protect ethnic minority children from injustice. The community and the family can filter out destructive racist messages, and parents can present alternative frames of reference to those presented by the majority. The extended family also can serve as an important buffer to stress (McAdoo, 1999, 2002; Wakschlag, Chase-Lansdale, & Brooks-Gunn, 1996). To read further about ethnic minority parenting, see the Sociocultural Worlds of Development box on page 286.

Socioeconomic Status   In America and most Western cultures, differences have been found in child rearing among different socioeconomic (SES) groups (Hoff, Laursen, & Tardif, 2002):

- Lower-SES parents (1) are more concerned that their children conform to society's expectations, (2) create a home atmosphere in which it is clear that

What are some characteristics of families within different ethnic groups?

Family Diversity

Acculturation and Ethnic Minority Parenting

Cynthia Garcia Coll and Lee Pachter (2002) recently described how the cultural context influences ethnic minority parenting. A summary of their views is presented here.

Ethnic minority children and their parents are expected to transcend their own cultural background and incorporate aspects of the dominant culture into their development. Young children's expectations and opportunities for acculturation (the process through which cultural adaptation and change occurs) are mainly influenced by their parents and the extended-family system. The level of family acculturation can affect parenting style by influencing expectations for children's development, parent-child interactions, and the role of the extended family. The appropriateness of caregiving practices may involve conflict or confusion between less acculturated and more acculturated family members. For example, in one study, the level of acculturation and maternal education were the strongest predictors of maternal-infant interaction patterns in Latino families (Perez-Febles, 1992).

In early childhood, the family's level of acculturation continues to influence caregiving practices and important decisions about day care and early childhood education. In day-care centers, school, church, and other community settings, ethnic minority children learn about the dominant culture's values and may be expected to adapt to unfamiliar cultural norms (such as being on the winning team, expressing emotions, and being responsible for one's self). For example, an African American mother might prefer to leave her children with extended-family members while she is at work because historically this has been seen as the best way to cope with an absent mother. However, this well-intentioned, culturally appropriate decision might place the child at an educational and social disadvantage relative to other children of the same age who benefit from preschool experiences that support the transition into the elementary school years.

In middle and late childhood and adolescence, disparity between the acculturation of children, their parents, and the extended family can become magnified. In adolescence, individuals often make decisions about their acculturation status more independently from their family. When immigrant adolescents choose to adopt the values of the dominant U.S. culture (such as unchaperoned dating), they often clash with those of parents and extended-family members who have more traditional values.

It is important to recognize the complexity and individual variation in the acculturative aspects of ethnic minority parenting. This complexity and variation involve the generation of the family members, the recency of their migration, their socioeconomic status, national origin, and many aspects of the social context of the dominant culture in which they now live (such as racial attitudes, quality of schooling, and community support groups).

How is acculturation involved in ethnic minority parenting?

parents have authority over children, (3) use physical punishment more in disciplining their children, and (4) are more directive and less conversational with their children.

- Higher-SES parents (1) are more concerned with developing children's initiative and delay of gratification, (2) create a home atmosphere in which children are more nearly equal participants and in which rules are discussed rather than being laid out in an authoritarian manner, (3) are less likely to use physical punishment, and (4) are less directive and more conversational with their children.

There also are socioeconomic differences in the way that parents think about education (Magnuson & Duncan, 2002; Hoff, Laursen, & Tardiff, 2002). Middle- and upper-income parents more often think of education as something that should be mutually encouraged by parents and teachers. By contrast, low-income parents are more likely to view education as the teacher's job. Thus, increased school-family linkages especially can benefit students from low-income families.

Review and Reflect

2 Explain how families can influence young children's development

REVIEW

- What aspects of parenting are linked with young children's development?
- How are sibling relationships and birth order related to young children's development?
- How is children's development affected by having two wage earning parents, having divorced parents, and being part of a particular cultural, ethnic and socioeconomic group?

REFLECT

- Which style or styles of parenting did your mother and father use in rearing you? What effects do you think their parenting styles have on your development?

3 PEER RELATIONS, PLAY, AND TELEVISION

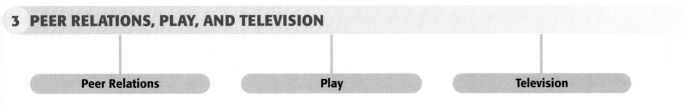

| Peer Relations | Play | Television |

The family is an important social context for children's development. However, children's development also is strongly influenced by what goes on in other social contexts, such as peer relations, play, and television.

Peer Relations

As children grow older, peer relations consume an increasing amount of their time. What is the function of a child's peer group?

Peers are children of about the same age or maturity level. Same-age peer interaction fills a unique role in our culture. Age grading would occur even if schools were not age graded and children were left alone to determine the composition of their own societies. One of the most important functions of the peer group is to provide a source of information and comparison about the world outside the family. Children receive feedback about their abilities from their peer group. Children evaluate what they do in terms of whether it is better than, as good as, or worse than what other children do. It is hard to do this at home because siblings are usually older or younger.

Are peers necessary for development? When peer monkeys who have been reared together are separated, they become depressed and less advanced socially (Suomi, Harlow, & Domek, 1970). The human development literature contains a classic example of the importance of peers in social development. Anna Freud (Freud & Dann, 1951) studied six children from different families who banded together after their parents were killed in World War II. Intensive peer attachment was observed. The children formed a tightly knit group, dependent on one another and aloof with outsiders. Even though deprived of parental care, they neither became delinquent nor developed serious mental disorders.

Thus, good peer relations can be necessary for normal social development. Special concerns focus on children who are withdrawn and aggressive (Coie, 1999; Ladd, 1999). Withdrawn children who are rejected by peers and/or victimized and feeling lonely are at risk for depression. Children who are aggressive with their peers are at

mhhe ●com/
santrockld9

Peer Relations

And that park grew up with me; that small world widened as I learned its secrets and boundaries, as I discovered new refuges in its woods and jungles: hidden homes and lairs for the multitudes of imagination, for cowboys and Indians. . . . I used to dawdle on half holidays along the bent and Devon-facing seashore, hoping for gold watches or the skull of a sheep or a message in a bottle to be washed up with the tide.

—DYLAN THOMAS
Welsh Poet , 20th Century

risk for developing a number of problems, including delinquency and dropping out of school. We will have much more to say about peer relations in chapter 11, "Socioemotional Development in Middle and Late Childhood."

Play

An extensive amount of peer interaction during childhood involves play. Although peer interaction can involve play, social play is but one type of play. *Play* is a pleasurable activity that is engaged in for its own sake. Our coverage of play includes its functions, Parten's classic study of play, and types of play.

Play's Functions   Play is essential to the young child's health. As today's children move into the twenty-first century and continue to experience pressure in their lives, play becomes even more crucial (Van Hoorn & others, 1999). Play increases affiliation with peers, releases tension, advances cognitive development, increases exploration, and provides a safe haven in which to engage in potentially dangerous behavior. Play increases the probability that children will converse and interact with each other. During this interaction, children practice the roles they will assume later in life (Sutton-Smith, 2000).

According to Freud and Erikson, play is an especially useful form of human adjustment, helping the child master anxieties and conflicts. Because tensions are relieved in play, the child can cope with life's problems. Play permits the child to work off excess physical energy and to release pent-up tensions. *Play therapy* allows the child to work off frustrations. Through play therapy, the therapist can analyze the child's conflicts and ways of coping with them. Children may feel less threatened and be more likely to express their true feelings in the context of play.

Piaget (1962) believed that play advances children's cognitive development. At the same time, he said that children's cognitive development *constrains* the way they play. Play permits children to practice their competencies and acquired skills in a relaxed, pleasurable way. Piaget thought that cognitive structures need to be exercised, and play provides the perfect setting for this exercise. For example, children who have just learned to add or multiply begin to play with numbers in different ways as they perfect these operations, laughing as they do so.

Vygotsky (1962), whose developmental theory was discussed in chapter 8, also believed that play is an excellent setting for cognitive development. He was especially interested in the symbolic and make-believe aspects of play, as when a child substitutes a stick for a horse and rides the stick as if it were a horse. For young children, the imaginary situation is real. Parents should encourage such imaginary play, because it advances the child's cognitive development, especially creative thought.

Daniel Berlyne (1960) described play as exciting and pleasurable in itself because it satisfies our exploratory drive. This drive involves curiosity and a desire for information about something new or unusual. Play is a means whereby children can safely explore and seek out new information—something they might not otherwise do. Play encourages this exploratory behavior by offering children the possibilities of novelty, complexity, uncertainty, surprise, and incongruity.

Parten's Classic Study of Play   Many years ago, Mildred Parten (1932) developed an elaborate classification of children's play. Based on observations of children in free play at nursery school, Parten arrived at these play categories:

- **Unoccupied play** is not play as it is commonly understood. The child may stand in one spot or perform random movements that do not seem to have a goal. In most nursery schools, unoccupied play is less frequent than other forms of play.
- **Solitary play** happens when the child plays alone and independently of others. The child seems engrossed in the activity and does not care much about anything else that is happening. Two- and 3-year-olds engage more frequently in solitary play than older preschoolers do.

unoccupied play Play in which the child is not engaging in play as it is commonly understood and might stand in one spot, or perform random movements that do not seem to have a goal.

solitary play Play in which the child plays alone and independently of others.

Mildred Parten classified play into six categories. *Study this photograph. Which of Parten's categories are reflected in the behavior of the children?*

- **Onlooker play** takes place when the child watches other children play. The child may talk with other children and ask questions but does not enter into their play behavior. The child's active interest in other children's play distinguishes onlooker play from unoccupied play.
- **Parallel play** occurs when the child plays separately from others but with toys like those the others are using or in a manner that mimics their play. The older children are, the less frequently they engage in this type of play. However, even older preschool children engage in parallel play quite often.
- **Associative play** involves social interaction with little or no organization. In this type of play, children seem to be more interested in each other than in the tasks they are performing. Borrowing or lending toys and following or leading one another in line are examples of associative play.
- **Cooperative play** consists of social interaction in a group with a sense of group identity and organized activity. Children's formal games, competition aimed at winning, and groups formed by the teacher for doing things together are examples of cooperative play. Cooperative play is the prototype for the games of middle childhood. Little cooperative play is seen in the preschool years.

Types of Play   Parten's categories represent one way of thinking about the different types of play. However, today researchers and practitioners who are involved with children's play believe other types of play are important in children's development. Whereas Parten's categories emphasize the role of play in the child's social world, the contemporary perspective on play emphasizes both the cognitive and the social aspects of play. Among the most widely studied types of children's play today are sensorimotor and practice play, pretense/symbolic play, social play, constructive play, and games (Bergin, 1988). We will consider each of these types of play in turn.

Sensorimotor and Practice Play   **Sensorimotor play** is behavior that is engaged in by infants to derive pleasure from exercising their existing sensorimotor schemas. The development of sensorimotor play follows Piaget's description of sensorimotor thought, which we discussed in chapter 6. Infants initially engage in exploratory and playful visual and motor transactions in the second quarter of the first year of life. For example, at 9 months of age, infants begin to select novel objects for exploration and play, especially those that are responsive, such as toys that make noise or bounce. At 12 months of age, infants enjoy making things work and exploring cause and effect.

onlooker play Play in which the child watches other children play.

parallel play Play in which the child plays separately from others, but with toys like those the others are using or in a manner that mimics their play.

associative play Play that involves social interaction with little or no organization.

cooperative play Play that involves social interaction in a group with a sense of group identity and organized activity.

sensorimotor play Behavior engaged in by infants to derive pleasure from exercising their existing Resensorimotor schemas.

Practice play involves the repetition of behavior when new skills are being learned or when physical or mental mastery and coordination of skills are required for games or sports. Sensorimotor play, which often involves practice play, is primarily confined to infancy, while practice play can be engaged in throughout life. During the preschool years, children often engage in play that involves practicing various skills. While practice play declines in the elementary school years, practice play activities such as running, jumping, sliding, twirling, and throwing balls or other objects are frequently observed on the playgrounds at elementary schools.

Pretense/Symbolic Play   **Pretense/symbolic play** occurs when the child transforms the physical environment into a symbol. Between 9 and 30 months of age, children increase their use of objects in symbolic play. They learn to transform objects—substituting them for other objects and acting toward them as if they were these other objects. For example, a preschool child treats a table as if it were a car and says, "I'm fixing the car," as he grabs a leg of the table.

Many experts on play consider the preschool years the "golden age" of symbolic/pretense play that is dramatic or sociodramatic in nature. This type of make-believe play often appears at about 18 months of age and reaches a peak at 4 to 5 years of age, then gradually declines.

Social Play   **Social play** is play that involves interaction with peers. Parten's categories, described earlier, are oriented toward social play. Social play with peers increases dramatically during the preschool years.

Constructive Play   **Constructive play** combines sensorimotor and practice repetitive activity with symbolic representation of ideas. Constructive play occurs when children engage in self-regulated creation or construction of a product or a problem solution. Constructive play increases in the preschool years as symbolic play increases and sensorimotor play decreases. In the preschool years, some practice play is replaced by constructive play. For example, instead of moving their fingers around and around in finger paint (practice play), children are more likely to draw the outline of a house or a person in the paint (constructive play). Some researchers have found that constructive play is the most common type of play during the preschool years (Rubin, Maioni, & Hornung, 1976). Constructive play is also a frequent form of play in the elementary school years, both in and out of the classroom. Constructive play is one of the few playlike activities allowed in work-centered classrooms. For example, having children create a play about a social studies topic involves constructive play. Whether children consider such activities to be play usually depends on whether they get to choose whether to do it (it is play) or whether the teacher imposes it (it is not play), as well as whether it is enjoyable (it is play(or not)it is not play) (King, 1982).

Constructive play also can be used in the elementary school years to foster academic skill learning, thinking skills, and problem solving. Many educators plan classroom activities that include humor, encourage playing with ideas, and promote creativity (Bergin, 1988). Educators also often support the performance of plays, the writing of imaginative stories, the expression of artistic abilities, and the playful exploration of computers and other technological equipment. However, distinctions between work and play frequently become blurred in the elementary school classroom. Think of constructive play as a midway point between play and work.

Games   Activities that are engaged in for pleasure. **Games** include rules and often competition with one or more individuals. Preschool children may begin to participate in social game play that involves simple rules of reciprocity and turn taking. However, games take on a much stronger role in the lives of elementary school children. In one study, the highest incidence of game playing occurred between 10 and 12 years of age (Eiferman, 1971). After age 12, games decline in popularity (Bergin, 1988).

practice play Play that involves repetition of behavior when new skills are being learned or when physical or mental mastery and coordination of skills are required for games or sports.

pretense/symbolic play Play in which the child transforms the physical environment into a symbol.

social play Play that involves social interactions with peers.

constructive play Play that combines sensorimotor/practice repetitive activity with symbolic representation of ideas. Constructive play occurs when children engage in self-regulated creation or construction of a product or a problem solution.

games Activities engaged in for pleasure that include rules and often competition with one or more individuals.

Television

Few developments in society in the second half of the twentieth century had a greater impact on children than television (Bryant & Bryant, 2001; Comstock & Scharrar, 1999; Murray, 2000). Many children spend more time in front of the television set than they do with their parents. Although it is only one of the many forms of mass media that affect children's behavior, television is the most influential. The persuasive capabilities of television are staggering (Kotler, Wright, & Huston, 2001). The 20,000 hours of television watched by the time the average American adolescent graduates from high school are greater than the number of hours spent in the classroom.

Television's Many Roles   Television can have a negative influence by taking children away from homework, making them passive learners, teaching them stereotypes, providing them with violent models of aggression, and presenting them with unrealistic views of the world. However, television can have a positive influence on children's development by presenting motivating educational programs, increasing their information about the world beyond their immediate environment, and providing models of prosocial behavior (Clifford, Gunter, & McAleer, 1995).

Amount of Television Watching by Children   Just how much television do young children watch? They watch a lot. In the 1990s, children watched an average of 26 hours of television each week, which is more than any other activity except sleep (National Center for Children Exposed to Violence, 2001). As shown in figure 9.8, considerably more children in the United States than their counterparts in other developed countries watch television for long periods. For example, seven times as many 9-year-olds in the United States as their counterparts in Switzerland watch television more than 5 hours a day.

Effects of Television on Children's Aggression and Prosocial Behavior   A special concern is the extent to which children are exposed to violence and aggression on television. Up to 80 percent of the prime-time shows include violent acts, including beatings, shootings, and stabbings. The frequency of violence increases on the Saturday morning cartoon shows, which average more than 25 violent acts per hour.

What are the effects of television violence on children's aggression? Does television merely stimulate a child to go out and buy a *Star Wars* ray gun, or can it trigger an attack on a playmate? When children grow up, can television violence increase the likelihood they will violently attack someone?

In one longitudinal study, the amount of violence viewed on television at age 8 was significantly related to the seriousness of criminal acts performed as an adult (Huesmann, 1986). In another study, long-term exposure to television violence was

"Mrs. Horton, could you stop by school today?"
Copyright © Martha F. Campbell.

Children's Television Workshop
Television and Violence
Television and Children

FIGURE 9.8 **Percentage of 9-Year-Old Children Who Report Watching More Than Five Hours of Television per Weekday**

Television is a medium of entertainment which permits millions of people to listen to the same joke at the same time, and yet remain lonesome.

—T. S. Eliot
*American-Born English Poet,
20th Century*

significantly related to the likelihood of aggression in 1,565 12- to 17-year-old boys (Belson, 1978). Boys who watched the most aggression on television were the most likely to commit a violent crime, swear, be aggressive in sports, threaten violence toward another boy, write slogans on walls, or break windows. These studies are *correlational,* so we cannot conclude from them that television violence *causes* aggressive behavior. In one experiment, children were randomly assigned to one of two groups: One group watched television shows taken directly from violent Saturday morning cartoon offerings on 11 different days; the second group watched television cartoon shows with all of the violence removed (Steur, Applefield, & Smith, 1971). The children were then observed during play at their preschool. The preschool children who saw the TV cartoon shows with violence kicked, choked, and pushed their playmates more than did the preschool children who watched nonviolent TV cartoon shows. Because the children were randomly assigned to the two conditions (TV cartoons with violence versus nonviolent TV cartoons), we can conclude that exposure to TV violence *caused* the increased aggression in the children in this investigation.

Television also can teach children that it is better to behave in positive, prosocial ways than in negative, antisocial ways (Dorr, Rabin, & Irlin, 2002; Wilson, 2001). Aimee Leifer (1973) demonstrated that television is associated with prosocial behavior in young children. She selected a number of episodes from the television show *Sesame Street* that reflected positive social interchanges. She was especially interested in situations that taught children how to use their social skills. For example, in one interchange, two men were fighting over the amount of space available to them. They gradually began to cooperate and to share the space. Children who watched these episodes copied these behaviors, and in later social situations they applied the prosocial lessons they had learned.

Some critics have argued that research results do not warrant the conclusion that TV violence causes aggression (Freedman, 1984). But many experts insist that TV violence can cause aggressive or antisocial behavior in children (Anderson & Bushman, 2002; Bushman & Huesmann, 2001; Perse, 2001). Of course, television violence is not the *only* cause of aggression. There is no *one* cause of any social behavior. Aggression, like all other social behaviors, has multiple determinants (Donnerstein, 2002). The link between TV violence and aggression in children is influenced by children's aggressive tendencies and by their attitudes toward violence and monitoring of children's exposure to it.

Television and Cognitive Development   Children bring various cognitive skills and abilities to their television viewing experience (Rabin & Dorr, 1995). Several important cognitive shifts take place between early childhood and middle and late childhood (Wilson, 2001). Preschool children often focus on the most striking perceptual features of a TV program and are likely to have difficulty in distinguishing reality from fantasy in the portrayals. As children enter elementary school, they are better able to link scenes together and draw causal conclusions from narratives. Judgments of reality also become more accurate in older children.

How does television influence children's creativity and verbal skills? Television is negatively related to children's creativity (Williams, 1986). Also, because television is primarily a visual modality, verbal skills—especially expressive language—are enhanced more by aural or print exposure (Beagles-Roos & Gat, 1983). Educational programming for young children can promote creativity and imagination, possibly because it has a slower pace, and auditory and visual modalities are better coordinated (Anderson & others, 2001). Newer technologies, especially interactive television, hold promise for motivating children to learn and become more exploratory in solving problems (Singer, 1993).

In one recent longitudinal study, viewing educational programs as preschoolers was associated with a host of desirable characteristics in adolescence: getting higher grades, reading more books, placing a higher value on achievement, being more creative, and acting less aggressively (Anderson & others, 2001). These associations were

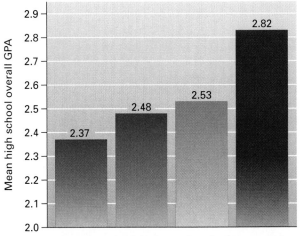

FIGURE 9.9 Educational TV Viewing in educational TV and High School Grade Point Average for Boys

When boys watched more educational television (especially *Sesame Street*) as preschoolers, they had higher grade point averages in high school (Anderson & others, 2001). The graph displays the boys' early TV viewing patterns in quartiles and the means of their grade point averages. The bar on the left is for the lowest 25 percent of boys who viewed educational TV programs, the next bar the next 25 percent, and so on, with the bar on the right for the 25 percent of the boys who watched the most educational TV shows as preschoolers.

more consistent for boys than girls. Figure 9.9 shows the results for boys' high school grade point average. However, girls who were more frequent viewers of violent TV programs in the preschool years had lower grades in adolescence than girls who infrequently watched violent TV programs in the preschool years.

Review and Reflect

3 **Describe the roles of peers, play, and television in young children's development**

REVIEW

- How do peers affect young children's development?
- What are some theories and types of play?
- How does television influence children's development?

REFLECT

- What guidelines would you recommend to parents that you believe would help them to make television a more positive influence on their children's development? Consider such factors as the child's age, the child's activities other than TV, the parents' patterns of interaction with the children, and types of TV shows.

Reach Your Learning Goals

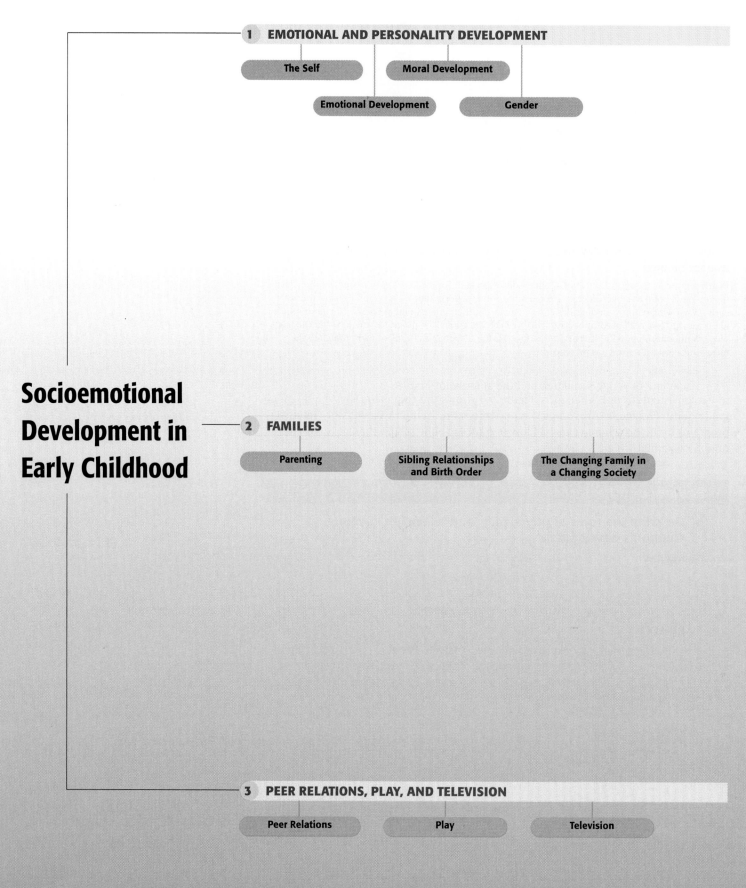

Socioemotional Development in Early Childhood

1 EMOTIONAL AND PERSONALITY DEVELOPMENT

- The Self
- Moral Development
- Emotional Development
- Gender

2 FAMILIES

- Parenting
- Sibling Relationships and Birth Order
- The Changing Family in a Changing Society

3 PEER RELATIONS, PLAY, AND TELEVISION

- Peer Relations
- Play
- Television

Summary

1 Discuss emotional and personality development in early childhood

- Erikson believed that early childhood is a period when development involves resolving the conflict of initiative versus guilt. While a rudimentary form of self-understanding occurs at about 18 months in the form of self-recognition, in early childhood the physical self, or active self, emerges.

- Preschoolers become more adept at talking about their own and others' emotions. Two- and 3-year-olds continue to increase the number of terms they use to describe emotion and learn more about the causes and consequences of feelings. At 4 to 5 years of age, children show an increased ability to reflect on emotions and understand that a single event can elicit different emotions in different people. They also show a growing awareness about controlling and managing emotions to meet social standards. Self-conscious emotions, such as pride, shame, and guilt, increase in early childhood.

- Moral development involves thoughts, feelings, and actions regarding rules and regulations about what people should do in their interactions with others. Developmentalists study how children think, behave, and feel about such rules and regulations. Piaget distinguished between the heteronomous morality of younger children and the autonomous morality of older children. Moral behavior is emphasized by behavioral and social cognitive theorists. They believe there is considerable situational variability in moral behavior and that self-control is an important aspect of understanding children's moral behavior. Freud's psychoanalytic theory emphasizes the importance of feelings with regard to the development of the superego, the moral branch of personality, which develops through the Oedipus conflict and identification with the same-sex parent. In Freud's view, children conform to societal standards to avoid guilt. Positive emotions, such as empathy, also are an important aspect of understanding moral feelings. In Damon's view, both positive and negative emotions contribute to children's moral development.

- Gender refers to the social and psychological dimensions of being male or female. Gender identity is acquired by 3 years of age for most children. A gender role is a set of expectations that prescribes how females or males should think, act, and feel. The 23rd pair of chromosomes may have two X chromosomes to produce a female, or one X and one Y chromosome to produce a male. The two main classes of sex hormones are estrogens, which are dominant in females, and androgens, which are dominant in males. Biology is not completely destiny in gender development; children's socialization experiences matter a great deal. Both psychoanalytic theory and social cognitive theory emphasize the adoption of parents' gender characteristics. Peers are especially adept at rewarding gender-appropriate behavior. Both cognitive developmental and gender schema theories emphasize the role of cognition in gender development.

2 Explain how families can influence young children's development

- Authoritarian, authoritative, neglectful, and indulgent are four main parenting styles. Authoritative parenting is the style most often associated with children's social competence. Physical punishment is widely used by U.S. parents but there are a number of reasons why it is not a good choice. An understanding of child abuse requires information about cultural and familial influences. Child maltreatment places the child at risk for a number of developmental problems. Coparenting has positive effects on children's development. In today's society, an unfortunate theme is that parenting can be done quickly. However, good parenting takes extensive time and effort.

- Siblings interact with each other in positive and negative ways. Birth order is related in certain ways to child characteristics, but some critics argue that birth order by itself is not a good predictor of behavior.

- Sociocultural and economic factors affect children's development in many ways. In general, having both parents employed full-time outside the home has not been shown to have negative effects on children. However, in specfic circumstances, when a mother works outside the home, such as when the infant is less than 1 year old, negative effects can occur. Divorce can have negative effects on children's adjustment, but so can an acrimonious relationship between parents who stay together for their children's sake. If divorced parents develop a harmonious relationship and practice authoritative parenting, children's adjustment improves. Authoritative parenting is the most widely used style around the world. Cultures vary on a number of issues regarding families. African American and Latino children are more likely than White American children to live in single-parent families and larger families and to have extended family connections. Lower-SES parents create a home atmosphere that involves more authority and physical punishment with children than higher-SES parents. Higher-SES parents are more concerned about developing children's initiative and delay of gratification.

3 Describe the roles of peers, play, and television in young children's development

- Peers are powerful socialization agents. Peers are children who are about the same age or maturity level. Peers provide a source of information and comparison about the world outside the family.

- Play's functions include affiliation with peers, tension release, advances in cognitive development, exploration, and provision of a safe haven. Parten developed the categories of unoccupied, solitary, onlooker, parallel, associative, and cooperative play. The contemporary perspective on play emphasizes both the cognitive and the social aspects of play.

Among the most widely studied aspects of children's play today are sensorimotor play, practice play, pretense/symbolic play, social play, constructive play and games.

- Television can have both negative influences (such as turning children into passive learners and presenting them with aggressive models) and positive influences (such as presenting motivating educational programs and providing models

of prosocial behavior) on children's development. Children watch huge amounts of television. TV violence is not the only cause of children's aggression, but it can induce aggression. Prosocial behavior on TV is associated with increased positive behavior by children. Children's cognitive skills influence their TV-viewing experiences. Television viewing is negatively related to children's creativity and verbal skills.

Key Terms

self-understanding 269
moral development 270
heteronomous morality 271
autonomous morality 271
imminent justice 271
gender 272
gender identity 272
gender role 272

psychoanalytic theory of gender 273
social cognitive theory of gender 273
cognitive developmental theory of gender 275
gender schema theory 275
authoritarian parenting 277

authoritative parenting 277
neglectful parenting 277
indulgent parenting 277
unoccupied play 288
solitary play 288
onlooker play 289
parallel play 289
associative play 289

cooperative play 289
sensorimotor play 289
practice play 290
pretense/symbolic play 290
social play 290
constructive play 290
games 290

Key People

Erik Erikson 268
Jean Piaget 270, 288
Sigmund Freud 272, 273

Lawrence Kohlberg 275
John Watson 276
Diana Baumrind 277

Lois Hoffman 283
Anna Freud 287
Lev Vygotsky 288

Daniel Berlyne 288
Mildred Parten 288

1. Doris and Ken are in the process of getting a divorce. Both of them want full custody of their two children, Kevin, age 10, and Chrissie, age 3. Although the divorce process has been very stressful for both of them, Doris and Ken share concerns about the effects their divorce might have on their children. What immediate effects can they expect, especially given the context of the custody battle? How might Kevin's reactions differ from Chrissie's? What might the long-term effects of the divorce be on their children?

2. Karen's mother is concerned about how to best help her daughter, Teresa, whose husband has abandoned her and their 5-year-old son. What are some of the challenges that Teresa may have to face and how can her mother help her through this difficult time?

3. Jonathan and Diedre want to shield their children from the violence on television, but they are not sure how to go about it—other than by not allowing any television viewing at all. What recommendations does the APA have for parents?

Connect to www.mhhe.com/santrockld9 to research the answers and complete these exercises.

To help you master the material in this chapter, you'll find a number of valuable study tools on the Student CD-ROM that accompanies this book. In addition, visit the Online Learning Center for *Life-Span Development*, ninth edition, where you'll find these valuable resources for chapter 9, "Socioemotional Development in Early Childhood."

- What might your parenting style be, based on what you've read in this chapter? Use the self-assessment, *My Parenting Style*, to get a better idea of what it might be.

- View video clips of key researchers, including Judy Dunn as she discusses her research on sibling relationships.
- Build your decision-making skills by trying your hand at the parenting and education "Scenarios."

Middle and Late Childhood

*Blessed be childhood,
which brings
something of heaven
into the midst of our
rough earthliness.*

—HENRI FREDERIC AMIEL
Swiss Poet, Philosopher, 19th Century

In middle and late childhood, children are on a different plane, belonging to a generation and feeling all their own. It is the wisdom of the human life span that at no time are children more ready to learn than during the period of expansive imagination at the end of early childhood. Children develop a sense of wanting to make things—and not just to make them, but to make them well and even perfectly. Their thirst is to know and to understand. They are remarkable for their intelligence and for their curiosity. Their parents continue to be important influences in their lives, but their growth also is shaped by successive choirs of friends. They don't think much about the future or about the past, but they enjoy the present moment. Section 5 consists of two chapters, "Physical and Cognitive Development in Middle and Late Childhood" (chapter 10) and "Socioemotional Development in Middle and Late Childhood" (chapter 11).

Every forward step we take we leave some phantom of ourselves behind.

—JOHN LANCASTER SPALDING
American Educator, 19th Century

Physical and Cognitive Development in Middle and Late Childhood

Chapter Outline

PHYSICAL CHANGES AND HEALTH

Body Growth and Proportion

Motor Development

Exercise and Sports

Health, Illness, and Disease

CHILDREN WITH DISABILITIES

Who Are Children with Disabilities?

Learning Disabilities

Attention Deficit Hyperactivity Disorder (ADHD)

Educational Issues

COGNITIVE CHANGES

Piaget's Theory

Information Processing

Intelligence

Creativity

LANGUAGE DEVELOPMENT

Vocabulary and Grammar

Reading

Bilingualism

Learning Goals

1 *D*escribe physical changes and health in middle and late childhood

2 *I*dentify children with disabilities and issues in educating them

3 *E*xplain cognitive changes in middle and late childhood

4 *D*iscuss language development in middle and late childhood

Images of Life-Span Development
Jessica Dubroff, Child Pilot

Some critics argue that Jessica Dubroff was not allowed to be a child. *Did her parents act irresponsibly?*

Many parents want their children to be gifted and provide them with many opportunities to achieve this status. Child psychologists believe that some parents go too far and push their children too much, especially when they try to get their children to be a child star in a particular area, like figure skating, tennis, or music. To think further about parents' efforts to get their children to achieve lofty accomplishments, let's examine the tragic story of Jessica Dubroff.

In 1996, Jessica Dubroff took off in cold rain and died when her single-engine Cessna nosedived into a highway. Seven-year-old Jessica was only 4 feet, 2 inches tall and weighed just 55 pounds. What was she doing flying an airplane, especially in quest of being the youngest person ever to fly across the continent?

Jessica's parents seemed determined to give their daughter independence from the beginning. She was delivered in a birthing tub without benefit of a doctor or midwife. Her parents' philosophy was that real life is the best tutor, experience the best preparation for life. As a result, they kept Jessica and her brother (age 9) and sister (age 3) at home without filing a home-schooling plan with local authorities. Jessica had no dolls, only tools. Instead of studying grammar, she did chores and sought what her mother called "mastery." Jessica had few, if any, boundaries. Parenting mainly consisted of cheerleading.

Jessica became interested in flying after her parents gave her an airplane ride for her sixth birthday, only 23 months before her fatal crash. Her father admitted that the cross-country flight was his idea, but claimed that he had presented it to Jessica as a choice. The father became her press agent, courting TV, radio, and newspapers to publicize her flight.

Did Jessica grow up too soon? Did her parents push her too much to achieve in a single activity? Should they instead have encouraged her to have a more well-rounded life and one more typical for her age? Were her parents living vicariously through her?

Later in this chapter, we will explore the real nature of giftedness in children. This chapter is about physical and cognitive development in middle and late childhood. To begin, we will explore some changes in physical development.

1 PHYSICAL CHANGES AND HEALTH

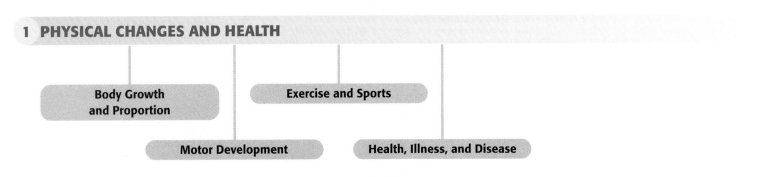

Body Growth and Proportion

Exercise and Sports

Motor Development

Health, Illness, and Disease

Continued change characterizes children's bodies during middle and late childhood and their motor skills improve. It is important for children to engage in regular exercise and avoid illness and disease.

Body Growth and Proportion

The period of middle and late childhood involves slow, consistent growth. This is a period of calm before the rapid growth spurt of adolescence. During the elementary school years, children grow an average of 2 to 3 inches a year until, at the age of 11, the average girl is 4 feet, 10¼ inches tall, and the average boy is 4 feet, 9 inches tall. During the middle and late childhood years, children gain about 5 to 7 pounds a year. The weight increase is due mainly to increases in the size of the skeletal and muscular systems, as well as the size of some body organs. Muscle mass and strength gradually increase as "baby fat" decreases. The loose movements and knock knees of early childhood give way to improved muscle tone. The increase in muscular strength is due to heredity and to exercise. Children also double their strength capabilities during these years. Because of their greater number of muscle cells, boys are usually stronger than girls.

Proportional changes are among the most pronounced physical changes in middle and late childhood. Head circumference, waist circumference, and leg length decrease in relation to body height (Wong & others, 2001). A less noticeable physical change is that bones continue to ossify during middle and late childhood but yield to pressure and pull more than mature bones.

Motor Development

During middle and late childhood, children's motor development becomes much smoother and more coordinated than it was in early childhood. For example, only one child in a thousand can hit a tennis ball over the net at the age of 3, yet by the age of 10 or 11 most children can learn to play the sport. Running, climbing, skipping rope, swimming, bicycle riding, and skating are just a few of the many physical skills elementary school children can master. In gross motor skills involving large activity, boys usually outperform girls.

As children move through the elementary school years, they gain greater control over their bodies and can sit and attend for longer periods of time. However, elementary school children are far from having physical maturity, and they need to be active. Elementary school children become more fatigued by long periods of sitting than by running, jumping, or bicycling. Physical action is essential for these children to refine their developing skills, such as batting a ball, skipping rope, or balancing on a beam. An important principle of practice for elementary school children, therefore, is that they should be engaged in *active,* rather than passive, activities.

Increased myelination of the central nervous system is reflected in the improvement of fine motor skills during middle and late childhood. Children's hands are used more adroitly as tools. Six-year-olds can hammer, paste, tie shoes, and fasten clothes. By 7 years of age, children's hands have become steadier. At this age, children prefer a pencil to a crayon for printing, and reversal of letters is less common. Printing becomes smaller. At 8 to 10 years of age, the hands can be used independently with more ease and precision. Fine motor coordination develops to the point at which children can write rather than print words. Letter size becomes smaller and more even. At 10 to 12 years of age, children begin to show manipulative skills similar to the abilities of adults. The complex, intricate, and rapid movements needed to produce fine-quality crafts or to play a difficult piece on a musical instrument can be mastered. Girls usually outperform boys in fine motor skills.

Exercise and Sports

How much exercise do children get? What are children's sports like?

Exercise   Are children getting enough exercise? In a 1997 national poll, only 22 percent of children in grades 4 through 12 were physically active for 30 minutes every day of the week (Harris, 1997). Their parents said their children were too busy watching TV, spending time on the computer, or playing video games to exercise much. Boys were more physically active at all ages than girls. In one historical comparison, the percentage of children involved in daily P.E. programs in schools decreased by 80 percent in 1969 to 20 percent in 1999 (Health Management Resources, 2001) (see figure 10.1).

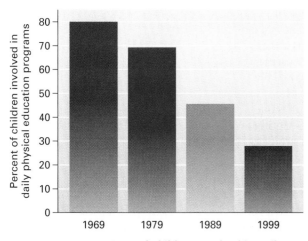

FIGURE 10.1 Percentage of Children Involved in Daily Physical Education Programs in the United States from 1969 to 1999

There has been a dramatic drop in the percentage of children participating in daily physical education programs in the United States from 80 percent in 1969 to only 20 percent in 1999.

mhhe ● com/
santrockld9

Child Health

Child Health Guide

Here are some ways to get children to exercise more:
- Offer more physical activity programs run by volunteers at school facilities.
- Improve physical fitness activities in schools.
- Have children plan community and school activities that really interest them.
- Encourage families to focus more on physical activity and parents to exercise more (in the national poll more than 50 percent of the parents engaged in no vigorous physical activities on a regular basis).

Sports   Sports have become an integral part of American culture. Thus, it is not surprising that more and more children become involved in sports every year. Both in public schools and in community agencies, children's sports programs that involve baseball, soccer, football, basketball, swimming, gymnastics, and other activities have grown to the extent that they have changed the shape of many children's lives.

Participation in sports can have both positive and negative consequences for children. Children's participation in sports can provide exercise, opportunities to learn how to compete, self-esteem, and a setting for developing peer relations and friendships. However, sports also can have negative outcomes for children: the pressure to achieve and win, physical injuries, a distraction from academic work, and unrealistic expectations for success as an athlete (Cheng & others, 2000; Committee on Sports Medicine and Fitness, 2000). Few people challenge the value of sports for children when conducted as part of a school physical education or intramural program. However, some critics question the appropriateness of highly competitive, win-oriented sports teams in schools and communities (Kelm & others, 2001; Washington & others, 2001).

The negative consequences of children's sports was tragically played out when Thomas Junta beat to death another father after their sons' ice hockey game in July 2001. He was sentenced to 6 to 10 years in prison in January 2002.

Six-year-old Zhang Liyin (*third from left*) hopes to someday become an Olympic gymnastics champion. Attending the sports school is considered an outstanding privilege; only 260,000 of China's 200 million children are given this opportunity. *What positive and negative outcomes might children experience from playing sports? Are some sports programs, such as China's sports schools, too intense for children? Should children experience a more balanced life? Is there too much emphasis on sports in the United States?*

Health, Illness, and Disease

For the most part, middle and late childhood is a time of excellent health. Disease and death are less prevalent in this period than in others in childhood and adolescence.

Accidents and Injuries The most common cause of severe injury and death in middle and late childhood is motor vehicle accidents, either as a pedestrian or as a passenger (Wong & others, 2001). The use of safety-belt restraints is important in reducing the severity of motor vehicle injuries (Bolen, Bland, & Sacks, 1999). The school-age child's motivation to ride a bicycle increases the risk of accidents. Other serious injuries involve skateboards, roller skates, and other sports equipment.

Most accidents occur in or near the child's home or school. The most effective prevention strategy is to educate the child about the hazards of risk taking and improper use of equipment. Appropriate safety helmets, protective eye and mouth shields, and protective padding are recommended for children who engage in active sports.

Cancer Cancer is the second leading cause of death (with injuries the leading cause) in children 5 to 14 years of age. Three percent of all children's deaths in this age period are due to cancer. In the 15 to 24 age group, cancer accounts for 13 percent of all deaths. Currently, 1 in every 330 children in the United States develops cancer before the age of 19. Morever, the incidence of cancer in children is increasing (Neglia & others, 2001).

Child cancers have a different profile from adult cancers. Adult cancers attack mainly the lungs, colon, breast, prostate, and pancreas. Child cancers mainly attack the white blood cells (leukemia), brain, bone, lymph system, muscles, kidneys, and nervous system. All are characterized by an uncontrolled proliferation of abnormal cells.

As indicated in figure 10.2, the most common cancer in children is leukemia, a cancer of the tissues that make blood cells. In leukemia, the bone marrow makes an abundance of white blood cells that don't function properly. They invade the marrow and crowd out normal cells, making the child susceptible to bruising and infection. Lymphomas arise in the lymph system. Childhood lymphomas spread to the central nervous system and bone marrow.

Child life specialists are among the health professionals who work to make the lives of children with diseases such as cancer less stressful. To read about the work of child life specialist Sharon McCleod, see the Careers in Life-Span Development insert.

Obesity In one recent analysis, the prevalence of being overweight from 6 to 11 years of age in the United States increased 325 percent from 1974 to 1999 (NHANES, 2001). Girls are more likely than boys to be obese. Obesity at 6 years of age results in approximately a 25 percent probability that the child will be obese as an adult; obesity at age 12 results in approximately a 75 percent chance that the adolescent will be obese as an adult.

Inadequate levels of exercise are linked with being overweight. A child's activity level is influenced by heredity but also by a child's motivation to

Careers in Life-Span Development

Sharon McLeod, Child Life Specialist

Sharon McLeod is a child life specialist who is clinical director of the Child Life and Recreational Therapy Department at the Children's Hospital Medical Center in Cincinnati ◀▥ p.37.

Under McLeod's direction, the goals of the Child Life Department are to promote children's optimal growth and development, reduce the stress of health-care experiences, and provide support to child patients and their families. These goals are accomplished through therapeutic play and developmentally appropriate activities, educating and psychologically preparing children for medical procedures, and serving as a resource for parents and other professionals regarding children development and health-care issues.

In McLeod's view, "Human growth and development, coping theory, and play provide the foundation for the profession of child life. My most beneficial moments as a student were during my fieldwork and internship when I experienced hands-on theories and concepts learned in courses."

Sharon McLeod, child life specialist, working with a child at Children's Hospital Medical Center in Cincinnati.

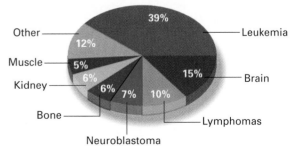

FIGURE 10.2 Types of Cancer in Children

**mhhe●com/
santrockld9**

Overweight Children

Heart Smart

Diseases and Illnesses

Medical Links

Cancer in Children

engage in energetic activities and caregivers who model an active lifestyle and provide children with opportunities to be active (French, Story, & Jeffery, 2001; Wardle & others, 2001).

The context in which children eat can influence their eating habits and weight. In one recent study, children who ate with their families were more likely to eat low-fat foods (such as low-fat milk and salad dressing and lean meats), more vegetables, and drank fewer sodas than children who ate alone (Cullen, 2001). In this study, overweight children ate 50 percent of their meals in front of a TV, compared to only 35 percent of normal-weight children.

Obesity is a risk factor for many medical and psychological problems (Kiess & others, 2001; Polivy & Herman, 2002). Obese children can develop pulmonary problems and hip problems. Obese children also are prone to have high blood pressure and elevated blood cholesterol levels. Low self-esteem and depression are common outgrowths of obesity. Furthermore, obese children often are excluded from peer groups. In chapter 14, we will discuss the most effective treatments for obesity, with a special focus on the importance of exercise.

Review and Reflect

1 **Describe physical changes and health in middle and late childhood**

REVIEW

- What are some changes in body growth and proportion in middle and late childhood?
- How do children's motor skills develop in middle and late childhood?
- What roles do exercise and sports play in children's lives?
- What are some characteristics of health, illness, and disease in middle and late childhood?

REFLECT

- Should parents be banned from coaching their children in sports and/or watching their children play in sports? Explain.

2 CHILDREN WITH DISABILITIES

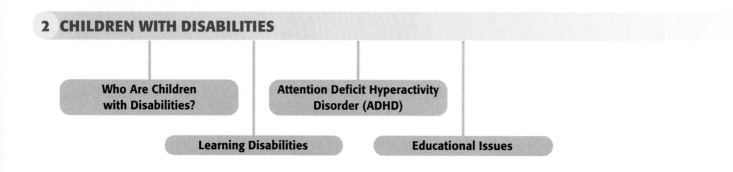

Who Are Children with Disabilities?

Attention Deficit Hyperactivity Disorder (ADHD)

Learning Disabilities

Educational Issues

The elementary school years are a time when children with disabilities become more sensitive about their differentness and how it is perceived by others.

Who Are Children with Disabilities?

Approximately 10 percent of all children in the United States receive special education or related services. Figure 10.3 shows the approximate percentages of children with

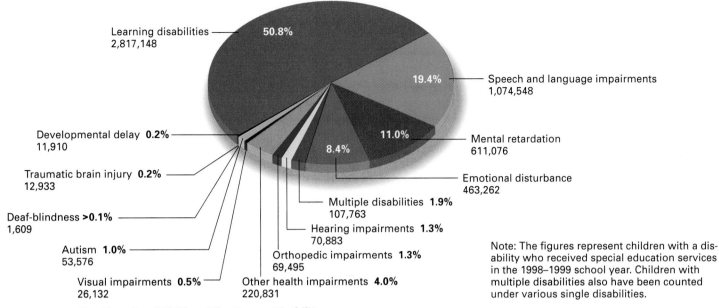

Learning disabilities — 2,817,148 — **50.8%**

Speech and language impairments 1,074,548 — **19.4%**

Developmental delay **0.2%** 11,910

Traumatic brain injury **0.2%** 12,933

Deaf-blindness **>0.1%** 1,609

Autism **1.0%** 53,576

Visual impairments **0.5%** 26,132

Mental retardation 611,076 — **11.0%**

Emotional disturbance 463,262 — **8.4%**

Multiple disabilities **1.9%** 107,763

Hearing impairments **1.3%** 70,883

Orthopedic impairments **1.3%** 69,495

Other health impairments **4.0%** 220,831

Note: The figures represent children with a disability who received special education services in the 1998–1999 school year. Children with multiple disabilities also have been counted under various single disabilities.

FIGURE 10.3 The Diversity of Children Who Have a Disability

various disabilities who receive special education services (U.S. Department of Education, 2000). Within this group, a little more than half have a learning disability. Substantial percentages of children also have speech or language impairments (19.4 percent of those with disabilities), mental retardation (11 percent), and serious emotional disturbance (8.4 percent).

Educators now prefer to speak of "children with disabilities" rather than "disabled children" to emphasize the person, not the disability. The term *handicapping conditions* is still used to describe impediments to the learning and functioning of individuals with a disability that have been imposed by society (Hallahan & Kaufman, 2003). For example, when children who use a wheelchair do not have adequate access to a bathroom, transportation, and so on, this is referred to as a handicapping condition.

Learning Disabilities

Children with a **learning disability** (1) are of normal intelligence or above, (2) have difficulties in at least one academic area and usually several, and (3) have a difficulty that cannot be attributed to any other diagnosed problem or disorder. The global concept of learning disabilities includes problems in listening, concentrating, speaking, and thinking.

About three times as many boys as girls are classified as having a learning disability (U.S. Department of Education, 1996). Among the explanations for this gender difference are a greater biological vulnerability of boys, as well as referral bias (boys are more likely to be referred by teachers for treatment because of their disruptive, hyperactive behavior).

The most common problem that characterizes children with a learning disability involves reading (Grigorenko, 2001; Siegel, 2003). Such children especially show problems with phonological skills (these involve being able to understand how sounds and letters match up to make words). **Dyslexia** is a severe impairment in the ability to read and spell (Pennington & Lefty, 2001).

Children with a learning disability often have difficulties in handwriting, spelling, or composition. Their writing may be extremely slow, their writing products may be virtually illegible, and they may make numerous spelling errors because of their inability to match up sounds and letters.

mhhe com/ santrockld9

Exploring Disabilities
Learning Disabilities
Learning Disabilities Association

learning disability A disability that involves (1) having normal intelligence or above; (2) having difficulties in at least one academic area and usually several; and (3) having no other problem or disorder, such as mental retardation, that can be determined as causing the difficulty.

dyslexia A category of learning disabilities involving a severe impairment in the ability to read and spell.

Many interventions have focused on improving the child's reading ability (Lyon & Moats, 1997; Snowling, 2002). For example, in one study, instruction in phonological awareness at the kindergarten level had positive effects on reading development when the children reached the first grade (Blachman & others, 1994).

Unfortunately, not all children who have a learning disability that involves reading problems have the benefit of appropriate early intervention. Most children whose reading disability is not diagnosed until the third grade or later and who receive standard interventions fail to show noticeable improvement (Lyon, 1996). However, intensive instruction over a period of time by a competent teacher can remediate the deficient reading skills of many children. For example, in one study, 65 severely dyslexic children were given 65 hours of individual instruction in addition to group instruction in phonemic awareness and thinking skills (Alexander & others, 1991). The intensive intervention significantly improved the dyslexic children's reading skills.

Attention Deficit Hyperactivity Disorder (ADHD)

mhhe●com/
santrockld9

ADHD

Attention deficit hyperactivity disorder (ADHD) is a disbility in which children consistently show one or more of these characteristics over a period of time: (1) inattention, (2) hyperactivity, and (3) impulsivity. Children who are inattentive have difficulty focusing on any one thing and may get bored with a task after only a few minutes. Children who are hyperactive show high levels of physical activity, almost always seeming to be in motion. Children who are impulsive have difficulty curbing their reactions and don't do a good job of thinking before they act. Depending on the characteristics that children with ADHD display, they can be diagnosed as (1) ADHD with predominantly inattention, (2) ADHD with predominantly hyperactivity/impulsivity, or (3) ADHD with both inattention and hyperactivity/impulsivity (Whalen, 2001).

The U.S. Office of Education figures on children with a disability shown in figure 10.3 include children with ADHD in the category of children with specific learning disabilities, an overall category that comprises slightly more than one-half of all children who receive special education services. The number of children diagnosed and treated for ADHD has increased substantially, by some estimates doubling in the 1990s. The disorder occurs as much as four to nine times more in boys than in girls. There is con-

attention deficit hyperactivity disorder (ADHD) A disability in which children consistently show one or more of the following characteristics: (1) inattention, (2) hyperactivity, and (3) impulsivity.

Many children with ADHD show impulsive behavior, such as this child who is jumping out of his seat and throwing a paper airplane at other children. *How would you handle this situation if you were a teacher and this were to happen in your classroom?*

troversy about the increased diagnosis of ADHD (Terman & others, 1996), however. Some experts attribute the increase mainly to heightened awareness of the disorder. Others are concerned that many children are being diagnosed without undergoing extensive professional evaluation based on input from multiple sources.

Definitive causes of ADHD have not been found. For example, scientists have not been able to identify cause-related sites in the brain. However, a number of causes have been proposed, such as low levels of certain neurotransmitters (chemical messengers in the brain), prenatal abnormalities, and postnatal abnormalites (Schweitzer, Cummins, & Kant, 2001). Heredity also may play a role, as 30 to 50 percent of children with ADHD have a sibling or parent who has the disorder (Faraone & Doyle, 2001; Woodrich, 1994).

Students with ADHD have a failure rate in school that is two to three times that of other students. About one-half of students with ADHD have repeated a grade by adolescence and more than one-third eventually drop out of school.

Many experts recommend a combination of academic, behavioral, and medical interventions to help students with ADHD learn and adapt more effectively (Rapport & others, 2001; Whalen, 2001). This intervention requires cooperation and effort on the part of the parents of students with ADHD, school personnel (teachers, administrators, special educators, and school psychologists), and health-care professionals (Whalen, 2001).

It is estimated that about 85 to 90 percent of students with ADHD are taking stimulant medication such as Ritalin to control their behavior (Denney, 2001). Although Ritalin is a stimulant, in many children with ADHD it has the opposite effect, slowing down their nervous system and behavior (Greenhill & others, 2002; Johnson & Leung, 2001). Researchers have found that a combination of medication (such as Ritalin) and behavior management improves the behavior of children with ADHD better than medication alone or behavior management alone (Swanson & others, 2001).

The use of Ritalin and other stimulants to treat ADHD continues to be controversial. Critics argue that physicians are too quick to prescribe Ritalin, especially for mild cases of ADHD, and that long-term studies of the effects of Ritalin on children with ADHD have not been conducted to determine possible negative effects.

Educational Issues

The legal requirement that schools serve all children with a disability is fairly recent. Beginning in the mid 1960s to mid 1970s, legislatures, the federal courts, and the United States Congress laid down special educational rights for children with disabilities. Prior to that time, most children with a disability were either refused enrollment or inadequately served by schools. In 1975, *Public Law 94-142*, the Education for All Handicapped Children Act, required that all students with disabilities be given a free, appropriate public education and be provided the funding to help implement this education.

In 1990, Public Law 94-142 was renamed the *Individuals with Disabilities Education Act (IDEA)*. The IDEA spells out broad mandates for services to all children with disabilities. These include evaluation and eligibility determination, appropriate education and the individualized education plan (IEP), and the least restrictive environment (LRE) (Martin, Martin, & Terman, 1996).

The IDEA requires that students with disabilities have an **individualized education plan (IEP),** a written statement that spells out a program that is specifically tailored for the student with a disability. In general, the IEP should be (1) related to the child's learning capacity, (2) specifically constructed to meet the child's individual needs and not merely a copy of what is offered to other children, and (3) designed to provide educational benefits.

Under the IDEA, a child with a disability must be educated in the **least restrictive environment (LRE),** which is a setting that is as similar as possible to the one in which children who do not have a disability are educated. The term **inclusion**

Public Law 94-142 mandates free, appropriate education for all children. *What are the aspects of this education?*

Education of Children Who Are Exceptional

Inclusion

individualized education plan (IEP) A written statement that spells out a program tailored to a child with a disability. The plan should be (1) related to the child's learning capacity, (2) specially constructed to meet the child's individual needs and not merely a copy of what is offered to other children, and (3) designed to provide educational benefits.

least restrictive environment (LRE) The concept that a child with a disability must be educated in a setting that is as similar as possible to the one in which children who do not have a disability are educated.

inclusion Educating a child with special education needs full-time in the regular classroom.

Family-Centered and Culture-Centered Approaches to Working with a Child Who Has a Disability

Best practices in service delivery to children with disabilities are moving toward a family-focused or family-centered approach (Lynch & Hanson, 1993). This approach emphasizes the importance of partnerships between parents and disability professionals and shared decision making in assessment, intervention, and evaluation. It also underscores the belief that services for children must be offered in the context of the entire family and that the entire family system is the partner and the client, not just the child (Lyytinen & others, 1994).

At the same time as services are becoming more family focused, the families served by many intervention programs are becoming increasingly diverse. Many families are characterized by attitudes, beliefs, values, customs, languages, and behaviors that are unfamiliar to interventionists. It is not uncommon for interventionists in some locations to work with families from as many as ten different cultures or more. In a large school district, as many as fifty languages may be spoken.

Who are these interventionists who work with children who have a disability or are at risk for one? They include educators, nurses, speech and language specialists, audiologists, occupational and physical therapists, physicians, social workers, and psychologists. Regardless of the agency, program, service, setting, or professional discipline, having the attitudes and skills that facilitate effective cross-cultural interactions is needed for competent intervention.

Ideally, families in need of services for their children receive assistance from professionals who are knowledgeable and competent in their discipline, who speak the same language as family members, and have the ability to establish rapport and work in partnership with family members to implement interventions for the child and family. However, the current match between many professionals and the families whom they serve is not perfect. This does not mean, though, that families cannot receive high-quality assistance. It simply means that interventionists need to be especially sensitive to the importance of developing cross-cultural competence and learning how to respond in sensitive and appropriate ways.

describes the education of a child with special education needs full-time in the general school program. Not long ago, it was considered appropriate to educate children with disabilities outside the regular classroom. However, today, schools must make every effort to provide inclusion for children with disabilities (Dettmer, Dyck, & Thurston, 2002; Hallahan & Kaufman, 2003). To read further about children with disabilities, see the Sociocultural Worlds of Development box.

Review and Reflect

2 **Identify children with disabilities and issues in educating them**

REVIEW

- Who are children with disabilities?
- What characterizes children with learning disabilities?
- How would you describe children with attention deficit hyperactivity disorder? What kind of treatment are they typically given?
- What are some issues in educating children with disabilities?

REFLECT

- Think back on your own schooling and how children with learning disabilities or ADHD either were or were not diagnosed. Were you aware of such individuals in your classes? Were they helped by specialists? You may know one or more individuals with a learning disability or ADHD. Ask them about their educational experiences and whether they believe schools could have done a better job of helping them.

3 COGNITIVE CHANGES

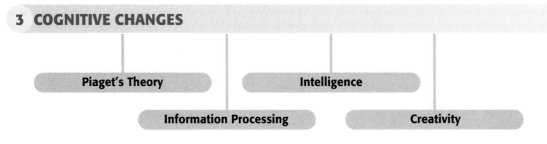

Piaget's Theory	Intelligence
Information Processing	Creativity

Do children enter a new stage of cognitive development in middle and late childhood? How do children process information in this age period? What is the nature of children's intelligence and creativity? Let's explore these questions.

Piaget's Theory

According to Piaget (1952), the preschool child's thought is preoperational ◀▥ p. 242. Preoperational thought involves the formation of stable concepts, the emergence of mental reasoning, the prominence of egocentrism, and the construction of magical belief systems. Thought during the preschool years is still flawed and not well organized. Piaget believed that concrete operational thought does not appear until about the age of 7, but, as we learned in chapter 8, Piaget may have underestimated some of the cognitive skills of preschool children. For example, by carefully and cleverly designing experiments on understanding the concept of number, it was demonstrated that some preschool children show conservation, a concrete operational skill (Gelman, 1969). In chapter 8, we explored concrete operational thought by describing the preschool child's flaws in thinking about such concrete operational skills as conservation; here we will cover the characteristics of concrete operational thought again, this time emphasizing the competencies of elementary school children. Piaget believed that concrete operational thought characterizes children from about 7 to 11 years of age. We will also consider applications of Piaget's ideas to children's education and an evaluation of Piaget's theory.

Remember that, according to Piaget, *concrete operational thought* is made up of operations—mental actions that allow children to do mentally what they had done physically before ◀▥ p. 242. Concrete operations are also mental actions that are reversible. In the well-known test of reversibility of thought involving conservation of matter, the child is presented with two identical balls of clay. The experimenter rolls one ball into a long, thin shape; the other remains in its original ball shape. The child is then asked if there is more clay in the ball or in the long, thin piece of clay. By the time children reach the age of 7 or 8, most answer that the amount of clay is the same. To answer this problem correctly, children have to imagine the clay rolling back into a ball. This type of imagination involves a reversible mental action. Thus, a concrete operation is a reversible mental action on real, concrete objects. Concrete operations allow the child to coordinate several characteristics rather than focus on a single property of an object. In the clay example, the preoperational child is likely to focus on height *or* width. The concrete operational child coordinates information about both dimensions.

Many of the concrete operations Piaget identified focus on the way children reason about the properties of objects. One important skill that characterizes the concrete operational child is the ability to classify or divide things into different sets or subsets and to consider their interrelationships. An example of the concrete operational child's classification skills involves a family tree of four generations (see figure 10.4) (Furth & Wachs, 1975). This family tree suggests that the grandfather (A) has three

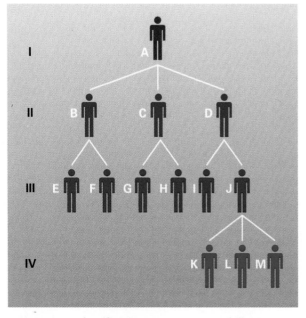

FIGURE 10.4 Classification: An Important Ability in Concrete Operational Thought

A family tree of four generations *(I to IV)*: The preoperational child has trouble classifying the members of the four generations; the concrete operational child can classify the members vertically, horizontally, and obliquely (up and down and across). For example, the concrete operational child understands that a family member can be a son, a brother, and a father, all at the same time.

children (B, C, and D), each of whom has two children (E through J), and that one of these children (J) has three children (K, L, and M). A child who comprehends the classification system can move up and down a level (vertically), across a level (horizontally), and up and down and across (obliquely) within the system. The concrete operational child understands that person J can at the same time be father, brother, and grandson, for example.

Some Piagetian tasks require children to reason about relations between classes. One such task is **seriation,** the concrete operation that involves ordering stimuli along a quantitative dimension (such as length). To see if students can serialize, a teacher might haphazardly place eight sticks of different lengths on a table. The teacher then asks the students to order the sticks by length. Many young children end up with two or three small groups of "big" sticks or "little" sticks, rather than a correct ordering of all eight sticks. Another mistaken strategy they use is to evenly line up the tops of the sticks but ignore the bottoms. The concrete operational thinker simultaneously understands that each stick must be longer than the one that precedes it and shorter than the one that follows it.

Another aspect of reasoning about the relations between classes is **transitivity,** which is the ability to logically combine relations to understand certain conclusions. In this case, consider three sticks (A, B, and C) of differing lengths. A is the longest, B is intermediate in length, and C is the shortest. Does the child understand that, if A > B and B > C, then A > C? In Piaget's theory, concrete operational thinkers do; preoperational thinkers do not.

mhhe com/
santrockld9

Piaget and Education

Piaget and Education Piaget was not an educator and never pretended to be. However, he provided a sound conceptual framework from which to view learning and education. Here are some more general principles in Piaget's theory that can be applied to teaching (Elkind, 1976; Heuwinkel, 1996):

- *Take a constructivist approach.* In a constructivist vein, Piaget emphasized that children learn best when they are active and seek solutions for themselves. Piaget opposed teaching methods which imply that children are passive receptacles. The educational implication of Piaget's view is that, in all subjects, students learn best by making discoveries, reflecting on them, and discussing them, rather than blindly imitating the teacher or doing things by rote.
- *Facilitate rather than direct learning.* Effective teachers design situations that allow students to learn by doing. These situations promote students' thinking and discovery. Teachers listen, watch, and question students to help them gain better understanding. Don't just examine *what* students think and the product of their learning. Rather, carefully observe them as they find out *how* they think. Ask relevant questions to stimulate their thinking and ask them to explain their answers.
- *Consider the child's knowledge and level of thinking.* Students do not come to class with empty heads. They have many ideas about the physical and natural world. They have concepts of space, time, quantity, and causality. These ideas differ from the ideas of adults. Teachers need to interpret what a student is saying and respond in a mode of discourse that is not too far from the student's level.
- *Promote the student's intellectual health.* When Piaget came to lecture in the United States, he was asked, "What can I do to get my child to a higher cognitive stage sooner?" He was asked this question so often here compared with other countries that he called it the American question. For Piaget, children's learning should occur naturally. Children should not be pushed and pressured into achieving too much too early in their development, before they are maturationally ready. Some parents spend long hours every day holding up large flash cards with words on them to improve their baby's vocabulary. In the Piagetian view, this is not the best way for infants to learn. It places too much emphasis on speeding up intellectual development, involves passive learning, and will not work.

seriation The concrete operation that involves ordering stimuli along a quantitative dimension (such as length).

transitivity The ability to logically combine relations to understand certain conclusions.

- *Turn the classroom into a setting of exploration and discovery.* What do actual class-rooms look like when the teachers adopt Piaget's views? Several first- and second-grade math classrooms provide some good examples (Kamii, 1985, 1989). The teachers emphasize students' own exploration and discovery. The classrooms are less structured than what we think of as a typical classroom. Workbooks and predetermined assignments are not used. Rather, the teachers observe the students' interests and natural participation in activities to determine what the course of learning will be. For example, a math lesson might be constructed around counting the day's lunch money or dividing supplies among students. Teachers encourage peer interaction because students' different viewpoints can contribute to advances in thinking.

Piaget with his wife and three children; he often used his observations of his children to provide examples of his theory.

Evaluating Piaget's Theory   What were Piaget's main contributions? Has his theory withstood the test of time?

Contributions   Piaget was a giant in the field of developmental psychology, the founder of the present field of children's cognitive development. Psychologists owe him a long list of masterful concepts of enduring power and fascination: assimilation, accommodation, object permanence, egocentrism, conservation, and others. Psychologists also owe him the current vision of children as active, constructive thinkers (Vidal, 2000).

Piaget also was a genius when it came to observing children ◀▥ p. 182. His careful observations showed us inventive ways to discover how children act on and adapt to their world. Piaget showed us some important things to look for in cognitive development, such as the shift from preoperational to concrete operational thinking. He also showed us how children need to make their experiences fit their schemas (cognitive frameworks) yet simultaneously adapt their schemas to experience. Piaget also revealed how cognitive change is likely to occur if the context is structured to allow gradual movement to the next higher level and that a concept does not emerge suddenly, fully blown but, rather, through a series of partial accomplishments that lead to increasingly comprehensive understanding (Haith & Benson, 1998).

Criticisms   Piaget's theory has not gone unchallenged. Questions are raised about estimates of children's competence at different developmental levels; stages; the training of children to reason at higher levels; and culture and education.

- *Estimates of children's competence.* Some cognitive abilities emerge earlier than Piaget thought (Meltzoff, 2001; Miller, 2001). For example, as previously noted, some aspects of object permanence emerge earlier than he believed. Even 2-year-olds are nonegocentric in some contexts. Some understanding of the conservation of number has been demonstrated as early as age 3, although Piaget did not think it emerged until 7. Young children are not as uniformly "pre" this and "pre" that (precausal, preoperational) as Piaget thought. Other cognitive abilities also can emerge later than Piaget thought. Many adolescents still think in concrete operational ways or are just beginning to master formal operations. Even many adults are not formal operational thinkers. In sum, recent theoretical revisions highlight more cognitive competencies of infants and young children and more cognitive shortcomings of adolescents and adults (Flavell, Miller, & Miller, 2002).
- *Stages.* Piaget conceived of stages as unitary structures of thought. Thus, his theory assumes developmental synchrony; that is, various aspects of a stage should emerge at the same time. However, some concrete operational concepts do not appear in synchrony. For example, children do not learn to conserve at the same time as they learn to cross-classify. Thus, most contemporary developmentalists agree that children's cognitive development is not as stagelike as Piaget thought.
- *Training children to reason at higher levels.* Some children who are at one cognitive stage (such as preoperational) can be trained to reason at a higher cognitive

We owe to Piaget the present field of cognitive development with its image of the developing child, who through its own active and creative commerce with its environment, builds an orderly succession of cognitive structures enroute to intellectual maturity.

—JOHN FLAVELL
Contemporary Developmental Psychologist, Stanford University

An outstanding teacher and education in the logic of science and mathematics are important cultural experiences that promote the development of operational thought. *Might Piaget have underestimated the roles of culture and schooling in children's cognitive development?*

stage (such as concrete operational). This poses a problem for Piaget's theory. He argued that such training is only superficial and ineffective, unless the child is at a maturational transition point between the stages (Gelman & Williams, 1998).

- *Culture and education.* Culture and education exert stronger influences on children's development than Piaget believed (Gelman & Brenneman, 1994). The age at which children acquire conservation skills is related to the extent to which their culture provides relevant practice. An outstanding teacher and education in the logic of math and science can promote concrete and formal operational thought.

Still, some developmental psychologists believe we should not throw out Piaget altogether. These **neo-Piagetians** argue that Piaget got some things right but that his theory needs considerable revision. In their revision of Piaget, more emphasis is given to how children process information through attention, memory, and strategies (Case, 1999). They especially believe that a more accurate vision of children's thinking requires more emphasis on strategies, the speed at which children process information, the particular cognitive task involved, and the division of cognitive problems into smaller, more precise steps (Case & Mueller, 2001; Demetriou, 2001).

Information Processing

Among the changes in information processing during middle and late childhood are those involving memory, critical thinking, and metacognition. Remember also, from chapter 8, that the attention of most children improves dramatically during middle and late childhood and that at this time children attend more to the task-relevant features of a problem than to the salient features ◀‖‖‖ p. 250.

Memory In chapter 8, we concluded that short-term memory increases considerably during early childhood but after the age of 7 does not show as much increase ◀‖‖‖ p. 251. Is the same pattern found for **long-term memory,** a relatively permanent and unlimited type of memory? Long-term memory increases with age during middle and late childhood.

neo-Piagetians Developmentalists who have elaborated on Piaget's theory, believing that more emphasis should be given to information processing, strategies, and precise cognitive steps.

long-term memory A relatively permanent type of memory that holds huge amounts of information for a long period of time.

Knowledge and Expertise   An especially important influence on memory is the knowledge that individuals have about a particular topic (National Research Council, 1999). The role of knowledge in memory has especially been studied in the context of experts and novices. Experts have acquired extensive knowledge that influences what they notice and how they organize, represent, and interpret information. This in turn, affects their ability to remember, reason and solve problems.

Expertise is a term that is used to describe organized factual knowledge about a particular content area. One child might have a great deal of knowledge about chess while another child is very knowledgeable about sports. When individuals have expertise about a particular subject, their memory also tends to be good regarding material related to the subject.

One study found that 10- and 11-year-olds who were experienced chess players ("experts") were able to remember more information about chess pieces than college students who were not chess players ("novices") (Chi, 1978) (see figure 10.5). In contrast, when the college students were presented with other stimuli, they were able to remember them better than the children were. Thus, the children's expertise in chess gave them superior memories, but only in chess.

There are developmental changes in expertise. Older children usually have more expertise about a subject than younger children do, which can contribute to their better memory for the subject.

Control Processes/Strategies   If we know anything at all about long-term memory, it is that long-term memory depends on the learning activities individuals engage in when learning and remembering information (Intons-Peterson, 1996; Mayer, 2003; Pressley, 2000). **Control processes** are cognitive processes that do not occur automatically but require effort and work. They are under the learner's conscious control and can be used to improve memory. They are also appropriately called *strategies*.

One research study found extensive variations in strategy instruction (Moely, Santulli, & Obach, 1995). Some teachers did try to help students with their memory and study strategies, but, overall, strategy instruction was low across a broad range of activities. Strategy instruction was most likely to occur in teaching math and problem solving. In many cases, children develop their own strategies.

Critical Thinking   Currently, both psychologists and educators have considerable interest in critical thinking, although it is not an entirely new idea (Santrock & Halonen, 2002). Famous educator John Dewey (1933) proposed a similar idea when he talked about the importance of getting students to think reflectively.

Critical thinking involves thinking reflectively and productively, as well as evaluating the evidence. In this book, the second part of the Review and Reflect sections of each chapter challenge you to think critically about a topic or an issue related to the discussion.

Jacqueline and Martin Brooks (1993, 2001) lament that so few schools really teach students to think critically and develop a deep understanding of concepts. For example, many high school students read *Hamlet* but don't think deeply about it, never transforming their prior notions of power, greed, and relationships. Deep understanding occurs when students are stimulated to rethink their prior ideas.

In Brooks and Brooks' view, schools spend too much time on getting students to give a single correct answer in an imitative way, rather than encouraging them to expand their thinking by coming up with new ideas and rethinking earlier conclusions. They believe that too often teachers ask students to recite, define, describe, state, and list, rather than to analyze, infer, connect, synthesize, criticize, create, evaluate, think, and rethink.

Brooks and Brooks point out that many successful students complete their assignments, do well on tests, and get good grades, yet they don't ever learn to think critically and deeply. They believe our schools turn out students who think too superficially, staying on the surface of problems rather than stretching their minds and becoming deeply engaged in meaningful thinking.

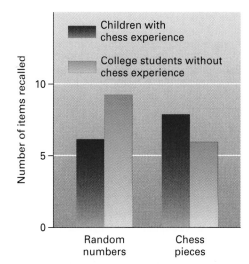

FIGURE 10.5 The Role of Expertise in Memory

Notice that when 10- to 11-year-old children and college students were asked to remember a string of random numbers that had been presented to them, the college students fared better. However, the 10- to 11-year-olds who had experience playing chess ("experts") had better memory for the location of chess pieces on a chess board than college students with no chess experience ("novices") (Chi, 1978).

control processes Cognitive processes that do not occur automatically but require work and effort. These processes are under the learner's conscious control and can be used to improve memory. They are also appropriately called *strategies*.

critical thinking Thinking reflectively and productively, as well as evaluating the evidence.

Careers in Life-Span Development

Laura Martin, Science Museum Educator and Research Specialist

After taking a psychology course as an undergraduate, Laura Martin obtained a master's degree from Bank Street College of Education in New York. Martin then worked as a teacher of young children for several years. That experience challenged her to learn more about how children think, so she applied to graduate school in child development and eventually obtained her Ph.D. from the University of California–San Diego. She later returned to Bank Street College and orchestrated projects on technology and learning. Then Martin joined Children's Television Workshop, which produces *Sesame Street,* as research director. Later, she became Vice President for Productions Research at Children's Television Workshop.

Interesting opportunities continued to be presented to her including offers from a software developer, the government, and colleges. She took a job as a science museum education and research specialist at the Arizona Science Center. At the center, Dr. Martin conceptualizes exhibits and researches whether the layout designs are communicating effectively. She organizes programs, classes, and resources. Martin says that as she does these things, her education and training in child development are extremely helpful.

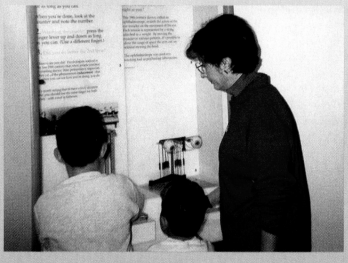

Laura Martin with children at the Arizona Science Center.

metacognition Cognition about cognition, or knowing about knowing.

Museums are settings that can stimulate children's thinking. To read about the work of Laura Martin, a science museum educator and researcher, see the Careers in Life-Span Development insert ◀‖‖ p. 30.

Metacognition **Metacognition** is cognition about cognition, or knowing about knowing (Flavell, 1999; Flavell, Miller, & Miller, 2002). One expert on children's thinking, Deanna Kuhn (1999), believes that metacognition should be a stronger focus of efforts to help children become better critical thinkers, especially at the middle school and high school levels. She distinguishes between first-order cognitive skills that enable children to know about the world (these have been the main focus of critical thinking programs) and second-order cognitive skills—*meta-knowing skills*—that entail knowing about one's own (and others') knowing.

The majority of developmental studies classified as "metacognitive" have focused on metamemory, or knowledge about memory (DeMarie, Abshier, & Ferron, 2001). This includes general knowledge about memory, such as knowing that recognition tests are easier than recall tests. It also encompasses knowledge about one's own memory, such as a student's ability to monitor whether she has studied enough for a test that is coming up next week.

By 5 or 6 years of age, children usually know that familiar items are easier to learn than unfamiliar ones, that short lists are easier than long ones, that recognition is easier than recall, and that forgetting is more likely to occur over time (Lyon & Flavell, 1993). However, in other ways young children's metamemory is limited. They don't understand that related items are easier to remember than unrelated ones and that remembering the gist of a story is easier than remembering information verbatim (Kreutzer, Leonard, & Flavell, 1975). By the fifth grade, students understand that gist recall is easier than verbatim recall. Young children also have an inflated opinion of their memory abilities. For example, in one study a majority of young children predicted that they would be able to recall all 10 items on a list of 10 items. When tested for this, none of the young children managed this feat (Flavell, Friedrichs, & Hoyt, 1970). As they move through the elementary school years, children give more realistic evaluations of their memory skills (Schneider & Pressley, 1997).

In the view of Michael Pressley (2000), the key to education is helping students learn a rich repertoire of strategies that result in solutions to problems. Good thinkers routinely use strategies and effective planning to solve problems. Good thinkers also know when and where to use strategies (metacognitive knowledge about strategies). Understanding when and where to use strategies often results from the learner's monitoring of the learning situation (McCormick, 2003).

Summarizing and getting the "gist" of what an author is saying are important strategies for improving one's reading skills. Planning, organizing, rereading, and writing multiple drafts are good strategies for improving writing skills.

Intelligence

Just what is meant by the concept of "intelligence"? Some experts describe intelligence as problem-solving skills. Others describe it as the ability to adapt to and learn from life's everyday experiences. Combining these ideas, we can arrive at a definition of **intelligence** as problem-solving skills and the ability to learn from and adapt to life's everyday experiences.

Interest in intelligence has often focused on individual differences and assessment. **Individual differences** are the stable, consistent ways in which people are different from each other. We can talk about individual differences in personality or any other domain, but it is in the domain of intelligence that the most attention has been directed at individual differences. For example, an intelligence test purports to inform us about whether a student can reason better than others who have taken the test. Let's go back in history and see what the first intelligence test was like.

The Binet Tests In 1904, the French Ministry of Education asked psychologist Alfred Binet to devise a method of identifying children who were unable to learn in school. School officials wanted to reduce crowding by placing students who did not benefit from regular classroom teaching in special schools. Binet and his student Theophile Simon developed an intelligence test to meet this request. The test is called the 1905 Scale. It consisted of 30 questions on topics ranging from the ability to touch one's ear to the ability to draw designs from memory and define abstract concepts.

Binet developed the concept of **mental age (MA),** an individual's level of mental development relative to others. Not much later, in 1912, William Stern created the concept of **intelligence quotient (IQ),** a person's mental age divided by chronological age (CA), multiplied by 100. That is:

$$IQ = \frac{MA}{CA} \times 100$$

If mental age is the same as chronological age, then the person's IQ is 100. If mental age is above chronological age, then IQ is more than 100. If mental age is below chronological age, then IQ is less than 100.

The Binet test has been revised many times to incorporate advances in the understanding of intelligence and intelligence tests. These revisions are called the Stanford-Binet tests (Stanford University is where the revisions have been done). By administering the test to large numbers of people of different ages from different backgrounds, researchers have found that scores on the Stanford-Binet approximate a normal distribution (see figure 10.6 on page 318). A **normal distribution** is symmetrical, with a majority of the scores falling in the middle of the possible range of scores and few scores appearing toward the extremes of the range.

The current Stanford-Binet is administered individually to people from the age of 2 through the adult years. It includes a variety of items, some of which require verbal responses, others nonverbal responses. For example, items that reflect a 6-year-old's performance on the test include the verbal ability to define at least six words, such as *orange* and *envelope,* as well as the nonverbal ability to trace a path through a maze. Items that reflect an average adult's intelligence include defining such words as *disproportionate* and *regard,* explaining a proverb, and comparing idleness and laziness.

The fourth edition of the Stanford-Binet was published in 1985. One important addition to this version was the analysis of the individual's responses in terms of four content areas: verbal reasoning, quantitative reasoning, abstract/visual reasoning, and short-term memory. A general composite score is still obtained to reflect overall intelligence. The Stanford-Binet continues to be one of the most widely used tests to assess a student's intelligence (Naglieri, 2000).

The Wechsler Scales Another set of widely used tests to assess students' intelligence is called the Wechsler scales, developed by David Wechsler. They include the

intelligence Problem-solving skills and the ability to learn from and adapt to the experiences of everyday life.

individual differences The stable, consistent ways in which people are different from each other.

mental age (MA) Binet's measure of an individual's level of mental development, compared with that of others.

intelligence quotient (IQ) A person's mental age divided by chronological age, multiplied by 100.

normal distribution A symmetrical distribution with most cases falling in the middle of the possible range of scores and a few scores appearing toward the extremes of the range.

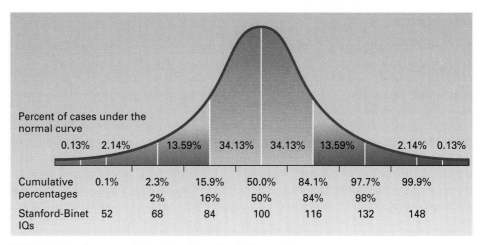

Percent of cases under the normal curve

	0.13%	2.14%	13.59%	34.13%	34.13%	13.59%	2.14%	0.13%

Cumulative percentages	0.1%	2.3%	15.9%	50.0%	84.1%	97.7%	99.9%	
		2%	16%	50%	84%	98%		
Stanford-Binet IQs	52	68	84	100	116	132	148	

FIGURE 10.6 The Normal Curve and Stanford-Binet IQ Scores

The distribution of IQ scores approximates a normal curve. Most of the population falls in the middle range of scores. Notice that extremely high and extremely low scores are very rare. Slightly more than two-thirds of the scores fall between 84 and 116. Only about 1 in 50 individuals has an IQ of more than 132, and only about 1 in 50 individuals has an IQ of less than 68.

Wechsler Preschool and Primary Scale of Intelligence–Revised (WPPSI-R) to test children 4 to 6½ years of age; the Wechsler Intelligence Scale for Children (WISC-III) for children and adolescents 6 to 16 years of age; and the Wechsler Adult Intelligence Scale (WAIS-III).

Not only do the Wechsler scales provide an overall IQ, but they also yield verbal and performance IQs. Verbal IQ is based on six verbal subscales, performance IQ on five performance subscales. This allows the examiner to quickly see patterns of strengths and weaknesses in different areas of the student's intelligence. Several of the Wechsler subscales are shown in figure 10.7.

Verbal Subscales

Similarities

A child must think logically and abstractly to answer a number of questions about how things might be similar.

Example: "In what way are a lion and a tiger alike?"

Comprehension

This subscale is designed to measure an individual's judgment and common sense.

Example: "What is the advantage of keeping money in a bank?"

Nonverbal Subscales

Block Design

An child must assemble a set of multicolored blocks to match designs that the examiner shows. Visual-motor coordination, perceptual organization, and the ability to visualize spatially are assessed.

Example: "Use the four blocks on the left to make the pattern on the right."

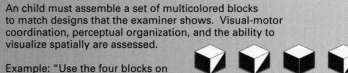

The Wechsler includes 11 subscales, 6 verbal and 5 nonverbal. Three of the subscales are shown here.

FIGURE 10.7 Sample Subscales of the Wechsler Intelligence Scale for Children (WISC-III)

Simulated items similar to those in the *Wechsler Intelligence Scale for Children*, Third Edition. Copyright © 1949, 1955, 1974, 1981, 1991 by The Psychological Corporation, a Harcourt Assessment Company. Reproduced by permission. All rights reserved.

Types of Intelligence Is it more appropriate to think of a child's intelligence as a general ability or as a number of specific abilities? Binet focused on a child's general intelligence. The IQ concept developed by William Stern was designed to capture this overall intellectual ability. Wechsler believed it was important to describe both a child's general intelligence and specific verbal and performance intelligences. This built on the ideas of Charles Spearman (1927), who said that people have both a general intelligence, which he called *g*, and specific types of intelligence, which he called *s*. As early as the 1930s, L. L. Thurstone (1938) said people have seven of these specific abilities, which he called primary abilities: verbal comprehension, number ability, word fluency, spatial visualization, associative memory, reasoning, and perceptual speed. More recently, the search for specific types of intelligence has heated up.

"You're wise, but you lack tree smarts."

© The New Yorker Collection, 1988, Donald Reilly from cartoonbank.com. All Rights Reserved.

Sternberg's Triarchic Theory Robert J. Sternberg (1986, 1999, 2002, 2003) developed the **triarchic theory of intelligence,** which states that intelligence comes in three forms:

- *Analytical intelligence.* This refers to the ability to analyze, judge, evaluate, compare, and contrast. Ann has high analytical intelligence. She scores high on traditional intelligence tests, such as the Stanford-Binet, and is a star analytical thinker.
- *Creative intelligence.* This consists of the ability to create, design, invent, originate, and imagine. Todd has high creative intelligence. He does not have the best test scores but has an insightful and creative mind.
- *Practical intelligence.* This involves the ability to use, apply, implement, and put ideas into practice. Art is high on practical intelligence. He is street-smart and has learned to deal in practical ways with his world, although his scores on traditional intelligence tests are average.

mhhe●com/
santrockld9

Sternberg's Theory

Sternberg (1999) says that children with different triarchic patterns "look different" in school. Students with high analytic ability tend to be favored in conventional schooling. They often do well in direct instruction classes, in which the teacher lectures and gives students objective tests. They often are considered to be "smart" students, who get good grades, show up in high-level tracks, do well on traditional tests of intelligence and the SAT, and later get admitted to competitive colleges. Children who are high in creative intelligence are often not in the top rung of their class. Sternberg says that many teachers have expectations about how assignments should be done, and creatively intelligent students may not conform to those expectations. Instead of giving conformist answers, they give unique answers, for which they might get reprimanded or marked down. No teacher wants to discourage creativity, but Sternberg believes that too often a teacher's desire to improve students' knowledge depresses creative thinking.

Like children high in creative intelligence, children who are practically intelligent often do not relate well to the demands of school. However, many of these children do well outside of the classroom's walls. They may have excellent social skills and good common sense. As adults, some become successful managers, entrepreneurs, or politicians, yet they have undistinguished school records.

Gardner's Eight Frames of Mind Howard Gardner (1983, 1993, 2002) believes there are eight types of intelligence. These are described here, with examples of the types of vocations in which they are reflected as strengths (Campbell, Campbell, & Dickinson, 1999):

- *Verbal skills:* the ability to think in words and to use language to express meaning (authors, journalists, speakers)

triarchic theory of intelligence Sternberg's theory that intelligence consists of analytical intelligence, creative intelligence, and practical intelligence.

Children in the Key School form "pods," in which they pursue activities of special interest to them. Every day, each child can choose from activities that draw on Gardner's eight frames of mind. The school has pods that range from gardening to architecture to gliding to dancing. *What are some of the main ideas of Gardner's theory and its application to education?*

- *Mathematical skills:* the ability to carry out mathematical operations (scientists, engineers, accountants)
- *Spatial skills:* the ability to think three-dimensionally (architects, artists, sailors)
- *Bodily-kinesthetic skills:* the ability to manipulate objects and be physically skilled (surgeons, craftspeople, dancers, athletes)
- *Musical skills:* sensitivity to pitch, melody, rhythm, and tone (composers, musicians, and sensitive listeners)
- *Interpersonal skills:* the ability to understand and effectively interact with others (teachers, mental health professionals)
- *Intrapersonal skills:* the ability to understand oneself and effectively direct one's life (theologians, psychologists)
- *Naturalist skills:* the ability to observe patterns in nature and understand natural and human-made systems (farmers, botanists, ecologists, landscapers)

Multiple Intelligence Links

Multiple Intelligences and Education

The Key School in Indianapolis immerses students in activities that closely resemble Gardner's frames of mind (Goleman, Kaufman, & Ray, 1993). Each day, every student is exposed to materials that are designed to stimulate a range of human abilities, including art, music, computing, language skills, math skills, and physical games. In addition, attention is given to students' understanding of themselves and others.

Evaluating the Multiple-Intelligence Approaches Sternberg's and Gardner's approaches have much to offer. They have stimulated teachers to think more broadly about what makes up children's competencies. And they have motivated educators to develop programs that instruct students in multiple domains. These approaches also have contributed to the interest in assessing intelligence and classroom learning in innovative ways that go beyond conventional standardized and paper-and-pencil memory tasks (Torff, 2000). One way this assessment is carried out is by evaluating students' learning portfolios.

Some critics say that classifying musical skills as a main type of intelligence is off base. They ask whether there are possibly other skill domains that Gardner has left out. For example, there are outstanding chess players, prizefighters, writers, politicians, physicians, lawyers, ministers, and poets, yet we do not refer to chess intelligence, prizefighter intelligence, and so on. Other critics say that the research base to support the three intelligences of Sternberg and the eight intelligences of Gardner as the best ways to categorize intelligence has not yet been developed.

There also are a number of psychologists who support Spearman's concept of *g* (general intelligence) and many of them believe that the multiple-intelligence views have taken the concept of *s* (specific intelligences) too far. For example, one expert on intelligence, Nathan Brody (2000) argues that people who excel at one type of intellectual task are likely to excel in others. Thus, individuals who do well at memorizing lists of digits are also likely to be good at solving verbal problems and spatial layout problems.

Controversies and Issues in Intelligence   The field of intelligence has its controversies. In chapter 3, "Biological Beginnings," we discussed the controversial issue of how extensively intelligence is due to heredity or environment ◀▥ p. 98. We concluded that intelligence is due to an interaction of heredity and environment (Sternberg & Grigorenko, 2001). Here, we will focus on several more issues, involving ethnicity and culture, as well as the use and misuse of intelligence tests.

Ethnicity and Culture   In the United States, children from African American and Latino families score below children from White families on standardized intelligence tests. Most comparisons have focused on African Americans and Whites. On the average, African American schoolchildren score 10 to 15 points lower than do White American schoolchildren (Neisser & others, 1996). Keep in mind that this figure of 10 to 15 points lower represents an average score. Many African American children score higher than many White children. Estimates are that 15 to 25 percent of all African American schoolchildren score higher than half of all White schoolchildren.

Are these differences based on heredity or environment? The consensus is environment (Brooks-Gunn, Klebanov, & Duncan, 1996). For example, in recent decades, as African Americans have experienced improved social, economic, and educational opportunities, the gap between White and African American children on conventional intelligence tests has narrowed (Jones, 1984). Between 1977 and 1996, as African Americans gained more educational opportunities, the gap between their SAT scores and those of their White counterparts shrank 23 percent (College Board, 1996). Also, when children from disadvantaged African American families are adopted by more advantaged middle-SES families, their scores on intelligence tests become closer to the national average for middle-SES children than to the national average for children from low-income families (Scarr & Weinberg, 1983).

Many of the early tests of intelligence were culturally biased, favoring urban children over rural children, children from middle-SES families over children from low-income families, and White children over minority children (Miller-Jones, 1989). The standards for the early tests were almost exclusively based on White middle-SES children. And some of the items were culturally biased. For example, one item on an early test asked what you should do if you find a 3-year-old in the street. The correct answer was "Call the police." However, children from impoverished inner-city families might not choose this answer if they have had bad experiences with the police. Children living in rural areas might not have police nearby. The contemporary versions of intelligence tests attempt to reduce such cultural bias.

Even if the content of test items is appropriate, another problem can characterize intelligence tests. Since many items are verbal, minority groups may encounter problems in understanding the language of the items.

Culture-fair tests are tests of intelligence that are intended to be free of cultural bias. Two types of culture-fair tests have been devised. The first includes items that are familiar to children from all socioeconomic and ethnic backgrounds, or items that at least are familiar to the children taking the test. For example, a child might be asked how a bird and a dog are different, on the assumption that all children have been exposed to birds and dogs. The second type of culture-fair test has no verbal questions. Figure 10.8 on page 322 shows a sample question from the Raven Progressive

culture-fair tests Tests of intelligence that are designed to be free of cultural bias.

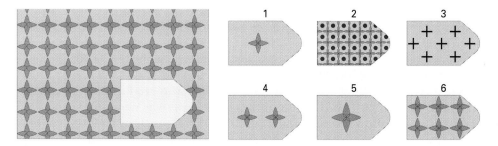

FIGURE 10.8 Sample Item from the Raven Progressive Matrices Test
Individuals are presented with a matrix arrangement of symbols, such as the one at the left of this figure, and must then complete the matrix by selecting the appropriate missing symbol from a group of symbols, such as the ones at the right.

Matrices Test. Even though tests such as the Raven Progressive Matrices are designed to be culture-fair, people with more education still score higher than those with less education do.

These attempts to produce culture-fair tests remind us that conventional intelligence tests probably are culturally biased, yet the effort to create a truly culture-fair test has not yielded a successful alternative. It also is important to consider that what is viewed as intelligent in one culture may not be thought of as intelligent in another (Serpell, 2000). In most Western cultures, children are considered intelligent if they are both smart (have considerable knowledge and can solve verbal problems) and fast (can process information quickly). By contrast, in the Buganda culture in Uganda, children who are wise, slow in thought, and say the socially correct thing are considered intelligent. And, in the widely dispersed Caroline Islands, one of the most important dimensions of intelligence is the ability to navigate by the stars.

The Use and Misuse of Intelligence Tests   Psychological tests are tools. Like all tools, their effectiveness depends on the knowledge, skill, and integrity of the user. A hammer can be used to build a beautiful kitchen cabinet, or it can be used as a weapon of assault. Like a hammer, psychological tests can be used for positive purposes, or they can be badly abused. Here are some cautions about IQ that can help you avoid the pitfalls of using information about a child's intelligence in negative ways:

- *Avoid stereotyping and expectations.* A special concern is that the scores on an IQ test easily can lead to stereotypes and expectations about students. Sweeping generalizations are too often made on the basis of an IQ score. An IQ test should always be considered a measure of current performance. It is not a measure of fixed potential. Maturational changes and enriched environmental experiences can advance a student's intelligence.
- *Not a sole indicator of competence.* Another concern about IQ tests occurs when they are used as the main or sole characteristic of competence. A high IQ is not the ultimate human value. As we have seen in this chapter, it is important to consider not only students' intellectual competence in such areas as verbal skills but also their creative and practical skills.
- *Caution in interpreting an overall IQ score.* In evaluating a child's intelligence, it is wiser to think of intelligence as consisting of a number of domains. Keep in mind the different types of intelligence described by Sternberg and Gardner. Remember that, by considering the different domains of intelligence, you can find that every child has at least one or more strengths.

The Extremes of Intelligence   Intelligence tests have been used to discover indications of mental retardation or intellectual giftedness, the extremes of intelligence. At times, intelligence tests have been misused for this purpose. Keeping in mind the theme that an intelligence test should not be used as the sole indicator of mental retardation or giftedness, we will explore the nature of these intellectual extremes.

Mental Retardation **Mental retardation** is a condition of limited mental ability in which an individual has a low IQ, usually below 70 on a traditional intelligence test, and has difficulty adapting to everyday life. About 5 million Americans fit this definition of mental retardation.

There are several classifications of mental retardation. About 89 percent of the mentally retarded fall into the mild category, with IQs of 55 to 70. About 6 percent are classified as moderately retarded, with IQs of 40 to 54; these people can attain a second-grade level of skills and may be able to support themselves as adults through some types of labor. About 3.5 percent of the mentally retarded are in the severe category, with IQs of 25 to 39; these individuals learn to talk and engage in very simple tasks but require extensive supervision. Less than 1 percent have IQs below 25; they fall into the profoundly mentally retarded classification and need constant supervision (Drew & Hardman, 2000).

Mental retardation can have an organic cause, or it can be social and cultural in origin:

- **Organic retardation** is mental retardation that is caused by a genetic disorder or by brain damage; the word *organic* refers to the tissues or organs of the body, so there is some physical damage in organic retardation. Down syndrome, one form of mental retardation, occurs when an extra chromosome is present in an individual's genetic makeup (see figure 10.9) ◀▥ p. 90. It is not known why the extra chromosome is present, but it may involve the health or age of the female ovum or male sperm. Most people who suffer from organic retardation have IQs that range between 0 and 50.
- **Cultural-familial retardation** is a mental deficit in which no evidence of organic brain damage can be found; individuals' IQs range from 50 to 70. Psychologists suspect that such mental deficits result from the normal variation that distributes people along the range of intelligence scores above 50, combined with growing up in a below-average intellectual environment.

Giftedness There have always been people whose abilities and accomplishments outshine others'—the whiz kid in class, the star athlete, the natural musician. People who are **gifted** have above-average intelligence (an IQ of 130 or higher) and/or superior talent for something. When it comes to programs for the gifted, most school systems select children who have intellectual superiority and academic aptitude. Children who are talented in the visual and performing arts (arts, drama, dance), athletics, or other special aptitudes tend to be overlooked (Olszewski-Kubilius, 2003).

There has been speculation that giftedness is linked with having a mental disorder. However, no relation between giftedness and mental disorder has been found. Recent studies support the conclusion that gifted people tend to be more mature, have fewer emotional problems than others, and grow up in a positive family climate (Davidson, 2000; Feldman, 2001).

What are the characteristics of children who are gifted? Lewis Terman (1925) conducted an extensive study of 1,500 children whose Stanford-Binet IQs averaged 150. A popular myth is that gifted children are maladjusted, but Terman found in his study that they were not only academically gifted but also socially well adjusted. Many of these gifted children went on to become successful doctors, lawyers, and professors, and scientists.

Ellen Winner (1996) described three criteria that characterize gifted children, whether in art, music, or academic domains:

1. *Precocity.* Gifted children are precocious. They begin to master an area earlier than their peers. Learning in their domain is more effortless for them than for ordinary children. In most instances, these gifted children are precocious because they have an inborn high ability in a particular domain or domains.
2. *Marching to their own drummer.* Gifted children learn in a qualitatively different way than ordinary children. One way that they march to a different drummer is that they need minimal help, or scaffolding, from adults to learn. In many

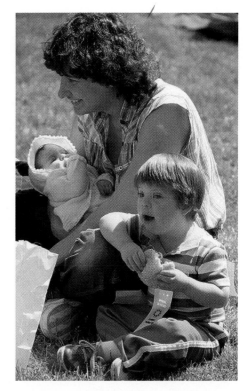

FIGURE 10.9 A Child with Down Syndrome
What causes a child to develop Down syndrome? In which major classification of mental retardation does the condition fall?

Mental Retardation
Children Who Are Gifted
Gifted Education

mental retardation A condition of limited mental ability in which an individual has a low IQ, usually below 70 on a traditional test of intelligence, and has difficulty adapting to everyday life.

organic retardation Mental retardation that involves some physical damage and is caused by a genetic disorder or brain damage.

cultural-familial retardation Retardation that is characterized by no evidence of organic brain damage, but the individual's IQ is between 50 and 70.

gifted Having above-average intelligence (an IQ of 130 or higher) and/or superior talent for something.

Careers in Life-Span Development

Sterling Jones, Supervisor of Gifted and Talented Education

Sterling Jones is program supervisor for gifted and talented children in the Detroit Public School System. Jones has been working with children who are gifted for more than three decades. He believes that students' mastery of skills mainly depends on the amount of time devoted to instruction and the length of time allowed for learning. Thus, he believes that many basic strategies for challenging children who are gifted to develop their skills can be applied to a wider range of students than once believed. He has rewritten several pamphlets for use by teachers and parents, including *How to Help Your Child Succeed* and *Gifted and Talented Education for Everyone.*

Jones has undergraduate and graduate degrees from Wayne State University and taught English for a number of years before becoming involved in the program for gifted children. He also has written materials on African Americans,

such as *Voices from the Black Experience*, that are used in the Detroit schools.

Sterling Jones with some of the children in the gifted program in the Detroit Public School System.

---

instances, they resist any kind of explicit instruction. They also often make discoveries on their own and solve problems in unique ways.

3. A *passion to master.* Gifted children are driven to understand the domain in which they have high ability. They display an intense, obsessive interest and an ability to focus. They are not children who need to be pushed by their parents. They motivate themselves, says Winner.

One career opportunity in life-span development involves working with children who are gifted as a teacher or supervisor. To read about the work of a supervisor of gifted and talented education, see the Careers in Life-Span Development insert.

Creativity

Creativity is the ability to think in novel and unusual ways and to come up with unique solutions to problems. Thus, intelligence and creativity are not the same thing. This was recognized in Sternberg's account of intelligence earlier in this chapter and by J. P. Guilford (1967). Guilford distinguished between **convergent thinking,** which produces one correct answer and characterizes the kind of thinking that is required on conventional tests of intelligence, and **divergent thinking,** which produces many different answers to the same question and characterizes creativity. For example, a typical item on a conventional intelligence test is "How many quarters will you get in return for 60 dimes?" By contrast, the following question has many possible answers: "What image comes to mind when you hear the phrase 'Sitting alone in a dark room' or 'Can you think of some unique uses for a paper clip?'"

Are intelligence and creativity related? Although most creative children are quite intelligent, the reverse is not necessarily true. Many highly intelligent children (as measured by high scores on conventional intelligence tests) are not very creative. And, if Sternberg were to have his way, creative thinking would become part of a broader definition of intelligence.

creativity The ability to think in novel and unusual ways and to come up with unique solutions to problems.

convergent thinking Thinking that produces one correct answer and is characteristic of the kind of thinking tested by standardized intelligence tests.

divergent thinking Thinking that produces many answers to the same question and is characteristic of creativity.

An important goal is to help children become more creative. What are the best strategies for accomplishing this goal?

- *Have children engage in brainstorming and come up with as many ideas as possible.* In **brainstorming,** individuals are encouraged to come up with creative ideas in a group, play off each other's ideas, and say whatever comes to mind. The more ideas children produce, the better their chance of creating something unique (Runco, 2000).
- *Provide children with environments that stimulate creativity.* Some settings nourish creativity; others depress it. People who encourage children's creativity often rely on their natural curiosity. They provide exercises and activities that stimulate children to find insightful solutions to problems, rather than asking a lot of questions that require rote answers.
- *Don't overcontrol.* Teresa Amabile (1993) says that telling children exactly how to do things leaves them feeling that any originality is a mistake and any exploration is a waste of time. Letting children select their interests and supporting their inclinations are less likely to destroy their natural curiosity than dictating which activities they should engage in (Csikszentmihalyi, 2000).
- *Encourage internal motivation.* The excessive use of prizes, such as gold stars, money, or toys, can stifle creativity by undermining the intrinsic pleasure children derive from creative activities. Creative children's motivation is the satisfaction generated by the work itself (Amabile & Hennessey, 1992).
- *Foster flexible and playful thinking.* Creative thinkers are flexible and play with problems, which gives rise to a paradox. Although creativity takes effort, the effort goes more smoothly if students take it lightly.
- *Introduce children to creative people.* Teachers can invite these people to their classrooms and ask them to describe what helps them become creative or to demonstrate their creative skills. A writer, poet, musician, scientist, and many others can bring their props and productions to the class, turning it into a theater for stimulating students' creativity.

Review and Reflect

3 Explain cognitive changes in middle and late childhood

REVIEW

- What characterizes Piaget's stage of concrete operational thought? What are some contributions and criticisms of Piaget?
- How do children process information in the middle and late childhood years?
- What is intelligence? What are some different forms of intelligence? What are some issues related to intelligence?
- What is creativity? What are some characteristics of creativity? What are some strategies for helping children to become more creative?

REFLECT

- A CD-ROM, *Children's IQ and Achievement Test*, now lets parents test their child's IQ and how well the child is performing in relation to his or her grade in school. What might be some problems with parents giving their children an IQ test?

brainstorming A technique in which individuals are encouraged to come up with creative ideas in a group, play off each other's ideas, and say practically whatever comes to mind.

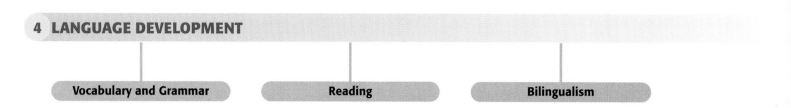

4 LANGUAGE DEVELOPMENT

Vocabulary and Grammar   **Reading**   **Bilingualism**

Children gain new skills as they enter school that make it possible to learn to read and write: these include increasingly using language in a displaced way, learning what a word is, and how to recognize and talk about sounds (Berko Gleason, 2002). They have to learn the alphabetic principle, that the alphabet letters represent sounds of the language. As children develop during middle and late childhood, changes in their vocabulary and grammar also take place (Hoff, 2003).

Vocabulary and Grammar

During middle and late childhood, a change occurs in the way children think about words. They become less tied to the actions and perceptual dimensions associated with words, and they become more analytical in their approach to words.

When asked to say the first word that comes to mind when they hear a word, young children typically provide a word that often follows the word in a sentence. For example, when asked to respond to "dog" the young child may say "barks," or to the word "eat" say "lunch." At about 7 years of age, children begin to respond with a word that is the same part of speech as the stimulus word. For example, a child may now respond to the word "dog" with "cat" or "horse." To "eat," they now might say "drink." This is evidence that children now have begun to categorize their vocabulary by parts of speech (Berko Gleason, 2002).

An important point needs to be made about vocabulary development. Children who begin elementary school with a small vocabulary are at risk when it comes to learning to read (Berko Gleason, 2002).

Children make similar advances in grammar. The elementary school child's improvement in logical reasoning and analytical skills helps in the understanding of such constructions as the appropriate use of comparatives *(shorter, deeper)* and subjectives ("If you were president . . . ").

Reading

What are some approaches to teaching children how to read? Education and language experts continue to debate how children should be taught to read (Combs, 2002). The debate is between those who advocate a basic-skill-and-phonetics approach and those who emphasize a whole-language approach.

- **Basic-skills-and-phonetics approach.** This approach involves teaching both phonemic awareness (breaking apart and manipulating sounds in words) and phonics (learning that sounds are represented by letters of the alphabet which can then be blended together to form words). Early reading materials should involve simple materials (Fox & Hull, 2002). Only after they have learned phonological rules should children be given books and poems.
- **Whole-language approach.** This approach assumes that reading instruction should parallel children's natural language learning. From the outset, reading materials should be whole and meaningful. That is, in early reading instruction, children should be presented with materials in their complete form, such as stories and poems. In this way, say the whole-language advocates, children learn to understand language's communicative function. The whole-language approach implies that all words are essentially "sight" words, which the child recognizes as

mhhe●com/
santrockld9

Reading Research
Reading
Children's Literature

basic-skills-and-phonetics approach The idea that reading instruction should teach both phonemic awareness and phonics.

whole-language approach An approach to reading instruction based on the idea that instruction should parallel children's natural language learning. Reading materials should be whole and meaningful.

a whole without detecting how the individual letters contribute to sounds. In the whole-language approach, reading should be connected with writing and listening skills. Also in this approach, reading is often integrated with other skills such as science and social studies. Most whole-language approaches have students read real-world, relevant materials, such as newspapers and books, and ask them to write about them and discuss them.

Which approach is best? Researchers have found that children can benefit from both approaches. They have found strong evidence that the basic-skills-and-phonetics approach should be used in teaching children to read but that students also benefit from the whole-language approach of being immersed in a natural world of print (Fox & Hull, 2002; Heilman, Blair, & Rupley 2002; Wilson & others, 2001).

These were the conclusions of the National Reading Panel (2000), which conducted the largest, most comprehensive review of research on reading ever conducted. The panel, which included a number of leading experts on reading, found that phonological awareness instruction is especially effective when it is combined with letter training and as part of a total literacy program. The most effective phonological awareness training involve two main skills: blending (listening to a series of separate spoken sounds and blending them, such as /g/ /o/ = go) and segmentation (tapping out/counting out the sounds in a word, such as /g/ /o/ = go, which is two sounds). Researchers also have found that phonological awareness improves when it is integrated with reading and writing, is simple, and is conducted in small groups rather than a whole class (Stahl, 2002). Other conclusions reached by the National Reading Panel (2000) suggest that children's reading benefits from guided oral reading (having them practice what they have learned by reading aloud with guidance and feedback) and applying reading comprehension strategies to guide and improve reading instruction. We will discuss a number of these strategies shortly.

In a recent study, Michael Pressley and his colleagues (2001) examined literacy instruction in five U.S. classrooms. Based on academic and classroom literacy performance of students, the effectiveness of classrooms was analyzed. In the most effective classrooms, teachers exhibited excellent classroom management based on positive reinforcement and cooperation; balanced teaching of skills, literature, and writing; scaffolding and matching task demands to students' skill level; encouragement of student self-regulation; and strong connections across subject areas. In general, the extensive observations did not support any particular reading approach (such as whole-language or basic-skills-and-phonetics approaches); rather, excellent instruction involved multiple, well-integrated components. An important point in this study is that effective reading instruction involves more than a specific reading approach—it also includes effective classroom management, encouragement of self-regulation, and other components (Pressley, 2003).

Reading is like other important skills that children need to develop. It takes time and effort to become a proficient reader. In a recent national assessment, children in the fourth grade had higher scores on a national reading test when they read 11 or more pages daily for school and homework (National Assessment of Educational Progress, 2000) (see figure 10.10). Thus, teachers who required students to read a great deal on a daily basis helped children develop their reading skills.

Bilingualism

As many as 10 million children in the United States come from homes in which English is not the primary language. One major concern regarding such children is to find the best way to help them to succeed in a culture where English is dominant, in school and beyond (Garcia & Willis, 2001; Nieto, 2002).

Bilingual education, which has been the preferred strategy of schools for the last two decades, aims to teach academic subjects to immigrant children in their native languages (most often Spanish), and slowly and simultaneously teach them English

What are the main approaches to teaching children how to read?

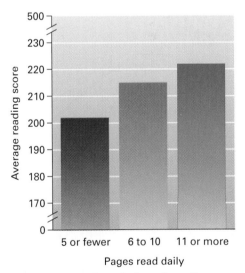

FIGURE 10.10 The Relation of Reading Achievement to Number of Pages Read Daily

In the recent analysis of reading in the fourth grade in the National Assessment of Educational Progress (2000), reading more pages daily in school and as part of homework assignments was related to higher scores on a reading test in which scores ranged from 0 to 500.

Careers in Life-Span Development

Salvador Tamayo, Bilingual Education Teacher

Salvador Tamayo teaches bilingual education in the fifth grade at Turner Elementary School in West Chicago. He recently was given a national educator award by the Milken Family Foundation for his work in bilingual education. Tamayo especially is adept at integrating technology into his bilingual education classes. He and his students have created several award-winning websites about the West Chicago City Museum, the local Latino community, and the history of West Chicago. His students also developed an "I Want to Be an American Citizen" website to assist family and community members in preparing for the U.S. Citizenship Test. Tamayo also teaches a bilingual education class at Wheaton College.

Salvador Tamayo working with students on technology in his bilingual education 5th grade class.

(Garcia & others, 2002). Bilingual education continues to be controversial. To read about the work of one bilingual education teacher, see the Careers in Life-Span Development insert.

Some states have passed laws declaring English to be their official language, eliminating the obligation for schools to teach minority children in languages other than English (Rothstein, 1998). In California, voters repealed bilingual education altogether.

How long does it take language minority students to learn English? Kenji Hakuta and his colleagues (2000) collected data on children in four different school districts to determine how long it takes language minority students to speak and read English effectively. Speaking proficiency took three to five years, while reading proficiency took four to seven years.

A common fear is that early exposure to English will lead to children's loss of their native language. However, researchers have found that bilingualism (the ability to speak two languages) is not detrimental to the child's performance in either language (Hakuta, 2000; Hakuta & Garcia, 1989). In studies of Latino American children, there was no evidence of a loss in Spanish proficiency (productive language, receptive language, and language complexity) for children attending a bilingual preschool (Rodriquez & others, 1995). Children who attended bilingual preschool, compared to those who remained at home, showed significant and parallel gains in both English and Spanish.

Is it better to learn a second language as a child or as an adult? Adults make faster initial progress but their eventual success in the second language is not as great as children's. For example, in one study Chinese and Korean adults who immigrated to the United States at different ages were given a test of grammatical knowledge (Johnson & Newport, 1991). Those who began learning English from 3 to 7 years of age scored as well as native speakers on the test, but those who arrived in the United States (and started learning English) in later childhood or adolescence had lower test scores (see figure 10.11). Children's ability to pronounce a second language with the correct accent also decreases with age, with an especially sharp decline occurring after the age

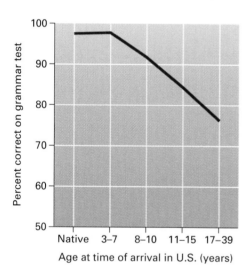

FIGURE 10.11 Grammar Proficiency and Age at Arrival in the United States

In one study, ten years after arriving in the United States, individuals from China and Korea took a grammar test (Johnson & Newport, 1991). People who arrived before the age of 8 had a better grasp of grammar than those who arrived later.

of about 10 to 12 (Asher & Garcia, 1969). Adolescents and adults can become competent at a second language but this is a more difficult task than learning it as a child.

The United States is one of the few countries in the world in which most students graduate from high school knowing only their own language. For example, in Russia schools have 10 grades, called forms, which roughly correspond to the 12 grades in American schools. Children begin school at age 7 in Russia and begin learning English in the third form. Because of the emphasis on teaching English in Russian schools, most Russian citizens under the age of 40 today are bilingual, able to speak at least some English in addition to their native language.

Review and Reflect

4 **Discuss language development in middle and late childhood**

REVIEW

- What are some changes in vocabulary and grammar in the middle and late childhood years?
- What controversy characterizes how to teach children to read?
- What is bilingualism? What issues are involved in bilingual education?

REFLECT

- What would be some of the key considerations in a balanced approach to teaching reading?

Reach Your Learning Goals

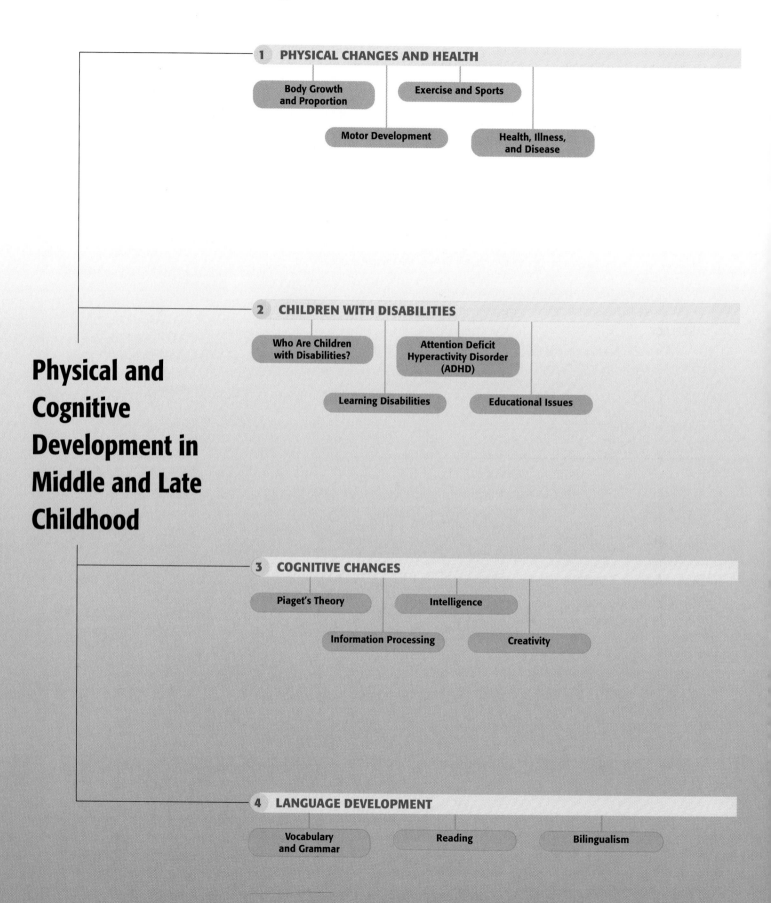

Physical and Cognitive Development in Middle and Late Childhood

1 PHYSICAL CHANGES AND HEALTH

Body Growth and Proportion

Exercise and Sports

Motor Development

Health, Illness, and Disease

2 CHILDREN WITH DISABILITIES

Who Are Children with Disabilities?

Attention Deficit Hyperactivity Disorder (ADHD)

Learning Disabilities

Educational Issues

3 COGNITIVE CHANGES

Piaget's Theory

Intelligence

Information Processing

Creativity

4 LANGUAGE DEVELOPMENT

Vocabulary and Grammar

Reading

Bilingualism

Summary

1 Describe physical changes and health in middle and late childhood

- The period of middle and late childhood involves slow, consistent growth. During this period, children grow an average of 2 to 3 inches a year. Muscle mass and strength gradually increase. Among the most pronounced changes in body growth and proportion are decreases in head circumference, waist circumference, and leg length in relation to body height.
- During the middle and late childhood years, motor development becomes much smoother and more coordinated. Children gain greater control over their bodies and can sit and attend for longer periods of time. However, their lives should be activity-oriented and very active. Increased myelination of the central nervous system is reflected in improved motor skills. Improved fine motor skills appear in the form of handwriting development. Boys are usually better at gross motor skills, girls at fine motor skills.
- Most American children do not get nearly enough exercise. Children's participation in sports can have positive (exercise and self-esteem) or negative (pressure to win and physical injuries) consequences.
- For the most part, middle and late childhood is a time of excellent health. The most common cause of severe injury and death in childhood is motor vehicle accidents, with most occurring at or near the child's home or school. Obesity in children poses serious health risks. Cancer is the second leading cause of death in children (after accidents). Childhood cancers have a different profile from adult cancers—they usually already have spread to other parts of the body and they typically are of a different type. Leukemia is the most common childhood cancer.

2 Identify children with disabilities and issues in educating them

- An estimated 10 percent of U.S. children with a disability receive special education or related services. Slightly more than 50 percent of these students are classified as having a learning disability (in the federal government classification, this includes attention deficit hyperactivity disorder, or ADHD). The term *children with disabilities* is now used instead of the term *disabled children*.
- Children with a learning disability are of normal intelligence or above, have difficulties in at least one academic area and usually several, and have a difficulty that is not attributable to another diagnosed problem or disorder. The most common learning disability in children involves reading. Dyslexia is a severe impairment in the ability to read and spell.
- ADHD is a disability in which children consistently show problems in one or more of these areas: inattention, hyperactivity, and impulsivity. Many experts recommend a combination of academic, behavioral, and medical interventions to help students with ADHD learn and adapt more effectively.
- Beginning in the mid 1960s to mid 1970s, the educational rights for children with disabilities were laid down. In 1975, Public Law 94-142, the Education for All Handicapped Children Act, required that all children be given a free, appropriate public education. In 1990, Public Law 94-142 was renamed the Individuals with Disabilities Education Act (IDEA). An IEP consists of a written plan that spells out a program tailored to a child with a disability. The concept of least restrictive environment, which is contained in the IDEA, states that children with disabilities must be educated in a setting that is as similar as possible to the one in which children without disabilities are educated. The term *inclusion* means educating children with disabilities full-time in the regular classroom.

3 Explain cognitive changes in middle and late childhood

- Piaget said that the stage of concrete operational thought characterizes children from about 7 to 11 years of age. This stage involves operations, conservation, classification, seriation, and transitivity. Thought is not as abstract as later in development. Piaget's ideas have been applied extensively to education. We owe Piaget the field of cognitive development; he was a genius at observing children. However, critics question his estimates of competence at different developmental levels, his stages concept, and other ideas. Neo-Piagetians believe that Piaget got some things right but that his theory needs considerable revision. Neo-Piagetians emphasize how children process information, strategies, speed of information processing, and more precise cognitive steps than Piaget did.
- Long-term memory increases in middle and late childhood. Knowledge and expertise influence memory. Control processes, also called strategies, can be used by children to improve their memory. Critical thinking involves thinking reflectively and productively, as well as evaluating the evidence. A special concern is the lack of emphasis on critical thinking in many schools. Metacognition is cognition about cognition, or knowing about knowing. Most metacognitive studies have focused on metamemory. Pressley believes the key to education is helping students learn a rich repertoire of strategies.
- Intelligence consists of problem-solving skills and the ability to adapt to and learn from life's everyday experiences. Interest in intelligence often focuses on individual differences and assessment. Binet and Simon developed the first intelligence test. Binet developed the concept of mental age and Stern created the concept of IQ as MA/CA X 100. The Stanford-Binet approximates a normal distribution. The Wechsler scales are widely used to assess intelligence and yield an

overall IQ, as well as verbal and performance IQs. Spearman proposed that people have a general intelligence (*g*) and specific types of intelligence (*s*). Sternberg proposed that intelligence comes in three main forms: analytical, creative, and practical. Gardner believes there are eight types of intelligence: verbal, math, spatial, bodily-kinesthetic, self-insight, insight about others, musical skills, and naturalist skills. The multiple-intelligence approaches have expanded our conception of intelligence, but critics argue that the research base for these approaches is not well established. Issues in intelligence include ethnicity and culture, and the use and misuse of intelligence tests. Mental retardation involves low IQ and problems in adapting to everyday life. One classification of mental retardation consists of organic or cultural-familial. A child who is gifted has above-average intelligence and/or superior talent for something. Terman contributed to our understanding that gifted children are not more maladjusted than nongifted children. Three characteristics of gifted children are precocity, individuality, and a passion to master.

- Creativity is the ability to think in novel and unusual ways and to come up with unique solutions to problems. Guilford distinguished between convergent and divergent thinking. A number of strategies can be used to encourage children's creative thinking, including brainstorming.

4 **Discuss language development in middle and late childhood**

- Children become more analytical and logical in their approach to words and grammar. They become less tied to the actions and perceptual dimensions associated with words, and they become more analytical in their approach to words. In terms of grammar, children now better understand comparatives and subjectives.
- A current debate in reading focuses on the basic-skills-and-phonetics approach versus the whole-language approach. The basic-skills-and-phonetics approach advocates phonetics instruction and giving children simplified materials. The whole-language approach stresses that reading instruction should parallel children's natural language learning and giving children whole-language materials, such as books and poems. The National Reading Panel (2000) concluded that both approaches can benefit children.
- Bilingual education aims to teach academic subjects to immigrant children in their native languages (most often in Spanish) while gradually adding English instruction. Researchers have found that bilingualism does not interfere with performance in either language. Success in learning a second language is greater in childhood than in adolescence.

Key Terms

learning disability 307
dyslexia 307
attention deficit hyperactivity
  disorder (ADHD) 308
individualized education plan
  (IEP) 309
least restrictive environment
  (LRE) 309
inclusion 309
seriation 312

transitivity 312
neo-Piagetians 314
long-term memory 314
control processes 315
critical thinking 315
metacognition 316
intelligence 317
individual differences 317
mental age (MA) 317
intelligence quotient (IQ) 317

normal distribution 317
triarchic theory of
  intelligence 319
culture-fair tests 321
mental retardation 323
organic retardation 323
cultural-familial
  retardation 323
gifted 323
creativity 324

convergent thinking 324
divergent thinking 324
brainstorming 325
basic-skills-and-phonetics
  approach 326
whole-language approach 326

Key People

Jean Piaget 311
John Dewey 315
Jacqueline and
  Martin Brooks 315
Deanna Kuhn 316

Michael Pressley 316, 327
Alfred Binet 317
Theophile Simon 317
William Stern 317
David Wechsler 317

Charles Spearman 319
L. L. Thurstone 319
Robert J. Sternberg 319
Howard Gardner 319
Nathan Brody 321

Lewis Terman 323
Ellen Winner 323
J. P. Guilford 324
Teresa Amabile 325

Taking It to the Net

1. Clarence wants to teach his fifth-grade students good diet, nutritional, and exercise habits. What lessons can they be taught now that will benefit them later in life?
2. Noah's parents are upset to hear that their fourth-grader may have dyslexia. Noah's father voices to his son's teacher his concern that people will think Noah is stupid. What should Noah's teacher tell these parents about the nature and causes of dyslexia?

3. Carla is the top student in mathematics. Mario displays exceptional talent in art class. Warren is very social and popular with his peers. What do these three students show us about different types of intelligence? How might traditional theories of intelligence miss the unique talents of these students?

Connect to www.mhhe.com/santrockld9 to research the answers and complete these exercises.

E-Learning Tools

To help you master the material in this chapter, you'll find a number of valuable study tools on the Student CD-ROM that accompanies this book. In addition, visit the Online Learning Center for *Life-Span Development,* ninth edition, where you'll find these valuable resources for chapter 10, "Physical and Cognitive Development in Middle and Late Childhood."

- Based on what you've read about Gardner's eight types of intelligence, what areas of intelligence are your strengths? In which are you least proficient? Use the self-assessment, *Evaluating Myself on Gardner's Eight Types of Intelligence,* to find out.
- Build your decision-making skills by trying your hand at the parenting and education "Scenarios."

Children are busy becoming something they have not quite grasped yet, something which keeps changing.

—ALASTAIR REID
American Poet,
20th Century

Socioemotional Development in Middle and Late Childhood

Chapter Outline

EMOTIONAL AND PERSONALITY DEVELOPMENT

The Self
Emotional Development
Moral Development
Gender

FAMILIES

Parent-Child Issues
Societal Changes in Families

PEERS

Friends
Peer Statuses
Social Cognition
Bullying

SCHOOLS

The Transition to Elementary School
Socioeconomic Status and Ethnicity
Cross-Cultural Comparisons of Achievement

Learning Goals

1 Discuss emotional and personality development in middle and late childhood

2 Describe parent-child issues and societal changes in families

3 Identify changes in peer relationships in middle and late childhood

4 Characterize the transition to elementary school and sociocultural aspects of schooling and achievement

Images of Life-Span Development
The Stories of Lafayette and Pharoah: The Tragedy of Poverty and Violence

Alex Kotlowitz (1991) followed the lives of two brothers, 10-year-old Lafayette and 7-year-old Pharoah, for two years. The boys lived in an impoverished housing project in Chicago. Their father had a drug habit and had trouble holding down a job.

Kotlowitz approached their mother, LaJoe, about the possibility of writing a book about Lafayette, Pharoah, and other children in the neighborhood. She liked the idea but hesitated. She then commented, "But you know, there are no children around here. They've seen too much to be children."

Over the two years, Lafayette and Pharoah struggled with school, resisted the lure of gangs, and mourned the deaths of friends. All the time they wondered why they were living in such a violent place and hoped they could get out.

Their older brother, 17-year-old Terrence, was a drug user. Lafayette told one of his friends, "You grow up 'round it. There are a lot of people in the projects who say they're not gonna do drugs, that they're not gonna drop out of school, that they won't be on the streets. But they're doing it now. Never say never. But I say never. My older brother didn't set a good example for me, but I'll set a good example for my younger brother."

A few days later, police arrested Terrence as a robbery suspect. They handcuffed him in the apartment in front of Lafayette and Pharoah. Pharoah told his mother, "I'm just too young to understand how life really is."

Several months later, shooting erupted in the housing complex, and their mother herded Lafayette and Pharoah into the hallway, where they crouched along the walls to avoid stray bullets. Lafayette said to his mother, "If we don't get away, someone's gonna end up dead. I feel it." Shortly thereafter, a 9-year-old friend of the boys was shot in the back of the head as he walked into his building just across the street. The bullet had been meant for someone else.

Poverty, stress, and violence were constants where Lafayette and Pharoah lived. There were so many shootings that many of them didn't even make the newspaper. Both boys wanted to move to a safe, quiet neighborhood, but their mother struggled just to make ends meet in the projects.

How might the stress of poverty and violence affect children's development? How might it affect the parent-child relationship? Although these kinds of circumstances are often harmful to children, might some children be resilient in the face of such stressors and have positive outcomes in life?

Some children triumph over life's adversities (Masten, 1999; Perkins & Borden, 2003). Norman Garmezy (1985, 1993) has studied resilience amid disadvantage for many years. He concluded that three factors help children become resilient to stress and disadvantage: (1) good cognitive skills, especially attention, which helps children focus on tasks, such as schoolwork; (2) a family—even if enveloped in poverty—characterized by warmth, cohesion, and a caring adult, such as a grandparent who takes responsibility in the absence of responsive parents or in the presence of intense marital conflict; and (3) external support, such as a teacher, a neighbor, a mentor, a caring agency, or a church. In one longitudinal study of resilient individuals from birth to 32 years of age in Kauia, these three factors were present in their lives (Werner, 1989). Later in this chapter we will focus on some of the strategies that can be used in schools to help children like Lafayette and Pharoah who live in impoverished conditions.

1 EMOTIONAL AND PERSONALITY DEVELOPMENT

> **The Self**
>
> **Emotional Development**
>
> **Moral Development**
>
> **Gender**

In chapter 9, we discussed the development of the self, emotional development, moral development, and gender in early childhood ◀▥ p. 268. Here, we will focus on these important dimensions of children's development in middle and late childhood.

The Self

What is the nature of the child's self-understanding and self-esteem in the elementary school years?

The Development of Self-Understanding   In middle and late childhood, self-understanding increasingly shifts from defining oneself through external characteristics to defining oneself through internal characteristics. Elementary school children are also more likely to define themselves in terms of social characteristics and social comparisons (Harter, 1999). This theme of self-definition will be discussed shortly.

In middle and late childhood, children not only recognize differences between inner and outer states but also are more likely to include subjective inner states in their definition of self. For example, in one study, second-grade children were much more likely than younger children to name psychological characteristics (such as preferences or personality traits) in their self-definition and were less likely to name physical characteristics (such as eye color or possessions) (Aboud & Skerry, 1983). For example, 8-year-old Todd included in his self-description, "I am smart and I am popular." Ten-year-old Tina says about herself, "I am pretty good about not worrying most of the time. I used to lose my temper, but I'm better about that now. I also feel proud when I do well in school."

In addition to the increase of psychological characteristics in self-definition during the elementary school years, the *social aspects* of the self also increase at this point in development. In one investigation, elementary school children often included references to social groups in their self-descriptions (Livesly & Bromley, 1973). For example, some children referred to themselves as Girl Scouts, as Catholics, or as someone who has two close friends.

Children's self-understanding in the elementary school years also includes increasing reference to *social comparison*. At this point in development, children are more likely to distinguish themselves from others in comparative rather than in absolute terms. That is, elementary-school-age children are no longer as likely to think about what they do or do not do but are more likely to think about what they can do *in comparison with others*. This developmental shift provides an increased tendency to establish one's differences from others as an individual.

Self-Esteem and Self-Concept   High self-esteem and a positive self-concept are important characteristics of children's well-being (Dusek & McIntyre, 2003; Harter, 1999). **Self-esteem** refers to global evaluations of the self. Self-esteem is also referred to as self-worth or self-image. For example, a child may perceive that she is not merely a person but a *good* person. Of course, not all children have an overall positive image of themselves. **Self-concept** refers to domain-specific evaluations of the self. Children can make self-evaluations in many domains of their lives—academic, athletic,

K̲now yourself.
—Socrates
Greek Philosopher, 5th Century B.C.

self-esteem The global evaluative dimension of the self. Self-esteem is also referred to as self-worth or self-image.

self-concept Domain-specific evaluations of the self.

appearance, and so on. In sum, *self-esteem* refers to global self-evaluations, *self-concept* to more domain-specific evaluations.

Investigators have not always made clear distinctions between self-esteem and self-concept, sometimes using the terms interchangeably or not precisely defining them. The distinction between self-esteem as global self-evaluation and self-concept as domain-specific self-evaluation should help you keep the terms straight.

Research on Self-Esteem   One research area explores whether self-esteem fluctuates from day to day or remains stable. Most research studies have found it to be stable at least across a month or so of time (Baumeister, 1993; Tesser, 2000). Self-esteem can change, especially in response to transitions in life. For example, when children go from elementary school to middle school, their self-esteem usually drops (Hawkins & Berndt, 1985).

As children grow through the elementary years, they increasingly engage in social comparison with their peers. This can lower their self-esteem when they evaluate themselves in a less favorable light than their peers (Damon & Hart, 1988; Harter, 1998).

Another research issue involves whether low self-esteem is linked with developmental problems. One area where the research has been consistent is depression—low self-esteem is related to depression (Harter, 1998).

An important point needs to be made about much of the research on self-esteem: It is correlational rather than experimental. Remember from chapter 2, "The Science of Life-Span Development," that correlation does not equal causation. Thus, if a correlational study finds an association between self-esteem and depression, depression might cause low self-esteem or low self-esteem might cause depression.

Increasing Children's Self-Esteem   Four ways children's self-esteem can be improved are listed here (Bednar, Wells, & Peterson, 1995; Harter, 1999):

- *Identify the causes of low self-esteem.* Intervention should target the causes of low-esteem. Children have the highest self-esteem when they perform competently in domains that are important to them. Therefore, children should be encouraged to identify and value areas of competence. These areas might include academic skills, athletic skills, physical attractiveness, and social acceptance.
- *Provide emotional support and social approval.* Some children with low self-esteem come from conflicted families or conditions in which they experienced abuse or neglect—situations in which support was not available. In some cases, alternative sources of support can be implemented either informally through the encouragement of a teacher, a coach, or another significant adult, or more formally, through programs such as Big Brothers and Big Sisters.
- *Help children achieve.* Achievement also can improve children's self-esteem. For example, the straightforward teaching of real skills to children often results in increased achievement and, thus, in enhanced self-esteem. Children develop higher self-esteem because they know the important tasks to achieve goals, and they have experienced performing them or similar behaviors.
- *Help children cope.* Self-esteem is often increased when children face a problem and try to cope with it, rather than avoid it. If coping rather than avoidance prevails, children often face problems realistically, honestly, and nondefensively. This produces favorable self-evaluative thoughts, which lead to the self-generated approval that raises self-esteem.

Industry Versus Inferiority   In chapter 2, we described Erik Erikson's (1968) eight stages of human development ◀▥ p. 46. His fourth stage, industry versus inferiority, appears during middle and late childhood. The term *industry* expresses a dominant theme of this period: Children become interested in how things are made and how they work. It is the Robinson Crusoe age, in that the enthusiasm and minute detail Crusoe uses to describe his activities appeal to the child's budding sense of industry.

When children are encouraged in their efforts to make, build, and work—whether building a model airplane, constructing a tree house, fixing a bicycle, solving an addition problem, or cooking—their sense of industry increases. However, parents who see their children's efforts at making things as "mischief" or "making a mess" encourage children's development of a sense of inferiority.

Children's social worlds beyond their families also contribute to a sense of industry. School becomes especially important in this regard. Consider children who are slightly below average in intelligence. They are too bright to be in special classes but not bright enough to be in gifted classes. They fail frequently in their academic efforts, developing a sense of inferiority. By contrast, consider children whose sense of industry is derogated at home. A series of sensitive and committed teachers may revitalize their sense of industry (Elkind, 1970).

Emotional Development

In chapter 9, we saw that preschoolers become more adept at talking about their own and others' emotions ◀▥ p. 270. They also show a growing awareness about controlling and managing emotions to meet social standards. Further developmental changes characterize emotion in middle and late childhood (Rubin, 2000; Saarni, 1999).

Developmental Changes   Here are some important developmental changes in emotions during the elementary school years (Kuebli, 1994; Wintre & Vallance, 1994):

- An increased ability to understand such complex emotions as pride and shame (Kuebli, 1994). These emotions become more internalized and integrated with a sense of personal responsibility.
- Increased understanding that more than one emotion can be experienced in a particular situation
- An increased tendency to take into fuller account the events leading to emotional reactions
- Marked improvements in the ability to suppress or conceal negative emotional reactions
- The use of self-initiated strategies for redirecting feelings ◀▥ p. 319

Emotional Intelligence   Both Sternberg's and Gardner's views, which were discussed in chapter 10, include categories of social intelligence. In Sternberg's theory the category is called "practical intelligence" and in Gardner's theory the categories are "insights about self" and "insights about others." However, the greatest interest in recent years in the social aspects of intelligence has focused on the concept of emotional intelligence. The concept of **emotional intelligence** initially was proposed in 1990 as a form of social intelligence that involves the ability to monitor one's own and others' feelings and emotions, to discriminate among them, and to use this information to guide one's thinking and action (Salovy & Mayer, 1990). However, the main interest in emotional intelligence was ushered in with the publication of Daniel Goleman's book *Emotional Intelligence* (1995). Goleman believes that when it comes to predicting an individual's competence, IQ as measured by standardized intelligence tests matters less than emotional intelligence. In Goleman's view, emotional intelligence involves these four main areas:

- *Developing emotional self-awareness* (such as the ability to separate feelings from actions)
- *Managing emotions* (such as being able to control anger)
- *Reading emotions* (such as taking the perspective of others)
- *Handling relationships* (such as the ability to solve relationship problems)

Some schools have begun to develop programs that are designed to help children with their emotional lives. For example, one private school near San Francisco, the

emotional intelligence A form of social intelligence that involves the ability to monitor one's own and others' feelings and emotions, to discriminate among them, and to use this information to guide one's thinking and action.

What are some effective strategies to help children cope with traumatic events, such as the terrorist attacks on the United States on 9/11/2001?

Nueva School, has a class in what is called "self science." The subject in self science is feelings—the child's own and those involved in relationships. Teachers speak to real issues, such as hurt over being left out, envy, and disagreements that could disrupt into a schoolyard battle. The list of the contents for self science matches up with many of Goleman's components of emotional intelligence.

Coping with Stress An important aspect of children's lives is learning how to cope with stress. As children get older, they are able to more accurately appraise a stressful situation and determine how much control they have over it. Older children generate more coping alternatives to stressful conditions and use more cognitive coping strategies (Compas & others, 2001; Saarni, 1999). For example, older children are better at intentionally shifting their thoughts to something that is less stressful than younger children are. Older children are better at reframing (changing one's perception of a stressful situation). For example, younger children may be very disappointed that their teacher did not say hello to them when they arrived at school. Older children may reframe this type of situation and think, "She might have been busy with other things and just forgot to say hello."

By 10 years of age, most children are able to use these cognitive strategies to cope with stress (Saarni, 1999). However, in families that have not been supportive and are characterized by turmoil or trauma, children may be so overwhelmed by stress that they do not use such strategies.

The terrorist attacks on the World Trade Center in New York City and the Pentagon in Washington, D.C., on September 11, 2001, raised special concerns about how to help children cope with such stressful events (La Greca & others, 2002). Children who have a number of coping techniques have the best chance of adapting and functioning competently in the face of such traumatic events. Here are some recommendations for helping children cope with the stress of these types of events (Gurwitch & others, 2001):

- *Reinforce ideas of safety and security.* This may need to be done a number of times.
- *Listen to and tolerate children retelling events.*
- *Encourage children to talk about confusing feelings, worries, daydreams, and disruptions of concentration.* Listen carefully and remind them that these are normal reactions following a scary event.
- *Help children make sense of what happened.* Children may misunderstand what took place. For example, young children may blame themselves. Children may believe things happened that did not happen, believe that terrorists are coming to their home or school, and so on. Gently help children to develop a realistic understanding of the stressful event.
- *Provide reassurance to children so that they will be able to handle stressful feelings over time.*
- *Protect children from reexposure to frightening situations and reminders of the trauma.* This includes limiting conversations about the event in front of children.

Traumatic events may cause individuals to think about the moral aspects of life. Hopelessness and despair may short-circuit moral development when a child is confronted by the violence of war zones and impoverished inner cities (Garbarino & others, 1992; Nadar, 2001). Let's further explore children's moral development.

Moral Development

Remember from chapter 9 our description of Piaget's view of moral development ◀▥ p. 271. Piaget believed that younger children are characterized by heteronomous morality but that, by 10 years of age, they have moved into a higher stage called "autonomous" morality. According to Piaget, older children consider the intentions of the individual, believe that rules are subject to change, and are aware that punishment does not always follow a wrongdoing.

A second major perspective on moral development was proposed by Lawrence Kohlberg. Kohlberg acknowledged that Piaget's cognitive stages of development (especially preoperational, concrete operational, and formal operational) serve as the underpinnings for his theory. However, Kohlberg believed there was more to moral development than Piaget's stages. Kohlberg especially emphasized the importance of opportunities to take the perspective of others and experiencing conflict between one's current stage of moral thinking and the reasoning of someone at a higher stage.

Kohlberg's Theory of Moral Development

Kohlberg stressed that moral development is based primarily on moral reasoning and unfolds in stages (Kohlberg, 1958, 1976, 1986). Kohlberg arrived at his view after 20 years of using a unique interview with children. In the interview, children are presented with a series of stories in which characters face moral dilemmas. Here is the most well-known Kohlberg dilemma:

> In Europe a woman was near death from a special kind of cancer. There was one drug that the doctors thought might save her. It was a form of radium that a druggist in the same town had recently discovered. The drug was expensive to make, but the druggist was charging ten times what the drug cost him to make. He paid $200 for the radium and charged $2,000 for a small dose of the drug. The sick woman's husband, Heinz, went to everyone he knew to borrow the money, but he could only get together $1,000 which is half of what it cost. He told the druggist that his wife was dying and asked him to sell it cheaper or let him pay later. But the druggist said, "No, I discovered the drug, and I am going to make money from it." So Heinz got desperate and broke into the man's store to steal the drug for his wife. (Kohlberg, 1969, p. 379)

This story is one of eleven that Kohlberg devised to investigate the nature of moral thought. After reading the story, the interviewee answers a series of questions about the moral dilemma. Should Heinz have stolen the drug? Was stealing it right or wrong? Why? Is it a husband's duty to steal the drug for his wife if he can get it no other way? Would a good husband steal? Did the druggist have the right to charge that much when there was no law setting a limit on the price? Why or why not? It is important to note that whether the individual says to steal the drug or not is not important in identifying the person's moral stage. What is important is the individual's moral reasoning behind the decision.

From the answers interviewees gave for this and other moral dilemmas, Kohlberg hypothesized three levels of moral development, each of which is characterized by two stages. A key concept in understanding moral development is **internalization,** the developmental change from behavior that is externally controlled to behavior that is controlled by internal standards and principles. As children and adolescents develop, their moral thoughts become more internalized. Let's look further at Kohlberg's three levels of moral development (see figure 11.1 on page 342).

Kohlberg's Level 1: Preconventional Reasoning

Preconventional reasoning is the lowest level in Kohlberg's theory of moral development. At this level, the individual shows no internalization of moral values—moral reasoning is controlled by external rewards and punishments.

- Stage 1. *Heteronomous morality* is the first stage in Kohlberg's theory. At this stage, moral thinking is often tied to punishment. For example, children and adolescents obey adults because adults tell them to obey.
- Stage 2. *Individualism, instrumental purpose, and exchange* is the second Kohlberg stage of moral development. At this stage, individuals pursue their own interests but also let others do the same. Thus, what is right involves an equal exchange. People are nice to others so that they will be nice to them in return.

Kohlberg's Level 2: Conventional Reasoning

Conventional reasoning is the second, or intermediate, level in Kohlberg's theory of moral development. At this

Lawrence Kohlberg, the architect of a provocative cognitive developmental theory of moral development. *What is the nature of his theory?*

mhhe com/
santrockld9

Kohlberg's Theory

internalization The developmental change from behavior that is externally controlled to behavior that is controlled by internal standards and principles.

preconventional reasoning The lowest level in Kohlberg's theory of moral development. The individual shows no internalization of moral values—moral reasoning is controlled by external rewards and punishment.

conventional reasoning The second, or intermediate, level in Kohlberg's theory of moral development. Internalization is intermediate. Individuals abide by certain standards (internal), but they are the standards of others (external), such as parents or the laws of society.

LEVEL 1
Preconventional Level
No Internalization

Stage 1
Heteronomous Morality

Children obey because adults tell them to obey. People base their moral decisions on fear of punishment.

Stage 2
Individualism, Purpose, and Exchange

Individuals pursue their own interests but let others do the same. What is right involves equal exchange.

LEVEL 2
Conventional Level
Intermediate Internalization

Stage 3
Mutual Interpersonal Expectations, Relationships, and Interpersonal Conformity

Individuals value trust, caring, and loyalty to others as a basis for moral judgments.

Stage 4
Social System Morality

Moral judgments are based on understanding of the social order, law, justice, and duty.

LEVEL 3
Postconventional Level
Full Internalization

Stage 5
Social Contract or Utility and Individual Rights

Individuals reason that values, rights, and principles undergird or transcend the law.

Stage 6
Universal Ethical Principles

The person has developed moral judgments that are based on universal human rights. When faced with a dilemma between law and conscience, a personal, individualized conscience is followed.

FIGURE 11.1 Kohlberg's Three Levels and Six Stages of Moral Development

level, internalization is intermediate. Individuals abide by certain standards (internal), but they are the standards of others (external), such as parents or the laws of society.

- Stage 3. *Mutual interpersonal expectations, relationships, and interpersonal conformity* is Kohlberg's third stage of moral development. At this stage, individuals value trust, caring, and loyalty to others as a basis of moral judgments. Children and adolescents often adopt their parents' moral standards at this stage, seeking to be thought of by their parents as a "good girl" or a "good boy."
- Stage 4. *Social systems morality* is the fourth stage in Kohlberg's theory of moral development. At this stage, moral judgments are based on understanding the social order, law, justice, and duty. For example, adolescents may say that, for a community to work effectively, it needs to be protected by laws that are adhered to by its members.

Kohlberg's Level 3: Postconventional Reasoning **Postconventional reasoning** is the highest level in Kohlberg's theory of moral development. At this level, morality is completely internalized and is not based on others' standards. The individual recognizes alternative moral courses, explores the options, and then decides on a personal moral code.

- Stage 5. *Social contract or utility and individual rights* is the fifth Kohlberg stage. At this stage, individuals reason that values, rights, and principles undergird or transcend the law. A person evaluates the validity of actual laws and social systems can be examined in terms of the degree to which they preserve and protect fundamental human rights and values.
- Stage 6. *Universal ethical principles* is the sixth and highest stage in Kohlberg's theory of moral development. At this stage, the person has developed a moral standard based on universal human rights. When faced with a conflict between law and conscience, the person will follow conscience, even though the decision might involve personal risk.

postconventional reasoning The highest level in Kohlberg's theory of moral development. Morality is completely internalized.

Kohlberg believed that these levels and stages occur in a sequence and are age related: Before age 9, most children reason about moral dilemmas in a preconventional way; by early adolescence, they reason in more conventional ways. Most adolescents reason at stage 3, with some signs of stages 2 and 4. By early adulthood, a small number of individuals reason in postconventional ways. Figure 11.2 shows the results of a longitudinal investigation of Kohlberg's stages (Colby & others, 1983). A review of data from 45 studies in 27 diverse world cultures provided support for the universality of Kohlberg's first four stages, although there was more cultural diversity at stages 5 and 6 (Snarey, 1987).

Kohlberg's Critics Kohlberg's provocative theory of moral development has not gone unchallenged (Helwig & Turiel, 2002; Rest, 1999). The criticisms involve the link between moral thought and moral behavior, inadequate consideration of culture's role and the family's role in moral development, and underestimation of the care perspective.

Moral Thought and Moral Behavior Kohlberg's theory has been criticized for placing too much emphasis on moral thought and not enough emphasis on moral behavior. Moral reasons can sometimes be a shelter for immoral behavior. Bank embezzlers and presidents endorse the loftiest of moral virtues when commenting about moral dilemmas, but their own behavior may be immoral. No one wants a nation of cheaters and thieves who can reason at the postconventional level. The cheaters and thieves may know what is right yet still do what is wrong.

Culture and Moral Development Yet another criticism of Kohlberg's view is that it is culturally biased (Banks, 1993; Miller, 1995). A review of research on moral development in 27 countries concluded that moral reasoning is more culture-specific than Kohlberg envisioned and that Kohlberg's scoring system does not recognize higher-level moral reasoning in certain cultural groups (Snarey, 1987). Examples of higher-level moral reasoning that would not be scored as such by Kohlberg's system are values related to communal equity and collective happiness in Israel, the unity and sacredness of all life forms in India, and the relation of the individual to the community in New Guinea. These examples of moral reasoning would not be scored at the highest level in Kohlberg's system because they do not emphasize the individual's rights and abstract principles of justice.

Family Processes and Moral Development Kohlberg believed that family processes are essentially unimportant in children's moral development. He argued that parent-child relationships are usually power-oriented and provide children with little opportunity for mutual give-and-take or perspective taking. Rather, Kohlberg said that such opportunities are more likely to be provided by children's peer relations (Brabeck, 2000).

Kohlberg likely underestimated the contribution of family relationships to moral development. Inductive discipline, which involves the use of reasoning and focuses children's attention on the consequences of their actions for others, positively influences moral development (Hoffman, 1970). Parents' moral values influence children's developing moral thoughts (Gibbs, 1993).

Gender and the Care Perspective Carol Gilligan (1982, 1992, 1996) believes that Kohlberg's theory of moral development does not adequately reflect relationships and concern for others. The **justice perspective** is a moral perspective that is built on the rights of the individual; individuals stand alone and make moral decisions independently. Kohlberg's theory is a justice perspective. By contrast, the **care perspective** is a moral perspective that views people in terms of their connectedness with others and emphasizes interpersonal communication, relationships with others, and concern for others. Gilligan's theory is a care perspective. According to Gilligan, Kohlberg greatly

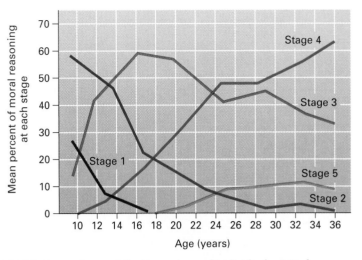

FIGURE 11.2 Age and the Percentage of Individuals at Each Kohlberg Stage

In one longitudinal study of males from 10 to 36 years of age, at age 10 most moral reasoning was at stage 2 (Colby & others, 1983). At 16 to 18 years of age, stage 3 became the most frequent type of moral reasoning, and it was not until the mid-twenties that stage 4 became the most frequent. Stage 5 did not appear until 20 to 22 years of age and it never characterized more than 10 percent of the individuals. In this study, the moral stages appeared somewhat later than Kohlberg envisioned and stage 6 was absent.

justice perspective A moral perspective that focuses on the rights of the individual; individuals independently make moral decisions.

care perspective The moral perspective of Carol Gilligan, that views people in terms of their connectedness with others and emphasizes interpersonal communication, relationships with others, and concern for others.

Carol Gilligan (third from right) is shown with some of the students she has interviewed about the importance of relationships in a female's development. *What is Gilligans's view of moral development?*

Gilligan's Care Perspective

underplayed the care perspective in moral development. She believes that this may have happened because he was a male, because most of his research was with males rather than females, and because he used male responses as a model for his theory.

Gilligan believes that girls reach a critical juncture in their development when they reach adolescence. Usually around 11 to 12 years of age, girls become aware that their intense interest in intimacy is not prized by the male-dominated culture, even though society values women as caring and altruistic. The dilemma is that girls are presented with a choice that makes them look either selfish or selfless. Gilligan believes that, as adolescent girls experience this dilemma, they increasingly silence their "distinctive voice."

Researchers have found support for Gilligan's claim that females' and males' moral reasoning often centers around different concerns and issues (Galotti, Kozberg, & Farmer, 1990). However, one of Gilligan's initial claims—that traditional Kohlbergian measures of moral development are biased against females—has been supported (Walker, 1991).

While females often articulate a stronger care perspective and males a stronger justice perspective, the gender difference is not absolute. For example, in one study, 53 of the 80 females and males showed either a care or a justice perspective, but 27 individuals used both orientations, with neither predominating (Gilligan & Attanucci, 1988).

Prosocial Behavior and Altruism Children's moral behavior can involve negative, antisocial acts—such as lying, cheating, and stealing—or it can involve their *prosocial behavior*—the positive aspects of moral behavior, such as showing empathy to someone or behaving altruistically (Hoffman, 2002). While Kohlberg's and Gilligan's theories have focused primarily on the cognitive, thinking aspects of moral development, the study of prosocial moral behavior has placed more emphasis on its behavioral aspects (Grusec, Davidov, & Lundell, 2002).

Altruism is an unselfish interest in helping someone else. Human acts of altruism are plentiful—the hardworking laborer who places $5 in a Salvation Army kettle; rock concerts to feed the hungry, help farmers, and fund AIDS research; the child who takes in a wounded cat and cares for it, and so on.

William Damon (1988) described a developmental sequence of children's altruism, especially of sharing. Most sharing during the first three years of life is done not for empathy reasons, but for the fun of the social play ritual or out of mere imitation. Then, at about 4 years of age, a combination of empathic awareness and adult encouragement produces a sense of obligation on the part of the child to share with others. This obligation forces the child to share, even though the child may not perceive this as the best way to have fun. Most 4-year-olds are not selfless saints, however. Children believe they have an obligation to share but do not necessarily think they should be as generous to others as they are to themselves.

By the start of the elementary school years, children genuinely begin to express more objective ideas about fairness. It is common to hear 6-year-old children use the word *fair* as synonymous with *equal* or *same*. By the mid to late elementary school years, children also believe that equity means special treatment for those who deserve it.

Missing from the factors that guide children's altruism is one that many adults might expect to be the most influential of all: the motivation to obey adult authority figures. Surprisingly, a number of studies have shown that adult authority has only a small influence on children's sharing (Eisenberg, 1982). Parental advice and prodding certainly foster standards of sharing, but the give-and-take of peer requests and arguments provides the most immediate stimulation of sharing.

Gender

In chapter 9, we discussed the biological, cognitive, and social influences on gender development ◀▥ p. 272. Gender is such a pervasive aspect of an individual's identity that we will further consider its role in children's development here. Among the

altruism Unselfish interest in helping another person.

gender-related topics we will examine are gender stereotypes, similarities, and differences; and gender-role classification.

Gender Stereotypes   **Gender stereotypes** are broad categories that reflect our general impressions and beliefs about females and males. How widespread is feminine and masculine stereotyping? According to a far-ranging study of college students in 30 countries, stereotyping of females and males is pervasive (Williams & Best, 1982). Males were widely believed to be dominant, independent, aggressive, achievement-oriented, and enduring, while females were widely believed to be nurturant, affiliative, less esteemed, and more helpful in times of distress. Other research continues to find that gender stereotyping is pervasive (Best, 2002; Kite, 2002; Spence & Buckner, 2000).

In a subsequent study, women and men who lived in more highly developed countries perceived themselves as more similar than women and men who lived in less developed countries (Williams & Best, 1989). In the more highly developed countries, the women were more likely to attend college and be gainfully employed. Thus, as sexual equality increases, male and female stereotypes, as well as actual behavioral differences, may diminish. In this study, the women were more likely to perceive similarity between the sexes than the men were (Williams & Best, 1989). And the sexes were perceived more similarly in the Christian than in the Muslim societies.

Gender Similarities and Differences   Let's now examine some of the differences between the sexes, keeping in mind that (1) the differences are averages—not all females versus all males; (2) even when differences are reported, there is considerable overlap between the sexes; and (3) the differences may be due primarily to biological factors, sociocultural factors, or both. First, we will examine physical differences, and then we will turn to cognitive and socioemotional differences.

Physical Similarities and Differences   From conception on, females have a longer life expectancy than males, and females are less likely than males to develop physical or mental disorders. Estrogen strengthens the immune system, making females more resistant to infection, for example. Female hormones also signal the liver to produce more "good" cholesterol, which makes females' blood vessels more elastic than males'. Testosterone triggers the production of low-density lipoprotein, which clogs blood vessels. Males have twice the risk of coronary disease as females. Higher levels of stress hormones cause faster clotting in males, but also higher blood pressure than in females. Women have about twice the body fat of men, most concentrated around breasts and hips. In males, fat is more likely to go to the abdomen. On the average, males grow to be 10 percent taller than females. Male hormones promote the growth of long bones; female hormones stop such growth at puberty.

Does gender matter when it comes to brain structure and function? Human brains are much alike, whether the brain belongs to a male or a female (Halpern, 2002). However, researchers have found some differences in the brains of males and females (Goldstein & others, 2001; Kimura, 2000) Among the differences that have been discovered are:

- One part of the hypothalamus responsible for sexual behavior is larger in men than in women (Swaab & others, 2001).
- Portions of the corpus callosum—the band of tissues through which the brain's two hemispheres communicate—is larger in females than males (Le Vay, 1994).
- An area of the parietal lobe that functions in visuospatial skills is larger in males than in females (Frederikse & others, 2000).
- The areas of the brain involved in emotional expression show more metabolic activity in females than in males (Gur & others, 1995).

Cognitive Similarities and Differences   In a classic review of gender differences, Eleanor Maccoby and Carol Jacklin (1974) concluded that males have better math and

There is more difference within the sexes than between them.
—IVY COMPTON-BURNETT
English Novelist, 20th Century

gender stereotypes Broad categories that reflect our impressions and beliefs about females and males.

"So according to the stereotype, you can put two and two together, but I can read the handwriting on the wall."

© 1994 Joel Pett. All Rights Reserved.

visuospatial skills (the kinds of skills an architect needs to design a building's angles and dimensions), while females have better verbal abilities. Subsequently, Maccoby (1987) revised her conclusion about several gender dimensions. She said that the accumulation of research evidence now suggests that verbal differences between females and males have virtually disappeared but that the math and visuospatial differences still exist.

Some experts in gender, such as Janet Shibley Hyde (1993; Hyde & Mezulis, 2002), believe that the cognitive differences between females and males have been exaggerated. For example, Hyde points out that there is considerable overlap in the distributions of female and male scores on math and visuospatial tasks.

In a national study boys did slightly better than girls at math and science (National Assessment of Educational Progress, 2001). Overall, though, girls were far superior students, and they were significantly better than boys in reading (see figure 11.3). In another recent national study, females had better writing skills than males in grades 4, 8, and 12 with the gap widening as students progressed through school (Coley, 2001; National Assessment of Educational Progress, 1998).

Socioemotional Similarities and Differences Two areas of socioemotional development in which gender similarities and differences have been studied extensively are aggression and the self-regulation of emotion.

One of the most consistent gender differences is that boys are more physically aggressive than girls are. The difference occurs in all cultures and appears very early in children's development (White, 2002). The physical aggression difference is especially pronounced when children are provoked. Both biological and environmental factors have been proposed to account for gender differences in aggression. Biological factors include heredity and hormones. Environmental factors include cultural expectations, adult and peer models, and social agents who reward aggression in boys and punish aggression in girls.

Although boys are consistently more physically aggressive than girls, might girls show as much or more verbal aggression, such as yelling, than boys? When verbal aggression is examined, gender differences often disappear or are sometimes even more pronounced in girls (Eagly & Steffen, 1986). Girls are much more likely than boys to engage in what is called *relational aggression*, which involves such behaviors as trying to make others dislike a certain child by spreading malicious rumors about the child or ignoring another child when angry at him or her (Crick, Grotpeter, & Bigbee, 2002; Crick & others, 2001; Underwood, 2002).

An important skill is to be able to regulate and control your emotions and behavior (Eisenberg, 2001). Males usually show less self-regulation than females, and this low self-control can translate into behavioral problems (Eisenberg, Martin, & Fabes, 1996). In one study, children's low self-regulation was linked with greater aggression, the teasing of others, overreaction to frustration, low cooperation, and inability to delay gratification (Block & Block, 1980).

Earlier in the chapter, we discussed Carol Gilligan's belief that many females are more sensitive about relationships and have better relationship skills than males do. In chapter 15, "Socioemotional Development in Early Adulthood," we will further explore this area of gender.

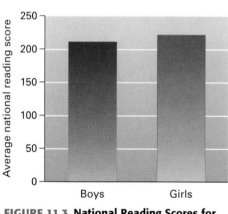

FIGURE 11.3 National Reading Scores for Boys and Girls

In the National Assessment of Educational Progress, data collected in 2000 indicated that girls did better in reading in the fourth grade (National Assessment of Educational Progress, 2001). An earlier study indicated that this gender difference holds for eighth- and twelfth-grade students as well (National Assessment of Educational Progress, 1998). Reading on the national assessment was scored on a scale from 0 to 500.

Gender-Role Classification Not very long ago, it was accepted that boys should grow up to be masculine and girls to be feminine, that boys are made of "frogs and snails" and girls are made of "sugar and spice and all that is nice." Let's further explore such gender classifications of boys and girls as "masculine" and "feminine."

In the past, a well-adjusted boy was supposed to be independent, aggressive, and powerful. A well-adjusted girl was supposed to be dependent, nurturant, and uninterested in power. The masculine characteristics were considered to be healthy and good by society; the feminine characteristics were considered undesirable.

In the 1970s, as both females and males became dissatisfied with the burdens imposed by their stereotypic roles, alternatives to femininity and masculinity were proposed. Instead of describing masculinity and femininity as a continuum in which more of one means less of the other, it was proposed that individuals could have both masculine and feminine traits. This thinking led to the development of the concept of **androgyny,** the presence of positive masculine and feminine characteristics in the same person (Bem, 1977; Spence & Helmreich, 1978). The androgynous boy might be assertive (masculine) and nurturant (feminine). The androgynous girl might be powerful (masculine) and sensitive to others' feelings (feminine). In one recent study it was confirmed that societal changes are leading females to be more assertive (Spence & Buckner, 2000).

Measures have been developed to assess androgyny. One of the most widely used measures is the Bem Sex-Role Inventory. To see whether your gender-role classification is masculine, feminine, or androgynous, see figure 11.4.

Gender experts, such as Sandra Bem, argue that androgynous individuals are more flexible, competent, and mentally healthy than their masculine or feminine counterparts. To some degree, though, deciding on which gender-role classification is best depends on the context involved. For example, in close relationships, feminine and androgynous orientations might be more desirable because of the expressive nature of close relationships. However, masculine and androgynous orientations might be more desirable in traditional academic and work settings because of the achievement demands in these contexts.

A special concern involves adolescent boys who adopt a strong masculine role. Researchers have found that high-masculinity adolescent boys often engage in problem behaviors, such as delinquency, drug abuse, and unprotected sexual intercourse (Pleck, 1995). Many of these boys, who present themselves as virile, macho, and aggressive, also do poorly in school. Too many adolescent males base their manhood on the caliber of gun they carry or the number of children they have fathered (Sullivan, 1991).

Gender in Context The concept of gender-role classification involves a personality trait–like categorization of a person. However, it may be helpful to think of personality in terms of person-situation interaction rather than personality traits alone.

*W*hat are little boys made of? Frogs and snails And puppy-dogs' tails. What are little girls made of? Sugar and spice And all that's nice.

—J.O. HALLIWELL
English Author, 19th Century

Androgyny

The following items are from the Bem Sex-Role Inventory. When taking the BSRI, a person is asked to indicate on a 7-point scale how well each of the 60 characteristics describes herself or himself. The scale ranges from 1 (never or almost never true) to 7 (always or almost always true).

EXAMPLES OF MASCULINE ITEMS	EXAMPLES OF FEMININE ITEMS
Defends open beliefs	Does not use harsh language
Forceful	Affectionate
Willing to take risks	Loves children
Dominant	Understanding
Aggressive	Gentle

Scoring: The items are scored on independent dimensions of masculinity and feminity as well as androgyny and undifferentiate classifications.

FIGURE 11.4 The Bem Sex-Role Inventory: Are You Androgynous?

Reproduced by special permission of the Distributor, Mind Garden, Inc., 1690 Woodside Road #202, Redwood City, CA 94061 USA www.mindgarden.com from the Bem Sex Role Inventory by Sandra Bem. Copyright 1978 by Consulting Psychologists Press, Inc. All rights reserved. Further reproduction is prohibited without the Distributor's written consent.

androgyny The presence of positive masculine and feminine characteristics in the same individual.

In China, females and males are usually socialized to behave, feel, and think differently. The old patriarchal traditions of male supremacy have not been completely uprooted. Chinese women still make considerably less money than Chinese men do, and, in rural China (such as here in the Lixian Village of Sichuan) male supremacy still governs many women's lives.

Thus, in our discussion of gender-role classification, we describe how different gender roles might be more appropriate, depending on the context, or setting, involved.

To see the importance of considering gender in context, let's examine helping behavior and emotion. The stereotype is that females are better than males at helping. But it depends on the situation. Females are more likely than males to volunteer their time to help children with personal problems and to engage in caregiving behavior. However, in situations in which males feel a sense of competence and involve danger, males are more likely than females to help (Eagly & Crowley, 1986). For example, a male is more likely than a female to stop and help a person stranded by the roadside with a flat tire.

"She is emotional; he is not"—that is the master emotional stereotype. However, like differences in helping behavior, emotional differences in males and females depend on the particular emotion involved and the context in which it is displayed (Shields, 1991). Males are more likely to show anger toward strangers, especially male strangers, when they feel they have been challenged. Males also are more likely to turn their anger into aggressive action. Emotional differences between females and males often show up in contexts that highlight social roles and relationships. For example, females are more likely to discuss emotions in terms of relationships, and they are more likely to express fear and sadness.

The importance of considering gender in context is nowhere more apparent than when examining what is culturally prescribed behavior for females and males in different countries around the world (Gibbons, 2000). While there has been greater acceptance of androgyny and similarities in male and female behavior in the United States, in many countries gender roles have remained gender-specific. For example, in many Middle Eastern countries, the division of labor between males and females is dramatic. Males are socialized and schooled to work in the public sphere, females in the private world of home and child rearing. The Islamic religion, which predominates in many Middle Eastern countries, dictates that the man's duty is to provide for his family and the woman's is to care for her family and household. China also has been a male-dominant culture. Although women have made some strides in China, the male role is still dominant. Androgynous behavior and gender equity are not what most males in China want to see happen.

Review and Reflect

1 **Discuss emotional and personality development in middle and late childhood**

REVIEW

- What changes take place in the self in the middle and late childhood years?
- How does emotion change in middle and late childhood?
- What is Kohlberg's theory of moral development and how has it been criticized? How do prosocial behavior and altruism develop in the middle and late childhood years?
- What are some important aspects of gender in middle and late childhood?

REFLECT

- What do you think about the following circumstance? A man who had been sentenced to serve 10 years for selling a small amount of marijuana walked away from a prison camp six months after he was sent there. He is now in his fifties and has been a model citizen. Should he be sent back to prison? Why or why not? At which Kohlberg stage should your response be placed?

2 FAMILIES

Parent-Child Issues

Societal Changes
in Families

As children move into the middle and late childhood years, parents spend considerably less time with them. In one study, parents spent less than half as much time with their children aged 5 to 12 in caregiving, instruction, reading, talking, and playing as when the children were younger (Hill & Stafford, 1980). This drop in parent-child interaction may be even more extensive in families with little parental education. Although parents spend less time with their children in middle and late childhood than in early childhood, parents continue to be extremely important socializing agents in their children's lives. What are some of the most important parent-child issues in middle and late childhood?

Parent-Child Issues

Parent-child interactions during early childhood focus on such matters as modesty, bedtime regularities, control of temper, fighting with siblings and peers, eating behavior and manners, autonomy in dressing, and attention seeking. While some of these issues—fighting and reaction to discipline, for example—are carried forward into the elementary school years, many new issues have appeared by the age of 7 (Maccoby, 1984). These include whether children should be made to perform chores and, if so, whether they should be paid for them; how to help children learn to entertain themselves, rather than relying on parents for everything; and how to monitor children's lives outside the family in school and peer settings.

School-related matters are especially important for families during middle and late childhood (Collins, Madsen, & Susman-Stillman, 2002). School-related difficulties are the number one reason that children in this age group are referred for clinical help. Children must learn to relate to adults outside the family on a regular basis—adults who interact with the child much differently than parents. During middle and late childhood, interactions with adults outside the family involve more formal control and achievement orientation.

Discipline during middle and late childhood is often easier for parents than it was during early childhood; it may also be easier than during adolescence. In middle and late childhood, children's cognitive development has matured to the point where it is possible for parents to reason with them about resisting deviation and controlling their behavior. By adolescence, children's reasoning has become more sophisticated, and they may be less likely to accept parental discipline. Adolescents also push more strongly for independence, which contributes to parenting difficulties. Parents of elementary school children use less physical discipline than do parents of preschool children. By contrast, parents of elementary school children are more likely to use deprivation of privileges, appeals directed at the child's self-esteem, comments designed to increase the child's sense of guilt, and statements indicating to the child that he or she is responsible for his or her actions.

During middle and late childhood, some control is transferred from parent to child, although the process is gradual and involves *coregulation* rather than control by either the child or the parent alone. The major shift to autonomy does not occur until about the age of 12 or later. During middle and late childhood, parents continue to exercise general supervision and exert control, while children are allowed to engage in

mhhe●com/
santrockld9

School-Family Linkages

How does living in a stepfamily influence a child's development?

mhhe●com/
santrockld9

Stepfamilies

Stepfamily Resources

Stepfamily Support

moment-to-moment self-regulation. This coregulation process is a transition period between the strong parental control of early childhood and the increased relinquishment of general supervision of adolescence.

Societal Changes in Families

As we discussed in chapter 9 ◀▥ p. 282, increasing numbers of children are growing up in divorced and working-mother families. But there are several other major shifts in the composition of family life that especially affect children in middle and late childhood. Parents are divorcing in greater numbers than ever before, but many of them remarry (Dunn & others, 2001). It takes time for parents to marry, have children, get divorced, and then remarry. Consequently, there are far more elementary and secondary school children than infant or preschool children living in stepfamilies.

Stepfamilies The number of remarriages involving children has grown steadily in recent years. Also, divorces occur at a 10 percent higher rate in remarriages than in first marriages (Cherlin & Furstenberg, 1994). As a result of their parents' successive marital transitions, about half of all children whose parents divorce will have a stepparent within four years of parental separation.

In some cases, the stepfamily may have been preceded by a circumstance in which the spouse died. However, by far the largest number of stepfamilies are preceded by divorce rather than death.

Three common types of stepfamily structure are (1) stepfather, (2) stepmother, and (3) blended or complex. In stepfather families, the mother typically had custody of the children and remarried, introducing a stepfather into her children's lives. In stepmother families, the father usually had custody and remarried, introducing a stepmother into his children's lives. In a blended or complex stepfamily, both parents bring children from previous marriages to live in the newly formed stepfamily.

Researchers have found that children's relationships with custodial parents (mothers in stepfather families, fathers in stepmother families) are often better than with stepparents (Santrock, Sitterle, & Warshak, 1988). Also, children in simple families (stepmother, stepfather) often show better adjustment than their counterparts in complex (blended) families (Anderson & others, 1999; Hetherington & Kelly, 2002).

As in divorced families, children in stepfamilies show more adjustment problems than children in nondivorced families (Hetherington, Bridges, & Isabella, 1998). The adjustment problems are similar to those in divorced children—academic problems and lower self-esteem, for example (Anderson & others, 1999). However, as with divorced children, it is important to recognize that a majority of children in stepfamilies do not have problems. In one recent study, 20 percent of children from stepfamilies showed adjustment problems compared to 10 percent in intact, never-divorced families (Hetherington & Kelly, 2002; Hetherington & Stanley-Hagan, 2002).

In terms of the age of the child, researchers have found that early adolescence is an especially difficult time for the formation of a stepfamily (Anderson & others, 1999). This may occur because the stepfamily circumstances exacerbate normal adolescent concerns about identity, sexuality, and autonomy.

Latchkey Children We concluded in chapter 9 ◀▥ p. 282 that when both parents work outside the home it does not necessarily have negative outcomes for their children. However, a certain subset of children from dual-earner families deserves further scrutiny: latchkey children. These children typically do not see their parents from the time they leave for school in the morning until about 6 or 7 P.M. They are called "latchkey" children because they are given the key to their home, take the key to school, and then use it to let themselves into the home while their parents are still at work. Latchkey children are largely unsupervised for two to four hours a day during each school week. During the summer months, they might be unsupervised for entire days, five days a week.

In one study, researchers interviewed more than 1,500 latchkey children (Long & Long, 1983). They concluded that a slight majority of these children had had negative latchkey experiences. Some latchkey children may grow up too fast, hurried by the responsibilities placed on them. How do latchkey children handle the lack of limits and structure during the latchkey hours? Without limits and parental supervision, latchkey children find their way into trouble more easily, possibly stealing, vandalizing, or abusing a sibling. Ninety percent of the juvenile delinquents in Montgomery County, Maryland, are latchkey children. Joan Lipsitz (1983), in testifying before the Select Committee on Children, Youth, and Families, called the lack of adult supervision of children in the after-school hours one of today's major problems. Lipsitz called it the "three-to-six o'clock problem" because it was during this time that the Center for Early Adolescence in North Carolina, when Lipsitz was director, experienced a peak of referrals for clinical help. And, in a 1987 national poll, teachers rated the latchkey children phenomenon the number one reason that children have problems in school (Harris, 1987).

While latchkey children may be vulnerable to problems, the experiences of latchkey children vary enormously, as do the experiences of all children with working parents (Belle, 1999). Parents need to give special attention to the ways in which their latchkey children's lives can be effectively monitored. Variations in latchkey experiences suggest that parental monitoring and authoritative parenting help the child cope more effectively with latchkey experiences, especially in resisting peer pressure (Galambos & Maggs, 1989; Steinberg, 1986). In one study, attending a formal after-school program that included academic, recreational, and remedial activities was associated with better academic achievement and social adjustment, in comparison with other types of after-school care (such as informal adult supervision or self-care) (Posner & Vandell, 1994). Practitioners and policymakers recommend that after-school programs have warm and supportive staff, a flexible and relaxed schedule, multiple activities, and opportunities for positive interactions with staff and peers (Pierce, Hamm, & Vandell, 1997).

Review and Reflect

2 **Describe parent-child issues and societal changes in families**

REVIEW

- What are some important parent-child issues in middle and late childhood?
- What are some societal changes in families that influence children's development?

REFLECT

- What was your relationship with your parents like when you were in elementary school? How do you think it influenced your development?

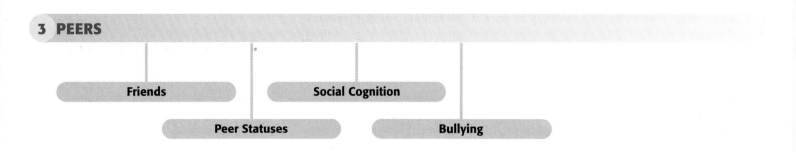

During middle and late childhood, children spend an increasing amount of time with their peers. First, we will explore children's friendships and then turn to other aspects of peer relations.

Friends

"My best friend is nice. She is honest and I can trust her. I can tell her my innermost secrets and know that nobody else will find out about them. I have other friends, but she is my best friend. We consider each other's feelings and don't want to hurt each other. We help each other out when we have problems. We make up funny names for people and laugh ourselves silly. We make lists of which boys we think are the ugliest, which are the biggest jerks, and so on. Some of these things we share with other friends, some we don't." This is a description of a friendship by a 10-year-old girl. It reflects the belief that children are interested in specific peers—not just any peers. They want to share concerns, interests, information, and secrets with them.

Why are children's friendships important? They serve six functions (Gottman & Parker, 1987:

- *Companionship.* Friendship provides children with a familiar partner and playmate, someone who is willing to spend time with them and join in collaborative activities.
- *Stimulation.* Friendship provides children with interesting information, excitement, and amusement.
- *Physical support.* Friendship provides time, resources, and assistance.
- *Ego support.* Friendship provides the expectation of support, encouragement, and feedback, which helps children maintain an impression of themselves as competent, attractive, and worthwhile individuals.
- *Social comparison.* Friendship provides information about where the child stands vis-à-vis others and whether the child is doing okay.
- *Intimacy and affection.* Friendship provides children with a warm, close, trusting relationship with another individual in which self-disclosure takes place.

Willard Hartup (1996, 2000, 2001; Hartup & Abecassis, 2002) has studied peer relations and friendship for more than three decades. He recently concluded that friends can be cognitive and emotional resources from childhood through old age. Friends can foster self-esteem and a sense of well-being. Although having friends can be a developmental advantage, not all friendships are alike. People differ in the company they keep—that is, who their friends are. Developmental advantages occur when children have friends who are socially skilled and supportive. However, it is not developmentally advantageous to have coercive and conflict-ridden friendships (Berndt, 1999).

Two of friendship's most common characteristics are intimacy and similarity. **Intimacy in friendships** is self-disclosure and the sharing of private thoughts. Research reveals that intimate friendships may not appear until early adolescence (Berndt & Perry, 1990). Also, throughout childhood, friends are more similar than dissimilar in terms of age, sex, race, and many other factors. Friends often have similar attitudes toward school, similar educational aspirations, and closely aligned achievement

intimacy in friendships Self-disclosure and the sharing of private thoughts.

orientations. Friends like the same music, the same kind of clothes, and the same kind of leisure activities.

Peer Statuses

Children often think, "What can I do to get all of the kids at school to like me?" or "What's wrong with me? Something must be wrong, or I would be more popular." What makes a child popular with peers? **Popular children** are frequently nominated as a best friend and are rarely disliked by their peers. Researchers have found that popular children give out reinforcements, listen carefully, maintain open lines of communication with peers, are happy, act like themselves, show enthusiasm and concern for others, and are self-confident without being conceited (Hartup, 1983).

Developmentalists have distinguished among three types of children who have a different peer status than popular children (Ladd, 1999; Wentzel & Asher, 1995):

- **Neglected children** are infrequently nominated as a best friend but are not disliked by their peers.
- **Rejected children** are infrequently nominated as someone's best friend and are actively disliked by their peers.
- **Controversial children** are frequently nominated both as someone's best friend and as being disliked.

What are some functions of children's friendships?

Rejected children often have more serious adjustment problems later in life than do neglected children (Kupersmidt & Patterson, 1993). For example, in one study, 112 fifth-grade boys were evaluated over a period of seven years until the end of high school (Kupersmidt & Coie, 1990). The key factor in predicting whether rejected children would engage in delinquent behavior or drop out of school later during adolescence was aggression toward peers in elementary school.

Not all rejected children are aggressive (Haselager & others, 2002; Hymel, McDougall, & Renshaw, 2002). Although aggression and its related characteristics of impulsiveness and disruptiveness underlie rejection about half the time, approximately 10 to 20 percent of rejected children are shy.

An important question to ask is how neglected children and rejected children can be trained to interact more effectively with their peers (Ladd, Buhs, & Troop, 2002). The goal of training programs with neglected children is often to help them attract attention from their peers in positive ways and to hold their attention by asking questions, by listening in a warm and friendly way, and by saying things about themselves that relate to the peers' interests. They also are taught to enter groups more effectively.

The goal of training programs with rejected children is often to help them listen to peers and "hear what they say" instead of trying to dominate peer interactions. Rejected children are trained to join peers without trying to change what is taking place in the peer group. Children may need to be motivated to use these strategies by being persuaded that they work effectively and are satisfying. In some programs, children are shown videotapes of appropriate peer interaction; then they are asked to comment on them and to draw lessons from what they have seen. In other training programs, popular children are taught to be more accepting of neglected or rejected peers.

Social Cognition

Social cognitions involve thoughts about social matters (Lewis & Carpendale, 2002). Children's social cognitions about their peers become increasingly important for understanding peer relationships in middle and late childhood. Of special interest are the ways in which children process information about peer relations and their social knowledge (Dodge, 2000).

A boy accidentally trips and knocks a peer's soft drink out of his hand. The peer misinterprets the encounter as hostile, which leads him to retaliate aggressively against the boy. Through repeated encounters of this kind, other peers come to

popular children Children who are frequently nominated as a best friend and are rarely disliked by their peers.

neglected children Children who are infrequently nominated as a best friend but are not disliked by their peers.

rejected children Children who are infrequently nominated as a best friend and are actively disliked by their peers.

controversial children Children who are frequently nominated both as someone's best friend and as being disliked.

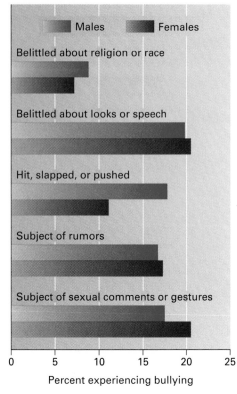

FIGURE 11.5 Bullying Behaviors Among U.S. Youth

This graph shows the type of bullying most often experienced by U.S. youth. The percentages reflect the extent to which bullied students said that they had experienced a particular type of bullying. In terms of gender, note that when they were bullied, boys were more likely to be hit, slapped, or pushed than girls were.

Reducing Bullying

perceive the aggressive boy as habitually acting in inappropriate ways. Kenneth Dodge (1983) argues that children go through five steps in processing information about their social world. They decode social cues, interpret, search for a response, select an optimal response, and enact. Dodge has found that aggressive boys are more likely to perceive another child's actions as hostile when the child's intention is ambiguous. And, when aggressive boys search for cues to determine a peer's intention, they respond more rapidly, less efficiently, and less reflectively than do nonaggressive children. These are among the social cognitive factors believed to be involved in the nature of children's conflicts.

Social knowledge is also involved in children's ability to get along with peers. An important part of children's social life involves knowing what goals to pursue in poorly defined or ambiguous situations. Social relationship goals, such as how to initiate and maintain a social bond, are also important. Children need to know what scripts to follow to get other children to be their friends. For example, as part of the script for getting friends, it helps to know that saying nice things, regardless of what the peer does or says, will make the peer like the child more.

Bullying

Significant numbers of students are victimized by bullies (Pellegrini, 2002; Rigby, 2002; Smith & others, 2002). In one recent national survey of more than 15,000 sixth-through tenth-grade students, nearly one of every three students said that they had experienced occasional or frequent involvement as a victim or perpetrator in bullying (Nansel & others, 2001). In this study, *bullying* was defined as verbal or physical behavior intended to disturb someone less powerful. Boys and younger middle school students were most likely to be affected. As shown in figure 11.5, being belittled about looks or speech was the most frequent type of bullying. Children who said they were bullied reported more loneliness and difficulty in making friends, while those who did the bullying were more likely to have low grades and to smoke and drink alcohol.

In one study, both bullying and victim behavior were linked to parent-child relationships (Olweus, 1980). Bullies' parents were more likely to be rejecting, authoritarian, or permissive about their son's aggression, whereas victims' parents were more likely to be anxious and overprotective.

To reduce bullying, these strategies can be adopted (Limber, 1997):

- Get older peers to serve as monitors for bullying and intervene when they see it taking place.
- Develop schoolwide rules and sanctions against bullying and post them throughout the school.
- Form friendship groups for adolescents who are regularly bullied by peers.
- Incorporate the message of the antibullying program into church, school, and other community activities where adolescents are involved.

Some children who are highly aggressive turn into juvenile delinquents and some become violent youth. We will discuss juvenile delinquency and violent youth in chapter 13, "Socioemotional Development in Adolescence." Next, we will turn our attention to the role of social cognition in peer relations. In part of this discussion, we will explore ideas about reducing the aggression of children in their peer encounters.

Review and Reflect

3 **Identify changes in peer relationships in middle and late childhood**

REVIEW

- What are children's friendships like?

- How does children's peer status influence their development?
- How is social cognition involved in children's peer relations?
- What is the nature of bullying?

REFLECT

- If you were a school principal, what would you do to reduce bullying in your school?

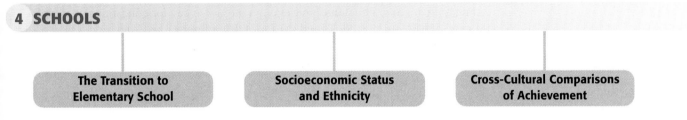

4 SCHOOLS

| The Transition to Elementary School | Socioeconomic Status and Ethnicity | Cross-Cultural Comparisons of Achievement |

It is justifiable to be concerned about the impact of schools on children: By the time students graduate from high school, they have spent 10,000 hours in the classroom. Children spend many years in schools as members of a small society in which there are tasks to be accomplished, people to be socialized and socialized by, and rules that define and limit behavior, feelings, and attitudes.

The Transition to Elementary School

For most children, entering the first grade signals a change from being a "homechild" to being a "schoolchild"—a situation in which new roles and obligations are experienced. Children take up a new role (being a student), interact and develop relationships with new significant others, adopt new reference groups, and develop new standards by which to judge themselves. School provides children with a rich source of new ideas to shape their sense of self.

A special concern about children's early school experiences is emerging. Evidence is mounting that early schooling proceeds mainly on the basis of negative feedback. For example, children's self-esteem in the latter part of elementary school is lower than it is in the earlier part, and older children rate themselves as less smart, less good, and less hardworking than do younger ones (Blumenfeld & others, 1981).

Children should be given opportunities to actively construct their learning. Let's examine two elementary school classrooms (Katz & Chard, 1989). In one, children spent an entire morning making identical pictures of traffic lights. The teacher made no attempt to get the children to relate the pictures to anything else the class was doing. In the other class, the children were investigating a school bus. They wrote to the district's school superintendent and asked if they could have a bus parked at their school for a few days. They studied the bus, discovered the functions of its parts, and discussed traffic rules. Then, in the classroom, they built their own bus out of cardboard. The children had fun, but they also practiced writing, problem solving, and even some arithmetic. When the class had their parents' night, the teacher was ready with reports on how each child was doing. However, all that the parents wanted to see was the bus because their children had been talking about it at home for weeks. Many contemporary education experts believe that this is the kind of education all children deserve. That is, they believe that children should be active, constructivist learners and taught through concrete, hands-on experience (Bonk & Cunningham, 1999).

mhhe.com/ santrockld9

ERIC Clearinghouse on Teachers
Elementary Education
Pathways to School Improvement

Socioeconomic Status and Ethnicity

Children from low-income, ethnic minority backgrounds have more difficulties in school than do their middle-socioeconomic status, White counterparts. Why? Critics argue that schools have not done a good job of educating low-income, ethnic minority students to overcome the barriers to their achievement (Scott-Jones, 1995). Let's further explore the roles of socioeconomic status and ethnicity in schools.

The Education of Students from Low-Socioeconomic Backgrounds Many children in poverty face problems at home and at school that present barriers to their learning (Bradley & Corwyn, 2002; Phillips & others, 1999). At home, they might have parents who don't set high educational standards for them, who are incapable of reading to them, and who don't have enough money to pay for educational materials and experiences, such as books and trips to zoos and museums. They might be malnourished and live in areas where crime and violence are a way of life (Ceballo, 1999).

Many of the schools that children from impoverished backgrounds attend have fewer resources than do the schools in higher-income neighborhoods (Bradley & Corwyn, 2002). Schools in low-income areas are more likely to have more students with lower achievement test scores, lower graduation rates, and smaller percentages of students going to college. And they are more likely to have young teachers with less experience than do schools in higher-income neighborhoods. In some instances, though, federal aid has provided a context for improved learning in schools located in low-income areas.

Schools in low-income areas also are more likely to encourage rote learning, while schools in higher-income areas are more likely to work with children to improve their thinking skills (Spring, 1998). Thus far too many schools in low-income neighborhoods provide students with environments that are not conducive to effective learning, and many of the schools' buildings and classrooms are old, crumbling, and poorly maintained.

Jonathan Kozol (1991) vividly described some of the problems that children of poverty face in their neighborhood and at school in *Savage Inequalities*. Here are some of his observations in one inner-city area. East St. Louis, Illinois, which is 98 percent African American, has no obstetric services, no regular trash collection, and few jobs. Nearly one third of the families live on less than $7,500 a year, and 75 percent of its population lives on welfare of some form. Blocks upon blocks of housing consist of dilapidated, skeletal buildings. Residents breathe the chemical pollution of nearby Monsanto Chemical Company. Raw sewage repeatedly backs up into homes. Lead from nearby smelters poisons the soil. Child malnutrition and fear of violence are common. The problems of the streets spill over into the schools, where sewage also backs up from time to time. Classrooms and hallways are old and unattractive, athletic facilities inadequate. Teachers run out of chalk and paper, the science labs are 30 to 50 years out of date, and the school's heating system has never worked correctly. A history teacher has 110 students but only 26 books.

Kozol says that anyone who visits places like East St. Louis, even for a brief time, comes away profoundly shaken. After all, these are innocent children who have done nothing wrong. Kozol's interest was in describing what life is like in the nation's inner-city neighborhoods and schools, which are predominantly African American and Latino. However, as indicated earlier, there are many non-Latino White children who live in poverty, although they often are in suburban or rural areas. Kozol argues that many inner-city schools are still segregated, are grossly underfunded, and do not provide adequate opportunities for children to learn effectively.

One trend in antipoverty programs is to conduct two-generational intervention (Huston, 1999; McLoyd, 1998, 1999, 2000). This involves providing both services for children (such as educational day care or preschool education) and services for parents (such as adult education, literacy training, and job skill training). Recent evaluations of the two-generational programs suggest that they have more positive effects on

mhhe•com/
santrockld9

**Urban Education and
Children in Poverty**

Interview with Jonathan Kozol

Diversity and Education

In his book *Savage Inequalities,* Jonathan Kozol (*above*) vividly portrayed the problems that children of poverty face in their neighborhood and at school. *What are some of these problems?*

parents than they do on children (St. Pierre, Layzer, & Barnes, 1996). Also discouraging for children is that, when the two-generational programs show benefits, they are more likely to be in the form of health benefits than cognitive gains.

Ethnicity in Schools   School segregation is still a factor in the education of children of color in the United States (Simons, Finlay, & Yang, 1991). Almost one third of all African American and Latino students attend schools in which 90 percent or more of the students are from minority groups.

The school experiences of students from different ethnic groups vary considerably (Nelson-LeGall & Kelly, 2001). African American and Latino students are much less likely than non-Latino White or Asian American students to be enrolled in academic, college preparatory programs and are much more likely to be enrolled in remedial and special education programs. Asian American students are far more likely than other ethnic minority groups to take advanced math and science courses in high school. African American students are twice as likely as Latinos, Native Americans, or Whites to be suspended from school. Ethnic minorities of color constitute the majority in 23 of the 25 largest school districts in the United States, a trend that is increasing (Banks, 1995). However, 90 percent of the teachers in America's schools are non-Latino White, and the percentage of minority teachers is projected to decrease even further in the coming years.

American anthropologist John Ogbu (1989) proposed the view that ethnic minority students are placed in a position of subordination and exploitation in the American educational system. He believes that students of color, especially African Americans and Latinos, have inferior educational opportunities, are exposed to teachers and school administrators who have low academic expectations for them, and encounter negative stereotypes of ethnic minority groups (Ogbu & Stern, 2001). In one study of middle schools in predominantly Latino areas of Miami, Latino and White teachers rated African American students as having more behavioral problems than African American teachers rated the same students as having (Zimmerman & others, 1995).

Like Ogbu, educational psychologist Margaret Beale Spencer (1990) says that a form of institutional racism permeates many American schools. That is, well-meaning teachers, acting out of misguided liberalism, fail to challenge children of color to achieve. Such teachers prematurely accept a low level of performance from these children, substituting warmth and affection for high standards of academic success.

Here are some strategies for improving relationships among ethnically diverse students (Santrock, 2001).

- *Turn the class into a jigsaw classroom.* When Eliot Aronson was a professor at the University of Texas at Austin, the school system contacted him for ideas on how to reduce the increasing racial tension in classrooms. Aronson (1986) developed the concept of "jigsaw classroom," in which students from different cultural backgrounds are placed in a cooperative group in which they have to construct different parts of a project to reach a common goal. Aronson used the term *jigsaw* because he saw the technique as much like a group of students cooperating to put different pieces together to complete a jigsaw puzzle. How might this work? Team sports, drama productions, and music performances are examples of contexts in which students cooperatively participate to reach a common goal.
- *Use technology to foster cooperation with students from around the world.* The Sociocultural Worlds of Development box on page 358 illustrates how to do this.
- *Encourage students to have positive personal contact with diverse other students.* Contact alone does not do the job of improving relationships with diverse others. For example, busing ethnic minority students to predominantly White schools, or vice versa, has not reduced prejudice or improved interethnic relations (Minuchin & Shapiro, 1983). What matters is what happens after children get to school. Especially beneficial in improving interethnic relations is sharing one's worries,

mhhe ● com/
santrockld9

Multicultural Education

The Global Lab

Traditionally, students have learned within the walls of their classroom and interacted with their teacher and other students in the class. With advances in telecommunications, students can learn from and with teachers and students around the world. The teachers and students might be from schools in such diverse locations as Warsaw, Tokyo, Istanbul, and a small village in Israel.

The Global Laboratory Project is one example that has capitalized on advances in telecommunications (Schrum & Berenfeld, 1997). It consists of science investigations that involve environmental monitoring, sharing data via telecommunication hookups, and placing local findings in a global context. In an initial telecommunications meeting, students introduced themselves and described their schools, communities, and study locations. The locations included Moscow, Russia; Warsaw, Poland; Kenosha, Wisconsin; San Antonio, Texas; Pueblo, Colorado; and Aiken, South Carolina. This initial phase was designed to help students develop a sense of community and become familiar with their collaborators from around the world. As their data collection and evaluation evolved, students continued to communicate with their peers worldwide and to learn more not only about science but also about the global community.

Classrooms or schools also can use fax machines to link students from around the country and world (Cushner, McClelland, & Safford, 1996). Fax machines transfer artwork, poetry, essays, and other materials to other students in locations as diverse as Europe, Asia, Africa, and South America. Students also can communicate the same day with pen pals through e-mail, where once it took weeks for a letter to reach someone in a faraway place. An increasing number of schools also use videotelephone technology

in foreign language instruction. Instead of simulating a French café in a typical French language class, American students might talk with French students who have placed a videotelephone in a French café in their country.

Such global technology projects can go a long way toward reducing American students' ethnocentric beliefs. The active building of connections around the world through telecommunications gives students the opportunity to experience others' perspectives, better understand other cultures, and reduce prejudice.

Global technology projects can help students become less ethnocentric. *What is the nature of some of these projects?*

successes, failures, coping strategies, interests, and other personal information with people of other ethnicities. When this happens, people are seen more as individuals than as a heterogeneous cultural group.

- *Encourage students to engage in perspective taking.* Exercises and activities that help students see others' perspectives can improve interethnic relations. This helps students "step into the shoes" of peers who are culturally different and feel what it is like to be treated in fair or unfair ways (Cushner, McClelland, & Safford, 1996).
- *Help students think critically and be emotionally intelligent when cultural issues are involved.* Students who think in narrow ways are prejudiced. Students who learn to think critically and deeply about interethnic relations are likely to decrease their prejudice. Becoming more emotionally intelligent includes understanding the causes of one's feelings, managing anger, listening to what others are saying, and being motivated to share and cooperate.
- *Reduce bias.* Teachers can reduce bias by displaying images of children from diverse ethnic and cultural groups, selecting play materials and classroom activities that encourage cultural understanding, helping students resist stereotyping, and working with parents (Derman-Sparks, 1989).
- *View the school and community as a team to help support teaching efforts.* James Comer (1988; Comer & others, 1996) believes that a community, team approach is the best way to educate children. Three important aspects of the Comer Project for

Careers in Life-Span Development

James Comer, Child Psychiatrist

James Comer grew up in a low-income neighborhood in East Chicago, Indiana, and credits his parents with leaving no doubt about the importance of education. He obtained a BA degree from Indiana University. He went on to obtain a medical degree from Howard University College of Medicine, a Master of Public Health degree from the University of Michigan School of Public Health, and psychiatry training at the Yale University School of Medicine's Child Study Center ◀||||| p. 32. He currently is the Maurice Falk Professor of Child Psychiatry at the Yale University Child Study Center and an associate dean at the Yale University Medical School. During his years at Yale, Comer has concentrated his career on promoting a focus on child development as a way of improving schools. His efforts in support of healthy development of young people are known internationally.

Dr. Comer, perhaps, is best known for the founding of the School Development Program in 1968, which promotes the collaboration of parents, educators, and community to improve social, emotional, and academic outcomes for children. His concept of teamwork is currently improving the educational environment in more than 500 schools throughout America.

James Comer (*left*) is shown with some of the inner-city African American children who attend a school that became a better learning environment because of Comer's intervention.

Change are (1) a governance and management team that develops a comprehensive school plan, assessment strategy, and staff development plan; (2) a mental health or school support team; and (3) a parent's program. Comer believes that the entire school community should have a cooperative rather than an adversarial attitude. The Comer program is currently operating in more than 600 schools in 26 states. To read further about Comer's work and his career, see the Careers in Life-Span Development insert.

- *Be a competent cultural mediator.* Teachers can play a powerful role as a cultural mediator by being sensitive to racist content in materials and classroom interactions, learning more about different ethnic groups, being sensitive to children's ethnic attitudes, viewing students of color positively, and thinking of positive ways to get parents of color more involved as partners with teachers in educating children (Banks, 1997; Cushner, 1999).

Cross-Cultural Comparisons of Achievement

American children are more achievement-oriented than their counterparts in many countries. However, in the past decade, the poor performance of American children in math and science has become well publicized. For example, in one cross-national comparison of the math and science achievement of 9- to 13-year-old students, the United States finished 13th (out of 15) in science and 15th (out of 16) in math

We [the United States] accept performances in students that are nowhere near where they should be.

—HAROLD STEVENSON
Contemporary Developmental Psychologist, University of Michigan

Asian grade schools intersperse studying with frequent periods of activities. This approach helps children maintain their attention and likely makes learning more enjoyable. Shown here are Japanese fourth-graders making wearable masks. *What are some differences in the way children in many Asian countries are taught compared to children in the United States?*

achievement (Educational Testing Service, 1992). In this study, Korean and Taiwanese students placed first and second, respectively.

Harold Stevenson's (1995, 2000; Stevenson & Hofer, 1999) research explores reasons for the poor performance of American students. Stevenson and his colleagues have completed five cross-cultural comparisons of students in the United States, China, Taiwan, and Japan. In these studies, Asian students consistently outperform American students. And the longer the students are in school, the wider the gap becomes between Asian and American students—the lowest difference is in the first grade, the highest in the eleventh grade (the highest grade studied).

To learn more about the reasons for these large cross-cultural differences, Stevenson and his colleagues spent thousands of hours observing in classrooms, as well as interviewing and surveying teachers, students, and parents. They found that the Asian teachers spent more of their time teaching math than did the American teachers. For example, more than one fourth of total classroom time in the first grade was spent on math instruction in Japan, compared with only one tenth of the time in the U.S. first-grade classrooms. Also, the Asian students were in school an average of 240 days a year, compared with 178 days in the United States.

In addition to the substantially greater time spent on math instruction in the Asian schools than the American schools, differences were found between the Asian and American parents. The American parents had much lower expectations for their children's education and achievement than did the Asian parents. Also, the American parents were more likely to believe that their children's math achievement was due to innate ability; the Asian parents were more likely to say that their children's math achievement was the consequence of effort and training (Stevenson, Lee, & Stigler, 1986) (see figure 11.6). The Asian students were more likely to do math homework than were the American students, and the Asian parents were far more likely to help their children with their math homework than were the American parents (Chen & Stevenson, 1989).

Critics of the cross-national comparisons argue that, in many comparisons, virtually all U.S. children are being compared with a "select" group of children from other countries, especially in the secondary school comparisons. Therefore, they conclude, it is no wonder that American students don't fare so well. That criticism holds for some international comparisons. However, even when the top 25 percent of students in different countries have been compared, U.S. students move up some, but not a lot (Mullis, 1999).

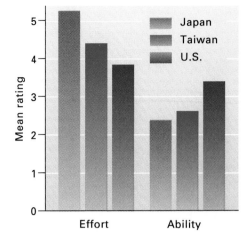

FIGURE 11.6 Mothers' Beliefs About the Factors Responsible for Children's Math Achievement in Three Countries

In one study, mothers in Japan and Taiwan were more likely to believe that their children's math achievement was due to effort rather than innate ability, while U.S. mothers were more likely to believe their children's math achievement was due to innate ability (Stevenson, Lee, & Stigler, 1986). If parents believe that their children's math achievement is due to innate ability and their children are not doing well in math, the implication is that they are less likely to think their children will benefit from putting forth more effort.

Review and Reflect

4 **Characterize the transition to elementary school and sociocultural aspects of schooling and achievement**

REVIEW

- What is the transition to elementary school like?
- How do socioeconomic status and ethnicity influence schooling?
- What are some cross-cultural comparisons of achievement?

REFLECT

- Should the United States be worried about the low performance of its students in mathematics and science in comparison to Asian students? Are Americans' expectations for students too low?

Reach Your Learning Goals

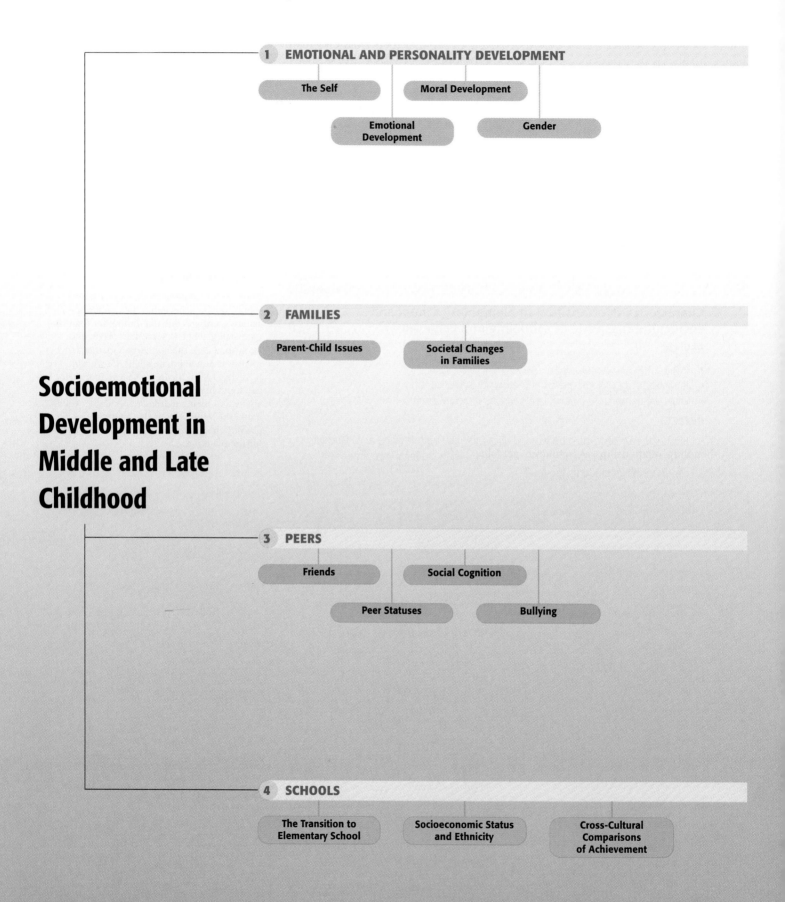

Socioemotional Development in Middle and Late Childhood

1 EMOTIONAL AND PERSONALITY DEVELOPMENT

- The Self
- Moral Development
- Emotional Development
- Gender

2 FAMILIES

- Parent-Child Issues
- Societal Changes in Families

3 PEERS

- Friends
- Social Cognition
- Peer Statuses
- Bullying

4 SCHOOLS

- The Transition to Elementary School
- Socioeconomic Status and Ethnicity
- Cross-Cultural Comparisons of Achievement

Summary

1 Discuss emotional and personality development in middle and late childhood

- The internal self, the social self, and the socially comparative self become more prominent in middle and late childhood. Self-esteem refers to global evaluations of the self and is also referred to as self-worth or self-image. Self-concept refers to domain-specific evaluations of the self. Four ways to increase self-esteem are to (1) identify the causes of low self-esteem, (2) provide emotional support and social approval, (3) help children achieve, and (4) help children cope. Erikson's fourth stage of development, industry versus inferiority, characterizes the middle and late childhood years.
- Developmental changes in emotion include increased understanding of such complex emotions as pride and shame, detecting that more than one emotion can be experienced in a particular situation, taking into account the circumstances that led up to the emotional reaction, improvements in the ability to suppress and conceal emotions, and using self-initiated strategies to redirect emotions. Emotional intelligence is a form of social intelligence that involves the ability to monitor one's own and others' feelings and emotions, to discriminate among them, and to use this information to guide one's own thinking and action. Goleman believes that emotional intelligence involves four main areas: emotional self-awareness, managing emotions, reading emotions, and handling relationships. As children get older, they use a greater variety of coping strategies and more cognitive strategies.
- Kohlberg developed a provocative theory of moral reasoning with three levels—preconventional, conventional, and post-conventional—and six stages (two at each level). Increased internalization characterizes movement to levels 2 and 3. Prosocial behavior involves positive moral behaviors. Altruism is an unselfish interest in helping others. Damon described a developmental sequence of altruism.
- Gender stereotypes are widespread around the world. A number of physical differences exist between males and females. Some experts, such as Hyde, argue that cognitive differences between males and females have been exaggerated. In terms of socioemotional differences, males are more physically aggressive than females while females regulate their emotions better. There is controversy about how similar or different males and females are in a number of areas. Gender-role classification focuses on how masculine, feminine, or androgynous individuals are. Androgyny means having both positive feminine and masculine characteristics. It is important to think about gender in terms of context.

2 Describe parent-child issues and societal changes in families

- Parents spend less time with children during middle and late childhood than in early childhood. New parent-child issues emerge and discipline changes. Control is more coregulatory.

- Like in divorced families, children living in stepparent families have more adjustment problems than their counterparts in nondivorced families. However, a majority of children in stepfamilies do not have adjustment problems. Latchkey children may become vulnerable when they are not monitored by adults in the after-school hours.

3 Identify changes in peer relationships in middle and late childhood

- Children's friendships serve six functions: companionship, stimulation, physical support, ego support, social comparison, and intimacy/affection. Intimacy and similarity are two common characteristics of friendship.
- Popular children are frequently nominated as a best friend and rarely disliked by their peers. Neglected children are infrequently nominated as a best friend but are not disliked by their peers. Rejected children are infrequently nominated as a best friend and are actively disliked by their peers. Controversial children are frequently nominated both as a best friend and as being disliked by peers. Rejected children are especially at risk for a number of problems.
- Social information-processing skills and social knowledge are two important dimensions of social cognition in peer relations.
- Significant numbers of children are bullied and this can result in short-term and long-term negative effects for the victim.

4 Characterize the transition to elementary school and sociocultural aspects of schooling and achievement

- Children spend more than 10,000 hours in the classroom as members of a small society in which there are tasks to be accomplished, people to be socialized and socialized by, and rules that define and limit behavior. A special concern is that early schooling too often proceeds on the basis of negative feedback to children.
- Children in poverty face problems at home and at school that present barriers to their learning. It is important that teachers have positive expectations for and challenge children of color to achieve.
- American children are more achievement-oriented than children in many countries, but are less achievement-oriented than many children in Asian countries, such as China, Taiwan, and Japan.

Key Terms

self-esteem 337
self-concept 337
emotional intelligence 339
internalization 341
preconventional
    reasoning 341

conventional reasoning 341
postconventional
    reasoning 342
justice perspective 343
care perspective 343
altruism 344

gender stereotypes 345
androgyny 347
intimacy in friendships 352
popular children 353
neglected children 353
rejected children 353

controversial children 353

Key People

Erik Erikson 338
Daniel Goleman 339
Lawrence Kohlberg 341
Carol Gilligan 343
William Damon 344

Nancy Eisenberg 344
Eleanor Maccoby 345
Carol Jacklin 345
Janet Shibley Hyde 346
Sandra Bem 347

Joan Lipsitz 351
Willard Hartup 352
Kenneth Dodge 354
Jonathan Kozol 356
John Ogbu 357

Margaret Beale Spencer 357
Eliot Aronson 357
Harold Stevenson 360

Taking It to the Net

1. Ling, a third-grade teacher, overheard a talk show discussion on emotional intelligence. She has seen several books on the subject in the local library but was unaware of its impact on learning. What is emotional intelligence and how can Ling and her students' parents facilitate this type of development in children?

2. Frank is researching the latest information on bullying after his younger brother told him of his recent experiences with bullies at his junior high school. What information is available on the prevalence of bullying, the makeup of the children who bully, and why this type of behavior is increasing?

Connect to www.mhhe.com/santrockld9 to research the answers and complete these exercises.

E-Learning Tools

To help you master the material in this chapter, you'll find a number of valuable study tools on the Student CD-ROM that accompanies this book. In addition, visit the Online Learning Center for *Life-Span Development,* ninth edition, where you'll find these valuable resources for chapter 11, "Socioemotional Development in Middle and Late Childhood."

- How well do you remember your own socioemotional development? Complete the self-assessment, *My Socioemotional Development as a Child.*

- View video clips of key developmental psychology experts, including Robert Emery discussing his research on children and divorce.
- Build your decision-making skills by trying your hand at the parenting and education "Scenarios."